IFIP Advances in Information and Communication Technology

652

Editor-in-Chief

IFIP – The International Federation for Information Processing

IFIP was founded in 1960 under the auspices of UNESCO, following the first World Computer Congress held in Paris the previous year. A federation for societies working in information processing, IFIP's aim is two-fold: to support information processing in the countries of its members and to encourage technology transfer to developing nations. As its mission statement clearly states:

> IFIP is the global non-profit federation of societies of ICT professionals that aims at achieving a worldwide professional and socially responsible development and application of information and communication technologies.

IFIP is a non-profit-making organization, run almost solely by 2500 volunteers. It operates through a number of technical committees and working groups, which organize events and publications. IFIP's events range from large international open conferences to working conferences and local seminars.

The flagship event is the IFIP World Computer Congress, at which both invited and contributed papers are presented. Contributed papers are rigorously refereed and the rejection rate is high.

As with the Congress, participation in the open conferences is open to all and papers may be invited or submitted. Again, submitted papers are stringently refereed.

The working conferences are structured differently. They are usually run by a working group and attendance is generally smaller and occasionally by invitation only. Their purpose is to create an atmosphere conducive to innovation and development. Refereeing is also rigorous and papers are subjected to extensive group discussion.

Publications arising from IFIP events vary. The papers presented at the IFIP World Computer Congress and at open conferences are published as conference proceedings, while the results of the working conferences are often published as collections of selected and edited papers.

IFIP distinguishes three types of institutional membership: Country Representative Members, Members at Large, and Associate Members. The type of organization that can apply for membership is a wide variety and includes national or international societies of individual computer scientists/ICT professionals, associations or federations of such societies, government institutions/government related organizations, national or international research institutes or consortia, universities, academies of sciences, companies, national or international associations or federations of companies.

More information about this series at https://link.springer.com/bookseries/6102

Ilias Maglogiannis · Lazaros Iliadis ·
John Macintyre · Paulo Cortez (Eds.)

Artificial Intelligence Applications and Innovations

AIAI 2022 IFIP WG 12.5 International Workshops

MHDW 2022, 5G-PINE 2022, AIBMG 2022
ML@HC 2022, and AIBEI 2022
Hersonissos, Crete, Greece, June 17–20, 2022
Proceedings

Editors
Ilias Maglogiannis
University of Piraeus
Piraeus, Greece

Lazaros Iliadis
Democritus University of Thrace
Xanthi, Greece

John Macintyre
University of Sunderland
Sunderland, UK

Paulo Cortez
Universidade do Minho
Guimaraes, Portugal

ISSN 1868-4238   ISSN 1868-422X (electronic)
IFIP Advances in Information and Communication Technology
ISBN 978-3-031-08343-3   ISBN 978-3-031-08341-9 (eBook)
https://doi.org/10.1007/978-3-031-08341-9

This Springer imprint is published by the registered company Springer Nature Switzerland AG
The registered company address is: Gewerbestrasse 11, 6330 Cham, Switzerland

Preface

Artificial Intelligence (AI) is a relatively new scientific area that emerged from the efforts of a handful of scientists from diverse fields, approximately 70 years ago. The achievements of AI in the era of the 4th Industrial Revolution are amazing and the expectations are continuously rising. Today AI applications are found in almost all areas of human activities.

Healthcare, finance, industry, security, robotics, molecular biology, autonomous vehicles, are only a small sample of the domains that have been influenced by artificial intelligence. However, serious ethical matters have emerged (e.g., privacy, surveillance, bias-discrimination, elimination of entire job categories) requiring corrective legislative actions.

The 18th International Conference on Artificial Intelligence Applications and Innovations (AIAI 2022) offered insight into all timely challenges related to technical, legal, and ethical aspects of intelligent systems and their applications. New algorithms and potential prototypes employed in diverse domains were also introduced.

AIAI is a mature international scientific conference that has been held all over the world and it is well established in the scientific area of AI. Its history is long and very successful, following and propagating the evolution of intelligent systems.

The first event was organized in Toulouse, France, in 2004. Since then, it has had a continuous and dynamic presence as a major global, but mainly European scientific event. More specifically, it has been organized in China, Greece, Cyprus, Australia, and France. It has always been technically supported by the International Federation for Information Processing (IFIP) and more specifically by the Working Group 12.5, which is interested in AI applications.

Overall, seven workshops were organized under the auspices of the 18th AIAI 2022 as satellite events.

Following tradition, this Springer volume belongs to the IFIP AICT Series. It contains original research papers that were accepted after a peer review process to be presented orally at the following five workshops that were organized under the framework of the 18th AIAI 2022 conference:

- The 11th Mining Humanistic Data Workshop (MHDW 2022),
- The 7th Workshop on 5G-Putting Intelligence to the Network Edge (5G-PINE 2022)
- The 1st Workshop on AI in Energy, Building and Micro-Grids (AIBMG 2022)
- The 1st Workshop/Special Session on Machine Learning and Big Data in Health Care (ML@HC 2022)
- The 2nd Workshop on Artificial Intelligence in Biomedical Engineering and Informatics (AIBEI 2022)

The following paragraphs contain a brief description of the aforementioned five workshops.

- The 11th Mining Humanistic Data Workshop (MHDW 2022)

MHDW 2022 was organized by the University of Patras and the Ionian University, Greece. It aimed to bring together interdisciplinary approaches that focus on the application of innovative as well as existing artificial intelligence, data matching, fusion and mining and knowledge discovery and management techniques to data derived from all areas of humanistic sciences.

- The 7th Workshop on 5G-Putting Intelligence to the Network Edge (5G-PINE 2022)

5G-PINE 2022 workshop was organized by the research team of the Hellenic Telecommunications Organization (OTE) in cooperation with many major partner companies. The 5G-PINE workshop was established to disseminate knowledge obtained from ongoing EU projects as well as from any other action of EU-funded research, in the wider thematic area of "5G Innovative Activities – Putting Intelligence to the Network Edge" and with the aim of focusing on artificial intelligence in modern 5G telecommunications infrastructures. This is achieved by emphasizing results, methodologies, trials, concepts and/or findings originating from technical reports/deliverables, related pilot actions, and/or any other relevant 5G-based applications, intending to enhance intelligence to the network edges.

- The 2nd Workshop on Defense Applications of AI (DAAI 2022)

The 2nd DAAI workshop was organized by the European Defense Agency (EDA), a European Union (EU) organization. Defense and security systems are becoming more and more complicated and at the same time equipped with a plethora of sensing devices which collect an enormous amount of information both from their operating environment as well as from their own functioning. Considering the accelerating technology advancements of AI, it is likely that it will have a profound impact on practically every segment of daily life, from the labor market to business and service provision. The security and defense sectors will not remain idle or unaffected by this technological evolution. On the contrary, AI is expected to transform the nature of future defense and security domains, because by definition defense and security forces are highly dependent on (accurate) data and (reliable) information. DAAI 2022 aimed at presenting recent evolutions in artificial intelligence applicable to defense and security applications.

- The 1st Workshop on AI in Energy, Buildings and Micro-Grids (AIBMG 2022)

This workshop was organized by the Center for Research and Technology), Greece. Sustainable energy is hands down one of the biggest challenges of our times. As the EU sets its focus on reaching its 2030 and 2050 goals, the role of artificial intelligence in the energy domain at building, district and micro-grid level becomes more prevalent. The EU and member states are increasingly highlighting the need to complement IoT capacity (e.g., appliances and meters) with artificial intelligence capabilities (e.g., building management systems, proactive optimization, prescriptive maintenance).

Moreover, moving away from the centralized production schema of the grid, novel approaches are needed not just for reducing energy consumption but also for the optimal management and/or balancing of local (or remote aggregated net metering) generation and consumption.

The aim of the AIBMG workshop was to bring together interdisciplinary approaches that focus on the application of AI-driven solutions for increasing and improving energy efficiency of residential and tertiary buildings without compromising the occupants' well-being. Applied directly at either the device, building or district management system level; the proposed solutions should enable more energy efficient and sustainable operation of devices, buildings, districts and micro-grids. The workshop also welcomed cross-domain approaches that investigate how to support energy efficiency by exploiting decentralized, proactive, plug-n-play solutions.

- The 2nd Workshop on Artificial Intelligence in Biomedical Engineering and Informatics (AIBEI 2022)

Artificial intelligence (AI) is gradually changing the routine of medical practice, and the level of acceptance by medical personnel is constantly increasing. Recent progress in digital medical data acquisition through advanced biosignal and medical imaging devices, machine learning and high-performance cloud computing infrastructures, push health-related AI applications into areas that were previously thought to be only the province of human experts. Such applications employ a variety of methodologies, including fuzzy logic, evolutionary computing, neural networks, or deep learning for producing AI-powered models that simulate human physiology.

- The 1st Workshop/Special Session on Machine Learning and Big Data in Health Care (ML@HC 2022)

In the present era, machine learning (ML) has been extensively used for many applications to real world problems. ML techniques are very suitable for big data mining, to extract new knowledge and build predictive models that given a new input can provide in the output a reliable estimate. On the other hand, healthcare is one of the fastest growing data segments of the digital world, with healthcare data increasing at a rate of about 50% per year. There are three primary sources of big data in healthcare: providers and payers (including EMR, imaging, insurance claims and pharmacy data), -omic data (including genomic, epigenomic, proteomic, and metabolomic data), and patients and non-providers (including data from smart phone and Internet activities sensors and monitoring tools).

The growth of big data in oncology, as well as other severe diseases (such as Alzheimer's Disease) can provide unprecedented opportunities to explore the biopsychosocial characteristics of these diseases and for descriptive observation, hypothesis generation, and prediction for clinical, research and business issues. The results of big data analyses can be incorporated into standards and guidelines and will directly impact clinical decision making. Oncologists and professionals from related medical fields can increasingly evaluate the results from research studies and commercial analytical products that are based on big data, based on ML techniques. Furthermore, all these applications can be Web-based, so are very useful for the post treatment of the patients.

The aim of this workshop/special session was to serve as an interdisciplinary forum for bringing together specialists from the scientific areas of computer and web engineering, data science, semantic computing, bioinformatics-personalized medicine, along with clinicians and caregivers. The focus of this special session was on current technological advances and challenges regarding the development of big data-driven algorithms, methods and tools; furthermore, it sought to investigate how ML-aware applications can contribute towards big data analysis on post-treatment follow up.

Moreover, the following two workshops, namely the 2nd AI & Ethics and the 2nd DAAI were organized as lecture and discussion events without a call for papers. The 2nd AIETH workshop aimed to discuss scientific responsibilities about global AI. Respective scientists must be prepared to act preemptively and ensure that our societies will avoid negative effects of AI and of 4th Industrial Revolution in general. The workshop on AI Ethics was organized at the University of Sunderland, UK, and it discussed potential major ethical issues that will arise in the near future. It was coordinated by John Macintyre.

The 18th AIAI was held during June 17–20, 2022, in Crete, Greece.

The diverse nature of papers presented demonstrates the vitality of AI algorithms and approaches. It certainly proves the very wide range of AI applications as well and it promotes the timely advances in this area on both theoretical and application level.

The response of the international scientific community to the workshops of the AIAI 2022 call for papers was more than satisfactory, with 74 papers initially submitted. All papers were peer reviewed by at least two independent academic referees. Where needed, a third referee was consulted to resolve any potential conflicts. A total of 35 papers 47% of the submitted manuscripts) were accepted to be published as full papers (12 pages long) in the proceedings.

June 2022

Ilias Maglogiannis
Lazaros Iliadis
John MacIntyre
Paulo Cortez

Organization

Executive Committee

General Co-chairs

Ilias Maglogiannis	University of Piraeus, Greece
John Macintyre	University of Sunderland, UK

Program Co-chairs

Lazaros Iliadis	Democritus University of Thrace, Greece
Konstantinos Votis	Information Technologies Institute, Greece
Vangelis Metsis	Texas State University, USA

Steering Committee

Ilias Maglogiannis	University of Piraeus, Greece
Lazaros Iliadis	Democritus University of Thrace, Greece

Advisory Co-chairs

Panagiotis Papapetrou	Stockholm University, Sweden
Paulo Cortez	University of Minho, Portugal

Publication and Publicity Co-chairs

Antonios Papaleonidas	Democritus University of Thrace, Greece
Anastasios Panagiotis Psathas	Democritus University of Thrace, Greece

Liaison Chair

Ioannis Chochliouros	Hellenic Telecommunication Organization (OTE), Greece

Doctoral Consortium Chairs

Antonios Papaleonidas	Democritus University of Thrace, Greece
Harris Papadopoulos	Frederick University, Cyprus

Workshops Co-chairs

Panagiotis Kikiras	European Defense Agency, Belgium
Phivos Mylonas	Ionian Univesity, Greece
Katia Kermanidis	Ionian University, Greece

Special Sessions and Tutorials Co-chairs

Spyros Sioutas	University of Patras, Greece
Christos Makris	University of Patras, Greece

Program Committee

Aiello Salvatore	Politecnico di Torino, Italy
Aldanondo Michel	IMT Mines Albi, France
Alexandridis Georgios	University of the Aegean, Greece
Alexiou Athanasios	Novel Global Community Educational Foundation, Australia
Aloisio Angelo	University of L'Aquila, Italy
Alonso Serafin	University of León, Spain
Amato Domenico	University of Palermo, Italy
Anagnostopoulos Christos-Nikolaos	University of the Aegean, Greece
Badica Costin	University of Craiova, Romania
Bezas Napoleon	Centre for Research and Technology Hellas, Greece
Bobrowski Leon	Bialystok University of Technology, Poland
Bozanis Panayiotis	International Hellenic University, Greece
C. Sousa Joana	NOS Inovação SA, Portugal
Campos Souza Paulo Vitor	Federal Center for Technological Education of Minas Gerais, Brazil
Caridakis George	National Technical University of Athens, Greece
Cavique Luis	University of Aberta, Portugal
Chamodrakas Ioannis	National and Kapodistrian University of Athens, Greece
Chochliouros Ioannis	Hellenic Telecommunications Organization S.A. (OTE), Greece
Delibasis Konstantinos	University of Thessaly, Greece
Demertzis Konstantinos	Democritus University of Thrace, Greece
Dimara Asimina	Centre for Research and Technology Hellas, Greece
Diou Christos Harokopio	University of Athens, Greece
Dominguez Manuel	University of Leon, Spain
Drakopoulos Georgios	Ionian University, Greece
Drousiotis Efthyvoulos	University of Liverpool, UK
Ferreira Luis	Polytechnic of Porto, Portugal
Fiannaca Antonino	National Research Council, Italy
Frittoli Luca	Politecnico di Milano, Italy
Fuertes Juan J.	University of León, Spain
Gaggero Mauro	National Research Council, Italy
Georgopoulos Efstratios	University of Peloponnese, Greece
Giancarlo Raffaele	University of Palermo, Italy
Giarelis Nikolaos	University of Patras, Greece
Giunchiglia Eleonora	University of Oxford, UK

Gonzalez-Deleito Nicolas	Sirris, Belgium
Grivokostopoulou Foteini	University of Patras, Greece
Hága Péter	Ericsson Research, Hungary
Hajek Petr	University of Pardubice, Czech Republic
Haralabopoulos Giannis	University of Nottingham, UK
Hatzilygeroudis Ioannis	University of Patras, Greece
Hichri Bassem	GCL International, Luxembourg
Hristoskova Anna	Sirris, Belgium
Humm Bernhard	Darmstadt University of Applied Sciences, Germany
Iakovidis Dimitris	University of Thessaly, Greece
Iliadis Lazaros	Democritus University of Thrace, Greece
Ishii Naohiro	Aichi Institute of Technology, Japan
Islam Shareeful	University of East London, UK
Ivanovic Mirjana	University of Novi Sad, Serbia
Jeannin-Girardon Anne	University of Strasbourg, France
Kalamaras Ilias	Centre for Research and Technology Hellas/Information Technologies Institute, Greece
Kallipolitis Athanasios	University of Piraeus, Greece
Kanakaris Nikos	University of Patras, Greece
Kanavos Andreas	University of Patras, Greece
Kapetanakis Stelios	University of Brighton, UK
Karacapilidis Nikos	University of Patras, Greece
Karatzas Kostas	Aristotle University of Thessaloniki, Greece
Karpouzis Kostas	National and Kapodistrian University of Athens, Greece
Kassandros Theodosios	Aristotle University of Thessaloniki, Greece
Kefalas Petros	CITY College, Greece
Kermanidis Katia Lida	Ionian University, Greece
Kokkinos Yiannis	University of Macedonia, Greece
Kollia Ilianna	IBM/National Technical University of Athens, Greece
Kontos Yiannis	Aristotle University of Thessaloniki, Greece
Koprinkova-Hristova Petia	Bulgarian Academy of Sciences, Bulgaria
Korkas Christos	Democritus University of Thrace/Centre for Research and Technology, Greece
Kosmopoulos Dimitrios	University of Patras, Greece
Kotis Konstantinos	University of the Aegean, Greece
Kotsiantis Sotiris	University of Patras, Greece
Koukaras Paraskevas	Centre for Research and Technology Hellas, Greece
Koussouris Sotiris	Suite5 Data Intelligence Solutions Ltd., Cyprus
Koutras Athanasios	University of Peloponnese, Greece
Krejcar Ondrej	University of Hradec Kralove, Czech Republic
Krinidis Stelios	Centre for Research and Technology Hellas, Greece
Kyriakides George	University of Macedonia, Greece
La Rosa Massimo	National Research Council, Italy
Lalas Antonios	Centre for Research and Technology Hellas/Information Technologies Institute, Greece

Lazaridis Georgios	Centre for Research and Technology Hella/Information Technologies Institute, Greece
Lazic Ljubomir	UNION University, Serbia
Lederman Dror	Holon Institute of Technology, Israel
Leon Florin	Technical University of Iasi, Romania
Likas Aristidis	University of Ioannina, Greece
Likothanassis Spiros	University of Patras, Greece
Livieris Ioannis	University of Patras, Greece
Lo Bosco Giosuè	University of Palermo, Italy
Logofatu Doina	Frankfurt University of Applied Sciences, Germany
Longo Luca	Technological University of Dublin, Ireland
Maghool Samira	University of Milan, Italy
Maglogiannis Ilias	University of Piraeus, Greece
Magoulas George	University of London, Birkbeck College, UK
Magri Luca	Politecnico di Milano, Italy
Makris Christos	University of Patras, Greece
Malialis Kleanthis	University of Cyprus, Cyprus
Maragoudakis Manolis	Ionian University, Greece
Marano Giuseppe Carlo	Politecnico di Torino, Italy
Margaritis Konstantinos	University of Macedonia, Greece
Martins Nuno	NOS Inovação SA, Portugal
Melnik Andrew	Bielefeld University, Germany
Menychtas Andreas	University of Piraeus, Greece
Mezaris Vasileios	Centre for Research and Technology Hellas, Greece
Michailidis Iakovos	Centre for Research and Technology Hellas, Greece
Mitianoudis Nikolaos	Democritus University of Thrace, Greece
Morán Antonio	University of León, Spain
Moutselos Konstantinos	University of Piraeus, Greece
Muhr David	Johannes Kepler University Linz, Austria
Müller Wilmuth	Fraunhofer IOSB, Germany
Munk Michal	Constantine the Philosopher University in Nitra, Slovakia
Mylonas Phivos	National Technical University of Athens, Greece
Nikiforos Stefanos	Ionian University, Greece
Ntalampiras Stavros	University of Milan, Italy
Oprea Mihaela	Petroleum-Gas University of Ploiesti, Romania
Papadopoulos Symeon	Centre for Research and Technology Hellas/Information Technologies Institute, Greece
Papadourakis Giorgos	Hellenic Mediterranean University, Greece
Papaioannou Vaios	University of Patras, Greece
Papaleonidas Antonios	Democritus University of Thrace, Greece
Papastergiopoulos Christoforos	Centre for Research and Technology Hellas/Information Technologies Institute, Greece
Papatheodoulou Dimitris	KIOS Research and Innovation Center of Excellence, Cyprus
Passalis Nikolaos	Aristotle University of Thessaloniki, Greece

Paulus Jan	Nuremberg Institute of Technology, Germany
Pérez Daniel	University of León, Spain
Perikos Isidoros	University of Patras, Greece
Pimenidis Elias	University of the West of England, UK
Pintelas Panagiotis	University of Patras, Greece
Prada Miguel Ángel	Universidad de León, Spain
Pradat-Peyre Jean-François	Paris Nanterre University and LIP6, France
Psathas Anastasios	Panagiotis Democritus University of Thrace, Greece
Racz Andras	Ericsson Research, Hungary
Rankovic Dragica	UNION University, Serbia
Reitmann Stefan	TU Bergakademie Freiberg, Germany
Rosso Marco Martino	Politecnico di Torino, Italy
Ryjov Alexander Lomonosov	Moscow State University, Russia
Sarafidis Michail	National Technical University of Athens, Greece
Scheele Stephan	Fraunhofer IIS/University of Bamberg, Germany
Scherrer Alexander	Fraunhofer ITWM, Germany
Seferis Manos	National Technical University of Athens, Greece
Serrano Will	University College London, UK
Shi Lei	Durham University, UK
Siccardi Stefano	University of Milan, Italy
Spyrou Evaggelos	Technological Educational Institute of Sterea Ellada, Greece
Staiano Antonino	University of Naples Parthenope, Italy
Stamate Daniel	Goldsmiths, University of London, UK
Stefanopoulou Aliki	Centre for Research and Technology Hellas, Greece
Stucchi Diego	Politecnico di Milano, Italy
Stylianou Nikolaos	Aristotle University of Thessaloniki, Greece
Theocharides Theo	University of Cyprus, Cyprus
Theodoridis Georgios	Aristotle University of Thessaloniki, Greece
Timplalexis Christos	Centre for Research and Technology Hellas/Information Technologies Institute, Greece
Trakadas Panagiotis	National and Kapodistrian University of Athens, Greece
Treur Jan	VU Amsterdam, The Netherlands
Trovò Francesco	Politecnico di Milano, Italy
Tsadiras Athanasios	Aristotle University of Thessaloniki, Greece
Tsaknakis Christos	Democritus University of Thrace, Greece
Van-Horenbeke Franz Alexander	Free University of Bozen-Bolzano, Italy
Versaci Mario	University of Reggio Calabria, Italy
Vidnerová Petra	Czech Academy of Sciences, Czech Republic
Vilone Giulia	Technological University Dublin, Ireland
Vonitsanos Gerasimos	Ionian University, Greece
Votis Kostas	Centre for Research and Technology Hellas, Greece

Vougiatzis Georgios   Information Technologies Institute/Centre for Research
                             and Technology Hellas, Greece
Wan Cen Birkbeck   University of London, UK
Yang Xin-She   Middlesex University London, UK
Zender Alexander   Darmstadt University of Applied Sciences, Germany
Zervas Panagiotis   University of Peloponnese, Greece
Zimmermann Tobias   Fraunhofer ITWM, Germany

Abstracts of Keynote/Invited Talks

What Neuroimaging Can Tell About Human Brain Function

Riitta Salmelin

Department of Neuroscience and Biomedical Engineering Aalto University,
Finland
riitta.salmelin@aalto.fi

Abstract. Over the past few decades, real-time tracking of cortical current flow (magneto/electroencephalography, MEG/EEG) and accurate localization of blood oxygenation changes (functional magnetic resonance imaging, fMRI) have offered windows to the functional architecture of the human brain. The neuroimaging domain has reached its first level of maturity: we now know how to measure and quantify different types of signals and, phenomenologically, we know what type of group-level functional effects to expect in a large variety of experimental conditions. Specific brain areas, networks and electrophysiological dynamics have been proposed to be linked with various perceptual, motor and cognitive functions and their disorders. To reach the next phase in human neuroscience, we need to advance from group-level descriptions to quantitative model-based individual-level predictions. These developments will be illustrated with focus on language function for which descriptive models, largely based on observations of patients with language disorders, are being supplemented by computationally explicit models of mechanisms and representations. Machine learning approaches are essential tools in this endeavor.

Socially Interactive Artificial Intelligence: Perception, Synthesis and Learning of Human-Like Behaviors

Elisabeth Andre

Human-Centered Artificial Intelligence, Institute for Informatics,
University of Augsburg, Germany
andre@informatik.uni-augsburg.de

Abstract. The automatic analysis and synthesis of social signals conveyed by voice, gestures, mimics, etc., will play a vital role for next-generation interfaces as it paves the way towards a more intuitive and natural human-computer interaction with robots and virtual agents. In my talk, I will present computational methods to implement socially interactive behaviors in artificial agents, focusing on three essential properties of socially interactive interfaces: Social Perception, Socially Aware Behavior Synthesis, and Learning Socially Aware Behaviors. I will highlight opportunities and challenges that arise from deep learning approaches that promise to achieve the next level of human-likeness in virtual agents and social robots. I will illustrate my talk with examples from various applications with socially interactive characters or robots, including art and entertainment, cultural training and social coaching, and personal well-being and health.

Responsible Conversational AI: Trusted, Safe and Bias-Free

Verena Rieser

School of Mathematical and Computer Sciences (MACS) at Heriot Watt
University, Edinburgh
V.T.Rieser@hw.ac.uk

Abstract. With recent progress in deep learning, there has been an increased interest in learning dialogue systems from data, also known as "Conversational AI". In this talk, I will focus on the task of response generation, for which I will highlight lessons learnt and ongoing challenges, such as reducing 'hallucinations for task-based systems, safety critical issues for open-domain chatbots, and the often-overlooked problem of 'good' persona design. I will argue that we will need to solve these challenges to create trusted, safe and bias-free systems for end-user applications.

Is Big Tech Becoming the Big Tobacco of AI?

John Macintyre

Dean of the Faculty of Applied Sciences and Pro Vice Chancellor at University of Sunderland
John.Macintyre@sunderland.ac.uk

Abstract. The future of AI is being shaped by many forces – politics, economics, and technology all play their part. Whilst science and academia continue to push forward the boundaries of knowledge, private sector investment in AI is growing exponentially, with commercial revenues from AI expected to exceed $500 billion in the near future. At the forefront of this commercial boom in AI is so-called "Big Tech" – the biggest technology companies driving the commercialization of AI products and systems for profit. These companies have vast R&D budgets, and employ an increasingly large fraction of the AI R&D workforce globally. The question is: are they living up to their responsibilities to develop AI for the good of society, or are they just pursuing profit? Will Big Tech follow the very negative pattern of huge companies prepared to inflict harms on society to boost their profits and shareholder dividends? Professor John MacIntyre's talk will look at the emerging issues in AI and examine what impact the behaviour of Big Tech is having on the whole field of AI.

Contents

**The 2nd Workshop on "Artificial Intelligence in Biomedical
Engineering and Informatics"**

**The 1st Workshop on AI in Energy, Buildings and Micro-Grids
Workshop (AIBMG)**

The 11th Workshop on "Mining Humanistic Data" (MHDW)

The 7th Workshop on "5G – Putting Intelligence to the Network Edge" (5G-PINE)

Preface to 5G-PINE'2022

The seventh, in turn, 5G-PINE Workshop following to the great success and the wider impact of its predecessors, has been established and organized in a concrete and fully efficient way to disseminate knowledge obtained from actual 5G EU-funded projects as well as from other actions of research, in the wider thematic area of "5G Innovative Activities – Putting Intelligence to the Network Edge" and with the aim of focusing upon Artificial Intelligence (AI) in modern 5G-oriented telecommunications infrastructures.

Based on its selected research papers, the 7th 5G-PINE Workshop is once again assesses to have a strong impact on the broader context of the AIAI-2022 International Conference in Aldemar Knossos Royal, Hersonissos, Crete, Greece (scheduled for June 17-20, 2022). Fore once again, the preparatory work has mainly been driven by the hard organizational effort and the dynamic coordination and supervision of **Dr. Ioannis P. Chochliouros** (Hellenic Telecommunications Organization S.A. - OTE, Greece). Support has been provided by: **Dr. Latif Ladid** (President of IPv6 Forum and Researcher of SnT/University of Luxembourg, Luxembourg), **Dr. George Lyberopoulos** (COSMOTE Mobile Telecommunications S.A., Greece), **Mr. Daniele Porcu** (ENEL Global Infrastructure and Networks S.r.l., Italy) also coordinator of the 5G-PPP project "Smart5Grid", **Dr. John Vardakas** (Iquadrat Informatica S.L., Spain) also coordinator of the 5G-PPP project "MARSAL", **Prof. Pavlos Lazaridis** (University of Huddersfield, UK), **Dr. Zaharias Zaharis** (Aristotle University of Thessaloniki, Greece), **Dr. Slawomir** Kukliński and Dr. Lechosław Tomaszewski (Orange Polska, Poland), **Prof. Nancy Alonistioti** (National and Kapodistrian University of Athens, Greece), **Mrs. Christina Lessi** (Hellenic Telecommunications organization S.A., Greece), Prof. Oriol Sallent and Prof. Jordi Pérez-Romero (Universitat Politècnica de Catalunya, Spain) and Dr. Michail-Alexandros Kourtis (National Centre for Scientific Research "DEMOKRITOS", Greece).

Apart from the above members of the Workshop Organising Committee, the entire process has also been supported by more than 80 European experts, several of which coming from the relevant EU-funded H2020/5G-PPP projects **"Smart5GRID"**, **"MARSAL"** and **"5G-ERA"** as well as from the H2020-MCSA-RISE **"RECOMBINE"** project. These projects have formed the "core" of the corresponding effort towards realizing a "joint" 5G-PINE 2022 Workshop, purely 5G oriented.

The 7th 5G-PINE Workshop promotes, inter-alia, the context of modern 5G network infrastructures and of related innovative services in a complex and highly heterogeneous underlying Radio Access Network (RAN) ecosystem, strongly enhanced by the inclusion of cognitive capabilities and intelligence features, with the aim of improving network management. Furthermore, based upon the well-known Self-Organizing Network (SON) functionalities, the 7th 5G-PINE Workshop promotes network planning and optimization processes through Artificial Intelligence- (AI-) based tools, able to smartly process input data from the environment and come up with knowledge that can be formalized in terms of models and/or structured metrics, so that to "depict" the network behavior to a satisfactory level. This allows for gaining in-depth and detailed knowledge about the whole underlying 5G ecosystem, understanding hidden patterns, data structures and relationships and, ultimately, using them for a more efficient network management. In parallel related Key Performance Indicators (KPIs) have also been evaluated, to demonstrate progress implicated by 5G growth. The Workshop also supports delivery of intelligence directly to network's edge, by exploiting the emerging paradigms of Network Functions Virtualisation (NFV), Software Defined Networking (SDN), Network Slicing and Edge Cloud Computing. Moreover, it supports promotion of rich virtualization and multi-tenant capabilities, optimally deployed close to the end-user.

Among the pillars of the 7th 5G-PINE Workshop has been the innovative background of the ongoing 5G-PPP/H2020 **"Smart5Grid"** project, where emphasis has been put both on the description of the corresponding project objectives for the demonstration of 5G solutions to serve smart energy grids as well as upon the description of related use cases coming from the energy vertical industry that may have significant impact on the broader 5G market sector. Two papers have been presented, shortly discussed as follows: (i) Based on the original framework of the Smart5Grid context, one work has examined several fundamental features of the related platform being able to affect 5G implementation as well as the intended NetApps (Network Applications). Therefore this paper has examined: (a) the specific context of smart energy grids, enhanced by the inclusion of ICT and also supported by 5G connectivity; (b) the cloud native context, together with the example of the cloud native VNF modelling, and; (c) the MEC context as a 5G enabler for integrating management, control and orchestration processes. Each among them has been assessed and compared to the actual state of the design and implementation of the Smart5Grid platform. As a step further, a preliminary framework for the definition of the NetApps has been proposed, following to the way how the previous essential features are specifically incorporated within the project processes. (ii) The second accepted paper has been about the detailed presentations of two Smart5Grid use cases of significant interest for the corresponding energy verticals: These are the millisecond level precise distributed generation monitoring and the real-time wide area monitoring. Both use cases have been described, conceptually assessed and evaluated as of their proposed services, their main business goals and their benefits in various sections, with specific emphasis given on the need for the inclusion of 5G facilities.

Moreover, the thematic context of the 7th 5G-PINE Workshop has also been upon the progress of the ongoing 5G-PPP/H2020 **"5G-ERA"** project, aiming to develop an enhanced 5G experimentation facility and relevant Network Applications (NetApps) for 3rd party application developers so as to provide them with a 5G experimentation playground to test and qualify their applications. Taking into account the present state of this project, two papers have been accepted and presented: (i) One paper has been about intent-based networking for 5G enhanced robot autonomy. A detailed work flow of four tools has been proposed comprising of: (a) Action Sequence Generation; (b) Network Intent Estimation; (c) Resource Usage Forecasting, and; (d) OSM Control Policy Generation. All of these have been further discussed with specific function descriptions, inputs, outputs and semantic models/Machine Learning tools that have been used, together with corresponding QoE considerations. (ii) The second paper has been about the use of robotics in critical use cases. 5G-ERA's ambition is to propose robotic solutions targeting vertical sectors such as transport, healthcare, Public Protection and Disaster Relief and Industry 4.0. These sectors require intensive data transmission and processing in order to implement robot collective intelligence approaches, that are technically impossible without the use of 5G networks capabilities. 5G-ERA promotes at a user-centered approach, where the main focus is on the Quality of Experience (QoE) offered for vertical customers. The work of the paper focuses on the description and the evaluation of suitable use cases, in parallel with the network design and corresponding requirements.

An interesting part of the actual Workshop has been around the progress of the ongoing 5G-PPP/H2020 **"LOCUS"** project, where a corresponding accepted paper was about the discussion of a 5G-based architecture, for localization accuracy purposes. LOCUS aims to design and implement an innovative location management layered platform, being able to improve localization accuracy and taking into consideration localization security and privacy concerns, to extend localization with physical analytics and finally to extract value out from the combined interaction of localization and analytics, while guaranteeing users' privacy.

Furthermore, another remarkable area has been the one correlated to the ongoing 5G-PPP/H2020 **"MARSAL"** project, targeting the development and evaluation of a complete framework for the management and orchestration of network resources in 5G and beyond, by utilising a converged optical-wireless network infrastructure in the access and fronthaul/midhaul segments. Upon this core objective, a related paper has presented a conceptual view of the MARSAL architecture, as well as a wide range of corresponding experimentation scenarios, based on latest progress.

The scope of the approved works also included an interesting paper coming from the ongoing 5G-PPP/H2020 **"5G!Drones"** project, discussing potential application of mobile networks (5G and beyond) in Precision Agriculture (PA) to facilitate related use cases. After the requirements assessment and 5G network capabilities analysis, the assignment of currently defined slice types to the typical PA services has been proposed. Moreover, the readiness of the 5G network as well as several missing features with regards to PA, have also identified. Contrary to the stereotypical vision that equates PA with the "low-end" IoT class, the needs of this sector will be a big challenge for the Mobile Network Operators (MNOs) in terms of the required QoS, involving a variety of service architectures and Network Slices Instances (NSIs).

The 7th 5G-PINE Worksop has also hosted a selected paper coming from the 5G-PPP/H2020 **"5G-COMPLETE"** project that focuses on delivering Beyond 5G (B5G) technology innovations in the edge and orchestration domains (among others), that can support highly demanding vertical services/applications and relevant use cases such as Advanced Surveillance along with holistic 5G deployment paradigms and experimentation deployments for testing and evaluation. The related paper has discussed the service and technical requirements and provided a detailed overview of the proposed technologies and deployment solutions, allowing for service lifecycle management based on an application and network orchestration framework.

In a parallel approach, a paper coming from the ongoing 5G-PPP/H2020 **"Int5-Gent"** project has also been accepted. The 5G and beyond advancements will impact significantly the evolution of many vertical industries such as the Public Protection and Disaster Recovery (PPDR) sector. Int5Gent aims at delivering a complete beyond 5G

solution suitable for various PPDR operational scenarios, namely for day-today operations and for disaster scenarios, simultaneously with experimentation deployments for
testing and evaluation. The corresponding paper has discussed the service and technical
requirements and provided an overview of the proposed technologies and deployment
solutions.

The Workshop has also included a detailed paper coming from the H2020
"DataPorts" project. This has discussed a framework for efficient data management
and interoperability middleware in business-oriented smart port use cases. Ports will
play key role in the new information system model, as in-house marketplaces will be
developed, for companies to disseminate and exploit their data and services. The
DataPorts context, through data-centric by design approach, presents a solution where
SMEs, telecom operators, data providers, service content creators and port authorities
can collaborate and coexist into a friendly data-sharing environment. That accomplishment is – and should be – the main goal of platforms that have the ambition to
build and populate an ecosystem, able to attract companies, startups and individual
developers.

Some interesting focus of the 7th 5G-PINE Workshop has also been the framework
promoted by the ongoing H2020-MCSA-RISE **"RECOMBINE"** project, discussing a
variety of aspects about the comparison of a deterministic adaptive beamforming
technique with two different types of Neural Network implementations; these are the
non-linear autoregressive network with exogenous inputs (NARX) and the recurrent
NN (RNN) with long short-term memory units. Using grid search, the authors find the
best architecture for both NNs. Then, they train the final models and evaluate them by
comparing their accuracy to that of the minimum variance distortionless algorithm
(MVDR) algorithm.

The set of the accepted works also include a paper based on the context of the
"ARTIST" project, funded by the Spanish Ministry of Science and Innovation. This
paper proposed the use of deep reinforcement learning to optimally split the traffic
among cells when multi-connectivity is considered in a heterogeneous 4G/5G networks
scenario. Obtained results revealed a promising capability of the proposed Deep Q
Network solution to select quasi-optimum traffic splits depending on the current traffic
and radio conditions in the considered scenario. Moreover, the paper has analysed the
robustness of the obtained policy in front of variations with respect to the conditions
used during the training.

Last but not least, an independent paper has been accepted, describing an intent-
lean AI chatbot solution that handles user queries posed in natural language upon
business related documents of a single-domain of the Hellenic Telecommunications
Organization S.A. Unlike other traditional chatbot solutions that strictly rely on intent
identification, the proposed approach has considered the implicit user need in order to
provide the most relative documents and text snippets within, as the "proper" answer.
The effectiveness of the proposed solution has been measured and identified features
for improvement have been presented.AI chatbots is a promising technology constantly
evolving in the next years with significant academic interest and potential applications
in various enterprises.

As mentioned above, the accepted papers have focused upon several innovative
findings coming directly from modern European research in the area, that is from:

Seven (-7-) 5G-PPP/H2020 projects coming from the current "Phase 3"(i.e.: "Smart5Grid","5G-ERA","MARSAL", "LOCUS", "5G!Drones","5G-COMPLETE" and "Int5Gent); one (-1-) H2020 project (i.e.: "DataPorts"); one (-1) H2020 MCSA-RISE project (i.e.: "RECOMBINE") and; one (-1-) national Spanish project ("ARTIST") also implicating for 5G beneficial uses, *per case*. All the above projects cover a wide variety of technical and business aspects and explicitly promote options for growth and development in the respective market(s). All accepted papers are fully aligned to the objectives of the 7th 5G-PINE scope and purely introduce innovative features, able to "influence" a 5G/B5G effective deployment.

Organization

Co-chairs

Ioannis P. Chochliouros	Hellenic Telecommunications Organization S.A. (OTE), Greece
Latif Ladid	IPv6 Forum and University of Luxembourg, Luxembourg
George Lyberopoulos	COSMOTE - Mobile Telecommunications S.A., Greece
Daniele Porcu	ENEL Global Infrastructure and Networks S.r. l., Italy
John Vardakas	Iquadrat Informatica S.L., Spain
Pavlos Lazaridis	University of Huddersfield, UK
Zaharias Zaharis	Aristotle University of Thessaloniki, Greece
Slawomir Kukliński	Orange Polska & Warsaw University of Technology, Poland
Lechosław Tomaszewski	Orange Polska, Poland
Nancy Alonistioti	National and Kapodistrian University of Athens, Greece
Christina Lessi	Hellenic Telecommunications Organization S.A., Greece
Oriol Sallent	Universitat Politècnica de Catalunya, Spain
Jordi Pérez-Romero	Universitat Politècnica de Catalunya, Spain
Michail-Alexandros Kourtis	National Centre for Scientific Research "DEMOKRITOS", Greece

Program Committee Members

Theodora Politi	Hellenic Telecommunications Organization (OTE), Greece
Alexandros Kostopoulos	Hellenic Telecommunications Organization (OTE), Greece
Anastasios Kourtis	National Centre for Scientific Research "Demokritos", Greece
Sebastien Ziegler	Mandat International, Switzerland
Hicham Khalifé	Thales SIX GTS France SAS, France
Anastasia Spiliopoulou	Hellenic Telecommunications Organization (OTE), Greece

Kelly Georgiadou	OTE, Greece
Nina Mitsopoulou	OTE, Greece
Konstantina Katsampani	OTE, Greece
George Tsiouris	OTE, Greece
George Goulas	OTE, Greece
Dimitrios Mouroukos	OTE, Greece
Elina Theodoropoulou	COSMOTE - Mobile Telecommunications S.A., Greece
Konstantinos Filis	COSMOTE - Mobile Telecommunications S.A., Greece
Ioanna Mesogiti	COSMOTE - Mobile Telecommunications S.A., Greece
Fotini Setaki	COSMOTE - Mobile Telecommunications S.A., Greece
Daniele Munaretto	Athonet S.R.L, Italy
Antonis Georgiou	ACTA Ltd., Greece
Simos Symeonidis	ACTA Ltd., Greece
Dimitrios Tzempelikos	Municipality of Egaleo, Greece
Evridiki Pavlidi	Municipality of Egaleo, Greece
Donal Morris	RedZinc Services, Ireland
Luis Cordeiro	OneSource Consultoria Informatica, LDA, Portugal
Panagiotis Kontopoulos	National & Kapodistrian University of Athens, Greece
Sotiris Nikoletseas	University of Patras, Greece
Vasilios Vlachos	University of Thessaly, Greece
Srdjan Krčo	DunavNET, Serbia
Nenad Gligoric	DunavNET, Serbia
Luca Bolognini	Italian Institute for Privacy, Italy
Camilla Bistolfi	Italian Institute for Privacy, Italy
Konstantinos Patsakis	University of Piraeus, Greece
Vasilios Vassilakis	University of West London, UK
Robert Kołakowski	Warsaw University of Technology, Poland
Sonia Castro	ATOS IT Solutions and Services Iberia SL, Spain
Borja Otura	ATOS IT Solutions and Services Iberia SL, Spain
Miquel Payaró	Centre Tecnològic de Telecomunicacions de Catalunya (CTTC), Spain
Irina Ciornei	University of Cyprus KIOS Research Centre, Cyprus
Nissrine Saraireh	Smart Mobile Labs AG, Germany
Oscar Carrasco	CASA Communications Technology SL, Spain
Nicola di Pietro	Athonet S.R.L, Italy
Konstantinos Tsagkaris	Incelligent, Greece

Dimitrios Brothimas   Independent Power Transmission Operator
                                   S.A., Greece
Nikolaos Tzanis   Independent Power Transmission Operator
                                   S.A., Greece
Ralitsa Rumenova   Entra Energy, Bulgaria
Antonello Corsi   Engineering-Ingegneria Informatica SpA, Italy
Stephanie Oestlund   University of Luxembourg, Luxembourg
Adam Flizikowski   IS-Wireless Pietrzyk Slawomir, Poland
Mike Iosifidis   Clemic Services S.A., Greece

5G for the Support of Smart Power Grids: Millisecond Level Precise Distributed Generation Monitoring and Real-Time Wide Area Monitoring

Ioannis P. Chochliouros[1(✉)] [ID], Daniele Porcu[2], Dimitrios Brothimas[3],
Nikolaos Tzanis[3], Nikolay Palov[4], Ralitsa Rumenova[5], Angelos Antonopoulos[6],
Nicola Cadenelli[6], Markos Asprou[7], Lenos Hadjidemetriou[7], Sonia Castro[8],
Pencho Zlatev[9], Bogdan Bogdanov[10], Thanassis Bachoumis[11], Antonello Corsi[12],
Helio Simeão[13], Michalis Rantopoulos[1], Christina Lessi[1], Pavlos Lazaridis[14],
Zaharias Zaharis[15], and Anastasia S. Spiliopoulou[1]

[1] Hellenic Telecommunications Organization (OTE) S.A., 99 Kifissias Avenue, 15124
Maroussi-Athens, Greece
ichochliouros@oteresearch.gr
[2] ENEL Global Infrastructure and Networks S.r.l., Rome, Italy
[3] Independent Power Transmission Operator S.A., Athens, Greece
[4] Software Company Ltd., Sofia, Bulgaria
[5] Entra Energy, Sofia, Bulgaria
[6] Nearby Computing SL, Barcelona, Spain
[7] University of Cyprus, Nicosia, Cyprus
[8] ATOS IT Solutions and Services Iberia SL, Madrid, Spain
[9] Yugoiztochnoevropeyska Tehnologichna Kompania OOD, Sofia, Bulgaria
[10] Bulgarska TelekominikaKompaniya EAD, Sofia, Bulgaria
[11] Ubitech Energy, Brussels, Belgium
[12] Engineering-Ingegneria Informatica SpA, Rome, Italy
[13] Ubiwhere LDA, Aveiro, Portugal
[14] The University of Huddersfield, Huddersfield, UK
[15] Aristotle University of Thessaloniki, Thessaloniki, Greece

Abstract. Smart grid deployment can strongly be supported and enhanced by the expansion of 5G infrastructures as the latter can offer immense opportunities to enable better efficiency, observability and controllability of the power systems, especially at the distribution side where the numbers of monitoring devices and automation equipment exponentially increase. Among the fundamental context of the original Smart5Grid EU-funded project, we focus upon two selected use cases of significant interest for the corresponding energy vertical sector. These are the millisecond level precise distributed generation monitoring and the real-time wide area monitoring. Both use cases are described, conceptually assessed and evaluated as of their proposed services, their main business goals and their benefits in various sections, with specific emphasis given on the need for the inclusion of 5G facilities.

I. Maglogiannis et al. (Eds.): AIAI 2022 Workshops, IFIP AICT 652, pp. 11–22, 2022.
https://doi.org/10.1007/978-3-031-08341-9_1

Keywords: 5G · Distributed generation monitoring · Energy management · Energy vertical ecosystem · Latency · Network Applications (NetApps) · Network slicing · Smart-grid · Ultra-reliable low latency communications (URLLC) · Wide area monitoring (WAM)

1 Introduction

Large and interconnected power systems are seen as the backbone of the critical infrastructures in any society. They are complex cyber-physical systems for which the communication layer plays an important role in monitoring, control and automation of the grid. So far, the communication networks dedicated to power systems' control and automation were hosted and managed by the electric utility itself. At the same time, telecom providers played little or no role in the communication infrastructure of the power grids, especially upstream the meter of the electricity consumers. However, this status quo is expected to drastically change in the smart grid era, a phase which has already started [1]. The smart grid concept and its deployment environment(s) are aiming to increase efficiency, resilience, reliability and security of the evolved and greener power grids, by means of increased digital automation and control [2]. In this respect, the traditional power grids need to be complemented with advanced communication and information technologies [3, 4], targeting to achieve efficiency and security, in a way that will "reshape" the modern landscape in the energy vertical. With the development of smart grids [5, 6], existing power networks fell short of the demanding requirements of industrial applications, especially with respect to bandwidth, end-to-end latency and reliability. Combining with vertical industry is a major development direction of 5G mobile communication technology, while its communication capacity of large bandwidth, low latency, high reliability as well as massive connection is matched with the service requirements of smart grid service.

The Fifth Generation (5G) of communication networks appears to possess the right features to allow the power grid to tackle the above-mentioned challenges [7, 8]. It is envisioned that 5G networks will play a significant role in the power grid transformation [9] to enable better efficiency, observability, and controllability of the power system, especially at the distribution side [10], where the number of monitoring devices and remote automation equipment is expected to dramatically increase [11, 12]. The vision for 5G is to not only provide better broadband with higher capacity and higher data rates at much lower cost, but also to address entirely new challenges, to enable new services, empower new types of user experiences, and connect new industries. With the continuous development of power grid information construction, 5G network is gradually applied to all aspects of power generation, transmission, transformation, distribution and use [13].

Specifications, such as high data rates and low latency across wide areas of coverage, flexible massive Machine Type Communication (mMTC) specific for dense urban areas, and Ultra-Reliable and Low Latency (URLL) communication are those which could enable a significant shift for the smart grid's communication layer. The flexibility of the 5G technology is the most valuable feature along with modularity and full programmability, allowing fast deployment of services to be tailored to the unique requirements of the energy vertical. This transition from a "horizontal" service model, specific for past mobile network versions such as 3G, 4G and LTE, towards a "vertical" dedicated service model opens the path for a plethora of innovative applications across a variety of industry- or community-related verticals, including the energy vertical [14, 15].

The present paper is composed by several distinct sections: Sect. 1 delineates the necessary introductory framework where the strong innovative correlation between smart grids and 5G is outlined. Section 2 serves as a brief overview of the full scope introduced by the ongoing Smart5Grid EU-funded project, practically structured around four selected use cases of practical market interest. Sections 3 and 4 discuss, in more detail, the corresponding use cases 3 (UC#3) and 4 (UC#4), by focusing on their conceptual descriptions, their proposed services that are related to UC-specific NetApps, their main business goals and services objectives, the need for involving 5G technology and their expected benefits. Section 5 provides some concluding remarks.

2   The Smart5Grid Concept

Taking into account the above concerns, the Smart5Grid EU-funded project [16] is focused on boosting innovation for the highly critical and challenging energy vertical, by providing an open 5G enabled experimentation platform customized to support the much promising smart grid vision for the benefit of the related market sector(s). The Open Smart5Grid experimental platform aims to be an ecosystem where stakeholders in the energy vertical, ICT integrators, Network Applications (NetApps) developers, actors in the telecom industry and/or network service providers in general, could "come together" fostering collaboration and innovation in a fully interactive way. The core goal of the project effort is to validate, both at the technical and business levels, the opportunities offered by the 5G technology [17], to be demonstrated in four meaningful use-cases, relevant to real scenarios of use [18], specifically targeting to the Renewable Energy Sources (RES) production and distribution of energy vertical ecosystem(s).

The proposed four use-cases (UCs) cover a broad range of operations for the power grids and a very diverse set of applications such as: (i) advanced fault-detection, isolation, and self-healing for the power distribution grids (UC#1, in Italy); (ii) enhanced safety tools for maintenance workers in high-voltage power substations (UC#2, in Spain); (iii) advanced and remote monitoring with millisecond precision for dispersed renewable-based power generation units (UC#3, in Bulgaria); and (iv) wide area monitoring of cross-border transmission power grids (UC#4, in Greece and Bulgaria). The UCs addressed by the Smart5Grid project are focused upstream the electricity meter, and more specifically at the power distribution and transmission system operators' sides, as well as at the power generation side, specifically multi-unit renewable generation owners.

These use-cases were specifically chosen in order to "capture" a wide range of operation scenarios for the power systems as well as to "reflect" scalable business needs at the European level for all stakeholders operating in the power distribution grids (e.g., electricity suppliers and Distribution System Operators (DSOs)), European Transmission System Operators (TSOs), owners, aggregators or operators of distributed, renewable-based power generation. The main outcomes from the use-cases analysis are a set of technical, business, and regulatory related requirements which are specific for the highly regulated and standardised energy vertical; and, a set of 5G network requirements which are particular to the Smart5Grid use cases. The requirements of these use cases also addressed the scope of the dedicated NetApps and their service objectives, the sequence diagrams of these services, as well as conditions and technologies involved, *per case.*

Through the effective adoption of 5G networks and the expected assistance of the respective NetApps that will be developed and validated on real power grid facilities, Smart5Grid facilitates the current energy sector stakeholders (i.e. DSOs and TSOs) as well as future smart grid shareholders (i.e.: Smart Grid Operators, Independent System Operators, Energy Aggregators, Regional Distribution Organisations and Energy Service Providers (ESPs), etc.) to: (i) Easily and effectively create and offer advanced energy services; (ii) interact in a dynamic and efficient way, with their surrounding environment (by assessing and considering multiple options), and; (iii) automate and optimise the planning and operation of their power and energy services, thus enhancing their market activity. In this way, Smart5Grid envisages towards providing a more secure, reliable, efficient and real-time communication framework for the modern smart grids.

The emerging 5G mobile cellular network, along with the celebrated new features introduced with it, (i.e.: URLLC, mMTC and enhanced Mobile Broadband (eMBB)) together with the innovative concept of MEC (Multi-Access Edge Computing) which extends the capabilities of cloud computing by bringing it to the edge of the network, provides a competent environment for the case of smart grids [19].

The Smart5Grid architecture which will accommodate and mediate the validation process of the demonstrators revolves around the Network Function Virtualisation (NFV) concept. The design targets an open experimentation facility for 3rd party NetApps developers, fully softwarised, and which integrates an Open Service Repository (OSR), a framework for Validation and Verification (V&V), and a flexible and modularized Management and Orchestration (M&O) framework.

The open testing platform built in the context of Smart5Grid will allow the implementation and experimentation with appropriate VNFs (Virtual Network Functions) [20] and NetApps, not only to Smart5Grid partners but also to third parties (i.e. entities outside the contractual Smart5Grid consortium). This will support and "give rise" to an experimental execution environment that increases reliability, availability and maintainability in smart grid energy networks, through application of specialised 5G solutions.

3   UC#3: Millisecond Level Precise Distributed Generation Monitoring

The scope of **UC#3** is the millisecond level precise distributed generation monitoring which addresses the domain of the distributed energy operation and maintenance with a specific focus on renewables [21]. Specifically, in the context of this UC, the real-time (RT) monitoring of a wind farm is to be performed, by using the emerging capabilities of 5G telecommunication networks. RT monitoring is vital for the proper operation of the wind farms, mainly for two reasons: (i) The owner, being aware of the RT condition of the farm, can predict and prevent on time potential future malfunctions that will cause significant financial losses, and; (ii) the wind farm owners, acting both as a BRP

(Balancing Responsible Party[1]) and BSP (Balancing Service Provider[2]), are account-able for the potential imbalances and for the provision of the committed services in the real-time market, respectively [22]. Hence, high granularity precise monitoring of the RT power production will offer the capability to wind farm owners to minimize their cost and, simultaneously, being eligible for provision of ancillary and innovative flexi-bility services (voltage regulation, congestion management, etc.) through flexible plant management. In addition, UC#3 intends to demonstrate a working solution of a dis-tributed Renewable Energy Sources (RES) generator/producer, which could be adopted and implemented on a bigger scale for other RES producers during the post project market exploitation stage [23]. The strict requirements set by power system operators for the service provision by RES, render essential the utilization of a highly reliable and secure telecommunication connection between the physical asset (wind farm) and the dispatch centre of the operator.

In the context of UC#3, the goal is to facilitate energy generation forecast for balanc-ing purposes and to enable energy cost optimization as well as visualization of end-users' behaviour to optimally manage their energy profile for operational availability, and provi-sion of flexibility services through respective electricity markets (intraday and balancing markets), in millisecond-level information exchange. Regarding operational availabil-ity, an illustrative example showing the benefits is the following one: it is important the wind farm owner, or aggregator or DSO to be confident if the power plant is currently in operation. Sometimes due to maintenance, inspection, or unforeseen circumstances, the power plant may not be in operation. In such a case, the power plant manager may for-get to notify the aggregator/DSO which can result in heavy balancing costs (unbalance penalties occur). In case of RT monitoring such mistake can be found in time, allowing cost optimization. Regarding the provision of flexibility services, the wind farm can pro-vide all its RT operational information to the system operators, allowing flexible plant management for procuring accurate and secure frequency and voltage control services [24] by the DSOs/TSOs.

Thus, *two services are targeted as part of UC#3 which are related to two distinct and UC-specific NetApps.* These are briefly described as follows:

- *Predictive maintenance:* gathering measurements from sensors capturing the perfor-mance of key components of the wind turbines, and thus offering to the wind farm owner information regarding the asset performance of the wind farm, and to the power system operator (i.e., TSO) information about operational availability of the asset.
- *Real-time energy production monitoring:* The wind farm owner and the power system operator (i.e., TSO) monitor RT energy production of the wind farm in a millisecond basis. On the one side, wind farm owner can increase efficiency and accuracy of both

---

[1] A BRP in the EU internal electricity market is a market participant or its chosen represen-tative responsible for its "imbalances" (i.e., deviations between generation, consumption and commercial transactions).

[2] A BSP in the EU internal electricity market is a market participant providing balancing ser-vices (here the term "balancing" stands for either or both balancing capacity and balancing energy) to its connecting TSO (Transmission System Operator) or in case of the TSO-BSP Model to its contracting TSO.

production control and forecasting, using also other information, such as weather data. On the other side, TSO can enhance power system stability through the supervision of RES production in hard-real-time.

From the vertical application point of view, there are three **main business goals or level objectives** about: (i) Offering predictive maintenance recommendation services in the wind farm (located in a rural area), by receiving RT measurements from multiple sensors; (ii) providing RT monitoring services of the energy generation of the controlled wind farm in hard RT conditions, and; (iii) providing the wind farm owner live monitoring features through a web-based dashboard and/or an application upon a smartphone device.

In order to accomplish the previous defined business level objectives, the following **technical objectives** are defined: (i) Collecting RT measurements from the sensors existing at different locations of the wind farm; (ii) forecasting the energy production of the wind farm in order to participate in the day-ahead, intra-day and balancing electricity markets; (iii) collecting RT measurements of the energy production in order to conduct RT control, and; (iv) analyzing data to offer data analytics services regarding predictive maintenance and RT operation of the wind farm.

The **need for 5G technology** for the development of this use case is based on the following reasons: (i) Previous generations of wireless technology do not fulfil the criteria for low-latency and high reliability in millisecond basis, as imposed by the UC3#'specifications; (ii) anticipating and foreseeing the massive deployment of Distributed Energy Resources (DERs) that are going to enter the grid, there is a need for new technology that could assist the transformation the grid is going to experience as well as the issues that will arise from that. The envision that more and more Internet of Things- (IoT-) enabled energy devices will be connected and also controlled by aggregators or system operators render necessary the investigation of robust solutions that consider the scalability aspect. In this case, we are talking about a widespread IoT ecosystem that includes millions or even billions of devices that operate on a range speed, have different bandwidth as well as a variety of quality and service (QoS) requirements. To achieve that, technologies before 5G cannot provide the needed coverage, latency, security, and cost optimization. Hence, scalability can be achieved through the utilization of 5G infrastructure, where more RES and IoT devices can be connected to the NetApp without deteriorating the performance of the services; (iii) compared to the optical fibre, 5G offers a more flexible and cost-efficient way of communication, with similar values of the above-mentioned metrics, and; (iv) the rural location of the RES significantly increases the capex in new projects, due to the high cost for dedicated investments in fibre infrastructure. Hence, the utilization of 5G can provide incentives to RES owners to further invest in new installations, by utilizing 5G networks even for the last mile network connection.

The **benefits** coming from UC#3 can be classified in several categories such as:

Business: Increased visibility in wind farm operation, not only from an energy production point of view but also from a multi-parameter wind turbine life cycle perspective provides the owners fertile ground to better manage their assets and offer innovative flexibility services. This is important as a well-functioning internal market in electricity should provide producers with appropriate incentives for investing in new power generation, including in electricity from renewable energy sources, while it should also provide consumers with adequate measures to promote more efficient use of energy, which presupposes a secure supply of energy.

Economic: Replacing parts of the wind turbines on time before the complete performance degradation of the wind farm, leads to continuous uninterruptible production, minimizing, at the same time, the maintenance cost. Having knowledge of the RT production in a millisecond basis, the system operator can minimize the overall system cost and the owner can benefit financially by providing innovative services to the operator, such as voltage regulation. In addition to that, better portfolio management of the BRPs can lead to lower deviations from the committed program and thus to lower needs and cost for balancing services.

Social: Secure and uninterruptible energy provision to the end-user.

Environmental: High visibility in RES production leads to better management of the power system and thus reducing the need for RES curtailment in order to alleviate congestion issues and imbalances. Higher participation rate of RES in the energy mix leads to cleaner energy production and lower levels of CO_2 emissions.

Technological: 5G is a relatively new technology and researching, testing and validating IoT devices to work over 5G in a real use case will pave the way for further adoption of IoT devices over 5G into energy sector and other industry verticals.

4 UC#4: Real-Time Wide Area Monitoring

The scope of **UC#4** is the real-time monitoring of a geographical wide area where cross-border power exchanges take place. UC#4 addresses the energy reliability and security domain of the broad energy vertical. Specifically, in the context of this UC, the interconnection flow between Greece and Bulgaria is monitored leveraging the advantages that the 5G telecommunication infrastructure provides. This function will be executed from the newly established Regional Security Coordinator (RSC) in Thessaloniki, Greece. The role of the RSC is to promote regional cooperation and to support the strengthening of the neighbouring power systems and market operations in the region. To achieve the enhancement of the interconnected power system operation, live monitoring of the power flows between the countries under its area of interest is of vital importance. Hence, this UC can be considered as the development of an additional element that increases the live monitoring capability of the RSC. Phasor Measurements Units (PMUs) located at the High Voltage network of Northern Greece, monitoring the interconnection area with Bulgaria, will be used as the input in the monitoring process of the RSC. By incorporating time-stamped synchronized PMU measurements high data granularity can be achieved (receiving the requested data 50 to 60 times per second, including positive, negative and zero sequence phasors of voltage and currents) [25–27]. A virtual Phasor Data Concentrator (vPDC) will be developed for the data gathering process. The utilization of 5G in UC#4 contributes to the connectivity between the PMUs and the vPDC, offering its low latency and high reliability needed, due to the criticality of the UC.

To give a broader perspective, it is worth mentioning that the continuous expansion of of the European high penetration rate of the Distributed Energy Resources (DERs) significantly increases the complexity of the power system making its RT operation and control functions demanding and difficult to handle. As the DER penetration rate increases, inverter-connected devices dominate, leading to the lack of physical inertia. The lack of inertia results in significant variations in the Rate of Change of Frequency (RoCoF), thus subsequently resulting in fundamental changes in the dynamic behaviour of the power system. Therefore, for the proper RT operation of the power system, the existence of a Wide Area Monitoring (WAM) system is essential [28, 29], that is capable of capturing and alleviating dynamic phenomena that create hazardous conditions for the stability of the entire interconnected European power system. Occurrences taking place at a specific location of the power system are able to create instability in the entire power system. WAM systems mainly leverage the high accuracy of PMUs and the low latency of the new era telecommunication networks [30]. Multiple control areas exist in the European power system, where each Transmission System Operator is responsible for the control of its system. For the proper coordination between neighbouring control areas, RSCs owned by adjacent TSOs were established. One of the RSC's goals is the coordinated security analysis in multiple timeframes (day-ahead, intraday and real-time). Regarding the RT monitoring of their area (including areas controlled by multiple TSOs), the RSCs provide advice to the TSOs for the proper operation of the power system. In addition, an RSC contributes by offering post-event feedback (in case of a major grid disturbance or frequency deviations) to the concerned TSOs in order to develop and improve guidelines for this kind of problematic situation. In the context of this UC, the RT monitoring function of the respective RSC from PMU measurements from Northern Greece monitoring the interconnection area is demonstrated. Afterwards, TSOs can leverage the information of their connected assets and the recommendations arriving from the RSC in order to perform better control actions and alleviate occurrences that threaten system stability.

Interconnected power systems often face frequency oscillations that tend to challenge their proper way of operation, even leading to instability of the system. A very effective way to monitor those events is the use of the synchronized measurements provided by the PMUs, which are placed near the borders of the connected power systems. These measurements are gathered by the PDCs in order to be sorted accordingly and get forwarded to the WAM service [31]. However, due to the vast amount of data provided by the PMUs and their criticality, a highly reliable means of communications is needed to ensure the flawless monitoring of the power system. This is where the 5G infrastructure can be utilized, offering that high reliability and low latency needed, as well as the flexibility to add more measurement units, without high cost and hard to move installations (e.g., optical fibre).

The UC#4 specific NetApps aim to cover *three types of services:*

- *vPDC Service:* The first service that this use case addresses is the vPDC that is responsible for data gathering from the PMUs placed in the broader interconnection area of Greece and Bulgaria. In that way, they are going to be comparable to each other. The vPDC receives and time-synchronizes phasor data from multiple PMUs to produce a RT, time-aligned output data stream. Virtualization of the PDC significantly minimizes communication and transfer delays in the network as it is closer to the PMUs. It also minimizes the implementation cost.

- *WAM Service:* Afterwards, the WAM service will present several status indicators and visualization features of the PMUs. Some of those features may be: (i) A map indicating the device's current location; (ii) the device's name, address, model, serial number and firmware version; (iii) the nominal grid frequency [Hz] and the current reporting speed [fps]; (iv) the phase diagram with voltage and current vectors displayed (updated in near-RT), and; (v) voltage magnitude and angle difference monitoring, derived from historical data of both sites.
- *Advisory Service:* The third service will provide advisory indications for RT operation to both TSOs, and ex-post analysis provision in case of severe event occurrence in the grid.

Business Goals: The Primary Actor of this use case can be considered the entity that monitors both concerned transmission grids. The RSC may be responsible for this task. Both TSOs (i.e., Greek and Bulgarian) involved in the use case can be considered as facilitators providing access to the measurement infrastructure (i.e., the PMUs). The business goal of the RSC is the RT monitoring of the supervision area and the provision to the TSOs of the information and strategies for the proper coordinated security analysis and operation of the system in RT conditions. By doing so, the power system in the greater region operates under secure conditions and is robust towards abnormal dynamic contingencies that threaten the overall system balance.

Service objectives: In terms of services, the goal is the monitoring of the PMUs' status and the visualisation of their features in such a way that efficient suggestions regarding power system control will be offered to the TSOs. Such indicators may be the voltage and current values as well as the angle between them, and, of course, the RoCoF value in both sides of the area to be monitored. The combination of different features and the comparison of each one with its symmetrical could also reveal hidden but useful results and deductions.

The **need for 5G technology** for the development of UC#4 is based on the following reasons: (i) Previous generations of wireless networks do not fulfil the latency, bandwidth, and reliability requirements imposed by the criticality of the application; (ii) compared to the optical fibre, 5G offers a more flexible and cost-efficient way of communication, with similar values for the aforementioned metrics.

Expected benefits are briefly discussed covering the following distinct categories:

Business: Better monitoring of the power system for the RSC leads both of the operators to have an enhanced monitoring ability and supervision of their area by being aware of the adjacent energy network condition.

Economic: By establishing an adequate level of coordination, faults leading to severe conditions in the transmission system such as outages can be captured and handled in time, saving TSOs from costs due to the energy not being provided to the customers. In addition to that, better network observability in the critical elements connecting Greece and Bulgaria can increase the energy transfer between the two countries, leading to stronger electricity market coupling between the countries and thus potential financial benefits for both.

Social: Secure and uninterruptible energy provision to the participating end-users.

Environmental: Higher share of renewable energy sources in the energy production mix significantly reduces the usage of fossil-dependent conventional power plants, thus leading to CO_2 emissions' reduction. However, the high penetration of RES increases security issues due to their intermittent stochastic nature and the inverter-based grid connection. This use case can be seen as a step to increase coordination security, an essential element for the further increase in the penetration rate of RES. Therefore, we can consider that this use case has indirect environmental benefits.

5   Concluding Remarks

A smart grid is a modernized power grid which uses information and communication technologies to collect information from the power grid. This information is used to adjust the production and distribution of electricity or to adjust power consumption in order to save energy, reduce losses and enhance the reliability of the power grid. In a normal power grid, devices are monitored manually onsite. With smart grids, these devices can be monitored and measured remotely and can automatically determine, adjust, and control power usage. Therefore, connecting these devices to the communications network is fundamental to smart grid construction and efficient operation.

As a representative example of the vertical industry, smart grid implicates for new and very important challenges to modern communications networks. In particular, the diversity of power grid services requires a flexible and orchestrated network, high reliability requires isolated networks and millisecond-level ultra-low latency requires networks with optimal capabilities. 5G networks constitute an ideal choice to enable smart grid services. 5G network slicing allows the power grid to flexibly customize specific slices with different network functions and different SLA (Service Level Agreement) assurances according to the needs, to meet different network requirements of various services. 5G also contributes to the effective integration of a multiplicity of devices to smart grids, it allows handling of immense data sets and permits for exact monitoring and management of energy needs of various underlying systems, thus providing benefits in a variety of applications and related services.

Being within this scope, the Smart5Grid project is a modern EU-funded research oriented initiative, around four distinct operational use cases scheduled to be implemented in four European countries. The core aim of the effort is to structure a modern platform able to serve high performance smart grids, especially with the implementation/experimentation of appropriate VNFs and corresponding NetApps.

In the present work we discuss, in more detail, two of the proposed uses cases, dealing with millisecond level precise distributed generation monitoring and RT wide area monitoring, correspondingly. The aim has been about explaining the relevant conceptual background as well as about discussing their proposed services related to UC-specific NetApps, their main business goals and the expected benefits in various categories, in parallel with support provided by the inclusion of 5G technology.

Acknowledgments. This work has been performed in the scope of the *Smart5Grid* European Research Project and has been supported by the Commission of the European Communities */5G-PPP/H2020, Grant Agreement No.101016912.*

References

1. Refaat, S.S., Ellabban, O., Bayhan, S., Abu-Rub, H., Blaabjerg, F., Begovic, M.M.: Smart Grid Standards and Interoperability. Smart grid and enabling technologies. Wiley-IEEE Press, Hoboken (2021)
2. Institute of Electrical and Electronic Engineers (IEEE): IEEE smart grid vision for vehicular technology 2030 and beyond reference model (webinar). In: Vehicular IEEE Smart Grid Vision for Vehicular Technology 2030 and Beyond Reference Model (Webinar), pp. 1–7 (2017)
3. Bakken, D.: Smart Grids—Cloud, Communications, Open Source, and Automation. CRC Press, Boca Raton (2014)
4. Gungor, V.C., Sahin, D., et al.: Smart grid technologies: Communication technologies and standards. Trans. Ind. Inf. **7**(4), 529–539 (2011)
5. Tuballa, M.L., Abundo, M.L.: A review of the development of smart grid technologies. Renew. Sustain. Energy Rev. **59**(c), 710–725 (2016)
6. Butt, O.M., Zulqarnain, M., Butt, T.M.: Recent advancement in smart grid technology: future prospects in the electrical power network. Ain Shams Eng. J. **12**(1), 687–695 (2021)
7. Liu, R., et al.: Application of 5G network slicing technology in smart grid. In: Proceedings of the 2021 IEEE 2nd International Conference on Big Data, Artificial Intelligence and Internet of Things Engineering (ICBAIE), pp. 740–743. IEEE (2021)
8. Li, W., Liu, R., Dai, Y., Wang, D., Cai, H., Fan. J., Li, Y.: Research on network slicing for smart grid. In: Proceedings of the 2020 IEEE 10th International Conference on Electronics Information and Emergency Communication (ICEIEC), pp. 107–110. IEEE (2020)
9. Matinkhah, S.M., Shafik, W.: Smart grid empowered by 5G technology. In: Proceedings of the 2019 IEEE Smart Grid Conference (SGC), pp. 1–6. IEEE (2019)
10. Li, W., Wu, Z., Zhang, P.: Research on 5G network slicing for digital power grid. In: Proceedings of the 2020 IEEE 3rd International Conference on Electronic Information and Communication Technology (ICEICT), pp. 679–682. IEEE (2020)
11. Cosovic, M., Tsitsimelis, A., Vukobratovic, D., Matamoros, J., Anton-Haro, C.: 5G Mobile cellular networks: Enabling distributed state estimation for smart grids. IEEE Commun. Mag. **55**(10), 62–69 (2017)
12. Meng, S., Wang, Z., Tang, M., Wu, S., Li, X.: Integration application of 5G and Smart Grid. In: Proceedings of the IEEE 2019 11th International Conference on Wireless Communications and Signal Processing (WCSP), pp. 1–7. IEEE (2019)
13. China Telecom Research Institute, et al.: 5G network slicing enabling the smart grid. https://www-file.huawei.com/-/media/CORPORATE/PDF/News/5g-network-slicing-enabling-the-smart-grid.pdf
14. Global System for Mobile Communications Association (GSMA): Smart grid 5G network slicing (2020). https://www.gsma.com/futurenetworks/wiki/smart-grid-5g-network-slicing/
15. Global System for Mobile Communications Association (GSMA): Powered by SA: Smart grid 5G network slicing. SGCC, China Mobile and Huawei (2020). https://www.gsma.com/futurenetworks/wp-content/uploads/2020/03/2_Powered-by-SA_Smart-Grid-5G-Network-Slicing_China-Telecom_GSMA_v2.0.pdf
16. Smart5Grid Project (Grant Agreement No.101016912). https://smart5grid.eu/
17. Chochliouros, I.P., Spiliopoulou, A.S., Lazaridis, P., Dardamanis, A., Zaharis, Z., Kostopoulos, A.: Dynamic Network Slicing: Challenges and Opportunities. In: Maglogiannis, I., Iliadis, L., Pimenidis, E. (eds.) AIAI 2020. IFIP AICT, vol. 585, pp. 47–60. Springer, Cham (2020). https://doi.org/10.1007/978-3-030-49190-1_5
18. Porcu, D., et al.: 5G communications as "Enabler" for smart power grids: the case of the Smart5Grid Project. In: Maglogiannis, I., Macintyre, J., Iliadis, L. (eds.) AIAI 2021. IFIP

AICT, vol. 628, pp. 7–20. Springer, Cham (2021). https://doi.org/10.1007/978-3-030-791 57-5_1

19. Chochliouros, I.P., et al.: Putting intelligence in the network edge through NFV and cloud computing: the SESAME approach. In: Boracchi, G., Iliadis, L., Jayne, C., Likas, A. (eds.) EANN 2017. CCIS, vol. 744, pp. 704–715. Springer, Cham (2017). https://doi.org/10.1007/978-3-319-65172-9_59

20. European Telecommunications Standards Institute: ETSI GS NFV 002 V1.2.1 (2014-12): Network functions virtualisation (NFV); architectural framework. ETSI. http://www.etsi.org/deliver/etsi_gs/NFV/001_099/002/01.02.01_60/gs_nfv002v010201p.pdf

21. International Renewable Energy Agency (IRENA): Global energy transformation: a roadmap to 2050. IRENA (2019)

22. European Commission (2017): Commission Regulation (EU) 2017/2195 of 23 November 2017 establishing a guideline on electricity balancing. Offic. J. L312, pp. 6–53

23. Alotaibi, I., Abido, M.A., Khalid, M., Savkin, A.V.: A comprehensible review of recent advances in smart grids: a sustainable future with renewable energy resources. Energies 13, 62–69 (2020)

24. Rebours, Y.G., Kirschen, D.S., Trotignon, M., Rossignol, S.: A survey of frequency and voltage control ancillary services—Part I: Technical features. IEEE Trans. Power Syst. 22(1), 350–357 (2007)

25. Phadke, A.G., Bi, T.: Phasor measurement units, WAMS, and their applications in protection and control of power systems. J. Mod. Power Syst. Clean Ener. 6(4), 619–629 (2018). https://doi.org/10.1007/s40565-018-0423-3

26. Phadke, A.G., Thorp, J.S.: Synchronized phasor measurements and their applications. Springer, Blacksburg (2008)

27. Göl, M., Abur, A.: A hybrid state estimator for systems with limited number of PMUs. IEEE Trans. Power Syst. 30(3), 1511–1517 (2015)

28. Appasani, B., Mohanta, D.K.: A review on synchrophasor communication system: communication technologies, standards and applications. Prot. Cont. Mod. Power Syst. 3(1), 1–17 (2018). https://doi.org/10.1186/s41601-018-0110-4

29. Zacharia, L., Asprou, M., and Kyriakides, E: Measurement errors and delays on wide area control based on IEEE Std C37.118.1-2011: Impact and compensation. IEEE Syst. J. 14(1), 422–432 (2020)

30. Institute of Electrical and Electronic Engineers (IEEE): IEEE guide for synchronization, calibration, testing, and installation of phasor measurement units (PMUs) for power system protection and control. IEEE Std C37.242-2013, pp. 1–107 (2013)

31. Zhu, K.: Data quality in wide-area monitoring and control systems: PMU data latency, completeness, and design of wide-area damping systems. Doctoral thesis. KTH Royal Institute of Technology (2013). https://www.diva-portal.org/smash/get/diva2:649889/FULLTEXT01.pdf

A 5G-Based Architecture for Localization Accuracy

Maria Belesioti[1]([✉]) [ID], Kostas Tsagkaris[2], Aristotelis Margaris[2], and Ioannis P. Chochliouros[1]

[1] Hellenic Telecommunications Organization (OTE) S.A., 99 Kifissias Avenue, 15124 Maroussi-Athens, Greece
mbelesioti@oteresearch.gr
[2] Incelligent, Athens, Greece

Abstract. Future communications technologies will radically transform the way we communicate, by introducing a vast array of capabilities and services. In current 5G networks, key elements such as increased bandwidth, smaller cells, high density, multiple radio access technologies and device-to-device (D2D) communication can offer great benefit in localization services. Telecom operators and ICT companies have accepted the challenge to develop and integrate mobile localization technologies, powered by AI algorithms and machine-learning techniques, which will exploit the location information while, at the same time, preserve end-users' privacy. The use of these technologies will enhance location-based communication and network management techniques as well as mobility and radio resource management. In this paper, we present the ambition coming from the framework of the LOCUS EU-funded project [1]. LOCUS aims to design and implement an innovative location management layered platform which will be able to improve localization accuracy, taking into consideration localization security and privacy concerns, to extend localization with physical analytics and finally to extract value out from the combined interaction of localization and analytics, while guaranteeing users' privacy.

Keywords: 5G · Artificial Intelligence (AI) · Localization analytics & services · Localization awareness · Machine learning (ML) · Network function (NF) · Privacy

1 Introduction

The deployment of 5G networks is expected to provide improvement in terms of capacity, number of connected devices and latency. Location awareness in mobile communication systems will enable many location-based applications and services while improving communication system performance [2]. However, the performance of these applications depends on the location accuracy [3]. Global Navigation Satellite System (GNSS), can offer in urban environments an approximate accuracy of five meters, when in dense urban areas, wireless local area network (WLAN) fingerprinting techniques can offer a

© IFIP International Federation for Information Processing 2022
Published by Springer Nature Switzerland AG 2022
I. Maglogiannis et al. (Eds.): AIAI 2022 Workshops, IFIP AICT 652, pp. 23–33, 2022.
https://doi.org/10.1007/978-3-031-08341-9_2

3–4 m accuracy. When it comes to 5G networks, the expectation have been risen to one meter or even below [4], with the adoption of disruptive technologies such as device-centric architectures, millimeter wave, massive multiple-in multiple-out (MIMO) and native support for machine-to-machine (M2M) communications [5]; this is significantly better than long term evolution (LTE) systems by observed time difference of arrival (OTDoA)-based techniques.

In addition, context-awareness is essential for many existing and emerging applications and it mainly relies on location information of people and things. Localization, together with analytics and their combined provision "as a service", will greatly increase the overall value of the 5G ecosystem, allowing network operators to better manage their networks and to dramatically expand the range of offered applications and services.

In the scope of the LOCUS vision, location information supplementary to context information will address several challenges in 5G networks by complementing already existing technologies. For instance, in 2G, user's position could be identified based on the cell serving his mobile phone with the accuracy ranging from tens of meters to dense urban areas to hundreds of meters to rural. However, in the 5G framework, seamless and ubiquitous location awareness will enforce the precision of location accuracy and will enable new services based on modern positioning technologies. To this respect, during the project's lifetime, integration of both 3GPP and non-3GPP technologies in 5G Core will be attempted and a virtualization and software platform that will enhance location accuracy and serve localization analytics for new service(s) will be developed.

The second Section of the paper provides an overview of 5G localization techniques and technologies, while the third one introduces the concept of locations awareness. Sections 4 and 5 refer exclusively to the context of the LOCUS project; its concept and dedicated objectives are highlighted and the proposed fundamental architecture along with the key functionalities is thoroughly analyzed. Section 6 is dedicated to privacy in localization-based services, while Sect. 7 concludes the paper.

2 Technologies for 5G Localization

Localization techniques become more accurate as cellular networks are evolving. In previous mobile networks generations, localization performed on user equipment (UEs) could not achieve high accuracy, especially concerning indoor environments. In Long Term Evolution (LTE) networks, positioning methods were dependent on radio access techniques (RATs) exploiting LTE signals or on using other signals such as Global Positioning System (GPS) which were independent of the RATs. The use of uplink time difference-of-arrival (UTDOA) allowed enhanced NodeBs (eNBs) to collect time difference-of-arrival (TDOA) measurements of the signal transmitted by UEs and esti-mate their exact position [6]. Future 5G devices will depend on ubiquitous location awareness, supported by accurate location information utilized by 5G networks across all layers of the communication protocol stack [7].

5G uses cases (cf. Fig. 1) are driven by the needs and requirements of Industry 4.0 ver-ticals, acting as key enablers, and are designed to "address" specific challenges of these verticals. In 5G, disruptive technologies such as device-centric architectures, mmWave, massive multiple-in multiple-out, smart devices, and native support for machine-to-machine (M2M) communications will be implemented in a way also to assist localization accuracy [5]. These technologies require wide bandwidths so as to meet capacity requirements and with the use of higher frequency bands such as mm waves, they can provide higher system capacity, especially in dense urban environments where the deployment of a large number of small cells enables massive MIMO and very accurate beamforming. The 5G networks shall exploit frequently transmitted uplink (UL) signals which, together with wide bandwidths enable accurate time of arrival (ToA) estimates which, in turn, provide an opportunity for positioning with remarkably high accuracy [8]. These features will enhance UE positioning accuracy both inside buildings and in dense urban areas, providing awareness of the current but also of the past UE location and in some cases, with the use of predictive algorithms, can even predict the UE location.

Related 3GPP specifications [9] analyze other access technologies, such as Wi-Fi, that can provide flexibility in the access of non-3GPP networks. As it is stated in Release 16 [10], non-3GPP access networks can use the same 5G Core for service provisioning, enhancing integration between these heterogeneous access networks as 3GPP ones.

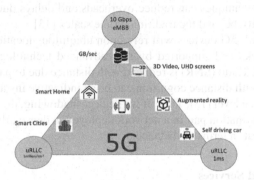

Fig. 1. 5G usage scenarios

As far as indoor location is concerned, Wi-Fi and Bluetooth are the most commonly used technologies providing high accuracy, but with significant shortcomings in terms of range and penetration. So, as it is evident, there is a need for a technology that "meets globally" the augmented demands of localization. 5G has all the potential to fulfill the requested requirements and, moreover, with the use of analytics and advanced location aware techniques can reduce overheads and delays, due to their ability to predict channel quality beyond traditional time scale.

3 Location Awareness in 5G Networks

The Global Positioning System (GPS) enabled smartphones to allow users locating their position, within accuracy of about 5 m, with a unidirectional flow of information meaning that the system cannot determine UEs location automatically and send this information to satellite [11]. Location awareness is the "key element" for a number of emerging applications in the 5G context and is expected to increase further in future 6G networks, receiving intense attention from both the business sector and the research community.

Location awareness is based on network's knowledge about the user's current location and can be utilized in many ways, in order to sufficiently meet 5G challenges. It is directly related with the use of information from a network owner—or an OTT (over-the-top) player—that provides information and services to specific user(s), all related to its current position [12]. In 5G and beyond networks, UEs will be able to determine their exact position in terms of coordinates with high accuracy, so specific information relevant to each user's position, in a given moment, can be forwarded to him/her.

Actually, location information is considered as one among the most important aspects in 5G networks and as the key enabler of location-based services. The performance of such services is purely dependent on the location accuracy. Location analytics are meant to exploit this information by incorporating it into dedicated network features, so as to utilize it in terms of real-time (RT) tracking of a UE location with high precision and accuracy. This sort of sophisticated spatial information will provide better knowledge related to processes as well as behavioral mechanism(s) to enhance predictive and coverage models and to enable the offering of application based on it. Location-aware resource allocation techniques can reduce overheads and delays due to their ability to predict channel quality beyond the traditional time scales [13].

On the other hand, 5G devices will rely upon ubiquitous location awareness, provided by 5G networks and supported by new advanced technological developments [14]. Signal-to-Noise Ratio (SNR) is reduced with distance due to path loss, so location awareness together with distance cognition can be an indicative instance of the received power and interference level [13]. Thus, if we neglect shadowing, the best multihop path between a source-destination pair in a network deployed in dense urban environment, is the one that is shortest in terms of distance.

3.1 Location Based Services

Location Based Services (LBSs) are in reality services that provide information to users exploiting the utilization of geographical raw data and processed information, in real time. The arrival of 5G cellular networks has contributed in the enhancement of LBS in terms of accuracy, speed and latency. Although, 3GPP distinguishes LBSs and location services, most times the terms are being confused. More specifically, location services deal with the automated localization of UEs and with the provision of location data to external stakeholders, without necessarily processing it. In addition, LBSs are often considered as context aware services, due to their ability to adapt their behavior [2].

5G uses massive MIMO beamforming and mmWave signals. The use of mmWave technology offers a two-fold advantage when it comes to LBSs, that is: the availability of large bandwidth and the ability to have many antenna elements even in small spaces [15].

The aim of achieving accurate location awareness in mobile networks implicates for the need of integration of sensing and communication where optimization, signal processing and data fusion will be under a common framework [16]. Since most 5G terminals will be associated with people, their mobility pattern could be considered to be predictable and this information could be exploited by a variety of LBSs.

4 The Fundamental LOCUS Concept

LOCUS aims to design and develop a location management layered infrastructure capable of improving localization accuracy and security as well as to extend it with physical analytics, extracting value out of it, meanwhile guaranteeing the end-users' right to privacy [17].

The project envisages to make localization and related analytics a first class priority in the cellular world; this is due to the appearing market trends that expected that evolution of 5G, both in the short and in the long term, shall address not only communication but also localization functionalities. Starting from the context of the 3GPP Release 16 [18], this is extending the functionality of 5G infrastructures to enable positioning reference signals, measurements and procedure information. Building on top of these components, adequate low complexity algorithms and scenario-dependent deployment designs can enable 5G and beyond networks to: (i) provide accurate and ubiquitous information on the location of physical targets as a network-native service, and; (ii) derive complex features and behavioral patterns from raw location and physical events, which can be exposed to application developers.

Localization, appropriate dedicated analytics and their combined provision "as a service" will greatly increase the overall value of the 5G ecosystem and beyond, and will allow network operators to dramatically expand their range of offered services, enabling holistic sets of user-, location- and context-targeted applications.

Moreover, LOCUS localization solutions, aim to extend the 3GPP Rel.16 positioning service levels, meeting the enhanced requirements in terms of accuracy, availability and latency dictated by 5G challenges, and in addition to develop new applications or improve already existing ones that are based on high location accuracy and low response times. Currently, outdoor localization depends on the accuracy of GNSS. The LOCUS ecosystem is expected to improve both outdoor and indoor accuracy with the use of analytics tools for processing huge amounts of target-based and/or context-based location information and with the exploitation and coexistence of wireless and cellular networks. As far as 5G is concerned, LOCUS will exploit the benefits of 5G networks for localization and analytics services as follows:

- 5G network devices can easily derive both time- and environment-related information and exploit them to strongly improve localization accuracy.
- 5G network devices are expected to be very close to users, hence they can provide low-latency location services, much faster than remote servers in the Internet.
- 5G will avail itself of virtualization tools for network functions and services.
- 5G virtualization platforms can be exploited to perform localization and the related analytics; primitive virtualized functions can also be specialized to match the requirements of vertical applications in a multi-tenancy scenario.

5 The LOCUS Architecture

The convergence of 5G systems and non-3GPP access networks is expected to have significant impact in the field of Information and Communication Technology. What is new in 5GCN (5G Core Network), compared to 4G/Evolved Packet Core (EPC) is that the 5G Core can be consider as a collection of Network Functions (NFs) which provide the specific core functionalities. More specifically, each NF can expose its services to other NFs, thus acting as a service provider. Additionally, as a consumer, a NF can utilize the services provided by other related NFs. This ability to expose and make services available, characterizes the Service-Based Architecture [20].

The proposed LOCUS architecture [19] integrates localization and analytics functions within a 5G Core architectural approach, as it is defined in 5G. LOCUS provides a platform for localization analytics to be offered and exposed to smart network management and new services and/or 3rd party applications, and makes use of 3GPP technologies combined with analytics and Machine Learning (ML)/Artificial Intelligence (AI) techniques.

Localization enablers are responsible for providing the user device location data (e.g. coordinates, velocity, direction) needed by the other LOCUS functions. They utilize data such as network data or user device outside the LOCUS system, providing an estimation about user's device location. This function employs analytics, data fusion and ML mechanisms, to achieve high accuracy as well as to ensure data reliability for the detection and mitigation of attacks against location data and for correction of the aforementioned data. The information acquired from the external sources, as well as the expected positioning-related output, is stored in the LOCUS Persistence Entity. This Entity is responsible for the storage of all relevant data, as well as analytics/ML results and metadata.

Localization & Analytics for Smart Network Management (SNM) block, as it is depicted in Fig. 2 is responsible for the use of Analytics and ML mechanisms in conjunction with the position-related information provided by the Localization Enablers, so as to offer localization analytics services related to KPIs' (Key Performance Indicators) monitoring and knowledge building, network planning, management, optimization and diagnostics purposes. The results are exposed outside of LOCUS through the LOCUS APIs (Application Programming Interfaces) and can be used by other external SNM applications and, given availability of the appropriate APIs, can be applied towards OSS (Operations Support Systems) / BSS (Business Support Systems). Intermediate results can be stored internally within the LOCUS platform and re-fed to the various subcomponents, enabling the internal communication of the various subcomponents.

Analytics functions and ML models such as clustering, anomaly detection, classification, regression and time-series modelling are employed for the derivation of localization analytics. Data privacy and security are of high importance in the context of the LOCUS architecture. Thus, functions related to these aspects are applied horizontally to all data and externally as well as internal interfaces for ensuring privacy regulations and for triggering alarm functionalities.

All the above-mentioned LOCUS functions are subject to automated lifecycle management through dedicated LOCUS MANO (Management and Orchestration) features which enable automated instantiation, configuration, and operation of the various localization and analytics; the latter are deployed in the form of virtualized network functions (VNFs) on top of the virtualized infrastructure, following the ETSI NFV (Network Functions Virtualization) principles for functions virtualization and their management.

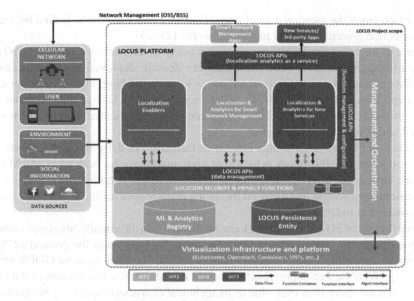

Fig. 2. LOCUS high level architecture

The virtualized platform is implemented as a 5G-enabled edge and core virtualized infrastructure, capable to offer isolated running environments for the various LOCUS functions.

6 Privacy in Location Based Services

In 5G networks, localization accuracy is unprecedented, especially in mmWave networks. 5G includes protocols for estimating, elaborating, and distributing the location information [21]. During the past four generations of mobile networks, LBSs were applied especially in cases of emergencies. Information related to user's location was retained only by telecom operators and could not be shared to any third parties. In 5G networks, location information can be disclosed to OTT market players, causing extra threat in already existing privacy concerns. As it is obvious, location privacy is a serious concern not only in current but in future networks as well, like 6G networks [22].

Location services by themselves are not the actual problem. The information/data that they can potentially store and provide to network operators and/or the third parties are the key concern for privacy. When mobile networks locate millions of UEs automatically on an ongoing basis, they generate an enormous amount of sensitive data. The control of access to this sensitive information is a high level, but deeply accurate, definition of privacy in LBSs.

The knowledge of the serving cell of a mobile user can disclose information about the end-user's exact location, especially in urban 5G environments with dense deployment. So, the main focus is given on the management of this location information. Threats such as semantic information attacks [23] (i.e., the use of incorrect information to cause harm) often target the location data of users. Location data can also be leaked by access point selection algorithms in 5G mobile networks [24, 25].

Since 5G networks radio planning requires many smaller antennas (small cells) and base stations, compared to 4G/LTE, which are densely deployed in order to ensure adequate coverage, the main issue in privacy is location tracking, identity, and personal data safeguarding. However, with 5G, although users will be able to achieve faster and easier communication as well as location addresses, this implicates that privacy may be affected and potentially be disrupted.

Privacy in 5G networks brings huge transformation in daily life applications and access modes of digital services, which is of high importance for both users and Mobile Network Operators (MNOs). New enhancements in terms of architectural and service requirements are brought and the need for strong privacy policies and regulations should be considered as indebtedness.

User privacy of 5G mobile network can be divided into three main categories namely: data, location and identity privacy [26]. The main focus is upon the context of "personal data", according to the General Data Protection Regulation (as in GDPR article 4, §1 [27]). With the fast deployment of the 5G infrastructures, the amount of data will rapidly increase more than ever, due to its technical characteristics; thus, 5G networks are expected to serve a wide range of applications and sectors supporting 100 times more devices if compared to the prior 4G/LTE networks [28].

As of the case of location privacy, with the advent of 5G technology, LBSs are increasingly expanded as users demand services based on their location [13]. So, UEs—and consequently the involved users- can continuously be tracked not only from the networks owners but from the service providers as well, causing serious concerns regarding their privacy, in general.

Recently, the promotion of LBSs has significantly been increased in several verticals, for instance, government, entertainment, transportation, healthcare, food delivery and others. Indeed, any corresponding LBSs make users' life easier and more enjoyable but also bring a plethora of privacy-related issues. In some cases, the individuals may be unaware of the potential risks graveled, the implications of how their location is being determined and to whom is permitted access to that information. In addition, service providers would like not to share the information gathered from their application to the providers of other services.

As far LBSs are concerned, two types of location privacy are acknowledged: personal subscriber level privacy and corporate level privacy [29]. Personal subscriber-level privacy is subjected to GDPR, giving also options to users related to their location control and the use of their location data as well as the option to unsubscribe from applications that use their UE location. Corporate level privacy refers to the use of data from service providers, in order to gain benefit from it.

With respect to identity, International Mobile Subscriber Identity (IMSI) catching attacks can reveal the identity of mobile subscribers. By seizing the IMSI of the subscriber's device, an attacker intercepts mobile traffic in a defined area to monitor an individual's activity. While an attacker can see the number of outgoing calls or text messages sent, they still cannot see the contents of those messages. However, even after an individual has left the attack area, the attacker can still monitor the number of past and future calls or messages.

Data collection is another major concern for 5G users. Virtually all smartphone applications require users' personal information before or during installation. App developers rarely mention how and where they store that data and what they will use it for. 5G networks have no physical boundaries and use cloud-based data storage. Subsequently, 5G operators cannot protect or control user data stored in cloud environments. As each country has different levels of privacy measures and enforcement, user privacy is seriously challenged if and when the data is stored in the cloud of a different country.

In order to protect mobile user's privacy several techniques that prevent disclosure of sensitive location information have been proposed such as privacy policies [30], anonymity-based techniques and systems where the users' true identity can be hidden, with the use of a pseudonym. Also differential privacy [31] or k-anonymity [32], or even the introduction of mix zones [33], meaning the interference a middle-ware between UE and LBS will enhance the anonymization of location information.

7 Conclusion

5G will provide super-high data rates, better quality of service and very low latency through dense base station deployments, serving increased huge number—compared to current networks—of connected devices. To fulfill these increased demands in terms of location based services, that benefit from precise and accurate location information, this paper proposed a novel 5G based architecture with integrated localization and analytics functions, which at the same time fulfill adequate privacy standards. This ecosystem, implemented during the lifetime of LOCUS project, incorporates advanced localization techniques and provides the potential for addressing 5G challenges related to location awareness, offering thus the opportunity of new applications development based on seamless and ubiquitous localization information.

Acknowledgments. This paper has been based on the context of the *LOCUS* ("*LOCalization and analytics on-demand embedded in the 5G ecosystem, for Ubiquitous vertical applicationS*") Project, and has been supported by the Commission of the European Communities / *H2020, Grant Agreement No.871249.*

References

1. LOCUS Project (Grant Agreement No.871249), https://www.locus-project.eu/
2. Küpper, A.: Location-Based Services: Fundamentals and Operation. Wiley, Munich (2005)
3. Koivisto, M., Hakkarainen, A., Costa, M., Kela, P., Leppanen, K., Valkama, M.: High-efficiency device positioning and location-aware communications in dense 5G networks. IEEE Commun. Mag. **55**(8), 188–195 (2017)
4. El Hattachi, R., Erfanian, J.: NGMN 5G White Paper. Next Generation Mobile Networks Alliance (2015). https://www.ngmn.org/work-programme/5g-white-paper.html
5. Boccardi, F., Heath, R.W., Lozano, A., Marzetta, T.L., Popovski, P.: Five disruptive technology directions for 5G. IEEE Commun. Mag. **52**(2), 74–80 (2014)

6. The 3rd Generation Partnership Project (3GPP): LTE Release 11, https://www.3gpp.org/spe cifications/releases/69-release-11
7. Slock, D.: Location aided wireless communications. In: Proceedings of the 2012 5th International Symposium on Communications Control and Signal Processing (ISCCSP), pp. 1–6. IEEE (2012)
8. Werner, J., Costa, M., Hakkarainen, A., Leppanen, K., Valkama, M.: Joint user node positioning and clock offset estimation in 5G ultra-dense networks. In: Proceedings of the 2015 IEEE Global Communications Conference (GLOBECOM), pp. 1–7. IEEE (2015)
9. European Telecommunications Standards Institute (ETSI): ETSI TS 124.502 V16.7.0: 5G; Access to the 3GPP 5G Core Network (5GCN) via non-3GPP access networks (3GPP TS 24.502 version 16.7.0 Release 16), (2021, April)
10. The 3rd Generation Partnership Project (3GPP): TR 21.916 V0.1.0: Release 16 Description; Summary of Rel-16 Work Items (release 16) (2019, September)
11. https://www.gps.gov/systems/gps/performance/accuracy/
12. Worboys, M.F., Duckham, M.: GIS: A Computing Perspective, 2nd edn. CRC Press, Boca Raton, FL (2004)
13. Di Taranto, R., Muppirisetty, S., Raulefs, R., Slock, D., Svensson, T., Wymeersch, H.: Location-aware communications for 5G networks: How location information can improve scalability, latency, and robustness of 5G. IEEE Signal Process. Mag. 31(6), 102–112 (2014)
14. Liao, D., Li, H., Sun, G., Zhang, M., Chang, V.: Location and trajectory privacy preservation in 5G-enabled vehicle social network services. J. Netw. Comput. Appl. 110, 108–118 (2018)
15. Chukhno, N., Trilles, S., Torres-Sospedra, S., Iera, A., Araniti, G.: D2D-Based cooperative positioning paradigm for future wireless systems: a survey. IEEE Sens. J. 22(6), 5101–5112 (2022)
16. Wang, Z., Liu, Z., Shen, Y., Conti, A., Win, M.Z.: Location awareness in beyond 5G networks via reconfigurable intelligent surfaces. IEEE J. Sel. Areas Commun. (2022)
17. Blefari-Melazzi, N., et al.: LOCUS: Localization and analytics on-demand embedded in the 5G ecosystem. In: Proceedings of the 2020 European Conference on Networks and Communications (EuCNC), pp. 170–175 (2020)
18. The 3rd Generation Partnership Project (3GPP): Release 16. https://www.3gpp.org/release-16
19. LOCUS Project: Deliverable 2.4: System architecture: Preliminary version (2020). https://www.locus-project.eu/results/deliverables/
20. Mayer, G.: RESTful APIs for the 5G service based architecture. J. ICT Stand. 6(1), 101–116 (2018)
21. Tomasin, S., Centenaro, M., Seco-Granados, G., Roth, S., Sezgin, A.: Location-privacy leakage and integrated solutions for 5G cellular networks and beyond. Sensors 21(15), 5176 (2021)
22. Fang, D., Qian, Y.: 5G wireless security and privacy: Architecture and flexible mechanisms. IEEE Veh. Technol. Mag. 15, 58–64 (2020)
23. Schneier, B.: Inside risks: Semantic network attacks. Commun. ACM 43(12), 168 (2000)
24. Kumar, G.V., Chigarapalle, S.B.: A study on access point selection algorithms in wireless mesh networks. Int. J. Adv. Netw. Appl. 6, 2158–2167 (2014)
25. Farhang, S., Hayel, Y., Zhu, Q.: PHY-layer location privacy-preserving access point selection mechanism in next-generation wireless networks. In: Proceedings of the 2015 IEEE Conference on Communications and Network Security (CNS), pp. 263–271. IEEE (2015)
26. Kumar, T., Liyanage, M., Ahmad, I., Braeken, A., Ylianttila, M.: User privacy, identity and trust in 5G. In: Liyanage, M., Ahmad, I., et al. (eds.) A Comprehensive Guide to 5G Security, pp. 267–279. Wiley, Hoboken (2018)
27. Intersoft Consulting: Art.4 GDPR—Definitions. https://gdpr-info.eu/art-4-gdpr/
28. Liyanage, M., Ahmad, I., Abro, A.B., Gurtov, A., Ylianttila, M.: A Comprehensive Guide to 5G Security. Wiley, Hoboken, NJ (2018)

29. Wang, T., Liu, L.: From data privacy to location privacy. In: Yu, P.S., Tsai, J.J.P. (eds.) Machine Learning in Cyber Trust, pp. 217–246. Springer, Berlin (2009)
30. Bamba, B., Liu, L., Pesti, P., Wang, T.: PrivacyGrid: Supporting anonymous location queries in mobile environments. In: Proceedings of the 2008 International World Wide Web Conference (WWW), pp. 237–246. ACM (2008)
31. Yin, C., Xi, J., Sun, R., Wang, J.: Location privacy protection based on differential privacy strategy for big data in industrial Internet of Things. IEEE Trans. Industr. Inf. **14**, 3628–3636 (2018)
32. Li, F., Chen, Y., Niu, B., He, Y., Geng, K., Cao, J.: Achieving personalized k-anonymity against long-term observation in location-based services. In: Proceedings of the 2018 IEEE Global Communications Conference (GLOBECOM), pp. 1–6. IEEE (2018)
33. Beresford, A., Stajano, F.: Mix zones: User privacy in location-aware services. In: Proceedings of the Second 2004 IEEE Annual Conference on Pervasive Computing and Communications Workshops, pp. 127–131. IEEE (2004)

A Deep Q Network-Based Multi-connectivity Algorithm for Heterogeneous 4G/5G Cellular Systems

Juan Jesús Hernández-Carlón[✉], Jordi Pérez-Romero, Oriol Sallent, Irene Vilà, and Ferran Casadevall

Department of Signal Theory and Communications, Universitat Politècnica de Catalunya (UPC) Barcelona, 08034 Barcelona, Spain
{juan.jesus.hernandez,jordi.perez-romero, irene.vila.munoz}@upc.edu, {sallent,ferranc}@tsc.upc.edu

Abstract. Multi-connectivity, which allows a user equipment to be simultaneously connected to multiple cells from different radio access network nodes that can be from a single or multiple radio access technologies, has emerged as a useful feature to handle the traffic in heterogeneous cellular scenarios and fulfill high data rate and reliability requirements. This paper proposes the use of deep reinforcement learning to optimally split the traffic among cells when multi-connectivity is considered in a heterogeneous 4G/5G networks scenario. Obtained results reveal a promising capability of the proposed Deep Q Network solution to select quasi optimum traffic splits depending on the current traffic and radio conditions in the considered scenario. Moreover, the paper analyses the robustness of the obtained policy in front of variations with respect to the conditions used during the training.

Keywords: Multi-connectivity · Deep reinforcement learning · Deep Q Network · Heterogeneous networks

1 Introduction

With the advent of 5G Mobile Network Operators (MNOs) face further increase in network deployment heterogeneity with different cell types (e.g. macrocells, indoor and outdoor small cells) based on multiple Radio Access Technologies (RATs) (e.g., 2G, 3G, 4G and 5G New Radio (5G NR)), operating in different spectrum bands (e.g. sub 6 GHz bands used by all RATs and millimeter wave (mmW) bands used by 5G New Radio). In this context, Multi-Connectivity (MC) technology enables a User Equipment (UE) to be simultaneously connected to multiple nodes of the Radio Access Network (RAN), e.g. eNodeBs (eNB) operating with LTE and/or gNodeBs (gNB) operating with 5G NR [1, 2]. There is one master node (MN) responsible for the radio-access control plane and one, or in the general case multiple, secondary node(s) (SN) that provide additional user-plane links. In this way, a UE can aggregate the radio resources from multiple eNBs/gNBs, which allows efficiently achieving the 5G requirements of high

© IFIP International Federation for Information Processing 2022
Published by Springer Nature Switzerland AG 2022
I. Maglogiannis et al. (Eds.): AIAI 2022 Workshops, IFIP AICT 652, pp. 34–43, 2022.
https://doi.org/10.1007/978-3-031-08341-9_3

data rate and ultra-reliability. The literature has considered different problems in relation to MC, such as the resource allocation in [3, 4] or the traffic split [5–8].

This paper addresses the traffic split multi-connectivity problem in multi RAT scenarios by exploiting Deep Q Network (DQN) technique [9] to obtain a policy that allows optimally distributing the traffic of a UE across the different RATs and cells while fulfilling the QoS requirements and optimizing the bandwidth consumption of the UE, so that overload situations are avoided in the involved cells. Deep reinforcement learning techniques such as DQN are useful for optimizing dynamic decision-making problems that depend on a large number of input variables taking a wide range of possible values. This is the case of the MC problem formulated in this paper, for which a DQN solution is presented and assessed by means of simulations. In addition, the results presented in this paper pay particular attention to the capability of the solution to generalize the knowledge learnt during the training phase. In this direction, the robustness of the learnt policy is analyzed when the conditions experienced by the algorithm differ from the ones that were considered during the training.

The rest of the paper is organised as follows. Section 2 presents the system model and formulates the considered multi-connectivity problem. The proposed DQN-based solution is presented in Sect. 3 and different performance results are provided in Sect. 4. Finally, Sect. 5 summarises the conclusions.

2   System Model and Problem Definition

Let us consider a heterogeneous RAN where different UEs with multi-connectivity capabilities are camping. A given UE u considers M different RATs and N different cells per RAT as candidates for the multi-connectivity. Then, let us denote as $A_u = \{C_{m,n}\}$ the set of candidate cells detected by the UE u. $C_{m,n}$ denotes the n-th cell of the m-th RAT with $n = 1, \ldots, N$ and $m = 1, \ldots, M$. It is worth mentioning that, due to the mobility of the UE, the specific cells that the UE detects in a given RAT may change with time. In this respect, it is assumed that the N cells of a RAT correspond to the best N cells detected by the UE at a certain time based on measurements averaged during a time window ΔT.

Through the use of multi-connectivity, the traffic of the u-th UE is split across multiple RATs/cells of the set A_u. It is assumed that, at a certain time, the UE can be simultaneously connected to a maximum of N_{max} cells among the $M \cdot N$ candidates. The multi-connectivity configuration for the u-th UE can be expressed as the $M \times N$ matrix $\mathbf{B} = \{\beta_{m,n}\}$ where $\beta_{m,n} \in [0,1]$ defines the fraction of total traffic of UE u that is delivered through the n-th cell of the m-th RAT. Then, the objective is to find the optimal configuration $\mathbf{B} = \{\beta_{n,m}\}$ to be applied in a time window of ΔT s that allow ensuring the Quality of Service (QoS) requirements with minimum resource consumption and avoiding overload situations in the different RATs/cells. In this respect, it is assumed that the QoS requirements of the user u are expressed in terms of a required bit rate R_u (b/s) to be provided.

To formalize the problem, let us denote as $T_u(\mathbf{B})$ the total throughput or bit rate obtained by user u during the last time window period ΔT with the multi-connectivity configuration $\mathbf{B}$. Let us also denote $a_{m,n}(\beta_{m,n})$ as the number of physical resource blocks (PRBs) in the m-th cell and n-th RAT assigned to the u-th UE to transmit the traffic corresponding to $\beta_{m,n}$. Considering that $b_{m,n}$ corresponds to the bandwidth of one PRB in the m-th cell and n-th RAT, the bandwidth allocated to the user u in this RAT, denoted as $\gamma(\beta_{m,n})$, is given by:

$$\gamma(\beta_{m,n}) = a_{m,n}(\beta_{m,n}).b_{m.n} \tag{1}$$

In addition, the total fraction of occupied PRBs in a RAT/cell accounting for all the UEs connected to that cell is denoted as $\rho_{m,n}(\beta_{m,n})$. Then, the considered problem to be solved for the u-th UE is formally defined as:

$$\mathbf{B} = \underset{\mathbf{B}}{argmin}\left[\frac{1}{w_{max}}\sum_{m=1}^{M}\sum_{n=1}^{N}\gamma(\beta_{m,n})\right] \tag{2}$$

$$\text{s.t. } T_u(\mathbf{B}) \geq R_u \, , \rho_{m,n}(\beta_{m,n}) \leq \rho_{max} \, \forall m, n$$

$$\sum_{m=1}^{M}\sum_{n=1}^{N}\beta_{m,n} = 1$$

where w_{max} is the maximum possible bandwidth to be assigned to the user u and ρ_{max} $\in [0,1]$ is the maximum threshold established to avoid overload situations in a cell.

Figure 1 depicts the architectural components to enforce the multi-connectivity configuration $\mathbf{B}$ in the network, obtained as a result of the above problem. The figure illustrates an example for the downlink traffic transmitted to a UE served by two cells of RAT $m = 1$ (e.g., 5G). The cell $n = 1$ is handled by the MN and the cell $n = 2$ by the SN. The traffic between these cells is split at the Packet Data Convergence Protocol (PDCP) layer of the MN using dual connectivity feature. The multi-connectivity configuration is determined by an MC controller that takes as an input different measurement from the RATs/cells as it will be explained in Sect. 3. The output of the MC controller is the configuration $\mathbf{B} = \{\beta_{m,n}\}$ with the weights $\beta_{m,n}$ to be configured at the PDCP layer of the MN to split the traffic between cells 1 and 2. Finally, the Medium Access Control (MAC) scheduler in each 5G NR or LTE cell will allocate the necessary amount of PRBs $a_{m,n}(\beta_{m,n})$ to the UE to transmit the fraction of traffic $\beta_{m,n}$ corresponding to the cell. The specific design of the MAC scheduler is out of the scope of this work, but in general it will consider aspects such as the propagation and interference conditions observed by the UE, the QoS requirements, the amount of UEs in the cell, etc.

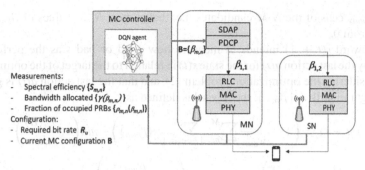

Fig. 1. Architectural components of the considered approach

3 DQN-Based Solution

A DQN approach is considered in this paper for solving the MC problem formulated in previous section. In this approach, the learning process is conducted dynamically by a DQN agent at the MC controller of Fig. 1 that makes decisions for the different UEs. The agent operates in discrete times with granularity equal to the time window duration ΔT. These discrete times are denoted as $t, t + 1, \ldots, t + k, \ldots$ At time t the DQN selects an action $a(t)$ that contains the MC configuration to be applied for a given UE in the next time window. The action selection is based on the current state at time t, denoted as $s(t)$ and on the decision-making policy available at this time. Then, as a result of applying the selected MC configuration, a reward signal $r(t + 1)$ is provided to the DQN agent at the end of the time window. This reward signal measures how good or bad was the last performed action and therefore it is used to improve the decision-making policy. The different components of this process are detailed in the following.

3.1 State, Action and Reward Specification

The state $s(t)$ is a vector that includes the following components for a given UE u:

- Requirements of UE u: R_u.
- Spectral efficiency per RAT/cell $\{S_{m,n}\}$ of UE u.
- Current configuration $\mathbf{B} = \{\beta_{m,n}\}$, which corresponds to the configuration applied at time $t - 1$.
- Bandwidth occupied by the UE u in each RAT/cell $\{\gamma(\beta_{m,n})\}$.
- Fraction of total occupied resources in each RAT/cell $\{\rho_{m,n}(\beta_{m,n})\}$.

All the values $S_{m,n}$, $\gamma(\beta_{m,n})$ and $\rho_{m,n}(\beta_{m,n})$ are average values measured during the last time window of duration ΔT, i.e. between discrete times $t - 1$ and t.

Each action $a(t) \in \mathcal{A}$ represents a matrix $\mathbf{B} = \{\beta_{m,n}\}$ that corresponds to the MC configuration to be applied during the next time window ΔT. The action space $\mathcal{A}$ includes all the MC configurations and is defined by considering that the possible $\beta_{m,n}$ values are discretized with granularity $\Delta \beta$ and the aggregate of all $\beta_{m,n}$ values in matrix $\mathbf{B}$ equals 1. Moreover, the action space considers that the UE can be simultaneously connected to at most N_{max} cells of the $N \cdot M$ candidates, i.e. that at most N_{max} values of $\beta_{m,n}$ can be different from 0.

The reward $r(t + 1)$ intends to measure how good or bad was the performance obtained by the last action $a(t)$ for the state $s(t)$ in relation to the target of the optimization. Then, considering the optimization problem (2), and that the last action $a(t)$ is given by MC configuration $\mathbf{B} = \{\beta_{m,n}\}$, the reward is defined as:

$$r(t + 1) = \left(1 - \frac{1}{w_{max}} \sum_{m=1}^{M} \sum_{n=1}^{N} \gamma(\beta_{m,n})\right) \cdot min\left(1, \frac{T_u(\mathbf{B})}{R_u}\right) \tag{3}$$

$$\cdot \prod_{\substack{m,n \\ \beta_{m,n} > 0}} min\left(1, \frac{\rho_{max}}{\rho_{m,n}(\beta_{m,n})}\right)$$

The first term in $r(t + 1)$ captures the total bandwidth assigned to the UE u in all the cells/RATs, so the lower the amount of bandwidth assigned the higher will be the reward. The second term represents a penalty introduced when the achieved throughput $T_u(\mathbf{B})$ is lower than the minimum requirement R_u. The last term introduces a penalty for each cell/RAT in which the UE has transmitted traffic (i.e. $\beta_{m,n} > 0$) and the cell is overloaded. Note that the values of $\gamma_{m,n}(\beta_{m,n})$, $\rho_{m,n}(\beta_{m,n})$ and $T_u(\mathbf{B})$ correspond to the averages obtained during the time window ΔT between discrete times t and $t + 1$.

3.2 Policy Learning Process

The DQN agent dynamically learns the decision-making policy π used to select the different actions based on the rewards obtained from previous decisions. This is done by means of the DQN algorithm of [9] particularised to the state, action and reward signals presented above. In summary, the algorithm aims at finding the optimal policy that maximises the discounted cumulative expected reward by approximating the optimum action-value function with a deep neural network (DNN) denoted as $Q(s, a, \theta)$, where s is the observed state, a is one of the possible actions that can be selected and θ are the weights of the interconnections between the different neurons in the DNN. Given the DNN, the decision making policy consists in selecting the action a with the highest value of $Q(s, a, \theta)$ for a given state.

The decision-making policy is updated progressively by modifying the weights θ based on the experiences gathered by the DQN agent. For this purpose, at a certain time t the DQN agent observes the state of the environment $s(t)$ for a given UE and it triggers an action by selecting with probability $1 - \varepsilon$ the action $a(t)$ with the highest value of $Q(s,a,\theta)$ and with probability ε a random action. As a result, the DQN agent gathers the obtained reward and the new state at time $t + 1$ and stores this experience (i.e., $s(t)$, $a(t)$, $r(t + 1)$, $s(t + 1)$) in an experience dataset. The information collected in this dataset is then used to update the weights θ of the DNN using the expressions detailed in [9].

4 Performance Evaluation

This section evaluates the performance of the proposed solution by means of system level simulations.

4.1 Scenario Description

The considered scenario is a square area of 500 m × 500 m composed by four 5G NR cells and two LTE cells. The relevant parameters of the cells are presented in Table 1. The scenario assumes a non-homogeneous traffic distribution with MC-capable UEs moving at 1 m/s along the scenario and have an active session during the whole simulation duration with a required bit rate $R_u = 50$ Mb/s. The candidate cells of the UEs can connect to $M = 2$ RATs and $N = 2$ cell per RAT, and the maximum number of cells that the UE can be connected to using MC is $N_{max} = 2$. Additional background traffic is considered, with UEs generating Poisson session arrivals with aggregate generation rate 0.8 sessions/s and exponentially distributed session duration with average 120s. A background UE remains static during a session. 50% of the background UEs are randomly located inside a square hotspot of 250 m × 250 m centred at the middle of the scenario. The rest of background UEs are randomly distributed in the whole scenario. Background UEs connect to the RAT/cell with the highest Signal to Interference and Noise Ratio (SINR). To capture the different bit rates achievable by the two technologies, when a background UE is connected to LTE, its serving cell allocates the needed resource blocks to achieve a bit rate of 2.5 Mb/s, and when it is connected to 5G NR, the allocation is to achieve a bit rate of 40 Mb/s.

The DQN model parameters are detailed in Table 2. The DQN model has been developed in Python using the *TF-agents* library [10].

Table 1. Cell configuration parameters

Parameter	Value	
Type of RAT	LTE	5G NR
Cells position [x, y] m	[62, 250] [437,250]	[187, 125] [187,375] [312,125] [312,375]
Frequency	2100 MHz	26 GHz
Subcarrier separation	15 kHz	60 kHz
Nominal channel bandwidth	20 MHz	50 MHz
Number of available PRBs	100	66
Base station transmitted power	49 dBm	21 dBm
Base station antenna gain	5 dB	26 dB
Base station height	25 m	10 m
UE antenna gain	5 dB	10 dB
Overload threshold ρ_{max}	0.95	0.95
UE noise figure	9 dB	
UE height	1.5 m	
Path loss model	Model of Sect. 7.4 of [11]	
w_{max}	95.04 MHz (corresponds to the case when MC is done with 2 cells of 5G NR)	

Table 2. DQN algorithm parameters

Parameter	Value
Initial collect steps	5000
Number of policy updates during learning	1e6
Experience Replay buffer maximum length (l)	1e5
Mini-batch size (J)	256
Discount factor(γ)	0.9
Learning rate (τ)	0.0003
ε value (ε-Greedy)	0.1
DNN architecture	Input layer: 17 nodes Two hidden layers: 100 and 50 nodes Output layer: 58 nodes
Time window (ΔT)	1 s
Granularity $\Delta\beta$	0.1

4.2 Training Evolution

The training process of the DQN algorithm is performed by considering a MC-capable UE moving along the scenario following trajectories according to random walk and with required bit rate $R_u = 50$ Mb/s, while at the same time background UEs also generate traffic as explained in Sect. 4.1. The DQN agent decides the MC connectivity configuration of the UE and, based on the obtained rewards, the decision making policy is progressively updated as explained in Sect. 3.2. In order to illustrate this learning process, the policies that are obtained every 2500 weight updates (i.e. training steps) are applied to an evaluation scenario in which an illustrative MC-capable UE follows a specific trajectory of duration 400 s, starting from point [$X_1 = 50$, $Y_1 = 300$] and following a straight trajectory up to the point [$X_2 = 450$, $Y_2 = 300$] at 1 m/s. Figure 1 presents the evolution of the average reward obtained with the application of these policies as a

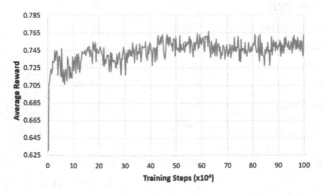

Fig. 2. Evolution of the average reward as a function of the training steps

function of the number of training steps. The results of Fig. 2 show that as the number of training steps increase average reward values tend to increase until 40×10^4 training steps, when the average reward values stabilize.

4.3 Performance Evaluation of the DQN-Based Strategy

In order to assess the benefits brought by the proposed DQN-based MC strategy, this sub-section compares the performance obtained by the proposed approach against two benchmarking approaches, namely the *optimum strategy* and the *SINR-based strategy*. The former consists of applying an exhaustive search process to select in each time step the MC configuration with the maximum reward, while the later considers that all the traffic of a UE is served by the cell with the highest SINR.

The comparison is performed by simulating a UE of interest following one hundred different trajectories of duration 400 s in the evaluation scenario and applying in each time window the MC configuration according to each of the evaluated schemes. For the DQN approach, the results correspond to the policy learnt by the DQN agent after a training consisting of 1E6 policy updates according to the procedure of Sect. 3.2.

Figure 3 shows the obtained average reward for each one of the trajectories with all the considered strategies. It is observed that the DQN-based strategy achieves a performance very close to the optimum one in all the studied cases, which confirms the good behavior of the proposed approach. In turn, Fig. 3 also shows that the DQN-based strategy outperforms the classical SINR-based strategy in all the studied cases thanks to the better distribution of the traffic of the UE among the cells that avoids overload and enhances the obtained bit rate.

Fig. 3. Average reward for different trajectories.

4.4 Analysis of the Robustness of the Learnt DQN-Policy

This section aims at evaluating the robustness of the DQN-policy when it is applied under conditions that differ from the ones that were considered during the training. For this purpose, considering that the training process has been done with a required bit rate

$R_u = 50$ Mb/s, the following results assess the generalization capability of the learnt policy when it is applied to different R_u values ranging between 15 and 65 Mb/s.

As a relevant metric for this assessment, a DQN-policy efficiency metric is considered, defined as the ratio between the reward of the DQN policy and that of the optimum strategy. Figure 4 depicts the DQN-policy efficiency as a function of the required bit rate R_u value. The results of policy efficiency correspond to the average for the one hundred trajectories considered in the study. For the R_u value of 50 Mb/s that was considered during the training it is observed in Fig. 4 that the efficiency of the original policy is around 95.75%. Then, it tends to decrease for higher and lower values of required bit rate. In fact, it is worth mentioning the effects of decreasing R_u, because even when the amount of required radio resources is less, the efficiency losses are higher. For example, the policy efficiency with $R_u = 15$ Mb/s is 13.42% less than with 50 Mb/s. From the red line in Fig. 4, we can realize that efficiency variations lower than 1% are observed when the R_u value changes from 40 Mb/s up to 65 Mb/s, i.e. $-10/ + 15$ Mb/s with respect to the value used for training. This reflects that the learnt DQN policy is robust in front of variations of around 20–30% of the R_u value used in the training.

Based on these results, another training process has been conducted with the same parameters of Table 2 but now changing the R_u value during training. Specifically, R_u at the beginning of the training is 50 Mb/s and then it is changed between 5 and 60 Mb/s with steps of $\pm 10\%$. Moreover, the number training steps has been increased up to 3E6 in order to account for a higher number of possible situations to learn. The green line in Fig. 4, shows the obtained efficiency with the new learnt policy (denoted as retrained policy) in comparison to the original policy. It is clearly observed that the new policy achieves a good efficiency for all the considered RBR values.

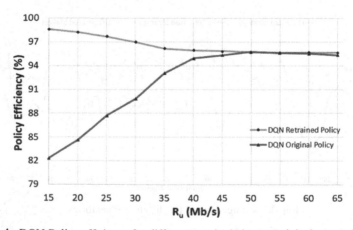

Fig. 4. DQN-Policy efficiency for different required bit rate (original vs retrained)

5   Conclusion

This paper has presented a novel approach based on Deep Q- Network for splitting the traffic of a UE among cells when using multi-connectivity depending on the current traffic and radio conditions experienced by the UE in the involved cells. The strategy intends to minimize the bandwidth consumption, the overload situations in the cells and enhancing throughput. The proposed strategy has been evaluated and compared against the optimum case and against a classical SINR-based approach. Results have shown the capability of the DQN agent to learn a quasi-optimal policy that in certain conditions outperforms the SINR-based approach in up to 33% in terms of reward, obtaining as a result better throughput performance with an optimized bandwidth assignment.

This paper has also analyzed the robustness of the learnt policy when being applied with a required bit rate value different than the one that was considered during the training stage. It has been observed that the learnt policy is able to work properly with variations of the required bit rate of around 20–30% of the value considered in the training. In turn, by conducting a training that considers a wider range of values of required bit rate, it is possible to increase the performance of the obtained policy.

Acknowledgement. This paper is part of ARTIST project (ref. PID2020-115104RB-I00) funded by MCIN/AEI/10.13039/ 501100011033. The work is also funded by the Spanish Ministry of Science and Innovation under grant ref. PRE2018-084691.

References

1. Maeder, A. et al.: A scalable and flexible radio access network architecture for fifth generation mobile networks. IEEE Communications Magazine, November (2016). https://doi.org/10.1109/MCOM.2016.1600140CM
2. Dahlman, E., Parkvall, S., Sköld, J.: 5G NR the Next Generation Wireless Access Technology. Academic Press Elsevier (2018)
3. Yan, M., Feng, G., Zhou, J., Qin, S.: Smart multi-RAT access based on multiagent reinforcement learning. IEEE Trans. Veh. Technol. 67(5), 4539–4551 (2018). https://doi.org/10.1109/TVT.2018.2793186
4. Monteiro, V.F., et al.: Distributed RRM for 5G multi-RAT multiconnectivity networks. IEEE Syst. J., 13(1), March (2019). https://doi.org/10.1109/JSYST.2018.2838335
5. Gerasimenko, M., et al.: Adaptive resource management strategy in practical multi-radio heterogeneous networks. IEEE Access, February (2017). https://doi.org/10.1109/ACCESS.2016.2638022
6. Taksande, P.K., Roy, A., Karandikar, A.: Optimal traffic splitting policy in LTE-based heterogeneous network. IEEE Wireless Communications and Networking Conference (WCNC) (2018). https://doi.org/10.1109/WCNC.2018.8377096
7. Zhang, B. et al.: Goodput-aware traffic splitting scheme with non-ideal backhaul for 5G-LTE multi-connectivity. IEEE Wireless Communications and Networking Conference (WCNC) (2019). https://doi.org/10.1109/WCNC.2019.8885728
8. Elias, J., Martignon, F. Paris, S.: Optimal split bearer control and resource allocation for multi-connectivity in 5G new radio. Joint European Conference on Networks and Communications & 6G Summit (EuCNC/6G Summit), pp. 187–192 (2021). https://doi.org/10.1109/EuCNC/6GSummit51104.2021.9482505
9. Mnih, V., et al.: Human-level control through deep reinforcement learning. Nature 518(7540), 529–533 (2015)
10. Guadarrama, S., et al.: TF-agents: A library for reinforcement learning in TensorFlow (2018)
11. 3GPP TS 38.901 v16.1.0: Study on Channel Model for Frequencies From 0.5 to 100 GHz (Release 16) Dec. 2019

A Framework to Support the Deployment of PPDR Services Across Edge and Cloud Domains

Janez Sterle[1] , Ioanna Mesogiti[2(✉)] , Luka Korsic[1], Eleni Theodoropoulou[2],
Fotini Setaki[2], George Lyberopoulos[2], Francesca Moscateli[3], Konstantina Kanta[4],
Giannis Giannoulis[4], Panagiotis Toumasis[4], Dimitris Apostolopoulos[4],
Hercules Avramopoulos[4], John Avramidis[5], Yigal Leiba[6], and Dimitris Klonidis[7]

[1] Internet Institute Ltd., Ljubljana, Slovenia
[2] COSMOTE Mobile Telecommunications S.A, Athens, Greece
imesogiti@cosmote.gr
[3] Nextworks S.R.L, Pisa, Italy
[4] National Technical University of Athens, Athens, Greece
[5] INTRASOFT International S.A, Luxemburg, Luxembourg
[6] SIKLU Communication LTD, Petach Tikwa, Israel
[7] UBITECH, Athens, Greece

Abstract. The 5G and beyond advancements will impact significantly the evolution of many vertical industries such as the Public Protection and Disaster Recovery (PPDR) sector. To this end, the requirements posed by PPDR operations and services can be satisfied to a certain great degree by 5G network capabilities associated with network slicing and incorporation of edge computing, while network coverage and availability even in disaster situations still remains a critical issue. However, the flexibility of 5G networks and the beyond 5G developments related to network and service orchestration can further lead the PPDR service provisioning. The 5G-PPP project Int5Gent aims at delivering a complete beyond 5G solution suitable for various PPDR operational scenarios, namely for day-to-day operations and for disaster scenarios; along with experimentation deployments for testing and evaluation. This paper discusses the service and technical requirements and provides an overview of the proposed technologies and deployment solutions.

Keywords: 5G · Public protection and disaster recovery · Edge computing · Vertical services

1 Introduction

In general terms, 5G and beyond networks move from network-driven to service-driven approaches, and this leads to a service provisioning transformation in terms of individualized services and user classification, and necessitates the shift to 5G and beyond distributed network deployments across cloud and edge domains. Of course, this transformation is also reflected in Standardization as we come across a number of 3GPP TRs

© IFIP International Federation for Information Processing 2022
Published by Springer Nature Switzerland AG 2022
I. Maglogiannis et al. (Eds.): AIAI 2022 Workshops, IFIP AICT 652, pp. 44–52, 2022.
https://doi.org/10.1007/978-3-031-08341-9_4

focusing on vertical industries requirements and Key Performance Indicators (KPIs), layered service provisioning etc., such as those in [1–4].

Focusing on the Public Protection and Disaster Relief (PPDR) sector as key vertical industry, communications have for a long time relied on narrowband networks (TETRA - Terrestrial Trunked Radio, TETRAPOL- Terrestrial Trunked Radio POLice, etc.), mainly utilizing mission-critical voice and, in certain cases, low-speed data services as PPDR services were limited to voice communications what is called "the lifeline of the PPDR" [9]. From this point, PPDR Communications are increasingly being complemented by Intelligence ([8–10]) as they follow Information and Communication Technology (ICT) advances. In particular, advanced PPDR services are enabling more effective operations from the PPDR responders as well as more effective mitigation of disaster events, incidents etc. Such advanced services are search and rescue support using emergency robots and Unmanned Aerial Vehicles - drones (UAVs), sensing of the affected areas using high definition (real-time) video streaming and massive Internet of Things (IoT), Situational – Contextual awareness, multimedia messaging, high accuracy location services and mapping, etc. ([5–7]). The advanced PPDR service requirements, result in rendering traditional voice-centric network solutions tailored for PPDR incapable to effectively deliver modern PPDR services. 5G networks are considered the candidate technology for future PPDR services as they promise the required network performance and enable the necessary architectural options incorporating Edge Computing. At the same time, certain aspects such as automation and adoption of IT advancements are part of beyond 5G networks research, which can further elevate PPDR service availability and resilience.

A number of projects and programs (EU, national funded, equipment vendor supported, etc., e.g. [5, 11],) are focusing on the technical realization of the PPDR concepts and principles over 5G networks. In this landscape, the 5G-PPP Int5Gent project [12] focuses on delivering two implementation paradigms for future PPDR service provisioning. This paper aims at providing an overview of the PPDR services that drive future network deployments, such those to be demonstrated at a field testbed in Athens, Greece.

This paper is organized as follows: initially, the service and network deployment requirements and options are discussed on the basis of main PPDR operational scenarios. An overview of the Int5Gent deployment options -covering these requirements- and technologies is presented in the subsequent section. Following these, aspects related to the operational adoption of such solutions are discussed, while conclusions are drawn at the end.

2 PPDR Service and Network Deployment Requirements

The advanced PPDR services pose very stringent requirements to the network, such as low latency and quality guarantees for the support of these services. These come along with the technical requirement to have a deployment of applications/services close to the affected area in order to provide the necessary performance and availability requirements. At the same time, the ever since requirements for availability and reliability pose requirements for coverage augmentation, extremely high availability and reliability, isolated operation and network resilience during disaster scenarios. These come along with the technical requirements for on-demand network extension, as well as resilience at various network segments.

5G networks promise the required network performance in terms of latency, data rates, and architectural options by enabling Mobile Edge Computing (MEC), while certain aspects such as automation and adoption of Information Technology (IT) advancements are part of beyond 5G networks research. Int5Gent aims to deliver a solution for the PPDR sector addressing key deployment and operational models required for the successful commercial delivery of advanced PPDR services over the 5G-based deployments.

In particular, PPDR day-to-day operations require on-demand but scheduled provisioning of mission critical services even in areas lacking public network coverage. At network level, this can be translated into the need for supporting automated deployment of 5G Radio Access Network (RAN) to connect to public 5G Core network (5GC) wherever needed for a specific time period, supporting slicing for meeting the versatile PPDR services performance requirements. At application level, given the spatio-temporal character of the operations in this scenario, it poses the requirement for supporting automatic deployment and life-cycle management of mission critical services. Although these deployments do not pose strict KPIs with regard to the network and application deployment times, the service performance -latency and datarates- KPIs can be very strict depending on the application/ services (as appear in [1–4]).

In case of disaster situations when we can have total or partial unavailability of the public infrastructure (core network, cloud infrastructure etc.), a resilient solution for all network segments is required to enable the PPDR service provisioning. This can be translated into the need for supporting automated deployment of complete 5G network and applications wherever needed for a specific time period, supporting slicing for meeting the versatile PPDR services performance requirements. Given the time-criticality of operations, disaster situations scenarios pose strict requirement regarding the deployment times for the network and the mission critical applications, the target being less than 5 min. Similarly to the previous scenario, the service performance -latency and datarates- KPIs can be very strict depending on the application/ services.

Considering, also the fact that PPDR services in many cases are consumed at specific locations possibly from a small group of end-users, makes private network deployments for PPDR is a valid option. As aforementioned, currently, private networks –of various technologies- serve part of the PPDR sector needs however public telecom networks are also heavily used where private networks are not available; the latter option coming with the availability, resilience, isolation constraints. To meet the PPDR service requirements and KPIs, novel architectural solutions and network deployment options need to be considered, exploiting the 5G network service provisioning – e.g. slicing- and ICT capabilities. Apparently, there is no single solution to address such environment.

Other business factors may as well lead to public networks being extended for PPDR service provisioning. In these cases, a distributed core network deployment allowing service deployment and processing at edge compute resources, and traffic offloading at MEC components can serve well the purpose of meeting the performance requirements (especially for low latency), while optimizing public network utilization and performance. Latter trends are visible in many contexts, as presented in [17].

In other cases, the performance requirements and the diversity of PPDR services set as well as the need to support multiple tenants on top of a single infrastructure necessitates the adoption of the 5G concept of network slicing at service and tenant level. In general, PPDR services can be well-mapped to the 3GPP distinction of services to uRLLC (ultra-Reliable Low Latency), and eMBB (enhanced Mobile Broadband), as basis for network layer slicing, over either a single private network deployment or a distributed public one.

3   Int5Gent Architecture and Deployment Options for PPDR

Int5Gent aims to deliver a solution for the PPDR sector addressing key deployment and operational models required for the successful commercial deployment of the advanced PPDR services over the 5G. The solution is based on a disaggregated, layered, architectural approach, allowing for different deployment options depending on the situation [18].

In particular, PPDR day-to-day operations require on-demand but scheduled provisioning of network coverage and the enablement of mission critical services even in areas lacking public network coverage. Int5Gent proposes a solution of ad-hoc automatic deployment of 5G access network segments -namely the gNB and the MEC - dedicated to the PPDR sector at a compact server (an edge box as portable Infrastructure-as-a-Service), as an extension of the public network. The solution also includes the deployment/ configuration of a resilient wireless transport network segment. On top of this, the solutions allows for quick and automated deployment of reliable PPDR services exploiting cloud native principles and placing Artificial Intelligence- (AI) processing at network edge.

Secondly, in case of disaster situations when we can have total or partial unavailability of the public core network, PPDR services require a resilient solution for all network segments. Int5Gent solution proposes an ad-hoc automatic deployment of complete 5G-assured network -including all 5G network segments- dedicated to the PPDR sector at a compact server (edge box) − in the form of Non-Public-Network (NPN in 5G terminology). On top of this, as in the previous case, the solutions allow for quick and automated deployment of reliable PPDR services using cloud native principles and AI-based edge processing. The two main, Int5Gent deployment options are presented in Fig. 1.

Access Network Layer: The deployments imply the installation of the necessary Remote-Radio Units (RRU) at the location where the coverage extension is needed for both scenarios. For the Int5Gent experimental setup, there will be used RRUs optically connected to an (enhanced Common Public Radio Interface) eCPRI-based BBU (Base-band Unit) deployed at network edge capable to provide New-Radio (NR) in Stand-Alone (SA) mode, operating at N78 (Time-Division-Duplex, TDD).

Last Mile Transport: The deployment includes a multi-technology last mile transport network, taking into consideration cases where fiber deployment is expensive or eve not possible.

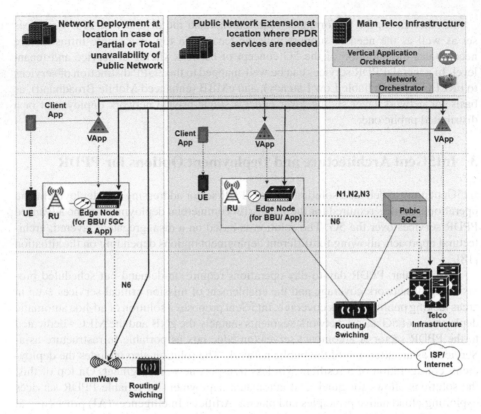

Fig. 1. Blueprint of Int5Gent deployments for PPDR services

Thus, besides the typical fiber network connectivity between the RRUs and the BBU (at edge compute resources), or/and from the edge towards a main switching point of the telco infrastructure, a number of millimeter-Wave (mmWave) mesh nodes supporting point-to-multipoint are deployed and configured at the transport network segment. The mmWave mesh nodes operate in the 60 GHz spectrum band and they use antennas with 360° total coverage, connecting in this way multiple low-cost client nodes which are used as the endpoints of the wireless transport network. In the disaster scenario this is particularly relevant, as these mmWave solutions aim to provide the necessary resilience this network segment.

Edge Computing: For the deployment of services, the central cloud infrastructure of a Telco could be considered for the day-to-day scenario. However, to meet the PPDR service requirements and to cater for the case of telecom operator (Telco) infrastructure unavailability, edge computing is considered in various ways - deployed at the location of the areas to be served. In the day-to-day scenario, edge computing will be used for the deployment of the necessary BBU functions, and edge applications with low latency and high resource requirements such as Artificial-Intelligent (AI) – based video services. In the disaster scenario, edge resources can be used for the deployment of the complete 5GC and applications.

For this purpose, the 3GPP network deployment shall be based on radio and network functions in the form of Cloud-Native Network Function (CNFs), namely: gNBs prepared as virtual BBU (vBBU) (extended with eCPRI-based RRU), 5GC prepared as a single CNF - that is integrating 3GPP Access and Mobility Management Function (AMF), Session Management Function (SMF), User Plane Function (UPF) and Authentication Server Function (AUSF) and that is exposing 3GPP interfaces N2 and N3).

Virtualization of the edge resources allows their use for automated deployment of the necessary network functions and applications via appropriate orchestration layers.

In the context of Int5Gent project, the implementation is based on a portable Network Functions Virtualization Infrastructure (NFVI) prepared to be deployed at the network edge (edge box), at hardware level including Commercial off-the-shelf server (COTs) (x86 architecture extendable with eCPRI processing cards) over which various virtualisation frameworks can be deployed such as OpenStack and Kubernetes.

Network Management, Orchestration and Slicing: Adhering to the Int5Gent architecture [14], a network management (based on Open Source Management and Orchestration (MANO) (OSM) [15]) and service orchestration framework will support highly reliable and fully automated PPDR services and network deployment, and their life cycle management. In particular the network management framework includes, a number of SDN controllers and number of network orchestration functionalities providing the following functionalities/capabilities:

- mmWave backhaul transport network management and control
- CNFs and VNFs (Virtual Network Functions) lifecycle management including: Radio Network Slice components (vBBU) orchestration at the Portable NFVI (Edge), 5GC Slice components orchestration at the Portable NFVI (Edge)
- Exchange of information with Portable NFVI and Telco cloud for: application's quota arbitration and reservation, application's quota management,
- 5G Network Slices' modelling
- Application's high-level requirements mapping into 5GQI (5G NR Standardized QoS Identifier)
- End-to-End (E2E) Network Slice composition and orchestration

On the other hand, the Application Orchestration framework is compatible with state-of-the-art cloud orchestrators (k8s or OpenStack) undertaking the application lifecycle management, including:

- (User Interface) UI-based application onboarding
- UI-based application policy definition
- Automated application graph composition
- Application components' lifecycle management, orchestration, scaling
- Data analytics and monitoring dashboard

PPDR Applications at Network Edge: At application level, the PPDR services can be versatile; one of the most commonly targeted is drone-based real-time video streaming services enhanced with video processing capabilities and visualization of processed outcomes and extracted results. For such applications, Int5Gent considers the deployment of AI-based edge processing functions for the advanced functionalities. In the context of Int5Gent, a drone-based real-time video streaming service is used that exploits the network edge for delivering:

- live transcoding to various formats and resolutions depending on user type (e.g., field unit, dashboard/tactical command, AI),
- video source to leverage AI capabilities,
- core AI/ML (Machine Learning) (learning/inference) functions.

4 Further Challenges and Requirements

Apparently, different network architecture designs and various deployment options (e.g. extension of public networks, provisioning of network slices over public networks and NPNs etc.) are feasible for offering PPDR services. However, as aforementioned relying on public networks availability may not be the option especially in disaster situations, while extending public networks may no be feasible due to inexistence or inadequate resources of transport network deployment. In such cases, the deployment of NPN can provide the necessary connectivity for PPDR services.

In such niche 5G networks (NPN) deployed by the vertical at issue, additional challenges may arise, that need to be tackled. Indicatively, the deployment options to be followed at the access and fronthaul network layer entail significant network planning challenges that depend on the area morphology/cluster, the coverage area size, the services to be deployed etc. For instance, in some cases point-to-point fiber (p2p) between the access network equipment and the edge node can be a solution, however in cases where multiple access network sites are needed, the transition towards beyond p2p topologies is required. Deployment-oriented challenges are associated with these p2mp fiber distribution network connections between the radio and baseband resources though, such as the high-precision synchronization and the strict packet delay requirements [19]. In deployment scenarios where fiber is not an option, wireless fronthaul technologies need to be considered. In the latter case, on the other hand, wireless fronthaul links pose their own requirements related to their wireless signal propagation characteristics. On the other hand, services may pose significant challenges related to coverage and performance that need to be tackled at network deployment time; for instance, UAV applications imply spatial coverage in three dimensions.

For services that are not locally restricted to disaster area, it is needed to ensure continuity outside the boundaries of the niche 5G systems (NPN), which will involve the interconnection or even tighter interoperability with public ones (e.g. in the form of networks' roaming, or even in the form of service migration across networks). In other cases, for PPDR NPNs that aim to provide also public services in disaster situations, Multi-Operator Core Network (MOCN) or Shared RAN configurations may need to be considered. At this point, a policies framework fostering the deployment and operation of small-scale networks is key.

5 Conclusions

This paper has provided an overview of key PPDR operational scenarios -namely the day-to-day operations and the disaster situation- and the relevant service requirements. These requirements have been used as a basis for the definition of system specifications of the Int5Gent solution. The solution addressing this vertical is based on a resilient, automatically deployed network layer that entails the incorporation of edge computing at the proximity to service area. Edge computing serves for placing the necessary virtualized network functions –ranging from vBBU, to specific data plane Network Functions, and further to complete 5G network- and for processing intensive service intelligence (AI/ML) functions. The solution is completed with a cutting-edge network orchestration framework, with intelligent service allocation and management capabilities.

To this end, specifications have been nailed down to an experimentation deployment for testing and evaluation of the PPDR scenarios and drone-based real-time video streaming services. Future work will focus on evaluating the capabilities of the solution in a real setup and on identifying the challenges related to the operation of the solution.

Acknowledgements. The research leading to these results has received funding from the European Union's Framework Programme Horizon 2020 under grant agreements (1) No. 957403 and project name "Integrating 5G enabling technologies in a holistic service to physical layer 5G system platform".

References

1. 3rd Generation Partnership Project (3GPP) Technical Specification 22.179, Mission Critical Push to Talk (MCPTT); Stage 1, Rel. 17
2. 3rd Generation Partnership Project (3GPP) Technical Specification 22.280, Mission Critical Services Common Requirements (MCCoRe); Stage 1, Rel.18
3. 3rd Generation Partnership Project (3GPP) Technical Specification 22.281, Mission Critical (MC) video, Rel.16
4. 3rd Generation Partnership Project (3GPP) Technical Specification 22.282, Mission Critical (MC) data, Rel. 16
5. Volk, M., Sterle, J.: 5G experimentation for public safety: technologies, facilities and use cases. IEEE Access **9**, 41184–41217 (2021). https://doi.org/10.1109/ACCESS.2021.3064405
6. SNS Telecom & IT. The Public Safety LTE & 5G Market: 2020 – 2030 – Opportunities, Challenges, Strategies & Forecasts, May 2020
7. SNS Telecom & IT. LTE & 5G for Critical Communications: 2020 – 2030 – Opportunities, Challenges, Strategies & Forecasts, October 2020
8. Bhatia, B.: Status and Trends of Public Protection and Disaster Relief (PPDR) Communications. https://www.itu.int/dms_pub/itu-r/oth/0a/0E/R0A0E0000CB0001PDFE.pdf
9. Bhatia, B.: Evolving and modernizing PPDR radiocommunications, 31 July 2019. https://news.itu.int/evolving-and-modernizing-ppdr-radiocommunications/
10. Saafi, S., Hosek, J., Kolackova, A.: Enabling next-generation public safety operations with mission-critical networks and wearable applications. Sens. (Basel, Switz.) **21**(17), 5790 (2021). https://doi.org/10.3390/s21175790

11. Golob, K.: Information Society Directorate, Ministry of Public Administration, Slovenia, Slovenian 5G pilot projects. ITU regional seminar on 5G Implementation, Budapest, 3 July 2018. https://www.itu.int/en/ITU-D/Regional-Presence/Europe/Documents/Events/2018/5GHungary/S2%20Kory%20Golob.pdf
12. Chochliouros, I.P., et al.: 5G for the support of public safety services. Wirel. Pers. Commun. **120**(3), 2321–2348 (2021). https://doi.org/10.1007/s11277-021-08473-5
13. 5G-PPP Project Int5Gent. https://int5gent.eu/
14. Klonidis, D., et al.: Int5Gent: an integrated end-to-end system platform for verticals and data plane solutions beyond 5G. In: 2021 Joint European Conference on Networks and Communications & 6G Summit (EuCNC/6G Summit), pp. 604–609 (2021). https://doi.org/10.1109/EuCNC/6GSummit51104.2021.9482436
15. Int5Gent Project. Deliverable D2.2, Marketable use case scenarios and related end user, standardization, and industrial requirements, January 2022
16. ETSI OpenSource MANO (OSM). https://osm.etsi.org/
17. Guillen, A., et al.: Edge computing for 5G networks - white paper. Zenodo (2020). https://doi.org/10.5281/zenodo.3698117
18. Int5Gent Project Deliverable D2.1, Complete 5G system architecture and requirements, October 2021
19. Liu, J., Xu, S., Zhou, S., Niu, Z.: Redesigning fronthaul for next-generation networks: beyond baseband samples and point -to-point links. IEEE Wirel. Commun. **22**(5), 90–97 (2015). https://doi.org/10.1109/MWC.2015.7306542

Advancements in Edge Computing and Service Orchestration in Support of Advanced Surveillance Services

Ioanna Mesogiti[1]([✉]) [iD], Eleni Theodoropoulou[1], Fotini Setaki[1],
George Lyberopoulos[1], Francesca Moscateli[2], Konstantina Kanta[3],
Giannis Giannoulis[3], Panagiotis Toumasis[3], Dimitris Apostolopoulos[3],
Hercules Avramopoulos[3], Lukasz Lopacinski[4], Jesús Gutiérrez Teran[4],
Anastasios Nanos[5], Yigal Leiba[6], Markos Anastasopoulos[7], and Anna Tzanakaki[7]

[1] COSMOTE Mobile Telecommunications S.A., Athens, Greece
imesogiti@cosmote.gr
[2] Nextworks S.R.L., Pisa, Italy
[3] National Technical University of Athens, Athens, Greece
[4] IHP - Leibniz-Institut für Innovative Mikroelektronik, Frankfurt, Germany
[5] Nubificus Ltd., Athens, Greece
[6] SIKLU Communication LTD., Petach Tikwa, Israel
[7] National and Kapodistrian University of Athens, Athens, Greece

Abstract. The 5G and beyond advancements will impact significantly the evolution of many vertical industries such as the Surveillance and Safety sector. To this end, the requirements posed by its associated services can be satisfied to a certain degree by 5G network slicing and by control and user plane separation -allowing for exploitation of edge computing-, while aspects related to network deployment resilience and end-to-end service orchestration of infrastructure, network and applications across edge and cloud domains are still under investigation. The 5G-COMPLETE project focuses on delivering Beyond 5G technology innovations in the edge and orchestration domains (among others), that can support highly demanding vertical services/applications and relevant use cases such as Advanced Surveillance; along with holistic 5G deployment paradigms and experimentation deployments for testing and evaluation. This paper discusses the service and technical requirements and provides an overview of the proposed technologies and deployment solutions.

Keywords: 5G · Advanced Surveillance Services · Edge computing · Vertical services · Network orchestration

1 Introduction

5G and beyond networks aim to transform traditional network service provisioning into the provision of a holistic infrastructure and network services tailored to individual service and user requirements. To this end, these networks enable the deployment of various

I. Maglogiannis et al. (Eds.): AIAI 2022 Workshops, IFIP AICT 652, pp. 53–60, 2022.
https://doi.org/10.1007/978-3-031-08341-9_5

services for key vertical industries (smart cities, industry 4.0, automotive, multimedia, etc.) that traditionally relied on closed, private infrastructures. This paradigm shift relies on the capability for distributed network deployments across cloud and edge domains.

During the last years, Surveillance Services have gradually evolved from human-based camera feeds monitoring to Advanced Surveillance (AS) applications [2]; then from AS applications based on local processing to applications deployable on cloud infrastructures [3–5]; and lately to distributed applications deployable across cloud and edge infrastructures [6, 7]. Other enhancements have focused on utilizing advanced (local) compute frameworks for the deployment of the processing-power-demanding (parts of) surveillance applications [8]. Overall, Surveillance Services are increasingly being featured with intelligence, following Information and Communication Technology (ICT) breakthroughs especially in the fields of cloud and edge computing and service deployment [9].

However, network service requirements of these applications entail the use of network frameworks beyond traditional centralized networks and the centralized cloud infrastructures. Delivering these services over 5G network slices spanning across edge and cloud domains can be considered the next step in this sector. At the same time, from 5G network perspective 5G advanced aspects such as automation and adoption of IT advancements can further elevate surveillance services provisioning (such as those described in [13]). In this landscape, the 5G-PPP 5G-COMPLETE project [1] focuses on delivering an implementation paradigm for AS service provisioning. This paper aims at providing an overview of this paradigm to be demonstrated at a field testbed in Athens, Greece.

This paper is organized as follows: initially, the service and network deployment requirements and options of AS services are discussed. An overview of the 5G-COMPLETE deployment paradigm -covering these requirements- and technologies is presented in the subsequent section. Following these, aspects related to the operational adoption of such solutions are discussed, while conclusions are drawn at the end.

2 Advanced Surveillance/Physical Security Services' Requirements

Provisioning of AS to various Service Customer segments (a.k.a. vertical industries) may include functionalities such as object detection/classification, object tracking, smart alerting, etc. Such services are especially relevant for vertical industries operating distributed, possibly unattended sites such as network sites, energy utilities sites etc., as well as for Industry 4.0 monitoring operations, for smart cities and state services providing public safety services, etc.

To render a solution attractive to the stakeholders, a long list of requirements shall be met. Such requirements refer to [11]:

- Usability including ease of installation/operation,
- Fast service deployment including
- Scalability
- Interoperability with various camera vendor models (e.g., wired and wireless, bullet and PTZ (Pan Tilt Zoom), indoor and outdoor cameras supported),

- Application functionalities including: 24 h × 7 days monitoring, visualization of in various ways of versatile information (e.g. sites' info over maps, snapshots/videos per site and per camera, statistics, playback, live streaming, camera configuration), automated storage in secure backend infrastructure, smart alerting, including enhanced notifications voice announcements, etc.
- Cost referring to low-cost deployment and operation; i.e. reuse of existing cameras, without additional hardware at site and associated support costs, reduced need for human resources for monitoring purposes, etc.,

On the other hand, specific functionalities/features pose highly demanding performance requirements. Such functionalities are:

- Object detection, classification and smart tracking; the list of objects (e.g., vehicles, humans) to be detected/tracked must be customized by the end-user and can be quite large.
- Synchronization of multiple cameras' and devices, considering cases in which a camera's movement needs to be triggered not only by information generated from its own feeds' processing (motion or object detection events), but also by external sources e.g., by a signal sent by an activity detector, another camera etc.

Such application functionalities require high availability, low latency for the actuation part of the service, and adequate user data rates for the relevant camera streams. Deploying such services at scale can pose highly demanding Key Performance Indicator (KPI) targets for the network deployment.

Currently, commercial surveillance/physical security solutions are mainly based on closed platforms (to support live streaming, video/snapshots storage, line/area crossing, remote configuration, cloud storage, etc.), followed by limitations for instance in terms of local processing (camera or site-level), flexibility in service provisioning, scalability in terms of number of cameras, maintenance and support overhead. From a network perspective, solutions rely on local private networks and utilization of own storage/cloud infrastructure. Latter deployments incur high Total Cost of Ownership (TCO) related to the purchase cost of the equipment and the operational cost of the network and compute infrastructure. 5G technologies incorporating network slicing and edge capabilities may address well such use cases.

3   5G-COMPLETE Technologies and Proposed Deployment

3.1   5G-COMPLETE Overview

5G-COMPLETE builds upon a well-defined layered architecture integrating novel networking and compute blocks, forming a common heterogeneous infrastructure where service-driven slice management can facilitate realistic deployment options [10, 14]. In particular, 5G-COMPLETE focuses on delivering novel physical and software technological blocks at network and compute domains for the on-demand deployment of services [11], exploiting:

- Beyond 5G wireless transport technologies, such as Software Defined Networking (SDN)-enabled millimeter Wave (mmWave) nodes for resilient point-to multipoint (P2MP) edge networking, and wideband sub-THz (sub-Tera Hertz) nodes featuring multi-core parallel processing baseband architectures.
- Various 3GPP network layer deployment options including centralized public 5G networks, distributed 5G networks and NPNs (non-Public-Networks), Disaggregated Radio Access Node (RAN) structures etc.

These are complemented with a compute domain based on powerful Mobile Edge Computing (MEC) platforms addressing the need for multiple virtualization frameworks (VMs, containers and unikernels) on a single edge resource pool, security and advanced processing capabilities at the edge. The Edge and Cloud domains will be reachable through 5G network connectivity offering 3GPP-compliant performance guarantees. For services such as ultra-reliable low latency communications (URLLC) or critical Machine-Type Communication (mMTC), with very low latency and high reliability requirements, deployment may span across these domains.

On top of these, 5G-COMPLETE solution includes a multi-layer, cross-domain network management and orchestration (MANO) layer that can functionally deploy the innovations of its technological blocks and perform their life-cycle-management (LCM), enabling the service-driven slice management in realistic deployment options [12]. 5G-COMPLETE multi-layer MANO layer is also designed with the aim of supporting the dynamic provisioning, configuration, and automation of virtualized vertical services for the service customers in tailored end-to-end 5G Network Slices, and is based on ETSI MANO OSM (Open Source MANO [15]).

3.2 5G-COMPLETE Deployment for Advanced Surveillance Services

Based on this set of technologies, 5G-COMPLETE aims to deliver a paradigm for the support of AS services and their lifecycle management [11]. The 5G-COMPLETE deployment is presented in Fig. 1. The proposed solution will include a multi-domain deployment consisting of distinct Edge and Cloud compute domains providing:

- Advanced infrastructure security at Edge Cloud deployment (e.g. trusted boot and secure execution for Workloads) [10] addressing the user requirement for high security.
- Diversification in terms of resources selection and capabilities, by exposing Hardware Acceleration (HA) functions for the AS service workloads that need low processing delay and low end-to-end network latency.

For the cases of (remote or urban) sites lacking fiber deployment, wireless transport network technologies are considered for the transport network domain. Considering also the service/business requirements for maximizing performance, availability and resilience these will be addressed by the following 5G-COMPLETE technologies:

- High capacity, self-organizing, resilient mmWave mesh architectures, based on Software Defined Networking (SDN)-enabled mmWave nodes.

- High capacity, SDN-enabled THz nodes.

These domains are orchestrated by an Orchestration framework that is capable of:

- Collecting and processing the network topology as well as the capabilities and characteristics of the multiple compute domains.
- (Co-)Provisioning the mmWave transport network resources on-demand, with specific QoS characteristics reflecting the slice requirements and taking into consideration the actual placement of service components (SCs) that have to be interconnected.
- (Co-)Provisioning connectivity over the THz link.
- Performing service lifecycle management across the multiple application and network service provisioning layers.

In addition, it shall be possible from the 5G-COMPLETE orchestration layer to interoperate with the 5G core (5GC) in order to define and provision the 5G network slice characteristics.

In the context of 5G-COMPLETE, an AS application [16] will be used to offer advanced functionalities on top of commodity Pan-Tilt-Zoom cameras and sensors. The application comprises various surveillance-related functionalities including:

- Functionalities such as Artificial Intelligence (AI)-based Smart Tracking requiring low end-to-end latency (including low network latency and fast processing) for real-time video processing and camera motion/zoom control so that it continuously monitors the target object, as well as high availability;
- Functionalities such as non-Real Time Processing (e.g. storage of captures, offline object detection/ classification, visualization, statistics generation, etc.), which might have high storage and processing requirements but lower latency requirements.

The application will be packaged in two chainable Service Components (SCs). One SC (SC1) is the Fast Video Processing component, comprising the performance-critical functionalities, and a second (SC2) is the non-Real Time Processing component, comprising functionalities with lower performance requirements.

The 5G-COMPLETE deployment will enable:

a. Vertical Service On-boarding: The vertical service will be on-boarded using the vertical service blueprint that describes the service (i.e. the service components, their attributes and high-level requirements).
b. Application Placement based on a Placement Service that will compute the optimized network paths for providing the necessary connectivity along with an optimal placement of the service components at the available compute resources (Network Function Virtualization Infrastructure (NFVI) Layer); matching the service requirements with the resources and capabilities. The suitable hardware resources and virtualized framework will be selected.
c. Transport Network (TN) Slice management (given a 5G network deployment): The Placement Service will also take care of the actual provisioning of the TN resources of the mmWave and the THz links.

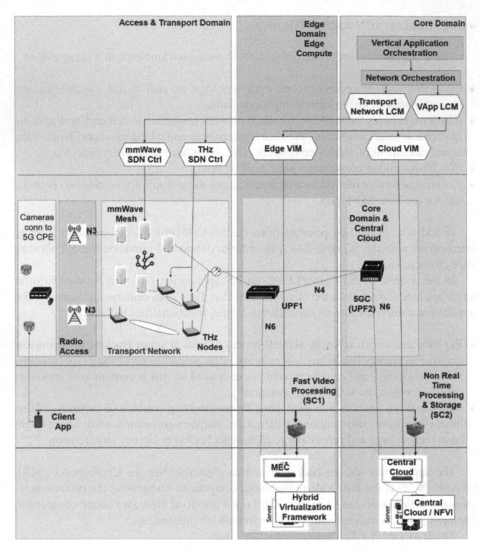

Fig. 1. 5G-COMPLETE, experimentation deployment for surveillance services.

4 Conclusions

Following the evolution in the field of surveillance services over the latest years in terms of application functionalities as well as in terms of deployment options on compute infrastructures this paper has focused on the exploitation of 5G and beyond deployments for the support of Advanced Surveillance services. To this end, the deployment paradigm of 5G-COMPLETE project tailored to AS services has been presented.

The 5G-COMPLETE solution is based on a resilient, self-optimized transport network layer complementing an existing 5G network deployment in areas lacking fiber deployment, and entails the incorporation of edge and cloud computing for the deployment of AS services components. Edge computing serves for placing the necessary application functionalities that are latency critical and processing intensive (e.g. AI-based functions), while the cloud resources can be used for storage demanding application functionalities/ components. The solution allows for service lifecycle management based on an application and network orchestration framework. Future work will focus on evaluating the capabilities of the 5G-COMPLETE solution in a real setup.

Acknowledgements. The research leading to these results has received funding from the European Union's Framework Programme Horizon 2020 under grant agreements (1) No. 871900 and project name 5G-COMPLETE - "A unified network, Computational and storage resource Management framework targeting end-to-end Performance optimization for secure 5G muLti-tEchnology and multi-Tenancy Environments".

References

1. 5G-PPP Project 5G-COMPLETE. https://5gcomplete.eu/
2. Mierzwiński, D., Walczak, D., Wolski, M., Wrzos, M.: Surveillance system in service-oriented manner. In: 12th International Symposium on Symbolic and Numeric Algorithms for Scientific Computing, pp. 427–433 (2021). https://doi.org/10.1109/SYNASC.2010.83
3. Usman Ullah, A.W., Shah, J.A., Kadir, K., Wahid, A.: Development of smart surveillance system using cloud for security application. In: IEEE International Instrumentation and Measurement Technology Conference (I2MTC), pp. 1–6 (2021). https://doi.org/10.1109/I2MTC5 0364.2021.9459817
4. Zhang, H., Ma, H., Fu, G., Yang, X., Jiang, Z., Gao, Y.: Container based video surveillance cloud service with fine-grained resource provisioning. In: IEEE 9th International Conference on Cloud Computing (CLOUD), pp. 758–765 (2016). https://doi.org/10.1109/CLOUD.2016. 0105
5. Usman Ullah, A.W., Shah, J.A., Kadir, K., Wahid, A.: Development of smart surveillance system using cloud for security application. In: 2021 IEEE International Instrumentation and Measurement Technology Conference (I2MTC), pp. 1–6 (2021). https://doi.org/10.1109/I2M TC50364.2021.9459817
6. Xu, X., Wu, Q., Qi, L., Dou, W., Tsai, S.-B., Bhuiyan, M.Z.A.: Trust-aware service offloading for video surveillance in edge computing enabled internet of vehicles. IEEE Trans. Intell. Transp. Syst. **22**(3), 1787–1796 (2021). https://doi.org/10.1109/TITS.2020.2995622
7. Nikouei, S.Y., Chen, Y., Faughnan, T.R.: Smart surveillance as an edge service for real-time human detection and tracking. In: IEEE/ACM Symposium on Edge Computing (SEC), pp. 336–337 (2018).https://doi.org/10.1109/SEC.2018.00036
8. Yan, W.Q.: Surveillance computing. In: Introduction to Intelligent Surveillance. TCS, pp. 195–212. Springer, Cham (2019). https://doi.org/10.1007/978-3-030-10713-0_9
9. Guillen, A., et al.: Edge computing for 5G networks - white paper. Zenodo (2020). https://doi.org/10.5281/zenodo.3698117
10. Tzanakaki, A., et al.: 5G-COMPLETE Deliverable D2.1, Initial report on 5G-COMPLETE network architecture, interfaces and supported functions (2021)
11. 5G-COMPLETE Project. Deliverable D6.1, Report on the Testing Methodologies and Testbed Setup (2021)

12. Moscatelli F., et al.: 5G-COMPLETE: service-driven slice management over heterogeneous 5G infrastructures. In: IEEE 26th International Workshop on Computer Aided Modeling and Design of Communication Links and Networks (CAMAD), pp. 1–6 (2021). https://doi.org/10.1109/CAMAD52502.2021.9617774
13. Gkatzios, N., Anastasopoulos, M., Tzanakaki, A., Simeonidou, D.: Optimized placement of virtualized resources for 5G services exploiting live migration. Photon Netw. Commun. **40**(3), 233–244 (2020). https://doi.org/10.1007/s11107-020-00905-9
14. Alevizaki V.M., Manolopoulos A.I., Anastasopoulos M., Tzanakaki A.: Dynamic user plane function allocation in 5G networks enabled by optical network nodes. In: European Conference on Optical Communication (ECOC), pp. 1–4 (2021).https://doi.org/10.1109/ECOC52684.2021.9606154
15. ETSI OpenSource MANO (OSM). URL: https://osm.etsi.org/
16. Lyberopoulos G., et al.: Unified e2e smart home/building solution for energy management, home comfort and security. In: (Demo) Proceedings of 2021 IEEE International Mediterranean Conference on Communications and Networking (MeditCom) (2021)

AI-Driven Intent-Based Networking for 5G Enhanced Robot Autonomy

Marios Sophocleous[1](✉) (iD), Christina Lessi[2], Zhao Xu[3], Jakub Špaňhel[4] (iD), Renxi Qiu[5], Adrian Lendinez[5], Ioannis Chondroulis[6], and Ioannis Belikaidis[6]

[1] Arch. Makariou III and Mesaorias 1, eBOS Technologies Ltd, 2090 Lakatamia, Nicosia, Cyprus
marioss@ebos.com.cy
[2] Hellenic Telecommunications Organization (OTE) S.A, 99 Kifissias Avenue, 15124 Maroussi, Athens, Greece
[3] NEC Laboratories Europe, Kurfürsten-Anlage 36, 69115 Heidelberg, Germany
[4] Faculty of Information Technology, Brno University of Technology, Brno, Czech Republic
[5] School of Computer Science, University of Bedfordshire, Luton, UK
[6] WINGS ICT Solutions, 189 Siggrou Avenue, 17121 Athens, Greece

Abstract. Innovative 5G orchestration architectures so far, have been mainly designed and optimized for Quality of Service (QoS), but are not aware of Quality of Experience (QoE). This makes intent recognition and End-to-End interpretability an inherited problem for orchestration systems, leading to possible creation of ineffective control policies. In this paper, an AI-driven intent-based networking for autonomous robots is proposed and demonstrated through the 5G-ERA project. In particular, to map an intent from individual vertical action to a global OSM control policy, a workflow of four tools is proposed: i) Action Sequence Generation, ii) Network Intent Estimation, iii) Resource Usage Forecasting, and iv) OSM Control Policy Generation. All of these tools are described in the paper with specific function descriptions, inputs, outputs and the semantic models/Machine Learning tools that have been used. Finally, the paper presents the developed intent-based dashboard for the visualization of the tools' outputs, whilst taking QoE into consideration.

Keywords: 5G · Intent-based networking · Enhanced robot autonomy · 5G-ERA · Machine learning · Semantic models · Autonomous robots

1 Introduction

5G technology has received a significant interest from the scientific and industrial community in the last decade. The advantages of the 5G technology are especially attractive for a variety of sectors, such as the robotics industry. Currently, innovative 5G orchestration architectures have been mainly designed for service delivery [1–3] without vertical-specific knowledge. Information models are the basis of the architectures on managing

© IFIP International Federation for Information Processing 2022
Published by Springer Nature Switzerland AG 2022
I. Maglogiannis et al. (Eds.): AIAI 2022 Workshops, IFIP AICT 652, pp. 61–70, 2022.
https://doi.org/10.1007/978-3-031-08341-9_6

the life cycle of the services and resources [3, 4]. Those models are largely based on the concept of Anaemic Domain Models [5] optimized for creating, reading, updating, and deleting (CRUD) services in a procedural style. As a result, implicit intents of the services are not really taken into consideration in the approach hence, orchestrators are optimized only for Quality of Service (QoS) without taking Quality of Experience (QoE) into consideration. This makes intent recognition and End-to-End (E2E) interpretability an inherited problem for orchestration systems, leading to the possible creation of ineffective control policies [6]. This issue has been partially addressed in some existing 5G vertical applications by limiting the number of technology stacks. However, robotic verticals normally require components from multiple vendors with multiple technology stacks [7–10]. 5G experimental facilities need a solution that maintains intent recognition and maps the user requirement into measurable network KPIs when multiple technology stacks are involved.

In this paper, AI-driven intent-based networking, from the semantic models and machine learning tools to the visualization dashboard, for 5G enhanced robot autonomy is presented. The intent-based networking is to capture users' (vertical customers) intent and to align continuously the E2E networking to the recognized intents. It aims to improve QoE for 5G-based autonomous robots. 5G robotic applications have received considerable attention in recent years. While most of the research has been focused on closed-loop control; the effectiveness of this approach alone is questionable in the robotics community as it overlooks a key experience of autonomous robots - the need for robot autonomy, particularly, in real-world robotic applications. By shifting knowledge and learning from individual robots to the edges and the central cloud, 5G is able to establish connected robotic intelligence, and subsequently realize and enhance robot autonomy with the connected intelligence.

2 Concept of Intent-Based Networking for Autonomous Robots

The aim of the intent-based networking for autonomous robots is to optimize the QoE of 5G orchestrators for vertical applications. For optimized experience on individual 5G-based autonomous robots, 5G needs to specify and optimally allocate resources required by the connected intelligence. The intent-based networking predicts the need for intelligence from the intents and specifies policy on individual applications to deliver management, topology, placement, and resource optimization within 5G and cloud environments. The autonomous use cases under the connected intelligence require computing and storage to be shifted dynamically and repeatedly among robots, edges, and the central cloud. Partial information will be replicated among Network Services (NSs) deployed in different locations. To tailor NSs under the intent-based networking, different configurations of Virtual Network Functions (VNFs) and slices are required [11–13]. The creation of slices, at the level of complexity of the use cases, is still problematic for exiting testbeds. 5G experimental facilities need to be adapted towards cloud-native approach for efficient service delivery on the enhanced robot autonomy. Meanwhile, the intent-based networking also enhances the existing NSs using cloud native approach, with respect to the scalability, availability and feature velocity of the NSs as expected by autonomous robots. Therefore, the development of the intent-based networking fills the gaps between existing 5G product vision and cloud native deployment required by the robot autonomy enhancement. Overall, the development of intent-based networking for autonomous robots reveals how operational processes of essential robotic capabilities can be integrated into a rich domain model on supporting advanced orchestration.

In this paper vertical specific QoE models will be identified as the basis of contexts for service interoperability and service topology. The patterns and contexts will be realized life cycle management. The contexts enable patterns to be tangible in their specific sub-domains for further verification. The innovation leads to an automated and interpretable mechanism for deriving the placement of network functions, order of component instantiation. The innovation paves the way for application-driven approaches toward automatic configuration on testbeds using Machine Learning (ML) and Artificial Intelligence (AI). The concept also led to a cloud native service delivery under Microservices architecture. Computing would be shifted among the robots, Multi-Access Edge Computing (MECs) and the central cloud under connected intelligence. The models will be optimized for MEC and central cloud for NSs' synchronization with data consistency. The conceptual design illustrated in the following sections enables the composition a distributed application from separately deployable services as required by Edgy DevOps [6] The innovation enables NetApps and Orchestrators to access the robotic resources by translating QoS of VNFs (instantiation, scaling, updating and termination) to efficient robot control policy.

3   Semantic Models and Machine Learning Tools

To achieve the QoE oriented networking for 5G-based autonomous robots, a set of semantic models and Machine Learning tools were developed. By design, each tool can fulfill a function independently with inputs from other functions, and in the meanwhile, all the functions are linked together as a loop to continuously align the network management with the identified behaviors of 5G enhanced robots. In particular, to map an intent from individual vertical action to a global Open-Source MANO (OSM) control policy, we propose a workflow with the following four tools, illustrated in Fig. 1. With the designed workflow, the network management and orchestration can be extended to stay aligned with the actions of robots, which enhances their capability, and facilitates the autonomous robots to carry out different vertical-specific tasks.

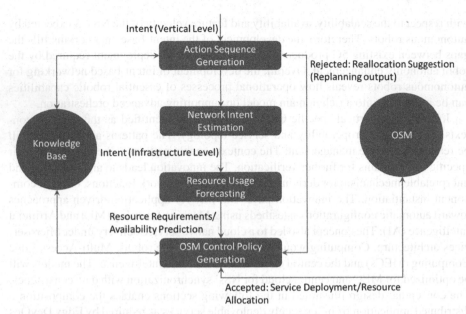

Fig. 1. AI-driven intent-based management workflow with the semantic and ML tools.

3.1 Action Sequence Generation

The semantic tool Action Sequence Generation maps the intent of a given task (e.g., go-to-kitchen) under the vertical application to a sequence of robot actions. This is learned from historical data, and integrates domain knowledge. The results are stored in a knowledge base. High level unstructured task requirement from users will be translated into specific and structured requirement of tangible actions. The actions can be retrieved from predefined containers or physical functions for instantiation, scaling and management. They lead to a scalable approach that translates vertical intent on capabilities into a network intent on resources. The vertical intents are defined in the semantic model based on "How do we store the intent within semantic model?". A task table is prepared in the Semantic Knowledge Base (KB) to hold the intent selected by domain driven design. It records:

1. The robots, which are running for a particular task/intent.
2. The time at which they were assigned to the intent.
3. The status of the execution of the intent.

Table 1. Semantic interpretation of robot tasks

Semantic tool: action sequence generation	
Function description	Predicting potential actions involved in a pre-defined task
Inputs	*From end users:* Name of the task Outputs of ML Tool: OSM Control Policy Generation Approval or Rejection of the task Feedback from OSM policy, in case it is rejected *From Semantic Knowledge Base:* Historical information of actions (successful rate, quality of experience, and blocked experience) Historical information of actors (Robot, Cloud, or Edge) and NetApps (placement of the containers, availability of the slices, completion of the actions)
Outputs	Expected action sequence for completing the task. Corresponding actor for the actions
Methods	State Based Decision Process & Experience Blocking Index

3.2 Network Intent Estimation

The function Network Intent Estimation is implemented with both semantic and ML tools. They aim to learn the mapping between the identified robot actions and the demanded network resources in a local site. Every provided robotic service has its own QoS requirements with respect to its purpose and implementation. The QoS demands may differ based on the placement location of this service even based on the requester. The semantic tool will look up the pre-defined static mappings and probabilistic distributions of the actions. The ML tool will learn new mappings from the existing ones. A basic description of the toolbox interface is provided in Table 2.

Methods Description: The semantic and machine learning tool performs individual resource planning through two independent mechanisms.

Static Mapping: The default variant based on deterministic table lookup according to pre-defined information in the KB with respect to the requested service and actor. The mean value for each metric part is used in case of multiple records or historical data available.

Forecasted QoS: This method exploits multiple records for each service with respect to the timeline order of these records (time-series), their seasonality, influence of holidays and forecast uncertainty.

Table 2. Description of the tool for mapping intent to resource usage

Semantic & machine learning tools: mapping intent to resource usage	
Function description	Translate expected action sequence into expected QoS and placement of the Kubernetes-based VNF (KNF)
Inputs	Action sequence from Tool 1 Actors from Tool 1 Table of QoS expectation per action stored in KB Historical data about real measured requirements by Actors/Services (optional)
Outputs	Placement of the KNFs/VNFs and expected resources per network function for an individual robot
Methods	Deterministic table lookup based on pre-defined information in KB Forecasted QoS based on pre-defined information in KB and historical data

3.3 Resource Usage Forecasting

The ML tool Resource Usage Forecasting analyses resource usage of a VNF/KNF associated with the robot. It will forecast the confidence of achieving the network intent in the near future. The basic function and technical details of the tool are summarized as the table below:

Table 3. Resource usage forecasting description

Machine learning tool: resource usage forecasting	
Function description	Analyze the historical resource usage, traffic load and other related telemetry, to forecast the future resource usage, and thus estimate the confidence of satisfying the intent, i.e., the allocated resource
Inputs	Intents: a set of numbers, e.g., allocated resources (CPU/memory usage) and required latency and throughput Time series data about traffic load and other related telemetry, e.g., channel quality etc Time series data about CPU usage etc
Outputs	Probabilistic distribution (confidence) that the intents can still be satisfied in the near future
Methods	Probabilistic models with uncertainty estimation

3.4 OSM Control Policy Generation

The ML tool OSM Control Policy Generation learns an OSM control policy. It makes decisions to accept/reject resource allocation plan or trigger a replanning request. Please refer to the following table for the technical details of the tool:

Table 4. OSM control policy generation description.

Machine learning tool: OSM control policy generation	
Function description	Analyze the historical data of the infrastructure to predict its behavior according to the predicted resource usage. Estimate the deployment feasibility to accept or reject the resource allocation plan
Inputs	Resource usage estimation Resource availability prediction Infrastructure-level resource usage/availability (historical data)
Outputs	OSM input: Accepted resource allocation plan Tool 1 input: new resource allocation suggestion (rejected resource allocation plan - replanning)
Methods	AI-algorithms (Q-learning, clustering, etc.)

4 Intent-Based Visualization Tools

An Intent-based, front-end Dashboard (IBD) has been developed to enable the use of the Semantic & Machine Learning (ML) tools, described in the previous section, for the better resource management of the network. Although each robot vendor might have an existing User Interface (UI) in order to control and communicate with their robots, there is no UI for the 5G-ERA's unique ML tool for resource usage prediction based on the user's intent and providing better performance, Quality of Service (QoS) and Quality of Experience by the dynamic control of the network resources. Network orchestrators, such as Open-Source MANO (OSM) usually have their own dashboard however, that dashboard only shows the network's resources hence, the results of the ML tool can't be integrated onto that interface.

IBD development can be separated into two parts, the back-end and the front-end. The back-end, responsible to communicate with the database to obtain and format the data was developed using .NET CORE [14] 3.1 framework and C#. The main purpose of the back-end is to connect to the database through an Application Programming Interface (API) and obtain the required data. Once the data is obtained from the database, the format that the data must have to be pushed to the front-end is also edited by the back-end. Additionally, the back-end is responsible to connect to the SQL server that has all the user login information with assigned access levels and site access. The main idea is that specific users will have different access levels, i.e., one user can only be an observer and another user can have higher authorization levels with full access to the IBD. The front-end was developed using HTML, CSS JavaScript, and jQuery technologies. The front-end is responsible to obtain the formatted data from the back-end and present them in a specific format/way e.g., a graphical representation of the data.

4.1 Intent-Based Dashboard Architecture

The general architecture of the IBD is based on the standard Model-View-Controller (MVC) approach. The actual architecture of the IBD is shown in Fig. 2 below. In this implementation, another component is introduced, the business logic that is responsible to communicate with the database's API and obtain the required data.

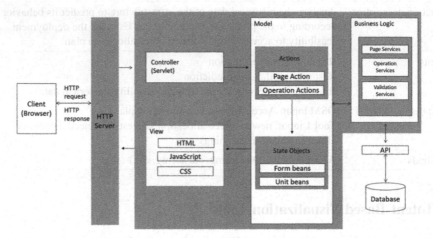

Fig. 2. IBD architecture and connectivity to the database.

4.2 Functionalities

Through the developed IBD users have their own login details to be used on the login page (Fig. 3) and each user will have his/her own access rights, specific use case (UC), and access to specific controls and these will be stored along with the user's login details. Each user can save their own customization formats and see data from the specific use case they are involved. Other than the authorization levels and direct link of an account with a specific UC, the developed IBD is capable of some visual customizations from the user such as the light or dark mode as well as the choice of changing the background colors. In terms of login security, the authentication security system from.NET Core framework (Microsoft) was used.

IBD is divided into four sections highlighting the four stages of the semantic & ML tools described in the previous section. Other than just the 4-sections, IBD has a navigation pane on the left. Although IBD was not intended to replace the proprietary HMIs of the UC executors and the robot users, based on the obtained UC requirements, it was proposed that such privileges would be very useful in the execution of the trials (Fig. 4). In terms of security, the same level of security implemented for the IBD login, will be valid for the HMI too.

Fig. 3. Login page.

Fig. 4. Portal from the IBD to a vendors' web-based HMI.

5   Conclusions

In this paper, the semantic models and the machine learning tools for 5G enhanced robot autonomy were presented. The tools, orchestrating the diverse resources to align with intents of the autonomous robots, are sequentially connected into a loop, including: the semantic tool Action Sequence Generation that maps the intent of a given task under the vertical application to a sequence of robot actions, the tool Net-work Intent Estimation which is responsible for the mapping, and the ML tool Resource Usage Forecasting that analyses resource usage of a VNF/KNF associated with the robot, as well as the tool OSM Control Policy Generation to estimate the deployment feasibility of a resource allocation plan. Additionally, the IBD development was presented and its separation into two parts, the back-end and the front-end, was described.

Acknowledgments. This project has received funding from the European Union's Horizon 2020 research and innovation programme under the Grant Agreement No 101016681.

References

1. Open-source Management and Orchestration (OSM). https://osm.etsi.org/. Accessed 01 Feb 2005
2. Cloudify, https://cloudify.co/. Accessed 01 May 2020
3. Trakadas, P., Karkazis, P., Leligou, H.C, et. al.: Comparison of management and orchestration solutions for the 5G Era. J. Sens. Actuator Netw. **4**(9), (2020)
4. OSM Experience with NFV Architecture, Interfaces and Information Models, May 2018. https://osm.etsi.org/wikipub/index.php/Release_notes_and_whitepapers. Accessed 01 May 2020
5. Anaemic Domain Models, M. Fowler. https://martinfowler.com/bliki/AnemicDomainModel.html. Accessed 01 May 2020
6. Desot, T., Portet, F., Vacher, M.: Towards end-to-end spoken intent recognition in smart home. In: SpeD 2019 – The 10th Conference on Speech Technology and Human Computer Dialogue, Timisoara, Romania, pp. 1–8, October 2019
7. Soldani, D., et al.: 5G mobile systems for healthcare. In: 2017 IEEE 85th Vehicular Technology Conference (VTC Spring), pp. 1–5 (2017). https://doi.org/10.1109/VTCSpring.2017.8108602
8. Zhihan, L.V., Qiao, L., Wang, Q.: Cognitive robotics on 5G networks. ACM Trans. Internet Technol. **21**(4), 92, 18 (2021). https://doi.org/10.1145/3414842
9. Yu, H., Lee, H., Jeon, H.: What is 5G? emerging 5G mobile services and network requirements. Sustainability **2017**, 9 (1848). https://doi.org/10.3390/su9101848
10. Raunholt, T., Rodriguez, I., Mogensen, P., Larsen, M.: Towards a 5G mobile edge cloud planner for autonomous mobile robots. In: 2021 IEEE 94th Vehicular Technology Conference (VTC2021-Fall), pp. 01–05 (2021). https://doi.org/10.1109/VTC2021-Fall52928.2021.9625208
11. Leivadeas, A., Falkner, M.: VNF placement problem: a multi-tenant intent-based networking approach. In: 2021 24th Conference on Innovation in Clouds, Internet and Networks and Workshops (ICIN), pp. 143–150 (2021). https://doi.org/10.1109/ICIN51074.2021.9385553
12. Paganelli, F., Paradiso, F., Gherardelli, M., Galletti, G.: Network service description model for VNF orchestration leveraging intent-based SDN interfaces. In: 2017 IEEE Conference on Network Softwarization (NetSoft), pp. 1-5 (2017). https://doi.org/10.1109/NETSOFT.2017.8004210
13. Rafiq, A., Mehmood, A., Ahmed Khan, T., Abbas, K., Afaq, M., Song, W.-C.: Intent-based end-to-end network service orchestration system for multi-platforms. Sustainability **12**, 2782 (2020). https://doi.org/10.3390/su12072782
14. ETSI White Paper on Developing Software for Multi-Access Edge Computing, https://www.etsi.org/images/files/ETSIWhitePapers/etsi_wp20ed2_MEC_SoftwareDevelopment.pdf. Accessed 01 May 2020

Application of Mobile Networks (5G and Beyond) in Precision Agriculture

Lechosław Tomaszewski[1](✉) [ID], Robert Kołakowski[1,2] [ID],
and Mirosław Zagórda[3] [ID]

[1] Orange Polska S.A., ul. Obrzeżna 7, 02-691 Warszawa, Poland
Lechoslaw.Tomaszewski@orange.com
[2] Warsaw University of Technology, ul. Nowowiejska 15/19,
00-665 Warszawa, Poland
[3] University of Agriculture in Kraków, al. Mickiewicza 21, 31-120 Kraków, Poland

Abstract. The multiple capabilities offered by the 5G network have significantly accelerated the expansion of the service portfolio of telecommunication operators. The future mobile network is expected to elevate these possibilities to an even higher level. Enormous data rate, near-to-zero latency and huge density of devices will allow for building robust and innovative ecosystems providing specialized services to the vertical industries. Moreover, the progress in network expansion towards the edge has facilitated the provisioning of services with stringent requirements much closer to the interested parties. One of such demanding field of services, which is recently gaining much economic significance, is Precision Agriculture (PA). The goal of the paper is to present and assess the possibility of application of 5G and next-generation mobile networks to facilitate PA use cases. After the requirements assessment and 5G network capabilities analysis, the assignment of currently defined slice types and 5G Quality Indicators (5QIs) to the typical PA services is proposed. Moreover, the readiness of the 5G network as well as missing features with regards to PA are identified and addressed to 5G-Advanced and future 6G mobile networks.

Keywords: 5G · 6G · Precision agriculture · Smart agriculture · Vertical services · Network slicing · UAV · V2X · MIoT · URLLC · eMBB · Augmented Reality · mMTC · HMTC · Sensors · MEC

1 Introduction

The 5G System (5GS), since its very first vision formulated by the International Telecommunication Union (ITU) [1], has been expected to introduce massive benefits to wireless communication-based services. One of the main targets of the new mobile generation was to provide one common solution that could address

Supported by the Horizon 2020 project 5G!Drones (Grant Agreement No. 857031).

I. Maglogiannis et al. (Eds.): AIAI 2022 Workshops, IFIP AICT 652, pp. 71–86, 2022.
https://doi.org/10.1007/978-3-031-08341-9_7

stringent and robust requirements of different vertical sectors. Several innovative mechanisms have been proposed by the Standards Developing Organizations (SDOs), with the most notable and revolutionary concept of network slicing – splitting a mobile network into a federation of several ones, each architecturally adapted to support a specific service. So far, five Slice/Service Type (SST) categories have been defined, each targeting a specific range of services characterised by common priority requirements, namely, Enhanced Mobile Broadband (eMBB), Ultra-Reliable Low-Latency Communication (URLLC), Massive Internet of Things (MIoT), Vehicle to Everything (V2X) and High-Performance Machine-Type Communications (HMTC) [2]. Additionally, the mechanisms that allow for data processing at the edge of the network have also been devised. The ETSI Multi-access Edge Computing (MEC) platform [3], integrated with the networks slicing-enabled 5GS, opens up a plethora of new possibilities regarding local-level provisioning of the low-latency and high-bandwidth services. This trend is expected to be further enhanced by the introduction of the 6G System (6GS) featuring near-to-zero latencies, Tbps data rates and advanced mechanisms supporting even the most demanding use cases.

One of the relatively new fields of application of 5G-based communication – important in the context of the continuous improvement of the efficiency of food production with minimization of its environmental footprint – is Precision Agriculture (PA). Its main goal is to utilize high-end technologies, including wireless communication, as well as control loop-based systems to optimize agricultural processes, e.g. by avoiding excessive fertilization or pest management and optimizing the agrotechnical treatments, thus contributing to sustainable use of natural resources and limiting the natural environment contamination.

The goal of the paper is to outline the application of the 5G and future mobile communication technologies in the field of PA emphasising demands heterogeneity – so far poorly recognized in the telecommunications sector – and a need to integrate multiple communication approaches to enable implementation of efficient End-to-End (E2E) systems. The paper is structured as follows. In Sect. 2, the specificity of the PA sector is presented. Section 3 describes the work related to the 5G advancements relevant to this sector. In Sect. 4, the characteristics of the PA processes and related data exchange are outlined. Section 5 is devoted to the 5GS applicability to PA and identification of gaps. Section 6 concludes the paper.

2   Specificity of the Sector of Precision Agriculture

PA is a relatively new trend in the field of agricultural science and practice, proposed at the beginning of the 1990s, which is based on the computer-aided process of planning, conducting and analyzing the efficiency of plant production. However, the fundamental paradigm of PA is relinquishing from treating the field as a uniform area in terms of properties, and therefore also subjected to agrotechnical treatments in a uniform manner, in favor of observing and measuring the spatial variability – with high resolution and accuracy of the order of single centimeters – of the properties of arable land (e.g. soil type, its abundance, reaction, the influence of the neighbourhood, terrain slope and its exposure, water conditions, microclimate, etc.), the occurrence of phenomena (e.g. properties of cultivated plants, their yield, presence of pests, damage due to violent weather conditions or caused by wildlife, etc.) and then adjusting the local point response to this variability. Consequently, e.g. the sowing rate can be adjusted locally to the soil properties, fertilizers' doses – to the nutritional requirements of plants, and pesticides' doses – to the local scale of infection or infestation [4]. PA is enabled primarily by the proliferation of Geographic Information Systems (GISs) and Global Navigation Satellite Systems (GNSSs), but also by the development of electronics (in particular, agriculture parameters metrology and ubiquity of embedded microprocessor systems), mechatronics, Artificial Intelligence (AI), and wireless data transmission technology to ensure continuous communication within the entire technical system of PA, thanks to which the spatial conditioning of agriculture and its processes is not an acute challenge.

PA is not an artificially sophisticated concept, but has strong economic, legal and social conditions and its development and implementation are motivated by an increase in: (i) efficiency of using the means of production in agriculture (10% fuel savings, even 85% pesticides' reduction [5]), (ii) yield, with a simultaneous reduction of production costs (100–300 EUR per hectare [6]), (iii) productivity of people and equipment (20–30% work time savings [6]), (iv) sustainability of the cultivation system by adjusting the treatments or dose of the means of production to the microhabitat, (v) quality of agricultural produce, and (vi) environmental protection by avoiding the unnecessary or excessive application of fertilizers or pesticides. It is worth a mention that in the European Union, agriculture is under strong regulatory and legal pressure, e.g. control of the use of fertilizers [7] and pesticides [8]. In addition, the production of the chemical industry for agriculture is extremely energy-intensive. Therefore, in the current situation in geopolitics and the global energy carriers market, more efficient use of agricultural inputs and filling gaps in the supply of food and fertilizers from outside the European Union will be of vital importance for food security. These factors imply a rapid growth of the PA significance in the coming years.

Apart from plant production, the concept of PA may also apply (with appropriate modifications) to livestock production, forest management, and even fish farms [9]. Sometimes, the term Smart Agriculture (or "Agriculture 4.0"), in which the emphasis is on the rapid exchange of completely digitized information at all stages of agricultural production and also with external partners, as well as on advanced decision support by cloud-based expert systems, is presented as the next stage of the technological revolution in agriculture after PA. In this paper, both stages will be considered together.

3   Related Work

The early visions of 5GS by ITU identified three fundamental usage scenarios: eMBB, Massive Machine Type Communications (mMTC), and URLLC –

further commonly followed by the industry [1]. However, among the example applications, agriculture is not indicated, although previously listed as one of the fields of Internet of Things (IoT). The majority of scientific efforts and papers on the borderland of telecommunications and PA, share that vision and associate the PA needs and applications with "low-end" sensoric IoT, i.e. mMTC. Works beyond this approach are rare. The automated radio network planning framework for nomadic 5G campus networks, which optimizes the base station downlink (DL) coverage, is presented [10] for several receiver altitudes (0.1–1.5–3.5 m) relevant in an agricultural scenario. A platform of drones [11] constituted a flying *ad hoc* 5G network and provides acquisition of data from the agricultural IoT sensors located in rural areas with poor coverage. The drones can also be equipped with cameras and sensors for remote crop inspection. An iterative optimization method [12] to find the optimal drone's altitude and location, the antenna beamwidth, and the variable power and block length allocated to each robot inside the circular cell to minimize the average overall decoding error has been proposed for drone-assisted relay systems supporting the URLLC services for agricultural robots. In [13], the system for a big dairy farm (1000 cows), consisting of drones with cameras and 5G connectivity, the image recognition-based system for Real-Time (RT) individual dairy cow monitoring, behavior analysis and feeding, is presented. An electronic fence with 5G-connected cameras and image recognition is proposed for RT detection of unauthorized persons' access for reduction of damages and thefts on farms [14].

Within the EU Horizon program, there are several projects to deal with the PA needs. The IoF2020 project [15] has demonstrated the applications of IoT technologies in 19 agriculture use-cases around five trials (arable, dairy, fruits, meat and vegetables) in an operational farm environment all over Europe, but the connectivity for trials was provided with Radio Access Technology (RAT) types as LoRa and 3G/4G mobile network. The 5G-HEART project [16] deploys digital use cases involving healthcare, transport and aquaculture, i.a. (i) high bandwidth in-vehicle situational awareness and see-through for platooning based on bidirectional 80 Mbps Vehicle to Vehicle (V2V) connectivity with 99.99999% reliability, 5 ms latency, and 100 signalling messages per second; (ii) tele-operated driving based on 20 Mbps/20 ms connectivity; and (iii) remote monitoring of water and fish quality in aquaculture using eMBB, URLLC, and mMTC service slices for aquaculture remote health, sensoric and camera data monitoring as well as automation and actuation functionalities. The 5GENESIS project has shown the exemplary implementation of an agricultural use case, in which a 5G-connected camera in a drone or autonomous robot was feeding the image recognition system with crop images for weed detection and application of herbicide by a robot [17]. The 5G!Drones project [18] demonstrates an integrated ecosystem of aviation (drone control and traffic management) and telecommunications in a number of scenarios, i.a. infrastructure inspection, drone-enhanced IoT data collection and connectivity extension by a flying nomadic 5G base station. It is worth a mention that there is growing awareness in the EU bodies that the transformative 5G solutions in agriculture should go beyond the IoT area [19] and include Augmented Reality (AR), RT automation and remote operation.

The mobile network SDOs present different approaches. The 3rd Generation Partnership Project (3GPP) has not decided to separate the agricultural sector, in opposite to e.g. unmanned aviation or automotive sectors, but the general service requirements for 5GS [20] should be mapped on the PA needs. The most demanding PA use cases may be additionally addressed in the field of cyber-physical control applications in vertical domains [21] and video, imaging and audio for professional applications [22], both commonly classified by 3GPP as "Industrial IoT" supported by New Radio (NR), i.e. 5G RAT. The most important gap in the 5GS is related to location accuracy (30 cm precision/1 s latency, still far insufficient). The GSM Alliance (GSMA) presented the "Future of farming" case study in PA as the field of IoT, promoting 4G NB-IoT RAT (featuring low data rates and high latency) [23]. They also present the later case study, in which the image data captured by the on-board cameras are sent from the autonomous agriculture robot to a cloud-based edge computing server via a 5G connection for AI-based weed recognition preceding the selective application of herbicide. The decision cycle duration was ~250 ms, where the transmission took 20–25 ms and the peak upload data rate was 120 Mbps [24].

In summary, it can be concluded that in the field of telecommunications, there is no comprehensive, sectoral approach to PA to allow the identification and dimensioning of its needs, as well as preparing network operators to the provisioning of services, and the scattered approach obscures the picture. Moreover, many of the mechanisms that have already been proposed by SDOs and are direly needed in the field of PA have not been implemented yet in carrier-grade networks [25], which is another obstacle for creating E2E, 5G-based Precision Agriculture Support System (PASS).

4 Characteristics of Processes, Touchpoints and Data Exchange in Precision Agriculture

The system of PA is related to a production process in which actions must be taken in response to numerous factors of varying variability in time and space. While soil properties change over a very long period of time, other phenomena, e.g. the nutritional status and hydration of plants, and especially the occurrence of an infestation with a pathogen, may require a very quick response. Additionally, the possibility of a reaction may depend on external factors (e.g. suitable weather, soil moisture, time of day, temporary legal limitations) and the availability of resources (e.g. personnel, farming machinery, production means). Moreover, in agriculture, there is a strong spatial condition related to the structure of the farm's land (concentrated or highly dispersed). Therefore, logistics will also affect the limitations of possible reaction scenarios.

PASS can be described by the classic model Monitor-Analyse-Plan-Execute based on Knowledge (MAPE-K) [26] (cf. Fig. 1) with highly spatially dispersed and diverse touchpoints, i.e. sources of process monitoring information and effectors used to influence the process. As PA acts within various perspectives (multi-year, growing season, the life cycle of the cultivated plant and RT), there will also be many management levels with individual MAPE-K loops, but based on a common knowledge module integrated with GIS, covering the spatially described current situation and history of land and crops, including the history of agrotechnical treatments, as well as models of analytics, inferences, solutions and execution orchestration, the goals of all time perspectives and the rules of arbitration between them. The data produced by lower level (short-term) MAPE-K loops will also feed the higher level (longer-term) ones.

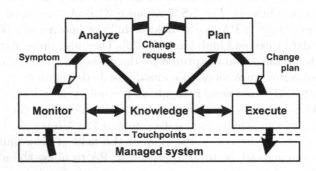

Fig. 1. IBM MAPE-K autonomous management loop (based on [26])

The basic requirement of PASS with regard to the responsiveness of the communication layer will therefore be that the communication between the MAPE-K chain and the touchpoints must not noticeably slow down, lengthen or stop MAPE-K processes at the level of their individual time scale, or force their rearrangement or additional logistic operations (e.g. passings, transits, etc.). Hence, the general principle is to avoid as much as possible manual data exchange, e.g. transferring data via USB memory, and to provide on-line connectivity for all elements of PASS.

The characteristics of the PA touchpoints and their data exchange are essential for determining the service requirements for the communication layer implemented by the mobile network. The use cases described below may refer to objects that are stationary or provide geospatially-stamped data ("on-the-go" acquisition). The majority of the PA equipment exposes the data after the end of the acquisition session (burst-like exchange of the acquired data files). Successive transmission of agricultural measurement data from PA objects is rather not used nowadays, but there are also cases of continuous transmission (RT processes, multimedia streaming).

UC1 Position Sensing: As the typical Global Navigation Satellite System (GNSS) accuracy of several meters is inadequate, the positioning correction has to be applied. The most commonly used is the Real-Time Kinematic (RTK) technology providing the accuracy of less than 3 cm. The typical maximum position readout frequency of GNSS receivers 10 Hz, which corresponds to ~13.9 cm spots spacing at 5 km/h. RTK enables RT position correction based on the information from the RTK reference station over the IP network using the RTCM SC-104 or CMR/CMR+ protocols. The required data rate typically ranges from 150 to 2400 bps.

UC2 Soil Properties Mapping: The class includes measurements of electrical conductivity (used to assess salinity, soil grain size and type, the depth of rock or hardly permeable layers and groundwater), reaction [pH], organic carbon content, and compactness (mechanical measurement, "stop-and-go" approach). Their common feature is the spot measurement of certain soil properties directly in the field with spot coordinates tagging. The typical time intervals between measurements are 1–25 s, so the approximate distances between measurement spots are 1.4–34.7 m at 5 km/h. There are also machines for automated collection of soil samples for laboratory analysis, but since the samples need to be unloaded on the farm, the spots information data transfer may also be performed there.

UC3 Contactless Evaluation of Soil and Crop Properties: The evaluation utilizes the image spectral analysis in the range of visible light (350–700 nm) and mainly near infrared (IR) (700–1000 nm, less often 700–2500 nm) resulting from the reflection of solar radiation (passive) or forced one (active). Depending on the shape of the spectral characteristics (so-called "signature"), it is possible to find the presence of a healthy plant, a dying plant, a dead plant, heavy and light mineral soil or peat soil within the image area, e.g. a pixel. The spectral analysis is based in particular on the observed phenomenon of a sharp change in reflection at the border of the red and near IR range ("red edge") characteristics of healthy plants. Spectral signatures will be specific for the plant species and the stage of their vegetation period, but the red edge effect always occurs. It is also possible to use thermography (9–14 μm) or the Light Detection and Ranging (LIDAR) technique (precise scanning of the shape of the land surface and evaluation of spatial variability of the shape and composition of the soil).

Image acquisition is done separately for narrow sub-ranges by means of narrow-band sensors included in a specialized camera (simplified solutions recording the image in RGB visible light channels and the IR range channel are also available), thus creating a set of images of the same area (bands) to make orthophotomaps for further analysis with specialized software to deliver a land map showing qualitatively and/or quantitatively the occurrence of some phenomenon of interest. The process of such a map delivery is multi-stage and computationally complex. In particular, various vegetation indices with different and complementary properties can be used for better identification.

Contactless sensing with the use of aerophotography can be carried out with the use of various flying objects, but from the point of view of this paper, important is the use of drones taking pictures along an optimal flight route adapted to the shape of the field, and then transmitting them for further processing in the terrestrial information system. Alternative local contactless sensing with the use of sensors operating at close range (passive or active, manual or mounted on a tractor or a cultivation set, e.g. on booms) is usually associated with an immediate calculation of the selected vegetation index by the device; this value with a time-spatial signature may be continuously transmitted to PASS. In the case of the autonomous RT MAPE-K loop in the on-board subsystem during the trip (e.g. a sprayer with an infestation detector), both the spot values of the tested indicator and of the applied product will be recorded, thus creating the legally required documentation of the procedure.

UC4 Yield Mapping: Used for evaluation of the final efficiency of all agrotechnical treatments in a season, will depend on the specifics of the harvested crop and the combine-harvester design, but may consist of multiple on-board sensors (1–5 s readout resolution) to measure various yield and harvesting process parameters. The yield monitors are implemented as on-board subsystems of combine-harvesters to visualize current process data and even show current maps against the background of archival maps. The continuous transmission of yield monitoring data may be irrelevant or required by the farm management model – in large farms, central monitoring of all activities within the farm may be necessary.

UC5 Telemetry and Telematics: Collecting telemetry data other than previously discussed is aimed at continuous remote monitoring of the machinery operation in the field, RT collection of diagnostic importance data, as well as fleet management. Moreover, communication will be bi-directional and may enable the following functions (depending on the manufacturer's policy): (i) mapping the current and historical location of the fleet components for the continuous optimization of its use; (ii) optimization of travel routes, adapting them to e.g. the location of a petrol station in case of prediction of soon refueling; (iii) reporting the working mode (driving, stopping, idling, loading/unloading, etc.) and the load weight; (iv) geo-fencing and working hours limitation; (v) informing about the following events: starting/stopping the engine, vehicle movement (including unauthorized use and location), opening the fuel filler, occurrence of diagnostic events represented by appropriate codes; (vi) insight to the machine's dashboard and its basic operating parameters: battery voltage, engine speed, operating fluids and fuel tank levels, ambient and machine system temperatures (engine oil, coolant, oil in the hydraulic system, air in tires), pressure in the hydraulic system; (vii) RT insight into CAN bus communication of the machine [27] and live transmission from information panels installed in the machine; (viii) identification and registration of the operator driving the machine. In most cases, the information from the machine (measurements, events) can be time/geospatially tagged to enable mapping their occurrence, advanced analysis against the background of maps describing the work area or route, etc.

UC6 Stationary or Quasi-Stationary Sensing: In a PA farm, sensors installed permanently in the fields may also be used, enabling continuous, independently to agricultural treatments, remote insight into the local situation, e.g. weather stations or soil moisture sensors arranged in a grid (they can also cooperate with an irrigation system installed in the field). In the case of free grazing animals on pastures, monitors of life processes (e.g. temperature, heart rate, etc.) may be worn. It is also potentially possible to install cameras providing situational awareness with a 360° viewing angle in remote fields. Apart from the latter case, stationary and quasi-stationary data sources will be data from IoT sources with a discontinuous, cyclical pattern of daily activity, a relatively low required transmission speed and relatively small data volume.

UC7 Effectors' Programming: Considering the agrotechnical operations, the effectors will be all mechatronic elements and systems, i.e. electronically controlled sprayer valves, actuators for the gate or tilt of the trailer's load box, spreader motors, etc. However, their direct remote control is rare, and they are controlled by the on-board machine controller, executing an operation program to send the appropriate control signals at the appropriate machine location or time. The same logic will also apply to programs or maps of routes, application or sampling spots. Communication with effectors takes the form of uploading the configuration file at an arbitrary moment and should be completed within a subjectively and contextually short time, i.e. not causing a downtime.

UC8 Drones: The use of drones in PA is a fragment of the overall area of their possible applications; some general characteristics will apply. In the case of large-scale farms or ones with spatially dispersed land structure, Beyond Visual Line of Sight (BVLOS) flights will be of particular importance, thus requiring a ubiquitous communication platform for: (i) Command and Control (C2) aspect: directly controlled flight or autonomic one along the uploaded route (cardinal points, azimuth, altitude, etc.) with in-flight drone parameters monitoring and with direct control – providing the pilot with First Person View (FPV), i.e. RT video streams from the high-definition (4K/8K) camera with a 360° viewing angle; (ii) active connection to the Unmanned Aircraft Systems Traffic Management (UTM) system for airspace management and flight coordination (telemetry data transmission: position, azimuth and flight speed, etc.); (iii) use case-specific data transmission (photogrammetric data collection, crop and infrastructure monitoring, crop pest control by air discharges of pest antagonists, etc.).

UC9 Communication Between Machines: The complementary functionality applicable to large farms may be the synchronous operation of multiple machines, e.g. in line formation of a group of combine-harvesters with the simultaneous transfer of the threshed grain to the next machine, and finally to a truck at the end of the array. In consequence, the use of machinery is optimized through minimizing stoppage during unloading and U-turning, and the excessive soil compaction by loaded machines is avoided. To enable this approach, mechanisms for communicating between machines are necessary, e.g. broadcasting their location, azimuth and ground speed information, and optionally FPV.

UC10 Autonomous Agricultural Robots: With mechanisms of autonomy (detection of plant rows or driving on the basis of a plant map from sowing, supported by high-precision GNSS positioning), the manual remote control is not required for their operation. The communication will be needed for e.g.

remote transmission of the action plan, changes in the base knowledge (patterns of weeds, pests or infestations to be detected), use of remote computing in the cloud for off-loading the local processing as well as sending information (including video stream) to the operator. In terms of the model of communication needs, there are similarities to drones. The difference will be the speed of movement (the maximum speed is much lower than in the case of drones), as well as work near the ground, as opposed to drone flights at altitudes of up to 120 m.

UC11 Support for People Performing Agrotechnical Activities in the Field: To support field workers, AR technology may be used. For a simple workaround, a personal terminal (e.g. a tablet), based on the current position, would receive information from Geographic Information System (GIS) of the farm in the form of maps of soil properties and water relations, sown plants, history of treatments, photos taken previously, etc., to quickly familiarize the farm worker with the current situation even without prior on-site presence. True AR allows adding contextual information to the observed image, e.g. names or legends of recognized objects, information about their properties, instructions on how to proceed, etc. The transmission requirements for AR are characterized by a very high quality of RT video streaming and a maximum Round-Trip Time (RTT) of 20 ms for good Quality of Service (QoS) perception [28]; for RTT >40 ms a cybersickness may occur, significantly intensified for RTT >75 ms [29].

UC12 Architecture and Implementation Approach to PASS: At present, there are no comprehensive solutions to cover 100% of all functional needs of a PA farm; it is necessary to use various PASSs and interchange data, using commonly recognized formats. There exist PASSs prepared for local installation and – more and more popular – network ones run in the cloud. In the latter approach, the system architecture aims to optimize the information processing and data transferring, leading to distributed computing, in particular edge computing.

Table 1. Examples of burst-type data exchange at various PA touchpoints

Use case type	Data volume per spot	Data volume per hectare	Notes
Soil properties mapping	384 B	37,5 kB	Conductometer, induction-based measurement, 100 spots per hectare
Soil properties mapping	143 B	–	Tensometric frame, possible different working widths
Contactless crop evaluation	255 B	51,9 kB	Handheld vegetation index meter, ~200 spots per hectare
Effector programming	303 B	41,6 kB	Mineral fertilizer application map, 140 spots per hectare
Yield mapping	115 B	166,3 kB	Wheat combine-harvester, 5 s intervals
Drone photogrammetry	–	37,4 GB	1 cm per pixel, 42.4 MP RGB+IR camera, 14 bits per band, necessary images overlapping included

In Table 1, the exemplary characteristics of selected PA touchpoints with burst-type data exchange is presented for comparison.

5   Precision Agriculture Use Cases' Support by 5G System

Based on the general assumptions and descriptions of the use cases presented in Sect. 4, an analysis of service requirements was carried out against the background of the relevant 3GPP Stage 1 documents for 5GS [20,30,31]. The results have been presented in Table 2. The intensity and type of data exchange (burst/stream), required data rate, maximum delay and reliability were determined for individual use cases through mapping to identified service classes defined by 3GPP. On that basis, it was proposed to assign the relevant SST to each of the use cases.

Table 2. PA use cases' requirements mapping to 5GS service requirements

Use case ID		Exchange intensity	Exchange type	Data rate	Max. delay	Reliability	SST
UC1		High	Stream	2.4 kbps	–	High	URLLC
UC2		Low	Burst	≤1 kbps	–	Low	MIoT
UC3	Photogram-metry	High	Burst	~1 Gbps	200 ms	Low	eMBB
	Local sensing	Low	Burst	≤1 kbps	–	Low	MIoT
UC4		Low	Burst	≤1 kbps	–	Low	MIoT
UC5		High	Stream	1 Mbps	20 ms	High	eMBB
UC6	Sensors	Low	Burst	≤1 kbps	–	Low	MIoT
	Video streaming	High	Stream	120 Mbps	20 ms	99.99%	eMBB
UC7		Low	Burst	~ Mbps	–	Low	eMBB
UC8	C2	High	Stream	28 kbps	40 ms	99.9%	URLLC
	UTM	Low	Stream	~ kbps	500 ms	99.9%	URLLC
	FPV, video streaming	High	Stream	120 Mbps	20 ms	99.99%	eMBB
UC9		High	Stream	65 Mbps	20 ms	99.99%	V2X
UC10		High	Burst	1.1 Gbps	2 ms (1)	99.9%	HMTC
UC11		High	Stream	0.1–1 Gbps	10 ms	99.99%	eMBB

(1) Achievable in low area campus networks only

The primary observation based on the analysis is the huge data rates variety range as well as the appearance of immensely challenging delay limits. Moreover, for UC8–UC11, these very and extremely high data rates are associated with the uplink (UL) transmission. Compared to other applications, e.g. medical monitoring or smart grids, the required levels of reliability are not particularly high. However, the support of all use cases by the mobile network will require the use of all SST classes, and due to the further differentiation of the QoS requirements for use cases mapped to some SST, the separate Network Slice Instances (NSIs) with use case-relevant QoS parameters – traffic priority, (non-)guaranteed data rate, packet error rate and delay budget, etc. [2] – will have to be implemented, particularly for different tenants or differentiated User Plane (UP) architectures. Creation of NSIs implies the 5G Stand-Alone (SA) architecture [2] (almost all 5G networks in the world are still working in the 5G Non-SA architecture) and advanced automated network management algorithms for which the 3GPP standardization is currently still not advanced enough. The proposal for allocation of 5G QoS Identifiers (5QIs) to analysed PA use cases has been presented in Table 3. In each case except UC10, the relevant 5G QoS Identifier (5QI) can be assigned. It has to be noted that 3GPP does not provide the 5QI that ensures delay <5 ms, which might be an obstacle in demanding URLLC cases.

Table 3. 3GPP 5QIs [2] supporting the analysed PA use cases

5QI	Resource type	Priority level	Delay	Packet error	Max. data burst volume	Use case ID
6	Non-Guaranteed Bit Rate (GBR)	60	300 ms	10^{-6}	N/A	UC2 UC4 UC7
7	Non-GBR	70	100 ms	10^{-3}	N/A	UC3: photogrammetry
8	Non-GBR	80	300 ms	10^{-6}	N/A	UC3: local sensing
70	Non-GBR	55	200 ms	10^{-6}	N/A	UC8: UTM UC6: sensors
80	Non-GBR	68	10 ms	10^{-6}	N/A	UC6: video streaming UC8: FPV UC10 UC11
82	Delay-critical GBR	19	10 ms	10^{-4}	255 B	UC1 UC5
83	Delay-critical GBR	22	10 ms	10^{-4}	1354 B	UC9 UC8: C2

The above requirements are in fundamental contradiction to the 3GPP basic service requirements for rural macro scenarios (cf. [20], clause 7.1) where the maximum user-experienced data rates are 50 Mbps for DL and 25 Mbps for UL, while the traffic capacities are 1 Gbps per km^2 for DL and 0.5 Gbps per km^2 for UL. The DL and UL traffic capacities for urban macro scenarios are 100 Gbps per km^2 and 50 Gbps per km^2, respectively; for dense urban scenario 750 Gbps per km^2 and 125 Gbps per km^2, respectively. Thus, according to the current 3GPP vision, rural areas will be too impaired in capacity to cope with some PA use cases, as well as those for some drone applications. This seems to be the evidence of how far the complexity of sectoral service needs of agriculture, in particular of PA, is unrecognized, which may have general economic consequences. It is also an expression of the need for SDOs in the field of telecommunications to transform the approach to the agriculture sector into a comprehensive one.

The application layer support by edge cloud computing (UC12 for UC2–UC4, UC6, UC8, UC10–UC11) can be provided by the European Telecommunications Standards Institute (ETSI) MEC [3] implementation. It should be remarked, however, that the standardization of MEC integration with 5GS is still ongoing. Moreover, important issues related to the necessary adaptation of both architectural frameworks, taking into account the problems of duplicated functionalities and their potential conflicts or competition, scalability, simplification of the integrated architecture, etc. [32], have still not been resolved.

From the above considerations, it can be noted that for the implementation of 5G services for PA in a rural environment, the density of PA-related devices will not be a problem. The main barriers will be the network capacity, the maximum achieved data rates and latency levels. Hence, the provided support can become insufficient especially for latency-critical and extremely high UL data rate use cases (e.g. UC3, UC8, UC10, UC11). Moreover, the typically adopted network planning strategy in rural areas (high diameter macro-cells) as well as operation in "rural" sub-GHz frequency bands having inherently low capacity (e.g. in Europe the 700 MHz band with maximum channel width of 15 MHz) result in limited resources and non-100% coverage. The temporary palliative solution for the rural coverage and capacity issues may be the advance of integration of Non-Terrestrial Networks (NTNs) – especially High Altitude Platform Systems (HAPSs), having relatively low delays – with the 5GS as well as UL coverage enhancements, which are currently envisioned in the scope of the 3GPP Release 18, named "5G-Advanced" (to be concluded in the first quarter of 2024) [33].

According to the early visions, 6GS will not only fulfill the above gaps, but also promises the headroom for the development of future PA services. One of the expected benefits is network ubiquity and full convergence of fixed, mobile networks and NTNs, which can significantly contribute to service provisioning in rural areas. New service classes targeting more specialized use cases are proposed, i.a. Human-Centric Services (HCS), Multi-Purpose Services (MPS), reliable eMBB, Mobile Broadband Reliable Low Latency (MBRLLC), Massive Ultra-Reliable Low Latency Communication (mURLLC) [34]. Also, a considerable boost of system performance is anticipated – 10× lower latency (0.1 ms in radio link) and 10× better spectrum efficiency implying the respective capacity growth [35].

6   Conclusions

In this paper, the application of mobile networks in the field of PA has been discussed, presenting the complexity and variety of needs and use cases of this economic sector, the importance of which will grow dynamically in the coming years. Based on the use case analysis, the service requirements related to the communication layer of PASS have been identified. Contrary to the stereotypical vision that equates PA with the "low-end" IoT class, the needs of this sector will be a big challenge for the Mobile Network Operators (MNOs) in terms of the required QoS, involving a variety of service architectures and NSIs. Additionally, the approach of SDOs to PA should be changed to a comprehensive sectoral one, and the development of standardization of 5G networks and the next generations should take into account the PA service needs to fill the gaps identified here that may hinder the support of PA by MNOs' communication services.

References

1. ITU-R: IMT Vision – Framework and overall objectives of the future development of IMT for 2020 and beyond. Recommendation ITU-R M.2083 (09/15), International Telecommunication Union – Radiocommunication Sector (September 2015). https://www.itu.int/rec/R-REC-M.2083
2. 3GPP: System architecture for the 5G System (5GS). Technical Standard TS 23.501, ver. 17.4.0, 3rd Generation Partnership Project (March 2022)
3. ETSI: Multi-access Edge Computing (MEC). https://www.etsi.org/technologies/multi-access-edge-computing. Accessed 22 Apr 2022
4. Adamchuk, V.I.: Precision agriculture: does it make sense? Better Crops Plant Food **94**(3), 4–6 (2010)
5. European Parliament, Directorate-General for Parliamentary Research Services, Schrijver, R., Poppe, K., Daheim, C.: Precision agriculture and the future of farming in Europe: scientific foresight study. Publications Office of the European Union (2019). https://doi.org/10.2861/175493
6. Auernhammer, H.: Precision farming – the environmental challenge. Comput. Electron. Agric. **30**(1–3), 31–43 (2001). https://doi.org/10.1016/S0168-1699(00)00153-8
7. European Communities: Council Directive 91/676/EEC of 12 December 1991 concerning the protection of waters against pollution caused by nitrates from agricultural sources. Official Journal of the European Communities, L 375, pp. 1–8 (31 December 1991). https://eur-lex.europa.eu/eli/dir/1991/676/oj
8. European Union: Directive 2009/128/EC of the European Parliament and of the Council of 21 October 2009 establishing a framework for Community action to achieve the sustainable use of pesticides (Text with EEA relevance). Official Journal of the European Union, L 309, pp. 71–86 (24 October 2009). https://eur-lex.europa.eu/eli/dir/2009/128/oj
9. Beluhova-Uzunova, R.P., Dunchev, D.M.: Precision farming – concepts and perspectives. Zagadnienia Ekonomiki Rolnej/Probl. Agric. Econ. **3**(360), 142–155 (2019). https://doi.org/10.30858/zer/112132
10. Krause, A., Anwar, W., Martinez, A.B., Stachorra, D., Fettweis, G., Franchi, N.: Network planning and coverage optimization for mobile campus networks. In: 2021 IEEE 4th 5G World Forum (5GWF), pp. 305–310 (2021). https://doi.org/10.1109/5GWF52925.2021.00060
11. Faraci, G., Raciti, A., Rizzo, S., Schembra, G.: A 5G platform for unmanned aerial monitoring in rural areas: design and performance issues. In: 2018 4th IEEE Conference on Network Softwarization and Workshops (NetSoft), pp. 237–241 (2018). https://doi.org/10.1109/NETSOFT.2018.8459960
12. Ranjha, A., Kaddoum, G., Dev, K.: Facilitating URLLC in UAV-assisted relay systems with multiple-mobile robots for 6G networks: A prospective of Agriculture 4.0. IEEE Trans. Ind. Inform. (early access) 1–18 (2021). https://doi.org/10.1109/TII.2021.3131608

13. Zhang, J., Zhang, R., Yang, Q., Hu, T., Guo, K., Hong, T.: Research on application technology of 5G Internet of Things and Big Data in dairy farm. In: 2021 International Wireless Communications and Mobile Computing (IWCMC), pp. 138–140 (2021). https://doi.org/10.1109/IWCMC51323.2021.9498643
14. Hsu, C.K., Chiu, Y.H., Wu, K.R., Liang, J.M., Chen, J.J., Tseng, Y.C.: Design and implementation of image electronic fence with 5G technology for smart farms. In: 2019 IEEE VTS Asia Pacific Wireless Communications Symposium (APWCS), pp. 1–3 (2019). https://doi.org/10.1109/VTS-APWCS.2019.8851659
15. Internet of Food & Farm 2020 (IoF2020). https://www.iof2020.eu/. Accessed 22 Apr 2022
16. 5G HEalth AquacultuRe and Transport validation trials (5G HEART). https://5gheart.org/. Accessed 22 Apr 2022
17. Fornes-Leal, A., et al.: Deployment of 5G experiments on underserved areas using the Open5GENESIS suite. In: 2021 International Conference on Smart Applications, Communications and Networking (SmartNets), pp. 1–4 (2021). https://doi.org/10.1109/SmartNets50376.2021.9555428
18. 5G!Drones: Unmanned Aerial Vehicle Vertical Applications' Trials Leveraging Advanced 5G Facilities. https://5gdrones.eu/. Accessed 22 Apr 2022
19. Gilles, F., Toth, J.: Accelerating the 5G transition in Europe: how to boost investments in transformative 5G solutions (main report for the European Commission). Eur. Invest. Bank (2021). https://doi.org/10.2867/252427
20. 3GPP: Service requirements for the 5G system; Stage 1. Technical Standard TS 22.261, ver. 18.6.0, 3rd Generation Partnership Project (March 2022)
21. 3GPP: Service requirements for cyber-physical control applications in vertical domains; Stage 1. Technical Standard TS 22.104, ver. 18.3.0, 3rd Generation Partnership Project (December 2021)
22. 3GPP: Service requirements for Video, Imaging and Audio for Professional Applications (VIAPA). Technical Standard TS 22.263, ver. 17.4.0, 3rd Generation Partnership Project (June 2021)
23. GSMA: The future of farming: How mobile IoT technologies can help agriculture feed the world. GSM Association (2018). https://www.gsma.com/iot/resources/chunghwa-nhr-agriculture-iot-case-study/
24. GSMA: Smart Farming: Weed elimination with 5G autonomous robots. GSM Association (2020). https://www.gsma.com/iot/resources/smart-farming-weed-elimination-with-5g-autonomous-robots/
25. Tomaszewski, L., Chochliouros, I.P., Kołakowski, R., Kukliński, S., Kourtis, M.A.: High mobility 5G services for vertical industries - network operator's view. IFIP Adv. Inf. Commun. Technol. **628**, 71–84 (2021). https://doi.org/10.1007/978-3-030-79157-5_7
26. IBM: An architectural blueprint for autonomic computing. IBM Autonomic Computing White Paper, Fourth Edition (June 2006)
27. Stevan, S.L., Jr., Farinelli, F.A.: CAN-bus remote monitoring: standalone CAN sensor reading and automotive diagnostics. SAE Int. J. Connect. Autom. Veh. **2**(1), 27–46 (2019). https://doi.org/10.4271/12-02-01-0003
28. Hou, X., Lu, Y., Dey, S.: Wireless VR/AR with edge/cloud computing. In: 2017 26th International Conference on Computer Communication and Networks (ICCCN), pp. 1–8 (2017). https://doi.org/10.1109/ICCCN.2017.8038375
29. Caserman, P., Garcia-Agundez, A., Gámez Zerban, A., Göbel, S.: Cybersickness in current-generation virtual reality head-mounted displays: systematic review and outlook. Virtual Real. **25**(4), 1153–1170 (2021). https://doi.org/10.1007/s10055-021-00513-6

30. 3GPP: Unmanned Aerial System (UAS) support in 3GPP. Technical Standard TS 22.125, ver. 17.6.0, 3rd Generation Partnership Project (April 2022)
31. 3GPP: Service requirements for enhanced V2X scenarios. Technical Standard TS 22.186, ver. 17.0.0, 3rd Generation Partnership Project (April 2022)
32. Tomaszewski, L., Kukliński, S., Kołakowski, R.: A new approach to 5G and MEC integration. In: Maglogiannis, I., Iliadis, L., Pimenidis, E. (eds.) AIAI 2020. IAICT, vol. 585, pp. 15–24. Springer, Cham (2020). https://doi.org/10.1007/978-3-030-49190-1_2
33. 3GPP: Release 18. https://www.3gpp.org/release18. Accessed 22 Apr 2022
34. Yazar, A., Doğan Tusha, S., Arslan, H.: 6G vision: an ultra-flexible perspective. ITU J. Futur. Evol. Technol. 1(1), 121–140 (2020). https://doi.org/10.52953/IKVY9186
35. Imoize, A.L., Adedeji, O., Tandiya, N., Shetty, S.: 6G enabled smart infrastructure for sustainable society: opportunities, challenges, and research roadmap. MDPI Sens. 21(5), 1709 (2021). https://doi.org/10.3390/s21051709

Building a Knowledge-Intensive, Intent-Lean, Question Answering Chatbot in the Telecom Industry - Challenges and Solutions

Antonios Misargopoulos[1], Filippos Nikolopoulos-Gkamatsis[1],
Konstantinos Nestorakis[1], Alexandros Tzoumas[2],
Georgios Giannakopoulos[3], Christos-Antonios Gizelis[1(✉)],
and Michalis Kefalogiannis[1]

[1] Hellenic Telecommunications Organization S.A. (HTO), Marousi Attiki, Greece
{amisargopo,fnikolop,knestorak,cgkizelis,mkefalogiannis}@ote.gr
[2] SciFY PNPC, Ag. Paraskevi Attiki, Greece
a.tzoumas@scify.org
[3] National Centre of Scientific Research "Demokritos", Ag. Paraskevi Attiki, Greece
ggianna@iit.demokritos.gr

Abstract. Artificial Intelligence (AI) is one of the most emerging technologies of the past decade, leading the way towards human and machine interactions in terms of efficiency, accuracy and the overall value gained. This paper describes an intent-lean AI chatbot solution that handles user queries posed in natural language upon business related documents of a single-domain of Hellenic Telecommunications Organization S.A. (HTO). Unlike other traditional chatbot solutions that strictly rely on intent identification, our approach infers the implicit user need in order to provide the most relative documents and text snippets within, as the proper answer. To do this, we proceeded with a custom implementation based on Elasticsearch engine and most common NLP techniques tailored to our needs; i.e., tokenization, lowercase filtering, stop words removal, stemming, fuzzy searching, synonyms, etc. The main challenges as well as the architectural models that thrive to overcome them are being described in detail. Finally, the effectiveness of the proposed solution is being measured and the identified features for improvement are being presented.

Keywords: Artificial Intelligence (AI) · NLP · Chatbot · Intent-lean · Lemmatization · Stemming · Synonyms · Elasticsearch

1 Introduction

Artificial Intelligence (AI) technologies have been evolving in a tremendous pace during the past few years expanding research opportunities and multi-domain

© IFIP International Federation for Information Processing 2022
Published by Springer Nature Switzerland AG 2022
I. Maglogiannis et al. (Eds.): AIAI 2022 Workshops, IFIP AICT 652, pp. 87–97, 2022.
https://doi.org/10.1007/978-3-031-08341-9_8

capabilities in large enterprises. AI chatbots offer profound contribution acting as interactive agents to handle costly user requests; i.e., place a new order, open a trouble ticket or navigate in a knowledge base.

The Hellenic Telecommunications Organization S.A. (HTO), as the largest telecommunications provider in Southeast Europe, serves its customers with a wide variety of ICT services addressing a large customer base. HTO owns a vast amount of official corporate documents governed by BPMN Specification [1] in Greek & English language; i.e., policies, procedure, processes, work instructions etc., that support the core operation on a daily basis. At the moment, this knowledge base is published to a custom intranet portal and utilized via a simple searching mechanism based on keywords filtering; but lacks to answer user *questions*. As a result, users fail to retrieve the required information; and so, seniors and subject-matter experts SMEs get involved inflicting an undesirable effort and labor expenses overhead.

This work proposes a knowledge-intensive, intent-lean AI chatbot solution to tackle the need to handle openly-posed queries *inferring* the implicit user need so that to provide correct and adequate answers; i.e., pairs of a relative document and text snippet within. In Sect. 2 we discuss the limitation of other chatbot implementations that strictly rely on intent identification; while in Sects. 3 and 4 we highlight some challenges and present our methodology and technical architecture in detail based on a custom implementation over *Elasticsearch* [2] functionality and other well-known AI Natural Language Processing (NLP) techniques. Later, in Sect. 5 we present our experimental results and in Sect 6 we conclude with some potential future work to enhance the algorithms' effectiveness and improve the overall user experience.

2   Related Work

AI has drawn the immense attention of both the academic community and the industry during last decade worldwide. One of the AI-based applications expected to have the most emerging development in near future, is conversational agents [3]. Conversational agents, also known as chatbots, or chatterbots, are machine conversation systems that interact with human users through natural conversational language. The Bank of America announced in December 2019 that its AI-driven virtual financial assistant Erica has surpassed 10mil users since its nationwide roll-out in 2018 [4]. Back in 2011 Apple Inc. introduced AI-powered virtual assistant *Siri* as part of all Apple devices operating systems, while Google came up with *Google Assistant* with advanced two-way conversations capabilities [5]. Moreover, chatbot applications leave influential imprint on multiple other domains such as education [6] or healthcare [7].

During the past years numerous research and academic publications aimed to designate the challenges around chatbot implementations and propose sustainable solutions. As already mentioned, they are based mainly on intent identification [8] to manage specific flow-based business cases like opening a fault ticket or placing a new order [9]. In this paper we present an end-to-end solution that is not based in strict intent detection and can be deployed within industries with diversity in knowledge domain almost transparently.

3   Challenges and Problem Definition

The existing corporate portal in place supports keyword-based search functionality upon specific document attributes, like title or description; but is totally incapable of handling free-text questions. In 2020, more than 300 incidents have been recorded, where users experienced inadequate search response. To handle those cases, SMEs have to be involved in an expensive and time-consuming effort overhead. Thus, a sophisticated, custom chatbot solution has been promoted to eliminate this operational cost. Some of the most critical challenges, that need to be addressed, are presented below.

Challenge 1. Data Diversity Makes Data Modelling Difficult: The knowledge base consists of hundreds of documents mapped to approximately 10 different domains like Human Resource (HR), IT, Technology, Legal etc. The documents in each domain embed different vocabulary, notation or even formatting type, i.e., plain text, tabular, or images.

Challenge 2. Complexity on the Type of Questions Asked by the Users: Based on the questions that Procurement & Finance domain SMEs handle in daily basis, we concluded the following challenges:

(a) variety in the type of questions that can be made by the users; i.e., (i) simple questions that can be answered from a single and inseparable portion of the text inside one document, (ii) complex questions where the desired answer can be found in different locations inside one or more documents.
(b) diverse vocabulary and wording used by users of different expertise or role in the company
(c) vast number of semantically different questions. As already stated in the Challenge 1 above, this is a multi-domain knowledge base; consequently, the queries can vary in linguistic meaning dramatically.

Challenge 3. Variety of User Intents: Traditional chatbot engines focus on serving answers based on user intents. The user query is analyzed and fragmented into one or more intents to describe distinct scenarios and different business logic each; e.g., in case of a vacation leave request, the chatbot would prompt a specific absence form to be filled in by the requestor, while if a user asks how much a new service costs, the chatbot would need more information about specific service features. The large number of documents and the diversity in the domains made it very challenging to a-priori define the full list of intents expected to be faced throughout the system use. Thus, a more generic solution should be introduced.

3.1 Problem Definition

The aforementioned challenges form an information retrieval problem, where given a user query the chatbot engine should identify and return the related set of documents and text paragraphs (snippets) of the knowledge domain(s) in scope where the answers reside. We introduce a method that calculates the *similarity relevance* of two text arguments and concludes a matching performance result. In our case as Eq. (1) depicts, given an initial user query q, consider f_match as the function that returns a set of $\{d_i, sp_j\}$ pairs, where sp_j is a snippet located in document d_i of the knowledge base Ω in scope and sp_j matches user query q with a matching performance $score_j$.

$$f_match(q, \Omega) = \bigcup_{i,j=1}^{k} (d_i, sp_j, score_j), sp_j \in d_i \cap d_i \in \Omega \tag{1}$$

To assure the highest level of performance, we filter out the result set to remove the snippets with $score_j$ lower than a threshold, defined with respect to business needs. Eq. (2) depicts that for a given user query q and a threshold $thres$, in $res(q, \Omega, thres)$ the chatbot would use f_{match} and retrieve all $\{d_i, sp_j\}$ pairs where the matching performance $score_j$ satisfies the performance threshold.

$$res(q, \Omega, thres) = f_{match}(q, \Omega), thres \leq score_j \tag{2}$$

In the following section, the entire solution and all implemented architecture modules are presented in detail.

4 Methodology and Proposed Solution

The methodology consists of the following main components:

1. Definition of a Generic Data model (related to challenge 1 in Sect. 3), see Sect. 4.1.2.
2. Definition of an evaluation model to measure performance each time changes are made, see Sect. 4.3.1.
3. Focus on term-based question answering first (related to challenges 2, 3 in Sect. 3), see Sects. 4.1.3, 4.2.1 and 4.2.2.
4. Innovation in User Interface design (related to challenge 3 in Sect. 3), see Sect. 4.2.3.
5. Support for feedback from the experts (related to challenge 3 in Sect. 3), see Sect. 4.3.2.
6. Ontology engineering (related to challenge 3 in Sect. 3), see Sect. 4.2.1.
7. Query classification (related to challenges 2, 3 in Sect. 3), see Sect. 4.2.1.
8. Definition of frequently asked questions (FAQs) (related to challenge 2 in Sect. 3). For questions that cannot be answered directly by the content of the document.

In the sections below, the aforementioned components are described in detail.

4.1 Data Management

The first component of our architecture is the *data management* that consists of three main modules as Fig. 1 depicts.

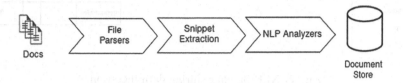

Docs

File Parsers

Snippet Extraction

NLP Analyzers

Document Store

Fig. 1. High level overview

4.1.1 File Parsers

HTO has documents from multiple domains. The approach was to first incorporate one of the most complex domains; i.e., Finance & Procurement, and provided that the results are satisfying, incorporate more and more domains. The input dataset consists of 32 word documents (with information related to activities and processes), 6 excel spreadsheets (that contain FAQs and manuals), and 3 powerpoint presentations (that contain manuals). The Word documents which contain the core process information are being revised over time, iteratively. Thus, not all documents follow the same template. The same applies for Excel spreadsheets and the PowerPoints presentations.

In order to incorporate and ingest all the available data into the database, five distinct parsers have been implemented to accommodate the different file formats and templates. The parsers split the document into smaller chunks of information (e.g., parsing a document as an *html* page) and discard portion of text that is out of scope, like footers, headers etc. Moreover, all documents have been classified into categories based on a set of regular expressions rules; i.e. a) FAQ, b) Processes, c) Manuals, d) Definitions and Abbreviations.

4.1.2 Snippet Extraction

The string chunks generated from the previous step are transformed into a custom common data model that consists of the following fields: Filename, Document Title, Document Summary, Document Text, Snippet Title, Snippet Body, Snippet Type, Document Summary, Snippet Additional Info, Snippet Hash.

4.1.3 NLP Analyzers

Finally the snippets are processed via a NLP Pipeline, before their storage into the database, as demonstrated in Fig. 2. The NLP Pipeline follows the common and standard procedures of tokenization (standard tokenizer), lowercase filter,

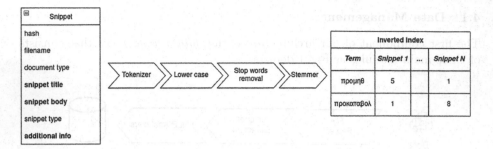

Fig. 2. NLP pipeline during data ingestion

stop words removal and stemmer. The outcome of this pipeline is the creation of an inverted index [11]. Not all fields of the snippet data model are being processed. Those that undergo processing are those that carry the important information (snippet title, snippet body and additional info) that will be queried to answer the users' questions.

4.2 Chatbot Engine/Question Answering System

The high-level overview of the question answering system is depicted in Fig. 3. The user submits a query via the custom User Interface (UI), then the query gets processed and executed; and finally the result set is displayed back to the user.

4.2.1 Query Processing

Query processing module follows a similar pipeline with Sect. 4.1.3, with the addition of *query expansion* and *query classification*. Query expansion is based on a flat ontology and associates the query with synonyms, translations, abbreviations and business-related terms. The ontology was created by business matter experts and information extracted by web scrappers. Query classification was built with the goal to classify questions to a predefined list of categories (similar to intents) [12]. It is based on simple regex rules that identify terms in the query and assign a category.

4.2.2 Query Execution

During this step the chatbot engine utilizes information from the previous step and creates multiple requests to the document database implemented in the ELK[1] stack [13]. In general, snippets are filtered first by their generic type (Sect. 4.1.2) and a set of term-based queries are executed towards the related

---

[1] *ELK* stands for three open source projects: Elasticsearch, Logstash, and Kibana.

inverted index. Then these results are ranked, filtered and grouped in categories by their data type. A set of custom rules define the filters and the type of requests that will be made depending on the classification type of the query. Furthermore, the search type, defines the different weights at corresponding snippet fields. The specification of those weights has been derived via a machine learning process that used the initial test queries in order to determine the proper weights depending on the search type. Our model was based on the gradient descent algorithm. In addition, the searches include an approximate string-matching feature; i.e., *fuzzy searching* [14], which allows the user to make spelling errors without negatively impacting the results. In essence, the user query returns documents that contain terms similar to the search terms. Similarity is defined by a maximum threshold of the *Levenshtein edit distance* [14] between the query term and the document terms. Furthermore, Query execution utilizes the query expansion information from Sect. 4.2.1 in order to perform phrase matching for business related terms (e.g. 'sap expense order') that is important to be searched as a whole phrase, instead of each term individually. As a last step the TF-IDF score of each retrieved snippet is normalized into the [0,1] range. Snippets with score less than 60%[2], are filtered out to reduce the size of the result set. The results are categorized based on their type as discussed in Sect. 4.1.2 and handled in an intelligent manner by the UI, as explained in the following section.

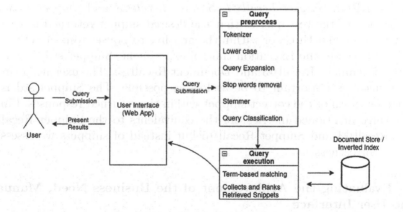

Fig. 3. Chatbot core engine

4.2.3 Innovative User Interface

At challenge 3 in Sect. 3 we argued about the difficulty of a-priori defining the user intents. Having no insights on which kind of intents will be more valuable for the business led to the implementation of more generic, intent-agnostic user-interface that is different from traditional chatbot based systems. Let's consider

---

[2] 60% threshold has been chosen after experimentation with the test questions at hand.

a sample question *"What does 'R' mean in the second digit of the payment code"*. Even though the intent of the user is agnostic to the chatbot i.e., not recognized by the Query classification component, the chatbot engine performs a search in every snippet available and returns a ranked list of potential answers. A single concrete answer is intentionally avoided. Instead, the response is generic, displaying a set of suggested documents found, and inviting the users to explore and identify the information requested themselves. Selecting one the available answers, opens an embedded pdf document viewer that scrolls automatically to the page where the answer is identified.

4.3   Evaluation System

The evaluation system described below allowed us to immediately compare different versions and understand if the changes have a positive or negative effect to the desired results of the test set.

4.3.1   Evaluating the Chatbot Engine Automatically

The automatic evaluation framework was exploited with the usage of 100 test questions along with their "gold standard" answers. For every new chatbot version, the evaluation framework was executed to quantify the impact of the change. The evaluation framework measured the following Key Performance Indicators (KPIs): *Snippet Recall@1, Snippet Recall@3* and *Snippet Recall@5*, the percentage of the test queries that the desired snippet returned in the first place, within the first three, or within the first five responses respectively. Other valuable metrics are the Execution time of experiment, Snippet std, Document Recall@1, Document Recall@3 and Document Recall@5. The execution time of the experiment is important to be as low as possible. The Snippet std is the standard deviation of the correct snippet within the returned responses. Finally, the last three mentioned metrics are the equivalents to the Snippet Recall@1, Snippet Recall@3 and Snippet Recall@5 but instead of snippets we assess the document correctness.

4.3.2   Evaluating the Achievement of the Business Need, Manually, via the User Interface

During an extensive period of User Acceptance Tests (UATs), SMEs evaluated the performance of the chatbot, as well as the overall level of satisfaction with respect to the initial business need; i.e., "How satisfied are you from the results? - The chatbot: a) Helped you find the quickly the correct information b) Gave you the correct information, but not in the first order c) Helped you slightly d) Did not help you at all". The results are presented extensively in Sect. 5 below.

5   Experiments and Discussion

For the automatic evaluation of the chatbot engine (see Sect. 4.3.1) 100 test questions have been collected and 41 documents from the domain in scope have been processed, resulting into about 1500 snippets in our database. We measured the performance for two distinct iterations (chatbot versions) as presented at Table 1. "Baseline" iteration included the first implementation of the NLP pipeline (see Sect. 4.1.3) and term-based matching. "Enhanced" iteration included improvements in the NLP pipeline (utilization of *Skroutz* Greek stemmer [10]), query classification, fuzziness search, expansion of term-based matching to take into account phrases, query expansion and weights of the search fields; as anticipated, a significant performance improvement has been measured.

Table 1. Comparing iteration results

Iteration	Doc. Recall@1	Doc. Recall@3	Doc. Recall@5	Snippet Recall@1	Snippet Recall@3	Snippet Recall@5	Execution time
Baseline	35%	55%	62%	27%	45%	51%	0.05 s
Enhanced	70%	87%	91%	65%	84%	88%	0.14 s

It is important to note that during both iterations a set of *irrelevant documents*[3] have also been included and evaluated in order to monitor the KPIs values variation. The hypothesis was denied by the results, indicating that the solution is quite stable and unbiased.

The technology stack consisted of Python and related libraries (Natural Language Toolkit NLTK, Scikit-Learn, Numpy, Pandas etc.) for the chatbot NLP engine, Elasticsearch for storing the snippets and performing term-based matching and MySQL for storing the feedback from the users.

Moreover, a user study has been conducted via a series of User Acceptance Test (UAT) sessions (see Sect. 4.3.2). User perception is subjective comprising performance, responsiveness and reliability. In the question "How satisfied are you from the results?-, the SMEs gave positive feedback for 75% of the questions they submitted, neutral: 11% and negative: 14%, as demonstrated in Table 2.

Table 2. UAT evaluation results

Test queries	Helped to find quickly the correct info	Gave the correct info but not in the first place	Helped slightly	Did not help at all
180	41%	34%	11%	14%

6 Next Steps

Following the UAT results, the future work about the chatbot would include new documents from other domains like HR. In addition the NLP engine will

---

[3] Documents not related to the Procurement & Finance domain in scope.

be enhanced with *entity recognition* capabilities, trained to identify products, references to internal systems, monetary values and arithmetic operators in the snippets and the user query. This will allow us to build a dialog system asking for disambiguation of terms and to further expand the mechanism in Sect. 4.2.2 with business rules like "if an product entity is recognized in the user query, give preferences to snippets that contain information related with this product family". Finally, given the initial positive response from the users, UI enhancements will be evaluated to replace the 'Process Web' portal completely.

7   Conclusion

In this paper we have analyzed the methodology to build a question answering chatbot that does not strictly rely on intent identification. We described the NLP components, the user interface approach and the evaluation mechanisms to measure performance. The challenges presented at Sect. 3 along with the iterative approach of building the chatbot engine led us to the following lessons learned, that we would like to share with the reader as a conclusion: a) when building a system that encapsulates knowledge that is hard to model, start with the simplest approach possible and increment it gradually, b) user interface design should be an integral part of any AI application acting as an ally towards facilitating the user c) the system performance should be measured independently from any technical KPIs and should based on business-related human-centric goals. In principal, it is clear that AI chatbots is a promising technology constantly evolving in the next years with significant academic interest and potential applications in various enterprises.

References

1. Business Process Model and Notation (BPMN) Homepage. https://www.bpmn. org/
2. Elasticsearch Homepage. https://www.elastic.co/what-is/elasticsearch
3. Carter, D.: How real is the impact of artificial intelligence. Bus. Inf. Rev. (Bus. Inf. Surv.) **35**(3), 99–115 (2018)
4. Bank of America: Bank of America's Erica®Surpasses 10 Million Users (2019). https://newsroom.bankofamerica.com/press-releases/consumer-banking/bank-americas-ericar-surpasses-10-million-users-introduces-new
5. López, G., Quesada, L., et al.: Alexa vs. Siri vs. Cortana vs. Google Assistant: a comparison of speech-based natural user interfaces. In: Nunes, I. (ed.) AHFE 2017. AISC, vol. 592, pp. 241–250. Springer, Cham (2017). https://doi.org/10.1007/978-3-319-60366-7_23
6. Kerly, A., Hall, P.D., Bull, S.: Bringing chatbots into education: towards natural language negotiation of open learner models. In: International Conference on Innovative Techniques and Applications of Artificial Intelligence, pp. 179–192 (2006). https://doi.org/10.1007/978-1-84628-666-7_14
7. Oh, K.-J., Lee, D., Ko, B.: A chatbot for psychiatric counseling in mental healthcare service based on emotional dialogue analysis and sentence generation. In: 18th IEEE International Conference on Mobile Data Management MDM (2017). https://doi.org/10.1109/MDM.2017.64

8. Ngai, E.W.T., Lee, M.C.M., et al.: An intelligent knowledge-based chatbot for customer service. Electron. Commerce Res. Appl. (2021). https://doi.org/10.1016/j.elerap.2021.101098
9. Hussain, S., Sianaki, O.A., Ababneh, N.: A survey on conversational agents/chatbots classification and design techniques. Artif. Intell. Netw. Appli. Proc. 946–956 (2019). https://doi.org/10.1007/978-3-030-15035-8_93
10. Skroutz Greek Stemmer Homepage. https://github.com/skroutz/greek_stemmer/blob/master/README.md
11. Cutting, D., Pedersen, J.: Optimization for dynamic inverted index maintenance. In: Proceedings, pp. 405–411 (1980). https://doi.org/10.1145/96749.98245
12. Kang, Y., Cai, Z., et al.: Natural language processing (NLP) in management research: a literature review. J. Manag. Anal. 139–172 (2020). https://doi.org/10.1080/23270012.2020.1756939
13. ELK Stack Homepage. https://www.elastic.co/what-is/elk-stack
14. Siahaan, A.P.U., Aryza, A., et al.: Combination of Levenshtein distance and Rabin-Karp to improve the accuracy of document equivalence level. Int. J. Eng. Technol. **7**, 17–21 (2018). http://dx.doi.org/10.14419/ijet.v7i2.27.12084

Comparative Study of a Deterministic Adaptive Beamforming Technique with Neural Network Implementations

Ioannis Mallioras[1,2]($\boxtimes$) (iD), Zaharias D. Zaharis[1] (iD), Pavlos Lazaridis[3] (iD),
Traianos V. Yioultsis[1], Nikolaos V. Kantartzis[1] (iD), and Ioannis P. Chochliouros[4] (iD)

[1] School of Electrical and Computer Engineering, Aristotle University of Thessaloniki,
54124 Thessaloniki, Greece
mallioras@auth.gr
[2] Maggioli S.P.A., 47822 Santarcangelo di Romagna, Italy
[3] School of Computing and Engineering, University of Huddersfield, Huddersfield H1 3DH, UK
[4] Hellenic Telecommunications Organization S.A. Member of the Deutsche Telekom Group of
Companies, 15122 Athens, Greece

Abstract. Future wireless networks depend on the development of new mechanisms that can increase the efficiency of the network. Antenna array adaptive beamforming (ABF) is an antenna operation that can be significantly improved with the use of machine learning. In this paper, a deterministic beamforming technique is compared with two different types of neural networks (NNs). These are the non-linear autoregressive network with exogenous inputs (NARX) and the recurrent NN (RNN) with long short-term memory (LSTM) units. To train the NNs, we produce a dataset using the minimum variance distortionless algorithm (MVDR) applied to a realistic antenna array. Using grid search, we find the best architecture for both NNs. Then, we train the final models and evaluate them by comparing their accuracy to that of the MVDR algorithm. We demonstrate how the use of NNs is preferable to that of deterministic algorithms as they appear to maintain high accuracy while having a much lower response time than that of deterministic algorithms. The RNN with LSTM units is the most promising out of the two NN models as it achieves higher accuracy with a slightly shorter training time.

Keywords: Adaptive beamforming · Antenna array · Long short-term memory (LSTM) · Neural network (NN) · Non-linear autoregressive network with exogenous inputs (NARX) · Recurrent neural network (RNN)

1 Introduction

The complexity of a modern telecommunications environment is constantly changing and becoming increasingly demanding in terms of response time and data management. There is a huge need for new mechanisms that could elevate the efficiency of the network

I. Maglogiannis et al. (Eds.): AIAI 2022 Workshops, IFIP AICT 652, pp. 98–107, 2022.
https://doi.org/10.1007/978-3-031-08341-9_9

and allow it to handle the demands of current and future network traffic. Given the continuous increase of data load, older and high-complexity algorithms are not able to respond properly and therefore they become less reliable for future use. Already, neural networks (NNs) and other machine learning techniques have proven to be a fast and reliable alternative to many high-complexity algorithms of different scientific fields and so their use in the field of wireless networks is very promising and has already shown a lot of potential [1–6]. By training our models using pre-recorded data from the application of deterministic algorithms, we can create reliable and accurate machine learning alternatives that can replace current mechanisms and improve the overall quality of service.

1.1 Antenna Array Adaptive Beamforming

In this regard, we aim to improve the efficiency of smart antennas and specifically one of their most important operations, i.e., adaptive beamforming (ABF). By applying ABF, a smart antenna can dynamically adapt its feeding weights to maintain high gain towards the direction of a desired user while eliminating signals of interference. By steering the main lobe of its radiation pattern towards the direction of a desired incoming signal (i.e., signal of interest or SoI) while placing nulls towards the directions of respective interfering signals (i.e., signals of avoidance or SoAs) the antenna establishes a reliable connection with the desired source and a high signal to interference-plus-noise ratio (SINR). The radiation pattern produced by the antenna array can be altered to fit the desired criteria by tweaking the feeding weight of each array element appropriately. This can be done using an algorithm, also known as a beamformer, to which we give information about the directions of arrival (DoAs) of new incoming signals, and it calculates the appropriate feeding weights. To achieve the same task using NNs, we must train the network to accurately map the angles of arrival (AoAs) of the incoming signals to the desired weight vectors, thus bypassing the high-complexity and time-consuming operations that deterministic algorithms come with. To compare the performance of the NN approach with a deterministic algorithm, we test two types of NNs, namely the non-linear autoregressive network with exogenous inputs (NARX), and a recurrent neural network (RNN) both of which have already been used in the field [3, 6, 7].

2 Theoretical Background

2.1 Theoretical MVDR Beamformer

For this study, we utilize the minimum variance distortionless algorithm (MVDR) as the deterministic beamforming algorithm for comparison. This beamformer keeps the incoming signal undistorted at the output and minimizes the output signal variance, which practically translates into reducing the output power due to the unwanted signal component thus maximizing SINR. If we consider an M-element linear antenna array and $N + 1$ incoming signals (where the first is SoI and the rest N are SoAs), the desired weights are calculated using the following expression:

$$\mathbf{w}_{MV} = \mathbf{R}_{xx}^{-1}\mathbf{a}(\theta_1, \varphi_1) \tag{1}$$

where $\mathbf{R}_{xx}$ is the input correlation matrix of the beamformer, and $\mathbf{a}(\theta_1, \varphi_1)$ is the steering vector that corresponds to the desired signal, which arrives at the antenna from DoA described in the spherical coordinate system by (θ_1, φ_1). This steering vector is calculated considering an antenna array composed of isotropic point sources, but in order to pursue a more realistic approach we use a modified version as shown below.

2.2 Realistic Version of MVDR Beamformer

Modifying the previous equation for a more realistic approach (as seen in [8]) we use the following equation for calculating the desired feeding weights:

$$\mathbf{w}_{MV} = (\mathbf{E}_\varphi \mathbf{E}_\varphi^{\mathrm{H}} + \mathbf{R}_{nn})^{-1} \mathbf{e}_\varphi(\theta_1, \varphi_1) \tag{2}$$

where $\mathbf{E}_\varphi$ is a $M \times (N+1)$ matrix representing the total realistic steering matrix, $\mathbf{R}_{nn}$ is the noise correlation matrix and $\mathbf{e}_\varphi(\theta_1, \varphi_1)$ is the realistic steering vector that corresponds to DoA of the desired signal. All matrices and vectors shown in Eq. (2) are calculated given that the incoming AoAs are known. These calculations can be found in [8] and [9], and are beyond the scope of this paper.

2.3 NARX as a Beamformer

A NARX is a type of NN that differs from the common feed-forward operation in that it utilizes values of its previous outputs to improve future predictions. As shown in Fig. 1, the outcome of each NARX training iteration, is calculated using the previous attempt's output. This way, this type of NN can process incoming data in a sequential manner and produce an output by having each new input "affecting" the previous prediction.

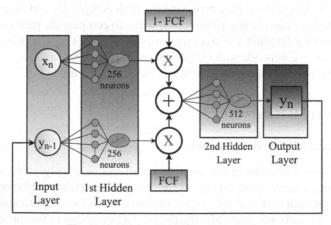

Fig. 1. Two-layer NARX implementation

To use a NARX as a beamformer, the incoming AoAs x_n(n=0, 1,...,N) enter the NN in series and at each prediction step n the outcome of the network y_n is calculated using both the current input x_n and the feedback of the output y_{n-1} derived during the previous iteration. The only exception to this process is of course the first input x_0, which also represents the SoI, as it enters the first layer of the network without the additional feedback information, since there is no y_{-1}.

For this application we also introduce another parameter, called as the *feedback contribution factor* (FCF), and it is used to regulate the compromise between the contribution of the feedback over the current input during the prediction process. The utilization of this parameter can also be seen in Fig. 1 and its value is decided after grid searching within the range [0, 1] as shown in Fig. 2. For this purpose, we use 10^4 records for training and another 10^3 records for testing, while considering the root mean square error (RMSE) as a cost function and performing a 3-fold cross validation to further validate our findings. The results in Fig. 2 show that the most promising value for this parameter is 0.4.

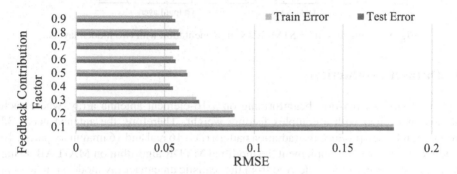

Fig. 2. Grid search to adjust the feedback contribution factor

2.4   RNN as a Beamformer

RNNs belong to another type of NNs, which are mostly used for processing sequential data. This type of NN uses its processing units not only to process the current input, but also to use valuable information from previous inputs. For this study, we build an RNN with long short-term memory (LSTM) processing units.

In this scenario (as shown in Fig. 3), at each time step $(t = 0, 1, ..., N)$, the current AoA input x_t is processed by the LSTM units to influence their hidden states, which are consequently passed on to the next time step's units. In this way, each input affects the outcome of the RNN. Once all inputs are processed, and the output y_N has been produced, we pass it through a linear transformation layer, which is also included in the training process, in order to have the correct weight vector size. The idea behind this approach is to have the weight vector initially configured based on AoA of SoI (x_0) and then, to let the interferences $(x_n, n = 1,..,N)$ shape the final form of the RNN output.

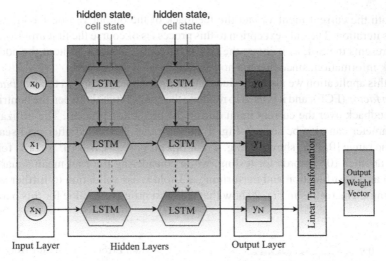

Fig. 3. Example of the LSTM- RNN implementation with two hidden layers.

3 Dataset Production

For this study, we perform beamforming on a 16-element antenna array, where each element is excited with a complex feeding weight. Therefore, the antenna needs 32 weight numbers to produce the radiation pattern (i.e., 16 real and 16 imaginary parts). To produce the dataset, we implement the modified MVDR algorithm on MATLAB, using the realistic steering vectors derived from the realistic antenna array model simulated in CST [10]. Further restrictions are applied to the produced records so that the NN models are trained based on realistic and demanding circumstances. AoAs of the incoming signals must lie within the angular sector [30°, 150°] and have a minimum distance of $\Delta\theta = 6°$ between each other, while the signal to noise ratio (SNR) of the incoming signals is considered to be equal to 0 dB, thus considering high noise conditions.

Hence, each record consists of $N + 1$ AoAs (with the first one corresponding to SoI and the rest of them to SoAs), and 32 weight numbers created by the MVDR algorithm for the specified AoAs. To make the process of searching the best architecture for each type of NN faster, we assume the simple case of 1 SoI and 2 SoAs. Additionally, we normalize both AoAs and output weights in the range [0,1] to improve the performance of the optimization algorithm. Thus, we produce two datasets, one with 1.1×10^4 records (10^4 for training and 10^3 for testing) to be used for the purpose of finding each best NN architecture, and one with 1.1×10^6 records (10^6 for training and 10^5 for testing) for the training and evaluation of the final NN models.

4 Training and Evaluation of NNs

4.1 NARX

We start by investigating the best architecture for NARX. We test upon a two and a three-hidden layer approach with different values for the layer size. These variations are shown in Fig. 4 using the following notation: [Size of 1st hidden layer, Size of 2nd hidden layer, ..., Size of last hidden layer]. To train these models, we use the smaller dataset we produced (as explained in Sect. 3) with a 3-fold cross validation to confirm our findings. Each configuration has been trained for 500 epochs with a learning rate of 0.001 and a batch size of 512. Figure 4 demonstrates that the two hidden layer architecture described as [256, 512] (also depicted in Fig. 1) has the most satisfactory results with good train and test error values. It also appears that the increase in the network depth, and thus in its complexity and training time, does not come with a significant decrease in test RMSE values. Therefore, the three-layer approach is disregarded.

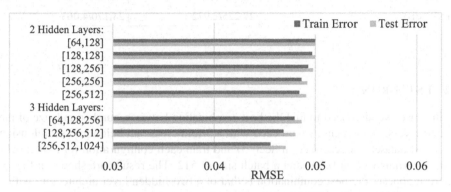

Fig. 4. Comparison between 2 and 3-hidden layer NARX implementations

Now that we know the best architecture for this type of NN, we proceed to train the final model using the big dataset of 1.1×10^6 records (as explained in Sect. 3), a batch size of 512, and a learning rate of 0.001. Moreover, we use the Pytorch function *ReduceLRonPlateau*, which reduces the learning rate by a factor of 0.8 if the training RMSE is decreasing at a very slow rate. This function increases the training performance by a factor between 2 and 10 [11]. When the learning rate has dropped to a point where it no longer contributes to the training process, or when the test error does not seem to improve over time, we stop the training process. The results are presented in Table 1.

Table 1. NARX training and test results

Epochs	Training RMSE	Test RMSE	Final learning rate	Training time (hours)
380	0.0256	0.0257	0.0003	3.5

We can now test the trained model in terms of beamforming accuracy using 10^4 triads of AoAs (1 SoI and 2 SoAs) on which the trained model has no prior "experience". In Table 2, we present a statistical analysis of the performance of the NARX in comparison to that of the MVDR algorithm. It is evident that this model is accurate regarding the placement of the main lobe with similar accuracy to that of the MVDR algorithm, but faces some difficulty in placing nulls at DoAs of SoAs as shown by the higher mean value of nulls divergence. This also explains the lower SINR mean value achieved by the NARX compared to that of the MVDR algorithm.

Table 2. Comparison between MVDR and NARX

	MVDR [Mean/Std]	NARX [Mean/Std]
Divergence of main lobe (°)	0.429/0.320	0.411/0.317
Divergence of nulls (°)	0.000/0.000	0.856/0.773
SINR (dB)	27.225/2.972	24.170/4.063

4.2 LSTM-RNN

In this case, we also need to find the best combination between number and size of the hidden layers. Once again, we proceed with a 3-fold cross validation grid search using the small dataset (as described in Sect. 3) and train each configuration for 500 epochs with a learning rate of 0.001 and a batch size of 512. The results are shown in Fig. 5, where it appears the best combination is that of a two-hidden layer architecture with a layer size of 256.

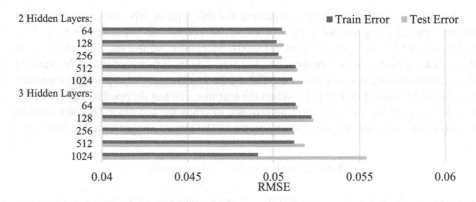

Fig. 5. Comparison between 2 and 3-hidden layer LSTM-RNN implementations

We proceed to train the final model using the big dataset and the same configurations used in the training of the NARX model, as shown in Sect. 4.1. The training results are provided in Table 3.

Table 3. LSTM-RNN training and test results

Epochs	Training RMSE	Test RMSE	Final learning rate	Training time (hours)
245	0.0133	0.0133	0.0005	3.2

Once more, we evaluate the trained model in terms of beamforming accuracy using 10^4 triads of AoAs on which the trained model has no prior "experience". The comparison in terms of performance between the MVDR algorithm and the trained model can be seen in Table 4. It appears that the LSTM-RNN is very precise regarding the placement of the main lobe and demonstrates significant accuracy regarding the placement of the nulls. The competence of this model as a beamformer can also be validated by the mean SINR value, which is very similar to that of the MVDR algorithm.

Table 4. Comparison between MVDR and LSTM-RNN

	MVDR [Mean/Std]	LSTM-RNN [Mean/Std]
Divergence of main lobe (°)	0.429/0.320	0.422/0.314
Divergence of nulls (°)	0.000/0.000	0.309/0.353
SINR (dB)	27.225/2.972	26.665/3.113

5 Comparison Between the Beamformers

In this section, we compare the performances of the different NN beamformers with that of the MVDR algorithm. In Table 5, we see the summary of the performance of each beamformer, so that we can easily compare them. It is evident that the LSTM-RNN implementation is the most promising model as it outperforms the NARX model in terms of both null placement accuracy and SINR values. We observe that both NN models are much faster than the MVDR algorithm (see mean response time). All measurements have been performed in the Google Colaboratory environment, using an Intel® Xeon® CPU @2.30 GHz with 12 GB of RAM (assigned by the Google Colaboratory environment).

We additionally provide a radiation pattern comparison in Fig. 6 for AoAs equal to 100°, 60°, and 140°. Here, we see that all beamformers have accurately placed the main lobe towards the direction of 100°, but the pattern produced by the LSTM-RNN is much closer to that of the MVDR algorithm, as it appears to almost coincide with it. It is also obvious that the LSTM-RNN model has been slightly more accurate at the null placement at 60°.

Table 5. Comparison between MVDR, NARX and LSTM-RNN

	MVDR	NARX	LSTM-RNN
Mean divergence of main lobe (°)	0.429/0.320	0.411/0.317	0.422/0.314
Mean divergence of nulls (°)	0.000/0.000	0.856/0.773	0.309/0.353
SINR (dB)	27.225/2.972	24.170/4.063	26.665/3.113
Training time (hours)	–	3.5	3.2
Mean response time (sec)	1.48	0.0010	0.0048

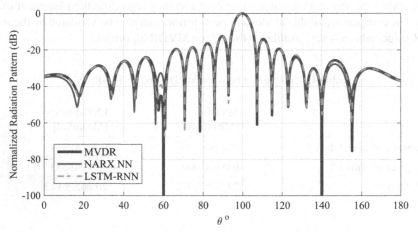

Fig. 6. Radiation patterns produced by MVDR, NARX and LSTM-RNN beamformers for a SoI received at 100° and two SoAs received at respective AoAs equal to 60° and 140°.

6 Conclusion

In this study, we have compared two different types of NNs, namely a NARX and a LSTM-RNN, with a conventional deterministic ABF technique, i.e., MVDR, to find which one provides better behavior in the ABF operation. The comparative results shown in Table 5 prove that the most promising model is the LSTM-RNN with two hidden layers, and a size of 256 per hidden layer. Even though the NARX implementation has a slightly faster response time, the LSTM-RNN model achieves higher levels of accuracy with less training time. Given the results, it seems that the implementation of ABF using LSTM-RNN models has great potential and is highly recommended.

Acknowledgements. This research was supported by the European Union, partially through the Horizon 2020 Marie Skłodowska-Curie Innovative Training Networks Programme "Mobility and Training for beyond 5G Ecosystems (MOTOR5G)" under grant agreement no. 861219, and partially through the Horizon 2020 Marie Skłodowska-Curie Research and Innovation Staff Exchange Programme "Research Collaboration and Mobility for Beyond 5G Future Wireless Networks (RECOMBINE)" under grant agreement no. 872857.

References

1. Senthilkumar, K.S., Pirapaharan, K., Hoole, P.R.P., Hoole, H.R.H.: Single perceptron model for smart beam forming in array antennas. Int. J. Electr. Comput. Eng. **6**(5), 2300– 2309 (2016)
2. Ramezanpour, P., Rezaei, M.J., Mosavi, M.R.: Deep-learning-based beamforming for rejecting interferences. IET Sign. Process. **14**, 467–473 (2020)
3. Che, H., Li, C., He, X., Huang, T.: A recurrent neural network for adaptive beamforming and array correction. Neural Netw. **80**, 110–117 (2016)
4. Zaharis, Z., Gotsis, K., Sahalos, J.N.: Comparative study of neural network training applied to adaptive beamforming of antenna arrays. Prog. Electromagn. Res **126**, 269–283 (2012)
5. Zaharis, Z.D., et al.: Implementation of antenna array beamforming by using a novel neural network structure. In: International Conference Telecommunications and Multimedia (TEMU), Heraklion, Greece (2016)
6. Bhadauria, P., Kumar, R., Sharma, S.: Performance dependency of LSTM and NAR beamformers with respect to sensor array properties in V2I scenario. arXiv (2021)
7. Mallioras, I., Zaharis, Z.D., Lazaridis, P.I., Chochliouros, I.P., Mistry, K.K., Loh, T.H.: A novel approach based on recurrent neural networks applied to adaptive beamforming. In: International Conference COMPUMAG, Cancun, Mexico (2021)
8. Zaharis, Z.D., Gravas, I.P., Lazaridis, P.I., Yioultsis, T.V., Antonopoulos, C.S., Xenos, T.D.: An effective modification of conventional beamforming methods suitable for realistic linear antenna arrays. IEEE Trans. Antennas Propag **68**(7), 5269–5279 (2020)
9. Godara, L.C.: Smart Antennas, 1st edn. CRC Press, Boca Raton (2004)
10. CST Studio Suite. https://www.3ds.com
11. Dauphin, Y.N., Pascanu, R., Gulcehre, C., Cho, K., Ganguli, S., Bengio, Y.: Identifying and attacking the saddle point problem in high-dimensional non-convex optimization. Adv. Neural Inf. Process. Syst. 2933–2941 (2014)

Efficient Data Management and Interoperability Middleware in Business-Oriented Smart Port Use Cases

Achilleas Marinakis[1] , Matilde Julian Segui[2] , Andreu Belsa Pellicer[2] ,
Carlos E. Palau[2] , Christos-Antonios Gizelis[3](✉) ,
Anastasios Nikolakopoulos[1] , Antonios Misargopoulos[3] ,
Filippos Nikolopoulos-Gkamatsis[3] , Michalis Kefalogiannis[3] ,
Theodora Varvarigou[1], Konstantinos Nestorakis[3] , and Vrettos Moulos[1]

[1] School of Electrical and Computer Engineering, National Technical University
of Athens, 9 Iroon Polytechniou St., 15780 Athens, Greece
{achmarin,tasosnikolakop,vrettos}@mail.ntua.gr, dora@telecom.ntua.gr
[2] Department of Communications, Universitat Politécnica de Valéncia,
Camino de Vera, s/n, 46022 Valencia, Spain
{majuse,anbelpel}@upv.es, cpalau@dcom.upv.es
[3] IT Innovation Center OTE Group, 99 Kifissias Avenue, 15124
Marousi, Athens, Greece
cgkizelis@cosmote.gr,
{amisargopo,fnikolop,mkefalogiannis,knestorakis}@ote.gr

Abstract. The interoperability of critical infrastructures, such as ports, has become a primary concern of EU in recent years. Information systems that have the control of these infrastructures are continuously evolving and handle heterogeneous collections of data, processes, and people. Moreover, cross-infrastructure dependencies may give rise to cascading and escalating data model discrepancies across interconnected systems. In this article, we present a data model -following the newest technology standards- that tries to consolidate APIs and services of highly complex infrastructures. Port environments are a characteristic example of them, since massive amount of data and services from different sources are processed and used. We adopt a bottom-up approach, considering every service interconnection as an independent entity, which must be aligned with the proposed common vocabulary and data model. The strict guidelines that are injected into the lifecycle of a service/component development, lead to explicitly enforce interoperability between each one service that lives inside the ecosystem of the port. That is -and should be- a step towards "the cognitive port of the future", where developers, SMEs and huge vendors can exchange and reuse data from a shared repository. Consequently, ports will play key role in the new information system model, as in-house marketplaces will be developed, for companies to disseminate and exploit their data and services.

Supported by DataPorts EU Project – 871493.

I. Maglogiannis et al. (Eds.): AIAI 2022 Workshops, IFIP AICT 652, pp. 108–119, 2022.
https://doi.org/10.1007/978-3-031-08341-9_10

Keywords: Smart Ports · Marketplaces · Interoperability · Smart Data Model · Data virtualization

1   Introduction

Seaports constitute a cornerstone of the global economy, since they serve as the connecting tissue between all the other modes of transport. Ports activity in terms of international shipping trade has exploded in the recent decades, resulting in the dynamic evolution of the harbours and the increasing degree of complexity of their management [1]. In order to support port management process under transparency, data-driven intelligence is introduced. The latter requires the aggregation of miscellaneous data that can be gathered from the port itself, as well as any stakeholders that are involved in its operations. In fact, the maritime domain involves data sources of a high magnitude that may include information about vessels, oceans, wave stations, observations from environmental conditions, fishing and maritime biodiversity, routes, trajectories, and incidental or voluntary oil spill events [18]. Furthermore, concerning Smart Ports and the interrelated IoT technology, the rapidly growing presence of smart logistics mechanisms and smart sensing systems in ports, realize the automation of the port's functionality and thus the generation of large amounts of data. The range of this generated information is wide while involving a plethora of communication, sensor systems and control technologies to facilitate data collection throughout the supply chain for decision-making in real time and information sharing between the various stakeholders of the port [6]. Moreover, the collection of maritime data is performed through a variety of ways and stored in many different data formats, while the harvested data itself might be structured, semi structured or unstructured.

Big Data techniques applied to this huge amount of data could provide ports the necessary tools for automating decision processes and controlling job queues. Those techniques would allow -for example- dynamic job assignment for container handling, integrating not only operational data but also global data coming from other actors along the value chain. In other words, unleashing the potential power of the existing data derived from port operations could optimize the usage of its resources and infrastructure. However, this scenario is far from being real, due to the lack of interoperability among data combined with efficient data management schemes, which is preventing ports from adopting data-driven solutions in their production environments. This is where DataPorts project [4] kicks in, and more specifically its data processing middleware that is introduced in this paper.

From business perspective, increasing data interoperability is a way to assist seaport authorities to optimize their passengers' facilitation, improve traffic around the port region and by that improve the approach routes, the embarkation and disembarkation processes aiming to have a positive economic effect for the Port (potential increase of the serving ships), as well as for the shipping

Port Authorities	•New Services.
Shipping Companies	•New Services for Customer support
Cargo Companies	•Need for data and also provide data
Transport Companies	•Interest on mobility (goods and people)
Logistics Companies	•Can share data they own. Interested in new
Research Institutes / Academia / Unis / Colleges	•Interested in data in order to provide algorithms and services, Online courses in Shipping, Maritime, etc., to be added as data in the Platform
Startups/ SMEs	•Interested in data in order to provide services (ready to do business)
Municipalities / Public Sector Organizations	•Need for data, regarding mobility, traffic, in order to have a better view of the region
Commerce Associations / Trade Unions	•Need of data, regarding mobility, traffic, in order to manage their advertising approach.
Culture Associations / Museums / Special Interest Groups	•Potential interest of newcomers. Manage visiting hours / increase visitors
Transportation Authorities	•Need of data to dynamically optimize routing plans and schedules. Can also provide data
LEAs / Medical Bodies	•Need of data and services. Identify potential areas of interest that they might be needed.
Public Authorities / Policy Makers	•Need data analytics to define policies (eg. over tourism, increase visitors, improve services and facilities).

Fig. 1. External potential beneficiaries

companies (cost reduction). Potentially, besides the economic benefits for the port authorities, various stakeholders can be beneficiaries from the data interoperability, in order to improve their services. Telecom operators, by exploiting their vast amounts of data, are considered as a valuable player in this emerging data-driven market. Offering data, or services through APIs, can provide great insights for improved decision making to external interested stakeholders (e.g. Public authorities, Municipalities, Shipping Companies, Transportation Authorities, Cultural and Trade Associations, etc.). In many cases it is considered challenging to fuzz such data with streams coming from other sources and therefore the benefit is increased.

2   Business Model and Services

Envisage the following brief scenario: on the day of their travelling, passengers are going to use a mobile application that will inform them in real time about the best route to approach the port and board on ship. This approach may have as an outcome the orchestration of the passenger flow in an optimal way towards their boarding. In order to achieve this scenario, it needs to rely on historic and real-time data residing in mobile application, as well as web services. Several external stakeholders might be beneficiaries of such data-driven services. Some of them have no previous relation with shipping ports community. They are listed in Fig. 1, along with the potential benefit.

Concerning Telecom companies, they could generate revenues from the data and services offerings/usage and the respective fees and also benefit from customer loyalty and possible additional communication services sales. In principle, they need to take into account various assumptions both regarding the CAPEX/OPEX and the revenues parameters depending on the individual case (e.g. country, market size, penetration, income per capita, and prices). The business case analysis would be required in a long-term timeframe, for an estimation of the breakeven point and the expected profits that can be obtained. More specifically, based on the selected data market, the revenues and costs that are incurred should also be considered (e.g. number of customers and the increasing rate, average monthly volumes of data, H/W and S/W costs and the cost for upgrading/deployment of additional H/W, customer acquisition, etc.). Telecoms, collect, handle or own large amounts of data that usually are exploited internally. In a data-driven market, the Telecoms' involvement may include mobility and usage traffic, demographics, and other network related data that can be associated with the population density [13]. Such datasets fused with port authorities' available data, like the ship's arrival/departure schedules and the number of passengers of each ship provided by the shipping lines, will offer valuable cognitive information to be accessed and exploited by many shipping ports' ecosystem stakeholders, not excluding those that until now are not related to the ports. In such an emerging market the mobility data -real and non-real time ones- can be of significant value. Those datasets may be also used by Port Authorities, Shipping Companies, Cargo/Logistics Companies. These stakeholders may be considered as consumers of the Data as a Product service, where they can use the offered data as a source for decision support and new services. Similarly, available data might also be used by Research Institutes, Universities, Startups and SMEs in order to develop AI-based cognitive services that can be sold to various stakeholders in shipping port ecosystem, not excluding other non-shipping related ones. They may be considered as consumers or partners towards the development of Data bundle as a Service category.

Moreover, there are several other consumer categories such as, the Municipalities and other Public Sector Bodies, Commerce Associations, Cultural Heritage and Museum entities, Transportation (public or private), LEAs and Medical Bodies that can be considered as consumers to both categories (i.e. Data as a Product and Data bundle as a Service) by using offered datasets as information for their customers (e.g. citizens) or by fuzzing them with other services or develop new ones. Having so many heterogeneous stakeholders, a detailed data model should be developed in order to adapt, collect and safely store the data. On top of that interoperability analysis should take place forehand, as most of the services have to exchange information in such an interconnected environment.

3   Data Model and Interoperability

Interoperability is the ability to share data and services among different computer systems and depends on the ability of the involved systems to understand the structure and meaning of the data that they receive and present the data that they send in a way that can be interpreted by the others. Semantic interoperability is based on the definition of an unambiguous way to interpret the data that is being exchanged between computer systems. This can be achieved through the use of an ontology, which provides a vocabulary for a domain where the concepts present in that domain are defined without any ambiguity and may be related to each other or organized according to different criteria. Hence, an ontology provides a common understanding of the domain of interest [12].

However, in the case of DataPorts, enabling interoperability is not a trivial task because the different organizations in transportation and logistics do not follow a common standard. Instead, they usually have their own vocabularies, which may have a poor definition of semantics or no explicit semantic formulation at all. For this reason, the proper definition of a common vocabulary for this domain, following the appropriate guidelines and best practices, is necessary to enable interoperability. Moreover, the actual needs of the market must be taken into account during the definition of a common data model in order to be able to implement solutions that are valuable for the different stakeholders. The DataPorts project has developed a common data model for describing the data of the port domain in a systematic and standardized way, with mappings to standard vocabularies in order to facilitate interoperability with other solutions. The use of this common data model will enable the reuse and exploitation of the data in cognitive port applications, as well as the reuse of those applications.

The first step in the definition of the common data model was the identification and analysis of the different data sources that had to be integrated in the DataPorts platform. This analysis considered the meaning and format of the data, as well as the storage and data management mechanisms. From this analysis, the main concepts of the vocabulary were identified and classified as possible classes, attributes or relationships. Next, the existing ontologies and vocabularies related with the application domain were studied in order to identify which of their concepts could be reused in the DataPorts data model. In this step, the following ontologies and vocabularies have been analyzed in order to reuse the appropriate concepts in the DataPorts common data model: Fiware Smart Data Models [11], IDSA Information Model [15], United Nations Centre for Trade Facilitation and Electronic Business (UN/CEFACT) model, Blockchain in Transport Alliance (BiTAS) [2], DCSA Interface for Track & Trace [5], IPSO Smart Objects (OMA SpecWorks) [16] and Smart Applications REFerence (SAREF) ontology [22]. In particular, the Fiware Smart Data Models have been especially relevant for DataPorts because components of the Fiware platform [10] have been selected as part of the core elements of the DataPorts platform. The concepts from the identified vocabulary that were not found in the standard ontologies and vocabularies were defined following the Fiware Smart Data Models guidelines.

The Fiware Smart Data Models are based on open standards and real use cases and have been developed by a collaborative Fiware-related initiative focused on the definition of data models to facilitate interoperability in different application domains by the provision of harmonised formats and semantics for the data. Following those guidelines, the DataPorts common data model is compatible with Fiware NGSI v2 and the European Telecommunications Standards

Institute (ETSI) [7] standard NGSI-LD [20], which is an evolution of NGSI v2 to support Linked Data. NGSI defines an information model and an interface for sharing context information, while the use of Linked Data enables the automatic association of the data with an ontology.

The DataPorts common data model is hosted in a Git repository. Following the structure of Fiware Smart Data Models, the concepts in the DataPorts data model have been grouped under a set of subjects inside the Smart Ports domain (Fig. 2). Each subject contains the corresponding NGSI-LD context document, which describes how the data is interpreted according to the ontology, as well as other shared resources and information, and provides access to the different entity types that it contains. The representation of the entity types is described using JSON schema. In addition, the specifications of each entity type and the corresponding examples in NGSI v2 and NGSI-LD, as well as in plain JSON and JSON-LD, are provided. Thus, the data model is fully compatible with the Fiware ecosystem and the Smart Data Models initiative.

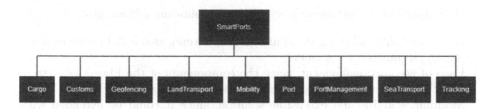

Fig. 2. Domain and subjects of the DataPorts common data model

The DataPorts platform enables semantic interoperability between the different data providers and data consumers through the definition of a unified semantic model and interface to access the data. In addition to the common data model, the necessary mechanisms and enablers to provide access to the data from the existing data sources were implemented. Since the data sources are heterogeneous in terms of their interfaces, data formats and data models, a set of agents was developed to connect each data source with the DataPorts platform. An agent is a piece of software able to obtain data from a source and translate it into the common data model and format. When certain conditions are met, the agent retrieves the data from the data source, translates it and sends it to the upper layers of the platform (Fig. 3). As a result, the data sent to the analytics services of the platform and any other potential data consumers that have the proper access permissions, follow the same format and semantic model, regardless of the particular aspects of the data source. The agents send the translated data to the Orion Context Broker, which provides a common API to access the data from the different data sources, and also to another component of the Fiware ecosystem, named Cygnus, which is designed to facilitate the management of historical data. The Orion Context Broker [9] and Cygnus [8] compose one of the building blocks of the Connecting Europe Facility (CEF)

[3] digital catalogue, which is known as the CEF Context Broker. In addition, the DataPorts platform provides mechanisms to enable security and data governance.

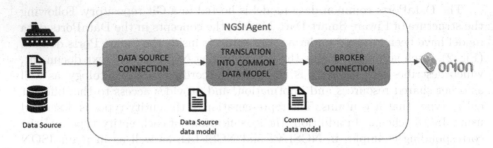

Fig. 3. NGSI agent

This approach to interoperability offers the following advantages:

- Interoperability, allowing the connection of heterogeneous data sources while offering a common data model.
- Ease of use and deployment, since the components of the Fiware ecosystem and the agents can be deployed on Docker.
- Modular, scalable and extensible solution, since it could be extended with added value tools, and it is also possible to scale the components on demand according to the needs of the users.
- Less development effort, since the data will be available through a common API following the same format and semantics regardless of the type of data source, thus decoupling the applications that consume the data from the data sources.
- Fully compatible with the Fiware ecosystem and common open-source software.

4   Data Processing and Virtualization

Given that the data are translated and harmonized according to the data model described in Sect. 3, the next step is to provide those data as a service, so that developers can build cognitive data-driven applications on top of the platform. Therefore, a data processing and virtualization middleware is needed, as an abstraction layer between data providers and consumers. The goal is to assist the application developers to focus only on the required data, relying on the proposed middleware to deliver them, thus encapsulating all the underlying technical complexity. In fact, data virtualization is a data integration technique that provides access to information via a virtualized service layer, regardless of the location of the data sources. It allows applications to access data through a unique endpoint, thus providing a unified, abstracted, and encapsulated view of information, while also being able to transform and process the data in order to prepare it for consumption. Furthermore, data-intensive applications, that use a virtualized data source, still expect certain quality of service guarantees from the system, such as performance, availability, etc.

DataPorts project attempts to deal with those challenges, putting emphasis on the quality of the data as well. For that reason, the so-called Data Abstraction and Virtualization (DAV) component has been developed, to simplify the data management in heterogeneous, complex, and distributed infrastructure, following the Data as a Service (DaaS) paradigm. More specifically, DAV is responsible for the proper pre-processing, cleaning, and filtering of the data coming from the agents, storing them to a secure and scalable data repository (data lake), and then making them available as data ponds to any potential recipients. Data ponds are created by applying specific filtering rules, defined by the users upon request. DAV also transforms and serves the data in a format selected by the developer, such as JSON, Parquet or CSV. Figure 4 depicts the internal structure of DAV, which is based on an already proposed information life cycle management framework [19]. The following subsections describe DAV's subcomponents from functional and technical point of view.

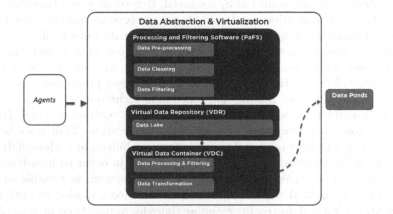

Fig. 4. Data abstraction and virtualization internal structure

4.1 Pre-processing and Filtering Software

PaFS is responsible for the initial pre-processing, cleaning and filtering of the datasets. It pre-processes the data by the means of fully collecting them, transforming into a Python code-friendly format and taking care of proper column/row structure. It cleans the data by detecting values such as NaNs, empty fields, outliers, wrong values, and finally filters the dataset by the means of eliminating all those values found, either by replacing, or removing them along with their respective rows. In more detail, to all the datasets available in the Data-Ports platform, PaFS applies the following generic pre-processing techniques:

- Removal of whitespaces from all string-type cells
- Conversion of empty cells and 'NULL' string values to 'nan' in all cells
- Removal of rows without datetime values, or with wrong ones
- Conversion of datetime values to UTC format

The scope of those techniques is to improve the quality of the data and thus to increase the performance of the applications that exploit them. Indeed, input data is a major concern for analytics services. For example, the quality of the data used to train the models has a huge impact on the efficiency, accuracy and complexity of machine learning tasks [14]. Furthermore, PaFS calculates a correlation matrix between the columns of each dataset. Last but not least, it detects outliers in numerical attributes, creating additional columns that indicate which corresponding column cell is considered as an outlier. The detection is implemented using the method of "three standard deviations from the mean", as a cut-off radius/threshold.

4.2 Virtual Data Repository

VDR is the distributed infrastructure where all the pre-processed, cleaned, and filtered datasets, coming from PaFS, are saved. It is constructed based on MongoDB, carrying modifications and custom parameters to comply with DAV's efficiency standards. MongoDB was selected due to its auto-scaling/sharding capabilities, as well as its allowance of vital modifications/custom configurations by the designer. VDR lives inside a Kubernetes cluster, which is the optimal solution and fits perfectly to the needs of DAV, as it achieves proper load balancing, whilst offering replication, scaling and scheduling techniques [17]. Since DAV's main functionality is data virtualization, MongoDB's co-existence with Kubernetes (as a container management tool) seems imperative. VDR goes beyond existing frameworks that offer real time scaling capabilities in a MongoDB cluster [21]. Such frameworks enable the cluster to scale in order to handle rapidly changing number of users. However, the proposed system is capable of scaling in a fully automated way according to the workload, aiming at optimizing resource utilization and decreasing response times for applications in need of high availability. In particular, VDR takes full advantage of the Kubernetes built-in monitoring system, in order to automatically increase or reduce the number of replicas in a sharded MongoDB cluster, when the nodes CPU usage is higher or lower than certain thresholds.

4.3 Virtual Data Container

VDC is the interface through which communication with data recipients is achieved, for data stored in VDR to be made available, as shown in Fig. 5. Its role is to further process and filter the data, by applying specific filtering rules defined by the data consumers via HTTP POST requests. The scope of those rules is twofold: i) to filter the datasets and thus to serve only the specific data pond that a user is interested in and ii) to detect and remove wrong values

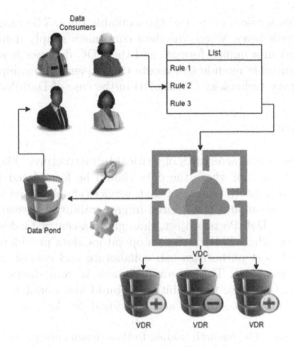

Fig. 5. Virtual data container information flow

(from columns where those values are not acceptable e.g., outdoor temperatures at minus 50 °C), which are most probably caused by sensors malfunction. Through that request, the data consumers also define the format (JSON, Parquet or CSV) in which they want to receive the data (data transformation). The filtering rules are structured as an Array of JSON Objects, which consist of three core elements:

- The "subject_column", which shall have the name of a dataset's column
- A logical "operator"
- The "object", which shall be a value in the same datatype as the "subject_column" or the name of another column that has the same datatype

Most of the common logical operators (greater than, less than, (not) equal, or, etc.) are supported by VDC and can be used by the rules' author (data scientist, application developer, end-user etc.). It is worth mentioning that a rule's main objective is to apply filters to only one subject column at a time and not combining subjects. If more than one columns are concerned as subjects in the same rule, then this step is considered more as a pre-processing and less as a filtering action, thus out of scope of VDC. The goal is to enable any potential DataPorts user to define a list of filtering actions on a requested dataset. For that reason, the rules structure is kept simple, so that they can be specified not only by data scientists and experts, but also by users with limited or no technical background within a ports ecosystem, who are nevertheless interested

in using analytics services on top of the available data. The tangible outcome
is a common access layer, where the data consumers simply define queries (in
the form of rules) in a unified format, and the VDC designer is responsible for
developing the suitable module to execute those queries, in compatibility with
the selected storage technology (MongoDB in the case of DataPorts).

5   Conclusion

The unique business characteristics of Critical Infrastructures -like ports- reveal
the need of a middleware where the data should be formulated in a way that
can be analysed accurately. On top of that, services should be refactored before-
hand in order to accomplish the desired interoperability between the interconnected components. DataPorts project, through data-centric by design approach,
presents a solution where SMEs, telecom operators, data providers, service content creators and port authorities can collaborate and coexist into a friendly
data-sharing environment. That accomplishment is -and should be- the main
goal of platforms that have the ambition to build and populate an ecosystem,
able to attract companies, startups and individual developers.

Acknowledgement. The research leading to these results has received funding from
the European Commission under the H2020 Programme's project DataPorts (grant
agreement No. 871493).

References

1. Benedicto, M.I., Morales, R.M.G., Marino, J., de los Santos, F.: A decision support
   tool for port planning based on Monte Carlo simulation. In: 2018 Winter Simulation Conference (WSC). IEEE (December 2018). https://doi.org/10.1109/wsc.
   2018.8632389
2. Blockchain in Transport Alliance. https://www.bita.studio/. Accessed 28 Mar 2022
3. CEF Digital Home. https://ec.europa.eu/cefdigital/wiki/display/CEFDIGITAL/.
   Accessed 28 Mar 2022
4. DataPorts H2020 EU Project. https://dataports-project.eu/. Accessed 28 Mar
   2022
5. DCSA Interface for Track & Trace. https://dcsa.org/standards/track-trace/.
   Accessed 28 Mar 2022
6. Douaioui, K., Fri, M., Mabrouki, C., Semma, E.A.: Smart port: design and perspectives. In: 2018 4th International Conference on Logistics Operations Management
   (GOL). IEEE (April 2018). https://doi.org/10.1109/gol.2018.8378099
7. European Telecommunications Standards Institute. https://www.etsi.org/
   committee/cim. Accessed 28 Mar 2022
8. FIWARE Cygnus. https://fiware-cygnus.readthedocs.io/en/latest/. Accessed 28
   Mar 2022
9. FIWARE Orion Context Broker. https://fiware-orion.readthedocs.io/en/master/.
   Accessed 28 Mar 2022
10. FIWARE Platform. https://www.fiware.org/. Accessed 28 Mar 2022

11. FIWARE Smart Data Models. https://github.com/smart-data-models. Accessed 28 Mar 2022
12. Ganzha, M., Paprzycki, M., Pawłowski, W., Solarz-Niesłuchowski, B., Szmeja, P., Wasielewska, K.: Semantic interoperability. In: Palau, C.E., et al. (eds.) Interoperability of Heterogeneous IoT Platforms. IT, pp. 133–165. Springer, Cham (2021). https://doi.org/10.1007/978-3-030-82446-4_5
13. Gizelis, C.-A., Mavroeidakos, T., Marinakis, A., Litke, A., Moulos, V.: Towards a smart port: the role of the telecom industry. In: Maglogiannis, I., Iliadis, L., Pimenidis, E. (eds.) AIAI 2020. IAICT, vol. 585, pp. 128–139. Springer, Cham (2020). https://doi.org/10.1007/978-3-030-49190-1_12
14. Gupta, N., et al.: Data quality for machine learning tasks. In: Proceedings of the 27th ACM SIGKDD Conference on Knowledge Discovery & Data Mining. ACM (August 2021). https://doi.org/10.1145/3447548.3470817
15. IDSA Information Model. https://github.com/International-Data-Spaces-Association/InformationModel. Accessed 28 Mar 2022
16. IPSO Smart Objects. https://omaspecworks.org/develop-with-oma-specworks/ipso-smart-objects/. Accessed 28 Mar 2022
17. Jawarneh, I.M.A., et al.: Container orchestration engines: a thorough functional and performance comparison. In: ICC 2019–2019 IEEE International Conference on Communications (ICC). IEEE (May 2019). https://doi.org/10.1109/icc.2019.8762053
18. Lytra, I., Vidal, M.E., Orlandi, F., Attard, J.: A big data architecture for managing oceans of data and maritime applications. In: 2017 International Conference on Engineering, Technology and Innovation (ICE/ITMC). IEEE (June 2017). https://doi.org/10.1109/ice.2017.8280019
19. Moulos, V., et al.: A robust information life cycle management framework for securing and governing critical infrastructure systems. Inventions 3(4), 71 (2018). https://doi.org/10.3390/inventions3040071
20. Privat, G., Medvedev, A.: Guidelines for modelling with NGSI-LD. ETSI White Paper (42) (2021)
21. Psomakelis, E., et al.: A scalable and semantic data as a service marketplace for enhancing cloud-based applications. Futur. Internet 12(5), 77 (2020). https://doi.org/10.3390/fi12050077
22. Smart Applications Reference Ontology. https://saref.etsi.org/. Accessed 28 Mar 2022

Experimentation Scenarios for Machine Learning-Based Resource Management

Alexandros Kostopoulos[1]([☒]) [iD], Ioannis P. Chochliouros[1] [iD], John Vardakas[2],
Miquel Payaró[3], Sergio Barrachina[3], Md Arifur Rahman[4], Evgenii Vinogradov[5],
Philippe Chanclou[6], Roberto Gonzalez[7], Charalambos Klitis[8],
Sabrina De Capitani di Vimercati[9], Polyzois Soumplis[10], Emmanuel Varvarigos[10],
Dimitrios Kritharidis[11], and Kostas Chartsias[11]

[1] Hellenic Telecommunications Organization (OTE) S.A., 99 Kifissias Avenue, 15124
Maroussi, Athens, Greece
alexkosto@oteresearch.gr
[2] Iquadrat Informatica SL, Barcelona, Spain
[3] Centre Tecnològic de Telecomunicacions de Catalunya (CTTC/CERCA), Barcelona, Spain
[4] IS-Wireless, Piaseczno, Poland
[5] Katholieke Universiteit Leuven, Leuven, Belgium
[6] Orange S.A., Paris, France
[7] NEC Laboratories Europe GmbH, Heidelberg, Germany
[8] EBOS Technologies Limited, Nicosia, Cyprus
[9] Universita degli Studi di Milano, Milan, Italy
[10] Institute of Communications and Computer Systems (ICCS), Athens, Greece
[11] Intracom S.A. Telecom Solutions, Peania, Greece

Abstract. 5G changes the landscape of mobile networks profoundly, with an
evolved architecture supporting unprecedented capacity, spectral efficiency, and
increased flexibility. The MARSAL project targets the development and evaluation of a complete framework for the management and orchestration of network
resources in 5G and beyond by utilizing a converged optical-wireless network
infrastructure in the access and fronthaul/midhaul segments. In this paper, we
present a conceptual view of the MARSAL architecture, as well as a wide range
of experimentation scenarios.

Keywords: 5G · Cell-free (CF) · Distributed cloud · Network automation ·
Machine learning (ML) · Secure multi-tenancy

1 Introduction

5G mobile networks will be soon available to handle all types of applications and to
provide services to massive numbers of users. In this complex and dynamic network
ecosystem, an end-to-end performance analysis and optimisation will be key features
in order to effectively manage the diverse requirements imposed by multiple vertical
industries over the same shared infrastructure.

© IFIP International Federation for Information Processing 2022
Published by Springer Nature Switzerland AG 2022
I. Maglogiannis et al. (Eds.): AIAI 2022 Workshops, IFIP AICT 652, pp. 120–133, 2022.
https://doi.org/10.1007/978-3-031-08341-9_11

To enable such a vision, the MARSAL [1] EU-funded project targets the development and evaluation of a complete framework for the management and orchestration of network resources in 5G and beyond, by utilizing a converged optical-wireless network infrastructure in the access and fronthaul/midhaul segments.

At the network design domain, MARSAL targets the development of novel cell-free (CF) based solutions that allows the significant scaling up of the wireless Access Points (Aps) in a cost-effective manner by exploiting the application of the distributed cell-free concept and of the serial fronthaul approach, while contributing innovative functionalities to the O-RAN project [2]. In parallel, in the fronthaul/midhaul segments MARSAL aims to radically increase the flexibility of optical access architectures for Beyond-5G (B5G) Cell Site connectivity via different levels of Fixed Mobile Convergence (FMC).

At the network and service management domain, the design philosophy of MARSAL is to provide a comprehensive framework for the management of the entire set of communication and computational network resources by exploiting novel ML-based algorithms of both edge and midhaul Data Centres (DCs), by incorporating the Virtual Elastic Data Centers/Infrastructures paradigm.

Finally, at the network security domain, MARSAL aims to introduce mechanisms that provide privacy and security to application workload and data, targeting to allow applications and users to maintain control over their data when relying on the deployed shared infrastructures, while AI (Artificial Intelligence) and Blockchain technologies will be developed in order to guarantee a secured multi-tenant slicing environment.

In this paper, we present a conceptual view of the MARSAL architecture (Sect. 2), as well as a wide range of experimentation scenarios (Sect. 3). The first domain includes a set of scenarios focused on *cell-free networking in dense and ultra-dense hotspot areas*. The second domain includes scenarios related to *cognitive assistance*, as well as *security and privacy implications* in 5G and beyond. We conclude our remarks in Sect. 4.

2 Architectural Framework

MARSAL aims to provide an evolved architecture towards B5G/6G, offering unprecedented degrees of flexibility and closed-loop autonomy at all tiers of the infrastructure, and significantly improved spectral efficiency via cell-free networking. The overall architecture and the structure of the envisioned B5G/6G MARSAL is depicted in the generic schematic of Fig. 1, and includes all the main infrastructure elements that are deployed within the MARSAL project. MARSAL adopts an evolved 3GPP NG-RAN (Next Generation - Radio Access Network) [3, 4] which is extended with emerging cell-free technologies for network densification. Moreover, the MARSAL architecture considers innovations at the optical transport domain and significant evolutions of the MEC (Multi-access Edge Computing) system [5] towards fully elastic Edge Computing. MARSAL deploys a distributed Edge infrastructure with DCs structured in 2 tiers, featuring Regional Edge and Radio Edge nodes. Radio Edge DCs will host the Network Functions (NFs) of the (virtualised) RAN, which fully aligned with the O-RAN specifications.

At the network level, the emphasis is on innovations at the RAN and fronthaul domains that will "unlock" the potential of cell-free networking in future B5G/6G networks. MARSAL envisions cell-free networking as a "key component" of B5G/6G

RANs, that will offer unprecedented spectral efficiency (SE) and performance, which is not constrained by inter-cell interference. The MARSAL network architecture is based on novel cell-free networking mechanisms that will allow the significant scaling up of AP deployment in a cost-effective manner, by exploiting the distributed processing cell-free concept. The novel mechanisms are based on the disaggregation of the traditional cell-free Central Processing Unit (CPU) in Distributed Units (DUs) and a Central Unit (CU) in line with the 3GPP NG-RAN architecture. Regarding the wireless fronthaul links, the MARSAL architecture is based on an innovative mmWave Hybrid MIMO (Multiple-Input, Multiple-Output) solution [6, 7], specifically targeting cell-free networks, with advanced beamforming and beamsharing capabilities. In this way, a new AP topology adaptation in cell-free networks and advanced scenarios can be supported, with APs reassigned to different DUs, on demand. MARSAL's cell-free innovations will be implemented and integrated with existing vRAN (virtualised RAN) elements for the first time and will be contributed back to the O-RAN project. Specifically, the MARSAL network architecture will be aligned with the O-RAN Alliance architecture, which represents an evolution of Cloud RAN (C-RAN) [8], further disaggregating and complementing the 3GPP 5G standards with a foundation of vRAN network elements and packet-based interfaces. Specifically, O-RAN disaggregates the BBU (Base Band Unit) in a DU with the real-time functions, and a CU with the non-real time functions. The latter is further disaggregated into the CU-User Plane (CU-UP) and the CU-Control Plane (CUCP). MARSAL's CU User Plane function (i.e., CU-UP) and DU will be deployed at MARSAL's Radio Edge, and the CU-CP Near-RT RIC (Radio Intelligent Controller) at the Regional Edge.

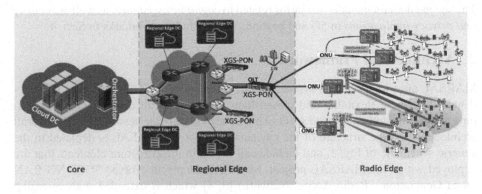

Fig. 1. The MARSAL network architecture

At the network service and management level, the MARSAL architecture will consider a novel hierarchical control plane solution, federating the SDN (Software Defined Network) controllers of the fixed and mobile segments of the network under a common orchestration subsystem. MARSAL proposes the disaggregation of the Non-RT (non-real-time) into Near-RT SDN Control function that will be hosted by the Near-RT RIC at the Regional Edge nodes. Thus, near real-time reaction to workload variations will be supported, at sub-second timescales. Moreover, MARSAL proposes the deployment of Software-Defined Transport Network Controllers (i.e., SDTNs) [9] at the Regional Edge to control the fixed segment. Both domains will be federated under MARSAL's Core Tier NFVO (Network Function Virtual Orchestrator), based on ETSI OSM (Open Source MANO) [10], which will provide Network Slicing as a Service (NSaaS) functionality as per 3GPP TR 28.801 [11] specifications. Thus, end-to-end (E2E) slicing with centralised orchestration is supported, while still allowing innovative closed-loop (or ML-driven) control of each individual domain. The MARSAL architecture also considers a novel Fixed Mobile Convergence solution, to facilitate integrated connectivity of mobile and fixed (i.e., fiber-to-the-home - FTTH) services. MARSAL's solution involves two transmission approaches seamlessly integrated at the Regional Edge node, including a standard Point-to-Point (PtP) connection with or without WDM (Wavelength-Division Multiplexing) and a very disruptive Point-to-Multipoint (PtMP) approach based on XGS-PON (passive optical network) modules [12].

In addition, while previous approaches adopted a common Virtual Machine- (VM-) based technology stack for MEC and NFV (Network Functions Virtualisation), MARSAL approach is based on Cloud-Native technologies (i.e., Docker Containers, Kubernetes Virtual Infrastructure Managers (VIMs)) which are widely regarded as the future of vertical application development [13]. While support for Kubernetes VIMs is gradually emerging in MEC platforms (e.g., in StarlingX [14]), there is currently a gap in supporting disaggregated Cloud-Native apps. To fill this gap, MARSAL proposes extensions to the Multi-access Edge Orchestrator (MEO) [15] to support the disaggregation of application functions, that will be defined as collections of helm charts, both horizontally (i.e., across Edge sites) and vertically (i.e., from the cell site towards the core cloud). MARSAL will consider the deployment of the aforementioned functions, either at the "bare metal" of the MEC hosts' NFVIs (Network Function Virtualisation Infrastructures), or within VNFs (Virtual Network Functions), as proposed in the NFV-IFA 029 [16], thus compatible with the NSaaS sub-system. Moreover, MARSAL will extend the Mobile Edge platform at the host level, to allow MEC apps to be accessed by any UE (User Equipment), irrespective of physical location. Dynamic Virtual Network Embedding algorithms will be explored, to determine the optimal disaggregation of application functions at any Edge DC, considering Compute, Networking, and Storage constraints, thus achieving increased resource utilisation.

In parallel, the MARSAL architecture is built by considering a novel, distributed approach that involves Analytic Engines (AEs) at all tiers of the Edge infrastructure, and Decision Engines (DEs) at the two Core-Tier orchestration subsystems. Analytic Engines, the first pillar of automation, analyse and federate measurements to achieve Context Awareness, and Decision Engines, as the second pillar, Plan and React to Context changes, delegating data-driven local control decisions to the lower tiers of the hierarchy. For the first pillar of automation, MARSAL will design and implement an innovative, decentralised approach to achieve global Context Awareness, using for the first time Representation Learning such as Embedding Propagation (EP) [17] or the GraphSage algorithms [18]. State-of-the-art (SoTA) context representation methods for 1D and 2D datasets are not appropriate for MARSAL's diverse network and application data, that can be best represented with a graph-like abstraction. To this end, network slices and

MEC applications will be represented as the nodes of a knowledge graph, along with their defining variables and parameters (e.g., SLA (Service Level Agreement) requirements, latency budgets, cost considerations, energy efficiency goals). MARSAL proposes to apply EP mechanisms to build the node representations (or embeddings) of the knowledge graph, iterating over the data and minimizing the differences among neighbouring embeddings in the graph. For the second pillar of automation, the resulting embeddings that represent the current state (or context) of the MARSAL infrastructure in a highly compressed form (i.e., encoded as multidimensional normalised arrays) can be transmitted to the Core Tier Decision Engines. The embeddings are fed to downstream ML algorithms implemented by the Decision Engines that jointly orchestrate Network Slices, Network Services and MEC applications continuously and automatically evaluating current context under required policy. Due to the high number of (potentially conflicting) parameters and policy requirements involved, MARSAL will consider multi-objective optimisation techniques that achieve different trade-offs between optimality and complexity.

Finally, at the network security level, MARSAL introduces mechanisms that guarantee privacy and security in multi-tenancy environments, targeting both end users and tenants. MARSAL aims to deliver a decentralised, blockchain-based platform that supports network slicing transactions via smart contracts, targeting multi-tenant infrastructures for the first time. In this platform, the MNO (Mobile Network Operator), MVNOs (Mobile Virtual Network Operators), and OTT (Over-The-Top) vertical application owners form a decentralised autonomous organisation, which can dynamically negotiate network slice contracts, flexibly integrating large and small players without the need for a centralised entity. Smart Contracts facilitate direct contracts among entities that can be dynamically renegotiated based on real-time supply and demand. MARSAL's smart contract platform will be implemented with a private, permissioned blockchain solution where tenants will co-own the validator nodes' network after approval and authentication. Going a step further, MARSAL will also incorporate new privacy-preserving context representations, which will allow MARSAL's data-driven NSaaS subsystem to operate without exposing tenants' business and operational data. Context awareness requires the exchange of local embeddings (via EP mechanisms) that represent the nodes of a knowledge graph, risking information leakage. These embeddings have inherent anonymisation properties, as they represent nodes as compressed, high-dimensional arrays, while the application of EP algorithms iteratively minimizes the differences among neighbouring embeddings, further decreasing the risk of re-identification of the original node. MARSAL will also integrate innovative techniques to guarantee that embeddings cannot be reversed and can be shared among competing partners and the NSaaS sub-system, without any risk of disclosing confidential information.

The MARSAL architecture will also incorporate an innovative NFS (Network File System) Gateway, controlled by the OTT application provider, to serve as the foundation of trust. The DCS gateway will be the intermediary between the (trusted) OTT application, and (untrusted) DCS (Distributed Cloud Solution) infrastructure. The NFS gateway will be extended to implement a novel data pipeline for the controlled sharing of data among different parties. The gateway will support for first time a policy language, extending SoTA solutions such as Open Digital Rights Language or JSON-LD (JavaScript Object Notation for Linking Data), effectively enforceable in the data protection context of different stakeholders that will permit the specification of sharing and processing restrictions over data. Finally, the NFS gateway will implement a novel probabilistic scheme that protects the integrity of computations based on the randomised injection of pre-computed and replicated computational tasks. Thus, a unified solution for data obfuscation and integrity assurance will be implemented for the first time, which varies the probability of randomised injections based on the degree of protection or performance required.

To improve the performance of current signature-based solutions for dealing with zero-day or evolving attacks, MARSAL considers hardware accelerated solutions for a decentralised Threat Detection Engine (TDE) and a centralised Threat Analysis Engine (TAE). ML-based threat detection, that has demonstrated an improved ability to extract complex non-linear relationships in attack data, will be leveraged for the design of MARSAL's TDE. Moreover, MARSAL will leverage the capabilities of a new generation of programmable SDN Switches, which allows MARSAL's data-plane to behave as a distributed barrier against threats, securing the entire transport infrastructure and intercepting cyber-attacks at a very early stage. Detected cyber-attacks can be isolated by the data-plane at the level of individual traffic flows, going beyond traditional slice-centric approaches and towards micro-segmentation.

Moreover, MARSAL's network security level also considers a centralised TAE, that operates as an ML Fusion Centre, collecting and correlating metadata and features extracted from the P4 pipeline of the decentralised TDE. This allows complex attacks such as Advanced Persistent Threats that simultaneously target multiple network nodes, to be detected. Furthermore, it provides system-wide consistency and correlation for events occurring within all the involved P4 pipelines. MARSAL will exploit the flows' destination IPs (Internet Protocols), and specifically their sequence, since this information is both unencrypted and readily available as part of the SDN Switches' telemetry framework. Thus, the TAE will associate observed flows (with unknown status) with malicious ones based on the sequence of IPs accessed. MARSAL's solution will involve feeding a Deep Neural Network (DNN) with sequences of IPs to build a vector representation of network flows; intuitively, flows with a small distance from Radio Edge DCs will host the Network Functions malicious flows should also be flagged as malicious.

3   Experimentation Scenarios

3.1   Dense User-Generated Content Distribution with mmWave Fronthauling

The main objective of this scenario is to demonstrate and evaluate MARSAL's distributed cell-free RAN in terms of increased capacity and spectral efficiency gains, and the adaptivity of dynamic clustering and RRM mechanisms in managing connectivity resources in a dynamic environment with varying hotspots areas. Furthermore, an additional objective of this scenario is to evaluate the Hybrid MIMO Fronthaul in terms of its ability to offer a dynamic AP topology.

This experimentation scenario will show the potential of deploying cell-free networking in 6G networks with massive AP deployments. The MARSAL innovations will focus on distributed processing, with clusters of APs and DUs coordinating via fronthaul links. In this experimentation scenario, we will evaluate the performance of dynamic data driven clustering algorithm. It will also explore and evaluate inter-DU coordination effect in Spectral Efficiency and propose dynamic adaptability of the coordination levels jointly addressing AP-DU and DU-DU coordination for the first time. The Cell-free vRAN components in this experimentation scenario will validate the design of cell-free enable virtual O-RAN Distributed Unit (O-DU), cell-free MAC (Medium Access Control) scheduler, PHY sub-layer. Moreover, it will also validate the appropriate modification of the CP protocols and O-RAN spo-duecified interfaces (i.e., E2, O1) [19] to support practical cell-free operation and fully distributed processing.

In CF networks, the environment around the user defines the set of APs serving it. These APs may: *i) be connected to different O-DU and ii) utilize different types of fronthaul links.* The latter, in its turn, defines the information to be shared between the APs and their O-DUs. Next, the involved O-DUs share necessary information with each other. The final MARSAL processing will also consider the fronthaul and midhaul constraints (feedback to the cluster formulation block).

We list below a generic description of the stakeholders involved in this experimental scenario:

Cell-free mMIMO Infrastructure Provider: An infrastructure provider is needed to validate the MARSAL solution, especially for a novel cell-free NG-RAN architecture. The relevant stakeholder, besides providing the infrastructure, can conduct research on the area of cell-free mMIMO (massive MIMO) and could be providing, e.g., cell-free clustering solutions. The cell-free clustering solutions are needed to cooperate with the CPUs (Central Processing Units) and the O-DUs via algorithms that integrate the cell-free RUs (Radio Units) with the O-DUs by using PHY API's (Application Programming Interfaces).

Cell-free vRAN VNFs Provider: The cell-free vRAN VNFs provider from the industrial stakeholder will be designing the cell-free vRAN architecture. The stakeholder will be further implementing the solution on 3GPP protocol stacks and provide the VNFs. The VNFs can be implemented in radio edge DCs and/or regional edge DCs based on the underlying user's requirements and their SLA. However, the solution provided by the stakeholders as a form of VNFs (i.e., the vO-DU and vO_CU-UP) can be deployed at the Radio Edge DCs as white-box servers.

RAN Intelligent Controller and xAPPs[1] Provider: The RAN intelligent controller and the xAPPs provider will be involving providing the cell-enabled solutions with the modifying the necessary O-RAN specified interfaces. The AI/ML models at the Near-RT RIC provided by the stakeholders will somehow provide the RAN functionalities of the underlying architecture. The stakeholder will be providing the resources of Non-RT RIC/SMO (Service Management and Orchestration), Near-RT RIC, and RAN nodes, and relevant O-RAN specified interfaces to enable cell-free in the traditional O-RAN

---

[1] Application available at RAN Controller for RAN Configuration, AI/ML model policy execution, Radio Resource Management (RRM) model, slice selection, etc., as per O-RAN compliance approved specifications specified by O-RAN WG-1 and WG-3.

architecture. The stakeholder solution of the Near-RT RIC and vCU_CP can be deployed at a Regional Edge white-box server, and it can be further connected to the radio edge DCs through optical network unit from other stakeholders.

mmWave Fronthaul Provider: Stakeholders can enable scalability through the flexible utilisation of a distributed cell-free approach and an mmWave fronthaul, by relying on optical technologies (PONs, WDM rings) for their interconnection with other components of MARSAL architecture. The mmWave transceivers and the beamforming solutions from the stakeholder can be integrated in Hybrid MIMO node that will be characterised via experiments (e.g., in terms of EIRP (Effective Isotropic Radiated Power), beam pattern, Field of View and beam directivity).

mmWave Transport Network: The stakeholder will contribute to design of the 6G x-haul networks and provide SDN-enabled wireless transport for the interconnection of distributed vRAN components of the MARSAL architecture. The Point-to-Point (PtP) mmWave solution of the stakeholders that can enable several deployment options (e.g., Co-located O-CU and O-DU: O-RAN split 7.2x, independent O-RU (O-RAN Radio Unit), O-CU (O-RAN Central Unit), O-DU locations: O-RAN split 7.2x, and O-RU and O-DU integration on cell site: O-RAN split 2), respectively[2].

Network Equipment Manufacturer: Apart from traditional network devices (e.g., routers and switches), VNF-based devices must be designed and manufactured to support the MARSAL architecture, including DCs and MEC platforms.

3.2 Ultra-dense Video Traffic Delivery in a Converged Fixed-Mobile Network

This scenario will showcase MARSAL's solution towards Fixed-Mobile Convergence in an ultra-dense indoors context (e.g., campus, stadium, malls, etc.). Mobile clients served by a distributed Cell-Free RAN will be sharing the Optical Midhaul with third party fixed clients. The Fixed-Mobile Convergence in an Ultra-dense indoors scenario will be operated based on two operation modes: *Fixed operation* (Passive Optical LAN (Local Area Network)) and *Mobile operation* (small/pico cell with optionally Distributed Antenna System), respectively. The mobile clients served by a distributed cell-free RAN will be sharing the Optical Midhaul with third party FTTH clients. The optical fiber access equipment (Optical Line Terminal - OLT) will relate to PON and PtP interfaces where the Network urbanism organisation, e.g., OLT and CU co-localised and DU at the end face of the optical termination.

5G carriers and equipment are emitted and localised at the regular antenna locations with 2G/3G/4G. The pressure of coverage based on the requirements of the regulator is the main reason to have such deployment engineering rules. Concerning the mobile backhaul, 5G deployment coincides with a massive use of optical fiber to achieve the required backhaul throughput up to 10GEth. The fixed access network is based on PtP (Point-to-Point) topology to achieve the connectivity between antenna site and the first

---

[2] Further information about O-RAN components' definitions can also be found at: https://docs.o-ran-sc.org/en/latest/architecture/architecture.html.

aggregation node (central office). Due to that in parallel of 5G, FTTH is under deployment, we have more and more central offices (COs) equipped with OLT shelf. 5G backhauling could be addressed either by direct PtP connection to aggregation switch/router or through OLT PtP ports and cards. In order to address the increase of 6G cells, the preferred fixed technology to collect multiple spots is the PtMP also named PON (Passive Optical Network) based on "tree" fiber infrastructure. 6G transport challenges concern the coordination between RAN and FAN (Radio and Fixed Access Network) networks to "address" throughput, latency and availability issues.

We list below a generic description of the stakeholders involved in this experimental scenario.

Optical Access Networks and Fiber Infrastructure Provider: This stakeholder will be providing the ONU (Optical Node Unit) and optical fiber infrastructure that will connect the Radio Edge nodes of the MARSAL architecture, which is hosting the vRAN elements. It will further enable an interconnection via PtP and PtMP (PON technology) midhaul links with the Regional Edge. The Regional Edge nodes of the MARSAL architecture will be interconnected in a WDM ring topology, will host the Radio Intelligent controller and the vCU_CP VNFs from the NVFs provider.

Radio Intelligent Controller Provider: The stakeholder will be providing Radio intelligent controller including the Near-RT RIC, SMO, relevant O-RAN specified interfaces to enable cell-free in the traditional O-RAN architecture.

The RAN Components Provider: The RAN components provider will be providing the CU and DU as monolithic VNFs that will be integrated with the cell-free RUs (APs). Furthermore, the stakeholder of the VNFs providers will modify and implement necessary interfaces to enable cell-free NG-RAN for the PoC (Proof-of-Concept) experimentation validation.

Network Equipment Manufacturer: Apart from traditional network devices (e.g., routers and switches), VNF-based devices, the ONU, optical fiber gateway must be designed and manufactured to support the MARSAL architecture.

3.3 Cognitive Assistance and Smart Connectivity for Next-Generation Sightseeing

In this scenario, the deployment of two real-time and interactive cloud-native applications for outdoors sightseeing supporting human-centered interaction via 3D cameras is envisioned in the MARSAL's multi-tenant elastic edge infrastructure. These applications would be offered to users equipped with untethered Augmented Reality (AR) glasses. Both applications would endure an enhanced strolling experience by showing overlaid information relevant to their surroundings (APP#1) and enabling virtual artifacts manipulation (APP#2), while considering background traffic from other applications and services. This experimentation scenario envisaged within MARSAL leverages smart glasses to furnish a full B5G/6G sightseeing experience. To better showcase the scope of the proposed scenario, let us conceive a general use case consisting of a next-generation sightseeing tour enhanced with AR in a big city. Throughout the tour, the user is provided with information of interest as she/he walks by the streets of the city (APP#1). The tour also proposes a predefined route where the user visits multiple points of interest (POI) empowered with artifact manipulation applications (APP #2).

This scenario would fit within the "Immersive smart city" use case under the category "Massive twinning" and also within the "Fully-merged cyber-physical worlds" use case under the category "Immersive telepresence for enhanced interactions" as described in [20]. In our vision: i) the sightseeing application (APP#1) could be part of the different services that would be managed under the Immersive smart city, e.g., under the ambience/environment (for example, climate, air quality) and cultural aspects. and; ii) the virtual artifact manipulation (APP#2) would be linked with the enhanced interactions to be addressed by B5G/6G networks. As explained in [20], the use of B5G/6G networks are needed in these use cases as they improve some existing KPIs (Key Performance Indicators) of 5G networks (such as service availability, coverage, and network energy efficiency); this also happens because B5G/6G networks bring new capabilities leading to new KPIs among which we highlight integrated sensing, local compute integration, integrated intelligence and flexibility (ability of the system to be adapted and tailored to specific use cases and environments as a consequence of disaggregation, softwarisation, and automation/orchestration, which are concepts dealt with in MARSAL).

Below we list a generic description of the stakeholders involved in this experimentation scenario. These are the following entities:

End-user: The end-user is the consumer of the applications, participating as a spectator and active player, in the respective applications.

User Equipment Manufacturer: These are the companies in charge of designing and manufacturing user equipment for VR (Virtual Reality) / AR (Augmented Reality) devices like smart glasses.

Network Equipment Manufacturer: Apart from traditional network devices (e.g., routers and switches), VNF-based devices must be designed and manufactured to support the MARSAL architecture, including DCs and MEC platforms.

Connectivity Provider: Large enterprises (such as telecom operators) play this role by offering resources (network, computing, and storage) in large-scale and cloud-based environments for service deployment. It is their duty to safeguard the integrity and long-term viability of their infrastructures in order to accommodate virtualised services. NFV Infrastructures are provided/leased by connectivity providers, where VIMs are in charge of the infrastructures, connected with the Service Virtualisation Platform (SVP) and controlled by the Service Platform Provider. The NFVIs address not only the requirements for a static, centralised cloud environment, but also the dynamic and mobility-related requirements.

Service Provider: This is a generic role that can be assigned to many types of companies, covering a plethora of services in vertical domains that may potentially be benefited from the MARSAL architecture. Service Providers are companies that offer services to end-users or other companies, considered as the consumers of a service, for example, a company offering a MEC platform for processing of video files captured through the smart glasses or charging end-users.

Service Virtualisation Platform Operator: This stakeholder is in charge of running and maintaining a secure, scalable, and efficient SVP for the deployment of media services. The SVP Operator's responsibilities include general control of daily operations, provisioning and maintenance processes, security practices, disaster recovery planning and execution. The SVP operator is also responsible for analysing and optimizing resource allocation, as well as ensuring that charges are made in accordance with agreed-upon SLAs.

Applications Developer: Companies that develop novel 6G-related applications (or services or functions that can be integrated to make a service). They may use the SVP's Service Development Kit (SDK) for deploying, configuring, and managing their services.

3.4   Data Security and Privacy in Multi-tenant Infrastructures

The goal of this scenario is to demonstrate and evaluate MARSAL's privacy and security mechanisms. They guarantee the isolation of slices and ensure collaboration of participants in multi-tenant 6G infrastructures without assuming trust. These mechanisms will also be evaluated in terms of their ability to mitigate the increased privacy risks of NGI (Next Generation identification) applications that process Personally Identifiable Information (PII). To this end, this scenario will demonstrate the application of security and privacy mechanisms in four different layers, namely: *secure and private sharing of information among tenants, legal security using smart contracts, security of the data stored in the cloud and security of the end-users.*

The development of each of the different layers presents different challenges ranging from the implementation of smart contracts among different tenants to the real time analysis of network data to allow the protection of the end-users in a timely manner.

We approach the security and privacy in 6G networks in a holistic way. Contrary to the previous scenarios, offering a solution tailored for the MARSAL architecture, here we present a modular design to offer four different layers of security and privacy that could be applied in very different contexts. Moreover, we adapt them to work in the context of the *Cognitive Assistance scenario in 5G and beyond* described above.

This scenario assumes a multi-tenant infrastructure with one MNO and two MVNOs, each serving an OTT application provider. MARSAL technology will ensure the isolation of the different slices while offering the possibility of collaboration among the different tenants. To this end, we will demonstrate how the usage of smart contracts can be paired with the private representation of data, allowing the sharing of information among different tenants and the owner of the infrastructure that can be interested in the optimisation of different ML models.

Moreover, the scenario will also cover the security (and privacy) at different levels of the MARSAL architecture. First, we will demonstrate how policies can be used to safely store data in the cloud (either at the core or the edge of the network), testing different allocation strategies that ensure the perpetual security of the data.

Then, we move our focus to the network, and we will demonstrate how the browsing patterns of users can be analysed in real time to alert end-users against malicious behaviours they may have, before they get in trouble.

We list below a generic description of the stakeholders involved in this experimentation scenario.

- **Network operator:** The network operator is in charge of the last 2 layers of security: the *security of the end-users* and the *security of the network itself*. It will be in charge of deploying the engines in charge of the protection.
- **Cloud providers:** The cloud providers should apply the storage policies defined by the users and tenants to ensure the security of the data.
- **Slice tenants:** The slice tenants will be responsible for the correct execution of the privacy transformation of the data and the signature of the smart contracts.
- **Network equipment manufacturers:** They should be able to generate equipment able to execute complex tasks, such as ML models execution or on-line rule adaptation to allow the protection of the end-users.
- **End-users:** They are the most benefited from the execution of the different privacy and security layers that allows them to use the MARSAL architecture in a safer way.

4 Discussion

In this paper, we presented a conceptual view of the MARSAL architecture, as well as a wide range of experimentation scenarios.

In particular, the *first domain* is focused on *cell-free networking in dense and ultra-dense hotspot areas*. The first experimentation scenario considers *dense User-Generated Content (UGC) distribution with mmWave fronthauling*. The main objective of this scenario is to demonstrate and evaluate MARSAL distributed cell-free RAN in terms of increased capacity and spectral efficiency gains, and the adaptivity of dynamic clustering and RRM mechanisms in managing connectivity resources in a dynamic environment with varying hotspots areas.

The second experimentation scenario investigates *ultra-dense video traffic delivery in a converged fixed-mobile network*. This scenario showcases MARSAL's solution towards Fixed Mobile Convergence in an ultra-dense indoors context. Mobile clients served by a distributed Cell-Free RAN will be sharing the Optical Midhaul with third party FTTH clients.

The *second domain* is focused on *cognitive assistance and its security and privacy implications in 5G and Beyond*. The third experimentation scenario is about *cognitive assistance and smart connectivity for next-generation sightseeing*. In this scenario, the deployment of two real-time and interactive cloud-native applications for outdoors sightseeing supporting human-centered interaction via 3D cameras is envisioned in the MARSAL's multi-tenant elastic edge Infrastructure. These applications would be offered to users equipped with untethered AR glasses. Both applications would endure an enhanced strolling experience by showing overlaid information relevant to their sur-roundings and enabling virtual artifacts manipulation, while considering background traffic from other applications and services.

The fourth experimentation scenario addresses *data security and privacy technical challenges in multi-tenant infrastructures.* We approach the security and privacy in 6G networks in a holistic way. We present a modular design to offer four different layers of security and privacy that could be applied in very different contexts.

Our future work will include a list of testing set-ups for the evaluation process, as well as a set of preliminary targeted KPIs. It should be noted here that these KPIs will be under continuous reconsideration. Furthermore, we will focus on the network architecture specifications, the requirements of management and security components, as well as the finalisation of MARSAL architecture.

Acknowledgments. The paper has been based on the context of the *"MARSAL"* (*"Machine Learning-Based, Networking and Computing Infrastructure Resource Management of 5G and Beyond Intelligent Networks"*) Project, funded by the EC under the Grant Agreement (GA) No. 101017171.

References

1. MARSAL (Machine Learning-based Networking and Computing Infrastructure Resource Management of 5G and Beyond Intelligent Networks) 5G-PPP/H2020 project, Grant Agreement No.101017171. https://www.marsalproject.eu/
2. Open RAN (O-RAN) Alliance. https://www.o-ran.org/
3. The 3rd Generation Partnership Project (3GPP): NG-RAN Architecture. https://www.3gpp.org/news-events/2160-ng_ran_architecture
4. The 3rd Generation Partnership Project (3GPP): Technical Specification (TS) 38.801 V14.0.0 (2017–03): Study on new radio access technology; Radio access architecture and interfaces (Release 14). 3GPPP (2017)
5. European Telecommunications Standartds Institute (ETSI): Multi-access Edge Computing (MEC). https://www.etsi.org/technologies/multi-access-edge-computing
6. Méndez-Rial, R., Rusu, C., et al.: Hybrid MIMO architectures for millimeter wave communications: phase shifters or switches? IEEE Access **4**, 247–267 (2016)
7. Heath, R.W., González-Prelcic, N., Rangan, S., Roh, W., Sayeed, A.M.: An overview of signal processing techniques for millimeter wave MIMO systems. IEEE J. Select. Top. Sign. Process. **10**(3), 436–453 (2016)
8. Prananto, B.H., Iskandar, B.H., Kurniawan, A.: Low split cloud RAN opportunities and challenges. In: Proceedings of the 2019 IEEE 13th International Conference on Telecommunication Systems, Services, and Applications (TSSA), pp.119–123. IEEE (2019)
9. Alvizu, R., et al.: Comprehensive survey on T-SDN: software-defined networking for transport networks. IEEE Commun. Surv. Tutorials **19**(4), 2232–2283 (2017)
10. European Telecommunications Standartds Institute (ETSI): Open Source MANO. https://osm.etsi.org/
11. The 3rd Generation Partnership Project (3GPP): Technical Specification (TS) 28.801 V2.2.0 (2017–09): Telecommunication management; Study on management and orchestration of network slicing for next generation network (Release 15). 3GPPP (2017)

12. International Telecommunication Union - Telecommunication Standardization Sector (ITU-T): Recommendation G.987: 10-Gigabit-capable passive optical network (XG-PON) systems: Definitions, abbreviations and acronyms. ITU-5 (2012)
13. 5G PPP Software Network Working Group, Cloud Native and 5G Verticals' services. https://5g-ppp.eu/wp-content/uploads/2020/02/5G-PPP-SN-WG-5G-and-Cloud-Native.pdf, February 2020
14. STARLINGX Platform website. https://www.starlingx.io/
15. European Telecommunications Standartds Institute (ETSI): ETSI GS MEC 003 V2.2.1 (2020–12): Multi-access Edge Computing; Framework and reference Architecture (2020)
16. European Telecommunications Standartds Institute (ETSI): ETSI GR NFV-IFA 029 V3.3.1 (2019–11): Network Functions Virtualisation (NFV) Release 3; Architecture; Report on the Enhancements of the NFV architecture towards "Cloud-native and PaaS. ETSI (2019)
17. Rodríquez, P., Laradji, I., Drouin, A., Lacoste, A.: Embedding Propagation: Smoother manifold for Few-Shot Classification (2020). https://arxiv.org/abs/2003.04151
18. Stanford University: GraphSAGE: Inductive reprsentation Learning on Large Graphs. http://snap.stanford.edu/graphsage/
19. O-RAN: O-RAN Architecture Overview. https://docs.o-ransc.org/en/latest/architecture.html
20. Hexa-X (A flagship for B5G/6G vision and intelligent fabric of technology enablers connecting human, physical, and digital objects), H5G-PPP/2020 project, Grant Agreement No.101015956: Deliverable D1.2: Expanded 6G vision, use cases and societal values – including aspects of sustainability, security and spectrum, April 2021. https://hexa-x.eu/wp-content/uploads/2021/05/Hexa-X_D1.2.pdf

Fundamental Features of the Smart5Grid Platform Towards Realizing 5G Implementation

Ioannis P. Chochliouros[1](✉) 🅳, Daniele Porcu[2], Sonia Castro[3], Borja Otura[3],
Paula Encinar[3], Antonello Corsi[4], Irina Ciornei[5], Rita Santiago[6],
Angelos Antonopoulos[7], Nicola Cadenelli[7], Nicola di Pietro[8], August Betzler[9],
Inmaculada Prieto[10], Fabrizio Batista[11], Elisavet Grigoriou[12], Georgios Ellinas[5],
Lenos Hadjidemetriou[5], Dimitrios Brothimas[13], Ralitsa Rumenova[14],
Athanasios Bachoumis[15], Anastasia S. Spiliopoulou[1], Michalis Rantopoulos[1],
Christina Lessi[1], Dimitrios Arvanitozisis[1], and Pavlos Lazaridis[16]

[1] Hellenic Telecommunications Organization (OTE) S.A., 99 Kifissias Avenue, 15124
Maroussi-Athens, Greece
ichochliouros@oteresearch.gr
[2] ENEL Global Infrastructure and Networks S.R.L., Rome, Italy
[3] ATOS IT Solutions and Services Iberia SL, Madrid, Spain
[4] Engineering - Ingegneria Informatica SpA, Rome, Italy
[5] University of Cyprus, Nicosia, Cyprus
[6] Ubiwhere LDA, Aveiro, Portugal
[7] Nearby Computing SL, Barcelona, Spain
[8] Athonet Srl, Bolzano Vicentino, Italy
[9] Fundació i2CAT, Barcelona, Spain
[10] EDistribución Redes Digitales, Madrid, Spain
[11] Gridspertise, Rome, Italy
[12] Sidroco Holdings Ltd., Nicosia, Cyprus
[13] Independent Power Transmission Operator S.A., Athens, Greece
[14] Entra Energy, Sofia, Bulgaria
[15] UBITECH Energy Sprl, Brussels, Belgium
[16] The University of Huddersfield, Huddersfield, UK

Abstract. Based on the original framework of the Smart5Grid EU-funded project,
the present paper examines some fundamental features of the related platform that
can be able to affect 5G implementation as well as the intended NetApps. Thus we
examine: (i) the specific context of smart energy grids, enhanced by the inclusion of
ICT and also supported by 5G connectivity; (ii) the cloud native context, together
with the example of the cloud native VNF modelling, and; (iii) the MEC context
as a 5G enabler for integrating management, control and orchestration processes.
Each one is assessed compared to the state of the design and the implementation of
the Smart5Grid platform. As a step further, we propose a preliminary framework
for the definition of the NetApps, following to the way how the previous essential
features are specifically incorporated within the project processes.

© IFIP International Federation for Information Processing 2022
Published by Springer Nature Switzerland AG 2022
I. Maglogiannis et al. (Eds.): AIAI 2022 Workshops, IFIP AICT 652, pp. 134–147, 2022.
https://doi.org/10.1007/978-3-031-08341-9_12

Keywords: 5G · Cloud computing · Cloud native · Distributed Energy Resources (DERs) · Energy vertical ecosystem · Latency · Multi-access Edge Computing (MEC) · Network Applications (NetApps) · Network Functions Virtualization (NFV) · Renewable Energy Sources (RES) · Smart grid (SG)

1 Smart Grids and Their Main Functionalities

The Smart5Grid project [1] constitutes a step forward in the integration of energy grids with the latest innovations in virtualization and communication technologies that 5G, the 5th Generation of mobile communications, brings. Smart5Grid is focused on boosting innovation for the highly critical and challenging energy vertical, by providing an open 5G enabled experimentation platform customized to support the smart grid vision. The Open Smart5Grid experimental platform aims to be an ecosystem where stakeholders in the energy vertical, ICT integrators, Network Applications (NetApps) developers, actors in the telecom industry and/or network service providers in general, could "come together" fostering collaboration and innovation. The final goal is to validate, both at the technical and business levels, the opportunities offered by 5G technology to the energy vertical, to be demonstrated in four meaningful use cases (UCs), relevant to real scenarios of use [2]. The use cases were specifically chosen to capture a wide range of operation scenarios for the power systems.

The present paper focuses on the description of the current state-of-the-art from the project's perspective, providing insights on the latest advancements in areas such as smart grids (SGs), the cloud native paradigm as well as the impact of Multi-access Edge Computing (MEC) in 5G networks. Each one is assessed as of its relevance to the state of the Smart5Grid platform design and/or implementation.

The energy sector represents undoubtedly one of the most significant "test cases" for 5G enabling technologies. This is linked to the need of addressing a huge range of very diverse requirements to deal with across a variety of applications, like the stringent capacity for smart metering/Advanced Metering Infrastructure (AMI) that is used as a two-way channel for communications between meter and users, versus the latency for supervisory control and fault localization. Moreover, to effectively support energy utilities along their transition towards more decentralized renewable-oriented systems, there are different open issues to be fully solved as, for example, the need for 5G networks to enable the management of automation, security, resilience, scalability, and portability of the smart grid energy services.

The application of the virtualization and service-oriented principles in network design enables network systems to be realized based on cloud technologies and network services to be provisioned following the cloud service model [3]. This emerging trend is often referred to as cloud native network design, which is expected to be widely adopted in future networks, including the design of 5G/6G networks. Thus, cloud native is an approach to build and run applications that fully exploit the benefits of the cloud computing model. Such approach refers to the way applications are created and deployed, not where they are executed. It includes things like service architectures, infrastructure as a code, automation, continuous integration/delivery pipelines, observability/monitoring tools, etc. Cloud native apps are designed and built to exploit the scale, elasticity, resiliency and flexibility the cloud provides.

MEC makes no assumptions on the underlying radio infrastructure, which makes it a highly flexible element in the communications networks. As the delivery technology – together with the underlying hardware of the MEC platform – remains open, this enables new levels of adaptability to the chosen deployment scenario. Therefore, Service Providers (SPs) can use MEC as a revenue generator and application test bed (including service producing applications) without being forced to wait for full ratification/deployment of the 5G standard and the associated capital investment. This approach allows SPs to offer third parties a cost-effective way to trial their applications.

The work is organised as follows: The present Sect. 1 serves as an introduction where some essential features of the Smart5Grid project platform have been identified, able to affect 5G implementation. These are further discussed in more details in the subsequent sections, that is: Sect. 2 presents the context of smart energy grids with the consideration of ICT for smart metering and for better managing collected data; Sect. 3 discusses the cloud native context together with the example of the cloud native VNF modelling, that can strongly affect the intended Smart5Grid architecture. Then, Sect. 4 is structured to elucidate aspects from the MEC context, in particular as 5G enabler for effectively integrating 5G management, control and orchestration processes. Each one among the above platform architectural features is also correlated to the ongoing Smart5Grid approach, as actually performed in the process of the project. Following to the previous discussion, Sect. 5 is dedicated to the description of the intended NetApps. Finally, Sect. 6 summarizes the paper with several concluding remarks.

2 Smart Energy Grids

The profound transformation driven by deeper and faster decarbonisation is changing the energy world and is also creating new challenges, both on the supply side and on the demand side. In particular, the energy infrastructure needs to be enhanced and digitalized in order to cope with the deployment of renewable sources, increased decentralization, electrification of end-user and active customers, ensuring, at the same time, energy network stability, security, and resilience [4, 5]. The electric grids, which are essentially massive interconnected physical networks, are the infrastructure backbone for energy supply and use of today [6].

Electricity generated from renewable sources is predominantly variable in nature; in this respect, grids will be required to manage power flows more promptly and efficiently to support the integration of less predictable energy production, while maintaining the quality of supply. Nonetheless, supporting the boost of Renewable Energy Sources (RESs), smart grids will deliver substantial benefits in terms of resource-efficient economic growth, global and local pollution reduction [7, 8].

Grid interoperability with distributed resources is one of the fundamental pillars of grids' development [9]. Shifting from demand and supply patterns towards more decentralized generation (connected at medium and low voltage grids) raises the need to properly manage congestions and multidirectional energy flows. Moreover, connecting customers equipped with smart meters to the distribution system will allow their active participation to the energy market through the provision of flexibility services (e.g. via a "demand response" approach). Energy consumption patterns are also changing, due to the growth of new forms of energy demand in building, transport and industry sectors, with a high variability and high-power rating. The smart integration of electricity with final uses will significantly decrease both greenhouse gas emissions and energy demand, in order to deliver equivalent services with less energy input and resources.

In this multi-challenging framework, energy system operators will have to be empowered with more advanced instruments to provide reliable electricity supply and quality of service (QoS) in the increasing challenging energy system. The goal is to allow the grid system to work as efficiently as possible [10], minimizing operating costs and environmental impacts while maximizing system stability and security. This is a "key issue" to ensure more resilient supply of electricity, through the use of solutions that improve fault detection and allow self-healing of the energy distribution grid, without the intervention of technician. Smart grids accomplish the required optimization of energy networks by using digital and other advanced technologies [11]. They are necessary for the integration of growing amounts of variable RESs (like solar and wind power), and of new loads (such as energy storage and charging of electric vehicles), while maintaining stability and efficiency of the system. Furthermore, smart grids enable the utilization of flexibilities that are currently available or that will become available in the future, to better match needs on the grid with respect to generation and demand [12].

On this regard, the Smart5Grid platform is structured in a way to support the energy transition by providing the needed digital layer to ensure the availability of the communication infrastructure, whenever is needed.

Smart grids are complex systems [6–8]. They aim to intelligently integrate the behaviors and actions of all the stakeholders in the energy supply chain to efficiently deliver sustainable, economic, and secure electric energy, and ensure economical and environmentally sustainable use. Key to the success of SGs is the seamless integration and interaction of the power network infrastructure as the physical systems, and information sensing, processing, intelligence, and control as the cyber systems. With respect to power transmission and distribution networks, SGs integrate interconnected and geographically wide distributed components, both hardware and software, both on the demand and on the supply side, and "pool" their resources to create higher functionalities [13, 14] such as the following:

- *Advanced metering and monitoring,* for close to real-time (RT) transmitting and receiving data for information, monitoring and control purpose on what goes on the energy network, in order to acquire/provide feedback for the grid operation and enable consumers to better manage consumptions.
- *Active network management,* for the operational optimization through predictive maintenance, energy network remote reconfiguration and recovery schemes activation in almost real time.
- *Flexibility services,* from Distributed Energy Resources (DERs) such as distributed generation, energy storage assets and demand side response, leveraging on end-user's flexibility. A DER is a small-scale unit of power generation that operates locally and is connected to a larger power grid at the distribution level. DERs can include solar panels, small natural gas-fuelled generators, electric vehicles, and controllable loads,

such as HVAC (Heating, Ventilation and Air Conditioning) systems and electric water heaters

- *Smart charging services,* such as vehicle-to-grid (V2G) or vehicle-to-home (V2H) solutions (for battery electric and plug-in hybrid vehicles) and additional growth of electrification grade (i.e.: heating and cooling), increasing RESs grid hosting capability. (V2G is a technology that enables energy to be pushed back to the power grid from the battery of an electric car; a V2H system enables customers to store home generated renewable energy in their leaf battery or fill their battery when energy tariffs are low or even free).

In this context, the Smart5Grid project is structured so that to effectively support most of the above functionalities, offering dedicated services not only for the energy system operators, but also for DERs providers and aggregators who are assessed as "the new emerging actors" of the energy industry ecosystem.

The following responses are identified to the fundamental smart grids' functionalities, as the latter are actually developed by the Smart5Grid effort:

- Regarding *advanced monitoring,* an innovative cross-border frequency monitoring system will be implemented to support the regional Transmission System Operators (TSOs) to provide the system stability in the Greek-Bulgarian demo (*as discussed in the context of the respective use case 4, UC#4*).
- Besides this, in the Spanish demo (*as examined in the specific framework of use case 2, UC#2*), an innovative *safety system* for people working in high-voltage power stations will also be implemented and tested, since electricity still represents a danger for workers if not properly approached, keeping the due physical distance from the live parts.
- The most advanced *active grid management system,* developed by Enel Distribuzione Italia (EDI), will be supported by a NetApp to provide RT communication monitoring, preparing the ground for further implementation of edge-based computing (*as examined in the specific framework of use case 1, UC#1*).
- The real-time monitoring and control of DERs compose the basis for the provision of *flexibility services* to the energy system operators.

3   The Cloud Native Context

Within the Smart5Grid framework a core aim is to embrace and adopt, where possible, the cloud native paradigm [15]. The concept of cloud native, in a simple way, can be defined as related to applications that are born in the cloud – as opposed to applications that are born and raised on-premises [16]. However, this definition is quite simple and not representative of what cloud native truly means, so it is better to introduce the concept by means of different examples extracted from [17]. Based on this approach, cloud native applications have the following characteristics:

- *They often need to operate at global scale:* While a simple website can be accessed anywhere given that internet is not blocked, the concept of global implies that the application's data and services are replicated in local data centres so that interaction latencies are minimized, and the integrity of the application is clear to the final user.

- *They must scale well with thousands of concurrent users:* This is another dimension of parallelism that is orthogonal to the horizontal scaling of data required for global-scale distribution and it requires careful attention to synchronization and consistency in distributed systems.
- *They are built on the assumption that infrastructure is fluid and failure is constant* so even in the case the failure rate is extremely small, the law of large numbers guarantees that in a global scale even a low probability event can happen.
- *Cloud-native applications are designed* so that upgrade and test occur seamlessly without disrupting production.

The above characteristics perfectly "match" the requirements of a smart grid's communication and application layers, consequently entailing the need of adopting 5G. Due to the need of addressing a huge range of very diverse requirements to deal with across a variety of applications, an approach based on microservices [18] and cloud nativeness is strongly needed with the consequent use of different techniques of virtualization, to help the power grid to truly become smart. Dedicated effort has been planned to realize this specific aim.

The current specifications for realizing network virtualization and softwarization in 5G change how network functions are realized and deployed (as software instances hosted on Virtual Machines (VMs) and/or containers) but not with regards to how the functions are designed [19]. In fact, the state-of-the-art of NFV (Network Functions Virtualisation) implementations [20] often replace monolithic hardware-based network functions with their software VNF (Virtual Network Functions) counterparts. This app-roach naturally brings for any project based on software virtualization the creation of a certain number of common functionalities that are repeated across different VNFs, and which causes evident repetition and lack of flexibility in the network infrastructure. Moreover, NFV and Software-Defined Network (SDN) architectures both comprise a set of predefined function blocks that are interconnected via standardized reference points so, whenever a new function block is added into the architecture, these features bring a further "ossification" of the network infrastructure.

A promising way to tackle this problem with the current NFV and SDN architec-tures is to enable finer granularity for network functions and a common interface for loose-coupling interaction among them. The Service-Oriented Architecture [21] (SOA), with its latest development as the Micro-Service Architecture (MSA), offers an effective approach to achieve this objective. In the European Telecommunications Standards Insti-tute (ETSI) NFV specifications, a network service refers to an ordered set of (virtual) Network Functions (NFs) specified by a service description (VNF forwarding graph [22]). In the SOA approach, this principle has been embraced by the NFV architecture in different level as NFVIaaS [23], VNFaaS [24], and NSaaS [25], which all adopt the SOA service concept, as specified in [26].

Cloud native is an approach to design, build and run applications/virtual functions that fully exploits the benefits of the cloud computing model. It refers to the way applications are created and deployed, not where they are executed, and it is based on the principle of decomposing an application into a set of microservices that can be developed and deployed independently to accelerate and optimize the DevOps strategies [27]. The microservices are packaged into light-weight containers which are scheduled to run on compute nodes by a container orchestrator. As regards data, we must underline that, to be properly classified as cloud native, microservices need to be "stateless", meaning that there must be a separation of the processing logic from the processed data and how it is stored in the cloud.

In framework of the actual Smart5Grid platform, the involved partners intend to embrace and adopt – where possible – the cloud native paradigm so that to "pave the way" towards the integration of the energy infrastructure and the 5G Core Network (CN) SBA (Service-Based Architecture). This 5G CN SBA will require several techniques being applied in unison, i.e., NFV and SDN that will require the deconstruction of VNFs into microservices. This effectively translates to the containerization of the 5G Core, and the gradual decoupling of network functions from VMs in support of containerized network functions. For this reason, the adoption in the early stage of a cloud native approach for the NetApp development will increase the compatibility between telco and vertical infrastructure.

For the purpose of cloud native VNF modelling and in order to understand the roadmap of the evolution of the VNFs towards a cloud native approach, we can rely on the 5G PPP "Cloud Native and 5G Verticals' services" White Paper [28], that conveys the point of view of the European Commission (EC) and the industry (as in Fig. 1). This figure shows the evolution from the classic solution based on VNF implemented to run inside VMs. It also depicts a possible evolution of the term VNF to CNF (Cloud Native Function) that is another way to indicate VNF but with strong emphasis on the cloud design. Observing the present phase, we can see that the classic solution is based on running VMs on top of bare metal/public cloud and on the use of hypervisors such as VMware [29] or VirtualBox [30]. At the same time, OpenStack [31] has been used as the *de facto* cloud computing platform. This architectural approach adopted in the Telecom sector follows the NFV MANO (Management and Orchestration) specification [32].

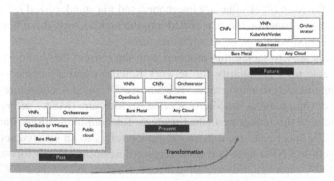

Fig. 1. Cloud native road path [26].

This early-stage approach brought several problems. For example, in multi-domain orchestration environments, as the ones used commonly in 5G services, the management of several Virtual Infrastructure Managers (VIM) (e.g.: OpenStack) in a multi-cloud environment is a complex and hard task not easy to solve. Another problem is that it is difficult to manage multiple VNFs in a consistent way because we are facing the hard dependency between the hardware and element management systems that exist in the real environments. Finally, at implementation level, it is also hard to combine different blocks from different vendors. These concerns can be solved if we move forward into a cloud native solution given their foundation principles.

By summarizing, we can extract four key ingredients that have to guide Smart5Grid project towards the development of cloud native applications. Consequently we shall need:

1) *Small, stateless microservices architecture, running in containers*, which are faster to get deployed and upgraded with the use of few cloud resources, with the purpose of deploying just what is needed instead of the entire network function.
2) *Open architecture and Application Programming Interfaces (APIs) so it is possible to continuously onboard innovation.* For example, the 5G Core uses an SBA with well-defined APIs for network functions to offer services or call on each other. This, merged with the cloud-native service mesh, enables rapid manipulation of the 5G Core, allowing the integration of new network functions, or rapidly scaling & deploying different slices.
3) *Cloud agnostic and infrastructure agnostic*, to eliminate the hardware dependencies.
4) *DevOps for automation and fast time to market.*

4 Multi-access Edge Computing as "Enabler" to 5G Adoption

Using an "edge cloud", SPs can host applications in a virtual retail space, test the revenue return and scale-up or remove as appropriate. So, starting out as a 4G edge test bed with limited deployments at first, MEC allows a smooth transition into the 5G network rollout, removing the need for major upgrades when the expected time for transition arrives [33, 34]. Another focus area for transitioning to the 5G networks is about re-using the existing deployed systems in the process. Due to the MEC's virtualised characteristics, it is very easy to monitor performance and resource needs of an application which, in turn, enables more accurate pricing for operators towards application providers for hosting the applications [35, 36].

The common feature set of providing much-improved capabilities at the edge of the network, improved intelligence about resources needed at the edge and the ability to charge for service delivered by cycles, memory, storage, and bandwidth delivered, makes it "quite attractive" to start the deployment in (early) 5G test sites. Taking into account the above considerations, MEC compatibility towards 5G networks may be about:

• Integrating the MEC data plane with the 5G system's one for routing traffic to the local data network and steering to an application.
• An Application Function (AF) interacting with 5G Control Plane Functions (CPFs) to influence traffic routing and steering, acquire 5G network capability information, and support application instance mobility.

- The possibility of reusing the edge computing resources and managing/orchestrating applications and/or 5G network functions, while MEC still orchestrates the application services (chaining).

MEC, as it is deployed in the 4th generation LTE (Long-Term Evolution) networks, is connected to the user plane. With LTE networks already having been deployed for a number of years, it was necessary to design the MEC solution as an add-on to a 4G network in order to offer services in the edge. Consequently, the MEC system – as defined in ETSI GS MEC 003 [37] and in the related interface specifications – is to a large extent self-contained, covering everything from management and orchestration down to interactions with the data plane for steering specific traffic flows. With 5G, the starting point is different, as edge computing is identified as one of the key technologies required to support low latency together with mission critical and future IoT (Internet of Things) services and to enable enhanced performance and quality of experience. The design approach taken by the 3GPP allowed the mapping of MEC onto AFs (Application Functions) that can use the services and information offered by other 3GPP network functions based on the configured policies [37, 38]. Several enabling functionalities can provide flexible support for different MEC deployments.

There is a growing consensus that in the long term, 5G deployments will increasingly integrate fixed-mobile networks infrastructures with cloud computing and MEC [39]. In these scenarios, the borders between cloud and MEC virtual resources will not be explicit, thus paving the way towards a sort of "continuum" of logical resources and functions, offering flexibility and programmability through global automated operations. This will require that the orchestration capabilities, which are already a key element for exploiting cloud computing capabilities, become an essential part of the operation of future 5G infrastructure.

The integration of 5G management, control & orchestration processes is expected to facilitate applications/services development by providing controlled access to high-level abstractions of 5G resources (e.g., abstractions of computing, memory/storage, and networking) thus enabling any vertical application. Moreover, as a real operating system, it should provide automated resource management, scheduling process placement, facilitating inter-process communication and simplifying installation and management of distributed functions/services, spanning from cloud computing to MEC. A shared data structure will to support multi-vendor systems and applications.

In the specific Smart5Grid framework, the core aim is to focus on the deployment of four selected UCs of strong market relevance for revolutionising the energy vertical industry, in parallel with the introduction of an open 5G experimental facility to support integration, testing and validation of existing and new 5G services and NetApps from third parties. MEC reduces latency to milliseconds and allows for constant connectivity. Plus, when the edge network experiences high traffic, the edge may offload data to the cloud to maintain a quick and reliable connection. MEC shall provide a multiplicity of explicit benefits for the provision of the related services to any participating market actor – especially to network operators – and also to support the effective transition towards a reliable 5G implementation.

5 Smart5Grid NetApps

This section presents the Smart5Grid NetApp which is proposed as a solution to the needs of Smart5Grid project and its UCs. In fact, the Smart5Grid NetApp provides a means for developers to define vertical applications by interconnecting together new and/or existing pieces of software in the form of VNFs. By splitting the functionality of the NetApp into decoupled VNFs, the reutilization of software functions is encouraged. This, however, is not something that the NetApp brings as a new concept. The ETSI NFV framework [32] describes the reference architecture, information models and tools required to manage this kind of applications. However, when introducing advanced networking such as 5G, this framework on its own requires a high level of expertise from developers, not only from the relevant field of the specific vertical application that is being developed, but also from the field of telecommunications if the building of End-to-End (E2E) application is the purpose. With this in mind, the Smart5Grid NetApp concept intends to provide a solution to this problem by abstracting the complexities of network deployment and configuration from the developers of vertical applications.

A Smart5Grid proposed NetApp is a cloud native application. Thus, it is made up of VNFs based on OS (Operating System) containers' technology. Consequently, a corresponding NetApp contains the necessary components to offer a service as a software (SaaS) application for the energy vertical (i.e., it is a complete and standalone (SA) vertical application). However, this does not imply that the service provided by this vertical application cannot be consumed by other external or legacy applications, e.g., from a north-facing API. Also, as shown in Fig. 2, a NetApp may directly expose other user interfaces, such as dashboards, open to design decisions made by the developer.

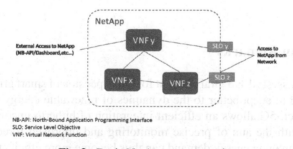

NB-API: North-Bound Application Programming Interface
SLO: Service Level Objective
VNF: Virtual Network Function

Fig. 2. Basic NetApp representation.

As already mentioned, NetApp components can be deployed as container-based VNFs. A NetApp can contain one or more VNFs. By splitting these components whenever possible in the implementation, the NetApp brings the opportunity to take advantage of the cloud/edge infrastructure. An example of this could be, in the case of a NetApp composed by two components (cf. Fig. 3), that the NetApp function that require low latency input or responses could be placed at the edge of the computing infrastructure, while the other function that may be resource-intensive, not suitable for an edge deployment and not requiring its benefits, should be placed in a cloud data centre where resources are not constrained.

Each NetApp is formally defined in a NetApp descriptor which will include the necessary information regarding the services that compose it, its topology and also the performance requirements of each component; this implicates that the infrastructure over which it is instantiated, can perform their intended functions, such as MEC offloading, VNF scaling, and traffic policy enforcement via its management and orchestration (M&O) systems. This information allows the M&O systems to create end-to-end slices that fulfil these requirements, allowing developers to design applications with strict performance demands and without needing the expertise to implement the networks that support them.

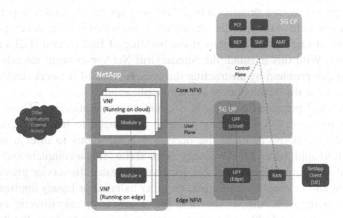

Fig. 3. NetApp deployment over a 5G network.

6   Concluding Remarks

5G networks are assessed as a vital element for the expansion of smart grid technologies, allowing the grid to adapt better to the dynamics of renewable energy and distributed generation. In fact, 5G allows an efficient integration of hitherto unconnected devices to smart grids with the aim of precise monitoring and improved forecasting of their energy needs. Managing energy demand can thus become more efficient, requiring less investments, as the smart grid has the ability to balance easier the energy load, reduce electricity peaks and, ultimately, reduce energy costs.

In this scope, the EU-funded Smart5Grid project intends to complement contemporary energy distribution grids with access to 5G network resources through an open experimentation 5G platform and innovative Network Applications (NetApps), focusing upon four meaningful use cases for the energy vertical ecosystem and aiming to demonstrate efficiency, resilience and elasticity provided by the 5G networks. In particular, the project proposes an innovative architecture [40, 41] and creates a dedicated platform to fulfill its innovative objectives, which is characterised by several essential features. In the present work we have discussed relevance to smart grid, correlation to the cloud native context and options for including – and promoting – MEC.

Smart5Grid foresees to deliver a more secure, reliable, efficient, and real-time communication framework for the modern smart grids. The project platform supports the current energy sector stakeholders to adopt smart grids so that to: (i) Easily and effectively create advanced energy services; (ii) interact in a dynamic and efficient way with their environment; and; (iii) automate and optimise the planning and operation of their power and energy services.

The Smart5Grid virtualisation framework is also based on cloud native applications that have been architected as a set of microservices running in Docker containers. This enhances the Smart5Grid platform with the ability to support applications designed specifically for cloud infrastructures that consist of loosely-coupled microservices and enabling zero-touch orchestration and agile DevOps practices, whereas each microservice will remain self-contained and will encapsulate its own code, data, and dependencies. Most importantly, the cloud native approach takes full advantage of the scalability and resiliency features found in modern serverless platforms.

Smart5Grid also "paves the way" for applying the key features of Multi-Access Edge Computing (MEC). The main target will be to push computation, storage, and network resources closer to the devices that consist the power grid to solve the resource limitation problem and to offload NetApps directly to edge servers. This will allow a significant reduction of latency for devices to access the network and to reduce energy consumption. MEC is also going to ensure data security and integrity by enabling ubiquitous last-mile service access to the smart grid devices, while at the same time, it will offer deployment of network slices within minutes, coupled with value-added capabilities for the smart grid NetApps, such as bandwidth assurance, life cycles management of network services, and overall balancing of service loads.

Following to the above, we have also presented the Smart5Grid NetApp intended scope which is actually proposed as a sort of solution to the needs of Smart5Grid project and its specific UCs. NetApps' main purpose is to hide the complexity of the 5G telco network to the energy application developers so that they can develop an application not having to deal with the underlying network. Smart5Grid will support most of smart grid´s functionalities by enabling an environment in which cloud-native NetApps can realize the integration between the energy vertical and 5G networks, with a special focus on deployments that leverage edge infrastructure.

Smart5Grid leverages on the concepts of 5G MEC, 5G SBA, network slicing, and ETSI MANO network management, in order to enable the vision of "5G empowering the energy sector" and to allow the roll-out of extended and highly demanding NetApps on top of a 5G mobile network infrastructure.

Acknowledgments. This work has been performed in the scope of the *Smart5Grid* European Research Project and has been supported by the Commission of the European Communities/5G-PPP/H2020, *Grant Agreement No. 101016912.*

References

1. Smart5Grid Project (Grant Agreement No. 101016912). https://smart5grid.eu/

2. Porcu, D., et al.: 5G communications as "Enabler" for smart power grids: the case of the Smart5Grid project. In: Maglogiannis, I., Macintyre, J., Iliadis, L. (eds.) AIAI 2021. IFIP AICT, vol. 628, pp. 7–20. Springer, Cham (2021). https://doi.org/10.1007/978-3-030-791 57-5_1
3. Javatpoint: Cloud Service Models (2021). https://www.javatpoint.com/cloud-service-models
4. Wu, J., Guo, S., Huang, H., Liu, W., Xiang, Y.: Information and communications technologies for sustainable development goals: state-of-the-art, needs and perspectives. IEEE Commun. Surv. Tutor. **20**, 2389–2406 (2018)
5. Chochliouros, I.P., et al.: Energy efficiency concerns and trends in future 5g network infrastructures. Energies (MDPI) **14**(17), 5932 (2021). https://doi.org/10.3390/en14175392
6. Yu, X., Cecati, C., Dillon, T., Simoes, M.G.: New frontier of smart grids. IEEE Ind. Electron. Mag. **5**(3), 49–63 (2011)
7. Refaat, S.S., Ellabban, O., Bayhan, S., Abu-Rub, H., Blaabjerg, F., Begovic, M.M.: Smart Grid Standards and Interoperability. Smart Grid and Enabling Technologies. Wiley-IEEE Press, Hoboken (2021)
8. Tuballa, M.L., Abundo, M.L.: A review of the development of smart grid technologies. Renew. Sustain. Energy Rev. **59**(c), 710–725 (2016)
9. Howell, S., Rezgui, Y., Hippolyte. J.-L., Jayan, B., Li, H.: Towards the next generation of smart grids: semantic and holonic multi-agent management of distributed energy resources. Renew. Sustain. Energy Rev. **77**, 193–214 (2017
10. Commission of the European Communities: Communication on "Addressing the challenge of energy efficiency through Information and Communication Technologies". COM (2008) 241 final (2008). https://eur-lex.europa.eu/legal-content/ga/ALL/?uri=CELEX%25+3A+520 08DC0241
11. Butt, O.M., Zulqarnain, M., Butt, T.M.: Recent advancement in smart grid technology: future prospects in the electrical power network. Ain Shams Eng. J. **12**(1), 687–695 (2021)
12. Bush, S.F., Goel, S., Simard, G.: IEEE vision for smart grid communications: 2030 and beyond roadmap. In: IEEE Vision for Smart Grid Communications: 2030 and Beyond Roadmap, pp. 1--19 (2013)
13. Yu, X., Xue, Y.: Smart grids: a cyber-physical systems perspective. Proc. IEEE **104**(5), 1058–1070 (2016)
14. Alotaibi, I., Abido, M.A., Khalid, M., Savkin, A.V.: A comprehensible review of recent advances in smart grids: a sustainable future with renewable energy resources. Energies **13**, 6269 (2020)
15. Kepler/Cannon: The Cloud-Native Paradigm. Evolving enterprises and the new business-IT convergence (2021). https://www.keplercannon.com/cloud-native-paradigm/
16. Linthicum, D.S.: Cloud-native applications and cloud migration: the good, the bad, and the points between. IEEE Cloud Comput. **4**(5), 1–14 (2017)
17. Gannon, D., Barga, R., Sundaresan, N.: Cloud-native applications. IEEE Cloud Comput. **4**(5), 16–21 (2017)
18. Newman, S.: Building Microservices: Designing Fine-Grained Systems. O'Reilly Media, Sebastopol (2015)
19. Imadali, S., Bousselmi, A.: Cloud native 5G virtual network functions: design principles and use cases. In: Proceedings of the 2018 IEEE 8th International Symposium on Cloud and Service Computing (SC2), pp. 91–96. IEEE (2018)
20. European Telecommunications Standards Institute: ETSI GS NFV 002 V1.2.1 (2014–12): "Network Functions Virtualisation (NFV); Architectural Framework". ETSI. https://www.etsi.org/deliver/etsi_gs/NFV/001_099/002/01.02.01_60/gs_nfv002v010201p.pdf
21. Hustad, E., Olsen, D.H.: Creating a sustainable digital infrastructure: the role of service-oriented architecture. Procedia Comput. Sci. **181**, 597–604 (2021)
22. OpenStack: VNF Forwarding Graph definition (2021). https://docs.openstack.org/tacker/lat est/user/vnffg_usage_guide.html

23. European Telecommunications Standards Institute (ETSI): ETSI GR NFV-IFA 028 V3.1.1 (2018–01): "Network Functions Virtualisation (NFV) Release 3; Management and Orchestration; Report on architecture options to support multiple administrative domains" (2018). https://www.etsi.org/deliver/etsi_gr/NFV-IFA/001_099/028/03.01.01_60/gr_NFV-IFA028v030101p.pdf

24. Carapinha, J., Di Girolamo, M., Monteleone, G., Ramos, A., Xilouris, G.: VNFaaS with end-to-end full service orchestration. In: Proceedings of the 2016 Fifth European Workshop on Software-Defined Networks (EWSDN), pp. 57–58. IEEE (2016)

25. Zhou, X., Li, R., Chen, T.: Network slicing as a service: enabling enterprises' own software-defined cellular networks. IEEE Commun. Mag. **54**(7), 146–153 (2016)

26. Duan, Q.: Intelligent and autonomous management in cloud-native future networks - a survey on related standards from an architectural perspective. Futur. Internet **13**(2), 42 (2021)

27. Bass, L., Weber, I., Zhu, L.: DevOps: A Software Architect's Perspective. Pearson Education, Inc., Old Tappan (2015)

28. 5G Public Private Partnership (5G PPP): 5G PPP Software Network WG Paper, "Cloud-Native and 5G Verticals' services" (2020). https://5g-ppp.eu/wp-content/uploads/2020/02/5G-PPP-SN-WG-5G-and-Cloud-Native.pdf

29. VMware website. https://www.vmware.com/

30. Virtualbox website. https://www.virtualbox.org/

31. OpenStack website. https://www.openstack.org/

32. European Telecommunications Standards Institute (ETSI): ETSI GS NFV MAN V1.1.1 (2014–12): "Network Functions Virtualisation (NFV); Management and Orchestration" (2014). https://www.etsi.org/deliver/etsi_gs/nfv-man/001_099/001/01.01.01_60/gs_nfv-man001v010101p.pd

33. European Telecommunications Standards Institute (ETSI): ETSI White Paper No.11: "Mobile Edge Computing: A key technology towards 5G" (2015). https://www.etsi.org/images/files/ETSIWhitePapers/etsi_wp11_mec_a_key_technology_towards_5g.pdf

34. Mao, Y., You, C., Zhang, J., Huang, K., Letaief, K.B.: A survey on mobile edge computing: the communication perspective. IEEE Commun. Surv. Tutor. **19**(4), 2322–2358 (2017)

35. European Telecommunications Standards Institute (ETSI): ETSI White Paper No.28: "MEC in 5G Networks" (2018). https://www.etsi.org/images/files/ETSIWhitePapers/etsi_wp28_mec_in_5G_FINAL.pdf

36. Chochliouros, I.P., et al.: Putting intelligence in the network edge through NFV and cloud computing: the SESAME approach. In: Boracchi, G., Iliadis, L., Jayne, C., Likas, A. (eds.) EANN 2017. CCIS, vol. 744, pp. 704–715. Springer, Cham (2017). https://doi.org/10.1007/978-3-319-65172-9_59

37. European Telecommunications Standards Institute (ETSI): ETSI GS MEC 003 V1.1.1, "Mobile Edge Computing (MEC); Framework and Reference Architecture" (2016). http://www.etsi.org/deliver/etsi_gs/MEC/001_099/003/01.01.01_60/gs_mec003v010101p.pdf

38. European Telecommunications Standards Institute (ETSI): ETSI GS MEC 011 V1.1.1, "Mobile Edge Computing (MEC); Platform Application Enablement" (2017). http://www.etsi.org/deliver/etsi_gs/MEC/001_099/011/01.01.01_60/gs_mec011v010101p.pdf

39. Nakazato, J., Nakamura, M., Yu, T., Li, Z., Tran, G.K., Sakaguchi, K.: Market analysis of MEC-assisted beyond 5G ecosystem. IEEE Access **9**, 53996–54008 (2021)

40. Porcu, D., et al.: Demonstration of 5G solutions for smart energy grids of the future: a perspective of the Smart5Grid project. Energies (MDPI) **15**(3), 839 (2022)

41. Smart5Grid Project: Deliverable 2.2: "Overall Architecture Design, Technical Specifications and Technology Enablers" (2021). https://smart5grid.eu/wp-content/uploads/2021/11/Smart5Grid_WP2_D2.2_V1.0.pdf

The Use of Robotics in Critical Use Cases: The 5G-ERA Project Solution

Christina Lessi[1]([✉]), George Agapiou[2], Marios Sophocleous[3],
Ioannis P. Chochliouros[1], Renxi Qiu[4], and Stelios Androulidakis[1]

[1] Hellenic Telecommunications Organization (OTE) S.A., 99 Kifissias Avenue,
15124 Maroussi, Athens, Greece
`clessi@oteresearch.gr`
[2] WINGS ICT Solutions, 189, Siggrou Avenue, 17121 Athens, Greece
[3] eBOS Technologies Ltd., Arch. Makariou III and Mesaorias 1, Lakatamia,
2090 Nicosia, Cyprus
[4] School of Computer Science, University of Bedfordshire, Luton, UK

Abstract. Lately, autonomous robots have been dynamically appearing in the foreground, being the solution to many problems that concern different areas of everyday life. 5G-ERA Project's ambition is to propose solutions based on robotic applications that are targeting vertical sectors such as transport, healthcare, Public Protection and Disaster Relief (PPDR), and Industry 4.0. These sectors require intensive data transmission and processing, offering services that could take advantage from 5G networks capabilities in order to implement robotic collective intelligence approaches that were impossible in the past. However, 5G-ERA does not target a provider-centric 5G architecture. The project aims at a user-centered approach, where the main focus is on the Quality of Experience offered for vertical customers. Based on this approach, the designers of the 5G experimental facility should take into consideration the requirements of vertical sectors in order to be able to meet the new challenges that will arise. In this paper, the 5G-ERA healthcare and PPDR use cases will be presented, providing the proposed solution and the scenario that is designed. Additionally, the network design and requirements will be analyzed based on the needs of the use case.

Keywords: Autonomous robots · 5G networks · Management and orchestration · Network functions virtualization (NFV) · Virtual network function (VNF) · Standalone architecture · Reliability

1 Introduction

The main characteristic of an autonomous robot is its ability to perform tasks with a high degree of autonomy. However, in a realistic case taking place in an environment that is unstructured and very complex, learning all possible navigation and manipulation tasks before deployments, is impossible. Therefore, the degree of autonomy will be adapted based on circumstances [1]. There will be scenarios pre-programmed, while others can

© IFIP International Federation for Information Processing 2022
Published by Springer Nature Switzerland AG 2022
I. Maglogiannis et al. (Eds.): AIAI 2022 Workshops, IFIP AICT 652, pp. 148–155, 2022.
https://doi.org/10.1007/978-3-031-08341-9_13

be executed collaboratively with a high level of intelligence on Cloud or with human operators, especially when the robots are not able to operate completely autonomously. For instance, a robot could support remote trajectory planning services on the cloud semi-autonomously for as much as possible, e.g., by ensuring collision-free motion or by assisting the remote operators when grasping an object. And then enhancing its capabilities through learning from this semi-autonomous experience.

Cloud-based robots are essential for realizing a high degree of autonomy for robotics. Supported by a "brain" in the cloud/edge, the robustness of autonomous robots will be improved significantly. The brain may be located in a data center, which makes use of Artificial Intelligence and other advanced software technologies to deal with resource-critical tasks or unexpected tasks. Traditionally, they are undertaken by a local, on-board controller due to connective constraints. Compared to robots running locally, "cloud robots will generate new value chains, new technologies, new architectures, new experiences, and new business models" [2]. The combination of cloud and robotics offers global libraries knowledge sharing and enables augmented human-robot interactions, as part of robotic services. Compared to traditional internet-based trajectory control, the key focus of cloud-based, autonomous robots is on knowledge collaboration. By shifting part of the cognitive capabilities from robots to the cloud, it enhances the potential of the robotic autonomous operations by utilizing the cloud's massive computation power and global knowledge. Many projects have been delivered in this field, such as [3–5].

In order to combine the capabilities of autonomous robots and clouds, the robot must be able to perceive and understand its environment. The perception enables the operational knowledge to be shared between both sides and digital data representing physical objects to be constructed on the cloud. This specifically includes the detection of objects relevant to semi-autonomous or autonomous manipulation and the perception of the environment by simultaneous localization and mapping (SLAM) objects and obstacles that could be in the way of navigation or grasping. Since it is hard to predict what objects the robot may face in the operational phase, it needs to be able to acquire all relevant knowledge about new objects and to update it continuously during operations.

The 5G-ERA will implement the above learning model, using the system architecture that is presented in Fig. 1. The main layers of the architecture are:

- Interface layer, which is responsible for accepting commands and presenting the information.
- Application Layer, which manages the activities and is responsible for performing tasks.
- Domain layer, which generates intent-based network policy based on specific domain knowledge pre-stored in semantic model and information model.
- Infrastructure enablement layer, which is responsible to manage virtualized hardware resources. It ensures the compatibility, scalability, and transparency of the testbeds.
- Infrastructure resource layer, which provides connectivity, computing resources, and storage.
- Smart event bus which connects event across the layers via event-based communication.

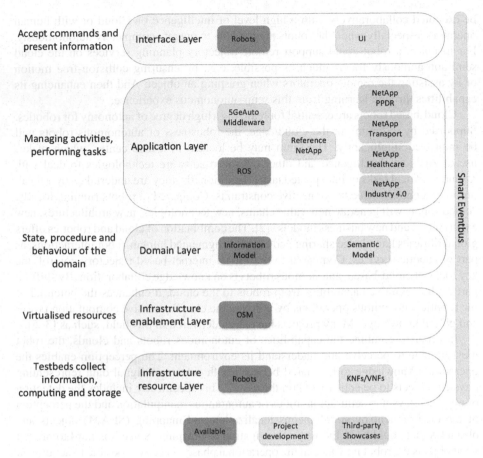

Fig. 1. 5G-ERA system architecture

2   Robotics in Healthcare Vertical Sector

In the healthcare use case, the Robot will replace the nurse in a representation of a hospital environment where a patient is in quarantine. More specifically, the robot will be able to carry the medical treatment to the appropriate spot, place them in a specific area inside the room and check the condition of the patient by streaming a video of his current state to the nurse or doctor who is responsible for him/her. When the patient will take the medicine, then the robot will move back to its original position [6].

To perform the above actions, the robot must be able to support some functionalities. It has to select and use a specific map of the room and navigate autonomously inside the desired room. Additionally, it will use perception to find and manipulate the treatment in a predefined space in the room and use human detection to find the patient. Finally, it will be able to stream live content of the patient and send it to an application.

In Fig. 2, the use case is presented in more detail: the robot enters the room and moves to the medicine cabinet, which is located in a pre-defined spot inside the room.

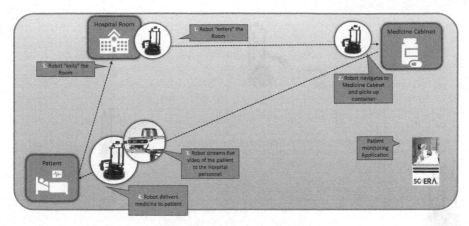

Fig. 2. Healthcare scenario

The robot detects and picks the proper medicine. At the same time, the robot streams a live video and health condition measurements of the patient (e.g., his/her temperature) allowing doctors to know the patient's condition. Finally, it approaches the patient and provides the medicine. Then, the robot exits the room and goes to its original position.

3 Robotics in PPDR Vertical Sector

In this use case the robot attempts to prevent a hazardous event to take place in order to avoid a catastrophic situation. In particular, a robot WX200 enters a dangerous place, where a gas switch is located in an indoor environment. The robot identifies the gas switch location and fixes the problem by closing the switch. After that, a detection routine starts to check if any person is inside the room and sends an alert if a human is identified. The series of events that take place are:

1. In cases of extreme natural phenomena, a person will trigger the robotic action or a sensor identifies a gas leakage and trigger the robot.
2. The robot will enter the "dangerous" room where e.g. a gas switch is located.
3. The robot scans the space, identifies the switch and goes to the gas switch.
4. Using the manipulator, closes the switch and secures the room
5. Robot starts human detection routine, if a human is identified an alert is sent.

This series of events is shown in the following Fig. 3.

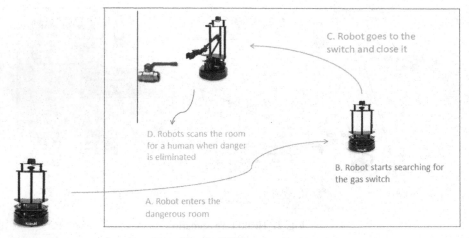

Fig. 3. PPDR scenario

4 Networks in 5G-ERA

Based on the description of the Healthcare and PPDR Use Cases, it is important to identify the characteristics of the network that will be able to support them. 5G networks are able to support heterogeneous requirements, offering network operators the capability to provide new services and fulfill the needs of the end-users. There are three generic services in 5G technology, which can include all the services that network providers design and implement for end-users [7, 8]:

- eMBB: Enhanced Mobile Broadband is used in use cases where very high peak rates across a wide coverage area are required. Its downlink speeds could be 1 Gbps in indoor environments and 300 Mbps in outdoor environments
- URLLC: Ultra-Reliable and Low Latency Communications supports low latency transmission of small payloads (in some cases latency could be 1 ms or less). At the same time, it offers high reliability, which could even be 99.99999%
- mMTC: Massive Machine Type Communications is used in use cases where a massive number of devices are required on a small area. For example, it could support 1M devices per km^2, unlike 4G which supports 1K devices per Km^2.

For the needs of 5G-ERA, a 5G Standalone (SA) Rel.16 network will be integrated. The end-to-end network will include both hardware (e.g., antennas, packet core) and software (e.g., VNFs) components. The high-level architecture of the network is presented in Fig. 4, where it is separated into five layers:

- The RAN includes the antenna, the Radio Unit and the Baseband Unit. It is based on the New Radio (NR) technology, allowing slicing on the RAN.
- The packet core is deployed based on the SA Rel. 16 architecture, as it is presented in Fig. 3, allowing the installation of core VNFs and supporting slicing.

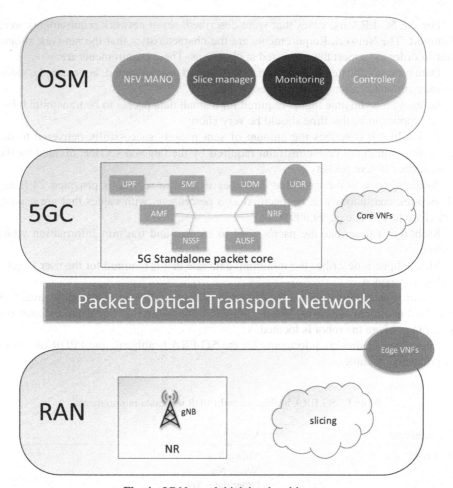

Fig. 4. 5G Network high level architecture

- The Multi-access Edge Computing, where the edge VNFs are installed, is a network architecture, which allows cloud computing features, introduced by ETSI [9]. MEC leads to lower latency communications and increases network reliability by decreasing errors and data packet loss:
- The transport network, which uses the packet optical networking solution
- The Orchestrator, which is deployed by using Open-Source Mano (OSM) [10–12] and is responsible for controlling the available resources.

Slicing is another important characteristic of the network since it allows the use of different types of services supporting the heterogeneous requirements of the use case that could not be fulfilled by one type of service. Slicing is the key feature of the 5G networks that offers flexibility and programmability, accommodating new applications requirements, such as the ultra-low latency and the high reliability at the same time.

For the 5G-ERA use cases that were described, seven network requirements were identified. The Network Requirements are the characteristics that the network should offer in order to support the requested applications. These requirements are:

Data type: it indicates the type of data that should be transmitted. For example, video or voice communication or other types of data.

Latency: it is the time that is required for a small data packet to be transmitted. For critical applications, this time should be very short.

Reliability: It describes the amount of sent packets successfully delivered to the destination within the time constraint required by the targeted service, divided by the total number of sent packets.

Availability: it is the term that describes whether a service is provided 24 h/day 7days/week continuously. It is specified as a percentage, with values that are usually very close to 100%, e.g., 99.999%.

Mobility: it describes the user's need to receive and transmit information while moving.

Throughput: it describes the minimum data rate that is required for the user to get a quality experience.

Location accuracy: it allows the detection of user equipment in a specific area. It is important in critical use cases, like the 5G-ERA one, since it is important to know the exact place where the robot is located.

The values of these requirements for the 5G-ERA healthcare and PPDR use cases are presented in Table 1.

Table 1. 5G-ERA healthcare and PPDR use cases requirements

Requirements	Value
Data type	Video: Yes Voice: No Other data: Yes
Throughput	100 Mbps < high ≤ 1.000 Mbps
Mobility	<walking-running-cycling speed
Location accuracy	High: ≤ 1 m
Latency	<25 ms
Reliability	High: 99.99999%
Availability	High: 99.99999%

5   Conclusion

In this paper the 5G-ERA healthcare and PPDR use cases were presented, as well as the 5G network design and requirements. The complexity of the environment where robots will be used, forces to a new approach on robot navigation and tasks manipulation deployment. Cloud-based robots are essential for realizing a high degree of autonomy in robots. However, in order to combine the capabilities of autonomous robots and clouds, the robot must be able to perceive and understand its environment. To do so, 5G-ERA proposes an architecture, which was presented in this paper, which will be used in a case where a robot will be used and requires a network's high reliability and availability and high location accuracy.

Additionally, taking into consideration the special characteristics of the use cases, the network that will be integrated was presented, which will be based on the 5G Standalone (SA) Rel.16 architecture. Finally, the network requirements were identified and analyzed. As a result of this analysis, it was identified that it is important to implement a network that will support large throughput and reliability, while the location accuracy must be less than one meter in order to be able to accurately locate the robot.

Acknowledgments. This work has been performed in the scope of the *5G-ERA* European Research Project and has been supported by the Commission of the European Communities (*Grant Agreement No. 101016681*).

References

1. Qiu, R., et al.: The development of a semi-autonomous framework for personal assistant robots - SRS project. Int. J. Intell. Mechatron. Robot. (IJIMR) **3**(4), 30–47 (2013). https://doi.org/10.4018/ijimr.2013100102
2. GTI 5G and Cloud Robotics White Paper (2017). https://www.huawei.com/uk/industry-insights/outlook/mobile-broadband/xlabs/insights-whitepapers/gti-5g-and-cloud-robotics-white-paper
3. RoboEarth Project (2015). http://roboearth.ethz.ch
4. KnowRob Project (2014). http://knowrob.org
5. SRS Project (2013). http://wiki.ros.org/srs_public
6. 5G-ERA project. https://www.5g-era.eu
7. Yu, H., Lee, H., Jeon, H.: What is 5G? Emerging 5G mobile services and network requirements. Sustainability **9**, 1848 (2017). https://doi.org/10.3390/su9101848
8. Soldani, D., et al.: 5G mobile systems for healthcare. In: 2017 IEEE 85th Vehicular Technology Conference (VTC Spring), pp. 1–5 (2017). https://doi.org/10.1109/VTCSpring.2017.8108602
9. ETSI Multi-access Edge Computing. https://www.etsi.org/technologies/multi-access-edge-computing
10. Open-source Management and Orchestration (OSM). https://osm.etsi.org
11. ETSI Open-source Management and Orchestration. https://www.etsi.org/technologies/open-source-mano
12. Rafiq, A., Mehmood, A., Ahmed Khan, T., Abbas, K., Afaq, M., Song, W.-C.: Intent-based end-to-end network service orchestration system for multi-platforms. Sustainability **12**, 2782 (2020). https://doi.org/10.3390/su12072782

The 2nd Workshop on "Artificial Intelligence in Biomedical Engineering and Informatics"

AI-BIOMED 2021 Workshop

Artificial Intelligence (AI) is gradually changing the routine of medical practice, and the level of acceptance by the medical personnel is constantly increasing. Recent progress in digital medical data acquisition through advanced biosignal and medical imaging devices, machine learning and high-performance cloud computing infrastructures, push health-related AI applications into areas that were previously thought to be only the province of human experts. Such applications employ a variety of methodologies, including fuzzy logic, evolutionary computing, neural networks, or deep learning for producing AI-powered models that simulate human physiology; often called digital twins. In this context, digital twins can also be used for modeling an individual's genomic makeup, physiological characteristics, and lifestyle to deliver personalized medicine. It is an ambitious paradigm looking at the human in an end-to-end approach, across all scales, unifying the virtual physiological human and the daily health behavior models and technologies. This approach is anticipated to disrupt clinical practice, since it offers a more individual focus than precision medicine, which typically involves specific groups within a greater population. Furthermore, twinning the human body can support medical diagnostics, follow-up monitoring, preventive medicine, therapy assessment, and many other domains.

These areas have been in recent years the subject of many research papers and research grants. Consequently, this workshop is devoted to the subject of artificial intelligence, in its broadest sense, in biomedical engineering and health informatics. The workshop is the second of a series organized within the 18th AIAI 2022 Artificial Intelligence Applications and Innovations conference. Topics of interest include, but are not limited to, the following:

- Wearable Systems
- Medical and Sensor Data Processing
- Machine Learning in eHealth
- Medical Image Analysis and Radiomics
- Robotics in Biomedical Engineering
- Quantified Self Technologies and Applications
- Intelligent Data Processing and Predictive Algorithms in eHealth
- Smart Homes and Assistive Environments
- Data Mining of Health Data on the Cloud
- Security, Safety, and Privacy in Intelligent eHealth Applications

Organization

The Organizers

Ilias Maglogiannis	University of Piraeus
Ioanna Chouvarda	Aristotle University of Thessaloniki
Spyretta Golemati	National and Kapodistrian University of Athens
Michail Sarafidis	National Technical University of Athens

Organization

An Automated 2D U-Net Segmentation Method for the Identification of Cancer Brain Metastases Using MRI Images

Vangelis Tzardis[1]([📧]) [iD], Efthyvoulos Kyriacou[1] [iD], Christos P. Loizou[1] [iD], and Anastasia Constantinidou[2,3] [iD]

[1] Department of Electrical Engineering, Computer Engineering and Informatics, Cyprus University of Technology, 3036 Limassol, Cyprus
em.tzardis@edu.cut.ac.cy, {efthyvoulos.kyriacou, christos.loizou}@cut.ac.cy
[2] University of Cyprus, 2029 Nicosia, Cyprus
constantinidou.anastasia@ucy.ac.cy
[3] Bank of Cyprus Oncology Centre, 2006 Nicosia, Cyprus

Abstract. In this study, we propose an automated system for the segmentation of cancer brain metastases (CBM) using MRI images. The goal is the correlation with regards to the primary cancer site. The segmentation of CBM is a challenging task due to their wide range in terms of number, shape, size and location in the brain. We experimented with the training of a modified U-Net convolutional neural network (CNN) using $N = 3474$ brain image slices for training, $N_v = 579$ for validation and $N_T = 579$ for testing from the public dataset BrainMetShare. The proposed model was evaluated on the testing data (N_T), on a lesion-cross section basis with areas from 2.8 to 1225.7 mm^2 and yielded a mean Sensitivity (SE) 0.70 ± 0.30, Specificity (SP) 0.77 ± 0.26 and Dice similarity coefficient (DSC) of 0.73 ± 0.29 across the entire dataset. The present results show the good agreement of the proposed method with the ground truth.

Keywords: Magnetic resonance imaging · Brain metastasis · Cancer brain metastasis · Automated image segmentation · Convolutional neural network · U-Net

1 Introduction

Cancer brain metastasis (CBM) is the most common intracranial malignant cancer in the adult population, by far outnumbering the primary brain tumors. According to [1], it is estimated that approximately 20% of the cancer patients will develop CBM. Breast cancer, lung cancer and melanoma are the most frequent sites to develop CBM. Breast cancer brain metastases (BCBM) accounts for 5–20% of all metastatic cancers, whereas CBM originating in lung and melanoma cancer appears in 20–56% and 7–16% of all cases respectively [1]. Additionally, CBM patients suffer from a poor quality of life,

© IFIP International Federation for Information Processing 2022
Published by Springer Nature Switzerland AG 2022
I. Maglogiannis et al. (Eds.): AIAI 2022 Workshops, IFIP AICT 652, pp. 161–173, 2022.
https://doi.org/10.1007/978-3-031-08341-9_14

a debilitating symptomatology and their future survival prognosis is often at one year [1]. These criteria necessitate the early detection of CBMs in order to select the best treatment option. Recent studies suggested that, along with systemic therapy, surgery and radiation, CBM patients' treatment should also be based on their overall performance status as well as the primary tumor site, its molecular subtype, the number, location and the size of the CBM [2].

Currently, the diagnosis of CBM is performed based on clinical information, magnetic resonance imaging (MRI) modalities and histopathological examination (biopsy). Even though biopsy is considered today as the gold standard for cancer diagnosis [1], it poses several challenges especially when discussing CBM and the risks during the biopsy procedure. MRI assessment of CBM in terms of localization and tissue characteristics, on the other hand, is a time-consuming and tedious procedure requiring the assistance of a medical professional, and typically including significant inter- and intra-reader variability. To cope with these issues, the research community has come up with computer-aided decision support systems to automate the segmentation and classification of CBM according to their primary cancer site, as described below.

For the segmentation task on CBM, a variety of Deep Learning (DL) methods has been identified as presented in [3–11]. More specifically, Liu et al. [4] and Charron et al. [5], both modified the known 3D DeepMedic convolutional neural network (CNN) [6], with the former adding an extra pathway for the local features, and the latter experimenting with the network hyper-parameters and data augmentation with virtual patients. Bousabarah et al. [7], demonstrated an ensemble of 2D U-Nets [8], with each one trained on a different subset of data or with a different loss function. In two other studies, Xue et al. [9] and Zhue et al. [10], cascaded two fully CNN, respectively 3D (full height) and 3-slice tall. Grøvik et al. [11], modified the DeepLab V3 method [12], in which they concatenated three MRI modalities as an input tensor, with five 2D slices per modality. In addition, the team made use of dilated convolutions and stochastic dropout of modalities. All above studies used a subset of the pre- and post-contrast T_1-weighted as well as fluid-attenuated inversion recovery MRI modalities. Their results showed insufficiency of the models for CBM, which were smaller than 6 mm in diameter. More specifically, in [10], a Dice similarity coefficient (DSC) $= 0.64 \pm 0.2$ for CBM between 3 and 6 mm was reported. Notably, the best DSC was reported at 0.84 ± 0.07 for CBM larger than 5 mm [9] and 0.81 ± 0.15 (averaged per CBM volume), for CBM in the range of 1–52 mm [10] respectively.

For the BCBM classification task, current methods proposed in the literature [13–15], using quantitative imaging features are not mature enough to be clinically applicable. More specifically Kniep et al. [13], showed that imaging features such as texture, shape, first-order statistics and wavelet decompositions are only complementary to the larger predictive power of age and sex data in BCBM. Ortiz-Ramón et al. [14], documented that only fair results (Area Under the Curve (AUC) $= 60\%$), could be achieved, for breast cancer in multi-class prediction mainly due to misclassifications with melanoma. Finally, in [15] Béresová et al. reported statistically significant differentiations between texture features both on images and local binary pattern maps (LBP) from CBM originating in breast and lung, whereas without developing a decision-making classifier.

Due to the aforementioned challenges, segmentation and identification of CBM, particularly in small ones, is still challenging and a work in progress. Through this study, we demonstrate the first steps towards the development of an integrated and fully automated system for CBM segmentation and BCBM classification.

2 Methodology

2.1 Proposed System Overview

In this study, we experimented with the segmentation of CBM, with results presented in Sect. 3. The proposed method for this task was based on our previous work [16], in which a modified 2D U-net was used (see also Fig. 1d). Also, the selection of this segmentation network for this study was based on the high accuracy results of U-Nets in brain tumors (gliomas). It was also based on the fact that it can achieve a DSC $= 0.90$ [17] as well as on the proposition that generalizable state of the art (as tested on gliomas) can be accomplished by optimizing the training hyper-parameters [18], without the need to develop elaborate architectures.

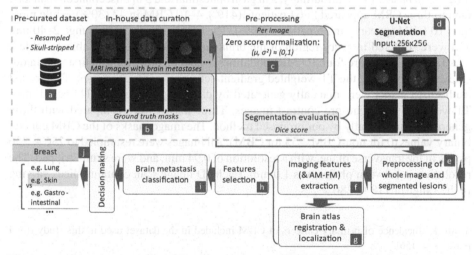

Fig. 1. Overview of the proposed integrated system for the automated brain metastasis segmentation and classification of the primary site of cancer. The light gray dashed boxes relates to the experimental implementation of the segmentation task as proposed in this work. (Color figure online)

The remaining system modules described in the following, are the main steps of our future work aiming at the BCBM classification. Based on Fig. 1, we propose to register and localize the segmented CBM lesions to existing brain atlases (see also Fig. 1g), such as to the Montreal Neurological Institute (MNI) 152 atlases database [13]. Then, the initial segmented images will be preprocessed (see Fig. 1e), and fed to various imaging feature extractors (see Fig. 1f), as the ones described in the previous paragraph. In addition, we also intend to use a new class of features based on amplitude modulation-frequency modulation (AM-FM) methods (see Fig. 1f), as it was also proposed by our group in [19]. AM-FM were applied in multiple sclerosis lesions which bear visual similarities with CBM. Out of all the extracted features, only a portion of the most statistically significant ones will be selected for the next step of classification (see Fig. 1h). For the features selection a variety of known methods will be used such as Gini- [13] and random forest-value importance [14]. Finally, the association of the segmentèd CBM with their primary cancer site will be modeled with both binary and multi-class classifiers such as random forests [13, 14] (see Fig. 1i), and then tested in unseen data (see Fig. 1j), based on the extracted imaging features (see Fig. 1h), along with the location of the CBM in the brain.

2.2 Image Dataset

The publicly available CBM image dataset BrainMetShare [20] was used (also used in [11]), which includes MRI scans of in total 156 patients, 105 females and 51 males, of mean age 63 ± 12 years old (range: 29 to 92 years), with at least 1 BM per patient and various primary cancers. More specifically, 99 of the patients have CBM originating in lung, 33 in breast, 7 in genitourinary, 5 in gastrointestinal and 5 in miscellaneous cancers. One to three CBM appeared in 64 patients (41%), 4–10 CBM in 47 (30%), while more than 10 CBM appeared in 45 patients (29%). The CBM sizes lie in the range 2–40 mm and were scattered in every region of the brain parenchyma (see also Table 1, Table 2 and Table 3). There are four 3D MRImodalities available, however as a first step in our study, we chose only the T1-weighted gradient-echo post-contrast images. The ground truth CBM masks were manually generated by different radiologists [11] based upon T1-weighted spin-echo pre-contrast images. These masks were compared with those generated automatically by our proposed method. The image masks of the CBM contain binary values (0 for non-CBM, 255 for CBM). All images were resampled to 256×256 pixels in the transverse plane, with a resolution of 0.94 mm, and were skull-stripped. The resolution in between planes was 1.0 mm. Each 3D image scan contains slices varying in the range of 118 to 286.

Table 1. Incidence of primary cancers of CBM included in the dataset used in this study (total patients = 156).

Primary cancer: Number of patients (% of total patients)
Lung: 99 (63%)
Breast: 33 (21%)
Melanoma: 7 (5%)
Genitourinary: 7 (5%)
Gastrointestinal: 5 (3%)
Miscellaneous: 5 (3%)

Table 2. Patients' age and CBM range

Mean patients' age: 63 ± 12 years old
Range: 29–92 years
CBM range in diameter: 2–40 mm

Table 3. Incidence of CBM with relation to number of CBM per patient.

Number of CBM: number of patients (% of total patients)
1 to 3: 64 (41%)
4 to 10: 47 (30%)
>10: 45 (29%)

2.3 Data Pre-processing

To pre-process the images and prepare them for further processing, we kept only the 2D image slices that contained CBM. We then randomly separated the dataset in training/validation and /testing in a ratio 70/15/15 respectively, thus ending up with 3474/579/579 slices respectively. Moreover, the only pre-processing that the images underwent was their intensity standardization [5, 7, 10] (zero score normalization) per slice, by subtracting the mean and dividing by the standard deviation of each slice. Also, the images of the CBM masks were set to the values 0 and 1 for non-CBM and CBM respectively.

2.4 Automated 2D Segmentation Model

The architecture of the 2D modified U-Net used in this study, was also proposed in [16], which was used for the binary brain metastasis segmentation (see also Fig. 2). It consists of six levels, with each level containing two convolution blocks of filter size 3 × 3, a Rectified Linear Unit (ReLU) as an activation function, and dropout layer where a percentage of its input units are randomly set to zero. The dropout rate ranges from 0.1 in the top level to 0.3 in the bottleneck of the network. The downsampling of the last feature maps of each encoding level was performed with max pooling of kernel size 2 × 2. The upsampling in the decoder path was done with transpose convolutions of kernel size 2 × 2. Starting from the input 256 × 256 image, the spatial dimensions got halved in each level until size 8 × 8, while the filters increased from 16 up to 512. The selection of this segmentation network for this study was based on the high accuracy results of U-Nets in brain tumors (gliomas) that can achieve DSC = 0.90 [17]. It was also based on the proposition that generalizable state of the art (as tested on brain tumors - gliomas), can be accomplished by optimizing the training hyper-parameters [18], without the need to develop elaborate architectures.

For the training, the binary cross entropy loss, with the Adam optimizer and learning rate 10^{-4} were used. The batch size was set to 10, due to GPU memory limitations. To determine the optimal number of epochs, the network was trained for 500 epochs and the losses on the training and validation data were noted. It was observed that after the 90th epoch, validation loss was virtually stagnant, therefore the final model presented in this study, was trained for 90 epochs. Furthermore, the threshold to discern between BM and non-BM pixels (to be applied to the predicted probability maps when evaluating the model) was experimentally determined, by evaluating the model on the training data (each slice) with different threshold values, using the DSC metric. The mean of the best DSCs yielded a threshold equal to 0.54 which was chosen. The training and testing of the model was performed on an NVIDIA RTX 3050 GPU (4 GB) and an AMD Ryzen 7 processor. For the training, each epoch was executed in approximately 40 s, thus resulting in 60 min for the whole experiment.

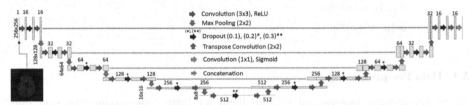

Fig. 2. Architecture of the proposed U-Net used in this study [16], which was implemented with the Tensorflow [21]-Keras [22] framework in Python.

2.5   Evaluation Metrics

In order to take into account the fact that each MRI slice contains CBM with multiple numbers and sizes, from each ground truth mask we extracted a separate bounding box around the sub-mask for every individual CBM cross section area. Also, for each extracted bounding box, we removed the corresponding area from the predicted mask. Then, the proposed segmentation model was evaluated in the training, validation and testing splits using the metrics SE, SP, PPV, IoU, and DSC [11]. All above metrics were implemented on the corresponding bounding boxes. Moreover, in each ground truth sub-mask, the area of the CBM cross section was calculated for comparison with the segmentation results. The evaluation metrics were calculated separately for every CBM cross section (see Fig. 3 for examples). The results of the metrics are presented both across the entire data (see also Table 2 and Fig. 4) as well as in 10 bins of 96 CBM cross sections each (see also Fig. 5). Below, the definitions of the proposed evaluation metrics are given:

$$SE = \frac{TP}{TP + FN} \tag{1}$$

$$SP = \frac{TN}{TN + FP} \tag{2}$$

$$PPV = \frac{TP}{TP + FP} \tag{3}$$

$$IoU = \frac{TP}{TP + FP + FN} \tag{4}$$

$$DSC = \frac{2 * TP}{2 * TP + FN + FP} \tag{5}$$

where TP, TN, FP and FN are the true positives, the true negatives, the false positives and the false negatives, calculated on a pixel basis respectively between the manual performed by an expert and the automated segmentations performed by the proposed method. Furthermore, for evaluating the performance of the segmentation method, box plots were used for graphically demonstrating the distribution of the proposed evaluation metrics (see Fig. 5).

3 Results

In Fig. 3, two representative segmentation results are shown, where in image A1, there are nine separate relatively small CBM cross sections ranging from approximately 10 to 30 mm^2. The segmentation results (see image A2 in Fig. 3), indicate both poor and good performance in this case. This is because the model fails to detect two areas completely, whereas in other areas the model reaches a DSC = 0.88. In Fig. 3, image B1 illustrates two CBM cross sections. In image B2, the automated segmentation results display an area (A = 56 mm^2) with a DSC = 0.86, whereas another relatively larger area (A =

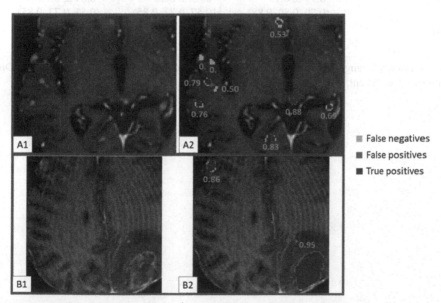

Fig. 3. Illustration of two representative examples of automatically segmented brain metastases from the testing dataset. Images are cropped for visual purposes. A1–B1) Images fed to the model. A2–B2) Segmentation results vs ground truths. Next to each cross section of brain metastasis, the DSC is noted in yellow, as calculated per cross section.

511 mm^2) gave a DSC $= 0.95$. In Table 2, the mean values ($\pm$standard deviations), and the 25th, 50th and 75th percentiles of the interquartile range (IQR) for all evaluation metrics are presented.

In Fig. 4 we present the results of the evaluation metrics on all images used in this study for comparing our proposed segmentation with the ground truth. Almost all evaluation metrics show a good agreement of the proposed segmentation method with the ground truth. Additionally, the mean values of all evaluation metrics for the different CBM cross section areas from the testing set are displayed in Fig. 5. Each point of the x-axis refers to the smallest of the areas of the CBM cross sections in the corresponding bin (see Fig. 5).

Table 4. Mean values with their standard deviations (mean $\pm$ std), and IQR percentiles (25th, 50th, 75th) for the segmentation evaluation metrics between the manual vs the automated results.

Evaluation metrics	Training dataset	Validation dataset	Testing dataset
Sensitivity	0.85 ± 0.15 (0.80, 0.89, 0.95)	0.71 ± 0.30 (0.62, 0.83, 0.93)	0.70 ± 0.30 (0.59, 0.82, 0.93)
Specificity	0.73 ± 0.26 (0.61, 0.80, 0.92)	0.76 ± 0.26 (0.65, 0.83, 1.00)	0.77 ± 0.26 (0.66, 0.85, 1.00)
PPV	0.89 ± 0.10 (0.85, 0.92, 0.97)	0.90 ± 0.10 (0.85, 0.92, 0.98)	0.90 ± 0.11 (0.85, 0.92, 0.98)
IoU	0.77 ± 0.15 (0.70, 0.80, 0.88)	0.65 ± 0.28 (0.57, 0.73, 0.85)	0.64 ± 0.28 (0.53, 0.72, 0.85)
DSC	0.86 ± 0.12 (0.82, 0.89, 0.94)	0.74 ± 0.28 (0.73, 0.84, 0.92)	0.73 ± 0.29 (0.70, 0.84, 0.92)

IQR: Interquartile range, PPV: Positive Predictive Value, IoU: Intersection over Union, DSC: Dice Similarity Coefficient. IQR shown in parentheses.

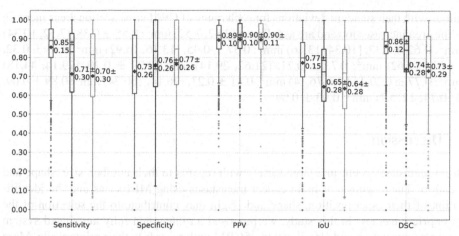

Fig. 4. Box plots for the evaluation metrics for the segmentation model across all CBM cross sections in the dataset. Red/Blue/Green boxes: Training/Validation/Testing data: Approximately 5700/900/900 individual cross section areas of CBM. DSC ± std is shown on the right of each box. (Color figure online)

The results of Fig. 5, show a large imbalance in the areas of the CBM cross sections across the dataset, with half of the data being in the range 2.8 mm² to 21.6 mm². The remaining half of the samples lies in the range 21.6 to 1225.7 mm². The mean DSC

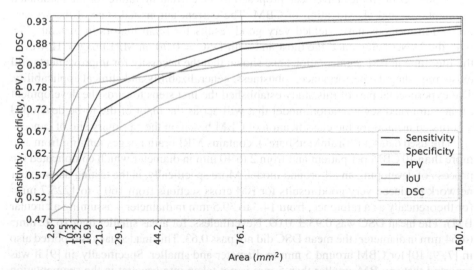

Fig. 5. Means of different segmentation evaluation metrics used in this study, for different range of sizes of cross sections of CBM (ground truth), as evaluated in the testing set. The areas were separated to 10 bins of equal number of measurements (N = 96). The displayed areas on the x-axis refer to the left edges. Last bin area = [160.7, 1225.7] mm². In each bin, the mean of each metric is calculated. For visual purposes, the plotted lines are smoothed with a gaussian filter of sigma = 0.75.

values with their standard deviations for each range of CBM cross section areas increase as the area increases too and are as follows: [2.82, 7.52) mm^2: 0.55 ± 0.38, [7.52, 10.34) mm^2: 0.62 ± 0.33, [10.34, 13.16) mm^2: 0.57 ± 0.35, [13.16, 16.92) mm^2: 0.63 ± 0.32, [16.92, 21.62) mm^2: 0.73 ± 0.21, [21.62, 29.14) mm^2: 0.79 ± 0.20, [29.14, 44.18) mm^2: 0.77 ± 0.20, [44.18, 76.14) mm^2: 0.81 ± 0.21, [76.14, 160.74) mm^2: 0.89 ± 0.09, [160.74, 1225.7) mm^2: 0.93 ± 0.09.

4 Discussion

Brain metastases occur in a large variety with regards to their number, size, shape and location. The diagnosis of brain cancer metastases using MRI scans and the identification of their exact position, shape and origin may contribute to the selection of the appropriate therapy. In this study, we proposed an integrated fully automated system for the segmentation and classification of CBM with regards to their primary site. More specifically, we also evaluated and experimented with our segmentation method as follows. We used a modified U-Net CNN using N = 3474 brain image slices for training, N_v = 579 for validation and N_T = 579 for testing from the public dataset BrainMetShare. The proposed model was evaluated on the testing data (N_T), on a lesion-cross section basis with areas from 2.8 to 1225.7 mm^2 and yielded a SE = 0.70 ± 0.30, a SP = 0.77 ± 0.26, a PPV = 0.90 ± 0.11, an IoU = 0.64 ± 0.28 and a DSC = 0.73 ± 0.29. The present results of this study show the good agreement of the proposed method with the ground truth.

A number of studies have been proposed in the current literature for the automated segmentation and classification of CBM. The current automated state-of-the-art segmentation methods have yielded very good results for brain tumors in general [17], with the U-Net being cited the most and with DSC = 0.90 on MRI images. However, the literature in BM segmentation have shown that the necessity for improvements still exists regarding the performance, robustness, generalizability and clinical applicability. The experimental part of this study established the first steps towards the development of an automated segmentation model that will act as the input of the to-be developed automated method for the classification of CBM based on their primary site of cancer.

The used dataset ("BrainMetShare"), contains MRI brain images ranging from 1 to more than 10 CBM per patient and from 2 to 40 mm in diameter which complicated the process of developing an all-around model. More specifically, in the testing dataset, our network produced very good results for BM cross sections from 160.7 to 1225.7 mm^2 (or theoretically as a reference, from 14.3 to 39.5 mm in diameter – assuming a circular BM). The mean DSC was 0.93 ± 0.09. Nevertheless, for areas smaller than 16.92 mm^2 (4.64 mm in diameter) the mean DSC did not pass 0.63. This inadequacy is reported also in [7, 9, 10] for CBM around 5 mm in diameter and smaller. Specifically, in [9] it was reported that any BM smaller than 5 mm is not taken into account in the segmentation evaluation with the DSC metric. Also, it is mentioned that a number of studies in the field of brain disease identification have set a minimum size for the measurable diseases and is equal to 5 mm. Moreover, the mean DSC across the entire testing dataset was 0.73 ± 0.29, which paves the way for further enhancement as much in the network architecture as in the optimization of a to-be generalizable preprocessing and training scheme. In the referenced CBM segmentation studies, all network architectures are different from the 2D U-Net. For comparison, in [4, 5] they used the 3D DeepMedic CNN and reported DSC equal to 0.67 and 0.79. Also, in [7] they used 3D U-Nets in an ensemble with different training datasets and loss functions for each model of the ensemble, resulting in mean DSC $= 0.71$. In [9, 10] a DSC equal to 0.84 and 0.81 respectively was reported. Furthermore, we report comparable results in this study in DSC as also in [11]. The same MRI dataset as in our study and a fully CNN trained with four MRI modalities in a 3D-to-2D scheme were used, achieving a DSC $= 0.79 \pm 0.12$. However, it is important to note that there is a difference in the calculation of the DSC metrics in our study and the aforementioned studies using 3D models. More specifically in the present study the DSC was averaged across the 2D CBM cross sections, as opposed to the averaged DSC across the CBM volumes of the datasets in the other studies. In all above studies, slightly better results but comparable to our study were reported. This can be due to the fact that different databases, type and number of modalities, pre-processing, data augmentation, post-processing and evaluation metrics criteria in terms of CBM volume were used as compared to our study.

In a future study, conditional random fields (CRF) will be also tested for the segmentation task to investigate if they can further reduce the FP islands of predicted lesions. Additionally, the proposed method will be further evaluated on a larger number of cases using additional network parameters, expert observers and evaluation metrics. The model proposed in this study did not use any elaborate techniques for dataset curation, image normalization, data augmentation and training schemes. Our next efforts towards these goals, will include a preprocessing step, where the images will be adaptively cropped in order to contain as much as brain information as possible in order to create a segmentation network with the smallest possible input patch for memory reasons. Also, data augmentation techniques such as non-rigid image transformations and simulations of different noise distributions such as changes in gamma, spatial intensity distributions, Gaussian and Rician noise, will be tested. Additionally, for datasets that have more than one modality available, it will be pursued to learn if the excess of such information facilitates or confuses the proposed CNN. Also, the multi-modal images will be examined as separate channels in the network or as a fused single channel. Moreover, a GPU of higher capacity will be used in order to be able to experiment will larger batch sizes and the training will be performed on a five-fold cross validation scheme. Finally, for a more direct comparison with other studies, the evaluation metrics will also be calculated on a CBM volume basis, where the metrics will be averaged across the volumes of the dataset. For this to be done, the testing dataset will include contiguous MRI image slices for every test patient.

References

1. Achrol, A.S., Rennert, R.C., Anders, C., Soffietti, R., et al.: Brain metastases. Nat. Rev. Dis. Primers. **5**(1), 1–26 (2019)
2. Mitchell, D., Kwon, H.J., Kubica, P.A., Huff, W.X., et al.: Brain metastases: an update on multi-disciplinary approach of clinical management. Neurochirurgie **68**(1), 69–85 (2021)
3. Tzardis, V., Kyriacou, E., Loizou, C., Constantinidou, A.: A review on breast cancer brain metastasis: automated MRI image analysis for the prediction of primary cancer using

radiomics. In: Tsapatsoulis, N., Panayides, A., Theocharides, T., Lanitis, A., Pattichis, C., Vento, M. (eds.) CAIP 2021. LNCS, vol. 13052, pp. 245–255. Springer, Cham (2021). https://doi.org/10.1007/978-3-030-89128-2_24

4. Liu, Y., Stojadinovic, S., Hrycushko, B., Wardak, Z., et al.: A deep convolutional neural network-based automatic delineation strategy for multiple brain metastases stereotactic radiosurgery. PLoS ONE 12(10), e0185844 (2017)

5. Charron, O., Lallement, A., Jarnet, D., Noblet, V., et al.: Automatic detection and segmentation of brain metastases on multimodal MR images with a deep convolutional neural network. Comput. Biol. Med. 95, 43–54 (2018)

6. Kamnitsas, K., Ledig, C., Newcombe, V.F.J., Simpson, J.P., et al.: Efficient multi-scale 3D CNN with fully connected CRF for accurate brain lesion segmentation. Med. Image Anal. 36, 61–78 (2017)

7. Bousabarah, K., Ruge, M., Brand, J.-S., Hoevels, M., et al.: Deep convolutional neural networks for automated segmentation of brain metastases trained on clinical data. Radiat. Oncol. 15(1), 1–9 (2020)

8. Ronneberger, O., Fischer, P., Brox, T.: U-Net: convolutional networks for biomedical image segmentation. In: Navab, N., Hornegger, J., Wells, W.M., Frangi, A.F. (eds.) MICCAI 2015. LNCS, vol. 9351, pp. 234–241. Springer, Cham (2015). https://doi.org/10.1007/978-3-319-24574-4_28

9. Xue, J., Wang, B., Ming, Y., Liu, X., et al.: Deep learning-based detection and segmentation-assisted management of brain metastases. Neuro. Oncol. 22(4), 505–514 (2020)

10. Zhou, Z., Sanders, J.W., Johnson, J.M., Gule-Monroe, M., et al.: MetNet: computer-aided segmentation of brain metastases in post-contrast T1-weighted magnetic resonance imaging. Radiother. Oncol. 153, 189–196 (2020)

11. Grøvik, E., Yi, D., Iv, M., Tong, E.A., et al.: Handling missing MRI sequences in deep learning segmentation of brain metastases: a multicenter study. NPJ Digit. Med. 4(1), 1–7 (2021)

12. Yi, D., Grøvik, E., Iv, M., Tong, E., et al.: MRI pulse sequence integration for deep-learning based brain metastasis segmentation. Med. Phys. 48(10), 6020–6035 (2019)

13. Kniep, H.C., Madesta, F., Schneider, T., Hanning, U., et al.: Radiomics of brain MRI: utility in prediction of metastatic tumor type. Radiology 290(2), 479–487 (2019)

14. Ortiz-Ramón, R., Larroza, A., Ruiz-España, S., Arana, E., Moratal, D.: Classifying brain metastases by their primary site of origin using a radiomics approach based on texture analysis: a feasibility study. Eur. Radiol. 28(11), 4514–4523 (2018). https://doi.org/10.1007/s00330-018-5463-6

15. Béresová, M., Larroza, A., Arana, E., Varga, J., Balkay, L., Moratal, D.: 2D and 3D texture analysis to differentiate brain metastases on MR images: proceed with caution. Magn. Reson. Mater. Phys., Biol. Med. 31(2), 285–294 (2017). https://doi.org/10.1007/s10334-017-0653-9

16. Georgiou, A., Loizou, C., Nicolaou, A., Pantzaris, M., Pattichis, C.: An adaptive semi-automated integrated system for multiple sclerosis lesion segmentation in longitudinal MRI scans based on a convolutional neural network. In: Tsapatsoulis, N., Panayides, A., Theocharides, T., Lanitis, A., Pattichis, C., Vento, M. (eds.) CAIP 2021. LNCS, vol. 13052, pp. 256–265. Springer, Cham (2021). https://doi.org/10.1007/978-3-030-89128-2_25

17. Bhalodiya, J.M., Lim Choi Keung, S.N., Arvanitis, T.N.: Magnetic resonance image-based brain tumour segmentation methods: a systematic review. Digit. Health 8, 20552076221074120 (2022)

18. Isensee, F., Kickingereder, P., Wick, W., Bendszus, M., Maier-Hein, K.: No new-net. In: Crimi, Alessandro, Bakas, Spyridon, Kuijf, Hugo, Keyvan, Farahani, Reyes, Mauricio, van Walsum, Theo (eds.) BrainLes 2018. LNCS, vol. 11384, pp. 234–244. Springer, Cham (2019). https://doi.org/10.1007/978-3-030-11726-9_21

19. Loizou, C.P., Pantzaris, M., Pattichis, C.S.: Normal appearing brain white matter changes in relapsing multiple sclerosis: texture image and classification analysis in serial MRI scans. Magn. Reson. Imaging. **73**, 192–202 (2020)
20. BrainMetShare. https://aimi.stanford.edu/brainmetshare, Accessed 04 Mar 2022
21. Abadi, M., Agarwal, A., Barham, P., Brevdo, E., et al.: TensorFlow: large-scale machine learn-ing on heterogeneous systems (2015). https://www.tensorflow.org
22. Chollet, F., et al.: Keras (2015). https://keras.io, Accessed 04 Mar 2022

An Intelligent Grammar-Based Platform for RNA H-type Pseudoknot Prediction

Evangelos Makris[1], Angelos Kolaitis[1], Christos Andrikos[1], Vrettos Moulos[1(✉)],
Panayiotis Tsanakas[1], and Christos Pavlatos[2]

[1] School of Electrical and Computer Engineering, National Technical University
of Athens, 9 Iroon Polytechniou Street, 15780 Athens, Greece
{vmakris,akolaitis,vrettos}@mail.ntua.gr, candrikos@cslab.ece.ntua.gr,
panag@cs.ntua.gr
[2] Hellenic Air Force Academy, Dekelia Air Base, 13671 Acharnes, Athens, Greece
christos.pavlatos@hafa.haf.gr

Abstract. Predicting the secondary structure of RNA sequences has been proved quite a challenging research field for bioinformatics. Predicting structures that encapsulate the pseudoknot motif highlights why it is an NP-complete problem. In this setting, researchers focus on accurately predicting this motif and its variations by leveraging heuristic methodologies that converge while decreasing the prediction time. Any accurate heuristic does not add significant value when it involves an extended execution period, specifically considering lengthy sequences. In this work, we introduce a novel, time-efficient method that employs grammar attributes, parallel execution, and pruning techniques to create an efficient prediction tool that is helpful for biologists, bioengineers, and biomedical researchers. This version of the proposed framework features a pruning technique to reduce the search space of the grammar. It eliminates trees derived from corner-case conditions to reduce execution time by 33% regarding the grammar-based methodology and 43% regarding the brute-force approach without sacrificing the initial accuracy percentage.

Keywords: RNA secondary structure · Pseudoknot · Syntactic pattern recognition · Context-free grammars

1 Introduction

RNA is the intermediate stage during the transition from DNA to proteins, consisting a significant factor in a variety of biological processes. The effect of RNA in protein synthesis, gene expression regulation, site recognition and catalysis illustrates its importance and attracts researchers from a wide range of scientific fields. Considering its valuable effect in these processes, many studies focus on its structural analysis, and specifically in a 2-D representation, which is called secondary structure. The prediction of this secondary structure is also

© IFIP International Federation for Information Processing 2022
Published by Springer Nature Switzerland AG 2022
I. Maglogiannis et al. (Eds.): AIAI 2022 Workshops, IFIP AICT 652, pp. 174–186, 2022.
https://doi.org/10.1007/978-3-031-08341-9_15

the core concept of this work. Even if the function of RNA is mainly depended on its 3-D or tertiary structure, the transformation of a primary structure of a molecule, which is a set of A(Adenine), U(Uracil), G(Guanine) and C(Cytosine) bases to a tertiary representation is a very difficult task. In that context, the intermediate secondary structure plays an important role in the prediction of an accurate and reliable tertiary structure prediction. Thus, the secondary structure of a molecule, which is a set of base pairing (A-U, C-G, G-U pairs) and the correct prediction of these pairs, is vital for the enlightenment of RNA operations.

The literature contains a substantial amount of publications dealing with the prediction of RNA secondary structure. Most of the methodologies are based on dynamic programming algorithms, such as Nussinov algorithm that predicts the maximum number of base pairings [44]. This algorithm is dominant but standalone, and it shows a lower prediction accuracy compared with other proposed methodologies in the literature. Secondly, thermodynamic models and specifically Zuker's minimum free energy algorithm is widely used. Zuker's thermodynamic model utilizes dynamic programming enriched by experimental parameters [42,43] . This approach leads to a stable structure with the minimum free energy and presents remarkable results in a variety of datasets. Other approaches incorporate stochastic methods, syntactic pattern recognition techniques, machine learning, other heuristic algorithms or a combination of the above. A detailed analysis of the related work is presented in Sect. 2.

For each secondary structure there is a set of possible motifs that can be formed such as stems, hairpins, bulges, interior loops, multibranch loops and pseudoknots. Nevertheless, the prediction of a pseudoknot motif is the most challenging, considering that only a few algorithms can predict it. The main reason is that dynamic programming and minimum free energy algorithms face difficulties to embrace the interconnection of pseudoknot motif and secondly, that the increase of the length of the molecule leads to an exponential execution time for those methods. Considering these difficulties and the utmost importance of this task, in this paper we present an improved version of Knotify, our intelligent grammar-based methodology of predicting H-type RNA pseudoknots, in terms of execution time using a pruning technique.

Initially, we analyze our dataset, searching for associated attributes in order to minimize the search space. Then, the RNA raw string is parsed via a Context-Free Grammar parser for all trees that include a pseudoknot to be produced in that optimized search space. Next, all trees are traversed to identify additional base pairs around the pseudoknot. Finally, the optimal tree is selected, maximizing the number of base pairs, while minimizing the free energy of the pseudoknot. For the first task, i.e. detecting possible pseudoknots, an alternative methodology is implemented as well using a brute force algorithm.

The proposed methodology does succeed in predicting the core stems of any RNA pseudoknot of test dataset by performing a 76.4% recall ratio. It achieves an F1-score equal to 0.774 and MCC equal 0.437. In [1], the methodology proposed by achieves a performance speed up of 3.45 and 7.75 compared to two well known platforms [6,10] using a dataset of 262 RNA sequences [39]. In this paper, the proposed methodology facilitates a pruning technique in search space of methodology presented in [1], by eliminating trees in corner conditions, which, in turn, maintains the initial accuracy percentage and at the same time, reduces execution time by 33%. By applying the same pruning methodology at brute force algorithm, an execution time reduction by 43% is achieved.

2 Related Work

As mentioned before, a significant number of algorithms utilize dynamic programming techniques, in order to predict the secondary structure with the minimum free energy, such as RNAfold [2], manifold [43]. More specialized approaches for H-type pseudoknot prediction as in [45] has been proposed, focusing on conformational entropy, stability, and the free-energy. Though, considering that the problem is NP-complete [5] and thus, the computational time is increasing exponentially to the molecule's length, stochastic and heuristic methods are deployed to overcome this constraint [7–9]. In that context, Knotty [6] predicts the secondary structure of a variety of RNA motifs including pseudoknots, with CCJ algorithm with sparsification, introducing at the same time a new class of structures called Three-Groups-of-Band (TGB). ProbKnot [11] on the other hand, utilizes the concepts of base pair probabilities and partition function. It computes probabilities of non-pseudoknotted substructures and then creates the secondary structure with the maximum expected accuracy, performing good results in a low runtime. Focusing on accuracy level, IPknot [10] outperforms the abovementioned approaches using integer programming, specific thresholds and base pair probabilities as optimization techniques.

SCFG-based frameworks have been also proposed in the literature such as Pfold [12,13], a multi threaded version of that, the PPfold [14], RNA-Decoder [15] and a variety of other implementations (Contrafold [16], Evfold [17], Infernal [18], Oxfold [19]), which leverage grammar's advantages. All these approaches embody a machine learning notion, considering that they search for common patterns and similarity measures, while they handle probabilities in their rules. That mathematical background combined with advanced computational methods and optimization algorithms lead to powerful prediction frameworks. Adding, also, information from biological concepts such as minimum free energy, as our framework proposes, we achieved a resilient and efficient grammar based prediction method.

The rise of machine learning has also affect this field of bioinformatics. Many machine learning algorithms has been partially adopted to predict the RNA secondary structure. Some of them focus on the base-pair prediction using deep learning and tertiary constraints [3], while others [22], predicts the secondary structure of RNA sequences, including pseudoknots by leveraging bidirectional-LSTM networks and Improved Base Pair Maximization principle (IBPMP) to choose the appropriate base pairs. Similarly, 2dRNA [20] applies a coupled two-staged deep neural network and a U-net architecture. Its bidirectional LSTM stage performs as an encoder in higher dimensions and in turn, a fully connected network acts as an decoder, which outputs the dot-bracket structure. Recently, ATTfold [21], an also deep learning framework was proposed, in the direction of predicting the secondary structure of RNA with pseudoknots. This approach encapsulates an attention mechanism, which operates as an encoder to a base pairing score matrix and a convolutional neural network as decoder. The whole system is trained with respect to hard biological rules, in order predict results that comply to basic folding principles.

3   Theoretical Background

In this section, basic theoretical issues regarding RNA, pseudoknot structure and parser implementations are analyzed, in order to introduce the reader to necessary basic concepts.

3.1   RNA

RNA secondary structure is the basis of various biological processes. By the use of four distinct nitrogenous bases: A (adenine), C (cytosine), G (guanine), and U (uracil), RNA manages to carry genetic information. In contrast to DNA, RNA forms a single-stranded molecule, while its bases bind in pairs known as the standard set of RNA base-pairs: A-U and G-C, which are the Watson–Crick base-pairs [26] and the less regularly showing off G-U wobble-base pairs. Depending on the way and the sequence base-pairs are created, various RNA-folding motifs are formed. The well known RNA-folding motifs are those of loops, kissing loops, bulges, hairpins and pseudoknots. In this paper, the proposed methodology is focused on H-type pseudoknots.

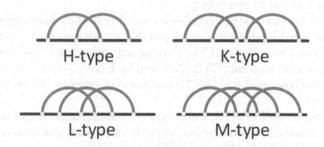

Fig. 1. H, L, K and M type of pseudoknots.

The Pseudoknot Pattern. One of the most-typical RNA-folding motif is that of the pseudoknot pattern. Pseudoknot motif was initially spotted in the *Turnip Yellow Mosaic virus* [24]. A pseudoknot motif consists of two helical segments that are bound by at least two single-stranded sections or loops. There may be various folding variations forming a pseudoknot motif. However, there are four main types [23] of pseudoknots known as the H-type, the K-type, the L-type, and the M-type that are shown in Fig. 1. In an H-type pseudoknot [25] the single-stranded RNA sequence folds into an "S" mode in order to construct two tangent loops, each one of arbitrary length.

3.2 Syntactic Pattern Recognition

In this paper, the proposed methodology facilitates a pruning technique in grammar's search space of presented methodology in [1]. In [1], the underlying model of the proposed methodology in order to predict H-types pseudoknots in RNA structures is that of Context Free Grammars using syntactic pattern recognition. The basic idea of syntactic pattern recognition is the definition of a language [27] which is a set of syntax rules, that may construct a parse tree having the examined string at the terminal nodes. The set of syntax rules along with a set of vocabulary consists of a grammar that may recognize if a string of symbols is belonging to the defined language or not. Noam Chomsky [28] divided the grammars into four specific classes, that are known as the Chomsky hierarchy. The proposed methodology is based on Context-free grammars (CFG), that are really helpful tools in natural language processing and programming languages [29].

Context Free Grammars. A CFG [38] may be defined by the use of four sets (quadruple). Consequently, $CFG = \langle NT, T, R, S \rangle$. Where S ($S \in NT$) is the root of the grammar, which is defined as the start symbol. The terminal symbols of the grammar compose set T, while the non-terminal symbols compose set NT. Set R consists of the syntactic rules. The syntax rules follow the formalism $K \rightarrow \gamma$, where $K \in NT$ and $\gamma \in (T \cup NT)^*$, denoting that non-terminal symbol K, can produce string of symbols γ.

CFG grammars have extensively been used, due to their high expressive capability, hence a considerable number of parsing algorithms have been presented in the literature. Two efficient CFG parsing algorithms are those presented by Cocke, Younger, and Kasami (CYK) [30] and by Earley [31]. Based on these two approaches numerous modified [32–34] and parallel versions [35,36] are proposed in the literature.

In this paper as well as in [1], the proposed system makes use of the most efficient Earley's parser implementation, capable of parsing ambiguous grammars, that of Yet Another Early Parser (YAEP) parser [37].

4 Proposed Methodology

In this paper, the proposed methodology facilitates a pruning technique in grammar's search space of the methodology presented in [1]. The proposed methodology as well as the methodology presented in [1] succeed in recognizing RNA H-type pseudoknots following three tasks: (i) construction of all parse trees that incorporate a pseudoknot by the use of a CFG parser; (ii) traversal of all produced trees in order to identify additional base pairs around the pseudoknot; and (iii) selection of the optimal tree by the use of the minimum free energy and the maximum number of base pairs of the pseudoknot criteria. The goal of the proposed methodology is to produce a base pairing in an extended dot-bracket notation given an input string representing an RNA.

The CFG G_{RNA} proposed in [1] is capable of detecting pseudoknots in strings where the first and last symbols of the sequence belong to the core stems group. However, this implies the parsing of subparts of the strings using a sliding-windows technique.

The sliding-windows technique divides the initial input string into substrings, starting from the one that starts with the first symbol and features the minimum potential length. Iteratively, the length of the examined substring is augmented by one symbol to finally include the entire initial RNA sequence. Then, using the same iterative fashion, starting symbol position is increased by one to exclude the previous set starting symbol.

Syntactic pattern recognition was chosen, having as future goal to augment the CFG with attributes, forming in this way an attribute (AG), aiming to augment system with probabilities and succeed in dynamically prune parse trees. However, the first task may be implemented using a brute-force algorithm which will enhance the performance of the presented system. The brute force algorithm traverses the RNA sequence in order to identify all possible base pairs and then examines all base pairs in order to locate couples of base pairs, that may potentially be parts of the core stems of a pseudoknot. The proposed methodology aims to facilitate a pruning technique in both grammar's and brute-force's methodology search space of methodology presented in [1]. This space elimination will affect only the first task of the implementation. The pruning technique is based on defining two thresholds regarding the minimum and maximum length an pseudoknot may have regarding the size of the whole RNA sequence. These two thresholds will be notated as *minimum_percentage* and *maximum_percentage*. Based on these two thresholds the number of substrings examined during the sliding-windows technique may dramatically be decreased.

It is implied from the analysis and Figs. 2 and 3 that there is room for improvement regarding the required time for the identification and description of the pseudoknot. Leveraging two heuristic thresholds (aka. features) suffice to improve the time by 33% at grammar based methodology and 43% at brute-force based methodology without trading accuracy. This finding was unveiled by observing the benchmark training set's statistical indicators, i.e. probability density, dispersion of a random variable, and mean value. This initial analysis highlights that hidden feature correlation could further improve the algorithm's performance. A dataset [39] of 262 RNA sequences was used in order to estimate the values of *minimum_percentage* and *maximum_percentage* thresholds. In Fig. 2 the percentage of pseudoknot length in RNA sequence (pseudoknot length/RNA sequence length) for all 262 RNA sequences is presented. As shown in this Figure, for all 262 RNA sequences the length of pseudoknot is limited

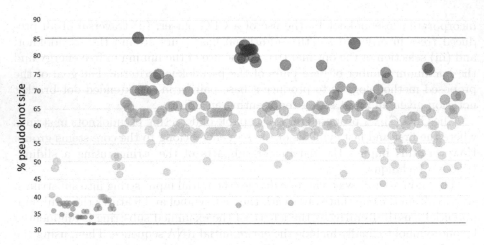

Fig. 2. Percentage of pseudoknot length in whole RNA sequence

between 32% and 85% of the length of the whole RNA sequence. One may come to the same conclusion observing the deviation of percentage of pseudo-knot length in RNA sequence for the same dataset in Fig. 3, where obviously there is no RNA sequence that has *minimum_percentage* smaller that 32% and *maximum_percentage* grater that 85%.

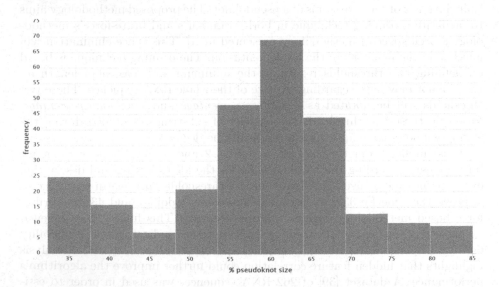

Fig. 3. Deviation of percentage of pseudoknot length in RNA sequence.

We argue that the modifications that have been observed can be mitigated directly through widely adopted AI methodologies. In particular, a) extracting new features and b) dynamically updating boundaries can be approximated with unsupervised distributed deep learning techniques. This observation can lead to structural changes in how we deal with pseudoknot algorithms for RNA. The DDL-friendly revision of the algorithm(s) will provide new artefacts on how we can deal the context-free grammar (CFG). At the same time, it will allow us to include extra functions and controls that previously were considered deterrents due to complexity limitations. The plethora of sub-cases forced us to re-implement/re-shape the brute-force (type) algorithm/s to deteriorate the search space that keeps growing exponentially to the length of the RNA sequence. To conclude, we envision the presented version (Knotify) to be the core platform where we would add processes, dictionaries and rules. These processes will snap onto the algorithm's platform by following whatever AI technique the researcher thinks is optimal. We argue that by extending and leveraging the features and functionalities that Knotify algorithm is offering, we will surpass the brute-force algorithm and apply it to extra/special cases with minimum changes.

5   Performance Evaluation

The same dataset [39] of 262 RNA sequences was used to evaluate our methodology's performance against other methodologies. It is composed of well-known RNA sequences; thus, it should be considered a perfect fit to compare our methodology against other highly respected implementations proposed in the literature, i.e., Hotknots, Iterative HFold (IHFold), IPknot, and Knotty [6,10,40,41].

Table 1. Execution time (secs) required per platform in entire dataset.

Platform	Average time	Total time
IHFold	0.030	8.096
Hotknots	0.169	44.432
IPknot	0.447	117.246
Knotty	1.004	263.303
Knotify_yaep	0.327	85.756
Knotify_bruteforce	0.129	33.894
Knotify_yaep_pruned	0.218	57.202
Knotify_bruteforce_pruned	0.073	19.377

As mentioned above, the limitation imposed to the sliding-window technique by the use of the *minimum_percentage* and *maximum_percentage* thresholds does not affect the accuracy. The proposed methodology succeed in predicting the core stems of any RNA pseudoknot of test dataset by performing a 76.4% recall ratio and it achieves an F1-score equal to 0.774 and MCC equal 0.437 which is

Table 2. Precision, Recall, F1-score, and MCC per platform in entire dataset.

Platform	tp	tn	fp	fn	Precision	Recall	F1-score	MCC
IHFold	3056	3556	1968	2196	0.608	0.582	0.595	0.226
Hotknots	4180	3632	1744	1220	0.706	0.774	0.738	0.452
IPknot	3872	3767	1522	1615	0.718	0.706	0.712	0.418
Knotty	5026	3352	1870	528	0.729	0.905	0.807	0.569
Knotify_yaep	4212	4102	1162	1300	0.784	0.764	0.774	0.543
Knotify_bruteforce	4214	4101	1160	1301	0.784	0.764	0.774	0.543
Knotify_yaep_pruned	4212	4102	1162	1300	0.784	0.764	0.774	0.543
Knotify_bruteforce_pruned	4214	4101	1160	1301	0.784	0.764	0.774	0.543

the initial accuracy of the methodology presented in [1], as shown in Table 2 as well. Consequently, the metric that was used in order to compare the proposed methodology with other platforms is that of execution time. In Table 1, the execution time required per platform to predict an existing pseudoknot in RNA sequences is provided. The third column of this table depicts the total execution time required by each platform to analyze all 262 RNA sequences, while the second column depicts the average execution time per RNA sequence. In this table the proposed methodologies are shown as Knotify_yaep_pruned and Knotify_bruteforce_pruned while methodologies presented in [1] are shown as Knotify_yaep and Knotify_bruteforce. Our methodology outperformed Knotty, which had worse results regarding the core stems prediction and the precision but better results regarding the F1-score and MCC. Knotify_bruteforce required 33.894 secs; Knotify_yaep required 85.756 secs; Knotify_bruteforce_pruned required 19.377 secs; Knotify_yaep_pruned required 57.202 secs; and Knotty required 263.303 secs. The proposed methodology knotify_yaep_pruned, achieved a speed up of 33% compared to the Knotify_yaep platform, while the methodology Knotify_bruteforce_pruned, achieved a speed up of 43% compared to the Knotify_bruteforce platform. Finally, IHFold recorded the lowest execution time; nonetheless, it had the poorest accuracy-evaluation profile as it is shown in [1]. The execution time required per platform is also shown in Fig. 4.

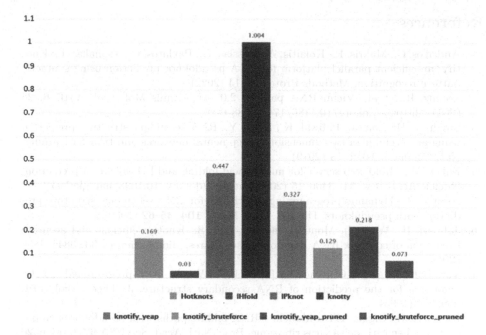

Fig. 4. Average execution time (sec) required per platform.

6   Conclusion

The prediction of RNA secondary structure is a useful tool for field experts to enhance their analysis toolkit and proceed to accurate results and innovative decision making in biology and medicine era. In that context, and considering the need of immediate requirements elicitation and decision making, as it arose from the thread of COVID-19 virus, the minimization of execution time, leveraging computation methods and search space optimization techniques, is of highly importance. To fulfill the above-mentioned crucial and imperative needs, we introduce a time-efficient, grammar-based algorithm and a brute-force one, which prune outlier parsing windows, based on data analysis. These optimized frameworks, eliminate trees in corner conditions, without any reduction in accuracy ratio. Specifically, compared to the initial implementation, we achieve an improvement in execution time by 33% in regards to the grammar-based methodology and by 43% in regards to the brute-force approach.

Acknowledgement. The research leading to the results presented in this article has received funding from the European Union's funded Project PolicyCLOUD under grant agreement No. 870675.

References

1. Andrikos, C., Makris, E., Kolaitis, A., Rassias, G., Pavlatos, C., Tsanakas, P.: Knotify: an efficient parallel platform for RNA pseudoknot prediction using syntactic pattern recognition. Methods Protoc. **5**, 14 (2022)
2. Lorenz, R., et al.: ViennaRNA package 2.0. Algorithms Mol. Biol. AMB **6**, 26 (2011). https://doi.org/10.1186/1748-7188-6-26
3. Singh, J., Hanson, J., Paliwal, K., Zhou, Y.: RNA secondary structure prediction using an ensemble of two-dimensional deep neural networks and transfer learning. Nat. Commun. **10**, 1–13 (2019)
4. Zuker, M.: Mfold web server for nucleic acid folding and hybridization prediction. Nucleic Acids Res. **31**, 3406–15 (2003). https://doi.org/10.1093/nar/gkg595
5. Akutsu, T.: Dynamic programming algorithms for RNA secondary structure prediction with pseudoknots. Discret. Appl. Math. **104**, 45–62 (2000)
6. Jabbari, H., Wark, I., Montemagno, C., Will, S.: Knotty: efficient and accurate prediction of complex RNA pseudoknot structures. Bioinformatics **34**, 3849–3856 (2018)
7. Van Batenburg, F., Gultyaev, A.P., Pleij, C.W.: An APL-programmed genetic algorithm for the prediction of RNA secondary structure. J. Theor. Biol. **174**, 269–280 (1995)
8. Isambert, H., Siggia, E.D.: Modeling RNA folding paths with pseudoknots: application to hepatitis delta virus ribozyme. Proc. Natl. Acad. Sci. USA **97**, 6515–6520 (2000)
9. Meyer, I.M., Miklos, I.: SimulFold: simultaneously inferring RNA structures including pseudoknots, alignments, and trees using a Bayesian MCMC framework. PLoS Comput. Biol. **3**, 149 (2007)
10. Sato, K., Kato, Y., Hamada, M., Akutsu, T., Asai, K.: IPknot: fast and accurate prediction of RNA secondary structures with pseudoknots using integer programming. Bioinformatics **27**, 85–93 (2011)
11. Bellaousov, S., Mathews, D.H.: ProbKnot: fast prediction of RNA secondary structure including pseudoknots. RNA **16**, 1870–80 (2010)
12. Knudsen, B., Hein, J.: RNA secondary structure prediction using stochastic context-free grammars and evolutionary history. Bioinformatics **15**, 446–454 (1999)
13. Knudsen, B., Hein, J.: Pfold: RNA secondary structure prediction using stochastic context-free grammars. Nucleic Acids Res. **31**, 3423–3428 (2003). https://doi.org/10.1093/nar/gkg614
14. Sukosd, Z., Knudsen, B., Vaerum, M., Kjems, J., Andersen, E.S.: Multithreaded comparative RNA secondary structure prediction using stochastic context-free grammars. BMC Bioinform. **12**, 103 (2011)
15. Pedersen, J.S., Meyer, I.M., Forsberg, R., Simmonds, P., Hein, J.: A comparative method for finding and folding RNA secondary structures within protein-coding regions. Nucleic Acids Res. **32**, 4925–4936 (2004)
16. Do, C.B., Woods, D.A., Batzoglou, S.: CONTRAfold: RNA secondary structure prediction without physics-based models. Bioinformatics **22**, e90–e98 (2006)
17. Pedersen, J.S., et al.: Identification and classification of conserved RNA secondary structures in the human genome. PLoS Comput. Biol. **2**, e33 (2006)
18. Nawrocki, E.P., Kolbe, D.L., Eddy, S.R.: Infernal 1.0: inference of RNA alignments. Bioinformatics **25**, 1335–1337 (2009)
19. Anderson, J.W.: Oxfold: kinetic folding of RNA using stochastic context-free grammars and evolutionary information. Bioinformatics **29**, 704–710 (2013)

20. Mao, K., Wang, J., Xiao, Y.: Prediction of RNA secondary structure with pseudoknots using coupled deep neural networks. Biophys. Rep. **6**(4), 146–154 (2020). https://doi.org/10.1007/s41048-020-00114-x
21. Wang, Y., et al.: ATTfold: RNA secondary structure prediction with pseudoknots based on attention mechanism. Front. Genet. **11**, 1564 (2020)
22. Wang, L., et al.: DMfold: a novel method to predict RNA secondary structure with pseudoknots based on deep learning and improved base pair maximization principle. Front. Genet. **10**, 143 (2019)
23. Kucharík, M., Hofacker, I.L., Stadler, P.F., Qin, J.: Pseudoknots in RNA folding landscapes. Bioinformatics **32**, 187–194 (2016)
24. Rietveld, K., Van Poelgeest, R., Pleij, C.W., Van Boom, J., Bosch, L.: The tRNA-Uke structure at the 3' terminus of turnip yellow mosaic virus RNA. Differences and similarities with canonical tRNA. Nucleic Acids Res. **10**, 1929–1946 (1982)
25. Staple, D.W., Butcher, S.E.: Pseudoknots: RNA structures with diverse functions. PLoS Biol. **3**, e213 (2005)
26. Watson, J., Crick, F.: Molecular structure of nucleic acids. Am. J. Psychiat. **160**, 623–624 (2003). https://doi.org/10.1176/appi.ajp.160.4.623
27. Hopcroft, J.E., Ullman, J.D.: Formal Languages and Their Relation to Automata. Addison-Wesley Longman Publishing Co., Inc., Boston (1969)
28. Chomsky, N.: Three models for the description of language. IRE Trans. Inf. Theory **2**, 113–124 (1956). https://doi.org/10.1109/TIT.1956.1056813
29. Sipser, M.: Introduction to the Theory of Computation, vol. 2. Thomson Course Technology, Boston (2006)
30. Younger, D.H.: Recognition and parsing of context-free languages in n^3. Inf. Control. **10**, 189–208 (1967)
31. Earley, J.: An efficient context-free parsing algorithm. Commun. ACM **13**, 94–102 (1970). https://doi.org/10.1145/362007.362035
32. Graham, S.L., Harrison, M.A., Ruzzo, W.L.: An improved context-free recognizer. ACM Trans. Program. Lang. Syst. **2**, 415–462 (1980)
33. Ruzzo, W.L.: General Context-Free Language Recognition. PhD Thesis, University of California, Berkeley, CA, USA (1978)
34. Geng, T., Xu, F., Mei, H., Meng, W., Chen, Z., Lai, C.: A practical GLR parser generator for software reverse engineering. JNW **9**(3), 769–776 (2014)
35. Pavlatos, C., Dimopoulos, A.C., Koulouris, A., Andronikos, T., Panagopoulos, I., Papakonstantinou, G.: Efficient reconfigurable embedded parsers. Comput. Lang. Syst. Struct. **35**, 196–215 (2009). https://doi.org/10.1016/j.cl.2007.08.001
36. Chiang, Y., Fu, K.: Parallel parsing algorithms and VLSI implementations for syntactic pattern recognition. IEEE Trans. Pattern Anal. Mach. Intell. **6**, 302–314 (1984)
37. https://github.com/vnmakarov/yaep , Accessed 25 Mar 2020
38. Aho, A.V., Lam, M.S., Sethi, R., Ullman, J.D.: Compilers: Principles, Techniques, and Tools, 2nd edn. Addison Wesley, London (2006)
39. https://bit.ly/dataset_pseudobase_knotify , Accessed 3 Jan 2022
40. Ren, J., Rastegari, B., Condon, A., Hoos, H.H.: HotKnots: heuristic prediction of RNA secondary structures including pseudoknots. RNA **11**, 1494–1504 (2005)
41. Jabbari, H., Condon, A.: A fast and robust iterative algorithm for prediction of RNA pseudoknotted secondary structures. MC Bioinform. **15**, 147 (2014)
42. Zuker, M.: Calculating nucleic acid secondary structure. Curr. Opin. Struct. Biol. **10**, 303–310 (2000)
43. Zuker, M.: Mfold web server for nucleic acid folding and hybridization prediction. Nucleic Acids Res. **31**, 3406–3415 (2003)

44. Nussinov, R., Jacobson, A.B.: Fast algorithm for predicting the secondary structure of single-stranded RNA. Proc. Natl. Acad. Sci. USA **77**, 6309–6313 (1980)
45. Cao, S., Chen, S.: Predicting structures and stabilities for H-type pseudoknots with interhelix loops. RNA (New York, N.Y.) **15**, 696–706 (2009). https://pubmed.ncbi.nlm.nih.gov/19237463

Deep Learning-Based Segmentation of the Atherosclerotic Carotid Plaque in Ultrasonic Images

Georgia D. Liapi[1] , Efthyvoulos Kyriacou[1(✉)] , Christos P. Loizou[1] ,
Andreas S. Panayides[2] , Constantinos S. Pattichis[2,3] ,
and Andrew N. Nicolaides[4]

[1] Department of Electrical Engineering, Computer Engineering and Informatics, Cyprus
University of Technology, 3036 Limassol, Cyprus
gd.liapi@edu.cut.ac.cy, efthyvoulos.kyriacou@cut.ac.cy
[2] Centre of Excellence, CYENS, Nicosia, Cyprus
[3] Department of Computer Science, University of Cyprus, Nicosia, Cyprus
[4] Vascular Screening and Diagnostic Center, Nicosia, Cyprus

Abstract. Early stroke risk stratification in individuals with carotid atherosclerosis is of great importance, especially in high-risk asymptomatic (AS) cases. In this study, we present a new computer-aided diagnostic (CAD) system for the automated segmentation of the atherosclerotic plaque in carotid ultrasound (US) images and the extraction of a refined set of ultrasonic features to robustly characterize plaques in carotid US images and videos (AS vs symptomatic (SY)). So far, we trained a UNet model (16 to 256 neurons in the contracting path; the reverse, for the expanding path), starting from a dataset of 201 (AS = 109 and SY = 92) carotid US videos of atherosclerotic plaques, from which their first frames were extracted to prepare three subsets, a training, an internal validation, and final evaluation set, with 150, 30 and 15 images, respectively. The automated segmentations were evaluated based on manual segmentations, performed by a vascular surgeon. To assess our model's capacity to segment plaques in previously unseen images, we calculated 4 evaluation metrics (mean ± std). The evaluation of the proposed model yielded a 0.736 ± 0.10 Dice similarity score (DSC), a 0.583 ± 0.12 intersection of union (IoU), a 0.728 ± 0.10 Cohen's Kappa coefficient (KI) and a 0.65 ± 0.19 Hausdorff distance. The proposed segmentation workflow will be further optimized and evaluated, using a larger dataset and more neurons in each UNet layer, as in the original model architecture. Our results are close to others published in relevant studies.

Keywords: Carotid ultrasound video · Atherosclerotic carotid plaques · Automated segmentation · Deep learning-based segmentation · Computer-aided diagnosis

© IFIP International Federation for Information Processing 2022
Published by Springer Nature Switzerland AG 2022
I. Maglogiannis et al. (Eds.): AIAI 2022 Workshops, IFIP AICT 652, pp. 187–198, 2022.
https://doi.org/10.1007/978-3-031-08341-9_16

1 Introduction

Carotid atherosclerosis, which may cause stroke [1] is a dangerous condition, with most studies assessing its risk of occurrence by detecting and analyzing developed plaques in carotid ultrasound (US) images. A recent meta-analysis study [2] estimated that, in 2020, approximately 28% of the global population, aged 30 to 79 years, would have abnormal carotid intima-media thickness (IMT), while 21% of the people would have carotid plaques detected. Multiple studies have associated presence, size and ultrasonic appearance of carotid arteries plaques with the risk of ischemic stroke [3–5], while 16% of all ischemic strokes occur due to carotid atherosclerosis [6]. Although carotid-IMT (c-IMT) has been a valuable marker of subclinical atherosclerosis [7], the focus is extended towards the automated detection and analysis of carotid atherosclerotic plaques and their association with future stroke events. In earlier studies, our group has identified carotid asymptomatic (AS) individuals at high risk [8] by analyzing US image features of plaques. Additionally, we had investigated how texture features of segmented plaques in carotid US videos vary among AS and symptomatic (SY) individuals, during the cardiac cycles [9].

In order to automate the process of localization and visualization of atherosclerotic plaques in carotid US images, a plethora of machine learning (ML) and deep learning (DL)-based studies have been presented, during the last 10 years, with convolutional neural networks (CNNs) frequently used to segment carotid plaques effectively, such as in [10, 11] and [12]. Lately, DL models, either trained from scratch or used under transfer learning (TL), have been widely used to classify atherosclerotic plaques in carotid US images and videos, into AS or SY [13–15]. Aside from DL-based carotid US plaque image classification studies, there is notable research on plaque motion characteristics in the current imaging modality, as well as on whether these characteristics are related to stable or unstable plaques [16, 17].

In most of the above-mentioned studies, there were multiple attempts to create work-flows for the accurate detection and characterization of atherosclerotic plaques in US images, a process crucial for early stroke risk assessment. Even though research in this area has been extensive over the years, the addition of extra features for better stroke risk estimation, such as video analysis parameters, is still an open research area.

In this study, we present the first steps towards the development of a new computer aided design (CAD) system for stroke risk assessment based on the analysis of US carotid images and videos. The aim of the currently presented work is to establish DL-based segmentation of US carotid plaques (see also Fig. 1, A, B and C), which is going to be part of the overall CAD system. The system presented in Fig. 1 will perform carotid US plaque analysis to support experts in decision making and stroke risk stratification. This is going to be the evolution of systems presented by our group [8, 9, 13, 17] and will be based on video analysis, extraction of new additional features and DL-based methods. More specifically, the proposed system will include: (a) a data preprocessing module (see Fig. 1, A), (b) a UNet-based model to automatically segment plaques in carotid US images (see Fig. 1, B and C), (b) extraction of ultrasonic image textural, morphological and motion features from the segmented plaque regions (see Fig. 1, D), (c) image feature selection (see Fig. 1, E), and (d) classification of selected mixed features into AS or SY, using a pre-trained ResNet50 [18] with TL (see Fig. 1, F). The ResNe50 (under Tl) has demonstrated a promising capacity to classify AS and SY plaques in US images, based on previous work of our group [13].

The rest of the paper is organized as follows. In Sect. 2, our methodology and materials are described. Section 3 summarizes the results, which are discussed in Sect. 4.

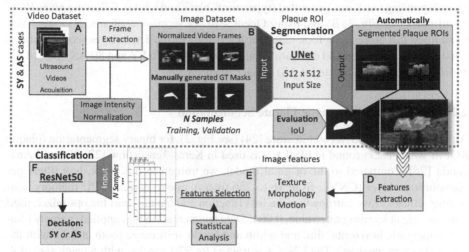

Fig. 1. General flow diagram illustrating the different modules in the CAD system proposed in this work for stroke risk stratification. **A**: Acquisition of carotid US B-mode videos, **B**: Video normalization and frame extraction, **C**: Automatic plaque ROI segmentation using a UNet and evaluation of the segmented area, **D**: Image-based textural, morphological and motion features extraction per segmented plaque ROI, **E**: Features selection based on statistical analysis, **F**: CNN-based image features classification to derive the plaque type. GT: Ground Truth, IoU: Intersection of Union; SY: Symptomatic, AS: Asymptomatic.

2 Materials and Methods

2.1 Video Dataset

A dataset of 201 carotid B-mode longitudinal US videos, from 196 subjects (123 males/73 females, AS = 108, SY = 88)), was used in this study. Five subjects had either 2 videos available or were presented with 2 plaques per video. The degree of stenosis in the subjects ranged between 50–95%. Overall, different carotid areas were included (Bifurcation, common carotid artery, external carotid artery, and internal carotid artery; both right and left sides). Plaque regions of interest (ROI) were manually selected on the first frame of each video, by an expert ultrasonographer, using a Matlab® [19]-based software created by our group. Each video was intensity-normalized, using the Video Despeckle Filtering (VDF) tool for carotid US video processing [20] (see also Fig. 1, A). Then, from each video the first frame was extracted (jpeg format, with the default OpenCv settings for the image quality), using OpenCv in Python [21–23] and resulting in a dataset of 201 different US images, with a total of 201 different plaque ROIs. Each of these images was cropped to include the plaque ROI at the image center, but also a part of the surrounding area (maximum number of included surrounding pixels was 70).

Then, black borders were added to all frames in order to reach 512 × 512 overall image size. The image input dimensions were set to 512 × 512, in order to accommodate plaque ROIs having width higher than 500 pixels (x-axis). For each of these new images, a corresponding mask was generated (type: uint8, black and white), following given ROIs coordinates (see Fig. 1, B) and using OpenCv to derive mask contours. It is important to mention that no resizing took place for the plaque ROIs. The images were separated into training, validation and evaluation subsets, with 156 (76 SY and 80 AS), 30 (14 SY and 16 AS) and 15 (6 SY and 9 AS) images, respectively.

2.2 Model for the Automatic Plaque Segmentation

An edited version of UNet architecture [24] (see Fig. 2), for binary segmentation (plaque ROI in white, background in black), was used in Keras-Tensorflow [22, 25], and Anaconda [26]. Compared to the original model, we trained in this work, less filters per convolutional layer (CNVL, from 16 to 256 filters), due to current GPU memory constraints. Binary cross-entropy was the loss function and 'Adam' was the optimizer, used with its default learning rate value, 0.001. Data augmentation was applied, namely rotation range (80), horizontal flip, and width and height shift range (both at 0.1), with the fill mode set to 'nearest'. The UNet was trained for 220 epochs, with a batch size of 4, an input size of 512 × 512 and an early-stopping callback of patience 30. We used a computer with an NVIDIA RTX 2060 GPU (6 GB), an i7 Intel Core processor and a 16 GB RAM. The best model version was saved when the validation loss had the lowest value.

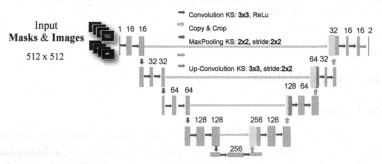

Fig. 2. The UNet architecture proposed in this work. The padding, in each convolutional layer, was set to 'same'. Kernel Size, KS.

2.3   Evaluation Metrics

In order to evaluate how similar the automatically segmented plaque ROIs were to their ground truth counterparts, we used the following evaluation metrics: 1. the Dice Similarity Coefficient (DSC), 2. the Intersection of Union (IoU), 3. the Cohen's Kappa Coefficient (KI) [27]. We also calculated the area under the receiver operating characteristic curve (AUC) and the directed Hausdorff distance (HD) [28] (see formula 4).

When evaluating model's capacity to segment, in order to obtain the segmented areas, the output of the model was thresholded (thresholding resulted probabilities), meaning that not all predictions were kept, as not all of them truly belonged to the given ROIs. To find the optimum probability threshold for the identification of the segmented ROIs, we performed predictions using all the training data, with 100 different threshold values (0.00 to 1.00) applied on the predictions and kept the threshold that yielded the highest DSC and IoU, as a guide. The metrics used to evaluate the automatic segmentations are:

$$DSC = \frac{2 * TP}{2 * TP + FN + FP} \tag{1}$$

$$IoU = \frac{TP}{TP + FP + FN} \tag{2}$$

$$KI = \frac{(2 * (TP * TN - FN * FP))}{((TP + FP) * (FP + TN) + (TP + FN) * (FN + TN))} \tag{3}$$

$$HD = \max_{a \in A} \left[\min_{b \in B} \{d(a, b)\} \right] \tag{4}$$

where TP are the true positives, TN are the true negatives, FN are the false negatives and FP are the false positives. In formula 4, a and b are points in the sets A and B, where A is the set of points forming a ground truth plaque ROI and B is the set of points of its predicted ROI counterpart, while d(a,b) is considered as the Euclidean distance between a and b.

3   Results

After training the model, 0.34 was the threshold that yielded the highest mean DSC and IoU values. In Fig. 3 the Interquartile Ranges (IQRs) for all our evaluation metrics for the 15 automatic plaque ROI segmentations are presented for the selected threshold. Also, the resulted AUC for all the examined probability thresholds on the evaluation images reached 0.80. Table 1 also shows the mean ± std values for all evaluation metrics. We reached a 0.736 ± 0.10 mean DSC, a 0.583 ± 0.12 mean IoU and a 0.728 ± 0.10 mean KI. Measurement of the Hausdorff distance showed an 8.18 ± 2.36 mean (normalized as 0.65 ± 0.19), suggesting that our segmentation methodology needs further refinement.

In Fig. 4, we present four out of the 15 cases of the automatically segmented plaque ROIs. We see that for the first two cases (see Fig. 4 A and B), there is an agreement (overlapping), higher than 70%, when comparing to the GT with the automatically segmented area, with the corresponding DSC values both being higher than 80%. In Fig. 4 B, we notice that the model falsely detects a small area (not part of the plaque), an overall segmentation that can be possibly refined with further optimization in the model's training process.

Table 1. Evaluation metrics of the proposed segmentation system based on four model performance metrics (N = 15).

Evaluation metrics	Average (±std)
DSC	0.736 ± 0.10
IoU	0.583 ± 0.12
KI	0.728 ± 0.10
HD	0.65 ± 0.19

DSC, Dice Similarity Coefficient; IoU, Intersection of Union; KI, Cohen's Kappa Coefficient; HD, Hausdorff Distance.

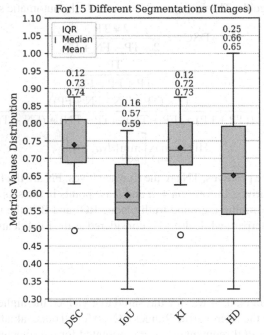

Fig. 3. Distribution of the segmentation performance evaluation metrics for all images (N = 15) investigated in this study. The ± IQR, the median and the mean values, per metric, are given at the top of each boxplot, while mean values are in red and median values are in dark blue. The HD values were normalized for visualization purposes. DSC: Dice similarity coefficient; HD, Hausdorff Distancce; IoU: Intersection of union; KI: Cohen's Kappa Coefficient. (Color figure online)

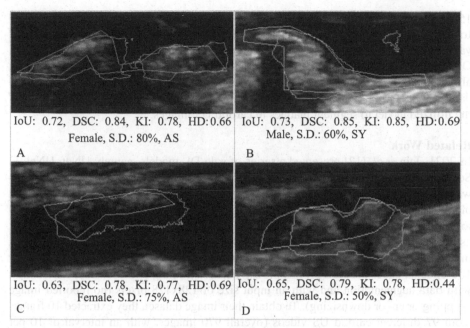

IoU: 0.72, DSC: 0.84, KI: 0.78, HD:0.66
Female, S.D.: 80%, AS
A

IoU: 0.73, DSC: 0.85, KI: 0.85, HD:0.69
Male, S.D.: 60%, SY
B

IoU: 0.63, DSC: 0.78, KI: 0.77, HD:0.69
Female, S.D.: 75%, AS
C

IoU: 0.65, DSC: 0.79, KI: 0.78, HD:0.44
Female, S.D.: 50%, SY
D

Fig. 4. Demonstration of the automatically segmented plaque versus the ground truth (GT) plaque ROIs in two different cases, AS and SY. The light-blue line is the GT plaque ROI, while the orange is the automatically segmented area, after thresholding. The DSC and the IoU values are given to depict the agreement of the GT with the automatically segmented areas, along with other patient information. For visualization purposes, the black borders were removed from each image. AS: Asymptomatic; DSC: Dice similarity coefficient; HD, Hausdorff Distancce; IoU: Intersection of union; KI: Cohen's Kappa Coefficient; S.D.: Stenosis Degree; SY: Symptomatic.

4 Discussion

Stroke risk stratification in individuals with atherosclerotic carotid plaques is of great importance, especially in cases considered as high risk, whether stenosis exists or there is a low risk. During the past ten years, there have been multiple attempts to identify valuable atherosclerotic plaque-derived features in carotid US images and videos in order to characterize the plaques based on DL methods. The two main processes, in which DL can facilitate stroke risk stratification in individuals with carotid atherosclerosis are: carotid plaque automatic segmentation and plaque classification. Studies have demonstrated the capacity of DL models to automatically segment plaque ROIs in US images or to classify plaques, in US images, into AS or SY.

In this study, we present the first step towards the development of a new CAD system for stroke risk stratification, using US carotid plaque images, along with the preliminary results we have obtained from automatic segmentation of atherosclerotic plaques in carotid US images, by training a UNet-based model. Our model is a UNet version that hosts fewer neurons per CNVL, compared to the original architecture. Initially, we applied image intensity normalization and prepared the image dataset such that no plaque ROI was resized; no plaque ROI content loss existed. With 220 epochs of training and

156 training samples, UNet segmented 15 previously unseen images, yielding DSC and IoU mean values at 0.736 ± 0.10 and 0.583 ± 0.12, respectively, with some of our DSC values being above 0.80, not very different from other relevant published results [10, 30]. Our IoU and HD resulting values suggest that our current approach needs improvement, although they might also be partially attributed to the level of image quality in our utilized dataset. Our current approach, although still premature, indeed depicts the capacity of the utilized model to segment plaques in carotid US images.

Related Work

In 2021, Jain *et al.* [12] presented a series of solo DL models, namely UNet, UNet +, SegNet, and hybrid DL models, namely SegNet-UNet and SegNet-UNet+. All models were trained with either DSC or binary cross-entropy loss to automatically segment plaques in carotid US images. They further quantified the segmented plaque ROIs (mm^2) to compare them with the GT ROIs. All models had the exact number of filters per CNVL as the standard UNet. The SegNet-UNet was their best-performing model, yielding a mean $\pm$ std IoU and DSC of 80.44 ± 1.59 88.98 ± 1.04, respectively, when trained for 100 epochs, under the K10 protocol (90% data for training and 10% data for testing), with data augmentation and with an input size of 128x128 pixels (no reported image cropping or up- or downsizing). To obtain their image dataset, they extracted 10 frames from 97 different carotid US videos (overall 970 images, with an interval of 10 per video). They have also stated that the 10 frames in each video were actually treated as different plaque ROI examples, although no metric for comparison of all GT ROIs per video was provided, in order to support their claim and despite their resulted IoU and DSC values from all their models. Also, no image intensity normalization was applied prior processing.

Zhou *et al.* [29], developed an automated plaque segmentation method, based on DL, in order to obtain the total plaque area automatically in carotid US images. They modified the original UNet architecture in terms of number of filters per CNVL, in a way similar to our UNet version, although they set 32 neurons in their first and last CNVL. They trained their model two times (two experiments, with GT masks from two different observers), for 500 epochs, using a dataset of 510 total images (2/3 used for training and 10% of the training data used for internal validation), with a batch size of 64 and used different input sizes among batches, as UNet can accept different input sizes, with the condition that the image size within each batch will be uniform. Where needed, they padded training examples to reach the mean required batch image size. They used data augmentations similar to those in our approach and they monitored the training process using the DSC loss. They used 1/3 of the primary data for testing. Their optimized model was finally trained on the whole first dataset and tested on another image US dataset. They reported a 0.05 ± 7.13 mm^2 and a 0.8 ± 8.7 mm^2 mean $\pm$ std TPA difference, when comparing each UNet with the manual segmentations. No image intensity normalization was reported.

In 2020, under a semantic segmentation approach, Xie *et al.* [30], introduced a method for plaque and vessel automatic segmentation in carotid US images based on UNet. They developed two types of UNet-based models, a two-stage model, where first a UNet architecture segments the lumen in carotid US images and its output is the input of a second UNet, which segments the plaque, and a dual-decoder, where instead of one main decoder unit in the UNet, they set a pair of decoders, one for the lumen ROIs and one for the plaque ROIs. In the two above-mentioned models, both the plaque and lumen areas were segmented on the same output image. They trained the models for 20 epochs, with carotid US images, cropped to remove specifications surrounding the US area and resized to 224 × 224 pixel size. They applied 10-fold cross validation and had a batch size of 4. Their images were not intensity-normalized. Their highest reported DSC was 0.69 for the dual-decoder model.

Finally, Meshram *et al.* [10] developed a fully- and a semi-automatic approach for plaque segmentation in carotid US images. They compared a standard UNet with a dilated UNet, hosting dilated CNVLs in its bottleneck. They overall performed 4 experiments. In their UNet models, they also started and ended with 32 filters in the CNVLs. Their semi-automatic approach allowed a sonographer to provide a bounding box as a guide to focus on plaque ROI, followed by an exterior 12.5% buffer added around the given box, on all sides, such that each input image had 75% plaque and 25% background included. They used 862 carotid US images, separated into 90% for training (from which 5% were used for internal validation) and 10% for testing and resampled to 512 × 512 pixels for the automatic approaches, while in the semi-automatic experiments, plaque ROI bounding boxes were resampled to 256 × 256 pixels. They reached a DSC of 0.84, when comparing semi-automatic plaque segmentations from the dilated UNet to their ground truth counterparts.

Compared to all studies described above, it is clear that our model's plaque segmentation performance was highly dependent on the size of the utilized dataset and the number of neurons trained per UNet CNVL, as well as on the batch size our hardware can currently support. For these reasons, at the moment, our model's full potential to segment plaque ROIs in carotid US images is not fully examined. Also, there is a possibility that in some images, the carotid anatomy is more complex than in others, which, accompanied also by speckle noise, might hinder model's ability to generate segmented areas with clear and smooth borders.

As in all DL-based classification tasks, preparation of the image dataset is of great importance, our primary focus in this study was to avoid content loss or resampling in the carotid US images we used as input to our UNet model. In contrast, in [12, 30] and [10], plaque ROIs were resized. More reliably, in [29], cropping and padding was applied in the input images, only where needed. Secondary, the preparation of our image dataset, where not all of the plaque ROI surrounding was included is similar to the data preparation approach in [29], in order to acquire the desirable input size, and to that in [10], regarding the area covered by the plaque in each image's carotid content.

As shown from the above-explained studies, it is still not clear if plaque automatic segmentation in carotid US images is improved when the input includes mainly the plaque ROI (with some carotid surrounding included) and when no intervention in the content occurs (resampling).

In our future steps, we will repeat the current segmentation experiment using carotid US whole images, the portable graphics format (png) for lossless data compression and a 5-fold cross validation workflow. We will have a larger dataset and a GPU of higher capacity, in order to optimize more parameters simultaneously, with a larger batch size. We will also extract segmentation metrics from a larger evaluation dataset, and we will investigate if speckle removal facilitates UNet-based automatic carotid plaque segmentation in US images. Finally, different comparison metrics between the automatically segmented and the GT total plaque areas will be included.

By following the above-described steps, we expect to have a robust UNet-based segmentation model that will be the heart of our developing CAD program, which will be used by experts for automated plaque characterization in carotid US images and videos, in clinical routine.

5   Limitations

Our current preliminary results for the automated plaque segmentation in carotid US images is accompanied by some limitations. Regarding the preparation of the dataset, the image intensity normalization (normalization applied on the video level), required a considerable amount of time and user interaction. Additionally, we had to prepare an automated workflow to acquire an appropriate dataset of a uniform size from plaques with quite different area sizes. For the training process of the segmentation model, we could obtain improved segmentation results by following the exact UNet architecture. It should be however noted that our current hardware is not designed for such an experiment, yet. In the automatically segmented plaque ROIs, after the thresholding process, the borders were noisy. This possibly implies that speckle noise or primary video quality play a role, both of which should be further investigated.

Funding – Acknowledgements. This study is funded by the project 'Atherorisk' "Identification of unstable carotid plaques associated with symptoms using ultrasonic image analysis and plaque motion analysis", code: Excellence/0421/0292, funded by the Research and In-novation Foundation, the Republic of Cyprus.

References

1. Flaherty, M.L., Kissela, B., Khoury, J.C., Alwell, K., et al.: Carotid artery stenosis as a cause of stroke. Neuroepidemiology **40**(1), 36–41 (2013)
2. Song, P., Fang, Z., Wang, H., Cai, Y., et al.: Global and regional prevalence, burden, and risk factors for carotid atherosclerosis: a systematic review, meta-analysis, and modelling study. Lancet Glob. Health **8**(2), 721–729 (2020)
3. Hollander, M., Bots M.L, Iglesias del Sol A., Koudstaal P.J et al.: Carotid plaques increase the risk of stroke and subtypes of cerebral infarction in asymptomatic elderly: The Rotterdam Study. Circulation 105(24), 2872–2877 (2002)
4. Paraskevas, K.I., Nicolaides, A.N., Kakkos, S.K.: Asymptomatic Carotid Stenosis and Risk of Stroke (ACSRS) study: what have we learned from it? Annals Translational Med. **8**(19), 1271 (2020)
5. Howard, D.P.J., Gaziano, L., Rothwell, P.M.: Risk of stroke in relation to degree of asymptomatic carotid stenosis: a population-based cohort study, systematic review, and meta-analysis. Lancet Neurol. **20**(3), 193–202 (2021)
6. Petty, G.W., Brown, R.D., Whisnant, J.P., Sicks, J.D., et al.: Ischemic stroke subtypes: a population-based study of incidence and risk factors. Stroke **30**(12), 2513–2516 (1999)

7. Stein, J.H., Korcarz, C.E., Hurst, R.T., Lonnet, E., et al.: Use of carotid ultrasound to identify subclinical vascular disease and evaluate cardiovascular disease risk: a consensus statement from the American Society of Echocardiography carotid intima-media thickness task force endorsed by the Society for Vascular Medicine. J. Am. Soc. Echocardiogr. **21**(2), 93–111 (2008)
8. Kyriacou, E.C., Petroudi, S., Pattichis, C.S., Pattichis, M.S., et al.: Prediction of high-risk asymptomatic carotid plaques based on ultrasonic image features. IEEE Trans. Inform. Technol. Biomed. **16**(5), 966–973 (2012)
9. Loizou, C.P., Pattichis, C.S., Pantziaris, M., Kyriacou, E.C., Nicolaides, A.: Texture feature variability in ultrasound video of the atherosclerotic carotid plaque. IEEE J. Transl. Eng. Health Med. **5**, 1–9 (2017)
10. Meshram, N.H., Mitchell, C.C., Wilbrand, S., Dempsey, R.J., Varghese, R.J.: Deep learning for carotid plaque segmentation using a dilated U-Net architecture. Ultrason. Imaging **42**(4–5), 221–230 (2020)
11. Del Mar Vila, M., Remeseiro, B., Grau, M., Elosua, R., et al.: Semantic segmentation with DenseNets for carotid artery ultrasound plaque segmentation and CIMT estimation. Artif. Intell. Med. **103**, 101784 (2020)
12. Jain, P.K., Sharma, N., Giannopoulos, A.A., Saba, L., et al.: Hybrid deep learning segmentation models for atherosclerotic plaque in internal carotid artery B-mode ultrasound. Comput. Biol. Med. **136**, 104721 (2021)
13. Panayides, A., Kyriacou, E.C., Nicolaides, A., Pattichis, C.S.: Stroke risk stratification using transfer learning. In: 41st Engineering in Medicine and Biology Conference (EMBC), Berlin, Germany (2019)
14. Guang, Y., He, W., Ning, B., Zhang, H., et al.: Deep learning-based carotid plaque vulnerability classification with multicentre contrast-enhanced ultrasound video: a comparative diagnostic study. BMJ Open **11**(8), 047528 (2021)
15. Sanagala, S.S., Nicolaides, A., Gupta, S.K., Koppula, V.K., et al.: Ten fast transfer learning models for carotid ultrasound plaque tissue characterization in augmentation framework embedded with heatmaps for stroke risk stratification. Diagnostics **11**(11), 2109 (2021)
16. Golemati, S., Patelaki, E., Gastounioti, A., Andreadis, I., et al.: Motion synchronisation patterns of the carotid atheromatous plaque from B-mode ultrasound. Sci. Rep. **10**(1), 11221 (2020)
17. Giannopoulos, A.A., Kyriacou, E., Griffin, M., Pattichis, C.S., et al.: Dynamic carotid plaque imaging using ultrasonography. J. Vasc. Surg. **73**(5), 1630–1638 (2021)
18. He, K., Zhang, X., Ren, S., Sun, J.: Deep residual learning for image recognition. arXiv:1512.03385 [cs] (2015)
19. MATLAB and Statistics Toolbox Release 2012b, The MathWorks, Inc., Natick, Massachusetts, United States (2012)
20. Loizou, C.P., Kasparis, T., Christodoulides, P., Theofanous, C., et al.: Despeckle filtering toolbox for medical ultrasound video. Int. J. Monitoring Surveillance Technol. Res. **1**(4), 61–79 (2013)
21. Bradski, G., Kaehler, A.: Learning OpenCV: Computer vision with the OpenCV library. Reilly Media, Inc. (2008)
22. Abadi, M., Agarwal, A., Barham, P., Brevdo, E., et al.: TensorFlow: large-scale machine learning on heterogeneous systems, Software available from tensorflow.org. (2015)
23. Raybaut, P.: Spyder-documentation. Available online at: pythonhosted org. (2009)
24. Ronneberger O., Fischer P., Brox T. U-Net: Convolutional networks for biomedical image segmentation. arXiv:1505.04597 [cs] (2015)
25. Chollet, F., et al.: Keras. Available at: https://github.com/fchollet/keras. (2015)
26. Anaconda Software Distribution. Computer software Version 2–2.4.0. Anaconda (2016)

27. Cohen, J.: A coefficient of agreement for nominal scales. Educ. Psychol. Measur. **20**(1), 37–46 (1960)
28. Taha, A.A., Hanbury, A.: An efficient algorithm for calculating the exact Hausdorff distance. IEEE Trans. Pattern Anal. Mach. Intell. **37**, 2153–2163 (2015)
29. Zhou, R., Azarpazhooh, M.R., Spence, J.D., Hashemi, S., et al.: Deep learning-based carotid plaque segmentation from B-Mode ultrasound images. Ultrasound Med. Biol. **47**(9), 2723–2733 (2021)
30. Xie, M., Li, Y., Xue, Y., Huntress, L., et al.: Two-stage and dual-decoder convolutional U-Net ensembles for reliable vessel and plaque segmentation in carotid ultrasound images. In: 19th IEEE International Conference on Machine Learning and Applications (ICMLA), pp. 1376–1381, Miami, FL, USA (2020)

On the Reusability of ISIC Data for Training DL Classifiers Applied on Clinical Skin Images

Konstantinos Moutselos[✉] [iD] and Ilias Maglogiannis[iD]

Department of Digital Systems, University of Piraeus, Athens, Greece
{kmouts,imaglo}@unipi.gr

Abstract. The ISIC archive is an open dermoscopy dataset containing thousands of images so that new Deep Learning skin classifiers can be trained. ISIC Challenges attract many participants to build a model that will bring the best performance to the ISIC test dataset. The question is whether such a model has consistent behavior in different datasets and other clinical images. In this work, we build and study the performance of a classifier trained in the ISIC 2019 dataset in three different cases: the performance during the cross-validation training process, the performance in the separate ISIC 2019 test dataset, and dermoscopy images taken from the SYGGROS skin disease hospital. The results show a stable performance compared to the metric F1 score for the categories in which there are more than 3000 images in the training dataset. In addition, we identify the factors that make it difficult to transfer and use classifiers from a competitive to a clinical setting.

Keywords: ISIC · Skin lesions · Deep learning classifiers

1 Introduction

Cutaneous melanoma is one of the most aggressive forms of cancer and in 2021 cases are expected to increase by about 5%, with a corresponding increase in mortality due to this disease [1]. Early diagnosis plays an important role in the progression of the disease. If diagnosed early, the 5-year survival rate for melanoma is 99% [1] while the normal statistic in the United States is 91.6% [2]. Therefore, great effort has been made to develop smart computing tools that use dermatoscopic images and can assist clinicians in their diagnosis [3]. The ever-better results of skincare diagnostic applications increase the acceptance of their use by the medical community and encourage dermatologists to provide more anonymous clinical data that further helps to develop better supporting applications. In this direction, the International Skin Imaging Collaboration (ISIC) has developed the ISIC Archive [4], an international repository of dermoscopic images. ISIC supports research toward automated algorithmic analysis by hosting the ISIC Challenges. The annual ISIC competitions [5], providing a common data set as a starting point, encourage competition in computing technologies to achieve better-performing algorithms in the classification of a skin lesion. In the context of these competitions, there is an opportunity to develop and test new techniques and architectures of deep learning that in recent years have recorded impressive results.

© IFIP International Federation for Information Processing 2022
Published by Springer Nature Switzerland AG 2022
I. Maglogiannis et al. (Eds.): AIAI 2022 Workshops, IFIP AICT 652, pp. 199–212, 2022.
https://doi.org/10.1007/978-3-031-08341-9_17

An important question, however, is whether a prognostic model trained in these competitions can respond similarly and consistently to new clinical data, obtained with different technical equipment and under different clinical conditions. To this question, there is a scarcity of publications that study the effectiveness of models trained in a specific dataset, upon different clinical data.

Valle et al. [6] conducted a thorough multifactorial analysis having as a starting point the ISIC2017 Challenge which involved considerably smaller image datasets (compared to ISIC2019) and three classes of skin lesions. They reported that the correlation of the results of ensembles on different datasets was far from perfect. E.g., the Spearman correlation between the ISIC2017/test and EDRA/dermo [7] datasets was .65 on melanoma AUC. As was reported, this was another example of the pitfalls of hyper-optimizing on specific datasets. To deal with vulnerabilities of hyper-optimizing and assess models on their generalization capabilities Maron et al. [8] proposed recently a benchmark skin dataset with unknown ground-truth labels, where the evaluation is provided by the authors themselves.

Nahata et al. [9] combined data from ISIC 2018 & 2019 to create a larger dataset, where the evaluation of the tested models, however, is done in the same dataset. This - as discussed in Discussion - carries an even greater risk of over-optimistic reports. In a different perspective, Lucius et al. [3] use a random split of the HAM10000 dataset [10] via the ISIC archive to train and evaluate the performance of eight different DL architectures with low/high image resolution modes and with/without clinical meta-data. The split is reported that resulted in completely disjoint train/test datasets. However, no action is described against the class imbalances of the initial dataset, and the two outcomes after the split. Moreover, most of the results are evaluated using the metric accuracy (and the complement: error rate) which, contestably, the authors report as measures suitable to evaluate performance on imbalanced datasets. Next, they compare the least performant classifier against the accuracy of diagnoses from non-dermatologist general practitioners and assess the use of the same classifier as a decision support tool for the physicians.

As an example of high performant classifiers over reduced confounding factors, Zhu et al. [11] study the performance of an enhanced DL skin-disease model in a clinical environment using, however, a controlled clinical dataset as well. Their images -spanning 14 skin conditions - are collected in the same Department, by the same technician, using the same dermoscopy system. Furthermore, all the patients were having the same skin type. Regarding the skin type, however, we should note that the HAM10000 dataset [10] and ISIC itself are also biased, consisting of samples from fair-skinned Caucasian population.

In this work, we use the data of the ISIC 2019 competition [12] which consists of about 25 thousand dermoscopy images, for the training of a DL classifier, without the use of other metadata. Next, we compare the effectiveness of the classifier in three cases: during the cross-validation training process, the result in the comparative test dataset of ISIC 2019 consisting of about 8 thousand images with unknown ground-truth labels and class distribution, and the performance in a new clinical dataset (SYGGROS) consisting of only 311 images. We chose the ISIC 2019 dataset due to the number of freely available images that include 8 categories of skin diseases, as well as the external evaluation and comparison procedures of the models that the 2019 ISIC challenge includes. A requirement for the participants is the submission of a report describing the construction of the submitted model. In the Discussion section, we compare our results with the best model of the competition that was trained in the same ISIC 2019 dataset.

Regarding the structure of the paper, after the Introduction follows the Materials & Methods where we describe the datasets of the work, the DL Architecture together with the methods of image pre-processing. Follows the reporting of the selected DL parameters as well as the performance metrics used. In the Results, the classifier is evaluated in the Cross-Validation training procedure, in the ISIC 2019 Test Dataset, and the new SYGGROS Dataset. Following is the Discussion where the results are compared, and last the Conclusions of the work.

2 Materials and Methods

Figure 1 shows the workflow for the comparison of the performance of a DL Classifier trained with the ISIC 2019 Training Dataset. On the left side of the figure with the thickest arrow, the training process of the model is represented. The other two arrows represent the prediction process of the trained model, for the SYGGROS and the ISIC 2019 Test Dataset. All three datasets contribute to an independent assessment of the classifier's performance in the 8 classes of skin conditions.

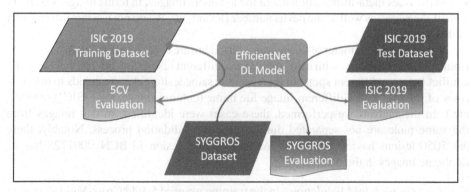

Fig. 1. Workflow for the comparison of the DL Model performance.

The dataflows of Fig. 1 represented by the arrows from their beginning up to the DL Model include the loading and preprocessing procedure of the images. Due to the TF2 efficient tf.data [13] pipeline, the data is consumed and processed in parallel which reduces the execution time of each training step. The 'online' image augmentation process is also handled inside the pipeline during the training stage.

The preprocessing and augmentation steps as well as the features of the DL architecture are described below. But first follows the description of the three image datasets along with their special features, on which the image pipeline applies.

2.1 Skin Datasets

ISIC 2019 Training Dataset. The ISIC 2019 dataset [10, 14, 15] consists of 25,331 dermoscopy images divided into 8 classes: Melanoma (MEL), Melanocytic nevus (NV), Basal cell carcinoma (BCC), Actinic keratosis (AK), Benign keratosis (solar lentigo/seborrheic keratosis/lichen planus-like keratosis) (BKL), Dermatofibroma (DF), Vascular lesion (VASC), Squamous cell carcinoma (SCC). The distribution of classes is given in Table 1.

Table 1. Class distribution in the ISIC 2019 training dataset

AK 867	BCC 3323
BKL 2624	DF 239
MEL 4522	NV 12875
SCC 628	VASC 253

The ISIC 2019 training dataset show great variation in terms of dimensions, the presence or not of the circle from the dermatoscope, the coloring, as well as additional objects (hairs, rulers, markings). Also, the dataset is accompanied by a metadata file, which provides meta-information about the available images, in terms of age, sex, body area of the nevus, as well as the nevus number (lesion_id). We do not use this information in this work.

An important parameter of the dataset is that there are cases where many images come from the same spot (e.g., with a different angle, different resolution, etc.) or there is an ID conflict between different spots. In this case, the same lesion_id corresponds to multiple rows of the file, with a different image file name (column Image, e.g., ISIC_0000002, etc.). In the analysis we performed, these cases were identified, so that images from the same mole are not separated during the cross-validation process. Notably, there are 5050 lesions having duplicates. As an example, lesion_id BCN_0001728 has 31 duplicate images in the dataset.

Stratified Group k-fold Validation. In the training we used 5-fold Cross-Validation with stratification of classes, so that all 5 folds contain -as much as possible- the same ratio of categories with skin diseases. As mentioned earlier, additional logic has been added so that multiple images of the same ID always belong to the same fold [16].

ISIC 2019 Test Dataset. The evaluation of the classifier in the ISIC 2019 challenge is done with the test dataset which consists of 8,238 images with an unknown distribution of classes. In addition to the 8 classes of the training dataset, images of moles belonging to other categories are also included (Unknown - UNK). The predicted image classes are submitted to the ISIC 2019 challenge server and the classifier is evaluated with the metric BAC: normalized multi-class accuracy metric (balanced across categories), and statistics are generated with ROC curves and other performance metrics.

SYGGROS Dataset. The dataset of dermatoscopic images used for the evaluation of the DL skin classifier is provided by Andreas SYGGROS Hospital and includes 311 dermatoscopic photographs with the corresponding labeling by dermatologists of the hospital. For automated classification, the images have been divided into 8 classes, as follows (Table 2). Regarding the technical description of the dataset, the digital dermatoscopy in the Oncology Department of Andreas SYGGROS Hospital was performed with the Digital Epiluminescence Microscopy system (MoleMaxHD 1.6) until 2017. From the beginning of 2018, the clinical and dermatological images of the suspected pigmented lesions are obtained with the digital imaging system FotoFinder Medicam 1000. The technical characteristics of the Medicam 1000 camera are: Full HD brilliance (CrystalView technology), continuous visual live-zoom with autofocus, suitable for dermatoscopy of skin, scalp and nail lesions, magnification up to 140X, control via a panel on the back of the camera.

Table 2. Class distribution in the SYGGROS dataset

AK 8	BCC 37
BKL 23	DF 1
MEL 33	NV 193
SCC 9	VASC 7

Additionally, a small number of shots have been taken with a special Nikon D300 dermatoscopic camera. Images from both systems are utilized within the project. All the dermatoscopic images are related to the histological features as they result from the biopsies of the patients that have been performed at Andreas SYGGROS Hospital and have been processed and evaluated by the Pathology/Anatomic Department.

2.2 DL Architecture

EfficientNets [17] were used as the basic Deep Learning architecture in our study. EfficientNets achieve top performances while utilizing lighter structures that reduce the complexity of the model. They also greatly facilitate the selection of hyperparameters, as the initial tests can be done in the B0 model, and then, depending on the availability of the GPU hardware, the B1-B7 models can be selected. As the code number of the model increases, so does the depth of the hidden levels, but also the resolution of the images as input. Their effectiveness on the ISIC challenge has been showcased by top performant submissions [18–20].

2.3 Image Preprocessing Functions

Image preprocessing is a fundamental step before the training and prediction stage of a classifier, and various techniques have been proposed in the literature [21] towards this scope. In this work, a set of pre-processing techniques frequently found in the ISIC challenges are applied. Image preprocessing functions include:

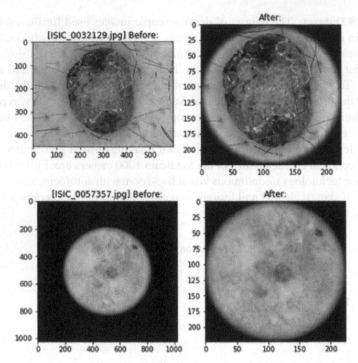

Fig. 2. Application of dermoscopy circle, nice crop and color constancy.

- Resizing and cropping, where we change the smallest dimension of the image to reach the desired size, while maintaining the ratio, and a cut is made to obtain a square table.
- Nice crop. Dermoscopy images from ISIC 2019 may contain the characteristic dermoscope cycle with numerous variations. This technique is applied so that the circle is exactly cut off, removing unnecessary black areas around the perimeter.
- Random erasing. This technique [22] randomly erases a small area of the image, to reduce overfitting in the classifier.
- Color constancy. This technique [23] is based on normalizing the color of dermoscopic images [24] and attempts to remove differences in images resulting from changes in lighting and cameras.
- Dermoscopy cycle. This technique adds the dermoscope circle to all images so that there is no variability in the images regarding this parameter. The technique, if applied during the model training, should also be applied to the images that are then inserted to predict the class. In Fig. 2 in the 1st column 2 images are displayed in their original form, while in the 2nd column the result after the application of nice_cropping, color constancy and dermoscopy circle. The result is square images of the same resolution ready for input for the training of the model. The application of this technique has the additional advantage that it removes the distortion of angles due to random rotations of the image.

2.4 Selected DL Parameters

All training images are converted to resolution 400×400 and caching is applied to make the process of importing the training fold faster in each epoch. The final resolution with which the training is done is 300×300 as the augmentation random cropping technique is applied as well. The parameter "DROP_CONNECT_RATE" corresponds to the drop-out during the construction of the layers and was set to 0.4, which is also a method to fight overfitting.

BATCH_SIZE is set to 16 images. This variable depends on the selected resolution of the training images as well as the available GPU memory. The training of the model was carried out, in our case, with the use of an NVIDIA 2080 Ti GPU card. We chose $CV = 5$ to be the number of folds in the cross-validation. Finally, each model is trained, for a maximum of 40 epochs.

The EfficientNet B3 architecture is introduced in our code headless (without the last layers), but by carrying the weights of the trained model in the ImageNet images. The Transfer Learning technique is used [25, 26], and it is set that the weights of the headless model will not be frozen during the training. Next, we add to the sequential model the GlobalMaxPooling layer and a Dense layer with 9 neurons (which are our data classes). The Softmax activation function is selected. Rectified Adam [27] is chosen as the optimizer, with a lookahead option, after many trials for better performance. The categorical cross-entropy is set as the loss function.

Also, the callback early_stop was set during the training, so that if the validation loss metric does not improve for 8 seasons (patience duration), the training process will stop and the weights with which the best value of the metric was observed will be kept.

As previously described, during the CV process, the dataset is divided into training and validation sets. An example of the distribution of the classes in the two sets for one of the 5 folds (which contains in the training set 20.262 images, and in the validation set 5.069 images), is shown in Table 3.

To deal with the class imbalanced dataset, a weight is assigned to each class, which is the inverse of the probability of occurrence in the dataset. As an example, the weights for the 1st fold are MEL: 0.700, NV: 0.246, BCC: 0.953, AK: 3.655, BKL: 1.207, DF: 13.260, VASC: 12.538, SCC: 5.045.

Table 3. Class distribution for a training fold

	Training	Validation
AK	693	174
BKL	2099	525
MEL	3617	905
SCC	502	126
BCC	2658	665
DF	191	48
NV	10300	2575
VASC	202	51

2.5 Performance Metrics

The sklearn.metrics.classification_report function was used to calculate the classifier performance in the case of CV training in the ISIC 2019 training dataset, as well as in the SYGGROS dataset [28]. The result tables report the metrics: precision, recall and f1-score for each class. If TP, FP, FN are the number of true positives, false positives, false negatives respectively, then:

- Precision = TP / (TP + FP)
- Recall = TP / (TP + FN)
- F1 = the weighted harmonic mean of the precision and recall

Average values are calculated in the following ways: micro, macro and weighted [29]. In the first way, the metrics are calculated by counting the total number of TP, FN, FP from all classes. In the second way, the metric is calculated for each class separately and thus the class imbalance is not considered. Finally, in the third way, the metric for each class is calculated but their participation in the average is weighted by the number of samples of each class.

3   Results

3.1   Classifier Evaluation by the CV Training Process

Table 4 shows the performance evaluation per class, and overall.

Table 4. CV classifiers performance

	Precision	Recall	f1-score	Support
MEL	0.69	0.59	0.64	4522
NV	0.86	0.90	0.88	12875
BCC	0.72	0.84	0.77	3323
AK	0.43	0.43	0.43	867
BKL	0.67	0.58	0.62	2624
DF	0.51	0.50	0.51	239
VASC	0.67	0.77	0.72	253
SCC	0.40	0.30	0.34	628
UNK	0.00	0.00	0.00	0.00
Micro avg	0.77	0.77	0.77	25331
Macro avg	0.55	0.55	0.55	25331
Weighted avg	0.76	0.77	0.76	25331

3.2   Classifier Performance in the ISIC 2019 Test Dataset

The performance of the model in the ISIC 2019 Test was Balanced Multiclass Accuracy (BAC): 0.524.

Figure 3 shows the table of metrics per class, as provided by the ISIC 2019 Challenge server [30].

	Category Metrics	Mean Value	Diagnosis Category								
			MEL	NV	BCC	AK	BKL	DF	VASC	SCC	UNK
Integral Metrics	AUC	0.891	0.915	0.947	0.934	0.899	0.874	0.967	0.918	0.916	0.649
	AUC, Sens > 80%	0.785	0.833	0.906	0.868	0.798	0.747	0.928	0.890	0.826	0.270
	Average Precision	0.525	0.747	0.906	0.698	0.330	0.482	0.453	0.512	0.283	0.314
Threshold Metrics	Accuracy	0.922	0.895	0.891	0.887	0.944	0.918	0.989	0.988	0.977	0.807
	Sensitivity	0.430	0.575	0.838	0.769	0.219	0.340	0.367	0.485	0.268	0.0120
	Specificity	0.969	0.960	0.917	0.904	0.983	0.973	0.997	0.995	0.992	0.996
	Dice Coefficient	0.461	0.648	0.833	0.639	0.285	0.419	0.452	0.521	0.329	0.0235
	PPV	0.567	0.744	0.829	0.547	0.408	0.547	0.589	0.563	0.429	0.447
	NPV	0.942	0.918	0.922	0.963	0.959	0.940	0.992	0.993	0.984	0.809

Fig. 3. Summary evaluation table in the ISIC 2019 test dataset

3.3   Classifier Performance in SYGGROS Dataset

The model that gave the best results from the 5-CV training at ISIC 2019 was then used to classify the SYGGROS images. Table 5 shows the classifier performance metrics in the SYGGROS Dataset.

Table 5. Classifier performance on the SYGGROS Dataset

	Precision	Recall	f1-score	Support
MEL	0.59	0.73	0.65	33
NV	0.91	0.75	0.82	193
BCC	0.73	0.65	0.69	37
AK	0.43	0.38	0.40	8
BKL	0.21	0.57	0.30	23
DF	0.00	0.00	0.00	1
VASC	0.75	0.43	0.55	7
SCC	1.00	0.22	0.36	9
UNK	0.00	0.00	0.00	0
Micro avg	0.68	0.68	0.68	311
Macro avg	0.51	0.41	0.42	311
Weighted avg	0.78	0.68	0.71	311

Compared to Table 4, in the F1-score column, we observe a correlation of the results, where the performances in the SYGGROS Dataset are slightly lower. In the analysis per class in the metric F1, we observe a performance deviation in the BKL and DF classes and a smaller one in VASC. The DF and VASC classes, however, have only 1 and 7 images in the SYGGROS Dataset respectively.

4   Discussion

In this work, we used a single architecture: EfficientNets, without ensemble models. The reason was to keep the complexity of the process relatively simple and focus on the transferability of the results by keeping a common baseline. Ensemble modeling is a common technique for increasing the classification performance and the scalability of EfficientNets makes them suitable candidates towards this end [31]. As was noted in [6], ensembles also alleviate the instability of performance across different datasets. In this work, we wanted to study the behavior of such instabilities and so we opted out from ensembles. A recent review on the types of DL architectures and cases with combinations of multiple techniques can be found in [32].

As previously reported, we study the performance of the model trained in the ISIC 2019 training dataset with the CV training process (F1 CV), the ISIC 2019 test (F1

ISIC) and the SYGGROS Dataset (F1 SYGGROS). Because both the ISIC 2019 training dataset and the SYGGROS dataset are severely class imbalanced, and the largest number of images are in the MEL, NV and BCC classes, Table 6 compares the performance in the metric F1 with only these three classes.

Table 6. Model performance comparison F1 metric

	CV	ISIC	SYGGROS	Best ISIC
MEL	0.64	0.64	0.65	0.68
NV	0.88	0.83	0.82	0.84
BCC	0.77	0.64	0.69	0.66

In addition, to be able to compare our model in the ISIC 2019 test dataset with the best performant model of the ISIC 2019 competition, for which the training was done without any additional external data [20], we include in the last column of Table 6 the results also on metric F1 (F1 Best ISIC).

Regarding the model with the best performance at ISIC 2019, its authors [20] report the largest improvement in the metric Normalized Multi-class Accuracy (BAC) from the 5-fold CV training process, using ensemble, by 0.014 points. The best performance in single architecture - se_resnext101 has a value of 0.739 (BAC) and very close is the performance of an efficientnet-B3. However, the authors also cite tests with ensembles that are inferior to the best single models. In the final ISIC 2019 test, they submitted three attempts, which had in the test results a difference of only 0.003 points from each other in the metric BAC, with the best value: 0.607.

From the first three columns of Table 6, we observe - for the metric F1 score - consistent performance of the model for the three categories that had the most dermoscopy images. The most stable behavior is in the melanoma category, while in the other two NV, BCC there is an overestimation in the CV process 6 and 9 mm of F1 respectively. For the other categories in which the available images (either in the ISIC 2019 dataset or in the SYGGROS dataset) are much smaller, the performances, as expected, show greater variations. We also observe an analogous performance, in these three categories (MEL, NV, BCC) with the performance in the ISIC 2019 Test dataset of the best performant model. The highest value F1 is achieved in class NV, while they are similar for MEL and BCC. The NV class is also the most numerous in the ISIC 2019 training dataset, having almost three times more images in this category compared to the immediately smaller MEL. We notice that although during the training of our model, weights were used - apart from online augmentation - to compensate for the class imbalance, still the most populous class gives the best results.

5   Conclusions

ISIC Challenges attract many participants and offer an environment where new techniques can be tested based on a common dataset for objective model comparison.

There are, however, many factors that make it difficult to generalize and use these models in a different/clinical setting. In a competitive environment, multiple techniques are used in combination to improve even a few millimeters of the final index, without considering the computational complexity and prediction time. In the ISIC 2019 competition, the submission of multiple attempts was allowed, so results from different models are submitted, in the hope that one of the attempts will succeed even slightly better in the unknown test dataset. This is like shooting in the dark.

Another factor that makes it difficult to directly compare the developed models is the specific conditions of each competition. In the ISIC 2019 challenge, while the training dataset had 8 categories, the test dataset contained -as previously mentioned in Methodology- an additional category - Unknown. Participants tried various ingenious methods for outlier detection, but the most common is to apply a threshold to the output of the classifier so that low-value predictions are assigned to the unknown class. This is the method used in the model of this work, as well as in the model that had the best estimate in the ISIC 2019 challenge (without the use of external data)) [20]. The use of this threshold, however, affects the performance metrics in the other 8 classes. In addition, as the distribution of the ISIC 2019 test dataset classes is unknown, it is no longer possible to compare models on equal terms. A classifier that performs best in a large class of the test dataset will perform better than another that is better in other classes with less representation in the test dataset.

However, apart from the characteristics of the terms of competition and the unknown distribution of classes in the test dataset, the peculiarities of the provided training dataset are also important. To ISIC 2019 training dataset is characterized by class imbalance and duplicate/ID conflict images as mentioned in the Methodology. Both characteristics affect the performance metrics we receive from the cross-validation process. Although the performance estimation with the CV method is considered robust, the fold construction process must consider the class distribution, as we saw in the Methodology, to be stratified. The existence of multiple images corresponding to the same mole (same ID), introduces another important consideration in the CV process. If not considered when creating the folds, it leads to an overly optimistic estimate of performance. A typical example is the paper [9], where the authors report a Normalized Multi-class Accuracy (BAC) and an F1 score of 0.91.

To summarize, even when there is a common set of dermoscopy images, factors such as the characteristics of the specific training dataset, the terms of the competition (e.g., the way of comparison/metric, the unknown class distribution in the test dataset, the existence of a requirement for outlier detection) add also complexity in comparing the performance of the models. In addition, such competition characteristics make it difficult to transfer these models to a clinical setting, either due to complexity or performance instability. In this work, we observed consistent performance of a classifier trained in the ISIC 2019 training dataset in three different and independent cases, for the skin categories in which there were over 3,000 images for each class. To avoid over-optimistic performance during the CV process, we paid special attention to dealing with class imbalance in the training dataset, and the existence of duplicate/ID collision cases.

Acknowledgments. We would like to thank Alexios Zarras MD and Professor Alexander J. Stratigos MD, at the Department of Dermatology-Venereology, University of Athens Medical

School, Andreas Sygros Hospital (Athens, Greece) for providing the SYGGROS Dataset used in this paper, as well as information on the technical specifications and collection procedures of the dataset.

Funding. This work was supported by the National Project TRANSITION – Translating the diagnostic complexity of melanoma into rational therapeutic stratification – Hellenic General Secretariat of Research and Technology, [T1EΔK-01385] co-funded by the European Union.

References

1. Skin Cancer Facts & Statistics, https://www.skincancer.org/skin-cancer-information/skin-can cer-facts. Accessed 08 Mar 2019
2. USCS Data Visualizations. https://gis.cdc.gov/Cancer/USCS/#/AtAGlance/. Accessed 09 Oct 2021
3. Lucius, M., et al.: Deep neural frameworks improve the accuracy of general practitioners in the classification of pigmented skin lesions. Diagnostics **10**, 969 (2020). https://doi.org/10. 3390/diagnostics10110969
4. ISIC Archive, https://www.isic-archive.com/#!/topWithHeader/tightContentTop/about/abo utIsicOverview. Accessed 08 Oct 2021
5. ISIC Challenge History, https://www.isic-archive.com/#!/topWithHeader/tightContentTop/about/isicChallengesHistory. Accessed 09 Oct 2021
6. Valle, E., et al.: Data, depth, and design: learning reliable models for skin lesion analysis. Neurocomputing **383**, 303–313 (2020). https://doi.org/10.1016/j.neucom.2019.12.003
7. Lio, P.A., Nghiem, P.: Interactive Atlas of Dermoscopy: Giuseppe Argenziano, H. Peter Soyer, Vincenzo De Giorgio, Domenico Piccolo, Paolo Carli, Mario Delfino, Angela Ferrari, Rainer Hofmann-Wellenhof, Daniela Massi, Giampiero Mazzocchetti, Massimiliano Scalvenzi, and Ingrid H. Wolfpages. J. Am. Acad. Dermatol. **50**, 807–808 (2004). https://doi.org/10.1016/j.jaad.2003.07.029.ISBN 88–86457–30–8
8. Maron, R.C., et al.: A benchmark for neural network robustness in skin cancer classification. Eur. J. Cancer. **155**, 191–199 (2021). https://doi.org/10.1016/j.ejca.2021.06.047
9. Nahata, H., Singh, S.P.: Deep learning solutions for skin cancer detection and diagnosis. In: Jain, V., Chatterjee, J.M. (eds.) Machine Learning with Health Care Perspective. LAIS, vol. 13, pp. 159–182. Springer, Cham (2020). https://doi.org/10.1007/978-3-030-40850-3_8
10. Tschandl, P., Rosendahl, C., Kittler, H.: The HAM10000 dataset, a large collection of multi-source dermatoscopic images of common pigmented skin lesions. Sci. Data. **5**, 180161 (2018). https://doi.org/10.1038/sdata.2018.161
11. Zhu, C.-Y., et al.: A deep learning based framework for diagnosing multiple skin diseases in a clinical environment. Front. Med. **8**, 626369 (2021). https://doi.org/10.3389/fmed.2021.626369
12. ISIC 2019, https://challenge2019.isic-archive.com/. Accessed 08 Oct 2021
13. Module: tf.data | TensorFlow Core v2.7.0, https://www.tensorflow.org/api_docs/python/tf/data. Accessed 03 Feb 2022
14. Codella, N.C.F., et al.: Skin Lesion Analysis Toward Melanoma Detection: A Challenge at the 2017 International Symposium on Biomedical Imaging (ISBI), Hosted by the International Skin Imaging Collaboration (ISIC). ArXiv171005006 Cs. (2017). https://arxiv.org/abs/1710.05006v3
15. Combalia, M., et al.: BCN20000: Dermoscopic Lesions in the Wild. ArXiv E-Prints. 1908, arXiv:1908.02288 (2019)

16. Wasikowski, J.: Stratified Group k-Fold Cross-Validation. https://www.kaggle.com/jakubw asikowski/stratified-group-k-fold-cross-validation

17. Tan, M., Le, Q.V.: EfficientNet: Rethinking Model Scaling for Convolutional Neural Networks. ArXiv190511946 Cs Stat. (2020). http://arxiv.org/abs/1905.11946

18. Ha, Q., Liu, B., Liu, F.: Identifying Melanoma Images using EfficientNet Ensemble: Winning Solution to the SIIM-ISIC Melanoma Classification Challenge. ArXiv201005351 Cs. (2020). http://arxiv.org/abs/2010.05351

19. Gessert, N., Nielsen, M., Shaikh, M., Werner, R., Schlaefer, A.: Skin lesion classification using ensembles of multi-resolution EfficientNets with meta data. MethodsX 7, 100864 (2020). https://doi.org/10.1016/j.mex.2020.100864

20. Zhou, S., Zhuang, Y., Meng, R.: Multi-Category Skin Lesion Diagnosis Using Dermoscopy Images and Deep CNN Ensembles (2019). https://challenge.isic-archive.com/leaderboards/2019/

21. Kontogianni, G., Maglogiannis, I.: A review on state-of-the-art computer-based approaches for the early recognition of malignant melanoma. In: Maglogiannis, I., Brahnam, S., Jain, L.C. (eds.) Advanced Computational Intelligence in Healthcare-7. SCI, vol. 891, pp. 81–101. Springer, Heidelberg (2020). https://doi.org/10.1007/978-3-662-61114-2_6

22. Random-Erasing-tensorflow, https://github.com/uranusx86/Random-Erasing-tensorflow/blob/master/random_erasing.py

23. Shawn, N.: Shades of Grey

24. Barata, C., Celebi, M.E., Marques, J.S.: Improving dermoscopy image classification using color constancy. IEEE J. Biomed. Health Inform. 19, 1146–1152 (2015). https://doi.org/10.1109/JBHI.2014.2336473

25. Delibasis, K., Georgakopoulos, S.V., Tasoulis, S.K., Maglogiannis, I., Plagianakos, V.P.: On image prefiltering for skin lesion characterization utilizing deep transfer learning. In: Iliadis, L., Angelov, P.P., Jayne, C., Pimenidis, E. (eds.) EANN 2020. PINNS, vol. 2, pp. 377–388. Springer, Cham (2020). https://doi.org/10.1007/978-3-030-48791-1_29

26. Georgakopoulos, S.V., Kottari, K., Delibasis, K., Plagianakos, V.P., Maglogiannis, I.: Detection of malignant melanomas in dermoscopic images using convolutional neural network with transfer learning. In: Boracchi, G., Iliadis, L., Jayne, C., Likas, A. (eds.) EANN 2017. CCIS, vol. 744, pp. 404–414. Springer, Cham (2017). https://doi.org/10.1007/978-3-319-65172-9_34

27. tfa.optimizers.RectifiedAdam|TensorFlow Addons, https://www.tensorflow.org/addons/api_docs/python/tfa/optimizers/RectifiedAdam. Accessed 08 Oct 2021

28. sklearn.metrics.classification_report, https://scikit-learn/stable/modules/generated/sklearn.metrics.classification_report.html. Accessed 08 Oct 2021

29. sklearn.metrics.precision_recall_fscore_support. https://scikit-learn.org/stable/modules/generated/sklearn.metrics.precision_recall_fscore_support.html. Accessed 08 Oct 2021

30. ISIC Challenge 2019 Leaderboard - Lesion Diagnosis - Images Only, https://challenge.isic-archive.com/leaderboards/2019/. Accessed 12 Oct 2021

31. Tziomaka, M., Maglogiannis, I.: Ensembles of deep convolutional neural networks for detecting melanoma in dermoscopy images. In: Nguyen, N.T., Iliadis, L., Maglogiannis, I., Trawiński, B. (eds.) ICCCI 2021. LNCS (LNAI), vol. 12876, pp. 523–535. Springer, Cham (2021). https://doi.org/10.1007/978-3-030-88081-1_39

32. Popescu, D., El-Khatib, M., El-Khatib, H., Ichim, L.: New trends in melanoma detection using neural networks: a systematic review. Sensors 22, 496 (2022). https://doi.org/10.3390/s22020496

The 1st Workshop on AI in Energy, Buildings and Micro-Grids Workshop (AIBMG)

2022 Workshop on AI in Energy, Buildings and Micro-Grids Workshop (AIBMG)

Sustainable energy is hands down one of the biggest challenges nowadays. As the EU sets its focus to reach its 2030 and 2050 goals, the role of artificial intelligence in the energy domain at building, district and micro-grid level becomes prevalent. The EU and member states are increasingly highlighting the need to complement IoT capacity (e.g. appliances and meters) with artificial intelligence capabilities (e.g. building management systems, proactive optimization, prescriptive maintenance, etc.). Moreover, moving away from the centralized production schema of the grid, novel approaches are needed for the optimal management/balancing of local (or remote aggregated net metering) generation and consumption rather than only reducing energy consumption for presuming communities.

The AIBMG Workshop aims to bring together interdisciplinary approaches that focus on the application of AI-driven solutions for increasing and improving energy efficiency of residential and tertiary buildings without compromising the occupants' well-being. Either applied directly on the device, building or district management system, the proposed solutions should enable more energy efficient and sustainable operation of devices, buildings, districts and micro-grids. The workshop also welcomes cross-domain approaches that investigate how to support energy efficiency by exploiting decentralized, proactiveness, plug-n-play, etc. solutions.

Topics of interest covered by AIBMG 2022 include, but are not limited to: AI-based energy management applications at building and district level; Smart digital building renovation solutions; AI-based assessment in smart-grid systems; Predictive modelling for energy consumption and indoor comfort; Prescriptive modelling for building asset maintenance; Non-Intrusive Load Monitoring (NILM)/energy disaggregation; Smart decentralized energy solutions; Grey- and black-box data-driven user profiling; Ontologies, ontology matching and alignment in the energy domain; Anomalies detection and data filtering; Visual analytics and recommendation systems. Accepted papers focus on the application of AI solutions for various aspects of the energy domain, from energy efficiency, heat pump performance, EV charging modelling, forecasting, maintenance, and more.

Organization of AIBMG 2022

Organizing Committee

Iakovos Michailidis	Centre for Research and Technology Hellas (CERTH)/Democritus University of Thrace (DUTH), Greece
Stelios Krinidis	International Hellenic University (IHU)/Centre for Research and Technology Hellas (CERTH), Greece
Elias Kosmatopoulos	Democritus University of Thrace (DUTH)/ Centre for Research and Technology Hellas (CERTH), Greece
Dimosthenis Ioannidis	Centre for Research and Technology Hellas (CERTH), Greece
Dimitrios Tzovaras	Centre for Research and Technology Hellas (CERTH), Greece

Program Committee

Christos Korkas	Democritus University of Thrace (DUTH)/ Centre for Research and Technology Hellas (CERTH), Greece
Christos Tsaknakis	Centre for Research and Technology Hellas (CERTH), Greece
Napoleon Bezas	Centre for Research and Technology Hellas (CERTH), Greece
Evdoxia-Eirini Lithoxoidou	Centre for Research and Technology Hellas (CERTH), Greece
Paraskevas Koukaras	International Hellenic University (IHU), Greece
Georgios Vougiatzis	Centre for Research and Technology Hellas (CERTH)/Democritus University of Thrace (DUTH), Greece
Aliki Stefanopoulou	Centre for Research and Technology Hellas (CERTH)/Democritus University of Thrace (DUTH), Greece
Asimina Dimara	Centre for Research and Technology Hellas (CERTH), Greece
Christos Timplalexis	Centre for Research and Technology Hellas (CERTH), Greece

PRECEPT and **Smart2B** have received funding from the European Union's Horizon 2020 research and innovation programme under grant agreement No. 958284 and No. 101004152 respectively

An Innovative Software Platform for Efficient Energy, Environmental and Cost Planning in Buildings Retrofitting

Andreas Seitaridis[1]([✉]), Ioannis Mamounakis[1], Nikolas Tagkoulis[1], Petros Iliadis[1,2], Evangelos Bellos[1], Christos Papalexis[1], Vasileios Sougakis[1], and Nikos Nikolopoulos[1]

[1] Centre for Research and Technology Hellas/ Chemical Process and Energy Resources Institute, 52, Egialias Street, 15125 Maroussi, Athens, Greece
{a.seitaridis,mamounakis,n.tagkoulis,iliadis,e.bellos, ch.papalexis,sougakis,n.nikolopoulos}@certh.gr
[2] Department of Electrical and Computer Engineering of Democritus University of Thrace, Xanthi, Greece

Abstract. Building stock renovation is a major challenge towards a sustainable energy transition. In this context, there is a need for accurate and holistic assessment of retrofitting solutions. While Life Cycle Assessment (LCA) and Life Cycle Costing (LCC) methods are typically used to quantify the outcomes of a retrofit solution, these methods are highly dependent on accurate data, which is often not available in the design phase. The work presented in this paper demonstrates a building renovation assessment platform that follows a holistic approach and enables rapid but accurate consideration of several renovation scenarios. The innovation lies in the integration of two specialized tools, namely VERIFY and INTEMA.building, for lifecycle and energetic calculations, respectively. The integration offers a solution for the case in which no operational data are available. After the detailed presentation of the platform, the architecture and the offered functionality, a building renovation problem is considered as a demo case. A typical low-efficiency Greek building is examined while interventions are assumed, such as insulation of external wall, replacement of glazing surfaces, as well as heat pump and photovoltaic installation. Results showcase a significant reduction in lifetime CO_2 emissions and primary energy of around 785 tons and 700 MWh, respectively. At the same time, the economic viability is ensured with estimated savings of 225 k€ during project lifecycle.

Keywords: Sustainability assessment · Life cycle · Energy modeling and simulation

1 Introduction

Globally, one third of the final energy consumption and almost 40% of total CO_2 emissions is attributed to building sector [1], while in the European Union (EU), around 75%

© IFIP International Federation for Information Processing 2022
Published by Springer Nature Switzerland AG 2022
I. Maglogiannis et al. (Eds.): AIAI 2022 Workshops, IFIP AICT 652, pp. 217–228, 2022.
https://doi.org/10.1007/978-3-031-08341-9_18

of the building stock is considered energy inefficient, accounting for 40% of the EU's total energy consumption, and 36% of the total greenhouse gas (GHG) emissions [2, 3]. As depicted in the European Green Deal, building renovation and energy efficiency measures offer a huge potential for energy savings and reaching the EU emissions reduction target of at least 55% by 2030 and achieving climate neutrality by 2050 [4]. Achieving sustainability in buildings requires the application of innovative and ecological building materials, integration of smart technologies and higher penetration of Renewable Energy Sources (RES) for energy transition and decarbonization of the building stock [5].

The concept of green buildings is strongly related to building sustainability due to its contribution to environmental preservation and better quality of life [6, 7]. LCA and LCC methodologies are powerful instruments for the sustainable design and viable future of buildings. The application of these techniques through the building renovation should be integrated for achieving a highly energy efficient, cost effective and decarbonized building stock with social benefits for its users [8]. A life cycle approach considers both environmental, and economic factors and allows for the estimation of materials and energy consumption, costs, as well as GHG emissions. Decision-making towards an optimal selection of building elements through the entire life cycle [9] needs to be planned, managed and evaluated with accessible and adaptable software tools.

Malmqvist et al. (2011) proposed, within the context of ENSLIC Building project, a simplified step-by-step method and guidelines for building LCA calculations in early design phases [10]. Rossi et al. (2012) [11] created a tool in excel format to perform simplified LCA calculations for the embodied energy and carbon as well as the operational energy and carbon, at a masonry house and a steel-framed house in three European locations. Fu et al. (2014) designed an LCA calculation tool in order to estimate the carbon emissions occurring in the construction phase of LCA analysis and compare different construction plans [12]. In another work, Jayathissa et al. [13] applied an open-source LCA software to assess the environmental impact of dynamic Building Integrated Photovoltaic (BIPV) systems. The tool was developed initially by Ciroth in 2007 [14], entitled "OpenLCA". Moreover, it is useful to state that Li et al. (2016) developed an automated tool for the estimation of life cycle carbon emissions in residential buildings in China, named "Carbon Emission Estimator for Residential Buildings (CEERB)" [15], using a database with national emission factors and a carbon estimator capitalizing on the standardized LCA theory.

In this context, the developed tool "VERIFY" offers a) an integrated LCA & LCC calculation methodology based on a holistic life cycle approach considering existing building performance, new building designs and building renovation projects; b) a detailed lifecycle analysis of the use phase concerning RES production and energy/fuel consumption components as well as degradation effects and replacement actions for long-term projects; c) personalized project setup and creation by capitalizing on country specificities, meteorological data, material data, building properties and specific user preferences; d) a private database for materials and energy production taking into account all energy consumption for components construction and their initial environmental footprints ('cradle-to-gate') e.g. primary energy and emissions; e) the ability to store a large amount of data in private data repositories through the use and function of a Data Lake; f) communication with external tools related to energy modelling and simulation in order to obtain synthetic energy data (i.e. energy simulation data) useful in the analysis of building components. A significant feature regards the case where there are no adequate data available for the building operation. For this case, an integration with the "Integrated Energy Management - building (INTEMA.building)" tool offers accurate synthetic data, based on which the LCA can be drawn. Coordination of the proposed tools allows the estimation of the impact of various renovation scenarios in terms of energy efficiency, environmental emissions and economic cost during the whole life cycle of the building.

The remainder of this paper is structured as follows: Sect. 2 gives a description about VERIFY and INTEMA architecture and main goals. Section 3 presents the proposed environmental and costing methodology for the building renovation sector. Section 4 describes the renovation scenario setup procedure through the proposed software tools. Section 5 presents the tool application for a typical building in Greece, gives the overall evaluation results and discusses the outcomes. Finally, conclusions are drawn in the Sect. 6.

2 Objectives and Architecture

Valid building renovation scenario requires multidisciplinary expertise and a large set of parameters in each domain. The followed approach tackles these issues by coupling two distinct specialized software applications under a single platform. After a short description for each of the tool main objectives, the integration architecture is presented.

2.1 VERIFY Goals and Objectives

VERIFY is a software developed by CERTH for conducting LCA and LCC analysis [16]. When assessing the performance of a building under renovation scenarios, VERIFY investigates the improvement in terms of renewable energy production, environmental emissions reduction, and cost optimization. The optimal renovation strategies are investigated leading to a balance of environmental impacts and costs. Depending on the climatic conditions, fuel prices and emission factors at the country of interest, VERIFY's methodology approach is to highlight the effects of choices during the installation and the use-phase of the building for: a) electrical production systems, b) thermal power components, c) building specifications and materials. VERIFY has been implemented based on open-access tools, to provide a) holistic LCA and LCC analysis under the umbrella of a single software tool, b) easy and friendly user interface through server-based access, c) connection with external software tools and/or platforms, d) connection with internal data repositories, e) personalized and safe environment, f) compliance with data ontologies (e.g. SAREF).

LCA methodological approach, established by the specific ISO standards ISO 14040 [17] and ISO 14044 [18]. In addition, LCC concept in building practice, set by the ISO 15686-5 [19] is followed and performed. LCA and LCC modelling approach can be applied for a single energy system, building and/or multiple buildings/blocks projects subject to planned interventions. Effective comparison of alternative scenarios is supported along with comparative graphs and tables.

2.2 INTEMA.Building Goals and Objectives

The need for reliable and accurate calculations for the building's energetic behaviour is critical to calculate properly the energy savings and the CO_2 emissions reduction when planning retrofitting solutions. INTEMA.building is a dynamic Building Performance Simulation (BPS) engine developed by CERTH providing physics-based simulations of high accuracy and validity in the results [20]. INTEMA.building offers among others multi-zone dynamics calculation, HVAC systems (e.g., boiler, heat-pump, solar thermal collector, storage tank), electrical generation and storage systems, thermal comfort calculation, as well as ancillary modules for load/RES forecasting and battery scheduling. The tool leverages the Modelica language [21] capabilities to implement high order dynamic models for both passive and active elements. At the same time, a web-based interface is provided for the non-expert users which besides fully supporting the building system definition, also supports automatic data import through BIM (.ifc) file.

2.3 VERIFY and INTEMA.Building Architecture

A significant advantage of the platform lies in the integration of two specialized software applications under a single platform. The developed architecture depicted in Fig. 1 enables all required functionality and interoperability among the tools, while taking into consideration security and scalability concerns.

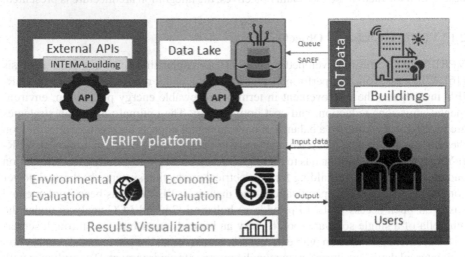

Fig. 1. VERIFY and INTEMA.building architecture

VERIFY constitutes a holistic software approach which enables the association of building modelling with energy consumption and production time series to evaluate and measure the building's performance through a graphical user interface. Time series data can originate through multiple sources as: 1) historical data manually provided by the user through.csv file upload, 2) synthetic data automatically provided by INTEMA.building tool and 3) real time data automatically gathered from the building's sensorial network. Real time data are stored in a large data repository which follows: 1) the Data Lake approach and 2) the Smart Applications REFerence (SAREF) ontology scheme [22]. VERIFY easily communicates with external software tools (e.g., Data Lake, INTEMA.building) using RESTful APIs. Environmental and economic computations are performed through smart Python algorithms in the core of the platform. Analysis results are presented through dynamic tables and graphs.

3 Environmental and Costing Methodology for Buildings

Typical LCA and LCC methodologies focus on evaluating the environmental and economic impact of a product or a service through its life cycle encompassing many stages of the value chain (raw materials extraction, manufacturing, distribution etc.) [23, 24].

A large variety of passive and active assets are included under the building structure. As a result, various direct and indirect interactions between them occur (e.g., the boiler consumption depends strongly on the quality of the wall insulation). Hence, even if the components are allocated to predefined suitable sectors (e.g., electrical production, active thermal) for easier manipulation, the analysis is performed regarding the building as an entity during its life cycle. According to the developed methodology, a building envelope consists of passive components (e.g., walls materials, insulation, glazing), thermal (e.g., heat/cool sources, thermal storage) and electrical components (e.g., appliances, PVs).

In order to simplify the project creation and provide the ability to users to create and modify different scenarios easily, VERIFY requires a relatively small set of scenario setup input information. The majority of environmental and costing initial data is provided by a private VERIFY's database. The dedicated database consists of multiple categories divided into: 1) energy production, 2) energy storage, 3) active thermal components and 4) passive thermal components capable to cover most of the building scenario needs. The analysis considers infrastructure energy of the components construction, initial environmental footprints and possible replacements; which are incorporated and automatically imported to the final computation procedure. In contrast to other methodologies where the use phase is analyzed using some average values [25] or the components maintenance [26, 27], the current methodology follows a more detailed approach regarding the use phase of the buildings. Specifically, accurate timeseries for assets consumption/production are retrieved either from the INTEMA.building tool after detailed dynamic simulations, or from installed sensors/meters in real pilot buildings (real time dispatch or stored data).

Finally, by applying the proposed methodology in the VERIFY tool, demanding in terms of time (performance time) building retrofit, is realized adequately fast and precisely.

4 Retrofitting Scenario Setup Procedure

The retrofitting scenario setup includes multiple steps, starting by: 1) importing specific scenario configurations preferences, 2) claiming synthetic/projected data from INTEMA.building tool, 3) performing the LCA and LCC analysis and 4) viewing the KPI computation results. The retrofitting procedure is depicted in Fig. 2 under the detail sequence diagram.

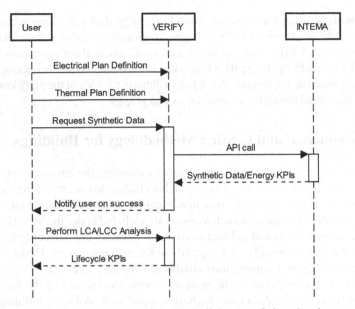

Fig. 2. Sequence diagram describing the building retrofitting planning steps

The modeling of a building and its infrastructure for both the current state and the planned renovations is achieved through the front-end layer of VERIFY and requires details regarding: 1) the building's envelope, 2) the electrical systems and energy storage devices and 3) the thermal systems. To do so, the user develops i) an electrical plan and ii) a thermal plan. The electrical plan setup consists of the energy generation (e.g. photovoltaics) and the storage systems (i.e. batteries) preferences definition. Furthermore, the location of the building and the analysis lifespan is also considered at this stage. Indicative annual consumptions (lighting and appliances) need also to be provided by the platform user. Following the configuration of the electrical plan, the thermal plan configuration includes the building envelope information and the comfort boundaries in terms of building's temperature during summer and winter periods. Moreover, details regarding the already installed or planned renovation thermal components are specified. Thermal components might be of two types: 1) active components, which contribute to electrical or fuel consumptions, and 2) passive components, which prevent energy losses.

After building set-up configuration is finalized (as represented by the electrical and thermal passive and active components) the operation data during the building use-phase is imported. These data can be either actual monitored data retrieved from the building sensorial network or synthetic data obtained through dynamic simulation. In the case of no available monitored data, synthetic data can be requested from INTEMA.building through restful API. Upon request, VERIFY forwards the relevant subset of the defined building's retrofitting scenario information to INTEMA.building. INTEMA's engine generates the Modelica system model of the particular building system. In the next step, the Modelica code is simulated in the Dymola environment based on the provided simulation date range (typically one year). While the simulation time may vary depending on the generation and storage systems present in the model, typical times do not exceed the two minutes mark. Timeseries synthetic data are generated and forwarded back to VERIFY in order to be stored and utilized in the LCA and LCC methodology. The last step involves the LCA or LCC analysis and the performance evaluation of the building. The analysis results are presented through interactive charts and table in the user interface of the platform.

5 Evaluation Scenario Results and Discussion

To highlight the main functionalities of the platform, Sect. 5 briefly presents an evaluation demo case scenario by analyzing a typical household building renovation in Greece, through the proposed software tools.

5.1 Scenario Description

A single-storey building has been chosen for the demonstration of the tool's functionality. The building is located in Athens, Greece, has a gross area of 170 m^2 and represents a typical low energy efficiency case. Heating is provided by a 24kW heating oil boiler and cooling is provided by 3 air-to-air heat pumps (mini split units). Table 1 includes the main geometric and thermal parameters of the studied building. It is useful to state that the envelope has no insulation and the windows are single-glazed with aluminum frame (without thermal break).

Table 1. Main envelope parameters

Type	Direction	Area (m^2)	Thermal transmittance – U value (W/m^{2}K)	Thickness (m)
External Wall	N-W	27.16	3.45	0.25
	N-E	13.94	3.45	0.25
	S-W	13.26	3.45	0.25
Window	N-E	8.8	5.74	–
	S-W	13.5	5.40	–
Internal Wall	–	16	3.85	0.25
Ceiling	–	70	4.00	0.23
Floor	–	70	4.20	0.23

The considered interventions are presented in Table 2. More specific, the interventions under evaluation include the replacement of the heating oil boiler with a natural gas one, insulation of the envelope and replacement of windows, as well the installation of a 10kW rooftop photovoltaic plant.

Table 2. Installed components

	Current	Planned
Thermal Active	Boiler Oil 24 kW	Boiler Natural Gas 24 kW
	Heat Pump (Cooling) 3x3.5 kW	Heat Pump (Cooling) 3x3.5 kW
Thermal Passive	No insulation	Insulation 75 mm, Expanded polysterene
	Glazing 1 layer, 10 mm, Aluminum frame	Glazing 2 layers, 10 mm, Aluminum frame
RES	–	Photovoltaic 10 kW, Monocrystalline

5.2 Results and Discussion

In this section the analysis results of the two scenarios (prior to and after the renovation) is described and presented.

In Table 3 the energy results regarding the electrical and thermal consumption/production for the two scenarios are depicted Table 4 presents a set of indicative environmental Key Performance Indicators (KPIs) from the LCA analysis for the current and the planned scenario. Considering the Lifetime CO2 emissions and Primary Energy (PE), reduction is achieved as a result of the interventions. The exact values of the emerging savings, which besides the energy reduction, also, include the environmental/energy profits that originate from the PV's operation, are also presented. The total savings through retrofitting lifetime are calculated based on Eq. 1. Lastly, the Energy Payback Time (EPBT) and the CO2 Payback Time (CPBT) for the photovoltaic (PV) installation are calculated to happen early in the building's lifespan.

$$
\begin{aligned}
\text{Savings} = {} & (\text{Infrastructure Costs} + \text{Functional Costs})_{\text{current}} - \\
& (\text{Infrastructure Costs} + \text{Functional Costs} - \text{Profits})_{\text{planned}}
\end{aligned}
\tag{1}
$$

The electricity import and export price were set to 0.167 and 0.5 €/kWh respectively. In addition, oil and natural gas price were set to 0.105 and 0.048 €/kWh respectively. Lifetime costs (infrastructure and functional), lifetime revenues (PV investment), electricity bills and fuel costs are significantly diminished due to the retrofitting of the building envelope and the boiler upgrade. Furthermore, considering the profit from the PV investment and the reduction of the functional costs, the savings achieved, which are calculated by Eq. 1, are considerably high. Similarly, Table 5 shows the costing KPIs extracted from the analysis. Finally, Table 6 contains three economic metrics regarding only the energy investment of the PV.

VERIFY also performs yearly environmental and cost savings comparison between the planned and the current scenario and presents the result into charts. Figure 3 presents the functional and infrastructure environmental emissions. Positive values indicate that the planned scenario achieves higher emissions reductions (e.g., lower fuel consumption). On the other hand, negative values, indicate worse performance. This can be noticed even during the first year of analysis, at which the components of the planned scenario have to be purchased and installed (heavy emissions and monetary costs), while in the case of the current scenario, the components are already installed (i.e. there are no extra costs and no additional embodied energy of new materials). Figure 4 presents the amount of avoided costs achieved, during the project lifetime. During the project initial

Table 3. Annual energy load and generation amounts

Value	Scenario	
	Current (kWh)	Planned (kWh)
Electrical consumption	11.574	11.199
Imported energy	11.574	6.916
Exported energy	0	5.119
PV generation	0	9.402
Heat consumption	96.036	91.982
Cool consumption	7.996	8.030

Table 4. Environmental KPIs

Scenario	KPIs			
	Lifetime CO2 Emissions (kg)	Lifetime PE (kWh)	Photovoltaic EPBT (years)	Photovol-taic CPBT (years)
Current	982.557	3.848.939	–	–
Planned	265.843	3.341.085	4,6	3,3
Savings	785.083	699.577	–	–

Table 5. Costing KPIs

Scenario	KPIs			
	Lifetime costs (€)	Lifetime revenues (€)	Annual El. Bills (€)	Annual fuel costs (€)
Current	391.170	0	1.948	12.896
Planned	225.690	60.290	1.158	4.419
Savings	225.770			

Table 6. RES Investment

Scenario	KPIs		
	IRR (%)	ROI (%)	LCOE (€/kWh)
Planned	20,5	494,25	0,0686

year negative cost reduction values appear due to the capital and installation expenditures. The remaining years of analysis accomplish economic gains ranging from 5 to 20 k€ per year.

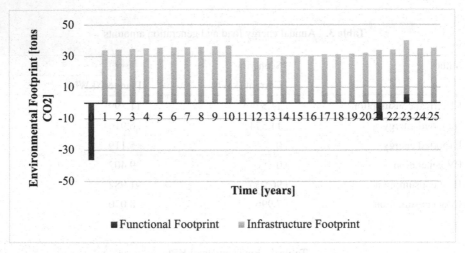

Fig. 3. CO_2 emissions reduced during project lifetime

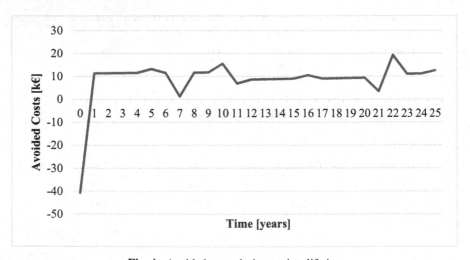

Fig. 4. Avoided costs during project lifetime

6 Conclusions

The current work presented a holistic environmental and economic evaluation tool for building retrofitting projects. The platform involves a set of innovative elements including the detailed LCA and LCC calculations based on the total building renovation. Furthermore, the tool goes beyond the classical life cycle methodologies that follow ISO 14040 and are based on aggregated yearly values and takes also into account real time data. Lastly, an integration scheme has been implemented with the INTEMA.building tool for the case of inadequate historical data.

A demo case has been presented to highlight the main functionalities of the platform, referring to the renovation of typical Greek building. Main interventions included replacement of the oil boiler with a natural gas one, insulation of the external surfaces, replacement of windows and installation of photovoltaic generation. Results indicated that a drastic environmental improvement can be achieved with 785 tons of CO_2 reduction and 700 MWh of primary energy savings during the project lifetime. In terms of economic benefits, the savings were estimated at 255 k€, the IRR at 20.5% and the ROI at 494.25%. Through the demonstrated renovation assessment, the platform capabilities became evident.

Acknowledgement. This work was funded by the European Union's Horizon 2020 Research and Innovation Programme through the RINNO project (https://rinno-h2020.eu/) under Grant Agreement Number 892071.

References

1. IEA: Buildings. A Source of Enormous Untapped Efficiency Potential, https://www.iea.org/topics/buildings
2. Filippidou, F., Jimenez Navarro, J.P.: Achieving the cost-effective energy transformation of Europe's buildings combinations of insulation and heating & cooling technologies renovations: methods and data (2019)
3. European Commission: Energy Performance of Buildings Directive, https://ec.europa.eu/energy/topics/energy-efficiency/energy-efficient-buildings/energy-performance-buildings-directive_en
4. European Commission: The European Green Deal, https://ec.europa.eu/info/strategy/priorities-2019-2024/european-green-deal/delivering-european-green-deal_en#documents (2019)
5. Kong, M., Hong, T., Ji, C., Kang, H., Lee, M.: Development of building driven-energy payback time for energy transition of building with renewable energy systems. Appl. Energy **271**, 115162 (2020). https://doi.org/10.1016/j.apenergy.2020.115162
6. Khan, J., et al.: Evolution to emergence of green buildings: a review. Admin. Sci. **9**, 6 (2019). https://doi.org/10.3390/admsci9010006
7. Del Rosario, P., Palumbo, E., Traverso, M.: Environmental product declarations as data source for the environmental assessment of buildings in the context of Level(s) and DGNB: how feasible is their adoption? Sustainability. **13**, 6143 (2021). https://doi.org/10.3390/su13116143
8. Lu, K., Jiang, X., Yu, J., Tam, V.W.Y., Skitmore, M.: Integration of life cycle assessment and life cycle cost using building information modeling: a critical review. J. Clean. Prod. **285**, 125438 (2021). https://doi.org/10.1016/j.jclepro.2020.125438

9. Di Maria, A., Eyckmans, J., Van Acker, K.: Use of LCA and LCC to help decision-making between downcycling versus recycling of construction and demolition waste. In: Advances in Construction and Demolition Waste Recycling, pp. 537–558. Elsevier (2020)

10. Malmqvist, T., et al.: Life cycle assessment in buildings: the ENSLIC simplified method and guidelines. Energy **36**, 1900–1907 (2011). https://doi.org/10.1016/j.energy.2010.03.026

11. Rossi, B., Marique, A.-F., Glaumann, M., Reiter, S.: Life-cycle assessment of residential buildings in three different European locations, basic tool. Build. Environ. **51**, 395–401 (2012). https://doi.org/10.1016/j.buildenv.2011.11.017

12. Fu, F., Luo, H., Zhong, H., Hill, A.: Development of a carbon emission calculations system for optimizing building plan based on the LCA framework. Math. Probl. Eng. **2014**, 1–13 (2014). https://doi.org/10.1155/2014/653849

13. Jayathissa, P., Jansen, M., Heeren, N., Nagy, Z., Schlueter, A.: Life cycle assessment of dynamic building integrated photovoltaics. Sol. Energy Mater. Sol. Cells **156**, 75–82 (2016). https://doi.org/10.1016/j.solmat.2016.04.017

14. Ciroth, A.: ICT for environment in life cycle applications openLCA — a new open source software for life cycle assessment. Int. J. Life Cycle Assess. **12**, 209–210 (2007). https://doi.org/10.1065/lca2007.06.337

15. Li, D.: Development of an Automated Estimator of Life-Cycle Carbon Emissions for Residential Buildings: A Case Study in Nanjing, China. Habitat I. (2016). https://doi.org/10.1016/j.habitatint.2016.07.003

16. CERTH/CPERI: VERIFY: An online platform for holistic Life Cycle Assessment and Costing in Energy Systems, https://www.cperi.certh.gr/en/component/content/article/55-projects-activities/projects-activities-sfta/186-verify

17. ISO/TC 207/SC 5: ISO 14040–2006 Environmental management — Life cycle assessment — Principles and framework (2006)

18. ISO/TC 207/SC 5: ISO 14044–2006 Environmental management — Life cycle assessment — Requirements and guidelines (2006)

19. ISO/TC 59/SC 14: ISO 15686–5–2008 Buildings and constructed assets - Service-life planning - Part 5: Life-cycle costing (2008)

20. CERTH/CPERI: INTEMA.building, https://www.cperi.certh.gr/en/component/content/article/55-projects-activities/projects-activities-sfta/195-2021-09-16-09-58-31?Itemid=161

21. The Modelica Association, https://modelica.org/

22. Smart Applications REFerence Ontology, and extensions, https://saref.etsi.org/

23. Ilgin, M.A., Gupta, S.M.: Environmentally conscious manufacturing and product recovery (ECMPRO): a review of the state of the art. J. Environ. Manage. **91**, 563–591 (2010). https://doi.org/10.1016/j.jenvman.2009.09.037

24. Shaikh, P.H., Shaikh, F., Sahito, A.A., Uqaili, M.A., Umrani, Z.: An Overview of the Challenges for Cost-Effective and Energy-Efficient Retrofits of the Existing Building Stock. In: Cost-Effective Energy Efficient Building Retrofitting, pp. 257–278. Elsevier (2017)

25. Fontaras, G., Franco, V., Dilara, P., Martini, G., Manfredi, U.: Development and review of Euro 5 passenger car emission factors based on experimental results over various driving cycles. Sci. Total Environ. **468–469**, 1034–1042 (2014). https://doi.org/10.1016/j.scitotenv.2013.09.043

26. Broun, R., Menzies, G.F.: Life cycle energy and environmental analysis of partition wall systems in the UK. In: Procedia Engineering, pp. 864–873 (2011)

27. Salehian, S., Ismail, M.A., Ariffin, A.R.M.: Assessment on embodied energy of non-load bearing walls for office buildings. Buildings **10**, 79 (2020). https://doi.org/10.3390/buildings10040079

Anomaly Detection in Small-Scale Industrial and Household Appliances

Niccolò Zangrando[1] , Sergio Herrera[1(✉)] , Paraskevas Koukaras[2,4] ,
Asimina Dimara[2,5] , Piero Fraternali[1] , Stelios Krinidis[2,3] ,
Dimosthenis Ioannidis[2] , Christos Tjortjis[4] ,
Christos-Nikolaos Anagnostopoulos[5] , and Dimitrios Tzovaras[2]

[1] Politecnico di Milano, 20133 Milano, Italy
{niccolo.zangrando,sergioluis.herrera,piero.fraternali}@polimi.it
[2] Information Technologies Institute, Centre for Research and Technology,
57001 Thessaloniki, Greece
{p.koukaras,adimara,krinidis,djoannid,dimitrios.tzovaras}@iti.gr
[3] Department of Management Science and Technology, International Hellenic
University, Kavala, Greece
[4] School of Science and Technology, International Hellenic University,
57001 Kavala, Greece
c.tjortjis@iti.gr
[5] Department of Cultural Technology and Communication, University of the Aegean,
Intelligent Systems Lab, Mytilene, Greece
canag@aegean.gr

Abstract. Anomaly detection is concerned with identifying rare
events/observations that differ substantially from the majority of the
data. It is considered an important task in the energy sector to enable
the identification of non-standard device conditions. The use of anomaly
detection techniques in small-scale residential and industrial settings can
provide useful insights about device health, maintenance requirements,
and downtime, which in turn can lead to lower operating costs. There are
numerous approaches for detecting anomalies in a range of application
scenarios such as prescriptive appliance maintenance. This work reports
on anomaly detection using a data set of fridge power consumption that
operates on a near zero energy building scenario. We implement a variety of machine and deep learning algorithms and evaluate performances
using multiple metrics. In the light of the present state of the art, the
contribution of this work is the development of a inference pipeline that
incorporates numerous methodologies and algorithms capable of producing high accuracy results for detecting appliance failures.

Keywords: Anomaly detection · Time series analysis · Machine
learning · Deep learning

© IFIP International Federation for Information Processing 2022
Published by Springer Nature Switzerland AG 2022
I. Maglogiannis et al. (Eds.): AIAI 2022 Workshops, IFIP AICT 652, pp. 229–240, 2022.
https://doi.org/10.1007/978-3-031-08341-9_19

1 Introduction

Predictive maintenance (PdM) aims to optimize the trade off between run-to-failure and periodic maintenance, by empowering manufacturers to improve the remaining useful life of their machines while at the same time avoiding unplanned downtime and decreasing planned downtime. At the core of PdM lies Anomaly Detection task (AD) whose primary focus is to find anomalies in the operation of working equipment at early stages and alert the supervisor to carry out maintenance activity. In addition, anomaly detection may stand as a core component for prescriptive maintenance (PsM) being a type of maintenance that gains popularity lately and poses as the evolution of PdM.

In recent years, AD has proved beneficial in different application scenarios and has acquired a prominent stance in the unsupervised machine learning research. AD finds use in different fields such as healthcare, where it applies to the analysis of clinical images [1] and of ECG data [2], in the cybersecurity field, where it is applied for malware identification [3] and in the energy field. In this latter area AD may be combined with energy load forecasting to improve accuracy [4], or integrated as a component for detecting non nominal energy fluctuations for enhancing decision making in energy transfer between microgrids [5]. AD has also been successfully employed for banking fraud detection [6].

However, the lack of public data sets for small scale industrial devices and household appliances makes it difficult to understand the applicability of the anomaly detection methods used for large industrial devices in other contexts such as domestic appliances or common service system in residential buildings (e.g. heating or air-conditioning systems).

This paper summarizes and evaluates the current status of the art on anomaly detection approaches with a focus on their applicability to the context of household appliances. The primary objective is to provide a comprehensive survey of the most important contributions, developments, and experimental approaches in the field. By implementing some of them for the specific use case of a fridge energy behavior, we assess the most relevant techniques and highlight the outstanding research problems for the specific target of house appliances and residential building systems.

The rest of the article is organised as follows: Sect. 2 overviews the state of the art in anomaly detection. Section 3 surveys the research design including the used data sets, the identified methods and the most common evaluation metrics. Section 4 summarizes the obtained results. Finally, Sect. 5 provides the conclusions.

2 Related Work

AD refers to the identification of rare events or observations which significantly deviate from the majority of the data [7].

This task spans different disciplines and is primarily applied in industrial IoT applications where data are collected as time series [8]. Time series data sets collect observations sampled at different times: recording can be continuous, when data are collected continuously in a given interval, or discrete, when data are recorded at set time intervals [9]. In the literature, anomalies for time series are classified into three different types [8, 10, 11]:

- *PointAnomaly*: represents data that abruptly deviates from the normal ones. With these anomaly types, the time series usually returns to its previous normal state within a very short time of only a few observations.
- *ContextualAnomaly*: represents an instance of a potential anomaly in a specific context. This means that the same data point in a different time period would not always indicate an anomalous behavior.
- *CollectiveAnomaly*: collection of observations that are anomalous with respect to the rest of the data. Individual observations within a collective anomaly may or may not be anomalous, but considered as a group they appear suspicious.

Based on the number of observations at each timestamp, the time series can be univariate or multivariate. Univariate time series log values generated by a single sensor, whereas multivariate time series record signals from multiple sensors simultaneously. Depending on the nature of the time series different algorithms and approaches have been applied, ranging from more classical and statistical techniques to the deep learning ones. Moreover, the different approaches can be categorized into three different types depending on their anomaly identification criteria as follow:

- *Reconstruction error*: this criterion applies to all those models whose objective is to generate an output as close as possible to the input. An example is the Autoencoder-based models, which reconstruct input data by extracting features from them. Anomalous data are identified based on the residuals between the input and the generated data: the higher the difference, the higher the probability of an anomaly.
- *Prediction error*: prediction models are used to identify anomalies based on the difference between the predicted value and the expected one. Like the models based on input reconstruction, the larger the residual, the higher the probability of anomalous data.
- *Dissimilarity*: this criterion consists of identifying outliers based on the difference between the input data and the distribution or clusters obtained from the analysis of normal data.

Statistical methods based on regressive models are used for the identification of the outliers in univariate time series, such as Autoregressive Moving Average models (ARMA) used for stationary time series [12] (i.e. time series whose properties do not depend on the time at which the series is observed), or Autoregressive Integrated Moving Average models (ARIMA) preferred for nonstationary time series [13, 14].

By exploiting a sliding window on the input data clustering methods have been applied for anomaly detection on time series, such as K-Means clustering

[15], DBSCAN [16] and Local Outlier Factor (LOF) [17]. Also machine learning based approaches have been employed such as Isolation Forest [18] and One-Class Support Vector Machine [19]. All these techniques rely on a dissimilarity criterion to identify anomalies.

With the advent of Deep Learning (DL), several algorithms have been applied to time series to identify anomalies. The results highlight that DL approaches overcome the difficulties of the more classical techniques [11]. Since time series data are related to a temporal context, the Recurrent Neural Networks (RNNs) [20] is one of the most widely used approaches. Due to the vanishing or exploding gradient problem that limits the ability of the network to model long temporal relationships between data, two variants are preferred, Long-Short Term Memory (LSTM) [21] and Gated Recurrent Unit (GRU) [22]. RNN-based techniques are used in two different ways for anomaly detection. The first consists in the prediction error criterion [23–25], and the second one is based on the reconstruction error criterion [26–28]. CNN-based methods have also been applied to time series analysis, despite they are not designed to identify temporal relationships they still manage to extract meaningful information in the data sequences. The methodologies applied to identify anomalies are, as for RNNs, based on the prediction error [29,30] or the input reconstruction error [31].

Although some data sets with the consumption of household appliances have been published, there are few works concerning anomaly detection in this field, also due to the absence of labelled anomalous data acting as ground truth. In [32], for example, the authors manually analysed and annotated potential anomalies concerning the energy consumption of appliances in the REFIT data set [33]; in [34], instead, the authors have annotated the anomalies in the AMPds2 data set [35] through an ensemble method and then have evaluated their LSTM-autoencoder implementation.

In this paper, we compare the performance of nine different anomaly detection techniques, summarized in Table 1, using a data set of fridge power consumption samples.

Table 1. The AD techniques assessed in this paper and their anomaly identification criterion.

Technique	Anomaly criterion
Local Outlier Factor (LOF)	Dissimilarity
One-Class SVM	Dissimilarity
Isolation Forest	Dissimilarity
CNN	Prediction error
GRU	Prediction error
LSTM	Prediction error
CNN-Autoencoder	Reconstruction error
GRU-Autoencoder	Reconstruction error
LSTM-Autoencoder	Reconstruction error

3   Research Design

3.1   Experimental Data Set

The CERTH data set represents the power consumption of a fridge in a household over a 4 month period, from 10th July 2019 until 3rd November 2019. The data were collected every minute, sampling in total 164,795 consumption values. The raw data were then analyzed and resampled every 10 min to remove sensor noise, obtaining the regular power consumption shown in Fig. 1 and reducing the total number of observations to 16,710.

To be able to evaluate and compare the performance of the different algorithms, we have manually analyzed the data set and we have annotated all the potential anomalies, by following the criterion used in [32]: data are flagged anomalous if the appliance's consumption has been found significantly different from its historical normal consumption. This analysis of the data set revealed two recurrent anomalous behaviors:

- An instant increment in power consumption (point anomaly).
- A continuous power consumption over time (contextual anomaly).

As shown in Fig. 2, these potential anomalies can occur simultaneously.

For the evaluation, the data until the 30–09-2019 has been cleaned from the anomalies and used for training, and the data from 01-10-2019 to 31–10-2019 has been used for testing the performance of the different algorithms.

Table 2 summarizes the CERTH data set information, regarding the anomalous data and the train-test split.

3.2   Methods and Algorithms

Based on the main criterion of anomaly identification, we implemented nine different techniques:

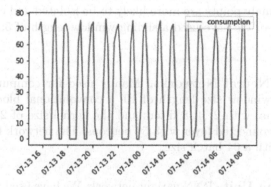

Fig. 1. Fridge normal consumption pattern.

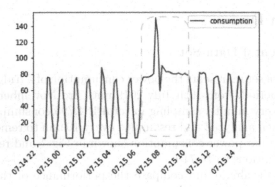

Fig. 2. Fridge potential anomaly consumption.

Table 2. CERTH data set: data points and anomalies.

	Total data	Anomaly data	% anomalies
Total	16710	1737	10.39%
Train set	10460	Not needed	Not needed
Test set	4464	488	10.93%

Local Outlier Factor (LOF). Clustering algorithm based on the identification of the nearest neighbors and local outliers. We have used a sliding window size of 10 and a k value of 400.

One-Class Support Vector Machine. Support vector machine used for novelty detection. In the implementation we have used a sliding window length of 5, the RBF kernel with a gamma value of 0.001 and a nu value of 0.025.

Isolation Forest. Ensemble method that creates different binary trees isolating data points. Anomaly points are more likely to be isolated and closer to the root of an isolation tree. We have used a sliding window length of 5 and 100 trees in the ensemble.

Convolutional Neural Networks. Mainly used for computer vision tasks. We have used a window size length of 10, a convolutional block with a ReLU activation function, with 2, 4, 8 filters and the kernel size of 2, a max pooling layer and a fully connected layer with 50 neurons. The network has been trained for 300 epochs with a 64 batch size.

Gated Recurrent Unit. RNN variant network. We have used a sliding window size of 10, 2 GRU layers with 8 hidden layers and a dropout of 0.2 respectively. The network was trained for 300 epochs with a batch size of 64.

Long Short Term Memory Networks. RNN variant network. We have used a sliding window size of 10, 2 LSTM layers with 8 hidden layers respectively and a dropout of 0.2. The network was trained for 300 epochs with a batch size of 64.

CNN-autoencoder. Hybrid implementation with autoencoder and CNN network. We used a sliding window size of 12 and, for the encoding-decoding phase two convolutional block with 16 and 8 filters and a kernel size of 2. The network has been trained for 300 epochs with a batch size of 64.

GRU-autoencoder. Hybrid implementation with autoencoder and GRU network. We used a sliding window size of 10 and, for the encoding-decoding phase two GRU layers with 16 and 8 hidden layers. The network has been trained for 300 epochs with a batch size of 64.

LSTM-autoencoder. Hybrid implementation with autoencoder and LSTM network. We used a sliding window size of 10 and, for the encoding-decoding phase two LSTM layers with 16 and 8 hidden layers. The network has been trained for 300 epochs with a batch size of 64.

3.3   Evaluation Metrics

In order to compare the implemented methods, we have evaluated them with the most widely used machine learning metrics, based on the true positives (TP), false positives (FP), false negatives (FN), and true negatives (TN): precision, recall, F1 score, false alarm rate (FAR) and miss alarm rate (MAR).

$$precision = \frac{TP}{TP + FP} \tag{1}$$

$$recall = \frac{TP}{TP + FN} \tag{2}$$

$$F1 = 2 * \frac{precision * recall}{precision + recall} \tag{3}$$

$$FAR = \frac{FP}{FP + TN} \tag{4}$$

$$MAR = \frac{FN}{FN + TP} \tag{5}$$

4   Results

Table 3 summarizes the results. The metrics described in the previous section (i.e., precision, recall, F1 score) are used to compare the performances of the tested algorithms. One-Class SVM and CNN have the highest precision (i.e., 0.76) while GRU-Autoencoder has the lowest (i.e., 0.62). Local Outlier Factor (LOF) showcases the highest recall (i.e., 0.92) and CNN-Autoencoder the lowest (i.e., 0.58).

Moreover, Isolation Forest attains the highest F1 score (i.e., 0.78), while the lowest one (i.e., 0.64) is achieved by CNN-Autoencoder. It may be observed that precision is only moderately good for all the tested algorithms, varying from 0.62 to 0.76. On the contrary, recall exhibits better performances and ranges from 0.58 to 0.92. The F1 score performs similarly to the precision metrics. Table 3 highlights the best algorithm for each group based on the adopted anomaly criterion.

From a quantitative evaluation standpoint, all the algorithms seem to achieve comparable performances. But if we analyze their behavior from a qualitative perspective, two observations emerge.

The first one is related to the CNN-Autoencoder, which has a high precision compared to the other approaches based on input reconstruction, but has a recall value rather low with respect to all the other algorithms. As shown in Fig. 3, this is due to the lack of identification of the anomaly in case the device stops working (i.e. the power consumption is zero), which can be a problem especially for household appliances such as the one analysed.

The second aspect refers to the overall performances of the implemented methods, which achieve good results. However, they have been evaluated considering only each single labelled anomalous point separately, but, as shown in Fig. 4, all algorithms correctly identified almost all the time windows in which the anomalies occur. The precise identification of the starting or ending point of them is the main difference among the different techniques.

Table 3. Results summary of implemented methods. For each one is specified the anomaly criterion (Dissimilarity, Prediction, Reconstruction).

Technique	Miss Alarm Rate	False Alarm Rate	Precision	Recall	F1 score
One-Class SVM (D)	0.24	0.03	0.76	0.76	0.76
Local Outlier Factor (D)	0.08	0.06	0.66	0.92	0.77
Isolation Forest (D)	0.16	0.04	0.73	0.84	**0.78**
CNN (P)	0.4	0.02	0.76	0.60	0.67
GRU (P)	0.38	0.03	0.73	0.62	0.67
LSTM (P)	0.38	0.03	0.73	0.62	**0.67**
CNN-Autoencoder (R)	0.42	0.03	0.72	0.58	0.64
GRU-Autoencoder (R)	0.17	0.06	0.62	0.81	0.70
LSTM-Autoencoder (R)	0.24	0.05	0.67	0.76	**0.71**

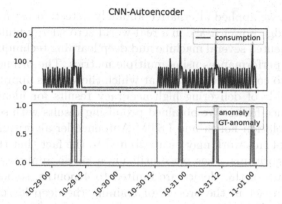

Fig. 3. CNN-Autoencoder anomaly identification lack example. The green line refers to the ground truth, while the red one to the model predictions. (Colore figure online)

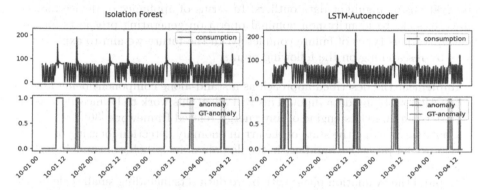

Fig. 4. Qualitative overall performances. The green line refers to the ground truth, while the red one to the model predictions. On the left are shown the Isolation Forest anomaly predictions, while on the right the LSTM-Autoencoder ones. (Color figure online)

5   Conclusion

The identification of anomalies focuses on recognizing unusual events/observations that deviate significantly from the rest of the data. Being able to recognize non-standard device operation is seen as a significant responsibility in the energy industry. AD in small-scale residential and industrial settings can benefit the insight into the device health, the maintenance requirements, and the experienced downtime and thus has the potential to reduce maintenance costs significantly. Several alternative techniques have been proposed and evaluated for AD in a variety of application contexts, also in the prescriptive maintenance scenario.

In this work, we applied alternative anomaly detection methods to data collected from a fridge power usage in a real-world zero-energy building prototype. We have implemented several machine and deep learning techniques and assessed their respective performances using multiple metrics. The primary contribution of this study is to compare the extent at which the various approaches and algorithms are capable of delivering high accuracy results for identifying device/-machine/appliance faults. We obtained promising results with several methods, among which Isolation Forest and LSTM-Autoencoder algorithms stand out.

Limitations of this work may be attributed to the fact that the evaluation of methods and algorithms takes place utilizing a single appliance (fridge). Also, the historical data of this device are limited to 4 months, something that may have negative impact in the process of training the deep learning algorithms. More data should be employed for a more thorough testing phase but also for producing more reliable and generic results.

All in all, anomaly detection seeks to identify anomalous behavior in data observations or highlight data outliers. In terms of appliance or device maintenance it seeks to identify non nominal operation generating prospects for preventing various types of failure completely. In the future we aim to expand this work by researching on the following points.

- Implement the described approach as a stand-alone component being able to function with any data input. This will allow this work to be incorporated as part of an analytics engine or any energy related framework [36].
- Continue tracking the state of the art in anomaly detection focusing on maintenance for proactive buildings in the domain of households or small industrial setups.
- Expand the evaluation phase with more data sets including small scale industrial units or household clusters containing more devices.

Acknowledgements. This work is supported by the project PRECEPT - A novel decentralized edge-enabled PREsCriptivE and ProacTive framework for increased energy efficiency and well-being in residential buildings funded by the EU H2020 Programme, grant agreement no. 958284.

References

1. Schlegl, T., Seeböck, P., Waldstein, S.M., Langs, G., Schmidt-Erfurth, U.: f-anoganL fast unsupervised anomaly detection with generative adversarial networks. Med. Image Anal. **54**, 30–44 (2019)
2. Chauhan, S., Vig, L.: Anomaly detection in ECG time signals via deep long short-term memory networks. In: 2015 IEEE International Conference on Data Science and Advanced Analytics (DSAA), pp. 1–7. IEEE (2015)
3. Sanz, B., Santos, I., Ugarte-Pedrero, X., Laorden, C., Nieves, J., Bringas, P.G.: Anomaly detection using string analysis for android malware detection. In: International Joint Conference SOCO 2013-CISIS 2013-ICEUTE 2013, pp. 469–478. Springer (2014)

4. Koukaras, P., Bezas, N., Gkaidatzis, P., Ioannidis, D., Tzovaras, D., Tjortjis, C.: Introducing a novel approach in one-step ahead energy load forecasting. Sustain. Comput. Inform. Syst. **32**, 100616 (2021)
5. Koukaras, P., Tjortjis, C., Gkaidatzis, P., Bezas, N., Ioannidis, D., Tzovaras, D.: An interdisciplinary approach on efficient virtual microgrid to virtual microgrid energy balancing incorporating data preprocessing techniques. Computing **104**(1), 209–250 (2021). https://doi.org/10.1007/s00607-021-00929-7
6. Zhou, X., et al.: A state of the art survey of data mining-based fraud detection and credit scoring. In: MATEC Web of Conferences, vol. 189, pp. 03002. EDP Sciences (2018)
7. Hawkins, D.M.: Identification of Outliers, vol. 11. Springer, Berlin (1980)
8. Cook, A.A., Mısırlı, G., Fan, Z.: Anomaly detection for IoT time-series data: a survey. IEEE Internet of Things J. **7**(7), 6481–6494 (2019)
9. Brockwell, P.J., Davis, R.A.: Time series: theory and methods. Springer Science & Business Media (2009)
10. Chalapathy, R., Chawla, S.: Deep learning for anomaly detection: a survey. arXiv preprint arXiv:1901.03407 (2019)
11. Choi, K., Yi, J., Park, C., Yoon, S.: Deep learning for anomaly detection in time-series data: review, analysis, and guidelines. IEEE Access (2021)
12. Pincombe, B.: Anomaly detection in time series of graphs using arma processes. Asor Bull. **24**(4), 2 (2005)
13. Moayedi, H.Z., Masnadi-Shirazi, M.A.: Arima model for network traffic prediction and anomaly detection. In: 2008 International Symposium on Information Technology, vol. 4, pp. 1–6. IEEE (2008)
14. Yaacob, A.H., Tan, I.K.T., Fong Chien, S., Tan, H.K.: Arima based network anomaly detection. In: 2010 Second International Conference on Communication Software and Networks, pp. 205–209. IEEE (2010)
15. Idé, T.: Why does subsequence time-series clustering produce sine waves? In: Fürnkranz, J., Scheffer, T., Spiliopoulou, M. (eds.) PKDD 2006. LNCS (LNAI), vol. 4213, pp. 211–222. Springer, Heidelberg (2006). https://doi.org/10.1007/11871637_23
16. Çelik, M., Dadaşer-Çelik, F., Şakir Dokuz, A.: Anomaly detection in temperature data using DBSCAN algorithm. In: 2011 International Symposium on Innovations in Intelligent Systems and Applications, pp. 91–95. IEEE (2011)
17. Oehmcke, S., Zielinski, O., Kramer, O.: Event detection in marine time series data. In: Hölldobler, S., Krötzsch, M., Peñaloza, R., Rudolph, S. (eds.) KI 2015. LNCS (LNAI), vol. 9324, pp. 279–286. Springer, Cham (2015). https://doi.org/10.1007/978-3-319-24489-1_24
18. Ding, Z., Fei, M.: An anomaly detection approach based on isolation forest algorithm for streaming data using sliding window. IFAC Proc. Vol. **46**(20), 12–17 (2013)
19. Ma, J., Perkins, S.: Time-series novelty detection using one-class support vector machines. In: Proceedings of the International Joint Conference on Neural Networks, 2003, vol. 3, pp. 1741–1745. IEEE (2003)
20. Medsker, L.R., Jain, L.C.: Recurrent neural networks. Design Appl. **5**, 64–67 (2001)
21. Hochreiter, S., Schmidhuber, J.: Long short-term memory. Neural Comput. **9**(8), 1735–1780 (1997)
22. Cho, K., et al.: Learning phrase representations using RNN encoder-decoder for statistical machine translation. arXiv preprint arXiv:1406.1078 (2014)
23. Malhotra, P., Vig, L., Shroff, G., Agarwal, P., et al.: Long short term memory networks for anomaly detection in time series. In: Proceedings **89**, 89–94 (2015)

24. Taylor, A., Leblanc, S., Japkowicz, N.: Anomaly detection in automobile control network data with long short-term memory networks. In: 2016 IEEE International Conference on Data Science and Advanced Analytics (DSAA), pp. 130–139. IEEE (2016)
25. Munir, M., Siddiqui, S.A., Dengel, A., Ahmed, S.: Deepant: a deep learning approach for unsupervised anomaly detection in time series. IEEE Access, **7**, 1991–2005 (2018)
26. Hsieh, R.J., Chou, J., Ho, C.H.: Unsupervised online anomaly detection on multivariate sensing time series data for smart manufacturing. In: 2019 IEEE 12th Conference on Service-Oriented Computing and Applications (SOCA), pp. 90–97. IEEE (2019)
27. Park, D., Hoshi, Y., Kemp, C.C.: A multimodal anomaly detector for robot-assisted feeding using an LSTM-based variational autoencoder. IEEE Robot. Autom. Lett. **3**(3), 1544–1551 (2018)
28. Guo, Y., Liao, W., Wang, Q., Yu, L., Ji, T., Li, P.: Multidimensional time series anomaly detection: a GRU-based gaussian mixture variational autoencoder approach. In: Asian Conference on Machine Learning, pp. 97–112. PMLR (2018)
29. Wen, T., Keyes, R.: Time series anomaly detection using convolutional neural networks and transfer learning. arXiv preprint arXiv:1905.13628 (2019)
30. Choi, Y., Lim, H., Choi, H., Kim, I.G.: Gan-based anomaly detection and localization of multivariate time series data for power plant. In: 2020 IEEE International Conference on Big Data and Smart Computing (BigComp), pp. 71–74. IEEE (2020)
31. Fu, X., Luo, H., Zhong, S., Lin, l.: Aircraft engine fault detection based on grouped convolutional denoising autoencoders. Chin. J. Aeronautics, **32**(2), 296–307 (2019)
32. Rashid, H., Stankovic, V., Stankovic, L., Singh, P.: Evaluation of non-intrusive load monitoring algorithms for appliance-level anomaly detection. In: ICASSP 2019– 2019 IEEE International Conference on Acoustics, Speech and Signal Processing (ICASSP), pp. 8325–8329. IEEE (2019)
33. Murray, D., Stankovic, L., Stankovic, V.: An electrical load measurements dataset of united kingdom households from a two-year longitudinal study. Sci. Data **4**(1), 1–12 (2017)
34. Weng, Yu., Zhang, N., Xia, C.: Multi-agent-based unsupervised detection of energy consumption anomalies on smart campus. IEEE Access **7**, 2169–2178 (2018)
35. Makonin, S., Ellert, B., Bajić, I.V., Popowich, F.: Electricity, water, and natural gas consumption of a residential house in Canada from 2012 to 2014. Sci. Data, **3**(1), 1–12 (2016)
36. Koukaras, P., et al.: A tri-layer optimization framework for day-ahead energy scheduling based on cost and discomfort minimization. Energies, **14**(12) (2021)

Chargym: An EV Charging Station Model for Controller Benchmarking

Georgios Karatzinis[1] , Christos Korkas[1,2](✉) , Michalis Terzopoulos[1],
Christos Tsaknakis[1,2], Aliki Stefanopoulou[1] , Iakovos Michailidis[1,2] ,
and Elias Kosmatopoulos[1,2]

[1] Democritus University of Thrace, 67100 Xanthi, Greece
[2] Center for Research and Technology, 57001 Thessaloniki, Greece
chriskorkas@iti.gr

Abstract. This paper presents Chargym, a Python-based openai-gym compatible environment, that simulates the charging dynamics of a grid connected Electrical Vehicle (EV) charging station. Chargym transforms the classic EV charging problem into a Reinforcement Learning setup that can be used for benchmarking of various and off-the-shelf control and optimization algorithms enabling both single and multiple agent formulations. The incorporated charging station dynamics are presented with a brief explanation of the system parameters and function of the technical equipment. Moreover, we describe the structure of the used framework, highlighting the key features and data models that provide the necessary inputs for optimal control decisions. Finally, an experimental performance analysis is provided using two different state-of-the-art Reinforcement Learning (RL) algorithms validating the operation of the provided environment.

Keywords: Electric vehicles · Charging optimization · Deep reinforcement learning · Benchmarking

1 Introduction

Current and upcoming introduction of plug-in hybrid electric vehicles (PHEVs) and fully electric vehicles (EVs) in markets, will introduce large amounts of electrical loads and storage capacity into the electric grid requiring many efforts for the sufficient integration and management. Moreover, the EV charging and discharging will introduce different load profiles not only in terms of quantity, but also in terms of timely change. In US and North America in general, the EV deployment and introduction of EVs is more mature compared to other countries and Europe. The deployment of EV vehicles results to large electrical loads that reach the 18% of the total energy consumption [1]. Moreover, the introduction of EV's also adds uncertainty in the grid since, with the Vehicle-to-Grid (V2G) functionality [2], they can also provide energy to the power grid by discharging

© IFIP International Federation for Information Processing 2022
Published by Springer Nature Switzerland AG 2022
I. Maglogiannis et al. (Eds.): AIAI 2022 Workshops, IFIP AICT 652, pp. 241–252, 2022.
https://doi.org/10.1007/978-3-031-08341-9_20

the battery. It is clear that developing appropriate algorithms to control and optimize the charging/discharging process is crucial in order to facilitate the smooth
integration of EV units in the current electrical grid. Numerous works can be
found in literature, focusing on optimal EV charging. Initial approaches for controlling the charging systems were formed by open loop strategies [6,11], but
the simple rule-based control approach that they follow, combined with possible
computational complexity that they introduce, can lead to sub-optimal control
behavior, since it is known that open-loop control strategies result to non-robust
solutions [12], e.g. they require to re-calibrate their decisions for different initial and exogenous conditions resulting to extensive and numerous simulations.
Therefore, introducing close-loop efficient charging control provides the tools to
reduce energy consumption, environmental impact and maximize the user satisfaction. Recent research approaches cover the fields of (robust) model predictive control (MPC) (see e.g., [9,10], adaptive or learning-based approaches (see
e.g., [3,4]), and reinforcement learning (RL); see e.g., [5,7]. A thorough review
on electric vehicle technologies, charging methods, standards and optimization
techniques can be found in [8].

1.1 Related Work

Alongside the recent developments in state-of-the-art RL and control algorithms
for optimal charging and scheduling of EVs and other smart grid nodes, large
efforts have been paid for the implementation of open-source tools and simulators
offering robust and ease to use platforms supporting new research. Many of
these platforms are focused on smart-grids, buildings and microgrid operation,
however the research community has also developed simulators focused on EV
operation and charging. In [16] the simulation aspects of energy consumption,
available charging stations and charging duration are considered. The problem
of the shortest path and travel planning is studied in [17], where the authors
designed an approximation scheme to calculate the most energy-efficient path.
In [18,21] traffic simulations are presented utilizing EVs and investigating the
optimal online charging based on highway available public chargers. Two of
the most used simulators are V2GSim [14] and EVLibSim [13]. However both
V2G-Sim and EVLibSim allow for precomputed charging schedules or simple
control strategies. Another recently developed simulator, called ACN-Sim [15] is
designed explicitly around evaluating online algorithms which adapt to changes
in the system state over time. However, ACN-Sim is more oriented towards,
energy system aspects of the problem rather than to the cost/penalty evaluation.

1.2 Contributions

The main contribution of this work is to provide a framework that simulates
the operation of a grid-connected EV charging station. Our main goal is to
provide a generalised environment for charging/discharging EVs under various
disturbances (weather conditions, pricing models, stochastic arrival-departure
EV times and stochastic Battery State of Charge (BOC) at arrival). Thereby,

by training multiple times in such generated environments, the controller will grasp/understand the underlining charging dynamics and leverage it to efficiently complete its goal, even in days/instances that it has never been trained. Moreover, Chargym offers control over multiple charging set-points (one per connected vehicle) enabling multi-agent formulations as well. Finally, both charging and discharging of the vehicles is offered, in order to achieve the optimal results. Within this work, a novel simulation environment for EV charging has been developed, based on the openai-gym format. All the core parameters and dynamics that describe and simulate a real EV charging setup have been included. Chargym (available at https://github.com/georkara/Chargym-Charging-Station (accessed on 20/4/2022), is a Python-based library, made for standardized comparison and evaluation of controller performances, based on predefined evaluation scenarios, and is inspired by the RL benchmarking library Gym. It should be emphasized that Chargym is one of the first simulators that provide highly realistic simulation of an EV charging station and it is also a framework upon where state of the art RL methods (and also other learning approaches) will be efficiently benchmarked in EV charging tasks aiming to optimize not only cost related rewards, but also penalties related to failing charge the EVs to the desired Battery State-of-Charge. Two state-of-the-art RL algorithms, namely DDPG and PPO, have been evaluated on the Chargym environment. To better comprehend these evaluation results, the average human-level performance (Rule-Based Controller) in the Chargym environment is also reported. However, the follow-up analysis utilizing the best-performing algorithm is not conducted with respect to the different levels of solar availability and pricing models and levels of performance, rather presents the easy integration of algorithms utilizing the station as a simulation environment.

The rest of this paper is organized as follow: Sect. 2 presents the physical description, characteristics and main assumptions of the charging station. Section 3 presents the details of the openai-gym/RL charging environment and formulation. Section 4 presents the main results of applying two state-of-the-art RL algorithms, evaluated against a Rule-Based-Controller, showcasing the integration and interoperability of Chargym with common RL libraries. Finally, Sect. 5 summarizes the main innovations of this work and the main future steps.

2   Charging Station Overview

Chargym simulates the operation of an electric vehicle charging station (EVCS) considering random EV arrivals and departures within a day. The main objective is to minimize the cost for the electricity absorbed by the power grid, while ensuring that all EVs reach their desired level of State of Charge (SoC) at departure. If an EV departs without reaching the desired SoC, a penalty cost is calculated and applied. The EVCS architecture is presented in Fig. 1. More specifically, the core components of the Chargym environment are given: i) a set of 10 charging spots; ii) one photovoltaic (PV) generation system; iii) power grid connection offering energy at a certain price and iv) the vehicle to grid operation

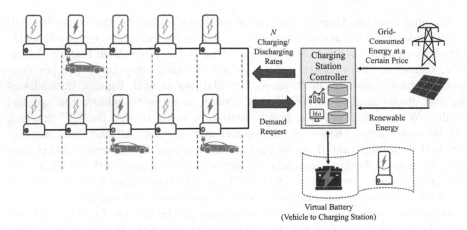

Fig. 1. Chargym interaction architecture

(V2G), which adds a Vehicle to Charging Station functionality, allowing the usage of energy stored in EVs for charging other EVs, when necessary.

Regarding the operational framework, the station is connected with the grid absorbing electricity at a fluctuating price, when the available amount of energy is inadequate. The station's available amount of energy (apart from the grid) is unfolded into two types:

- Stored energy in the cars that can be utilized under the V2G operation.
- Produced energy from the PV.

Note that the term *stored energy* refers to storage that is formed from the available energy storage of EVs in a Vehicle to Charging Station perspective. Therefore, the environment describes a case where the stored energy in EVs, can be utilized from the station (based on the control setpoints) to satisfy the demands of other EVs that have limited time until their departure time. In Table 1, the basic parameters related with EVCS and EVs are presented.

The following conditions describe the overall perception of the EVCS, providing clear insights concerning the implementation of the environment's operating framework.

Assumption 1 . All EVs that arrive to the station are assumed to share the same characteristics related with their battery (type, capacity, charging/ discharging rate, charging/ discharging efficiency, battery efficiency).

Assumption 2 : The desired State of Charge for every EV at departure time is 100%.

Assumption 3 : If an EV departs with less than 100% State of Charge, a penalty score is calculated.

Table 1. Charging station parameters.

Station Parameters	Value
Timestep length (dk) (h)	1
EV Battery Capacity(B_{max}) (kWh)	30
Charging and Discharging Eff. (η_{ch}) (%)	91
Maximum Charging Output $(P_{ch,max})$ (kW)	11

Stochastic parameter	Minimum	Maximum
Arrival State of Charge (%)	10	80
Arrival Time (hour)	0	22
Departure Time (hour)	Arrival+2	Next Day

Assumption 4 : There is no upper limit of supply from the power grid. This way, the grid can supply the Charging Station with any amount of requested energy.

Assumption 5 : The maximum charging/discharging supply of each EV is dictated by charging/discharging rate of the station.

Assumption 6 : Each charging spot, can be used more than once per day.

3   Framework Description

The real-time EVCS scheduling problem can be formulated, in a Reinforcement Learning context, as a Markov Decision Process (MDP) with a 4-tuple $(\mathbf{S}, \mathbf{A}, \mathbf{P}, \mathbf{R})$, where $\mathbf{S}$ is the set of states, $\forall s \in S$; $\mathbf{A}$ is a finite set of actions, $\forall a \in A$; $\mathbf{P}$ is the state transition probability with $P : S \times A \times S \to [0,1]$ being the transition function with the probability of the transition from state s by choosing action a to state s' at time $t+1$, such that $p_a(s,s') = p(s_{t+1} = s'|s_t = s, a_t = a)$; $R : S \times A \times S \to \mathbb{R}$ is the reward function, where $R_a(s,s')$ is the reward received by the agent after transition from state s to state s' occurs.

3.1   State

The EVCS state at each time step t is defined as:

$$
\begin{aligned}
s_t = (&G_t, pr_t, G_{t+1}, G_{t+2}, G_{t+3}, pr_{t+1}, pr_{t+2}, pr_{t+3}, \quad \cdots \\
&\cdots \quad SoC_t^1, SoC_t^2, ..., SoC_t^{10}, Tleave_t^1, Tleave_t^2..., Tleave_t^{10})
\end{aligned}
\tag{1}
$$

This vector contains four types of information: (i) G_t is current value of solar radiation and $(G_{t+1}, G_{t+2}, G_{t+3})$ implies solar radiation ahead predictions for the next three hours; (ii) pr_t is current value of electricity price that the utility company charges the station for a requested amount of energy and

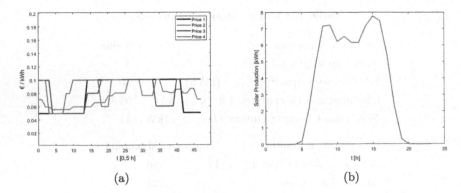

Fig. 2. Price and solar production simulation profiles. (a) Different profiles of dynamic pricing, used in test cases; (b) Solar production on a typical day.

$(pr_{t+1}, pr_{t+2}, pr_{t+3})$ are the three hour price predictions ahead. Although price changes dynamically throughout the day simulating tariff, it is not a function of supply and demand. Thus, price is dynamic but independent of the requested amount; (iii) SoC_t^i denotes the SOC of the EV at i_{th} charging spot at timestep t and (iv) $Tleave_t^i$ indicates the number of hours until departure for the EV at i_{th} charging spot. The latter states, SoC_t^i and $Tleave_t^i$, can be considered as the physical states of the EVCS. In Fig. 2(a), the four pricing profiles that are available for simulation are presented, whereas in Fig. 2(b) a typical day of electricity production is shown.

Regarding the states two main points should be highlighted:

- If charging spot i is empty at t, then SOC_t^i and $Tleave_t^i$ are 0.
- All the states presented in Eq. 1, are normalized between 0 and 1.

3.2   Action

As described above, the charging station is composed by 10 charging spots, all able to charge or discharge (V2G capability) the connected EVs. Therefore, there are 10 actions defining the charging or discharging rate of each vehicle spot. These 10 action set-points $(action^i)$ are defined as continuous variables, which are constrained in the $[-1, 1]$ space. The charging/discharging power for each vehicle i at timestep t is defined as :

$$MaxEnergy_t^i = \begin{cases} (1 - SOC_t^i) * B_{max} & action_t^i >= 0 \\ (SOC_t^i) * B_{max} & action_t^i < 0 \end{cases} \quad (2)$$

$$MaxEnergy_t^i <= P_{ch,max} * \eta_{ch} \quad (3)$$

$$P_t^{dem,i} = action_t^i * MaxEnergy_t^i \quad (4)$$

where SoC_t^i is the state of charge of each EV (i) at time t and B_{max}, $P_{ch,max}$, η_{ch} are given in Table 1.

Thus, the three equations above, describe the calculation of the demand for each charging spot in timestep t based on the actions that are taken by the controller. If action is a positive number, the $P_t^{dem,i}$ is positive (charging mode), whereas if action is negative $P_t^{dem,i}$ is negative (discharging mode). The value of $action^i$ affects directly the demand as shown in Eq. 4. Equations 3 and 2, describe the constraints on the maximum charging/discharging energy that can be allocated in one timestep.

3.3   Reward

The main objective of the EVCS's controller/agent is to adopt a scheduling policy towards minimizing the cost for the electricity absorbed by the power grid. The reward function observed at each timestep t is the electricity bill being payed by EVCS to the utility company. However, an additional term is incorporated in order to present a more realistic and complete description ensuring that the controller will exploit effectively the available resources as well as fulfil the defined requirements. The second term considers penalizing situations involving EVs that are not completely charged. The equation describing this specific formulation is the following:

$$r_t(S_t, A_t) = \sum_{i \in \Omega_t} (pr_t \cdot P_t^{dem}) + \sum_{i \in \Psi_t} [2 \cdot (1 - SoC_t^i)]^2 \tag{5}$$

where $P_t^{dem} \in \Omega_t$ stands for the total charging demand that the EVCS requests to receive from the utility company as mentioned above. The electricity price, pr_t, follows a varying bill profile that the utility company provides/charges the EVCS at each timestep in €/KWh and presented in Fig. 2(a). The second term is related with the state of charge of those EVs that are expected to departure the next hour. The goal is to fully charge the EVs that depart. However, in future realizations, the EV owner could choose the desired SOC at departure (to reduce the charging cost), making the formulation even more realistic.

4   Performance Evaluation

This section presents an experimental evaluation of the Chargym environment. The analysis begins with all the implementation details that are important for realizing the Chargym experimental setup. We employ two state-of-the-art Deep Reinforcement Learning algorithms, namely Deep Deterministic Policy Gradient (DDPG) [19] and Proximal Policy Optimization (PPO) [20], in order to evaluate their performances using the Chargym environment. Moreover, a simple rule based controller (RBC) is presented to perform as a baseline model providing a reasonable operational strategy, simulating human-operated decisions. However, as stated in introduction, the goal of this section is to evaluate the operation and the ease-of-use of Chargym environment, and not to perform a deep analysis on the performance of state-of-the-art algorithms.

4.1 Implementation Details and Key Experimental Attributes

Stable Baselines 3 framework [22] was utilized to perform all the experiments. The fact that Stable Baselines 3 is a well-documented, highly-robust library also eases the build-on developments (e.g., apply a different RL pipeline), as it follows a common framework. Furthermore, such an experimental setup may also leverage the interoperability with other powerful frameworks and showcases the ease-to-use nature of the Chargym environment.

On the other hand Chargym was designed to bridge the gap between realistic charging/discharging EV operations and powerful state-of-art control and RL solutions. The experiments/simulations that were conducted on Chargym, as well as, the whole formulation of the EVCS design were based on the following key attributes:

– **Schedule Diversity**: For each episode, the general dynamics and EV schedules are determined by a specific automated and random process. These levels correspond to the randomness in the number, arrival and departure rates, and schedules of the EVs, the initial SoC of each EV upon arrival and of course the different solar and pricing conditions. This approach forces the control algorithms to be trained and tested in multiple/diverse layouts, producing robust solutions which are of paramount importance in real-life applications where unknown schedules appear.
– **Partial Observability**: At each timestep, the EVCS is only aware of the attributes of the connected EVs, and the forecasts for the next three hours for the solar and pricing tariffs. The station can not utilize information of the EVs that are going to arrive in the future, therefore, any long-term plan should be agile enough to be adjusted on the fly, based on future information about the newly arrived vehicles.
– **Real Life Applicability**: One of the fundamental advantages of Chargym is that any learned policy can be straightforwardly applied to an appropriate EVCS case, since the whole problem formulation is using common and relevant EV knowledge and assumptions. Our goal is to create policies that calculate the optimal charging/discharging schedule based on the generic perception of the environment. Thus, assuming that a smooth integration with the sensor's readings, can be used to represent the environment as in Eq. 1, and no elaborate simulation model of the dynamics is required to adjust the RL algorithm into the specifics of the station.

4.2 Rule-Based Controller

The main comparison for the used RL algorithms, will be conducted with respect to a Rule-Based Controller (RBC), that makes human-based decisions regarding the charging-discharging of the EVs. The RBC offers simple and fast decisions, however far from optimal, decisions. The RBC consists of two simple rules that are presented in Eq. 6:

$$action_t^i = \begin{cases} 1 & Tleave_t^i <= 3 \\ \frac{(G_t + G_{t+1})}{2} & Tleave_t^i > 3 \end{cases} \tag{6}$$

The controller checks each charging spot and collects the Departure timeplan of each connected EV. If an EV is going to depart during the next three hours, then the station is charging in full capacity this specific EV. On the other hand, if an EV does not depart during the next three hours, the station checks the current availability of the solar energy and charges the EV, based on that availability. The three hour time-limit, is selected based on the EVCS attributes, since the EVs utilize 30kWh batteries, and the maximum charging ability of the station is 10kW. Thus, an EV needs three hours to charge from 0 to 100% SoC.

4.3   State-of-the-Art RL Algorithms Comparison

Regarding the training process, each episode concerns a different simulated day in terms of solar energy production, pricing profile and EV schedules and demands. Also the RL implementations, DDPG and PPO, are trained utilizing diverse training sets. The hyperparameter configurations of both RL algorithms are shown in Table 2. A larger hidden layer structure has been chosen for the case of DDPG. Figure 3(a) presents the transition learning performance from day to day between the adopted algorithms. As it can be noted, DDPG converges a little bit earlier achieving higher levels of reward in respect with PPO. In order to test the performance of the RL algorithms, we recall the trained models, indicatively after 940K episodes, and evaluate them in a new set of 100 simulated days with diverse configurations. The evaluation comparison between the RL algorithms and the RBC involves the same day configuration with identical operating conditions among algorithms for each episode, but different configurations between episodes (days). Both RL algorithms outperform the RBC, as depicted in Fig. 3(b) and Table 3, while also the DDPG implementation consistently attains higher reward versus PPO.

Table 2. DDPG and PPO hyperparameter configuration

DDPG		PPO	
Parameters	Value	Parameters	Value
Memory buffer size	1e5	Learning rate	3e-4
Batch size	100	Batch size	64
Optimizers	Adam	Optimizers	Adam
Layer structure	[400, 300]	Layer structure	[64, 64]
Actor, Critic learning rate	0.001	GAE lambda, Clipping ratio	0.95, 0.2
Discount factor (γ)	0.99	Discount factor (γ)	0.99
Target update factor (τ)	0.005	Entropy and value function coefficients	0, 0.5
Ornstein Uhlenbeck (μ, σ, θ)	$0_{1 \times 10}$, 0.5, 0.15	Max grad norm	0.5

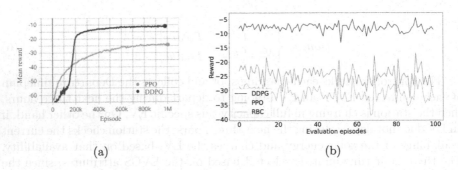

(a)   (b)

Fig. 3. Training and evaluation reward comparison. (a) Rolling mean of the average episodic reward of PPO and DDPG; (b) Evaluation reward over 100 days between RL algorithms and RBC.

Table 3. Mean evaluation reward

Approach	Mean Reward
RBC	−30.99
PPO	−24.64
DDPG	−7.93

5   Conclusions and Future Work

This paper presents a new simulation enviroment, called Chargym, based on openai-gym format that bridges the gap between reinforcement learning and the real-life charging/discharging strategies in the EV domain. The environment simulates the problem of EV charging/discharging under multiple stochastic parameters (weather, electricity pricing, EV arrival, departure, SOC) into a reinforcement learning setup that can be tackled by a wide range model-free and model based RL and optimal control algorithms. An experimental evaluation was also conducted and presented, with 2 state-of-the-art RL algorithms, namely DDPG and PPO evaluated in Chargym, and their training results were also compared with a Rule Based Controller's performance for the task at hand. Future work, will aim on extensive comparison tests between state of the art RL and control algorithms (such as MPC) for the optimal scheduling of charging/discharging set-points, and special effort will be given in multi-agent frameworks enabling distributed and coordinated control of the charging setpoints/slots.

Acknowledgements. We acknowledge support of this work by the European Commission H2020-EU.2.1.5.2., Turning traditional reactive buildings into proactive ones, under contract 958284 (PRECEPT).

References

1. Ma, Z., Callaway, D.S., Hiskens, I.A.: Decentralized charging control of large populations of plug-in electric vehicles. IEEE Trans. Control Syst. Technol. **21**(1), 67–78 (2011)
2. Han, S., Han, S.H., Sezaki, K.: Design of an optimal aggregator for vehicle-to-grid regulation service. In: 2010 Innovative Smart Grid Technologies (ISGT). IEEE (2010)
3. Korkas, C.D., Baldi, S., Michailidis, P., Kosmatopoulos, E.B.: A cognitive stochastic approximation approach to optimal charging schedule in electric vehicle stations. In: 2017 25th Mediterranean Conference on Control and Automation (MED), pp. 484–489. IEEE, July 2017
4. Korkas, C.D., Baldi, S., Yuan, S., Kosmatopoulos, E.B.: An adaptive learning-based approach for nearly optimal dynamic charging of electric vehicle fleets. IEEE Trans. Intell. Transp. Syst. **19**(7), 2066–2075 (2017)
5. Qian, T., Shao, C., Wang, X., Shahidehpour, M.: Deep reinforcement learning for EV charging navigation by coordinating smart grid and intelligent transportation system. IEEE Trans. Smart Grid **11**(2), 1714–1723 (2019)
6. Bhatti, A.R., et al.: Optimized sizing of photovoltaic grid-connected electric vehicle charging system using particle swarm optimization. Int. J. Energy Res. **43**(1), 500–522 (2019)
7. Wan, Z., Li, H., He, H., Prokhorov, D.: Model-free real-time EV charging scheduling based on deep reinforcement learning. IEEE Trans. Smart Grid **10**(5), 5246–5257 (2018)
8. Arif, S.M., Lie, T.T., Seet, B.C., Ayyadi, S., Jensen, K.: Review of electric vehicle technologies, charging methods, standards and optimization techniques. Electronics **10**(16), 1910 (2021)
9. Zheng, Y., Song, Y., Hill, D.J., Meng, K.: Online distributed MPC-based optimal scheduling for EV charging stations in distribution systems. IEEE Trans. Ind. Inf. **15**(2), 638–649 (2018)
10. Tang, W., Zhang, Y.J.: A model predictive control approach for low-complexity electric vehicle charging scheduling: optimality and scalability. IEEE Trans. Power Syst. **32**(2), 1050–1063 (2016)
11. Zhang, M., Chen, J.: The energy management and optimized operation of electric vehicles based on microgrid. IEEE Trans. Power Deliv. **29**(3), 1427–1435 (2014)
12. Bardi, M., Dolcetta, I.C.: Optimal Control and Viscosity Solutions of Hamilton-Jacobi-Bellman Equations, vol. 12. Birkhäuser, Boston (1997)
13. Rigas, E.S., Karapostolakis, S., Bassiliades, N., Ramchurn, S.D.: EVLibSim: a tool for the simulation of electric vehicles' charging stations using the EVLib library. Simul. Model. Pract. Theory **87**, 99–119 (2018)
14. Saxena, S.: Vehicle-to-grid Simulator (No. V2G-Sim; 005701MLTPL00). Lawrence Berkeley National Lab. (LBNL), Berkeley, CA (United States) (2013)
15. Lee, Z.J., Johansson, D., Low, S.H.: ACN-sim: an open-source simulator for data-driven electric vehicle charging research. In: 2019 IEEE International Conference on Communications, Control, and Computing Technologies for Smart Grids (SmartGridComm). IEEE (2019)
16. Díaz de Arcaya, A., et al.: Simulation platform for coordinated charging of electric vehicles (2015)
17. Strehler, M., Merting, S., Schwan, C.: Energy-efficient shortest routes for electric and hybrid vehicles. Transp. Res. Part B Methodol. **103**, 111–135 (2017)

18. Mou, Y., et al.: Decentralized optimal demand-side management for PHEV charging in a smart grid. IEEE Trans. Smart Grid **6**(2), 726–736 (2014)
19. Lillicrap, T.P., et al.: Continuous control with deep reinforcement learning (2015). arXiv preprint arXiv:1509.02971
20. Schulman, J., Wolski, F., Dhariwal, P., Radford, A., Klimov, O.: Proximal policy optimization algorithms (2017). arXiv preprint arXiv:1707.06347
21. Bae, S., Kwasinski, A.: Spatial and temporal model of electric vehicle charging demand. IEEE Trans. Smart Grid **3**(1), 394–403 (2011)
22. Raffin, A., Hill, A., Gleave, A., Kanervisto, A., Ernestus, M., Dormann, N.: Stable-Baselines3: reliable reinforcement learning implementations. J. Mach. Learn. Res. (2021)

Environmental Feature Correlation and Meta-analysis for Occupancy Detection - A Real-Life Assessment

Asimina Dimara[1,2(✉)] [ID], Alkiviadis Kyrtsoglou[1] [ID], Iakovos Michailidis[1,3] [ID], Stelios Krinidis[1,4] [ID], Elias B. Kosmatopoulos[1,3] [ID], Dimosthenis Ioannidis[1] [ID], Christos-Nikolaos Anagnostopoulos[2] [ID], and Dimitrios Tzovaras[1] [ID]

[1] Information Technologies Institute, Centre for Research and Technology Hellas, 57001 Thessaloniki, Greece
adimara@iti.gr
[2] Department of Cultural Technology and Communication, Intelligent Systems Lab, University of the Aegean, Mytilene, Greece
[3] Electrical and Computer Engineering Department, Democritus University of Thrace, 67000 Xanthi, Greece
[4] Management Science and Technology Department, International Hellenic University (IHU), Kavala, Greece

Abstract. Even though occupancy inference is of utmost importance for numerous real-time and real-life applications a widely-accepted approach to predict occupancy does not exist. In this paper, an assessment of widely-recommended approaches and data processing for occupancy is overviewed. Furthermore, the correlation and meta-analysis between various sensor features like motion sensing, temperature, humidity, and energy consumption were tested. Random Forest classifier a widely-applied artificial model for occupancy inference prediction is evaluated in 4 different real-life data sets including various features. The results of both a univariate and multivariate model are examined. Random Forest classifier results during an experimental phase are presented to reveal the best model. The outcomes of the current research indicate that even in similar spaces data analysis and correlation have different results while the multivariate model is more accurate than the bivariate model.

Keywords: Occupancy inference · Environmental sensors · Meta-analysis · Data correlation

1 Introduction

Occupancy inference is the process that estimates if a space is occupied or not. Occupancy either reports absence or presence in a room or space, or the number of occupants [1]. Occupancy factor is of key importance for many energy-related applications as it dictates the energy loads inside the building [2]. Specifically, most of the controllable energy saving actions are based on whether the room is

I. Maglogiannis et al. (Eds.): AIAI 2022 Workshops, IFIP AICT 652, pp. 253–264, 2022.
https://doi.org/10.1007/978-3-031-08341-9_21

occupied [3]. Furthermore, occupancy is important for occupants safety therefore many application are based on motion tracking and alerts [4]. Additionally, occupancy is highly related to Indoor Environmental Quality, occupants well-being and comfort [5].

Consequently, there exist numerous approaches, methods and technologies to infer occupancy for real-life and real-time applications. Furthermore, each of them depends on various and diverse type of data and information. Non Artificial Intelligence (AI) methods use specific devices or hardware means to sense occupancy (e.g., smart-phones, thermal cameras, motion sensors, camera sensor network, etc.) [5]. AI methods use data and information deriving from various environmental sensors (e.g., temperature, illuminance, CO_2 sensors) and energy meters to predict occupancy based on machine learning techniques and models (e.g., regression algorithms, neural networks, classification algorithms, supervised and unsupervised learning) [6].

Nonetheless, the plethora of methods does not reassure that occupancy prediction is a straightforward task and choosing one of the aforementioned methods will guarantee high accuracy. Primarily, sensor raw data is filled with prevalent errors, noise, duplicates, constant stack values and many other faults [7] making it almost impossible to be used as it is. As a result, data pre-processing is necessary to heal sensor data before using and saving it using cleaning tools and applications (e.g., imputation, erase duplicates) [8]. Furthermore, in a smart home there are many sensors installed and there is a huge amount of data streams. Therefore, a data correlation must be performed to facilitate feature selection [9]. There exist many data-driven models for occupancy prediction each using different features [10]. Finally, some methods use a univariate model to predict occupancy [11], while others use a multivariate model instead intro12.

Based on the previous analysis, the current paper intends to overview the basic assumptions of occupancy inference from a real-life use case scenario. Initially, data check will be performed to assess the quality and type of errors. Basic techniques like heat-maps and data correlation will be examined and applied on a raw data set [13]. Moreover, the same classification model will be tested using a univariate and a multivariate approach. Eventually, all findings will be analyzed and suggestions will be made for the best approach to use for an accurate occupancy prediction.

The remainder of the paper is structured as follows: Sect. 2 presents all the investigated approaches and widely used data-analysis methods. In Sect. 3 the aforementioned approaches are tested and results are presented. Subsequently, results are drawn in Sect. 4.

2   Investigated Approaches and Data Analysis

In this section commonly-used techniques for data pre-processing and data correlation are addressed. Moreover, feature selection methods are examined and the relationship between various environmental features and occupancy inference are evaluated. Eventually, two methods for classification models (i.e., univariate,

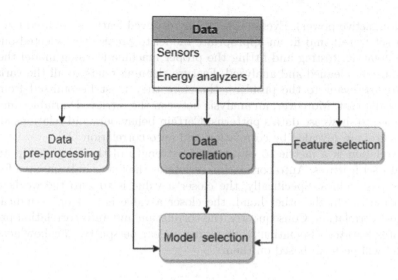

Fig. 1. Overview work flow

multivariate) is assessed. The overall work flow of the investigated approaches and data analysis is depicted in Fig. 1.

2.1 Data Pre-processing

Data pre-processing is a very important process implied in machine learning. Especially, if the data to handled is raw data and not simulated. Some of the most used techniques are:

Impute Missing Values. Imputation is the method used to handle all missing data (e.g., NaN, Null, missing timestamps, etc.). Every feature that appears in a data set demands a unique imputation technique based on its behaviour. Specifically, for continuous features (e.g., humidity, temperature, CO_2), gaps may be filled exploiting an interpolation method (e.g., linear interpolation, spline interpolation) [14]. On the other hand, boolean data may be filled with the backward filling technique [15].

Feature Encoding. Label encoding [16] is applied to the occupancy state feature to convert the occupants schedule to a numeric format as described below:

$$occupancy\ state = \begin{cases} 0, \text{Absent} \\ 1, \text{Presence} \end{cases} \quad (1)$$

2.2 Data Correlation

Every data set that is retrieved by a sensor monitoring network includes various features (e.g., temperature. humidity, illuminance, CO_2, window state, motion detection, active power). Eventually, all the retrieved features are used to create a data set to test and fit an appropriate model to predict the selected output. Before creating, testing and fitting the proper machine learning model the features must be cleaned and analyzed. Feature cleaning refers to all the variables that are irrelevant to the problem, therefore they must be omitted from the training data set. Moreover, an analysis between the retrieved variables must be performed to showcase data's patterns. Certain behaviours and relations among the features are revealed by correlation and auto-correlation [20].

Correlation is a metric to estimate the strength of the relationship among two data-set features. Auto-correlation estimates the linear link among a feature and its past values. Specifically, the closer a value is to zero the weakest the correlation is. On the other hand, the closer a value is to 1 or −1 indicates a strongest correlation. Consequently, the correlation and auto-correlation process facilitates features association while giving a clear perspective for how accurate a model will perform based on them.

2.3   Bivariate Random Forest Versus Multivariate Random Forest Classification for Occupancy

Random Forest (RF) is a widely-used and accurate tree-based machine learning algorithm. It is really popular for classification predictive modeling data sets especially for occupancy inference as it has proven efficient enough [17]. RF could be exploited for time-series prediction and inference, although a transformation of the timestamp (e.g., timestamp to unix) should be performed first. It could be used following two different approaches [19]:

Bivariate Time Series RF. Bivariate is a model that uses two features to predict the output. This type of model associates the relationship and strength of those two variables.

Multivariate Time Series RF. A multivariate model exploits multiple features to predict the output. This type of model associates the relationship and strength of multiple features.

3   Experimental Results

All the above were tested on a real-case scenario. In 4 almost similar offices (i.e., size, occupancy schedule), sensors and energy analyzers were installed as depicted in Fig. 2. Data streams from the sensors and equipment were pushed periodically every 5 min to a database. No further data process was handled before saving data to the database. As a result, all aforementioned approaches will be tested, using the sensors' and energy analyzers' raw data.

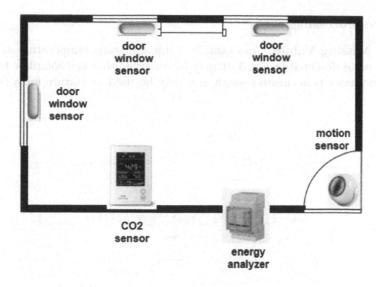

Fig. 2. Floor plan of the sensors and energy meters used

In Table 1 all sensors and equipment used for the experiments is presented. For each of the sensors an identifier was used to save data streams. As a result, a variable called co_temperature indicates that this values derives from the CO_2 sensor. Furthermore, if there are more than one of the indicate type sensor, a number is added after the identifier (e.g., dw1).

Table 1. Sensors and equipment used for the experiments

Type of equipment	Name	Values
Occupancy schedule	Occupancy	0,1 (presence, absence)
CO2 sensor	co_	Humidity
		Carbon_Dioxide
		Temperature
Motion sensor	ms_	Illuminance
		Temperature
		state: 0,1 (presence, absence)
Door window	dwXX_	Temperature
		state: 0,1 (close,open)
Smart meter	sm_	Consumption_total

3.1 Pre-processing

Impute Missing Values. An example of filling missing temperature values in the data-set is depicted in Fig. 3. It may be observed that the complete temperature time-series is accurate enough and may be used as feature for a training data set.

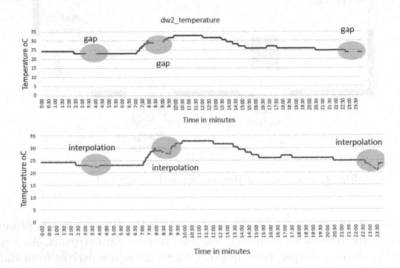

Fig. 3. Example of imputation of missing temperature values using interpolation

Feature Encoding. An example of feature encoding for occupancy schedule in the data-set is depicted in Fig. 4. It may be observed that the occupancy schedule from the offices was encoded to zero and one for absence and presence respectively.

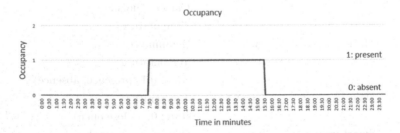

Fig. 4. Example of feature encoding for occupancy schedule

3.2   Data Correlation

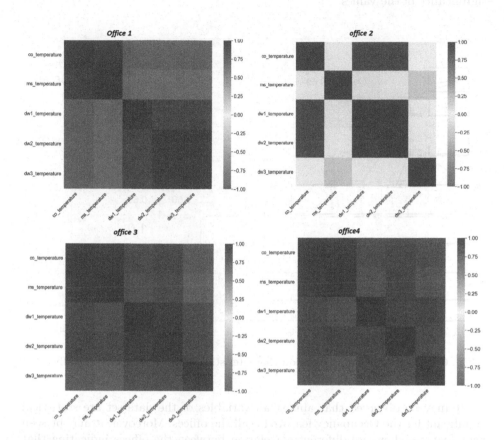

Fig. 5. Heat map of all temperature variables from all sensors for all the offices

Initially, a heat map is created for all the different temperatures received from the various sensors (i.e., door window, CO_2, motion sensor) depicted in Fig. 5. Highly correlated features of the same variable may be some how associated as they do not contribute more to the prediction. Specifically, they have the same information quality so merging those features will reduce running speed and storage needs. It may be observed, from Fig. 5, that temperatures in offices 1, 3 and 4 are highly correlated. As a result, the average temperature was used for these offices. On the contrary, in office 2 only temperatures from door window 1 and 2 were highly correlated, so all of the temperatures were used.

Two out of the four offices are depicted in Figs. 6 and 7 indicatively, and present the total analysis of the correlation among the retrieved features from the sensors. Specifically, the diagonal line presents each variable's distribution. While, under the diagonal line the bivariate scatter plots are presented. Moreover, over the diagonal line the probability of no relationship (significance level) and the correlation values are depicted. Finally, the stars indicate the statistical significance of the values.

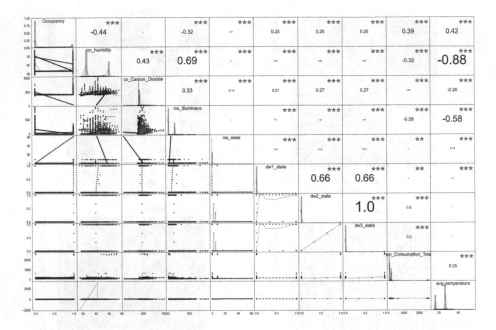

Fig. 6. Distribution and correlation characteristics between all features of office 1.

It may be observed that almost all variables of the data-set are statistical significant for the Occupancy feature for all the offices. Moreover, it may be seen that features showcase different correlation between the offices indicating that the features of each office must be selected separately for each one of them.

3.3   Bivariate Classification Results

Bivariate classification was implemented for all the offices and office 3 is indicatively presented here due to limited space. In more detail, the features of focus for this experiment were the timestamp and the occupancy information described in Sect. 3. Moreover, for the occupancy feature, its own two past values (lags) were also taken into account. Since we are dealing with time sensitive data, the information yielded by past values is necessary to preserve the feature's time dependence. In addition, due to the nature of the problem (supervised learning), a pre-processing step was mandatory. RF requires the conversion of some feature values in order for it to "understand" them.

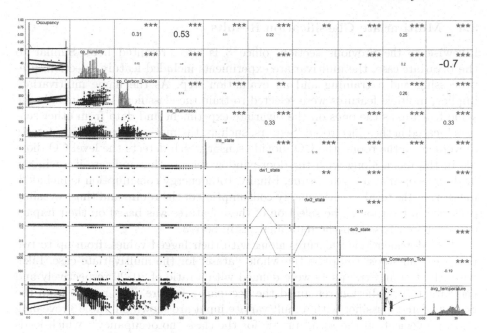

Fig. 7. Distribution and correlation characteristics between all features of office 4.

Specifically, the timestamp of the dataset was converted from python's datetime format to the unix format. For the occupancy, besides the addition of the two lagged versions of itself, all of their values were converted to integers. Before executing the classification, the data were split into train and test sets with a ratio of 80–20 respectively. The purpose of the classifier is to predict whether the office has occupants at a specific moment. For this purpose the RF classifier was used along with some metrics for the evaluation of the output results. The most commonly used features in a classification are the precision, recall and f1 score [21]. Table 2 depicts the results for the case of office 3. The high precision score and the very low score on recall metric, for the 'occupancy' class, indicates a small percentage of correctness for this class which means that further investigation is needed using these features.

Table 2. Random forest classifier results for the bivariate case

	Precision	Recall	f1-score
Not_occupancy	0.78	1	0.87
Occupancy	1	0.01	0.02
Accuracy			0.78
Macro avg	0.89	0.51	0.45
Weighted avg	0.83	0.78	0.68

3.4   Multivariate Classification Results

Likewise to the previous section, office 3 is also presented here. Similar to the bivariate case, the multivariate experiments included feature selection, pre-processing and a training and an evaluation step. As the name multivariate implies, multiple features were selected to train the classifier. These include the same features as the ones on the bivariate experiment and data from other sensors located in the office room. Sensors, such as, the motion sensor which detects movement in the room, the CO dioxide sensor which detects the level CO dioxide in the room, along with the door-window sensors that indicate if a window or door is open at a certain time. Finally, total energy consumption is included, measuring the total electric energy consumption of the room, and thus revealing presence in the room. The selection of these features was based on their impact on occupancy based on the data analysis in Sect. 3.

The aforementioned features along with their lagged values, from up to two previous timesteps, comprise the whole dataset for the multivariate case. Likewise, the test and train sets were defined with a ratio of 80–20 respectively and the target of prediction remained the occupancy feature. The results from the random forest classifier with a multivariate input are shown on Table 3 revealing an improvement on the recall metric for the class "no_occupancy", which leads to an improvement to the overall accuracy of the algorithm in comparison with the bivariate case.

Table 3. Random Forest Classifier results for the multivariate case

	Precision	Recall	f1-score
Not_occupancy	0.99	1	0.99
Occupancy	0.98	0.97	0.98
Accuracy			0.99
Macro avg	0.99	0.98	0.99
Weighted avg	0.99	0.99	0.99

4   Conclusions

The experiments on the occupancy detection as well as the data analysis of all the available sensor data yielded interesting results regarding the effect of similar datasets on different locations. One observation regarding the selection of features concerns the correlation between them. Typically, highly correlated features can be merged to one (e.g. average value) or can be discarded, as there is not additional information that can be shared. On the other hand, such correlation may or may not be observed on, intuitively, same data. Results indicate this statement, since office 2 temperature heatmap depicts temperature features with no correlation in contrast to the remaining offices, which have high correlated data.

A similar observation is based on the correlation results. Each office presents a different set of features which are affected by the occupancy attribute. In other words, although every office produces data from similar sensors, each case differs and thus the feature selection procedure cannot be the same for all of them.

In conclusion, the indicative classification results for the occupancy detection problem, are distinct between the two approaches, bivariate and multivariate. Using the date information and the past values of the occupancy feature produced not so satisfying results with an accuracy of 0.78 but a very low recall ratio. On the contrary the augmentation of the feature set with environmental and energy related features helped the random forest model raise its metrics indicating the importance of the additional information provided by the added features. Still, further research is required to compare different aspects of the whole procedure (e.g. different data imputation methods), to conclude to a more accurate outcome. Lastly, an undeniable observation is that when dealing with similar datasets, depending on the context, the behavior of the data may vary substantially, rendering separate investigation mandatory.

In the future, we intend to work on further improving and optimizing the data analysis procedures. One scope is the feature analysis automization, where highly correlated features will be merged automatically, and another scope is the feature selection automization where only relevant features will automatically be selected after analysis, meaning features with correlation above 0.5 or under -0.5.

Acknowledgements. The research leading to these results was partially funded by the European Commission "LC- EEB-07-2020 - Smart Operation of Proactive Residential Buildings" - PRECEPT H2020 project (Grant agreement ID: 958284) https://www.precept-project.eu/, accessed on 8 March 2022; and "LC-SC3-B4E-3-2020 Upgrading smartness of existing buildings through innovations for legacy equipment" - Smart2B H2020 project (Grant agreement ID: 101023666) https://www.smart2b-project.eu/, accessed on 2 March 2022.

References

1. Dimara, A., Krinidis, S., Tzovaras, D.: occupI: a novel non-intrusive occupancy inference tool. In: 2020 International Conferences on Internet of Things (iThings) and IEEE Green Computing and Communications (GreenCom) and IEEE Cyber, Physical and Social Computing (CPSCom) and IEEE Smart Data (SmartData) and IEEE Congress on Cybermatics (Cybermatics). IEEE (2020)
2. Salimi, S., Hammad, A.: Critical review and research roadmap of office building energy management based on occupancy monitoring. Energy Build. **182**, 214–241 (2019)
3. Jafarinejad, T., et al.: Bi-level energy-efficient occupancy profile optimization integrated with demand-driven control strategy: university building energy saving. Sustain. Cities Soc. **48**, 101539 (2019)
4. Luo, K., et al.: Safety-oriented pedestrian occupancy forecasting. In: 2021 IEEE/RSJ International Conference on Intelligent Robots and Systems (IROS). IEEE (2021)

5. Jung, W., Jazizadeh, F.: Human-in-the-loop HVAC operations: a quantitative review on occupancy, comfort, and energy-efficiency dimensions. Appl. Energy **239**, 1471–1508 (2019)
6. Rueda, L., et al.: A comprehensive review of approaches to building occupancy detection. Build. Environ. **180**, 106966 (2020)
7. Wang, X., Wang, C.: Time series data cleaning: a survey. IEEE Access **8**, 1866–1881 (2019)
8. Kenda, K., Mladenić, D.: Autonomous sensor data cleaning in stream mining setting. Bus. Syst. Res. Int. J. Soc. Adv. Innov. Res. Econ. **9**(2), 69–79 (2018)
9. Saha, H., et al.: Occupancy sensing in buildings: a review of data analytics approaches. Energy Build. **188**, 278–285 (2019)
10. Golestan, S., Kazemian, S., Ardakanian, O. : Data-driven models for building occupancy estimation. In: Proceedings of the Ninth International Conference on Future Energy Systems (2018)
11. Kutafina, E., et al.: Recursive neural networks in hospital bed occupancy forecasting. BMC Med. Inform. Decis. Mak. **19**(1), 1–10 (2019)
12. Hepler, S.A., Erhardt, R.J.: A spatiotemporal model for multivariate occupancy data. Environmetrics **32**(2), e2657 (2021)
13. Barter, R.L., Bin, Yu.: Superheat: an R package for creating beautiful and extendable heatmaps for visualizing complex data. J. Comput. Graph. Stat. **27**(4), 910–922 (2018)
14. Verma, V., et al.: Interpolation consistency training for semi-supervised learning. arXiv preprint arXiv:1903.03825 (2019)
15. Saad, M., et al.: Machine learning based approaches for imputation in time series data and their impact on forecasting. In: 2020 IEEE International Conference on Systems, Man, and Cybernetics (SMC). IEEE (2020)
16. Jia, B.B., Zhang, M.L.: Multi-dimensional classification via decomposed label encoding. IEEE Trans. Knowl. Data Eng. (2021)
17. Amayri, M., et al.: Estimating occupancy in heterogeneous sensor environment. Energy Build. **129**, 46–58. Zeigermann, Lars (2016)
18. TIMESTAMP: Stata module to obtain a UNIX timestamp and the current time of a user-specified timezone (2016)
19. Denis, D.J.: SPSS Data Analysis for Univariate, Bivariate, and Multivariate Statistics. John Wiley & Sons, Hoboken (2018)
20. Liebhold, A.M., Sharov, A.A.: Testing for Correlation in the Presence of Spatial Autocorrelation in Insect Count Data. Population and Community Ecology for Insect Management and Conservation, pp. 111–118. CRC Press, Boca Raton (2020)
21. Tharwat, A.: Classification assessment methods. Appl. Comput. Inform. **17**(1), 168–192 (2021). https://doi.org/10.1016/j.aci.2018.08.003

Non-intrusive Diagnostics for Legacy Heat-Pump Performance Degradation

Iakovos Michailidis[1,2], Georgios Vougiatzis[1], Aliki Stefanopoulou[1],
Asimina Dimara[1,4]([envelope]), Christos D. Korkas[1,2], Stelios Krinidis[1,3],
Elias B. Kosmatopoulos[1,2], Dimosthenis Ioannidis[1],
Christos-Nikolaos Anagnostopoulos[4], and Dimitrios Tzovaras[1]

[1] Information Technologies Institute, Centre for Research and Technology Hellas,
57001 Thessaloniki, Greece
adimara@iti.gr
[2] Electrical and Computer Engineering Department,
Democritus University of Thrace, 67000 Xanthi, Greece
[3] Management Science and Technology Department, International Hellenic
University (IHU), Kavala, Greece
[4] Department of Cultural Technology and Communication, Intelligent Systems Lab,
University of the Aegean, Mytilene, Greece

Abstract. Diagnosing abnormal behavior of different severity and convenience effects in a real-time manner is of paramount importance for energy-intensive building appliances. Both industrial and residential sectors suffer from post-incident maintenance where undetected faults occur for several days until the total breakdown of the equipment. To generate the necessary data set, a simulative test bed from Energym initiative was considered, exploiting an already validated residential environment. In this work, a Convolutional Neural Network (CNN) model was considered for classifying non-intrusive, low-cost temperature sensor embeddings in 3 categories with different abnormal heat pump severity levels. The features considered available derived from indoor zones temperatures and the outdoor/ambient temperature of the building; omitting intentionally readings from more elaborate sensors e.g., power analyzers or energy meters. The trained CNN model was eventually able to achieve very high accuracy i.e., around 95%; ensuring its high operational reliability by consuming real-time 15 min sequential temperature embeddings.

Keywords: Heat-Pump maintenance · Performance degradation diagnostics · Simulation data · Non-Intrusive malfunction classification

1 Introduction

Systems that heat and/or cool a space are used by the occupants to manage all temperatures, weather fluctuations, and seasons changing, while assessing a comfortable indoor environment. Almost 43% of the total energy consumption

© IFIP International Federation for Information Processing 2022
Published by Springer Nature Switzerland AG 2022
I. Maglogiannis et al. (Eds.): AIAI 2022 Workshops, IFIP AICT 652, pp. 265–275, 2022.
https://doi.org/10.1007/978-3-031-08341-9_22

is used for heating and cooling, while there is also an increasing of heating and cooling energy consumption by 32% during the last decade [1]. A proper heating and/or cooling system is really beneficiary for the occupants as it helps them deal with extreme weather conditions while regulating a convenient Indoor Environmental Quality (IEQ). Energy expenses, especially nowadays, are one of the biggest expenses for the occupants. As a result, heating and/or cooling systems that do not operate smoothly and perpetually may greatly increase energy costs [2].

A suitable heating system will preserve the desired thermal comfort levels during a short period of time. Nonetheless, malfunctions in the heating system have an enormous effect on exergy and energy efficiency [3]. Error and problems in the operation of heat pumps could result significant energy losses during the heating period [3]. Consequently, tools and applications that have the ability to predict and alert the occupants for upcoming heat pump faults, malfunctions or unusual behaviour are of utmost importance. On time notifications of potential faulty heat pump operation will ensure non delayed healing actions while reducing maintenance and repairing costs of a total system breakdown [4].

Literature points out that enormous performance losses occur in heat pumps in the building sector. Specifically, almost 20–50% of heat pumps operate with a lowest efficiency of at least 70–80% compared to their design efficiency [5]. Moreover, this faulty heat pump operation contributes in an increase of 40% in the energy consumption [5]. Nevertheless, there is lack of machine learning models and applications in the literature for early-diagnosis of heat pump errors, especially for the residential sector [6].

The current study is structured as follows:

- In Sect. 1, basic information about the energy efficiency of heating systems and the contribution of the study is addressed.
- In Sect. 2, the simulation test bed, the dataset synthesis and the fault diagnosis model are presented.
- In Sect. 3, the experimental results are given along with an evaluation.
- In Sect. 4, conclusions are drawn.

1.1 Contributions of the Study

Operational malfunctions and abnormal behaviors may result significant energy losses or even devastating breakdowns, since such dynamics may stay undetected for several days. Modern smart appliances are usually equipped with elaborate micro-sensorial and on-board processing capabilities [7], having the ability to detect and report errors and faults by using simplistic rule based engines for raising alerts. However, legacy conventional appliances usually do not have such capability [8]. Moreover, installing additional OEMS sensory equipment may conflict with the appliance guarantee; while in other non-intrusive approaches, quite elaborate sensors (e.g., power analyzers) may be a quite expensive solution surpassing the value of the appliance itself; especially in domestic or small-scale industrial use-cases. As a result low-cost non-intrusive approaches are often required in order to be able to monitor, detect, diagnose and even predict abnormal behaviour of the appliances themselves [9].

The current study exploits the performance of a supervised machine-learning approach for the accurate and early detection of heat pump performance degradation effects at different severity levels. The goal is to train such a model utilizing data from non-intrusive low-cost sensors [10] which are commonly used in building automation applications. For this reason, the current study considers the indoor zone temperatures of a simulative building plant - from Energym [11] initiative - and the ambient/outdoor temperature as the only available features (for more details see Sect. 2.1 and Sect. 2.2); such sensory readings can derive by cheap and easy to install (even wireless) sensors, enabling the application across different building types and use cases. It is important to note the current study focuses on one of the most energy-intensive end-use sectors with very high disruption potential (very important for occupants convenience) in buildings which is climating [12].

2 Experimental Setup

2.1 Simulation Testbed

The building where the simulation was applied consists of four floors, each of which is an apartment and has two thermal zones on each storey (in total 8 thermal zones). The building is located in Spain, specifically in Tarragona. The area of surface of building is $417.12\,\mathrm{m}^2$ and total volume is $1042.83\,\mathrm{m}^3$. Apartments thermal system consists of a centralized water-to-water geothermal heat pump (HP) system, which extracts heat from the ground through a vertical ground heat exchanger, and provides hot water for the indoor fan coil units (two units per apartment) and the Domestic Hot Water (DHW)[1]. The DHW system is composed by four storage systems, one for each household, and consist in a four node-stratified tank (see footnote 1). Heating loop circuit from the heat pump is connected to the bottom half part of the tanks and electrical heaters are placed on the top part acting as auxiliary systems (see footnote 1). Regarding the electrical part, apartments system includes a PV array, a community battery and an electric vehicle (EV) and in the thermal scenario, community battery and electric vehicle charging are disregarded (see footnote 1).

"ApartmentsThermal-v0" is a EnergyPlus model [13]. A description of the model's inputs and outputs is provided in Table 1 and Table 2 respectively. More information regarding inputs and outputs can be found in https://bsl546.github. io/energym-pages/sources/apt.html. It is noted that the evaluation process is carried out under predetermined weather conditions and for a specific period of time. The weather instantiation (i.e., outdoor temperature) considers conditions occurring between January and April. The main controllable inputs for the "ApartmentsThermal-v0" model are listed in Table 3.

---

[1] https://bsl546.github.io/energym-pages/sources/apt.html.

Table 1. Heat pump available information

Variable name	Type	Lower bound	Upper bound	# States	Description
Inputs					
P1_T_Thermolat_sp ... P4_T_Thermolat_sp	Scalar	16	26		Floor 1 Thermostat Setpoint (°C) ... Floor 4 Thermostat Setpoint (°C)
Bd_T_HP_sp	Scalar	35	55		Heat Pump Temperature Setpoint (°C)
P1_T_Tank_sp ... P4_T_Tank_sp	Scalar	30	70		Floor 1 Tank Temperature (°C) ... Floor 4 Tank Temperature (°C)
HVAC_onoff_HP_sp	Discrete	0	1	2	Heat Pump on/off Setpoint
Bd_Pw_Bat_sp	Scalar	−1	1		Battery Charging/Discharging Setpoint Rate
Bd_Ch_EVBat_sp	Scalar	0	1		EV Battery Charing Setpoint Rate

2.2 Dataset Synthesis

As already mentioned above, the dataset considers synthetically generated data from a simulative test bed. The energy consuming assets consider existing domestic appliances and a heat pump coupled with dedicated fan coils in different climate zones. In order to decouple the observed thermal dynamics of the building from the control strategy applied, the fan coil control thermostats were set constantly to 22 °C in order to preserve indoor thermal comfort between acceptable bounds.

The main goal was to simulate abnormal dynamics and behaviours during different realization conditions (external conditions) that would enable sampling and annotating accordingly. The application considered annotating/classifying different degradation effects imposed in the heating capacity of the heat pump during operation, considering only the indoor and outdoor temperature readings. The degradation effects were imposed by lowering the temperature set point of the heat pump (see Table 1).

The nominal behavior of the heat pump was acquired by setting the heat pump temperature (i.e., $Bd\_T\_HP\_sp$ in Table 1) to its maximum value, i.e., 55 °C. To generate enough data, the simulation tests considered two different degradation severity levels for the heat pump temperature: a) 35 °C, b) 45 °C. These two different events/incidents were simulated during three different

Table 2. Indicative outputs

Variable name	Type	Lower bound	Upper bound	Description
Outputs				
Ext_T	Scalar	−10	40	Outdoor Temperature (°C)
HVAC_Pw_HP	Scalar	0	120000.0	Heat Pump Power (W)
Z01_T ... Z08_T	Scalar	10	40	Zone 1 Temperature (°C) ... Zone 8 Temperature (°C)
P1_T_Thermostat_sp_out ... P4_T_Thermostat_sp_out	Scalar	16	26	Floor 1 Thermostat Setpoint (°C) ... Floor 4 Thermostat Setpoint (°C)

simulation days between January and April, while the degradation events were inserted at four different timeslots: early morning (4 p.m.), morning (9 p.m.), noon (14 a.m.), afternoon (18 p.m.).

The considered dataset presented a sampling rate of 180 s i.e., 480 samples per day. The indoor (i.e., 8 thermal zones) and outdoor temperature timeseries were hashed into slices of 5 consecutive timesteps i.e., $5 \times 180 \text{ s} = 15 \text{ min}$, lagged by 1 (stride) i.e., $1 \times 180 \text{ s} = 3 \text{ min}$; and annotated with three different labels:

- Nominal operation, considering Heat Pump temperature = 55 °C was annotated with 0,
- Operation with severe fault, considering Heat Pump temperature = 35 °C was annotated with 1,
- Operation with mild fault, considering Heat Pump temperature = 45 °C was annotated with 2,

Evidently, the abnormal heat pump behavior (vertical green line) is not easily detectable by visualizing the indoor temperature evolution as shown in Fig. 1.

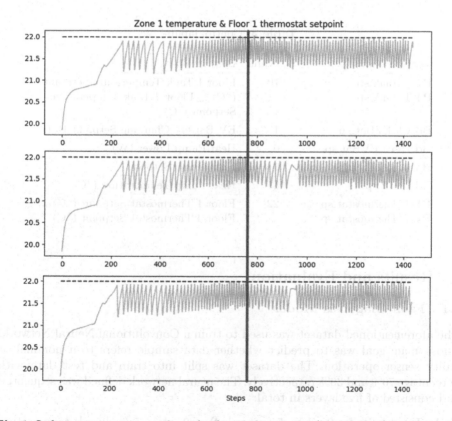

Fig. 1. Indoor temperature readings (red) and thermostat (blue dashed) from Zone01 during nominal operation, severe and mild heat pump malfunction. The vertical green line indicates the exact moment when the malfunction is imposed. (Color figure online)

The problem becomes even more complicated when the available temperature readings reduce to only one i.e., consider the case where the only available thermal zone temperature was from "Zone 1". Moreover, the severity of the heat pump malfunction is even more difficult to be determined visually only by considering the indoor temperature readings; facts which both suggest the adoption of an intelligent data-driven approach for this purpose.

The data set generated eventually was consisted of X-Y tuples, where the feature matrix X was formed by 9-by-5 = 45 features resulted by flattening the aforementioned hashed slices of length 5 and the annotation (label) matrix Y was formed by 0, 1 and 2 labels as already discussed.

In order to further reduce the intrusiveness of the approach and the number of features used, the same data set was reduced significantly omitting all indoor temperature readings but one; zone 1 (ground floor) in specific. As a result the reduced data set was consisted of X-Y tuples, where the feature matrix X was formed by 2-by-5 = 10 features resulted by flattening the aforementioned hashed slices of length 5 and the annotation (label) matrix Y was formed by the exact same 0, 1 and 2 labels with the extended data set case.

Table 3. Control inputs

Variable Name	Value	Description
P1_T_Tank_sp ... P4_T_Tank_sp	70	Floor 1 Tank Temperature Setpoint (°C) ... Floor 4 Tank Temperature Setpoint (°C)
Bd_Ch_EVBat_sp	1	EV Battery Charging Setpoint Rate
Bd_Disch_EVBat_sp	0	Heat Pump Power (W)
HVAC_onoff_HP_sp	1	Heat Pump Setpoint
Bd_T_HP_sp	55	Heat Pump Temperature (°C)
P1_T_Thermostat_sp ... P4_T_Thermostat_sp	22	Floor 1 Thermostat Setpoint (°C) ... Floor 4 Thermostat Setpoint (°C)

3   Results and Evaluation

3.1   Fault Diagnosis Model

The aforementioned dataset was used to train a Convolutional Neural Network, whose main goal was to predict whether data sample refers to a nominal or faulty sensor operation. The dataset was split into train and test data with percentage 70% and 30% respectively. The neural network defined was sequential and consisted of five layers in total:

  i An Input layer for $9 - by - 5$ (extended) or $2 - by - 5$ (reduced) temperature embeddings;
  ii A Convolution layer with "relu" activation functions

iii A Max Pooling layer;

iv A Fully Connected layer;

v An Output Layer implementing a "softmax" activation function of size 1 determining the class of the input embedding.

The convolution layer is the layer that a filter is applied to the data sample, to extract its features. For this layers we used 16 filters of size (3, 3), and "relu" as the activation function. After the Convolution layer, a Pooling layer was used to reduce the dimensions of the feature map, in order to preserve its important information and reduce computation time. The Max Pooling layer used was of size (2, 2) with a stride of 1. The next layer used was a fully connected layer of size 100 and activation function "relu", whose goal was to classify the input data into labels. This layer was fully connected to the output layer, aiming to classify the input data according to their type. The three different output types was "0", for a nominal sensor operation, "1" for an operation with mild fault and "2" for an operation with severe fault. The output layer's activation function was "softmax". For the compilation of the described model, "Adam" was used as an optimizer, "sparse categorical crossentropy" as a loss function and "accuracy" as a validation metrics function over the training set. Lastly, ten epochs were used in total to fit the model; enough to reach a very high training accuracy and avoid exhaustive optimization.

3.2 Model Inference Performance

Extended Model Case: *9-by-5* Input Size. The results of the model are depicted in Table 4. It is apparent that the model successfully diagnoses the type of error in the heat pump. The training accuracy of the model increases

Table 4. Training performance: extended model

Epochs	Data loss	Accuracy
1/10	0.2487	0.9332
2/10	0.2233	0.9407
3/10	0.2109	0.9443
4/10	0.1984	0.9478
5/10	0.1850	0.9515
6/10	0.1761	0.9541
7/10	0.1725	0.9555
8/10	0.1683	0.9564
9/10	0.1657	0.9570
10/10	0.1644	0.9576

Test loss: 0.1546788364648819

Test accuracy: 0.9591668844223022

with each epoch from 93.32% (Epoch 1) to 95.76% (Epoch 10). Data loss during training decreases consecutively, specifically from 24.87% to 16.44%. Focusing on the inference results on unknown data from the test set used, it can be observed that the performance results are comparable enabling the model to reach accuracy of 95.91% and reduce categorical cross entropy loss to 15.46%. In Figs. 2a and 2b the evolution of the aforementioned results is depicted across the different training epochs.

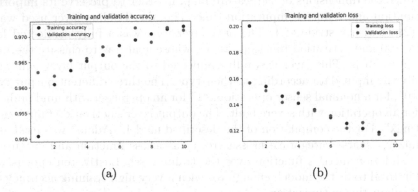

(a)   (b)

Fig. 2. (a) Training (blue) and Validation (red) Accuracy of the Extended Model (b) Training (blue) and Validation (red) Accuracy of the Extended Model (Color figure online)

Reduced Model Case: *2-by-5* Input Size. The results of the reduced model are depicted in Table 5. Evidently the reduced version of the model i.e., considering only one out of the eight indoor zone temperatures in the features matrix; was able to achieve comparable performance both on training and test sets. The training accuracy of the reduced model increased every epoch from 92.55% (Epoch 1) to 94.43% (Epoch 10). As expected the data loss during the training process descended, in specific from 30.85% to 21.86%. Focusing on the inference results on unknown data from the test set used, it can be observed that the performance results are comparable enabling the model to reach accuracy of 94.49% and reduce categorical cross entropy loss to 20.57%.

As expected the overall performance of the model both at training and inferencing evaluation stages is slightly worse than the one achieved when considering the extended data set case. However, the feasibility and practical value of such a reduced model surpasses the minor efficiency difference, since it utilizes one indoor temperature sensor instead of eight. In Figs. 3a and 3b the evolution of the aforementioned results is depicted across the different training epochs.

Table 5. Training performance: reduced model

Epochs	Data loss	Accuracy
1/10	0.3085	0.9255
2/10	0.2987	0.9255
3/10	0.2892	0.9255
4/10	0.2594	0.9333
5/10	0.2371	0.9400
6/10	0.2317	0.9418
7/10	0.2264	0.9427
8/10	0.2249	0.9425
9/10	0.2216	0.9437
10/10	0.2186	0.9443

Test loss: 0.2057267129421234

Test accuracy: 0.9449745416641235

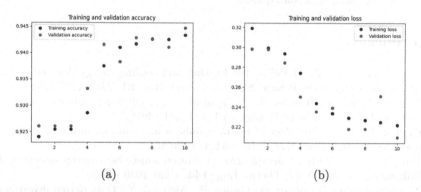

(a)   (b)

Fig. 3. (a) Training (blue) and Validation (red) Accuracy of the Reduced Model (b) Training (blue) and Validation (red) Loss of the Reduced Model (Color figure online)

4 Conclusions

In this work, a Convolutional Neural Network (CNN) model was considered for classifying non-intrusive, low-cost sensor embeddings as nominal or faulty. The features considered were derived from indoor zones temperatures and the outdoor/ambient temperature of the building: a) extended case: all 8 indoor temperature sensor readings are considered in the feature matrix; b) reduced case: only 1 indoor temperature sensor readings are considered in the feature matrix. In both data set cases, it was observed that such a CNN model was capable to classify unknown (test set) embeddings with very high accuracy i.e., around 95%; without any power or energy meter readings from the heat pump itself.

As a result, the CNN model once trained could be utilized in real-time inference applications where real-time 15 min sequential temperature embeddings (either from all or even one thermal zone) could be used to detect and diagnose the severity of the heat pump abnormal behavior; reducing excessive exergy, energy and capital expenditures as well as reducing the risk of total heat pump breakdown due to undetected incidents.

Indicative future research work topics have already been identified by the authors including: imposing heat pump faults in much higher granularity (i.e., create more annotated classes) as well as impose other types of malfunctions in the heat pump tanks to complicate the classification problem furthermore.

Acknowledgements. The research leading to these results was partially funded by the European Commission "LC-EEB-07-2020 - Smart Operation of Proactive Residential Buildings" - PRECEPT H2020 project (Grant agreement ID: 958284) https://www.precept-project.eu/, accessed on 8 March 2022; and "LC-SC3-B4E-3-2020 Upgrading smartness of existing buildings through innovations for legacy equipment" - Smart2B H2020 project (Grant agreement ID: 101023666) https://www.smart2b-project.eu/, accessed on 2 March 2022.

References

1. Frayssinet, L., et al.: Modeling the heating and cooling energy demand of urban buildings at city scale. Renew. Sustain. Energy Rev. **81**, 2318–2327 (2018)
2. Bye, B., Fæhn, T., Rosnes, O.: Residential energy efficiency policies: costs, emissions and rebound effects. Energy **143**, 191–201 (2018)
3. Ceylan, İ., et al.: The effect of malfunctions in air handling units on energy and exergy efficiency. Heat Transf. Res. **51**(11) (2020)
4. Han, Z., et al.: Study on design error of ground source heat pump system and its influencing factors. Appl. Therm. Eng. **144**, 1030–1036 (2018)
5. Narayanaswamy, B., Balaji, B., Gupta, R., Agarwal, Y.: Data driven investigation of faults in HVAC systems with model, cluster and compare (MCC). In: Proceedings of the 1st ACM Conference on Embedded Systems for Energy-Efficient Buildings, Memphis, TN, USA (2014)
6. A review of the fault behavior of heat pumps and measurements, detection and diagnosis methods including virtual sensors
7. Elmenreich, W., Egarter, D.: Design guidelines for smart appliances. In: Proceedings of the 10th International Workshop on Intelligent Solutions in Embedded Systems, pp. 76–82 (2012)
8. Egarter, D., Monacchi, A., Khatib, T., Elmenreich, W.: Integration of legacy appliances into home energy management systems. J. Ambient Intell. Humaniz. Comput. **7**(2), 171–185 (2015). https://doi.org/10.1007/s12652-015-0312-9
9. Gardner, G.T., Stern, P.C.: The short list: the most effective actions U.S. households can take to curb climate change. Environ. Sci. Policy Sustain. Dev. **50**(5), 12–25 (2008). https://doi.org/10.3200/ENVT.50.5.12-25
10. Meijer, G.C., Wang, G., Heidary, A.: Smart temperature sensors and temperature sensor systems (2018). https://doi.org/10.1016/B978-0-08-102055-5.00003-6
11. Scharnhorst, P., et al.: Energym: a building model library for controller benchmarking. Appl. Sci. **11**, 3518 (2021)

12. Carlson, D.R., Matthews, H.S., Berges, M.: One size does not fit all: averaged data on household electricity is inadequate for residential energypolicy and decisions. Energy Build. **64**, 132–144 (2013)
13. Crawley, D.B., Pedersen, C.O., Lawrie, L.K., Winkelmann, F.C.: EnergyPlus: energy simulation program. ASHRAE J. **42**, 49–56 (2000)

Performance Meta-analysis for Big-Data Univariate Auto-Imputation in the Building Sector

Aliki Stefanopoulou[1] , Iakovos Michailidis[1,2] , Asimina Dimara[1,4(✉)] ,
Stelios Krinidis[1,3] , Elias B. Kosmatopoulos[1,2] ,
Christos-Nikolaos Anagnostopoulos[4] , and Dimitrios Tzovaras[1]

[1] Information Technologies Institute, Centre for Research and Technology Hellas,
57001 Thessaloniki, Greece
adimara@iti.gr
[2] Electrical and Computer Engineering Department,
Democritus University of Thrace, 67000 Xanthi, Greece
[3] Management Science and Technology Department, International Hellenic
University (IHU), Kavala, Greece
[4] Department of Cultural Technology and Communication, Intelligent Systems Lab,
University of the Aegean, Mytilene, Greece

Abstract. Filtering refers to the process of defining, detecting and correcting errors in a given dataset, to achieve system reliability and minimize the impact of errors in data analysis. Automated and accurate tools for data filtering and healing are crucial to ensure reliability of the system. This study aims to investigate statistical and machine-learning-based methodologies for data gaps healing and missing values imputation. In total, five models are being investigated individually, the well known ARIMA model, Linear and Polynomial Interpolation, General Regression and Facebook Prophet. The raw data that are used to evaluate these methods are simulated, and artificial data gaps are imposed randomly within the dataset to evaluate the univariate imputation performance of the aforementioned models based on Mean Squared Error and Mean Absolute Error. As expected the evaluation results illustrate the efficiency of highly elaborate machine-learning Facebook Prophet against more simple statistic ARIMA in expense of time and computational efforts. However, for Big Data univariate imputation applications the study findings suggest that a combination of ARIMA and Facebook Prophet, depending on the data gap size, could balance out the required computational resources while maintaining highly accurate imputation results.

Keywords: Big data · Building application · Simulation data · Hybrid auto-imputation

© IFIP International Federation for Information Processing 2022
Published by Springer Nature Switzerland AG 2022
I. Maglogiannis et al. (Eds.): AIAI 2022 Workshops, IFIP AICT 652, pp. 276–288, 2022.
https://doi.org/10.1007/978-3-031-08341-9_23

1   Introduction

During 2020 almost 2.5 quintillion data bytes were created daily [1]. All these data are mostly unstructured and of low-density. Data streams of sensor-enabled devices, equipment and infrastructure generate tens of terabytes of information. Moreover, all this volume of data is transferred and received in fast rate while requiring real-time processing, action and evaluation [2]. Additionally, big data comes in a semi-structured or unstructured way while demanding an additional process to reinforce metadata [3]. As a result, handling, processing, saving, exploiting and development of big data is a thorny task that demands perplexing processes and methods.

One of the major problems when starting to assess big data is the missing values that generate lost sequences of valuable information [4]. This lack of information is crucial especially during the training process of machine learning models affecting the models' accuracy [5]. Specifically, even in small data-sets containing enormous gaps, missing data imputation may increase the algorithm's accuracy by at least 50% [4]. Furthermore, in numerous cases data are time-dependent as a result, forecasting the missing values is the one and only solution [6] to fit the time-series model to predict.

Numerous methodologies and technologies are exploited for missing data imputation in time-series data sets [7]. Some of these methods are of low complexity like averaging technique [8] or backward filling technique [9]. While others use more complicated methodologies like artificial neural networks [9]. To sum up, models of low complexity are of low accuracy but they are easy-to-use models and require low execution time and may be used for real-time applications [10]. Contrariwise, perplexing models offer higher accuracy and better results but they require longer execution time and further processing for big data [10].

1.1   Contributions of the Study

Based on the aforementioned discussion, the current study attempts to create an automated framework for big series data filtering. The study emphasizes on univariate imputation problems, which is a common issue in large data warehouses where continuous and reliable monitoring for long periods of time is not usual [11,12]. Reasonably, data warehouses usually present data gaps where data samples are missing, replaced with *NaN*, *Null* or even constant/frozen values instead. The root-cause and the size of such a problem may differ, depending on: the type of IoT/sensing infrastructure, the transmission channel bandwidth, power supply quality (constant supply or battery-based devices), the gateways operational reliability (freezing due to overloading and poor cooling), the protocol security (vulnerability to external cyber-attacks) and the data-storage management quality. Therefore, as data gaps may occur due to a large variety of causes; addressing such a problem usually suggests healing data gaps after their migration in the database/data-warehouse instead of trying to fix any or all aforementioned issues.

Several statistical approaches such as general regression (Gaussian mix imputation), linear interpolation, moving average (MA), auto-regressive MA (ARMA) and even ARIMA; have been proven capable of performing imputation in a quite robust manner [13,14], however their accuracy is gradually becoming poorer as the size of the data gap increases, where such lightweight mechanisms are called to impute large sequences of missing data. The main reason for such a performance degradation is their locally-driven nature [15], utilizing only neighboring data entries of the time-series which cannot replicate adequately the wide-scale trends and seasonalities of the entire time-series.

On the other hand, deep machine learning techniques, e.g., Convolutional Neural Networks (CNNs), Generative Adversarial Networks (GANs), Self Organizing Maps (SOMs); and applications have emerged over the recent past years due to the rapid emergence of cloud as well as distributed computational platforms (GPUs) providing adequate capacity to train such complex data-processing structures in a reasonable expense [16]. The usual approach for such mechanisms is to effectively fit a uni-variate forecasting deep-learning regression tool which can reliably impute missing values. Such complex mechanisms are trained over the entire available dataset in order to be able to generalize and adequately mimic the dynamic of the underlying time-series.

The current study utilizes simulative ground truth data and randomly generated data missing gaps in different time-series (see Sect. 3). Simulative data can provide a ground truth baseline which could support the performance assessment of the tested mechanisms. The data gaps imposed are of different sizes and were randomly applied at different time slots across the same series. The study investigates the performance of individually applied univariate imputation mechanisms of diverse complexity in order to assess their behavior in terms of accuracy (with respect to the ground truth data series) and in terms of computational/time expenses. Ultimately, the goal of the study is to identify an inventory of the most appropriate - both in terms of accuracy and time/complexity - big data imputation techniques to build an auto-imputation univariate engine based on automatically selected imputation mechanisms that depend on the size of the missing data sequences.

1.2   Study Structure

The current study is structured as follows:

- Section 1 includes a description of the objectives of this study, its possible application and contributions to the scientific community as well as a brief description of the approaches that are currently used for timeseries analysis and prediction.
- In Sect. 2, the investigated models are thoroughly described.
- In Sect. 3, the dataset synthesis is presented in depth.
- Section 4 includes the experimental ARIMA, Linear Interpolation, General Regression and Facebook Prophet results that are compared in detail in their overall performance with each other, in various cases of missing data gaps.

Finally, a hybrid model that makes use of both ARIMA and Facebook Prophet models is presented and evaluated ass well.
- In Sect. 5, the final conclusions of this study are drawn.

2   Investigated Approaches

2.1   ARIMA

One of the most widely used statistical methods for times series forecasting is the AutoRegressive Integrated Moving Average (ARIMA model). The key aspects of ARIMA model are:

- **AR:** *AutoRegression.* This model uses the dependent relationship between an observation and a predefined number of lagged observations in the time series.
- **I:** *Integrated.* It describes the differencing of observations that are used to make the time series stationary. If the time series is already stationary, this parameter is set to zero.
- **MA:** *Moving Average.* This model uses the dependent relationship between an observation and a residual error from a moving average model that is applies to lagged observations of the original time series.

The aforementioned components are specified in the model as parameters (p, d, q). These parameters are defined as follows:

- **p:** This parameter is mentioned as lag order and it defines the number of lagged observations that are used for the model.
- **d:** This parameter is mentioned as degree of differencing and it defines the number of times that the time series if differenced, in order for it to become stationary, to remove trend and seasonality.
- **q:** This parameter is mentioned as order of moving average and it defines the size of the moving average window.

For each of the elements, a value of 0 can be used to indicate that this element will not be used for the model, constructing a simpler model. In case that a value of 0 is used for the d parameter, the model performs the function of an ARMA model.

2.2   Linear Interpolation

Linear Interpolation is a method of curve fitting. According to this method, linear polynomials are used to construct new data points within the time series, to substitute possible missing values. Below is the algorithm for estimation of a value between two points of data, using linear interpolation.

- **Given Data X:** Independent variable for which the dependent variable is to be estimated.

– **Wanted Data Y_e:** Estimated dependent value for an independent given value **X**.

Linear Interpolation followed procedure:

1. Find the independent data in the records, with the highest value that is less than X. This will be $\mathbf{X_1}$. X_1 will give $\mathbf{Y_1}$, since they are associated in the time series.
2. Find the independent data in records, with the lowest value that is more than X. This will be $\mathbf{X_2}$. X_2 will give $\mathbf{Y_2}$, since they are associated in the time series.
3. These four values will give $\mathbf{Y_e}$ using the formula:

$$Y_e = Y_1 + \frac{(X - X_1)(Y_2 - Y_1)}{(X_2 - X_1)} \tag{1}$$

This method can be used for all missing values in between known data points in a time series.

2.3   General Regression

General regression is a method of statistical curve fitting. This method makes use of historical data for filling in the missing data and modeling. The aim of this method is to try to estimate a missing value Q_e, for a given value V, which denotes time, with the use of stored records:

$$Z_1, Z_2, Z_3...Z_n...Z_N$$
$$\updownarrow \tag{2}$$
$$(V_1, Q_1), (V_2, Q_2), (V_3, Q_3)...(V_n, Q_n)...(V_N, Q_N)$$

General Regression assumes that the closer V is to the given attributes of a stored record in the time series, V_n, the more similar the missing value Q_e will be, to the missing attribute of the same record in the time series Q_n. This means that the closer V is to V_n, the more the contribution of Q_n to Q_e will be (Eq. (3)).

$$Q_e = G(V) = \frac{\sum_{n=1}^{N} Q_n g(V - V_n, \sigma)}{\sum_{k=1}^{N} g(V - V_n, \sigma)}, \tag{3}$$

where g is the Gaussian window function:

$$G(V - V_n, \sigma) = \frac{1}{(\sqrt{2\pi}\sigma)^2} \epsilon^{\frac{-(V - V_n)^2}{2\sigma^2}}, \tag{4}$$

where σ is the standard deviation of the distribution.

2.4   Facebook Prophet

Facebook prophet is an open-source algorithm that makes for time series models generation. Facebook prophet model includes three main components, trend, seasonality and holidays. These components are combined to form the model's equation:

$$y(t) = g(t) + s(t) + h(t) + \epsilon_t, \tag{5}$$

where $g(t)$ is the piecewise linear or logistic growth curve for modeling non-periodic changes in a time series, $s(t)$ refers to the seasonality of the timeseries, $h(t)$ refers to the effect of holidays with irregular schedules and ϵ_t is the error term that describes any unusual changes that are not described in the model. Prophet's goal is to fit linear and non-linear functions of time as components, using time as a regressor.

3   Dataset Synthesis

As mentioned above, the dataset considers synthetically generated data from a simulative test bed. The simulative test bed comprises a commercial medium scale (3-thermal zone) building, equipped with indoor sensors for temperature, relative humidity, and energy consumption. The energy consumption relates to two different highly energy-intensive appliances, an electric heat pump for climating purposes coupled with DHW component. The control of the DHW and heat pump was undertaken by a simplified rule-based approach so as to maintain indoor thermal comfort between acceptable bounds. The considered dataset presented a sampling rate of one hour incorporating data from 12 months in total; for simplicity purposes only the available measurements from the first thermal zone were taken into account. To emulate missing values incidents, different data gaps were randomly imposed across timeseries with different descriptive statistical characteristics (e.g., minimum, maximum, mean value, variance): indoor temperature [$^\circ C$], relative humidity [%], heating load [kWh] and DHWs [kWh]. Initially only one short or one long data gap was imposed in order to individually evaluate the performance of the different imputation approaches mentioned above. Secondly both short and long incidents were randomly imposed in the considered timeseries evaluating again the performance of each individual univariate imputation technique. Eventually a hybrid approach, considering combinations of such techniques in order to exploit their different advantages/properties: lightness, complexity, data intensity, time required, accuracy achieved.

4   Evaluation of Results

All aforementioned methods where used in the datasets to impute the missing values. The models were evaluated using Mean Absolute Error, Mean Squared Error and Execution Time as metrics. They were evaluated in the data sets mentioned in Sect. 3, with a small number of consecutive missing values, in the same data sets with a large number of consecutive of missing values, and lastly in the same data sets with both a small number and a large number of consecutive missing values. The Results are presented below.

4.1 Two (2) Consecutive Missing Values

Table 1. Two missing values

Model	MSE	MAE	Execution Time (seconds)
Indoor Temperature			
ARIMA	0,00447	0,0659	26,8601
Linear Interpolation	0,0002	0,0116	0,0441
General Regression	0,00255	0,0424	19,6569
Facebook Prophet	0,1229	0,3395	29,7903
Indoor Relative Humidity			
ARIMA	0,176	0,3805	20,878
Linear Interpolation	0,1094	0,325	0,0437
General Regression	0,1227	0,3459	20,0882
Facebook Prophet	1,8674	1,3665	22,8563
Heating Load			
ARIMA	0	0,272	14,26
Linear Interpolation	0	0	0,0434
General Regression	1,046e–07	0,0002	19,96
Facebook Prophet	2,282	1,51	19,68
Cooling Load			
ARIMA	10	3,02	19,66
Linear Interpolation	3,2	1,79	0,0456
General Regression	6,61	2,18	20,436
Facebook Prophet	621,454	24,718	20,456

As illustrated in Table 1, in cases the data gap is comparatively small, linear interpolation manages to achieve the most accurate results, in and its execution time is significantly smaller that the execution time of the other investigated methods. However, as the data gap increases, it is evident that linear interpolation is unable to produce accurate results, because its predicted values depend only on the last value acquired right before the error and the first value acquired right after the error, and occasional trends are not considered.

4.2 Forty-eight (48) Consecutive Missing Values

As illustrated in Table 2, in cases the data gap is large, Facebook Prophet is able to achieve the most accurate results, in most of the datasets, however it is computationally expensive. ARIMA also manages to achieve notable results, and it is not as computationally expensive. General Regression does not manage to achieve accurate results in any of the studied datasets.

Table 2. Forty-eight consecutive missing values

Model	MSE	MAE	Execution Time (seconds)
Indoor Temperature			
ARIMA	0,3173	0,5113	25,255
Linear Interpolation	0,4832	0,5513	0,0671
General Regression	0,5046	0,5602	26,2536
Facebook Prophet	0,2762	0,461	28,6181
Indoor Relative Humidity			
ARIMA	2,4543	1,2754	23,1787
Linear Interpolation	1,6711	0,9774	0,0702
General Regression	14,6187	3,0567	27,1273
Facebook Prophet	101,512	9,8752	24,7457
Heating Load			
ARIMA	1,519	1,019	25,439
Linear Interpolation	6,554	2,109	0,065
General Regression	16,7	3,756	25,853
Facebook Prophet	0,348	0,436	20,183
Cooling Load			
ARIMA	4144,877	54,493	20,562
Linear Interpolation	9185,682	84,73	0,0693
General Regression	16124,449	90,898	25,895
Facebook Prophet	2829,142	48,661	21,772

4.3   Multiple Consecutive Missing Values

After investigating the accuracy of the previously mentioned models in small and large data gaps, a hybrid model that uses ARIMA model in comparatively small data gaps and Facebook Prophet in large data gaps was considered. We used an auto-detection gap technique to identify the gaps in the timeseries and then, we used ARIMA model for gaps that are of size fifteen at most, and Facebook Prophet for larger gaps. The Results are illustrated at Table 3 and Figs. 1, 2, 3 and 4.

Table 3. Multiple consecutive missing values

Model	MSE	MAE	Execution Time (seconds)
Indoor Temperature			
ARIMA	0,0066	0,0058	24,8823
Linear Interpolation	0,0047	0,0049	0,0775
General Regression	0,0057	0,0054	28,1362
Facebook Prophet	0,0032	0,0042	31,1767
ARIMA and Facebook Prophet	0.0043	0.0044	30.604
Indoor Relative Humidity			
ARIMA	0,3912	0,041	22,3956
Linear Interpolation	0,09133	0,01944	0,0789
General Regression	0,3132	0,0375	28,8337
Facebook Prophet	0,3029	0,04352	33,9757
ARIMA and Facebook Prophet	0.14733	0.0276	30.4774
Heating Load			
ARIMA	0,0543	0,0159	13,9703
Linear Interpolation	0,04414	0,0137	0,0776
General Regression	0,0485	0,01422	28,821
Facebook Prophet	0,0066	0,0054	18,7469
ARIMA and Facebook Prophet	0.0187	0.0082	18.5313
Cooling Load			
ARIMA	17,1138	0,2761	17,2349
Linear Interpolation	9,7903	0,1966	0,0777
General Regression	9,9738	0,1998	28,2922
Facebook Prophet	7,1788	0,2014	20,4320
ARIMA and Facebook Prophet	13.1541	0.2571	19.0174

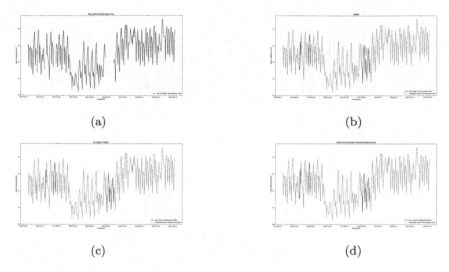

Fig. 1. (a) Raw Indoor Temperature Data with multiple missing values. (b) Indoor Temperature Data Univariate Imputation using ARIMA. (c) Indoor Temperature Data Univariate Imputation using Facebook Prophet. (d) Indoor Temperature Data Univariate Imputation using ARIMA on small gaps and Facebook Prophet on large gaps.

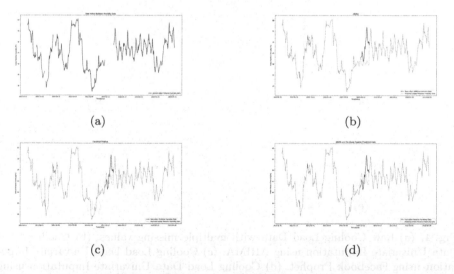

Fig. 2. (a) Raw Indoor Relative Humidity Data with multiple missing values. (b) Indoor Relative Humidity Data Univariate Imputation using ARIMA. (c) Indoor Relative Humidity Data Univariate Imputation using Facebook Prophet. (d) Indoor Relative Humidity Data Univariate Imputation using ARIMA on small gaps and Facebook Prophet on large gaps.

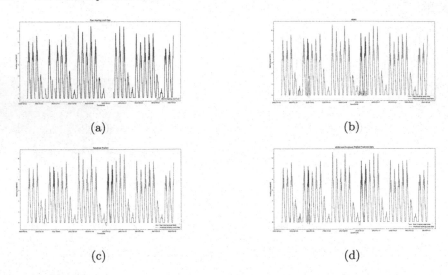

(a)   (b)

(c)   (d)

Fig. 3. (a) Raw Heating Load Data with multiple missing values. (b) Heating Load Data Univariate Imputation using ARIMA. (c) Heating Load Data Univariate Imputation using Facebook Prophet. (d) Heating Load Data Univariate Imputation using ARIMA on small gaps and Facebook Prophet on large gaps.

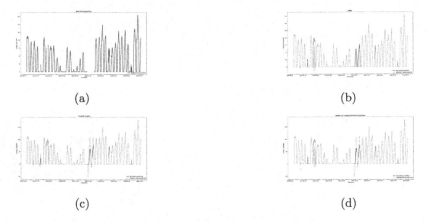

(a)   (b)

(c)   (d)

Fig. 4. (a) Raw Cooling Load Data with multiple missing values. (b) Cooling Load Data Univariate Imputation using ARIMA. (c) Cooling Load Data Univariate Imputation using Facebook Prophet. (d) Cooling Load Data Univariate Imputation using ARIMA on small gaps and Facebook Prophet on large gaps.

5   Conclusions

As indicated in Sect. 4 of this article, the longer the gap in the time-series, the more difficult it is for the models to accurately predict the missing values. In case the data gap is comparatively small, Linear Interpolation method predicts the missing values more accurately, outperforming all the other methods, especially when its execution time is taken under consideration. General Regression and ARIMA models are precise when the data gap is small, but their execution times are notably larger than the Linear Interpolation method's execution time. Facebook Prophet on the other hand is imprecise in small data gaps and its execution time is comparatively large as well. As the data gap increases, Linear Interpolation method's accuracy deteriorates, although its execution time remains significantly smaller than the execution time of the other methods. In large data gaps, Facebook Prophet tends to be the most accurate between all the aforementioned methods, however, its execution time is considerably large. To accommodate for that, we used a hybrid approach, using an auto-detection gap technique and we made use of the ARIMA model for the imputation of small data gaps, to take advantage of its accuracy and small execution time in such cases, and Facebook Prophet for the comparatively larger gaps, to take advantage of its high accuracy in such cases. The resulting model outperforms the ARIMA model when it comes to aggregated accuracy, and its execution time is slightly smaller than the execution time of Facebook Prophet model, in the same data sets.

Acknowledgements. The research leading to these results was partially funded by the European Commission "EEB-07-2017 Integration of energy harvesting at building and district level" - PLUG-N-HARVEST H2020 project (Grant agreement ID: 768735) https://www.plug-n-harvest.eu/, accessed on 22 February 2022; and "LC-SC3-B4E-3-2020 Upgrading smartness of existing buildings through innovations for legacy equipment" - Smart2B H2020 project (Grant agreement ID: 101023666) https://www.smart2b-project.eu/, accessed on 2 March 2022.

References

1. Roque, N.A., Ram, N.: tsfeaturex: an R package for automating time series feature extraction. J. Open Source Softw. **4**(37) (2019)
2. Olivera, P., et al.: Big data in IBD: a look into the future. Nat. Rev. Gastroenterol. Hepatol. **16**(5), 312–321 (2019)
3. Hancock, J.T., Khoshgoftaar, T.M.: CatBoost for big data: an interdisciplinary review. J. Big Data **7**(1), 1–45 (2020). https://doi.org/10.1186/s40537-020-00369-8
4. Schauer, J.M., et al.: Exploratory analyses for missing data in meta-analyses and meta-regression: a tutorial. Alcohol Alcohol. **57**(1), 35–46 (2022)
5. Bache-Mathiesen, L.K., et al.: Handling and reporting missing data in training load and injury risk research. Sci. Med. Footb. 1–13 (2021)
6. Kahale, L.A., et al.: Potential impact of missing outcome data on treatment effects in systematic reviews: imputation study. bmj 370 (2020)
7. Lin, W.-C., Tsai, C.-F.: Missing value imputation: a review and analysis of the literature (2006–2017). Artif. Intell. Rev. **53**(2), 1487–1509 (2019). https://doi.org/10.1007/s10462-019-09709-4
8. Flores, A., Tito, H., Silva, C.: Local average of nearest neighbors: univariate time series imputation. Int. J. Adv. Comput. Sci. Appl. **10**(8), 45–50 (2019)

9. Saad, M., et al.: Tackling imputation across time series models using deep learning and ensemble learning. In: 2020 IEEE International Conference on Systems, Man, and Cybernetics (SMC). IEEE (2020)

10. Saad, M., et al.: Machine learning based approaches for imputation in time series data and their impact on forecasting. In: 2020 IEEE International Conference on Systems, Man, and Cybernetics (SMC). IEEE (2020)

11. Zymbler, M., et al.: Cleaning sensor data in smart heating control system. In: 2020 Global Smart Industry Conference (GloSIC). IEEE (2020)

12. Brajković, H., Jakšić, D., Poščić, P.: Data warehouse and data quality-an overview. In: Central European Conference on Information and Intelligent Systems. Faculty of Organization and Informatics Varazdin (2020)

13. Chiu, P.C., Selamat, A., Krejcar, O.: Infilling missing rainfall and runoff data for Sarawak, Malaysia using gaussian mixture model based K-Nearest neighbor imputation. In: Wotawa, F., Friedrich, G., Pill, I., Koitz-Hristov, R., Ali, M. (eds.) IEA/AIE 2019. LNCS (LNAI), vol. 11606, pp. 27–38. Springer, Cham (2019). https://doi.org/10.1007/978-3-030-22999-3_3

14. Afrifa-Yamoah, E., et al.: Missing data imputation of high-resolution temporal climate time series data. Meteorol. Appl. **27**(1), e1873 (2020)

15. Chaudhry, A., et al.: A method for improving imputation and prediction accuracy of highly seasonal univariate data with large periods of missingness. Wirel. Commun. Mob. Comput. **2019**, 1–13 (2019)

16. Jan, B., et al.: Deep learning in big data analytics: a comparative study. Comput. Electr. Eng. **75**, 275–287 (2019)

Proactive Buildings: A Prescriptive Maintenance Approach

Paraskevas Koukaras[1,2] (iD), Asimina Dimara[1,5(✉)] (iD), Sergio Herrera[4] (iD),
Niccolò Zangrando[4] (iD), Stelios Krinidis[1,3] (iD), Dimosthenis Ioannidis[1] (iD),
Piero Fraternali[4] (iD), Christos Tjortjis[1,2] (iD),
Christos-Nikolaos Anagnostopoulos[5] (iD), and Dimitrios Tzovaras[1] (iD)

[1] Information Technologies Institute, Centre for Research and Technology,
57001 Thessaloniki, Greece
{p.koukaras,krinidis,djoannid,c.tjortjis,dimitrios.tzovaras}@iti.gr
[2] School of Science and Technology, International Hellenic University,
57001 Thessaloniki, Greece
[3] Department of Management Science and Technology,
International Hellenic University, Kavala, Greece
[4] Politecnico di Milano, 20133 Milano, Italy
{sergioluis.herrera,niccolo.zangrando,piero.fraternali}@polimi.it
[5] Department of Cultural Technology and Communication, University of the Aegean,
Intelligent Systems Lab, Mytilene, Greece
adimara@iti.gr, canag@aegean.gr

Abstract. Prescriptive maintenance has recently attracted a lot of scientific attention. It integrates the advantages of descriptive and predictive analytics to automate the process of detecting non nominal device functionality. Implementing such proactive measures in home or industrial settings may improve equipment dependability and minimize operational expenses. There are several techniques for prescriptive maintenance in diverse use cases, but none elaborates on a general methodology that permits successful prescriptive analysis for small size industrial or residential settings. This study reports on prescriptive analytics, while assessing recent research efforts on multi-domain prescriptive maintenance. Given the existing state of the art, the main contribution of this work is to propose a broad framework for prescriptive maintenance that may be interpreted as a high-level approach for enabling proactive buildings.

Keywords: Prescriptive maintenance · Time series analysis ·
Proactive buildings

1 Introduction

Prescriptive maintenance (PsM) is a type of data analytics that supports making better judgments by analyzing raw data. It takes into account information

© IFIP International Federation for Information Processing 2022
Published by Springer Nature Switzerland AG 2022
I. Maglogiannis et al. (Eds.): AIAI 2022 Workshops, IFIP AICT 652, pp. 289–300, 2022.
https://doi.org/10.1007/078_3_031-08341-9_24

about potential conditions or scenarios, available resources, previous and present performance, and recommends a plan of action that optimizes equipment maintenance. It may be used to make decisions across any time horizon, from the present to the long term. It uses Machine Learning (ML) to comprehend and advance from the data it collects, evolving as it goes. ML and Internet of Things (IoT) enable the processing of massive amounts of data, which are now available. PsM software solutions automatically adjust to make use of new or extra data as it becomes available, in a process that is exhaustive and faster than that afforded by human skills.

To be effective, PsM requires the training of a ML model using past sensor and service data. The more high-quality information supplied, the more accurate the ML model will be in detecting more maintenance requirements and failure signals, whilst providing fewer false positives. Before feeding data to the ML algorithm, it may be necessary to clean it. Sensor readings, for example, may need to be updated to account for changes in calibration or to standardize how various faults are recorded by human operators. When training a PsM algorithm, higher-level knowledge about an organization may be submitted to the ML algorithm. This enables the PsM software to analyze critical factors like maintenance costs and manufacturing downtime. Anomaly identification, residual usable life assessment and optimal algorithmic and metrics selection are common issues that impede PsM attempts.

Because of the equipment they employ, most systems are linked to signals, which are not always time series. Predictive maintenance (PdM) gets data from condition monitoring. Then, using complex algorithms, it detects a possible failure. A misalignment, for example, will be detected by vibration analysis around three months before it causes a breakdown. Nonetheless, asset managers must take action. They must analyze facts, make a decision, and develop a work order. In such situation, PsM would generate and submit a work order to technicians to repair the misalignment. It does not require asset managers' interaction and maintains equipment on its own. This results in increased availability and productivity, as well as the capacity to do remote maintenance.

Moreover, PsM offers the same advantages as PdM, but goes a step further. In general, once customized to meet the needs of a use case, it leads to i) less unplanned downtime and higher productivity as a result of maintenance optimization, ii) higher profitability as a result of higher productivity, iii) more virtual collaboration as data is available remotely, and finally, iv) digital PsM enables significant prospects for scalability.

This work examines PsM and proposes a framework that envisions practical implications that can be conceptualized within the context of proactive buildings. The goal is to predict and prescribe actions for minimizing operational costs and downtime of home appliances as a high-level approach (considering high data granularity). We believe that the proposed framework can facilitate processes supporting feature data requirements and system architecture for enabling prescriptive analytics in household and small-scale industrial solutions, while posing as an all around generic solution for modeling and enabling PsM.

The remainder of this article is structured as follows: Sect. 2 showcases related work, while Section 3 analyzes the developed concepts/methodology of the proposed PsM framework. The paper concludes with Sect. 4, discussing final thoughts, implications and future prospects.

2   Related Work

This section introduces different types of maintenance analytics and reviews recent attempts in PsM in a multi domain manner.

Electric utilities cover a wide geographic range of assets. They have been migrating from time-based maintenance planning to establishing a proactive and intelligent asset health management approach to address the conflicting constraints of decreasing customer downtimes, fulfilling regulatory standards, and managing increasing infrastructure. An advanced analytics strategy tries to model asset health and network dependability by projecting asset aging, determining the remaining lifespan, and computing network resilience. The analytics use data from business asset management, sophisticated metering infrastructure, weather systems, and other sources. The outcomes include a health score and risk ranking, as well as a proposed ideal maintenance approach based on cost limitations [1].

Big data analytics is quickly developing as a critical IoT endeavor aimed at giving valuable insights and assisting with optimal decision making despite time limitations. Prescriptive analytics seeks to make judgments that are adaptable, automated, limited, time-dependent, and optimum. Estimations, on the other hand, present major issues, due to the uncertainty resulting from improper user input, noisy data, and the non-stationarity of real-world data feeds. A suggested method solves sensor-driven learning issues linked to uncertainty arising from time dependent characteristics, such as user input, sensor noise, and gives estimates that lead to more trustworthy prescriptions [2].

One of the primary advantages of the railroads' digital transformation is the ability to improve asset management efficiency via the use of information modeling and decision support systems. Tracking circuits of an Italian urban railway network are used to demonstrate an actual railway signaling use case, covering from field data collecting through decision support and asset status. The acquired knowledge is then used to completely automate the prioritization of asset management actions using an optimization logic [3] and operational limitations. The goal is to improve i) maintenance activity scheduling, ii) service dependability, and iii) resource utilization and possession times while avoiding (or reducing) contractual fines and delays [4].

Nowadays, maintenance management methodologies are being turned into automated knowledge-based decision support systems. PriMa, which consists of four layers, is proposed. These are i) data management, ii) a predictive data analytics toolset, iii) a recommendation and decision support dashboard, and iv) an overarching layer for semantic-based learning and reasoning. As a result, two functional capabilities in a real-world production system are enhanced, i) efficiently processing large amounts of multi-modal and heterogeneous data, and ii) effectively producing decision support measures and suggestions for improving and optimizing upcoming scheduled maintenance, thereby reducing production downtime [5].

The digital revolution has had an influence on industrial processes and maintenance models, resulting in new needs, difficulties, and possibilities for ensuring and enhancing equipment utilization and process stability. A model is proposed that i) aids in the implementation of a PsM strategy and the assessment of its maturity level, ii) enables the integration of data-science techniques to predict future events, and iii) specifies intervention fields to achieve a higher target maturity condition and thus greater predictive accuracy [6].

PsM planning is a critical facilitator of intelligent, highly adaptable manufacturing processes. Traditional maintenance procedures are insufficient to meet today's production requirements due to rising complexity. Multimodal data analysis and simulation techniques are used in an unique method to analyze historical data, such as quality of product, machine malfunction, and production planning. Validation includes real-world applications in the automobile manufacturing field, where recognized data associations and real-time machine data are used to forecast system problems and provide fixes [7].

A dynamic maintenance plan is described that takes into account the amount of deterioration and aging, as well as the system failure rate. It is commonly expected that repair would always bring positive impact in the health of the system. Nevertheless, in the case of locomotive wheel-sets, restoration decreases the system age while increasing the deterioration levels. After conducting a dependability analysis it is observed that the best maintenance plan is achieved by reducing the long-run cost rate as a function of the repair cycle and dynamically determining the appropriate inspection time [8].

An end-to-end PsM approach that incorporates maintenance analysis, equipment, and operational data with predictive solutions and feedback to create actionable insights is offered. Workforce scheduling, supply chain optimization, field-replaceable unit control, process efficiency, and knowledge management are among the features used. The implementation has been validated in several datasets, including the data integration, feature reduction/selection, filling missing data, and noise removal stages. It detects faults at the individual equipment and fleet levels before offering a mechanism for full repair solutions, such as service staff scheduling and equipment downtime control. The findings result in an extendable PsM equipment maintenance architecture that achieves significantly decreased unexpected equipment downtime at an optimal cost [9].

Another framework is presented for achieving optimal future-failure awareness and safety-conscious production and maintenance plans while taking system complexity and resource allocation into account. Utilizing equipment condition data, ensembles of nonlinear support vector machine classification models were used to forecast the timing and probability of future equipment breakdown. To develop optimal processes and maintenance schedules, multi-objective optimization of predicted profit and a safety metric were also employed. Ensemble models had an average accuracy and an F1-score of 0.987 and they were 3% more accurate and sensitive than individual classifiers, and the Pareto-optimal process and maintenance schedules were established as equally acceptable alternative options for decision making [10].

One of the primary issues in smart manufacturing is interpreting information and deriving insights from data. A use case in the steel industry takes advantage of recent advances in ML in PdM and PsM analytics by utilizing corporate and operational data to assist operators on the shopfloor. Recurrent Neural Networks are used for predictive analytics, and Multi-Objective Reinforcement Learning is used for prescriptive analytics [11].

PsM is also used in the aviation sector finding application in a tire pressure indicator system, with the goal of lowering operating costs and boosting operational stability. However, research has been confined to calculating remaining usable lifespan while ignoring the influence on surrounding processes, changes in the aims of the associated stakeholders, and so on. The maturity level of the condition monitoring system must be considered when evaluating the potential of a fault diagnosis and failure prognosis system, including its implications on neighboring maintenance procedures. A PsM strategy is proposed by modeling the many stakeholders engaged in aircraft and line maintenance operations, as well as their functional connections. The findings are validated using an automated condition monitoring system that generates discrete-events and an agent-based simulation setup based on one-month's flight plan data [12].

Moreover, the aviation business is under increased competition to reduce operational costs, while features such as sustainability and customer experience are critical for differentiating from rivals. Aircraft maintenance accounts for about 20% of the total cost of airline operations. Consequently, maintenance providers must reduce their cost fraction and contribute to a more dependable and sustainable aircraft operation. The primary objective is to reduce costs while improving aircraft availability. A framework is established for the use case of an Airbus A320 tire pressure measuring task, allowing the optimization target for the proposed approach to be adjusted to integrate performance attributes other than the often used financial indicators [13].

In the PsM use case of a chemical complex system and a cooling water system, there is the possibility for anomalous operations and an unwanted increased occurrence of process safety events. A study proposes a multi-feature based paradigm for process control that is safety-aware, maintenance-aware, and disruption-aware. For fault detection, it employs ensemble classification using ML classifiers. Also, mixed integer nonlinear programming for integrated safety-aware production and maintenance scheduling, and hybrid multi-feature model predictive control for fault-tolerant set point tracking. In terms of fault detection accuracy, sensitivity, and specificity, the findings reveal that the ensemble classifier beats the individual classifiers. The designed controllers can alter control actions based on process disruption data [14].

The high equipment intensity and complexity of semiconductor manufacturing processes results in severe facility availability requirements in this competitive sector. A conceptual approach that enables PsM in the use case of etching equipment for semiconductor production addresses such issues. ML methods forecast time-to-failure periods, whereas Bayesian Networks identify the core cause of a malfunction. When these procedures are combined, prescriptions for maintenance planning routines are generated, while system availability is increased [15].

PsM is also used in protective coating systems against steel corrosion for tower components of big onshore wind turbines. The inspection, condition monitoring, and maintenance of such systems is an intensive and time-consuming task that necessitates a significant amount of human labor. The notion of a digital twin is introduced, with the initial guiding principle being an on-site virtual twin for producing reference regions for condition monitoring. The integration of an online picture annotation and processing tool, a maintenance strategy, corrosive resistance characteristics, structural load indicators, and sensor data is described in this study [16].

The state of the art in PsM finds applications in a variety of use cases. These include, but are not limited to energy sector and electric utilities, IoT and sensors, railway networks and circuit tracking, Industry 4.0 with deterioration, aging and equipment downtime, steel industry operations, aviation and the tire pressure measuring task, chemical complex systems with water cooling systems, semiconductor etching equipment and protective coating systems.

3   Framework Proposal

This section proposes a framework for prescriptive maintenance in proactive buildings, as depicted in Fig. 1. It consists of three main components, i) the IoT data storage that gathers all IoT device data into a central database, ii) a decision support system that implements the prescriptive maintenance engine, anomaly detection, failure diagnosis and suggests prescriptions and iii) the knowledge extraction that handles the graphical user interface of the proposed framework offering functionalities, such as device health monitoring, options for maintenance and maintenance scheduling.

3.1   Data Warehousing

The proposed approach will be implemented in various and heterogeneous buildings situated in four European countries: Greece, Spain, Germany and the Netherlands. The provided datasets will vary based on the actual, historical or forecasted [17] user energy habits, activities and also the climate. Indicatively, different climate zones result in different heating, cooling or ventilation systems and technologies.

Specifically, in Greece and Spain, due to high temperatures during the summer, Air Conditioning (AC) or Heating, Ventilation and Air Conditioning (HVAC) systems are more likely to exist compared to Germany and Netherlands. Furthermore, there are buildings that have a central heating system (e.g., central heat pump), while others have a heating system per apartment. A summary of the data that will be used is presented in Table 1.

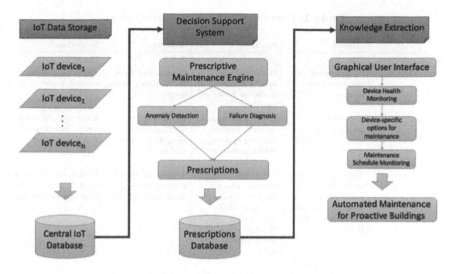

Fig. 1. Overview of framework architecture

3.2 Anomaly Detection

Anomalies are identified by detecting uncommon observations that differ considerably from the given dataset [18]. Recognizing non-standard device behavior is seen as a major duty in the energy business. Small-scale residential and industrial environments can benefit from anomaly detection on device condition, maintenance needs, and unavailability, which can lead to lower infrastructure costs.

Furthermore, anomaly detection is widely used in data pre-processing [19] to remove outliers from records. This is a procedure that is being carried out for a variety of reasons. For example, once anomalies are eliminated, data metrics, such as the mean and standard deviation become more accurate, but also data presentation may be improved. When implementing a supervised learning task, removing anomalous data usually results in a statistically significant increase in accuracy. Anomalies are typically the most essential findings to be uncovered in IoT [20].

There are numerous methods for detecting irregularities in a number of application scenarios, including prescriptive appliance maintenance. These may include machine and deep learning approaches such as Support Vector Machine (SVM), Convolutional Neural Networks (CNN), Long Short Term Memory Networks (LSTM), CNN-autoencoder, LSTM-autoencoder and more as well as their respective outcomes measured using a variety of common metrics such as Precision, Recall, F1 Score and more.

Table 1. Overview of the data warehousing

	Greece	Spain	Germany	Netherlands
Building structure	Concrete	Concrete	Brick	Brick
Domestic hot water	Solar system combined with electricity	Decentralized-local electric boiler or heat pump	Centralized from the building boiler room	Decentralized-local electric boiler or heat pump
Infrastructure	Electricity, heating, water system, internet and cable	Electricity, water system, central heating system, HVAC, internet and cable	Electricity, heating, water system, internet and cable	Electricity, heating, water, internet and cable
Home appliances	Television, fridge, AC, water heater, oven, microwave, washing machine, dishwasher and dryer	Television, fridge, electric water heater, oven, stove, HVAC splits, dish washer, washing machine and dryer	Television, fridge, electric stove, washing machine	Fridge, electric heater, electric oven, washing machine and dryer
Electrical vehicle	Two charging spots for electric vehicles	N/A	N/A	N/A

3.3 Failure Diagnosis and Prescriptions

Initially, an error is recognized in the device's regular behavior as a result of a specific problem. This error is classified to specific faults through a diagnostics process and then prescriptions are sent to the user. Such failures and recommended prescriptions are indicatively presented for widely-used home appliances (Table 2). The devices include faults (diagnosis) and course of action (prescriptions) for common household appliances like the fridge, the washing machine and the AC.

3.4 Knowledge Extraction

Knowledge extraction comes as a software-as-a-service implementation fostered by a graphical user interface that offers the following services. i) Device health monitoring, ii) device-specific options for maintenance, and iii) maintenance schedule monitoring. Generally, Knowledge Extraction and Application (KEA) methods intend to analyze all gathered information, data, models and methods to facilitate the decision making. KEA improves all available information and data by contextualizing information and knowledge. The result is an automated maintenance for proactive buildings. Taking into consideration infrastructures' current and historical information is the first step towards knowledge extraction.

Having a record of the devices' normal consumption pattern and behaviour under certain circumstances will facilitate detecting any anomalies and diagnosing any potential health device problems. Device health monitoring intends to keep a check on the devices behaviour and performance while detecting any perplexing motifs. Consequently, home appliances and devices are meant to constantly operate and perform well over the years. Proper devices' maintenance

Table 2. Failure diagnosis and prescriptions for widely-used home appliances

Device	Diagnosis	Prescription
Fridge	- Freezer is not cold enough - Unit is cycling too often - Frost buildup - Refrigerator is freezing food	- Check compressor and clean any dust - Set the temperature higher or remove the dust buildup or debris around the condenser coils - Inspect the damper door for air leakage - Replace the thermostat
Washing machine	- Washing machine moves around - Washing machine is noisy - Draining issues/Washing machine does not fill with water	- Level washing machine to the ground, check suspension rods - Remove items from the washing drum or contact a technician - Check the filter for blockages - Locate the hoses and check for blockages or kinks
AC	- Refrigerant leaks - Low performance - Cycle constantly or behave erratically - Drainage issues	- Contact a technician - Contact a technician for maintenance - Thermostat sensor problem - Check the condensate drain and clean it

will help the devices to extend their life-span. As a result, device-specific options for maintenance will alert the owner to take immediate actions that will maintain a smooth operation. Finally, a report about scheduled maintenance ensures that periodic maintenance actions will occur.

4 Conclusion

In reality, PsM is even more proactive than PdM. PdM forecasts when a failure is likely to occur so that repair may be scheduled ahead of time. PsM seeks to prevent particular types of failure completely. This paper investigates the state of the art in PsM reporting on multi-domain use cases and conceives a theoretical framework that enables PsM for proactive buildings that may also be considered as microgrids [21].

This work sets the grounds for the deployment and operation of proactive residential buildings. It will implement and test a prescriptive and proactive building energy management system that will learn and will be self-managed, -monitored and -optimized regarding the building operation. This research will focus on delivering supervised and unsupervised ML technologies capable of detecting and predicting the potential malfunctions in the building appliances, and to recommend appropriate actions.

At the current status of framework implementation limitations can be attributed to the fact that this research does not consider data granularity [22] due to the absence of open data sources for experimenting with the conceived approach. The absence of such details renders the conception of the PsM framework for proactive buildings, a theoretical approach. Therefore, an analytical and comparative analysis regarding the options of open dataset is not possible. Also, appropriate data gathering and extraction of features are beneficial in enhancing algorithm performance for classic ML algorithms, however for Deep Learning algorithms, deeper network architecture and larger dimensional feature vectors are more essential for achieving better metric evaluation scores.

PsM can detect capital expenditure requirements considerably sooner than human perception would. PsM tools, for example, can act as a digital testing environment, particularly when combined with a digital twin architecture, allowing the consequences of adding or replacing equipment to be simulated before making a purchase. This enables asset managers to arrange purchases and acquisitions more intelligently, decreasing both appliance downtime and operational expenses.

To sum up, this paper acts a as concrete baseline for experimenting with real data for generating prescriptions for proactive buildings. The main outcome of this work conceptualizes a theoretical framework as a PsM tool that enables building pro-activeness. It poses as a generic solution when engaging in PsM and considering building assets. The aim is to improve this study investigating the following aspects.

- Continue tracking the growth of PsM and analytics with a focus on household appliances. Improve the implement the conceived PsM framework by addressing constraints and extending our understanding of the data granularity, that is necessary for more informed prescriptions.
- Improve the proposed PsM framework by further automating the process of outputting prescriptions so that it may function as a stand-alone program with only the necessary input datasets.
- Examine and integrate environmental Key Point Indicators (KPIs) such as energy bills, water bills, purchase records, emissions to air, emissions to water, emissions to land, and resource usage while offering appliance prescriptions.
- Elevate the proposed PsM framework's business viewpoint by addressing additional practical applications as well as expanding the evaluation to small scale industrial setups.

Acknowledgements. This work is supported by the project PRECEPT - A novel decentralized edge-enabled PREsCriptivE and ProacTive framework for increased energy efficiency and well-being in residential buildings funded by the EU H2020 Programme, grant agreement no. 958284.

References

1. Goyal, A., et al.: Asset health management using predictive and prescriptive analytics for the electric power grid. IBM J. Res. Dev. **60**(1), 4:1–4:14 (2016)

2. Bousdekis, A., Papageorgiou, N., Magoutas, B., Apostolou, D., Mentzas, G.: Sensor-driven learning of time-dependent parameters for prescriptive analytics. IEEE Access **8**, 92383–92392 (2020)
3. Koukaras, P., et al.: A tri-layer optimization framework for day-ahead energy scheduling based on cost and discomfort minimization. Energies **14**(12) (2021). https://www.mdpi.com/1996-1073/14/12/3599
4. Consilvio, A., et al.: Prescriptive maintenance of railway infrastructure: from data analytics to decision support. In: MT-ITS 2019–6th International Conference on Models and Technologies for Intelligent Transportation Systems. Institute of Electrical and Electronics Engineers Inc., June 2019
5. Ansari, F., Glawar, R., Nemeth, T.: PriMa: a prescriptive maintenance model for cyber-physical production systems. Int. J. Comput. Integr. Manuf. **32**(4–5), 482–503 (2019)
6. Nemeth, T., Ansari, F., Sihn, W., Haslhofer, B., Schindler, A.: PriMa-X: a reference model for realizing prescriptive maintenance and assessing its maturity enhanced by machine learning. Procedia CIRP **72**, 1039–1044. Elsevier B.V. (2018)
7. Matyas, K., Nemeth, T., Kovacs, K., Glawar, R.: A procedural approach for realizing prescriptive maintenance planning in manufacturing industries. CIRP Ann. **66**(1), 461–464 (2017). https://www.sciencedirect.com/science/article/pii/S0007850617300070
8. Liu, B., Lin, J., Zhang, L., Kumar, U.: A dynamic prescriptive maintenance model considering system aging and degradation. IEEE Access **7**, 94931–94943 (2019)
9. Choubey, S., Benton, R.G., Johnsten, T.: A holistic end-to-end prescriptive maintenance framework. Data-Enabled Discov. Appl. **4**(1), 1–20 (2020)
10. Gordon, C.A.K., Burnak, B., Onel, M., Pistikopoulos, E.N.: Data-driven prescriptive maintenance: failure prediction using ensemble support vector classification for optimal process and maintenance scheduling. Ind. Eng. Chem. Res. **59**(44), 19607–19622 (2020)
11. Lepenioti, K., et al.: Machine learning for predictive and prescriptive analytics of operational data in smart manufacturing. In: Dupuy-Chessa, S., Proper, H.A. (eds.) CAiSE 2020. LNBIP, vol. 382, pp. 5–16. Springer, Cham (2020). https://doi.org/10.1007/978-3-030-49165-9_1
12. Meissner, R., Meyer, H., Wicke, K.: Concept and economic evaluation of prescriptive maintenance strategies for an automated condition monitoring system. Int. J. Progn. Health Manag. **12**(3) (2021)
13. Meissner, R., Rahn, A., Wicke, K.: Developing prescriptive maintenance strategies in the aviation industry based on a discrete-event simulation framework for post-prognostics decision making. Reliab. Eng. Syst. Saf. 107812 (2021)
14. Gordon, C.A., Pistikopoulos, E.N.: Data-driven prescriptive maintenance toward fault-tolerant multiparametric control. AIChE J. e17489 (2021)
15. Biebl, F., et al.: A conceptual model to enable prescriptive maintenance for etching equipment in semiconductor manufacturing. Procedia CIRP **88**, 64–69 (2020)
16. Momber, A.W., Möller, T., Langenkämper, D., Nattkemper, T.W., Brün, D.: A digital twin concept for the prescriptive maintenance of protective coating systems on wind turbine structures. Wind Eng. 0309524X211060550 (2021)
17. Koukaras, P., Bezas, N., Gkaidatzis, P., Ioannidis, D., Tzovaras, D., Tjortjis, C.: Introducing a novel approach in one-step ahead energy load forecasting. Sustain. Comput. Inform. Syst. **32**, 100616 (2021). https://www.sciencedirect.com/science/article/pii/S2210537921001049
18. Hawkins, D.M.: Identification of Outliers, vol. 11. Springer, Heidelberg (1980). https://doi.org/10.1007/978-94-015-3994-4

19. Xu, S., Qian, Y., Hu, R.Q.: A data-driven preprocessing scheme on anomaly detection in big data applications. In: 2017 IEEE Conference on Computer Communications Workshops (INFOCOM WKSHPS), pp. 814–819 (2017)
20. Cook, A.A., Mısırlı, G., Fan, Z.: Anomaly detection for IoT time-series data: a survey. IEEE Internet Things J. **7**(7), 6481–6494 (2020)
21. Koukaras, P., Tjortjis, C., Gkaidatzis, P., Bezas, N., Ioannidis, D., Tzovaras, D.: An interdisciplinary approach on efficient virtual microgrid to virtual microgrid energy balancing incorporating data preprocessing techniques. Computing **104**(1), 209–250 (2021). https://doi.org/10.1007/s00607-021-00929-7
22. Zhou, Y., Ren, H., Li, Z., Pedrycz, W.: An anomaly detection framework for time series data: an interval-based approach. Knowl.-Based Syst. **228**, 107153 (2021). https://www.sciencedirect.com/science/article/pii/S0950705121004160

Probabilistic Quantile Multi-step Forecasting of Energy Market Prices: A UK Case Study

Petros Tzallas[(✉)] [iD], Napoleon Bezas[(✉)] [iD], Ioannis Moschos[iD],
Dimosthenis Ioannidis[iD], and Dimitrios Tzovaras[iD]

Information Technologies Institute, Centre for Research and Technology,
57001 Thessaloniki, Greecee
{ptzallas,bezas,imoschos,djoannid,Dimitrios.Tzovaras}@iti.gr

Abstract. The transition from traditional dispatchable generation units to intermittent supply from renewable energy sources, as well as the continuous rise in energy demand, partially due to the growing popularity of electric vehicles (EVs), has sparked an upsurge in research interest for energy related forecasting in recent decades. The heavy reliance on weather conditions adds unpredictability in energy generation, resulting in fluctuations in the electricity system and, as a result, in electricity prices. Therefore, in order to support more efficient energy management, high-quality forecasts are required not just for energy demand and generation, but also for energy market prices. While most approaches aim to achieve point forecasts for the energy market prices, a probabilistic forecast approach could further assist the decision making process. This paper proposes a lightweight forecasting model for accurate multi-step forecasts of day-ahead and intra-day prices of the UK electricity market, while providing different quantiles of the forecast in order to estimate the potential uncertainty of price forecasts. The methodology focuses heavily on the feature engineering step by utilizing features extracted from numerical weather values, load and generation forecasts of the respective region, temporal features and historical values of day-ahead and intra-day prices. Furthermore, new metrics for evaluating the forecasted quantile intervals are introduced and defined in the analysis, in addition to the commonly used evaluation metrics implemented in time series forecasting.

Keywords: Electricity price forecast · Time series forecasting ·
Probabilistic forecast · Quantiles forecasting · Feature engineering

1 Introduction

Electricity, transportation and heating are some of the most vital needs of humanity and their fulfillment is of vital importance. Thus, the economic process is highly dependent on the energy sources. Since the beginning of the century

© IFIP International Federation for Information Processing 2022
Published by Springer Nature Switzerland AG 2022
I. Maglogiannis et al. (Eds.): AIAI 2022 Workshops, IFIP AICT 652, pp. 301–313, 2022.
https://doi.org/10.1007/978-3-031-08341-9_25

a significant rise in the energy demand has been observed [1]. Additionally, the conventional energy resources, such as oil, coal, and natural gas, are starting to be depleted [2]. Finally, due to high CO_2 emissions, the aforementioned resources can cause certain environmental issues [3]. These three reasons have led stakeholders of the energy sector to explore more sustainable and environmentally friendly resources, which has boosted the focus on renewable energy research [4].

The transition from conventional energy sources to renewables that was observed in the electricity system, has inevitably affected the energy market, which introduced different kinds of markets that assist in facilitating more efficient generation and demand-side management [5].

Despite the large increase in investment and consumption of renewable energy sources, there is still a strong obstacle to almost all renewable energy holdings. This obstacle is the uncertainty of source supply. Renewable energy sources show significant sporadicity, variability, and randomness. The former, not only threatens the stability and reliability of these power plants, and inevitably the stability of the electricity grid but also, introduces uncertainties in energy market prices. As a result, precise energy market forecasting, as well as generation and demand forecasting, has become necessary for a dispatcher to optimally plan the energy related transactions, making the most profitable decisions [6].

While in most energy related forecasting problems, point predictions could be considered adequate for the optimal dispatch of the assets, in energy market forecasting, a probabilistic approach could further assist the decision making process. Therefore, in this paper, we propose a lightweight machine learning based model that provides quantile forecasts for energy price data. More specifically, forecasts are going to be made for the two main price values in EU electricity wholesale markets, the day-ahead price and the intra-day price.

The day-ahead market refers to the bidding process that occurs on day X, during which stakeholders commit to selling or buying particular amounts of power at each hour of day X+1. The price of energy is not established at the moment of bidding, but rather after all of the bids from energy generators have been released. The amount of energy that each participant sells or buys, as well as the price of power, are the results of the day-ahead market mechanism.

The day-ahead market bids submitted by each participant have a high level of variability, due to the unpredictable nature of renewable energy sources, as mentioned previously. To address this issue and provide more accurate price forecasts, the intra-day market was established as a complement to the day-ahead market. Participants can make adjustments in the transaction of energy that are committed from the day-ahead process closer to the actual time of energy delivery using this mechanism, and thus have more certain information about the availability of assets and needs.

2   Related Work

There is limited literature review regarding the probabilistic electricity price forecasting. Achieving an accurate point forecast can provide a solid foundation for flexible investment decisions, but does not take into account the possibility of extreme events, which can have huge implications for the business as a whole. In recent years, the topic of probabilistic electricity price forecasting research received a lot of attention. By quantifying the development of published papers from the first related article written in 2003 [7] until the year 2016, [8] was able to demonstrate this trend in detail

Some researchers have sought to address this problem in the past by evaluating and modeling the variance. Zhao used a heteroscedastic and non-linear model to compute the prediction intervals (PIs) for electricity prices in [9]. Zhao, in particular, provides a statistical forecasting model for SVM that explicitly models the mean and the variance of electricity models. Similar approach was proposed by [10], where a hybrid approach is used to construct the prediction intervals with a two-stage formulation. The first step includes the estimation of point forecasts based on an extreme learning machine (ELM) model, while the second step involves assessing model uncertainty and noise variance using a bootstrap approach and the maximum likelihood method, respectively. The bootstrap and ELM method of generating PIs has also been employed in other studies. For example, Chen et al. [11] use the same technique to construct half-hourly point and interval forecasts in the Australian energy market. Also, Rafiei et al. [12] uses a hybrid approach for probabilistic electricity price forecasting based on the concept of bootstrap. A two-layer neural network is developed using the clonal selection algorithm and extreme machine learning (ELM). A decomposition of the time series is performed prior to the application of the model to partition the time series into one approximation and three details series. Each of the is fitted with a neural network, and the bootstrap is used to estimate the model uncertainty. The data uncertainty for the aggregated series is then assessed using the bootstrap approach one more.

However, it has been proven that focusing on specific moments of the distribution, particularly the mean and variance, is insufficient on its own. Hence, modeling the whole-time dependent distribution function of prices was considered as an alternative solution to this problem. One of the most common approach is to construct PIs utilizing the quantile regression. The authors in [13, 14] use the notion of quantile regression and a pool of point forecasts generated by averaging individual models to achieve better results in the context of interval forecasts of electricity prices resulting to a Quantile Regression Averaging (QRA) model. The previous approach is extended in [15] by extracting important information from all the individual models using Principal Component Analysis (PCA) before utilizing quantile regression, whereby the authors refer to as Factor Quantile Regression Averaging (FQRA). A different approach is suggested by the authors of [16], that outperforms the two previous methods and is considered as a regularized variant of QRA. The model utilizes the Least Absolute Shrinkage and Selection Operator (LASSO) to automate the process of selecting the most appropriate regressors, resulting in much better results in terms of profitability during energy trading activities.

3   Methodology

The adopted forecasting framework is described in detail in this section. Multi-step forecasts were produced for both day-ahead and intra-day price forecasting, and more specifically, an individual forecast for each horizon of the entire day (day-ahead forecasts). The general methodology can be separated into four main steps, as shown in Fig. 1. The data was acquired from the online electricity price service offered by ELEXON [17]. Following data collection, missing values were addressed and handled accordingly, either by removing them or by utilizing interpolation techniques. The next step is the implementation of feature engineering techniques and the training of machine learning algorithms. Finally, the model's forecasting results are then assessed using the appropriate error metrics.

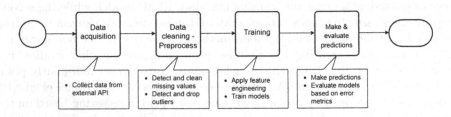

Fig. 1. Forecasting methodology flowchart

3.1   Forecasting Strategy and Feature Creation

Our approach is heavily centered in the feature engineering aspect of time series forecasting. For the multi-step point forecasting separate models were developed for each time-step of the forecast horizon, based on the approach described in [18], as seen in Fig. 2. In addition to the traditional model's mean point forecasts, three different quantiles are predicted, namely the 0.05 quantile, which is the lower limit of the interval, the 0.95 quantile which is the upper limit of interval, and the 0.5 quantile that corresponds to median of the interval. Hence, for each time-step four models are created, and for the whole day ahead horizon 96 models are created, when the data set is in hourly resolution, 24 for each of the four predictions.

There are three main categories that can separate the features used for energy forecasting, namely the historical energy price values, additional external features, and cyclical temporal features to capture time-series periodicity.

More specifically, we utilize the historical energy market prices values within a previously determined time range, referred to as history. As a result, in order to anticipate the $t + 1$ price, the models use historical load values from t through t-(history-1) time-steps. The history of the forecasting models of our approach is set to 24 h. More details for the energy market prices datasets are provided in Sect. 4.

The additional features consist of day-ahead generation and load forecasts and aggregated numerical weather values for the region of UK. The day ahead generation and load forecasts were retrieved from the online service of ENTSO-E [19]. They describe the total energy demand and energy generation predictions for the entire UK region.

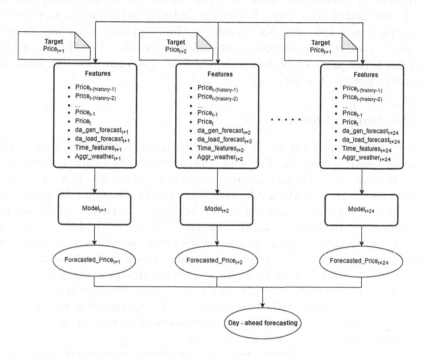

Fig. 2. Energy market price forecasting strategy

The aggregated numerical weather measurements are retrieved through the online weather data service Meteostat [20]. Meteostat is a public API that provide different weather measurements from the majority of the meteorological stations around the globe. In our approach, several weather measurements were received from the weather stations in the UK and their average was computed and used as a feature. The weather measurements that we used in this paper are temperature, dew point, relative humidity, total precipitation, wind direction, average wind speed, and finally sea-level air pressure.

3.2   Prediction Models

In our approach we decide to utilize common machine learning models, and more specifically tree based models, namely Random Forest Regressor (RF), Gradient Boosting Regressor (GBR), Light Gradient Boosting Machine (lightGBM), and Extra Trees Regressor. The selected models offer highly accurate results, without the need for a large dataset or data scaling [21]. In addition, as compared to deep learning models, their training and testing time is negligible. Lastly, these models offer easy to implement quantile predictions, either in their implementation in sklearn [22] library or in sklearn_quantile [23] library.

Grid search was conducted in order to tune the hyper-parameters of the models to achieve the most accurate results. More specifically, for Random Forest and Extra Trees Regressor and the hyper-parameters were set to n_estimators = 100 and max_depth = 9, for Gradient Boosting Regressor n_estimators = 100, max_features = auto and max_depth = 8 and finally, for Light GBM the hyper-parameters that we tuned were n_estimators = 100, num_leaves = 64, max_depth = -1, n_jobs = -1.

3.3   Evaluation Metrics

For the evaluation of the mean and median point results the most common evaluation metrics used in time series forecasting were utilized. More specifically, there are four distinct metrics utilized for the evaluation of the existing approaches, namely Mean Absolute Error (MAE) or Mean Absolute Deviation (MAD), Root Mean Square Error (RMSE), symmetric Mean Square Error (sMAPE) and MAD/Mean Ratio. Although, MAE and RMSE are the most commonly used and accepted metrics for regression problems, to consider them qualitatively significant, they must be compared to the data set mean and standard deviation. For easier interpretation of the results, percentage metrics, such as sMAPE and MAD/Mean Ratio are utilized that describe the absolute difference of the predicted and actual values divided by the absolute sum of their values and MAD metric divided by the arithmetical average of the observations respectively [24].

In order to evaluate the accuracy of the prediction interval, there are two factors that need to be examined. Initially, the target must be inside the limits of the forecasted intervals, thus the evaluation metric In Bounds was defined to showcase the percentage of the real values that fall within the intervals. By making the limits wide, the In Bounds metric can easily be very high, although the results is not the optimal. Thus, there is a need for metrics that highlight the error of the interval. In this approach the MAE of the upper and lower limit is utilized, together with the MAE of the interval, that corresponds to the average of the limit errors. Additionally, violin plots are provided to showcase the absolute error for each value.

4   Experimental Dataset

The two datasets used for our approach for quantile energy market was retrieved from Elexon API [17]. The datasets correspond to day-ahead and intra-day energy prices for the UK between 2021-01-04 and 2021-06-14. The measurement unit of the datasets is €/MWh and the time resolution was set on a hourly basis. Table 1 provides useful information about the two datasets and Fig. 3 provide indicative plots for the datasets. The two datasets were relatively clean, with some missing values that were filled using linear interpolation.

Table 1. Day-ahead and intra-day price data information.

	Day-ahead price	Intra-day price
Count	3888	3888
Mean	72.76	63.76
Std. deviation	38.49	27.63
Min	2.24	-40.30
Max	1192.33	369.51
Start date	2021-01-04	2021-01-04
End date	2021-06-14	2021-06-14

The additional data used as features in our approach, namely day ahead load and generation forecasts, and average weather values, correspond to the same time period and also have the same resolution.

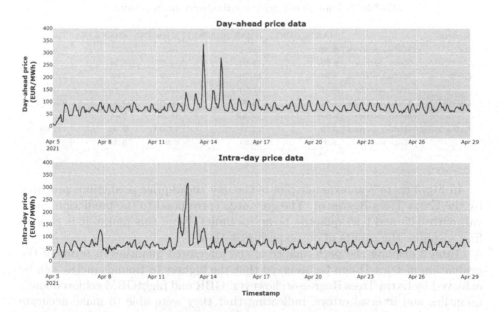

Fig. 3. Day-ahead price (upper) and intra-day price (lower) datasets example plots.

5   Results

As noted in Sect. 3.3, the review method for both day-ahead and intra-day price forecasts was divided into two stages. To begin, the aforementioned metrics were used to assess the mean and median results, as well as the training and testing execution time for each model. Violin plots were used to visualize the inaccuracies when evaluating the quantiles and intervals. The tables and figures required to demonstrate the accuracy of our findings are provided in the following sections.

5.1   Day-Ahead Price Results

In Table 2 we can observe the metrics for the predictions of the simple model that computes the mean value and the model that predicts the 0.5 quantile or median. Generally, the results of the selected tree-based models can be characterized adequate, with the best performing model being the Extra Tree Regressor, with Light Gradient Boosting Regressor and Random Forest Regressor also performing well. Furthermore, the required training time of the models is quite short, with the slowest model having a training and testing time of less than ten minutes. LightGBM was the fastest model, delivering results in under two minutes.

Table 2. Day-ahead price median and mean results.

Models		MAE (€/MWh)	RMSE (€/MWh)	MMR (%)	sMAPE (%)	Time (s)
RF	Median metrics	**8.59**	11.46	18.4	9.55	386.93
	Mean metrics	8.69	11.86	10.37	5.34	
GBR	Median metrics	8.84	11.73	19.09	9.86	570.8
	Mean metrics	8.64	11.99	10.3	5.31	
LightGBM	Median metrics	8.57	**11.35**	19.19	9.86	**93.17**
	Mean metrics	8.59	**11.32**	10.24	5.44	
Extra Trees	Median metrics	9.15	12.21	**17.93**	**9.35**	142.69
	Mean metrics	**8.3**	11.34	**9.9**	**5.18**	

In Fig. 4 there is an example plot of the day ahead price predictions provided by the Extra Trees Regressor. The grey area correspond to the prediction interval, with 0.05 and 0.95 quantile being its limits. From this figure, it is easy to first visualize the results of our experimentation.

Table 3 displays the performance of the forecasted quantiles in terms of the evaluation metrics. It can be observed that the highest In Bounds metric can be achieved by Extra Trees Regressor; however, GBR and LightGBM achieved lower quantiles and interval errors, indicating that they were able to make accurate prediction intervals without increasing the interval limits.

The violin plots in Fig. 5 demonstrate the absolute errors over the whole test set. We can see that the models have mostly low absolute errors, with the exception of the absolute error of the 0.95 quantile, which is the upper limit of the interval. The violin plots are a convenient way to visualize the errors in the test set and focus on the models that need further improvement.

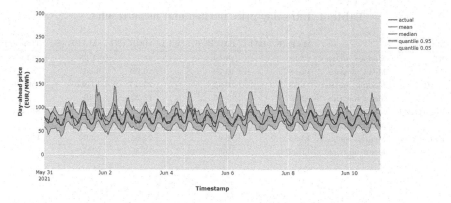

Fig. 4. Extra Trees Regressor day-ahead price quantile predictions example plot.

Table 3. Day-ahead price quantile metrics.

Models	In Bounds (%)	MAE (€/MWh)				
		0.05 quant	0.95 quant	Interval	Median	Mean
RF	92.5	22.2	28.48	25.34	8.59	8.69
GBR	80.5	26.6	**13.81**	20.21	8.84	8.64
LightGBM	80.75	**21.52**	18.8	**20.16**	**8.57**	8.59
Extra Trees	**95.0**	25.59	27.16	26.38	9.15	**8.3**

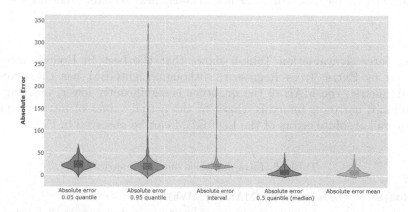

Fig. 5. Extra Trees Regressor day-ahead price quantile error violin plots.

5.2   Intra-day Price Results

LightGBM produced the best and fastest results for intra-day price forecasts, with Extra Trees Regressor also performing well. In Table 4 the final results of all the models are displayed for intra-day price forecasting, and in Fig. 6 an example plot is shown of the intra-day price predictions using LightGBM.

Table 4. Intra-day price median and mean results.

Models		MAE (€/MWh)	RMSE (€/MWh)	MMR (%)	sMAPE (%)	Time (s)
RF	Median metrics	12.18	16.69	21.7	11.73	363.9
	Mean metrics	12.15	16.79	16.72	9.36	
GBR	Median metrics	11.83	16.24	**21.17**	**11.41**	559.29
	Mean metrics	12.52	17.75	17.23	9.49	
LightGBM	Median metrics	**11.33**	**15.76**	21.63	11.47	**85.21**
	Mean metrics	**11.41**	**15.79**	**15.71**	**8.8**	
Extra Trees	Median metrics	12.33	16.41	22.05	12.03	146.0
	Mean metrics	11.89	15.9	16.36	9.24	

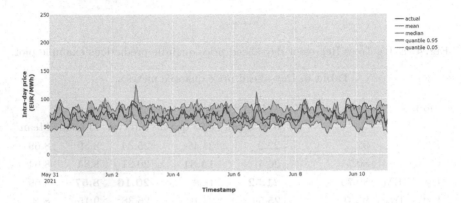

Fig. 6. Light Gradient boosting Machine intra-day price quantile predictions example plot.

For interval evaluation Table 5 shows that the best In Bounds metric is achieved by Extra Trees Regressor. Although LightGBM has the lowest In Bounds metric, the MAE of the quantiles is significantly lower, meaning that it produced narrower intervals, closer to the actual values of intra-day prices. The overall absolute errors of the LightGBM can be observed in Fig. 7.

Table 5. Intra-day price quantile metrics

Models	In bounds (%)	MAE (€/MWh)				
		0.05 quant	0.95 quant	Interval	Median	Mean
RF	87.875	31.94	26.70	28.77	12.18	12.15
GBR	78.25	26.91	17.04	21.98	11.82	12.51
LightGBM	75.88	**22.55**	**17.01**	**19.78**	**11.33**	**11.41**
Extra Trees	**91.25**	30.25	23.77	27.01	12.33	11.89

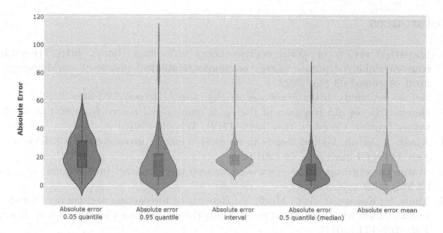

Fig. 7. LightGBM intra-day price quantile error violin plots.

6 Conclusion and Future Work

In our approach we presented simple and lightweight models for probabilistic quantile forecasting of energy market prices, which are heavily depended to the feature extraction techniques. Moreover, we provided a simple explanatory way to evaluate the intervals of our prediction, using the In Bounds metric together with MAE metrics for the interval and its limits, and violin plots to showcase the absolute error in all the data on our test sets.

The tree-based models performed adequately, without the need of a large dataset, in predicting all the requested values, namely the mean, median and 0.05 and 0.95 quantiles, in the 24-time-step ahead forecasting. In addition, a significant benefit of tree-based models is their short training period, which was highlighted in our study.

For future work, the experimentation in other machine learning and deep learning models for quantile forecasting could be beneficial. Our approach utilizes a plethora of features for energy market forecasting, but there are also more features to explore that could have a major impact on our results, namely the prices of gas or petrol in the UK, the day-ahead electricity generation from only renewable energy sources, numerical weather predictions, and more. Furthermore, the probability forecasting could provide an even richer information than the quantile forecasting, giving decision making tools the opportunity to make even more profitable decisions. Finally, different models could be utilized for the predictions of the interval's limits and the mean and median values, depending on the results of the experimentation.

Acknowledgements. This work is supported by the project IANOS - a novel for IntegrAted SolutioNs for the DecarbOnization and Smartification of Islands funded by the EU H2020 Programme, grant agreement no. 957810.

References

1. Statistical review of world energy–energy economics—home. https://www.bp.com/en/global/corporate/energy-economics/statistical-review-of-world-energy.html. Accessed 03 Mar 2022
2. Home—ecotricity. https://www.ecotricity.co.uk/. Accessed 03 Mar 2022
3. Bereiter, B., et al.: Revision of the epica dome c co2 record from 800 to 600 kyr before present. Geophys. Res. Lett. **42**(2), 542–549 (2015)
4. Ajadi, T., et al.: Global trends in renewable energy investment 2019. Bloomberg New Energy Finance, p. 76 (2019)
5. Status - enexgroup. https://www.enexgroup.gr/eu-market-in-tegration. Accessed 03 Mar 2022
6. Yuan, S., Kocaman, A.S., Modi, V.: Benefits of forecasting and energy storage in isolated grids with large wind penetration-the case of Sao Vicente. Renew. Energy **105**, 167–174 (2017)
7. Zhang, L., Luh, P.B., Kasiviswanathan, K.: Energy clearing price prediction and confidence interval estimation with cascaded neural networks. IEEE Trans. Power Syst. **18**, 99–105 (2003)
8. Nowotarski, J., Weron, R.: Recent advances in electricity price forecasting: a review of probabilistic forecasting. Renew. Sustain. Energy Rev. **81**, 1548–1568 (2018)
9. Zhao, J.H., Dong, Z.Y., Xu, Z., Wong, K.P.: A statistical approach for interval forecasting of the electricity price. IEEE Trans. Power Syst. **23**(2), 267–276 (2008)
10. Wan, C., Xu, Z., Wang, Y., Dong, Z.Y., Wong, K.P.: A hybrid approach for probabilistic forecasting of electricity price. IEEE Trans. Smart Grid **5**(1), 463–470 (2014)
11. Chen, X., Dong, Z.Y., Meng, K., Xu, Y., Wong, K.P., Ngan, H.W.: Electricity price forecasting with extreme learning machine and bootstrapping. IEEE Trans. Power Syst. **27**(4), 2055–2062 (2012)
12. Rafiei, M., Niknam, T., Khooban, M.H.: Probabilistic electricity price forecasting by improved clonal selection algorithm and wavelet preprocessing. Neural Comput. Appl. **28**(12), 3889–3901 (2016). https://doi.org/10.1007/s00521-016-2279-7
13. Nowotarski, J., Weron, R.: Merging quantile regression with forecast averaging to obtain more accurate interval forecasts of Nord pool spot prices. In: 11th International Conference on the European Energy Market (EEM14), pp. 1–5 (2014)
14. Nowotarski, J., Weron, R.: Computing electricity spot price prediction intervals using quantile regression and forecast averaging. Comput. Stat. **30**(3), 791–803 (2014). https://doi.org/10.1007/s00180-014-0523-0
15. Maciejowska, K., Nowotarski, J., Weron, R.: Probabilistic forecasting of electricity spot prices using factor quantile regression averaging. Int. J. Forecast. **32**, 957–965 (2016)
16. Uniejewski, B., Weron, R.: Regularized quantile regression averaging for probabilistic electricity price forecasting. Energy Econ. **95**, 105121 (2021)
17. Electricity data summary—bmrs. https://www.bmreports.com/bmrs/?q=eds/main. Accessed 03 Feb 2022
18. Xue, P., Jiang, Y., Zhou, Z., Chen, X., Fang, X., Liu, J.: Multi-step ahead forecasting of heat load in district heating systems using machine learning algorithms. Energy **188**, 116085 (2019)
19. Home. https://www.entsoe.eu/. Accessed 03 Feb 2022
20. The weather's record keeper—meteostat. https://meteostat.net/en/. Accessed 03 Feb 2022

21. Advantages of tree-based modeling. https://www.summitllc.us/blog/advantages-of-tree-based-modeling#:~:text=Are. Accessed 03 Oct 2022
22. scikit-learn: machine learning in python - scikit-learn 1.0.2 documentation. https://scikit-learn.org/stable/. Accessed 03 Mar 2022
23. jasperroebroek/sklearn-quantile.   https://github.com/jasperroebroek/sklearn-quantile. Accessed 03 Mar 2022
24. Kolassa, S., Schütz, W.: Advantages of the mad/mean ratio over the mape. Foresight: Int. J. Appl. Forecast. **6**, 40–43 (2007)

The 11th Workshop on "Mining Humanistic Data" (MHDW)

Preface MHDW 2021

Mining Humanistic Data Workshop

The abundance of available data, which is retrieved from or is related to the areas of Humanities and the human condition, challenges the research community in processing and analyzing it. The aim is two-fold: on the one hand, to extract knowledge that will help to understand human behavior, creativity, way of thinking, reasoning, learning, decision making, socializing and even biological processes; on the other hand, to exploit the extracted knowledge by incorporating it into intelligent systems that will support humans in their everyday activities.

The nature of humanistic data can be multimodal, semantically heterogeneous, dynamic, time and space-dependent, as well as highly complicated. Translating humanistic information, e.g. behavior, state of mind, artistic creation, linguistic utterance, learning and genomic information into numerical or categorical low-level data, is considered a significant challenge on its own. New techniques, appropriate to deal with this type of data, need to be proposed whereas existing ones must be adapted to its special characteristics.

The workshop aims to bring together interdisciplinary approaches that focus on the application of innovative as well as existing data matching, fusion and mining as well as knowledge discovery and management techniques (like decision rules, decision trees, association rules, ontologies and alignments, clustering, filtering, learning, classifier systems, neural networks, support vector machines, preprocessing, post processing, feature selection, visualization techniques, random sampling techniques for big data analysis) to data derived from all areas of Humanistic Sciences, e.g. linguistic, historical, behavioral, psychological, artistic, musical, educational, social, etc., Ubiquitous Computing as well as Bioinformatics.

Ubiquitous Computing applications (aka Pervasive Computing, Mobile Computing, Ambient Intelligence, etc.) collect large volumes of usually heterogeneous data in order to effect adaptation, learning and in general context awareness. Data matching, fusion and mining techniques are necessary to ensure human centered application functionality.

An important aspect of humanistic centers consists of managing, processing and computationally analyzing Biological and Biomedical data. Hence, one of the aims of this Workshop will be also to attract researchers that are interested in designing, developing and applying efficient data and text mining techniques for discovering the underlying knowledge existing in biomedical data, such as sequences, gene expressions and pathways.

Organization

Program Chairs

Andreas Kanavos	Ionian University, Greece
Christos Makris	University of Patras, Greece
Phivos Mylonas	Ionian University, Greece

Steering Committee Members

Ioannis Karydis	Ionian University, Greece
Katia-Lida Kermanidis	Ionian University, Greece
Spyros Sioutas	University of Patras, Greece

An Overview of MCMC Methods: From Theory to Applications

Christos Karras[1]([✉]) [iD], Aristeidis Karras[1] [iD], Markos Avlonitis[2] [iD],
and Spyros Sioutas[1] [iD]

[1] Computer Engineering and Informatics Department, University of Patras,
26504 Patras, Greece
{c.karras,akarras,sioutas}@ceid.upatras.gr
[2] Department of Informatics, Ionian University, 49100 Corfu, Greece
avlon@ionio.gr

Abstract. Markov Chain Monte Carlo techniques are used to generate samples that closely approximate a given multivariate probability distribution, with the function not having to be normalised in the case of certain algorithms such as Metropolis-Hastings. As with other Monte Carlo techniques, MCMC employs repeated random sampling to exploit the law of large numbers. Samples are generated by running a Markov Chain, which is created such that its stationary distribution follows the input function, for which a proposal distribution is used. This approach may be used for optimization tasks, for approximating solutions to non-deterministic polynomial time problems, for estimating integrals using importance sampling, and for cryptographic decoding. This paper serves as an introduction to the MCMC techniques and some of its applications.

Keywords: Metropolis-hastings · Markov Chains · Monte Carlo · MCMC methods · Gibbs sampling · Rejection sampling · Bayesian statistics

1 Introduction

Sampling across distributions is a significant concept in statistics, probability, systems engineering, and other fields that make use of stochastic models ([2, 8, 11, 20, 21]). Although sampling has long history, modern methods such as event detection and pattern recognition often rely to reservoir sampling methods as in [15] whereabouts the elements derived from a data stream are placed within a reservoir for further processing. Sampling from a multidimensional distribution is required for a variety of purposes, most notably to estimate sums and to approximate integrals that are highly insoluble analytically. However, typical sampling techniques such as rejection sampling are inadequate for this task, since they do not scale well with increasing dimensions, as the state space expands exponentially and hence rejection rates increase. *Markov Chain Monte Carlo*

© IFIP International Federation for Information Processing 2022
Published by Springer Nature Switzerland AG 2022
I. Maglogiannis et al. (Eds.): AIAI 2022 Workshops, IFIP AICT 652, pp. 319–332, 2022.
https://doi.org/10.1007/078-3-031-08341-9_26

(MCMC) techniques may be employed, given that their advanced variants are ideally suited for sampling from high-dimensional space. A brief introduction to MCMC methods is provided here to familiarise readers with the concept.

Moreover, an introduction to the mathematical underpinnings of *Markov Chains* is provided in order to aid in the comprehension of MCMC techniques. Following that, the fundamental concept behind *Monte Carlo* techniques is described. Based on this foundation, these two fundamental principles may be merged to form MCMC, with a particular emphasis on the popular *Metropolis-Hastings* algorithm (MH) [4] and the specific case of *Gibbs sampling* [7]. Following that, various elements such as parameter adjustment and convergence measurement are covered.

Finally, applications of these techniques are shown and described in further detail. It is feasible to decrypt encrypted documents [3], optimize functions [17], estimate integrals using generalized liner mixed models [22], and discover approximate solutions to non-deterministic polynomial-time (NP) hard problems using the Metropolis-Hastings algorithm [23].

2   Markov Chains

Stochastic processes are a series of random variables $(X_t)_{t \in T}$, that describe the states of a potentially infinitely vast state space S of a system at various points in time t. Only discrete time steps are considered in this case, hence $t \in \mathbb{N}_0$.

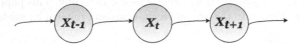

Fig. 1. A random variable X_t only depends on its immediate predecessor X_{t-1}, not on any others. With this Markov property, the structure of the dependence graph resembles a chain, hence the name Markov Chain.

Markov Chains are used to simulate stochastic processes in which the state of the next time step is determined by a small number of prior time steps. Only the final one is relevant in this paper, as seen in Fig. 1. The manner in which that condition was attained has no bearing on the subsequent state. This lack of memory in stochastic systems is often referred to as the Markov property:

$$\forall t \in \mathbb{N}_0, \forall i, j, k, \ldots \in S :$$

$$\Pr\left[X_{t+1} = j \mid X_t = i, X_{t-1} = k, \ldots\right] = \Pr\left[X_{t+1} = j \mid X_t = i\right] \tag{1}$$

A Markov Chain is composed of a collection of states S, a start distribution $q^{(0)}$, and the accompanying transition probabilities $p_{i,j} = \Pr\left[X_{t+1} = j \mid X_t = i\right]$

from one state to the next at a time step of t. Take note that transition probabilities are independent of time t in this case, implying that temporal invariance
is true:

$$\forall t, t' \in \mathbb{N}_0 : \Pr[X_{t+1} = j \mid X_t = i] = \Pr[X_{t'+1} = j \mid X_{t'} = i] \tag{2}$$

At each time step t, the stochastic process may be in just one state, which
does not have to be known. Thus, the distribution $q^{(t)}$ is introduced as a measure
of probability for states, where $q_i^{(t)}$ is the likelihood that the stochastic process
is in state $i \in S$ at time step t:

$$q_i^{(t)} = \Pr[X_t = i] \tag{3}$$

Thus, to satisfy the conditions for a probability distribution, $\forall i \in S, \forall t \in \mathbb{N}_0 : q_i^{(t)} \geq 0$ and $\Sigma_{i \in S} q_i^{(t)} = 1$, or $\int_{i \in S} q_i^{(t)} di = 1$, respectively. For the sake of
simplicity, the following computations will disregard the scenario when S is not
finite. Analogously, the continuous case follows.

Thus, assuming S is finite, the transition probabilities between states i and j
may be expressed as a matrix $P := (p_{i,j})$ and the distributions as vectors $q^{(t)} = \left(q_1^{(t)} \quad \cdots \quad q_n^{(t)} \right) \in \mathbb{R}^{|S|}$. As a result, the probabilities for the next state may be
determined using the current probabilities $q_i^{(t)}$ and the transition probabilities
$p_{i,j}$:

$$\begin{aligned} q_j^{(t+1)} &= \Pr[X_{t+1} = j] \\ &= \Sigma_{i \in S} \Pr[X_{t+1} = j \mid X_t = i] \times \Pr[X_t = i] \\ &= \Sigma_{i \in S} p_{i,j} \times q_i^{(t)} \end{aligned} \tag{4}$$

Equivalently this can be expressed using Matrix notation: $q^{(t+1)} = q^{(t)} \times P$.

Distributions π, which do not change after another iteration, are called stationary distributions: $\pi = q^{(t+1)} = q^{(t)}$ or $\pi = \pi \times P$.

If it is feasible to transition from any state to any (other) state, formally
$\forall (i,j) \in S^2, \exists n \in \mathbb{N} : p_{i,j}^{(n)} > 0$, the Markov Chain is said to be irreducible. This
is true if the state graph of the Markov Chain has a high degree of connectivity.

For irreducible Markov Chains a unique stationary distribution π exists.
Another sufficient condition for a unique π is satisfying detailed balance as in [1]:

$$\forall i, j \in S : \pi_i \times p_{i,j} = \pi_j \times p_{j,i} \tag{5}$$

A state $i \in S$ is said to be aperiodic if it is feasible to return to a state i
to it in any arbitrary number of steps after leaving it, as long as the number is
sufficiently big, hence:

$$\exists n_0 \in \mathbb{N} : \forall n \in \mathbb{N}, n \geq n_0 : p_{ii}^{(n)} > 0 \tag{6}$$

For instance, if a state i has a loop around itself, indicating that $p_{i,i} > 0$, it
is aperiodic.

If $\forall i \in S, i$ is aperiodic and irreducible, it is said to be ergodic. Regardless of the initial distribution $q^{(0)}$, an ergodic chain always converges to π. Formally:

$$\lim_{t \to \infty} q^{(t)} = \pi \tag{7}$$

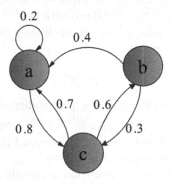

Fig. 2. This is a graphical example of a Markov Chain with three states a, b and c. The edges are annotated with the transition probabilities. The probabilities of the outgoing arrows of each state sum up to 1.

An example of a graphical depiction of an ergodic Markov Chain with three states as nodes and a transition matrix as edges is given in Fig. 2.

$$P = \begin{pmatrix} 0.2 & 0 & 0.8 \\ 0.4 & 0 & 0.6 \\ 0.7 & 0.3 & 0 \end{pmatrix}$$

3   Monte Carlo Simulations

Monte Carlo simulations are probabilistic processes that use repeated random sampling and the law of large numbers to numerically approximate solutions to complex problems. According to [12], given a random variable X, an $\epsilon > 0$ and a $\delta > 0$, the law of large numbers states: If $n \geq \frac{\text{Var}[X]}{\epsilon \delta^2}$ and $X_1, \cdots, X_n$ are random variables with the same distribution as X,

$$\Pr\left[\frac{X_1 + \cdots, + X_n}{n} - E[X] \geq \delta\right] \leq \epsilon \tag{8}$$

Thus, for any arbitrarily tiny positive precision and error probability, the expected value of X may be computed with a large enough n.

A well-known example is the approximation of the circular number π by sampling n times from a square of uniform distribution with length a. Thus, the number of samples c contained inside a circle with a radius of $\frac{a}{2}$ and centred in the centre of the square is tallied. Pythagoras' theorem may be used to assess if a sample (x, y) is included inside that circle. With the area of the square $A_{square} = a^2$ and the area of the circle $A_{circle} = \pi \times \left(\frac{a}{2}\right)^2$, the ratio of the areas equals the chance that a sample will be in the circle. Hence,

$$\lim_{n \to \infty} \frac{c}{n} = E\left[\frac{c}{n}\right] = \Sigma_{i=1}^{n} \frac{\Pr[\text{ sample i in the circle }]}{n} = \frac{A_{circle}}{A_{square}} = \frac{\pi}{4} \quad (9)$$

Thus, for sufficiently large n (at-least 1000 iterations), we have:

$$\pi \approx 4 \times \frac{\text{number of samples in circle}}{\text{total iterations}} =: \hat{\pi} \quad (10)$$

The approximation of π is done by counting samples inside the circle. The result is shown in Fig. 3.

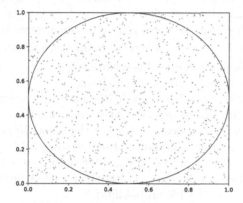

Fig. 3. Approximation of $\hat{\pi}$ by counting samples inside the circle. For $c = 789$ and $n = 1000$, $\hat{\pi} \approx 3.156$.

Monte Carlo techniques may be used with Markov Chains to generate random samples that adhere to a specified probability distribution p^*. The fundamental concept behind so-called Markov Chain Monte Carlo ($MCMC$) approaches is to construct a Markov Chain with a stationary distribution π that closely approximates the desired probability distribution. Following construction, the Markov Chain is executed and the visited states (or a portion of them) are returned as samples. Often, these distributions p^* are complex, and the procedures for building them use basic (proposal) distributions, such as a Gaussian or an unitary distribution [9].

4   Metropolis-Hastings Algorithm

Metropolis-Hastings algorithm is a Markov chain Monte Carlo (MCMC) method for obtaining a sequence of random samples from a probability distribution from which direct sampling is challenging. The Metropolis-Hastings algorithm, which serves as the foundation for many MCMC approaches, is one prominent method for creating such a Markov Chain that follows a particular probability distribution. It was first published in 1953 by Metropolis, who used it for computations in Physics [18] while Hastings introduced it in 1970 as an extension to the Metropolis algorithm [11].

4.1   Mathematical Underpinnings

Given any function $p : \mathbb{R}^n \to \mathbb{R}_0^+$, Metropolis-Hastings delivers samples that follow the distribution specified by that function [19]. Notably, there is no need that p has to be normalised, which means that $\int_{x \in \Omega} p(x)dx = 1$ does not have to hold. The samples continue to conform to the normalised probability distribution function $p^*(x) = \frac{p(x)}{Z}$, where Z is the normalising constant, so that $\int_{x \in \Omega} \frac{p(x)}{Z} dx = 1$. Take note that in this situation, $x = \left(x_1 \cdots x_n \right)$ is not a scalar, but a vector in case of multivariate distributions.

The Markov Chain is produced implicitly since no transition matrix is ever computed explicitly and the suggested next state x' and its transition probability are calculated on demand. Given a state $x^{(t)}$ the algorithm offers a subsequent state x' by sampling from a proposal distribution $q\left(x' \mid x^{(t)}\right)$. The proposal distribution q must assign a probability greater than zero to states in the target distribution p that has a probability greater than zero. A proposal x' is accepted as next state $\left(x^{(t+1)} := x'\right)$ with probability:

$$\min\left(1, \frac{p\left(x'\right) \times q\left(x^{(t)} \mid x'\right)}{p\left(x^{(t)}\right) \times q\left(x' \mid x\right)}\right) \tag{11}$$

and discarded otherwise, so that the current state will also be the next state $\left(x^{(t+1)} := x^{(t)}\right)$.

The Metropolis-Hasting pseudo code is described in algorithm 1. The primary distinction between Hastings and the Metropolis method is that whereas Metropolis employed only symmetric proposal distributions, Hastings devised the so-called Hastings adjustment, which allowed for non-symmetric proposal distributions as well.

Algorithm 1. Metropolis-Hastings Method

1: Initialize x_0
2: **for** $t = 0, 1, 2, \ldots$ **do**
3:   $x := x^{(t)}$
4:   sample $x' \sim q\left(x' \mid x\right)$
5:   acceptance probability $\alpha := \frac{p\left(x'\right) \cdot q\left(x \mid x'\right)}{p(x) \cdot q(x' \mid x)}$ $r := \min(1, \alpha)$
6:   sample $u \sim U(0, 1)$, where U is unitary distribution
7:   new sample $x^{(t+1)} := \begin{cases} x' & \text{if } u < r \\ x_t & \text{otherwise} \end{cases}$
8: **end for**

It can be proven that the resultant stationary distribution follows $p^*(x)$, since it meets the detailed balancing criterion indicted in equation (5).

This may be readily demonstrated in the situation when $x^{(t)} = i$ and q suggests a $j \neq i$ as in [1]. The proof of the preceding assumption is as follows:

$$
\begin{aligned}
&\Pr\left[x^{(t)} = i\right] \times \Pr\left[x^{(t+1)} = j \mid x^{(t)} = i\right] \\
&= \Pr\left[x^{(t)} = i\right] \times \Pr\left[j \text{ is proposed} \mid x^{(t)} = i\right] \\
&\qquad\qquad\qquad\quad \times \Pr\left[j \text{ is accepted} \mid x^{(t)} = i\right] \\
&= p^*(i) \times q(j \mid i) \times \min\left(1, \frac{p(j) \times q(i \mid j)}{p(i) \times q(j \mid i)}\right) \\
&= p^*(i) \times q(j \mid i) \times \min\left(1, \frac{p^*(j) \times q(i \mid j)}{p^*(i) \times q(j \mid i)}\right) \\
&= \min\left(p^*(i) \times q(j \mid i), p^*(j) \times q(i \mid j)\right) \\
&= \min\left(p^*(j) \times q(i \mid j), p^*(i) \times q(j \mid i)\right) \\
&= \Pr\left[x^{(t)} = j\right] \times \Pr\left[x^{(t+1)} = i \mid x^{(t)} = j\right]
\end{aligned}
\tag{12}
$$

Additionally, the constructed Markov Chain is irreducible and ergodic, the resultant distribution is unique, thus convergence to p^* is granted as in [19].

4.2 Optimizations and Challenges

Typically, as with the original Metropolis method, a symmetrical proposal distribution q is selected, of $q\left(x' \mid x\right) = q\left(x \mid x'\right)$ form. Frequently, a Gaussian distribution with constant or adaptive variance is utilised, centred on x so that:

$$
q\left(x' \mid x\right) \sim \mathcal{N}\left(x' \mid x, \Sigma\right)
\tag{13}
$$

The covariance matrix Σ must be optimized to produce acceptable acceptance rates that are neither too low (which results to a lot of duplicates) nor too high where the state space is explored very slowly). Murphy suggests aiming for acceptance rates of between 25% and 40% in [19].

However, the algorithm is not perfect or fine-tuned. Rather of being independent, as needed for samples, the states are strongly connected, or auto-correlated. Depending on the proposal function, states close i are more likely to be sampled than others. One solution is to return just a sample after every n-th step, which is termed thinning. This does not totally cure the issue, but it does reduce the association. Another issue is that the first samples heavily rely on the starting condition (or distribution). There is a "burn-in" phase when no samples are created for the first k steps. Forgetting the starting state assures the distribution of the Markov Chain is close to the true distribution p^*. For tiny Markov Chains that meet certain criteria of proximity to the true distribution some k can be computed. For larger Markov Chains, heuristics are used instead as in [14]. A trace plot may be made by running many chains. If the plots overlap and converge, the chain has mingled.

Tuning these parameters n and k is difficult, as there are trade-offs: The higher they are, the more steps are not considered, so it takes more steps and therefore time to create samples, which reduces computational efficiency. The lower they are, the more correlated and therefore of worse quality these samples are. To get sufficient samples, run numerous chains and sample their states. Murphy offers three 100.000-step chains, with half discarded and the remainder sampled. The more dimensions x has, the more likely suggested samples will be rejected. Bishop suggests picking the Gaussian scale based on the least standard deviation of each dimension, as seen in Fig. 4.

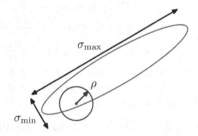

Fig. 4. A MH two-dimension function (red ellipse). A Gaussian with standard deviation $\rho \sim \sigma_{\min}$ is used as proposal distribution to avoid high rejection rates (blue circle) [1]. (Color figure online)

4.3   Gibbs Sampling

Gibbs Sampling, as explained in algorithm 2, is a common specific instance of MH that should not be overshadowed. The notion is that at each step, one (or a small subset) of the components i is updated by sampling from everything except i and replacing it with the most current values. Thus, to update the first component of $x^{(t)}, x_1^{(t+1)}$ is sampled from $p\left(x_1^{(t+1)} \mid x_2^{(t)}, \ldots, x_n^{(t)}\right)$. This is essentially MH, where every proposal is approved since $\alpha = 1$ is always true [19]. This simplifies the collection of samples, but their auto-correlation is increased.

Algorithm 2. Gibbs Sampling Method

1: Initialize x_0
2: **for** $t = 0, 1, 2, \ldots$ **do**
3:     sample: $x_1^{(t+1)} \sim p\left(x_1^{(t+1)} \mid x_2^{(t)}, \ldots, x_n^{(t)}\right)$

4:     $x_2^{(t+1)} \sim p\left(x_2^{(t+1)} \mid x_1^{(t+1)}, x_3^{(t)}, \ldots, x_n^{(t)}\right)$:

5:     $x_j^{(t+1)} \sim p\left(x_j^{(t+1)} \mid x_1^{(t+1)}, \ldots, x_{j-1}^{(t+1)}, x_{j+1}^{(t)}, \ldots, x_n^{(t)}\right)$:

6:     $x_n^{(t+1)} \sim p\left(x_n^{(t+1)} \mid x_1^{(t+1)}, \ldots, x_{n-1}^{(t+1)}\right)$
7: **end for**

---

5   Applications of MCMC Methods

MCMC methods have big advantages over other sampling methods like rejection sampling, as they scale well with higher dimensions. Therefore, sampling with MH has many applications, several of which are be presented in this paper. In this section the three major applications of MCMC methods we focus on are: integral estimation, simulated tempering and text decryption.

5.1   Estimation of Integrals

Particularly in Physics, where the Metropolis method originated, many integrals must be approximated, often with unknown normalisation factors for marginal likelihood calculations in order to detect gravitational waves [10]. A multidimensional integral may be estimated using Metropolis-Hastings [9]. For example, estimating the value of the following integral:

$$s := \int p(x) \times f(x)dx = E_p[f(x)] \tag{14}$$

with p being a normalized probability distribution. Then after using MH to draw samples $x^{(1)}, \ldots, x^{(n)}$ from p, s can be estimated by

$$\hat{s} = \frac{1}{n}\sum_{i=1}^{n} f\left(x^{(i)}\right) \tag{15}$$

One can show that the expectation value is the same:

$$E_p[\hat{s}] = E_p\left[\frac{1}{n}\Sigma_{i=1}^{n} f\left(x^{(i)}\right)\right] = \frac{1}{n}\Sigma_{i=1}^{n} E_p\left[f\left(x^{(i)}\right)\right] = \frac{1}{n}\Sigma_{i=1}^{n} s = s \tag{16}$$

So given only a function $g(x)$ and seeking an estimate for $s_g := \int g(x)dx$, a factorization $g(x) = f(x) \times p(x)$ with $p(x)$ being a valid probability distribution has to be found. Alternatively, one can sample from any probability distribution function $h(x)$ and use a technique called importance sampling.

As $g(x) = h(x) \times \frac{g(x)}{h(x)}$ the estimator can be modified:

$$\hat{s}_g = \frac{1}{n}\Sigma_{i=1}^n \frac{g\left(x^{(i)}\right)}{h\left(x^{(i)}\right)} \qquad (17)$$

Again, $E_h\left[\hat{s}_g\right] = s_g$ holds. Ideally, $h(x)$ is (up to a scaling factor) similar to $g(x)$ [9]. This proves to be powerful method for approximating any difficult integral. To illustrate it, an integral of the two dimensional function

$$g\left(x_1, x_2\right) = e^{-x_1^2 - x_2^2} \qquad (18)$$

will be estimated:

$$s := \int_{x_1 \in (0,1), x_2 \in (0,1)} g\left(x_1, x_2\right) dx1 dx2 \qquad (19)$$

For importance sampling, we set:

$$h\left(x_1, x_2\right) = (2 - x_1 - x_2) \qquad (20)$$

Note that: $\int_{x_1 \in (0,1), x_2 \in (0,1)} h\left(x_1, x_2\right) dx_1 dx_2 = 1$ and $h\left(x_1, x_2\right) > 0$ for the given integral. Thus h is a valid distribution function. Now, MH with a proposal function $q\left(x' \mid x\right) \sim \mathcal{N}\left(x' \mid x, 0.2\right)$ is used to draw 200 to 1000 samples from h. The algorithm is initialized by sampling from a normal distribution centred at $(0,0)$. This achieves an acceptance rate of 35.1% for $n = 200$ samples and 34.17% for $n = 1000$ samples. Using the samples and equation (17), the approximation results in $\hat{s}_h \approx 0.569$. This is relatively accurate, as the exact value is $s \approx 0.5677$. A visualization can be found in Figs. 5 and 6. The z-value of a sample x is $h(x)$ The density of the samples is higher in regions with high h-values and low in the others, as expected.

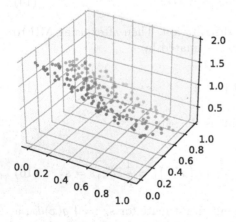

Fig. 5. MH on 200 samples.

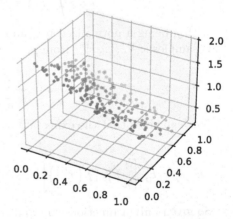

Fig. 6. MH on 1000 samples.

5.2 Simulated Tempering

However, MH may be utilised to solve optimization issues involving non-convex functions when a global minimum must be established and conventional gradient descent algorithms fail because they get caught in one of the several local minima [19]. To discover the minimum, one would use a distribution that assigns a high probability to f values that are small. A popular option is the Boltzmann distribution.

$$p(x) = e^{-\frac{f(x)}{T}} \qquad (21)$$

Utilizing the Boltzmann distribution here the requirement is to have an adjustable temperature T. This T value is lowered over time as Metropolis-Hastings executes the chain using a process called simulated annealing. This results in decreasing uphill movements over time, increasing the value of the function. The states converge to the global minimum as the probability of the chain being in the region with the greatest probabilities increases, without being trapped in a local minimum. Thus, analogous to physics, although huge motions are initially permitted to explore the state space, the system "cools down" and converges. At the conclusion of the random walk, the best x observation is returned. Once again, the starting temperature and the manner in which T is lowered are tuneable. Figure 7 shows a representation of various temperatures.

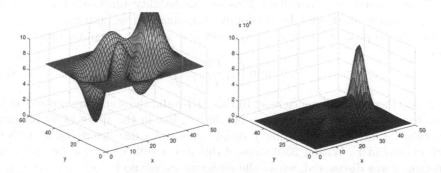

Fig. 7. Plot of the Boltzmann function for a function at a high temperature, where many areas have high values (left) and a low temperature, where only areas close to the optimal receive high values (right) [19].

Simulated tempering techniques, such as MH, may be used not just to continuous functions in $\mathbb{R}^n$, but also to discrete functions. This knowledge may be used to provide estimates for a given Traveling Salesman Problem (TSP) optimization [16]. TSP searches for the shortest route across a graph that visits each node precisely once. As a result, the states of this issue are represented by pathways across the graph that pass through each node precisely once. The length of these pathways added into the Boltzmann function is the function supplied to MH, which is no longer a legitimate probability distribution. Proposals are formed by rearranging the order in which two (or more) nodes in a given route are visited. This heuristic produces reasonable approximations, despite the fact that there is no optimum solution to the otherwise NP-hard issue.

5.3   Text Decryption

Another notable example of MH is interpreting documents, such as jail prisoners' secret code [6]. Given a text that has been ciphered by substituting other symbols Y for the letters S in the underlying text, it is feasible to learn the inverse f of the cypher function $c : S \to Y$ with remarkable accuracy.

By analysing the probabilities of each character y following another x in commonly used English texts, one may establish a decent estimate of a decode plausibility of a decipher function. This pre-supposes that the provided text is comparable to those, i.e. that the same language and proficiency level are employed. As a result, a transition matrix can be learned:

$$m_{x,y} = \Pr[\text{ next character is y} \mid \text{current character is } x] \tag{22}$$

Using this matrix M, a measure of plausibility for a decipher function f can be defined as:

$$Pl(f) = \prod_i m_{f(s_i),f(s_{i+1})} \tag{23}$$

Pl is entered into Algorithm 1 as the probability function. The proposal f' is created from state f by randomly swapping two assignments in f. As a result, the proposal distribution is symmetrical, and the acceptance probability decreases to:

$$\min\left(1, \frac{Pl(f')}{Pl(f)}\right) \tag{24}$$

However, there is a difference here: In this MH-walk, the states are possible decipher functions f, so the states are not in $\mathbb{R}^n$, but in the space of all bijective functions $\{f : Y \to S\}$. The first f simply allocates a distinct character in S to each symbol in Y. Within 2000 steps of this run, a sufficiently good deciphering function f was discovered, where the assignments are no longer often changing, indicating that the Markov Chain had converged. This is a surprising achievement, given there are around 40 potential functions in the search space for the approximately 40 distinct characters found in typical texts (letters, numerals, spaces, punctuation characters, etc.).

6   Conclusion

MCMC techniques seem to be quite beneficial in a wide variety of applications. The Metropolis-Hastings algorithm is among the top of the list of great algorithms of 20th century scientific computing [5], and its versions are critical for Bayesian statistics and machine learning. Nonetheless, MCMC approaches are approximate, and as a consequence of unpredictability, variations from the proper conclusions are possible. As a result, MCMC should be used sparingly and only in the absence of better alternatives, as no assurances can be made. Thus, assuming computing feasibility, this should be favoured over MCMC for integrals that can be solved analytically. For practical applications, more sophisticated variations of Metropolis-Hastings are employed as indicated in [13], since they need fewer steps and hence provide better samples, while also being tuned to avoid numerical difficulties, which are not discussed here. Alternatively, performance may be optimised by dynamically adjusting parameters, particularly the covariance matrix, without switching the distribution as the parameters vary over time. Additionally, various changes to Metropolis-Hastings are required for low correlations in higher dimensions.

References

1. Bishop, C.M.: Pattern Recognition and Machine Learning (Information Science and Statistics). Springer-Verlag, Berlin, Heidelberg (2006)
2. Brémaud, P.: Markov Chains: Gibbs Fields, Monte Carlo Simulation, and Queues, vol. 31. Springer, New York (2013). https://doi.org/10.1007/978-3-030-45982-6
3. Chen, J., Rosenthal, J.S.: Decrypting classical cipher text using Markov chain Monte Carlo. Stat. Comput. **22**(2), 397–413 (2012). https://doi.org/10.1007/s11222-011-9232-5
4. Chib, S., Greenberg, E.: Understanding the metropolis-hastings algorithm. Am. Stat. **49**(4), 327–335 (1995). https://doi.org/10.1080/00031305.1995.10476177
5. Cipra, B.A.: The best of the 20th century: editors name top 10 algorithms. SIAM News **33**(4), 1–2 (2000)
6. Diaconis, P.: The Markov chain Monte Carlo revolution. Bull. Am. Math. Soc. **46**(2), 179–205 (2009)
7. Gelfand, A.E.: Gibbs sampling. J. Am. Stat. Assoc. **95**(452), 1300–1304 (2000). https://doi.org/10.1080/01621459.2000.10474335
8. Geman, S., Geman, D.: Stochastic relaxation, Gibbs distributions, and the Baye sian restoration of images. IEEE Trans. Pattern Anal. Mach. Intell. PAMI **6**(6), 721–741 (1984). https://doi.org/10.1109/TPAMI.1984.4767596
9. Goodfellow, I., Bengio, Y., Courville, A.: Deep Learning. MIT press, Cambridge (2016)
10. Haasteren, R.V.: Marginal likelihood calculation with MCMC methods. In: Gravitational Wave Detection and Data Analysis for Pulsar Timing Arrays, pp. 99–120. Springer, Heidelberg (2014). https://doi.org/10.1007/978-3-642-39599-4_5
11. Hastings, W.K.: Monte Carlo sampling methods using Markov chains and their applications. Biometrika **57**, 97–109 (1970)
12. Huang, H., Yang, W.: Strong law of large numbers for Markov chains indexed by an infinite tree with uniformly bounded degree. Sci. China Ser. A: Math. **51**(2), 195–202 (2008)
13. Kaji, T., Ročková, V.: Metropolis-hastings via classification. J. Am. Stat. Assoc., 1–33 (2022). https://doi.org/10.1080/01621459.2022.2060836
14. Karras, C., Karras, A.: DBSOP: an efficient heuristic for speedy MCMC sampling on polytopes. arXiv preprint arXiv:2203.10916 (2022). https://doi.org/10.48550/arXiv.2203.10916

15. Karras, C., Karras, A., Sioutas, S.: Pattern recognition and event detection on IoT data-streams. arXiv preprint arXiv:2203.01114 (2022). https://doi.org/10.48550/arXiv.2203.01114
16. Kirkpatrick, S., Gelatt, C.D., Jr., Vecchi, M.P.: Optimization by simulated annealing. Science **220**(4598), 671–680 (1983)
17. Martino, L., Elvira, V., Luengo, D., Corander, J., Louzada, F.: Orthogonal parallel MCMC methods for sampling and optimization. Digital Signal Process. **58**, 64–84 (2016). https://doi.org/10.1016/j.dsp.2016.07.013
18. Metropolis, N., Rosenbluth, A.W., Rosenbluth, M.N., Teller, A.H., Teller, E.: Equation of state calculations by fast computing machines. J. Chem. Phys. **21**(6), 1087–1092 (1953)
19. Murphy, K.P.: Machine Learning: A Probabilistic Perspective. MIT press, Cambridge (2012)
20. Revuz, D.: Markov Chains. Elsevier, Amsterdam (2008)
21. Ripley, B.D.: Stochastic Simulation. John Wiley & Sons, Hoboken (2009)
22. Wolfinger, R., O'connell, M.: Generalized linear mixed models a pseudo-likelihood approach. J. Stat. Comput. Simul. **48**(3–4), 233–243 (1993). https://doi.org/10.1080/00949659308811554
23. Xu, J.-G., Zhao, Y., Chen, J., Han, C.: A structure learning algorithm for bayesian network using prior knowledge. J. Comput. Sci. Technol. **30**(4), 713–724 (2015). https://doi.org/10.1007/s11390-015-1556-8

Employing Natural Language Processing Techniques for Online Job Vacancies Classification

George Varelas[1(✉)], Dimitris Lagios[1], Spyros Ntouroukis[1], Panagiotis Zervas[1], Kenia Parsons[2], and Giannis Tzimas[1]

[1] Data and Media Laboratory, Department of Electrical and Computer Engineering, University of Peloponnese, Patras, Greece
g.varelas@go.uop.gr, {d.lagios,douroukis,p.zervas,tzimas}@uop.gr
[2] The World Bank, Washington, DC, USA
kparsons@worldbank.org

Abstract. With the advances in natural language processing and big data analytics, the labor market community has introduced the emerging field of Labor Market Intelligence (LMI). This field aims to design and utilize Artificial Intelligence (AI) algorithms and frameworks to analyze data related to the labor market information for supporting policy and decision-making. This paper elaborates on the automatic classification of free-text Web job vacancies on a standard taxonomy of occupations. In achieving this, we draw on well-established approaches for extracting textual features, which subsequently are employed for training machine learning algorithms. The training and evaluation of our machine learning models were performed with data extracted from online sources, pre-processed, and hand-annotated following the ISCO taxonomy. The results showed that the proposed model is very promising. The advantage is its simplicity. After its application to a relatively small and difficult to clean dataset, it achieved a good accuracy. Furthermore, in this paper we discuss how real-life applications for skill anticipation and matching could benefit from our approach.

Keywords: Natural language processing · Labor market · ISCO taxonomy prediction

1 Introduction

In a short period of time, the Internet has evolved into a powerful platform that has dramatically altered the way people do business and communicate. Even from the advent of the Internet, labor market stakeholders (including the employers and the job seekers) have used various online methods to advertise and search for jobs. In turn, this has led to the accumulation of a huge amount of data related to the labor market and the skills required. All these have resulted in researchers identifying the Web as a research platform and a data source, pointing out its value for labor market analysis.

© IFIP International Federation for Information Processing 2022
Published by Springer Nature Switzerland AG 2022
I. Maglogiannis et al. (Eds.): AIAI 2022 Workshops, IFIP AICT 652, pp. 333–344, 2022.
https://doi.org/10.1007/978-3-031-08341-9_27

Due to its nature as a data source, the Web contains a plethora of diverse digital sources available for extracting various kinds of information. This diversity imposes the need for the efficient identification of quality data sources. Various sources may be appropriate for extracting trends related to employer demands, job seekers' interests, and hard and soft-skills identification. Some sources can be considered as job-focused (i.e., EURES, National Public Employment Services Portals, and private sector online Job portals). In contrast, others can have generic content (i.e., Twitter user interaction data, YouTube post metadata and content, LinkedIn, etc.) or may have subjective content related to labor markets such as portals that hold public administrative microdata (i.e., ministries or public organizations reports), national statistical office microdata (i.e., data relevant to skills from statistical surveys, census of the population) and large-scale skills survey and skills measurement microdata (i.e., public and private organizations beyond national statistical offices undertake substantial enterprise skills surveys, CV analysis, etc.).

For extracting meta-information from textual data, natural language processing approaches have been explored and utilized. To this end, the term "Labor Market Intelligence" (LMI), is referring to the use and design of AI algorithms and frameworks for Labor Market Data to support decision-making.

In this paper, we describe how the problem of classifying and extracting practical knowledge from Web Labor Market Data has been addressed and formulated as a Text Classification problem. More specifically, our research contributes to addressing the problem of classifying textual data from online job vacancies in the ISCO-08 taxonomy (ISCO stands for International Standard Classification of Occupations). The remainder of this paper is structured as follows: Sect. 2 reviews in detail prior work in the areas of job vacancies data collection from web sources as well as machine learning approaches applied for text classification. In Sect. 3, data collection schemes and preparation methods are described. The methodology of our approach is presented in Sect. 4, while Sect. 5 discusses the implementation and the results. Finally, the concluding remarks of the paper are summarized in Sect. 6.

2 Related Work

Back in 1957, H. P. Luhn [1] published an article in which the foundations of NLP had been set. In this article, he was suggesting automatic system that would be able to classify documents according to a given topic. Nowadays, Natural Language Processing (NLP) is a subfield of linguistics, computer science, and artificial intelligence (AI) aiming at giving machines the ability to read, understand, and deliver meaning. There is a vast utilization of NLP approaches in various domains such as finance, media, and human resource. The NLP system needs to understand text, sign, and semantics properly. Since more than eighty percent of data about an entity are available only in unstructured form, many methods have been proposed for text and symbol understanding in an NLP workflow. Such methods are speech reorganization, probabilistic language models, word embedding, and text classification. Text clarification is the process of categorizing the text into a group of words. Using NLP, text classification can automatically analyze text and then assign a set of predefined tags or categories based on its context. Overall, NLP is used for sentiment analysis, topic detection, and language detection, among others.

Recently, text classification methods have been widely studied in extracting knowledge from unstructured online job postings. Job recommendation systems heavily depend on robust text classification modules for extracting knowledge related to the occupation code [2] of a job vacancy. In their work, Lu et.al [3] presented a recommender system for job seeking and recruiting employing graph modeling. Shalaby et.al in [4] have proposed a homogeneous Graph-Based architecture for job recommendation tasks. In [5] and [6] Boselli and et.al utilized machine learning approaches related to text classification for job web vacancies classification and other labor market intelligence tasks. Finally, in [7] the potential to assign occupations to job titles contained in administrative data using automated, machine-learning approaches was explored.

Bethmann et.al [8] applied Naive Bayes and Bayesian Multinomial to predict occupations from open-ended survey questions on respondents. They estimated correctness probabilities for every occupation category given the information in the training data. As labels, they used KldB2010 which is the German occupation code. Their results showed that in order to classify text relative to occupation correctly, one needs a large sample of quality data.

Russ Daniel, et.al [9] used Computer-based coding of free-text job descriptions to identify occupations in epidemiological studies efficiently. They used an ensemble classifier that automatically assigned SOC codes based on free-text job titles, free-text tasks, and SIC-1987. In external comparisons of jobs obtained from a case-control study, the classifier assignments had an overall agreement with expert coders that ranged from 45% at the 6-digit level to 76% at the 2-digit level.

Mukherjee et.al [10] compared the results of several algorithms to determine Standard Occupational Classification Codes from Job Descriptions in Immigration Petitions. They showed that TF-IDF n-gram (Term Frequency-Inverse Document Frequency) based support vector classifier with radial basis function (SVC-RBF) achieves the highest classification accuracy of 81%. However, they found also that doc2vec based random forest achieves the highest precision score. Their results are in agreement with our findings.

Adomavicius and Tuzhilin in [11] examine possible extensions. Content-Based methods read a user profile, extract a set of features, and determine if an item is appropriate for this profile as a recommendation. TF-IDF and clustering are common algorithms for this approach. In Hybrid methods of recommendation, different methods can be combined. For instance, one can implement separate collaborative and content-based systems. Then, the outputs obtained from individual recommender systems can be combined into one final recommendation using either a linear combination of ratings or a voting scheme. This approach was used in our paper.

Another article written by Amato, et.al [12] examined a different point of view. They exploited the affinity relation that the ISTAT occupation classifier (Italian standard classifier for Occupations) defines for some occupations. The rationale of this relationship is to express that a professional profile (e.g., programmer) is akin to another one, such as a software developer.

3   Corpora Pre-processing and Annotation

Having a set of four Greek online portals, web crawling was carried out, and a vast amount of content was gathered. The description of the overall process is schematically described in Fig. 1. The result of the initial procedure was a dataset having a considerable noise. With the term noise, we refer to objects that are irrelevant to the project's scope, such as city names. So, Data Cleansing was necessary in order to improve the results of the model. In this procedure, we removed characters like "*...etc.". and words the stop words (Example of stop words "mustn't, also, although etc.". From each vacancy, only 2 fields were kept: the title and the description of the job posting.

After the data collection and the data cleansing processes, the dataset was split into smaller sets and each one was assigned to an expert to label it with the correct occupation code manually. In our case, the job title concatenated with the job description was used as input text and the accuracy of the result, which is the ISCO occupation code, was measured. This procedure is the Document Classification.

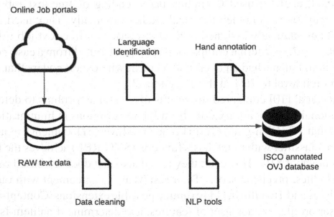

Fig. 1. Data preparation procedure

As a next step, we performed a lemmatization procedure that removes suffixes and leaves words in their root form.

Stemming was not used because it would not contribute considerably, and this way, we ended up in a simpler model. In the end, our resulting dataset contained 6,902 ads.

3.1   Exploratory Analysis

The distribution of Occupation Codes in our dataset is illustrated in Fig. 2. There are 113 different Codes. It is evident that the dataset is imbalanced. Greece is a tourist attraction, and subsequently, there is high demand for employees in this sector. The Occupation Code with the highest demand was that of a "Shop Sales Assistant". During the last decade, Greece has suffered an economic crisis. Many employers have chosen to work their shops by themselves (one should keep in mind that the majority of businesses in

Greece are family businesses or small companies). The job ads were collected during the reorganization of the Greek economy in which many measures to reduce unemployment were introduced.

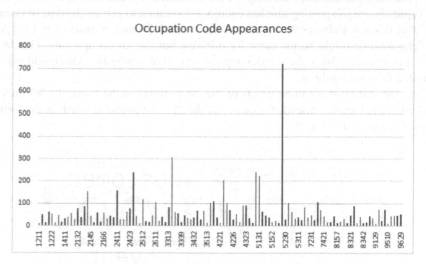

Fig. 2. Occupation Code label count in the dataset

The average number of words per Occupation Code is depicted in Fig. 3. That was a problem because it adds noise (irrelevant words) to the data. Additionally, it poses problems to all the algorithms involved.

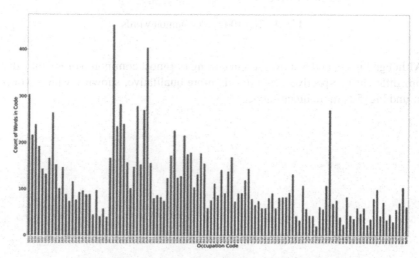

Fig. 3. Average number of words per Occupation Code

Cleaning this noise is one of the most challenging tasks in NLP. The irrelevant text was scattered throughout the job ads. There were many ads that had low levels of noise. After a lot of experimentation with the dataset the research team decided to keep the first 500 words (after document cleansing) of the combined title and description text data.

Typically, the job posting title has enough information to extract the type of occupation. But this is not always the case, as Amato et al. [13], and Marrara et al. [14] point out. The job title might be the same for different but similar occupations. The details of the occupation exist in the job description text. That is why the description was not excluded from the analysis.

The top 100 most common words of the job postings in the form of a WordCloud are depicted in Fig. 4, while the frequency of the 25 most common words in the form of bar plot is depicted in Fig. 5.

Fig. 4. Top 100 most common words

Although Figs. 4 and 5 show the same thing (topmost common words), they display it from different perspectives. Figure 4 is more qualitative, showing which words are there, and Fig. 5 is more quantitative.

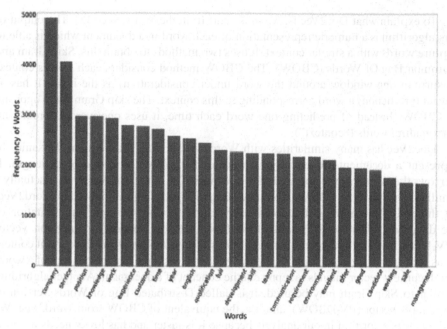

Fig. 5. Frequency of 25 most common words

4   Methodology

As mentioned in previous sections, a classifier aims to use a dataset of pre-classified documents for training a model that will be able to classify data having not seen yet. For implementing our text classification functionality, we followed the steps depicted in Fig. 6.

The first step in training a text classifier is that of feature extraction. By feature extraction, we refer to the task of representing a given text in a form that is suitable for applying it as input to a machine learning algorithm. A method that has been utilized successfully in NLP tasks is that of word-embedding. Although word-embedding can be considered as a language modeling tool, it also acts as a feature extraction method because it helps transform raw data (characters in text documents) to a meaningful alignment of word vectors in the embedding space that the model can work with more effectively (than other traditional methods such as TF-IDF, Bag of Words, etc., on a large corpus). Word embedding techniques help extract information from the pattern and occurrence of words and goes further than other traditional token representation methods to decode/identify the meaning/context of the words, thereby providing more relevant and important features to the model to tackle the underlying problem.

4.1   Feature Extraction

In our research for forming the feature vector of our dataset, we utilized Doc2Vec Word Embedding algorithm.

To explain what Doc2Vec is, we must start from the Word2Vec [15]. The output of this algorithm is a numeric representation of each word in a document which is able to capture words with a similar context. It uses two methods to obtain this. Skip Gram and Common Bag Of Words (CBOW). The CBOW method considers each word's context (a surrounding window around the word under consideration) as the input. It has as output (prediction) a word corresponding to this context. The skip Gram is the opposite of CBOW. Instead of predicting one word each time, it uses one word to predict all surrounding words ("context").

Doc2Vec has many similarities with Word2Vec, but the goal remains the same. To represent a document numerically as a vector but without considering its length. It borrows the Word2Vec vectors and adds one more. The Paragraph Vector. It is actually a small extension of the CBOW (Continues Bag of Words) algorithm used in Word2Vec. At the end of the training, the document vector D holds a numeric representation of the document. This model is called Distributed Memory version of Paragraph Vector (PV-DM). It acts as a memory that remembers what is missing from the current context or as the topic of the paragraph. While the word vectors represent the concept of a word, the document vector intends to represent the concept of a document. Another algorithm, similar to Skip-Gram may be used. It is called Distributed Bag of Words version of Paragraph Vector (PV-DBOW), and it is the equivalent of CBOW from Word2Vec. We utilized this algorithm in our analysis because it is faster and has lower needs in terms of memory, since the word vectors are not saved.

4.2 Methods

The SVM Linear, Random Forests, KNN, SGD (Stochastic Gradient Descent), and MLP Neural Network classifiers were implemented. These methods were used as the baseline for our Hard Voting ensembling model.

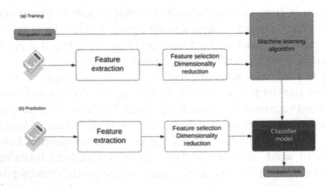

Fig. 6. (a) Training of text classification model, (b) Trained model utilization for prediction

In SVM we used Linear kernel with regularization equal to 10, in Random Forest we used 600 estimators, in MLP we used 512 units in 1 hidden layer with "Relu" activation and "Adam" solver, in KNN we took 10 neighbors depending on distance weights with Euclidean distance, and in SGD Classifier we used "modified_huber" as loss function and "L2" penalty. All these parameters came after experimentation.

4.3 Evaluation Metrics

The effectiveness of the classifiers has been evaluated based on their accuracy and the F1-score. Since the data are highly imbalanced, the F1 score is more appropriate as an index. The F1 score is the harmonic mean of precision and recall of the model. Its lowest value is 0, which means that no classification is accomplished with the model under consideration, and the highest value is 1, which means that the perfect classification has occurred. The weighted average of the precision of each class is calculated for this multiclass task.

Precision's meaning is: Within everything that has been predicted as a positive, precision counts the correct percentage.

Recall's meaning is: Within everything that actually is positive, how many did the model succeed to find.

$$Accuracy = \frac{true\ positives + true\ negatives}{total\ predictions}$$

$$Precision = \frac{true\ positives}{true\ positives + false\ positives}$$

$$Recall = \frac{true\ positives}{true\ positives + false\ negatives}$$

F1 score combines these two metrics into one and works well in imbalanced data. The F score is defined by the relationship:

$$F_\beta = \left(1 + \beta^2\right) \times \frac{precision \times recall}{\left(\beta^2 \times precision\right) + recall}$$

The β is a factor that indicates the importance of recall over precision. Here the β is set equal to 1 because the importance of precision is equal to the importance of recall.

5 Experiments and Results

The labeled dataset was randomly partitioned into training and test sets. The partition was performed to split the vacancies as: 80% in the training set and 20% in the test set (Table 1).

Table 1. Results of individual algorithms

Model	Test accuracy results	CV accuracy results	CV F1 score results
Random Forest	79%	75.69% (±0.63)	74.83% (±0.64)
MLP	85.69%	83.83% (±0.50)	83.27% (±0.51)
Knn	74.22%	70.39% (±1.29)	69.37% (±1.28)
SVM	82.91%	80.04% (±1.22)	79.99% (±1.16)
SGD	85.95%	83.39% (±0.37)	83.54% (±0.29)

Having the above results, we implemented an ensemble method. More specifically, we implemented a Hard Voting algorithm. The results were better than the ones above (Table 2).

Table 2. Results of the ensemble method

Model	Test accuracy results	CV accuracy results	CV F1 score results
Hard voting	88.85%	88.04% (±0.57)	87.9%

Moving one step further, we calculated the test accuracy on 3 and 2 digits of the occupation code (Table 3).

Table 3. The Sub-major and minor class of Occupation Code accuracy

Model	(3 digits Minor class)	(2 digits Sub-major Class)
Hard voting	89.93%	90.95%

The ensembling model of hard voting performed better than any other tested model, although some algorithms like MLP, SVD, and SGD performed so well that could be considered as standalone models that need better hyperparameter tuning and a more extensive training dataset.

6 Discussion

This problem of assessing the Occupation Code from job posting has singularities. It is highly dependent on the country and the distribution of different occupations in these postings. So, it results in different measurements of accuracy in modeling, and this is why one can find different accuracies in the literature.

In publication [5] the score of accuracy was 90.7%. During their scraping phase, they gathered 2,295,603 job vacancies. This a number large enough to help in the confidentiality of the results. One advantage these researchers had was that these job postings were written in English.

In this paper we presented an ensembling hard voting algorithm for the classification of job postings according to the ISCO Occupation Codes. The data was collected from job posting from Greek portals. The number of job postings in our case was not very extensive, but we are confident that our model would achieve higher accuracy if we had a larger volume of postings, this being the next step in our research.

Additionally, the model achieves high accuracy in the Minor and sub-major groups of ISCO-08. For example, it classifies a "Legislator" correctly under the "Legislators and senior officials" minor group with a probability of 89.93% and under the "Chief executive, senior official and legislator" sub-major group with a probability of 90.95%.

Nowadays, Deep Learning techniques are used in the vast majority of NLP tasks. This paper proves that simpler methods if they are combined properly can be equal or more powerful to deep learning. The advantage is that it can be computationally more efficient.

Checking our results under the context of another country and language is also the natural continuation of our research. It will be interesting to examine the performance of the model in other languages since most of the research in this sector is confined to the English language.

References

1. Luhn, H.P.: A statistical approach to mechanized encoding and searching of literary information. IBM J. Res. Dev. **1**, 309–317 (1957). https://doi.org/10.1147/rd.14.0309
2. International Labour Office, International Standard Classification of Occupations, International Labour Organization (2012)
3. Lu, Y., Helou, S. E., Gillet, D.: A recommender system for job seeking and recruiting website. In: Proceedings of the 22nd International Conference on World Wide (2013). https://doi.org/10.1145/2487788.2488092
4. Shalaby, W., et al.: Help me find a job: a graph-based approach for job recommendation at scale. In: IEEE International Conference on Big Data (BIGDATA) (2017). https://doi.org/10.1109/BigData.2017.8258088
5. Boselli, R., et al.: WoLMIS: a labor market intelligence system for classifying web job vacancies. J. Intell. Inf. Syst. **51**(3), 477–502 (2017). https://doi.org/10.1007/s10844-017-0488-x
6. Boselli, R., Cesarini, M., Mercorio, F., Mezzanzanica, M.: Using machine learning for labour market intelligence. In: Altun, Y., et al. (eds.) ECML PKDD 2017. LNCS (LNAI), vol. 10536, pp. 330–342. Springer, Cham (2017). https://doi.org/10.1007/978-3-319-71273-4_27
7. Ikudo, A., Lane, J., Staudt, J., Weinberg, B.: Occupational classifications a machine learning approach. In: IZA - Institute of Labor Economics, no. 11738, August 2018, 9th International Proceedings on Proceedings, pp. 1–2 (2010)
8. Bethmann, A., Schierholzy, M., Wenzig, K., Zielonka, M.: Automatic coding of occupations. using machine learning algorithms for occupation coding in several german panel surveys. In: Extensible Public Opinion : WAPOR 67th Annual Conference, Nice (2014)
9. Russ, D.E., et al.: Computer-based coding of free-text job descriptions to efficiently identify occupations in epidemiological studies. Occup. Environ. Med. (2016). https://doi.org/10.1136/oemed-2015-103152
10. Mukherjee, S., Widmark, D., DiMascio, V., Oates, T.: determining standard occupational classification codes from job descriptions in immigration petitions (2021). arXiv:2110.000 78v1, https://doi.org/10.48550/arXiv.2110.00078

11. Adomavicius, G., Tuzhilin, A.: Toward the next generation of recommender systems: a survey of the state-of-the-art and possible extensions. IEEE Trans. Knowl. Data Eng. **17**(6), 734–749 (2005). https://doi.org/10.1109/TKDE.2005.99
12. Amato, F., Boselli, R., Cesarini, M., Mercorio, F., Mezzanzanica, M., et al: Classifcation of web job advertisements: a case study. In: SEBD (2015)
13. Amato, F., Boselli, R., Cesarini, M., Mercorio, F., Mezzanzanica, M., et al: Challenge: processing web texts for classifying job offers. In: Proceedings of the 2015 IEEE 9th International Conference on Semantic Computing (IEEE ICSC 2015), pp. 460–463 (2015). https://doi.org/10.1109/ICOSC.2015.7050852
14. Marrara, S., et al.: A language modelling approach for discovering novel labour market occupations from the web. In: International Conference on Web Intelligence (2017). https://doi.org/10.1145/3106426.3109035
15. Mikolov, T., Chen, K., Corrado, G., Dean, J.: Efficient estimation of word representations in vector space. In: International Conference on Learning Representations (2013). https://doi.org/10.48550/arXiv.1301.3781

Maximum Likelihood Estimators on MCMC Sampling Algorithms for Decision Making

Christos Karras[1(✉)], Aristeidis Karras[1], Markos Avlonitis[3],
Ioanna Giannoukou[2], and Spyros Sioutas[1]

[1] Computer Engineering and Informatics Department, University of Patras,
26504 Patras, Greece
{c.karras,akarras,sioutas}@ceid.upatras.gr
[2] Department of Management Science and Technology, University of Patras,
26334 Patras, Greece
igian@upatras.gr
[3] Department of Informatics, Ionian University, 49100 Corfu, Greece
avlon@ionio.gr

Abstract. Monte Carlo simulations using Markov chains as the Gibbs sampler and Metropolis algorithm are widely used techniques for modelling stochastic problems for decision making. Like all other Monte Carlo approaches, MCMC exploits the law of large numbers via repeated random sampling. Samples are formed by running a Markov Chain that is constructed in such a way that its stationary distribution closely matches the input function, which is represented by a proposal distribution. In this paper, the fundamentals of MCMC methods are discussed, including the algorithm selection process, optimizations, as well as some efficient approaches for utilizing generalized linear mixed models. Another aim of this paper is to highlight the usage of the EM method to get accurate maximum likelihood estimates in the context of generalized linear mixed models.

Keywords: MCMC methods · Gibbs sampler · Maximum likelihood · Estimators · Generalized linear mixed models · Decision making

1 Introduction

Generalized linear mixed models (GLMMs) are variations of generalized linear models (GLMs) that include unobservable factors as extra components of variability. As a consequence, they have a variety of applications and practical relevance [3,4,12,16]. Typically, unobserved effects are handled by including random effects in the predictor of the generalised linear model. The marginal likelihood function of the GLM is then derived by integrating the likelihood of another GLM with regard to the mixing distribution, which is the anticipated

© IFIP International Federation for Information Processing 2022
Published by Springer Nature Switzerland AG 2022
I. Maglogiannis et al. (Eds.): AIAI 2022 Workshops, IFIP AICT 652, pp. 345–356, 2022.
https://doi.org/10.1007/978-3-031-08341-9_28

distribution of the random effects. While GLMMs are a robust family of statistical models, their practical use has been constrained by the complexity of the likelihood function. As a result, numerous techniques based on analytical approximations to the probability have been developed. In the context of this paper, we provide one distinct implementation of the Monte Carlo EM algorithm in which the intractable integral at the E-step (our S-step) is evaluated using simulation approaches. The first technique employs simulated random samples from the precise conditional distribution of the random effects vector u given the data y, which was derived by rejection sampling using the marginal distribution of u as the candidate distribution.

2   Related Work

Sampling is a crucial process across every discipline. With random sampling as indicated in [14], elements are taken in a probabilistic way for further processing. The underlying distribution of data is although hard to estimate requiring more accurate models. The capacity of conventional generalised linear models to accommodate non-Gaussian distributions and non-linear link processes is combined with the ability of classic (Gaussian) mixed models to express complicated dependent structures using random components. As a result, GLMMs appear to be well suited for many applications [1,5,6,16]. To be effective, GLMMs need more inference tools than ordinary statistical models.

For example, when doing probability inference, conditional probability values must be considered. Other integration simplifications used in conventional Gaussian mixed models (e.g., defining a Gaussian distribution on Gaussian random components that results in a Gaussian marginal distribution) are not applicable to GLMMs. The literature discusses several interpretative techniques, for example, [3,17] and [15] for a full study comparing different methods.

Many complicated stochastic systems may be simulated using Markov chain Monte Carlo [8,11,18]. Integrals may be calculated via simulation for various statistical inferences while there is a lot of study on Bayesian inference [2,7,8]. To describe stochastic processes, Markov chain Monte Carlo is a general-purpose technique that has been proved to be successful for sampling across difficult geometric objects [13] while it is also employed for probability inference. Several Monte Carlo approximation techniques have been created for complicated stochastic processes such as Markov random fields (Gibbs distributions) utilised in spatial statistics. One method is to use Monte Carlo simulations [9,10,21]. Another is to use stochastic models [19] and third, the likelihood situation [20]. Only the first allows for quick parametric bootstrapping and simulation experiments using a single Monte Carlo sample.

3   Methodology

3.1   Problem Definition

In this paper a clustering issue is examined. Assume there are n items, each of which has a binary answer of type:

$$Y_{ij} = 0, 1, \text{for } i = n, \ldots, 1, \text{for } j = n, \ldots, T \tag{1}$$

where n signifies all observed variables and T denotes the observation time. Typically, the time of observation varies across components; as a consequence, time points may also vary. For the purposes of this paper, we will assume that all elements are exactly equivalent in length and time points. Additionally, we suppose that these topics fall into two separate clusters. The dependent expectation of a variable for each cluster, responds as follows:

$$P_{1,ij} = \mathbb{E}(Y_{ij}|U_i, X_{1,ij}, Z_{1,i}) = f^{-1}(\beta_1 \cdot X_{1,ij} + Z_{1,i})$$
$$P_{2,ij} = \mathbb{E}(Y_{ij}|U_i, X_{2,ij}, Z_{2,i}) = f^{-1}(\beta_2 \cdot X_{2,ij} + Z_{2,i}) \tag{2}$$

where cluster membership is denoted by U, and fixed and random effects, are denoted by $X_{c,ij}$ and Z_c, i, $(c = 1, 2)$ respectively. The function of connection is specified as:

$$f^{-1}(x) = \frac{\exp(x)}{1 + \exp(x)} \tag{3}$$

Due to the fact that U is often unknown in a typical clustering scenario, it is treated as an effect of randomness. In (2), $u = 1$ for $P_{1,ij}$ while $u = 2$ for $P_{2,ij}$. For randomness, it is assumed:

$$Z_{c,i} \sim N(0, \sigma_c^2), \mathbb{P}(U) = 1 \tag{4}$$

Thus, $\Omega = \{\beta_1, \beta_2, \sigma_1, \sigma_2, \pi_1\}$ is the parameter to be assessed. By interpreting random effects as data missing, the function of likelihood for the whole set of data may be represented as in (5).

$$L(\Omega|Y_{ij}, U_i, Z_{U_i,i}) = \prod_{i=1}^{n}\prod_{c=1}^{2}\{\pi_c f_c(Z_{c,i})[\prod_{j=1}^{T} f_c(Y_{ij}|Z_{c,i})]\}^{w_{ic}} \tag{5}$$

where the normal distribution $f_c(Y_{ij}|Z_{c,i}) = \mathbb{P}^{Y_{ij}}(1 - \mathbb{P}_{ij})^{1-Y_{ij}}$ and $f_c(Z_{c,i})$ signifies the density of it. The dummy variable w_{ic} is associated with U_i, hence

$$w_{ic} = \begin{cases} 1, & \text{element belongs to cluster } c \\ 0, & \text{otherwise} \end{cases} \tag{6}$$

3.2   Generalized Linear Mixed Models (GLMMs)

Given the simulation parameters: n, T, β_1, β_2, π_1, σ_1, σ_2, we can obtain, Observed variables as Y

$$
Y = \begin{bmatrix} Y_{11} & Y_{12} & \cdots & Y_{1T} \\ Y_{21} & Y_{22} & \cdots & Y_{2T} \\ \vdots & \vdots & \ddots & \vdots \\ Y_{n1} & Y_{n2} & \cdots & Y_{nT}) \end{bmatrix} = \begin{bmatrix} \mathbf{Y}_1 \\ \mathbf{Y}_2 \\ \vdots \\ \mathbf{Y}_n \end{bmatrix}
$$

Additional unobserved or unobservable variables as U, Z

$$
\mathbf{U} = \begin{bmatrix} \mathbf{U}_1 \\ \mathbf{U}_2 \\ \vdots \\ \mathbf{U}_n \end{bmatrix}, \mathbf{Z} = \begin{bmatrix} \mathbf{Z}_{U_1,1} \\ \mathbf{Z}_{U_2,2} \\ \vdots \\ \mathbf{Z}_{U_n,n} \end{bmatrix}
$$

Explanatory variables (fixed effect) as X

$$
X = \begin{vmatrix} X_{U_1,11} & X_{U_1,12} & \cdots & X_{U_1,1T} \\ X_{U_2,21} & X_{U_2,22} & \cdots & X_{U_2,2T} \\ \vdots & \vdots & \ddots & \vdots \\ X_{U_n,n1} & X_{U_n,n2} & \cdots & X_{U_n,nT} \end{vmatrix}
$$

Computing Log-Likelihood. Given the necessary parameters for each element of Ω, the enhanced logged likelihood might be expressed as follows.

$$
L(\Omega|\mathbf{Y}_{ij}, \mathbf{U}_i, \mathbf{Z}_{1,i}, \mathbf{Z}_{2,i}) = \prod_{i=1}^{n}\prod_{c=1}^{2}\left\{ \pi_c f_c(Z_{c,i})[\prod_{j=1}^{T} f_c(Y_{ij}|Z_{c,i})] \right\}^{\omega_{ic}}
$$

$$
= exp\left\{ \sum_{i=1}^{n}\sum_{c=1}^{2}\omega_{ic}\left[ln\pi_c - ln(\sqrt{2\pi}\sigma_c) - \frac{Z_{c,i}^2}{2\sigma_c^2} \right. \right. \quad (7)
$$

$$
\left. \left. + \sum_{j=1}^{T}[Y_{ij}lnP_{ij}^{(c)} + (1-Y_{ij})ln(1-P_{ij}^{(c)})] \right] \right\}
$$

The logged likelihood could be expressed as in (8).

$$
l = \sum_{i=1}^{n}\sum_{c=1}^{2}\omega_{ic}\left[ln\pi_c - ln(\sqrt{2\pi}\sigma_c) - \frac{Z_{c,i}^2}{2\sigma_c^2} + \sum_{j=1}^{T}[Y_{ij}lnP_{ij}^{(c)} + (1-Y_{ij})ln(1-P_{ij}^{(c)})] \right]
$$

$$
(8)
$$

The result of (8) can be expressed in a simpler form as in (9)

$$l(\Omega|\mathbf{Y}, \mathbf{U}, \mathbf{Z}) = \sum_{i=1}^{n} \ln f_{(U_i, Z_{U_i,i})}(U_i, Z_{U_i,i}|\pi_c, \sigma_1, \sigma_2)$$

$$+ \sum_{i=1}^{n} \sum_{j=1}^{T} \ln f_{Y_{ij}|(U_i, Z_{U_i,i})}(Y_{ij}|(U_i, Z_{U_i,i}), \beta_1, \beta_2) \tag{9}$$

$$\overset{\triangle}{=} \ln f_{(\mathbf{U},\mathbf{Z})}(\mathbf{U}, \mathbf{Z}|\pi_c, \sigma_1, \sigma_2) + \ln f_{\mathbf{Y}|(\mathbf{U},\mathbf{Z})}(\mathbf{Y}|\mathbf{U}, \mathbf{Z}, \beta_1, \beta_2)$$

3.3   Monte Carlo Simulation Maximization

Simulation Maximization Algorithm. To perform maximization on the Monte Carlo method, the augmented logged likelihood must be approximated first. By taking expectation of $\mathbf{U}$ and $\mathbf{Z}$ given $\mathbf{Y}$ under the current estimate of the parameters $\Omega^{(m)}$, the expected augmented logged likelihood could be defined as:

$$Q(\Omega|\Omega^m) =$$

$$E(l|Y_{ij}, \Omega^{(m)}) = \frac{1}{N} \sum_{k=1}^{N} \sum_{i=1}^{n} \sum_{c=1}^{2} \omega_{ic}$$

$$\left[ln\pi_c - ln(\sqrt{2\pi}\sigma_c) - \frac{Z_{i,k}^2}{2\sigma_c^2} + \sum_{j=1}^{T} [Y_{ij}lnP_{ij}^{(c)} + (1 - Y_{ij}) \right. \tag{10}$$

$$\left. ln(1 - P_{ij}^{(c)})] \right].$$

Notice that in the expected log-likelihood, $\Omega^{(m)}$ could be decomposed into separate component as in (11).

$$Q(\Omega, \Omega^{(m)}) = \mathbb{E}_{(\mathbf{U},\mathbf{Z})|(\mathbf{Y},\Omega^{(m)})} \ln f_{(\mathbf{U},\mathbf{Z})}(\mathbf{U}, \mathbf{Z}|\pi_c, \sigma_1, \sigma_2)$$

$$+ \mathbb{E}_{(\mathbf{U},\mathbf{Z})|(\mathbf{Y},\Omega^{(m)})} \ln f_{\mathbf{Y}|(\mathbf{U},\mathbf{Z})}(\mathbf{Y}|\mathbf{U}, \mathbf{Z}, \beta_1, \beta_2) \tag{11}$$

$$\overset{\triangle}{=} P(\Omega, \Omega^{(m)}) + R(\Omega, \Omega^{(m)})$$

3.4   Monte Carlo Integration

In order to compute the integral above, we use Monte Carlo Integrating to approximate it. Suppose that $\{(\mathbf{U}_{(k)}, \mathbf{Z}_{(k)}, k = 1, 2, \cdots, K)\} \overset{i.i.d}{\sim} f_{(\mathbf{U},\mathbf{Z}|\mathbf{Y})}$ $(\mathbf{U}, \mathbf{Z}|\mathbf{Y}), \Omega)$ and we sample m times to approximate. Based on Mean Value Method we get:

$$Q\left(\Omega, \Omega^{(m)}\right) \approx \frac{1}{m} \sum_{k=1}^{m} \sum_{i=1, c=U_{(k),i}} \left[\ln \pi_c - \frac{1}{2} \ln (2\pi\sigma_c^2) - \frac{Z_{c,i}^2}{2\sigma_c^2} \right.$$

$$\left. + \sum_{j=1}^{T} [Y_{ij} (\beta_c X_{c,ij} + Z_{c,i}) - \ln (1 + \exp (\beta_c X_{c,ij} + Z_{c,i}))] \right] \tag{12}$$

Maximum Likelihood Estimators. To calculate the maximum likelihood estimators the partial derivatives must be approximated whose parameters are given by (13), (14), (15).

$$\frac{\partial Q(\Omega, \Omega^{(m)})}{\partial \pi_1} = \frac{1}{m} \sum_{k=1}^{m} \sum_{i=1}^{n} \mathbb{I}_{\{U_{(k),i}, i=1\}} \frac{1}{\pi_1} - \frac{1}{m} \sum_{k=1}^{m} \sum_{i=1}^{n} \mathbb{I}_{\{U_{(k),i}, i=2\}} \frac{1}{1 - \pi_1} \quad (13)$$

$$\frac{\partial Q(\Omega, \Omega^{(m)})}{\partial \sigma_c^2} = \frac{1}{m} \sum_{k=1}^{m} \sum_{i=1}^{n} \mathbb{I}_{\{U_{(k),i}=c\}} \left(-\frac{1}{2\sigma_c^2} + \frac{Z_{(k),c,i}^2}{2\sigma_c^4}\right) \quad (14)$$

$$\frac{\partial Q(\Omega, \Omega^{(m)})}{\partial \beta_c} = \frac{1}{m} \sum_{k=1}^{m} \sum_{i=1}^{n} \mathbb{I}_{\{U_{(k),i}=c\}} \sum_{j=1}^{T} \left[Y_{ij} X_{c,ij} - \frac{X_{c,ij} \exp(\beta_c X_{c,ij} + Z_{(k),c,i})}{1 + \exp(\beta_c X_{c,ij} + Z_{(k),c,i})}\right] \quad (15)$$

By setting the above partial derivatives to 0, we get the maximum likelihood estimators as in (16).

$$\hat{\pi}_1 = \frac{1}{mn} \sum_{k=1}^{m} \sum_{i=1}^{n} \mathbb{I}_{\{U_{(k),i}, i=1\}} \quad \hat{\sigma}_c = \sqrt{\frac{\sum_{k=1}^{m} \sum_{i=1}^{n} \mathbb{I}_{\{U_{(k),i}, i=c\}} Z_{(k),c,i}^2}{\sum_{k=1}^{m} \sum_{i=1}^{n} \mathbb{I}_{\{U_{(k),i}, i=c\}}}} \quad (16)$$

To compute the MLE of β_c, we use direct numerical maximization proposed by Newton-Raphson Method. The second order partial derivative of β_c is denoted as in (17).

$$\frac{\partial^2 Q(\Omega, \Omega^{(m)})}{\partial \beta_c^2} = -\frac{1}{m} \sum_{k=1}^{m} \sum_{i=1}^{n} \mathbb{I}_{\{U_{(k),i}=c\}} \sum_{j=1}^{T} \frac{X_{c,ij}^2 \exp(\beta_c X_{c,ij} + Z_{(k),c,i})}{(1 + \exp(\beta_c X_{c,ij} + Z_{(k),c,i}))^2} \quad (17)$$

3.5   Markov Chain Sampler

Since it difficult to sample directly from a multivariate distribution of the type $f_{(\mathbf{U},\mathbf{Z}|\mathbf{Y})}(\mathbf{U}, \mathbf{Z}|\mathbf{Y}), \Omega)$, we can use Gibbs Sampling, a Markov chain Monte Carlo (MCMC) algorithm to obtain a sequence of observations which are approximated from the multivariate distribution. First, we need to calculate the conditional distributions (18) and (19).

$$\frac{f_{(U_i, Z_{(U_i,i)}|\mathbf{Y}_i)}(U_i, Z_{U_i,i}|\mathbf{Y}_i, \Omega)}{f_{Z_{(U_i,i)}|\mathbf{Y}_i}(Z_{U_i,i}|\mathbf{Y}_i, \Omega)} = f_{U_i|(Z_{U_i,i}, \mathbf{Y}_i)}(U_i|Z_{U_i,i}, \mathbf{Y}_i) \quad (18)$$

$$\frac{f_{(U_i, Z_{(U_i,i)}|\mathbf{Y}_i)}(U_i, Z_{U_i,i}|\mathbf{Y}_i, \Omega)}{f_{U_i|\mathbf{Y}_i}(U_i|\mathbf{Y}_i, \Omega)} = f_{Z_{U_i,i}|(U_i,\mathbf{Y}_i)}(Z_{U_i,i}|(U_i, \mathbf{Y}_i)) \quad (19)$$

Then, suppose that $(U_{(k),i}, Z_{(k),U_{(k),i},i})$ is the i-th component of the k-th sample, we want to draw the i-th component of the $(k+1)$-th sample. We draw

$$U_{(k+1),i} \sim f_{U_i|Z_{U_i,i}, \mathbf{Y}_i}(u|Z_{U_i,i}, \mathbf{Y}_i, \Omega) \quad (20)$$

Algorithm 1. MCMC incorporated Metropolis-Hastings

1: **for** $i = 1, \cdots, n$ **do**
2:     Initialize($U_{(0),i}, Z_{(0),1,i}, Z_{(0),2,i}$)
3:     **for** c=1:2 **do**
4:         $k \leftarrow 0$
5:         **for** k **do**=1:K_2
6:             Draw $z^* \sim f_c(z|\Omega)$
7:             Accept z^* as $Z_{(k+1),c,i}$ with probability $A_{k,\mathbf{Y}_i}(z, z^*)$; otherwise, retain the original $Z_{(k),c,i}$
8:         **end for**
9:         Burn-in procedure and let the last K + 1 samples be the final samples $\{Z_{(k),c,i}, k = 0, 1, \cdots, K\}$
10:    **end for**
11:    $k \leftarrow 0$
12:    **for** k=1:K **do**
13:        Draw $U_{(k+1),i} \sim f_{U_i|Z_{U_i},i,\mathbf{Y}_i}(u|Z_{U_i}, i, \mathbf{Y}_i, \Omega)$
14:    **end for**
15:    Let the last m samples be the final samples $\{U_{(k),i}, k = 0, 1, \cdots, K\}$
16: **end for**
17: Burn-in procedure and return the m samples $\{(U_{(i),i}, Z_{(i),1,i}, Z_{(i),2,i}), k = 0, 1, \cdots, m\}$

$$Z_{(k+1),U_{(k+1),i},i} \tag{21}$$

where (21) can be approximated as:

$$f_{Z_{U_i},i|U_i,\mathbf{Y}_i}(z|U_i, \mathbf{Y}_i, \Omega). \tag{22}$$

Let (23) be a candidate distribution for (22).

$$h_{Z_{U_{(k)},i},i}(z) \tag{23}$$

Metropolis-Hastings Algorithm. To sample (21) from (22), we use (23). Since the candidate distribution should be similar to (22), we can choose $h_{Z_{U_{(k)},i},i}(z) = f_{U_i}(z|\Omega)$ and the acceptance function is

$$A_{k,\mathbf{Y}_i}(z, z^*) = \min\left[1, \frac{f_{Z_{U_i},i|U_i,\mathbf{Y}_i}(z^*|U_i, \mathbf{Y}_i, \Omega) f_{U_i}(z|\Omega)}{f_{Z_{U_i},i|U_i,\mathbf{Y}_i}(z|U_i, \mathbf{Y}_i, \Omega) f_{U_i}(z^*|\Omega)}\right] \tag{24}$$

where $\frac{f_{Z_{U_i},i|U_i,\mathbf{Y}_i}(z^*|U_i,\mathbf{Y}_i,\Omega) f_{U_i}(z|\Omega)}{f_{Z_{U_i},i|U_i,\mathbf{Y}_i}(z|U_i,\mathbf{Y}_i,\Omega) f_{U_i}(z^*|\Omega)}$ can be expressed as,

$$\frac{f_{Z_{U_i},i|U_i,\mathbf{Y}_i}(z^*|U_i,\mathbf{Y}_i,\Omega) f_{U_i}(z|\Omega)}{f_{Z_{U_i},i|U_i,\mathbf{Y}_i}(z|U_i,\mathbf{Y}_i,\Omega) f_{U_i}(z^*|\Omega)} = \exp\left[\sum_{j=1}^{T} Y_{ij}(z^* - z)\right] \prod_{j=1}^{T} \frac{1 + \exp(\beta_i X_{ij} + z)}{1 + \exp(\beta_i X_{ij} + z^*)} \tag{25}$$

We begin our Gibbs sampler incorporated a Metropolis-Hastings step as in Algorithm 1.

Monte Carlo Simulation Maximization. Unfortunately, we do know the $f_{(\mathbf{U},\mathbf{Z})|\mathbf{Y}}(\mathbf{U},\mathbf{Z}|\mathbf{Y},\Omega)$, so we use

$$f_{(\mathbf{U},\mathbf{Z})|\mathbf{Y}}(\mathbf{U},\mathbf{Z}|\mathbf{Y},\Omega^{(m)}) \tag{26}$$

in the $(m+1)$-*th* step from 2 to approximate the distribution so as to generate

$$\{(U_{(k)},Z_{(k)}),k=1,2,\cdots,m\} \overset{i.i.d}{\sim} f_{(\mathbf{U},\mathbf{Z})|\mathbf{Y}}(\mathbf{U},\mathbf{Z}|\mathbf{Y},\Omega^{(m)}) \tag{27}$$

The Monte Carlo Simulation-Maximization Algorithm we use in every experiment is given in Algorithm 2. Moreover, a flowchart of the proposed method is shown in Fig. 1.

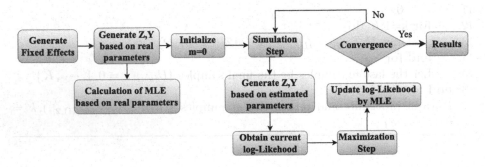

Fig. 1. Flow chart of the proposed method.

Algorithm 2. Monte Carlo Simulation Maximization (Proposed)

1: Start with the initial value for estimator $\Omega^{(0)}$. Set $m=0$.
2: SIMULATION-STEP:
3: a. Generate m samples $\{(U_{(i),i},Z_{(i),1,i},Z_{(i),2,i}),k = 0,1,\cdots,m\}$ from $f_{Z_{U_i,i}|U_i,\mathbf{Y}_i}(z|U_i,\mathbf{Y}_i,\Omega)$ throughAlgorithm 1
4: b. Calculate the partial derivatives of $Q(\Omega,\Omega^{(m)})$, the Monte Carlo estimator for every parameters.
5: MAXIMIZATION-STEP
6: $\Omega^{(m+1)} \leftarrow \arg\max_\Omega Q(\Omega,\Omega^{(m)})$
7: $m \leftarrow m+1$
8: Repeat step 2-6 until convergence and then output the maximum likelihood estimators $\Omega^{(m)}$.

---

4   Experimental Results

For $Y_{ij} = 0, 1$, for $i = n, \ldots, 1$, for $j = n$, $N = 100$, we start our experiments by setting the initial values of the parameter $\Omega = \{\beta_1, \beta_2, \sigma_1, \sigma_2, \pi_1\}$. For the first experiment we set Ω as $\beta_1 = 1.3$, $\beta_2 = 1.3$, $\sigma_1 = 2.0$, $\sigma_2 = 10$, $\pi_1 = 0.6$. These values are set after several experiments as they make the model operate smoothly. We perform variable step-size; we start the proposed Monte Carlo estimation with a modest sample size and gradually raise our sampling intervals as the Simulation Maximization (SM) iterates. We perform Gibbs sampling in each SM iteration. In each experiment, we repeat the SM iteration process for 50 times. We conduct 1000 tests with various random seeds and mark down the results of the first 100 experiments as well as the Mean Squared Error of the 1000 experiments. The results of the simulation (step 2 of Algorithm 2) are shown in Table 1. The aim here is to meet convergence for all values as close as possible in a relative short period of time. Next, we use the results derived from the previous process to perform the maximization step of 2. The results are shown in Table 1. Our convergences arc pretty good, as all parameters are converged in less than 50 steps, which costs about 1 min.

We monitor the convergence of the algorithm by plotting Ω^* vs. iteration number i and the plot reveals random fluctuation about the line $\Omega = \Omega^*$. So, we may continue with a large value of m to decrease the system variability. In Figs. 2, 3, 4 the convergence of β, σ and π is shown. The blue line represents the actual value while the orange represents the converged value.

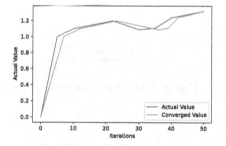

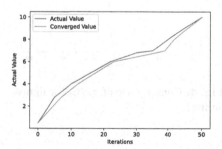

Fig. 2. Convergence of β. (Color figure online)

Fig. 3. Convergence of σ. (Color figure online)

As depicted in Figs. 2, 3 the converged value is relatively close to the true value at each given point across all 50 iterations while at some points they are even identical. Similarly the convergence of σ is relatively close to the true value across all iterations. Likewise, the convergence of π is close to the actual value as with the two previous results.

Table 1. True values and initial values vs converged values.

Variables	True value	Initial value	Converged value
β_1	1.3	0	1.2953680
β_2	1.3	0	1.3076125
σ_1	2	1	1.987342
σ_2	10	5	9.132040
π_1	0.6	0.8	0.480500

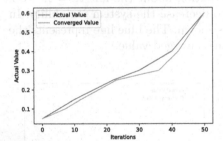

Fig. 4. Convergence of π. (Color figure online)

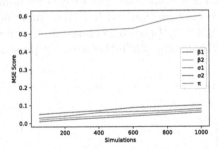

Fig. 5. MSE of parameters.

The simulations of the proposed algorithm are summarized in Table 2. The results show satisfactory performance across all five parameters of Ω.

Table 2. Simulations for $\beta_1 = 1.3$, $\beta_2 = 1.3$, $\sigma_1 = 2.0$, $\sigma_2 = 10$, $\pi_1 = 0.6$, $N = 100$.

N	β_1	β_2	σ_1	σ_2	π_1
100	1.2993	1.3045	1.9676	9.5722	0.4730
200	1.2983	1.3039	1.9675	9.5673	0.4731
300	1.2982	1.3059	1.9691	9.6156	0.4747
400	1.2982	1.3071	1.9681	9.6091	0.4744
500	1.2985	1.3059	1.9692	9.6096	0.4748
600	1.2984	1.3057	1.9683	9.6032	0.4746
700	1.2987	1.3054	1.9695	9.6325	0.4752
800	1.2985	1.3051	1.9683	9.6270	0.4749
900	1.2982	1.3047	1.9669	9.6238	0.4746
1000	1.2982	1.3051	1.9668	9.6233	0.4744

4.1 Evaluation

To evaluate the proposed method we use the Mean Squared Error Metric. The MSE is calculated as in (28).

$$MSE_\theta = \frac{1}{N} \sum_{n=1}^{N} (\theta^{(n)} - \hat{\theta}^{(n)})^2 \qquad (28)$$

where $\theta \in \Omega$, $\theta^{(n)}$ is the true MLE of θ in the n-th experiments and $\hat{\theta}^{(n)}$ is the estimator of $\theta^{(n)}$. The MSE score of β_1, β_2, σ_1, σ_2 and π is shown in Fig. 5. Generally MSE should be within the value range of 0–2 whereabouts zero value indicates that the model is perfect and the value of two indicates that the performance is marginally acceptable.

5   Conclusions and Future Work

In the context of this paper, the basic functions of MCMC methods were shown as well as the inner workings of these methods along with Gibbs sampling and a proposed method for Monte Carlo Simulation Maximization. The results show that the proposed method performed smoothly using the estimators created by our system. In respect to time, the system was capable to sample elements in a quite speedy way (approximately 1 min) for up to 1000 experiments. The MSE for 1000 experiments was also in relevantly low levels (approximately 0.5 for π) while the parameters β_1, β_2, σ_1, σ_2 and π_1 were simulated efficiently and effectively.

Future directions of this work include the integration of the proposed algorithm with a Bayesian Neural Network to better highlight the findings in a more accurate yet speedy way and to approximate the underlying evolving distributions in a more steady way. Another future scope is to increase the sampling rates and to reduce the MSE as low as possible compared to the existing method. One last but significant improvement could be the reduction of the difference among the real and estimated coefficients.

Acknowledgements. This paper is funded in the framework of THLEMAXOS project which is funded by the Ionian Region Islands with MIS code 5007986 in the context of Operational Program Ionian Islands 2014-2020.

References

1. Agresti, A.: Categorical Data Analysis. Wiley, Hoboken (2003)
2. Besag, J., York, J., Mollié, A.: Bayesian image restoration, with two applications in spatial statistics. Ann. Inst. Stat. Math. **43**(1), 1–20 (1991)
3. Breslow, N.E., Clayton, D.G.: Approximate inference in generalized linear mixed models. J. Am. Stat. Assoc. **88**(421), 9–25 (1993)
4. Clayton, D.G.: Generalized linear mixed models. Markov Chain Monte Carlo Pract. **1**, 275–302 (1996)
5. Demidenko, E.: Mixed Models: Theory and Applications (Wiley Series in Probability and Statistics). Wiley-Interscience, New York (2004)
6. Fahrmeir, L., Tutz, G., Hennevogl, W., Salem, E.: Multivariate Statistical Modelling Based on Generalized Linear Models, vol. 425. Springer, New York (1994). https://doi.org/10.1007/978-1-4899-0010-4
7. Gelfand, A.E., Smith, A.F.: Sampling-based approaches to calculating marginal densities. J. Am. Stat. Assoc. **85**(410), 398–409 (1990)
8. Geman, S., Geman, D.: Stochastic relaxation, Gibbs distributions, and the Bayesian restoration of images. IEEE Trans. Pattern Anal. Mach. Intell. PAMI **6**(6), 721–741 (1984). https://doi.org/10.1109/TPAMI.1984.4767596
9. Geyer, C.J.: Likelihood inference in exponential families and directions of recession. Electron. J. Stat. **3**, 259–289 (2009). https://doi.org/10.1214/08-EJS349
10. Geyer, C.J., Thompson, E.A.: Constrained Monte Carlo maximum likelihood for dependent data. J. Roy. Stat. Soc. Ser. B (Methodol.) **54**(3), 657–683 (1992)
11. Hastings, W.K.: Monte Carlo sampling methods using Markov chains and their applications. Biometrika **57**, 97–109 (1970)
12. Hedeker, D.: Generalized linear mixed models. Encyclopedia of statistics in behavioral science (2005)
13. Karras, C., Karras, A.: DBSOP: an efficient heuristic for speedy MCMC sampling on polytopes. arXiv preprint arXiv:2203.10916 (2022)
14. Karras, C., Karras, A., Sioutas, S.: Pattern recognition and event detection on IoT data-streams. arXiv preprint arXiv:2203.01114 (2022)
15. McCulloch, C.E.: Maximum likelihood algorithms for generalized linear mixed models. J. Am. Stat. Assoc. **92**(437), 162–170 (1997)
16. Mcculloch, C.E., Neuhaus, J.M.: Generalized Linear Mixed Models. Wiley (2014). https://doi.org/10.1002/9781118445112.stat07540
17. McCulloch, C.E., Searle, S.R.: Generalized, Linear, and Mixed Models. Wiley, Hoboken (2004)
18. Metropolis, N., Rosenbluth, A.W., Rosenbluth, M.N., Teller, A.H., Teller, E.: Equation of state calculations by fast computing machines. J. Chem. Phys. **21**(6), 1087–1092 (1953)
19. Moyeed, R., Baddeley, A.J.: Stochastic approximation of the MLE for a spatial point pattern. Scand. J. Stat., 39–50 (1991)
20. Ogata, Y., Tanemura, M.: Likelihood estimation of soft-core interaction potentials for Gibbsian point patterns. Ann. Inst. Stat. Math. **41**(3), 583–600 (1989)
21. Penttinen, A.: Modelling interactions in spatial point patterns: parameter estimation by the maximum-likelihood method. Comp. Sci. Econ. Statist. **7**, 1–107 (1984)

Simulating Blockchain Consensus Protocols in Julia: Proof of Work vs Proof of Stake

Georgios Drakopoulos[1]([⊠]) [iD], Eleanna Kafeza[2] [iD], Ioanna Giannoukou[3] [iD],
Phivos Mylonas[1] [iD], and Spyros Sioutas[3] [iD]

[1] Humanistic and Social Informatics Lab, Ionian University, Corfu, Hellas
{c16drak,fmylonas}@ionio.gr
[2] College of Technological Innovation, Zayed University, Dubai, UAE
eleana.kafeza@zu.ac.ae
[3] University of Patras, Patras, Hellas
igian@upatras.gr, sioutas@ceid.upatras.gr

Abstract. Consensus protocols constitute an important part in virtually any blockchain stack as they safeguard transaction validity and uniqueness. This task is achieved in a distributed manner by delegating it to certain nodes which, depending on the protocol, may further utilize the computational resources of other nodes. As a tangible incentive for nodes to verify transactions many protocols contain special reward mechanisms. They are typically inducement prizes aiming at increasing node engagement towards blockchain stability. This work presents the fundamentals of a probabilistic blockchain simulation tool for studying large transaction volumes over time. Two consensus protocols, the proof of work and the delegate proof of stake, are compared on the basis of the reward distribution and the probability bound of the reward exceeding its expected value. Also, the reward probability as a function of the network distance from the node initiating the transaction is studied.

Keywords: Blockchain simulation · Consensus protocols · Proof of work · Proof of state · Stakeholder delegate · Behavioral economics

1 Introduction

After the introduction of Bitcoin research interest focused not only on cryptocurrencies but also on the consensus protocols used to verify transactions. The latter are essential in achieving reward fairness, even approximately, and trust in the respective cryptocurrency by actively engaging nodes. A blockchain with reinforced trust in addition to the ability of global secure payments independent of the control of external parties is more attractive to potential stakeholders.

Since blockchain relies on massive peer-to-peer (p2p) network technology, it is difficult to predict the exact action course during a transaction sequence

Published by Springer Nature Switzerland AG 2022
I. Maglogiannis et al. (Eds.): AIAI 2022 Workshops, IFIP AICT 652, pp. 357–369, 2022.
https://doi.org/10.1007/978-3-031-08341-9_20

as well as the resulting blockchain state. One way to overcome this limitation is to probabilistically simulate the blockchain including the consensus protocol, network rewards, and the nodes themselves in terms of computing power.

The primary research objective of this conference paper is a highly parameterized node-level probabilistic blockchain simulation tool. As a concrete example, it has been applied to two common blockchain consensus protocols, namely proof of work (PoW) and proof of stake (PoS), and the results are analyzed.

The remainder of this conference paper is structured as follows. In Sect. 2 the recent scientific literature is briefly reviewed. Simulation in described in Sect. 3. The results are outlined in Sect. 4, while in Sect. 5 possible future research directions are given. Capital italic letters represent random variables and capital boldface letters matrices. In function definitions parameters follow arguments after a semi-colon. Finally, the notation is summarized in Table 1.

Table 1. Notation of this work.

Symbol	Meaning	First in
$\overset{\triangle}{=}$	Definition or equality by definition	Eq. (1)
$E[\mathcal{X}]$	Mean value of random variable $\mathcal{X}$	Eq. (8)
$Var[\mathcal{X}]$	Variance of random variable $\mathcal{X}$	Eq. (9)
$prob\{\Omega\}$	Probability of event Ω occurring	Eq. (3)
$\langle f \parallel g \rangle$	Kullback-Leibler divergence for f and g	Eq. (22)
$f^{(n)}(x)$	n-th derivative of function $f(x)$	Eq. (9)
$i \rightarrow j/(i \rightarrow j)^p$	Path of node i to j of any length/length p	Eq. (7)

2   Previous Work

Consensus protocols are instrumental in any blockchain [21]. Among the most widespread ones are proof of work [1] and proof of stake [19]. A recent survey is [6]. Algorithmic means for defending against rogue and powerful miners [15]. Game theoretic attacks for proof of work are analyzed in [4]. Blockchain applications include smart contracts [18], payments [13], and medical records [9]. Behavioral economics focus on the cognitive mechanisms for decision making [3] like cognitive bias [11], cognitive dissonance [12], and inducement prizes [10]. Such techniques have increased engagement in cultural content delivery [5] and prolonged the visiting times in cultural portals [8]. An important effect of consensus protocols is that they reinforce Web trust in a distributed and stateless environment where parties have no *a priori* reason to trust each other [20]. The latter is critical for Web services including e-commerce [2], database architecture selection [14], recommendation engines [16], and finding trusted candidates in LinkedIn [7]. Recently blockchains have been used in sensor networks [17].

3   Simulation of Consensus Protocols

Interested parties and stakeholders typically consider joining a blockchain in order to obtain certain rewards, whether tangible or intangible. Still, this work will deal in general with (*network*) *rewards* without further specialization.

This simulation aims to address the following fundamental questions:

- The reward distribution after a long transaction sequence, especially in terms of reward fairness and final node wealth distribution.
- How the costs of joining a blockchain and verifying transactions influence the wealth distribution and whether negate any initial incentives.
- The transaction initiation distribution after a large number of transactions. In the long run it reveals the true chances a node has for collecting rewards.

Note that the actual values of both the parameters discussed below and the internal fine tuning options are given in Table 2. The primary parameters are:

- The number of blockchain nodes N_0. It is the number of clients participating to the p2p network, each performing an identical set of roles.
- The processing power P_i, namely the number of processors and their power. They are identical, with factors like paging and caching policy ignored.
- The link capacity $C_{i,j}$ ignoring factors such as network technology, signal to noise (SNR) ratio, stack size, number of interfaces, and routing overhead.
- The node failure probability p_0. It is independent of local resiliency technologies like backup power sources, network drives, and RAID arrays.

The simulation consists of R_1 runs with the blockchain topology changing after each run. Each such run has R_0 rounds and each round has three steps:

- The initial transaction request and its propagation through the network.
- The transaction verification according to the consensus protocol.
- The verification propagation through the p2p network.

The number of rounds is determined as in Eq. (1). Each of the N_0 nodes is selected uniformly for a transaction. This in conjunction with R_0 implies that each node has on average γ_0 chances to collect network rewards.

$$R_0 \triangleq \lceil \gamma_0 N_0 \rceil \tag{1}$$

Blockchain topology plays a central role. In each run I_0 randomly selected links are created between the N_0 nodes. The density ρ_0 is defined as in (2):

$$I_0 \triangleq \lceil \rho_0 N_0 \rceil \tag{2}$$

Each node starts with a fixed amount of W_0 network reward units. In each round a node, called the *initiator* for brevity, requests a transaction claiming a randomly selected amount w_i. The latter is chosen uniformly in the interval between $w_l W_0$ and $w_h W_0$. The uniform distribution expresses the generic nature of the network rewards and it is by no means fit for every case. For instance, when the rewards are rare, the Poisson distribution might be more appropriate.

Network resiliency is expressed as the node failure probability p_0. In the context of the proposed simulation p_0 is the probability of a node failing to receive the request, process it, or send the reply. As each node operates independently, the probability that k nodes fail simultaneously is given by Eq. (3):

$$\pi_k \triangleq \text{prob}\{k \text{ failures}\} = \binom{N_0}{k} p_0^k (1 - p_0)^{N_0 - k} \tag{3}$$

Clearly π_k in the above equation follows a binomial distribution defined over a finite population N_0 with a success probability $1 - p_0$. When p_0 is very low, as it was chosen here, then Eq. (3) can be approximated as in (4):

$$\pi_k \approx \frac{(p_0 N_0)^k}{k!} e^{-p_0 N_0} = \frac{\lambda_0^k}{k!} e^{-\lambda_0}, \quad \lambda_0 \triangleq p_0 N_0 \tag{4}$$

Equation (4) is a Poisson distribution. This approximation is derived by (5). Each of the k simultaneous failures in every simulation round is independent and local as in a real p2p network there is no global failure knowledge.

$$\binom{N_0}{k} p_0^k \approx \frac{N_0^k}{k!} p_0^k = \frac{(p_0 N_0)^k}{k!}$$
$$(1 - p_0)^{N_0 - k} \approx (1 - p_0)^{N_0} \approx e^{-p_0 N_0} \tag{5}$$

The $N_0 \times N_0$ random symmetric link capacity matrix $\mathbf{C}$ is an instrumental parameter. Symmetry implies that the capacity in bits per second (bps) along any link is the same in both directions. The time $t_{i,i'}$ to transmit a packet of length L_0 in bits, complete with protocol headers and trailers, assuming that no failures or retransmission attempts take place is shown in Eq. (6):

$$t_{i,i'} = \frac{L_0}{\mathbf{C}_{i,i'}}, \quad \text{link } (i, i') \text{ exists} \tag{6}$$

The distribution of link capacity $\mathbf{C}_{i,j}$ is log-normal with its variance taking into account equipment technology, geographical distribution, and configuration differences among other factors. The network packets carrying the transaction verification request and the corresponding confirmation have length L_r and L_v respectively. Typically L_r is long since it contains the information necessary to verify the transaction. Additionally, both packets can be salted with cryptographic data so that neither a random or fake transaction request can be generated nor a phony verification. Capacity essentially imposes a network topology where the minimum distance between nodes i and j is the minimum weighted sum over all connecting paths $i \rightarrow j$. The minimum time $\mathbf{T}_{i,j}$ for a package is (7), which lends itself among others to dynamic programming solutions:

$$\mathbf{T}_{i,j}(L_0) \triangleq \min_{i \rightarrow j}\left[\sum_{(k,k')} t_{k,k'}\right] = \min_{i \rightarrow j}\left[\sum_{(k,k')} \frac{L_0}{\mathbf{C}_{k,k'}}\right] \approx \min_{(i \rightarrow j)^p}\left[\sum_{(k,k')} \frac{L_0}{\mathbf{C}_{k,k'}}\right] \tag{7}$$

In the simulation $\mathbf{T}_{i,j}$ is used, but in a real blockchain stack only local routing information in a neighborhood of depth p is used as in the right hand side of (7). The packet transmission times $\mathbf{T}_{i,j}$ depends on the link capacity distribution as shown in (6). Since the latter is stochastic, so are $\mathbf{T}_{i,j}$. This leads to the question of what can be deduced about them given the probabilistic properties of $\mathbf{C}$.

The mean values $\mathrm{E}\,[\mathcal{T}_{i,j}]$ of $\mathbf{T}_{i,j}$ can be computed as follows. If r.vs $\mathcal{X}$ and $\mathcal{Y}$ are connected through the measurable, not necessarily invertible function $h\,(\cdot)$, and if $f_X\,(\cdot)$ is the probability density function (pdf) of $\mathcal{X}$, then (8) holds:

$$\mathrm{E}\,[\mathcal{Y}] \triangleq \mathrm{E}\,[h\,(\mathcal{X})] = \int_{\Omega_f} h\,(x)\,f_X\,(x)\,dx \tag{8}$$

Concerning the variance $\mathrm{Var}\,[\mathcal{T}_{i,j}]$ the answer is not straightforward as the variance is invariant in the general case only to linear transforms. Thus an estimate by the *delta method* of Eq. (9) will be used which relies on a first order Taylor approximation of $\mathrm{Var}\,[\mathcal{Y}]$ around $\mathrm{E}\,[X]$. Specifically:

$$\mathrm{Var}\,[\mathcal{Y}] \approx \mathrm{Var}\,[\mathcal{X}] \left(h^{(1)}(\mathrm{E}\,[\mathcal{X}]) \right)^2 \tag{9}$$

Given (8) and (9) the mean and variance of $\mathcal{T}_{i,j}$ are as in Eq. (10):

$$\mathrm{E}\,[\mathcal{T}_{i,j}] \triangleq \frac{L_0}{\mathrm{E}\,[\mathcal{C}_{i,j}]} \quad \text{and} \quad \mathrm{Var}\,[\mathcal{T}_{i,j}] \approx \mathrm{Var}\,[\mathcal{C}_{i,j}] \frac{L_0^2}{\mathrm{E}\,[\mathcal{C}_{i,j}]^4} \tag{10}$$

Once a packet arrives at the destination node, it will be processed. Again time is a critical factor, but it is computed in a different way. The processing power P_i for each node is determined by the number and type of processors. The memory is assumed to be sufficiently high so that it does not interfere with thread or processor parallelism. Specifically, the processing power is given by Amdahl's law where each of the p_i processors is assumed to have s_i cores for a total of $P_i = p_i s_i$ cores. In this case Amdahl's speedup becomes:

$$\zeta_i \triangleq \frac{1}{(1 - \epsilon_0) + \dfrac{\epsilon_0}{P_i}} = \frac{1}{(1 - \epsilon_0) + \dfrac{\epsilon_0}{p_i s_i}} \tag{11}$$

In Eq. (11) $1 - \epsilon_0$ is the part of the verification transaction which cannot be parallelized and it is the same across nodes and runs. It has been determined based on observations and literature recommendations [19,21]. Also, p_i and c_i are uniformly selected among the respective number of possible choices.

The round trip time r_i for node i from initiator i^* is computed as in (12):

$$r_i \triangleq \begin{cases} \mathbf{T}_{i,i^*}\,(L_r + L_v) + T_b/\zeta_i, & \text{PoW/PoS I} \\ \mathbf{T}_{i,i^*}\,(L_r + L_v) + \max\,[\mathbf{T}_{i,j}\,(L_r + L_v) + T_b/\zeta_j], & \text{PoS II} \end{cases} \tag{12}$$

The first branch in (12) represents the time required for the request packet to reach i, to process it, and return the verification to i^* for PoW. This is mechanism also works for the original version PoS of PoS I, although the verifiers are selected in a specific probabilistic way. The second branch is the time under the delegate version of PoS or PoS II required for the request packet to reach i and be relayed to the witnesses, processing by the latter, return of the verifications from the witnesses to i, and the subsequent retransmission to i^*. T_b is the base task execution time which remains constant for every node and across runs.

3.1 Proof of Work

Under PoW the initiator is required to transmit a transaction verification request. The latter is approved only when a sufficient number of responder nodes approves the information the initiator has included in the request.

Algorithm 1. Consensus protocol simulation.

Require: The parameters of Table 2.
Ensure: The simulation objectives are achieved.
1: **for all** runs in the simulation **do**
2:      select topology, capacities, processors, and cores
3:      **for all** rounds in the current run **do**
4:          select initiator node and reward
5:          select responders or verifiers [and witness nodes]
6:          compute times and rank nodes based on time
7:      **end for**
8: **end for**
9: **return**

3.2 Proof of Stake

PoS relies on the principle that nodes which have accumulated more rewards are also more eager to contribute to the blockchain stability. In the original version (PoS I) η_0 verifier nodes are selected with a probability proportional to their rewards. To prevent rewards from being collected by a small group of nodes, in the delegate version (PoS II) each verifier contracts a witness, selected with a probability proportional to its computing power as shown in Eq. (13):

$$\delta_i \triangleq \text{prob}\{i \text{ is witness}\} = \frac{P_i}{\sum_{k=1}^{N_0} P_k} \tag{13}$$

Verifiers and witnesses each get a fraction τ_0 of the reward. The selection mechanism gives a chance to high power nodes in addition to the wealthier ones. Advanced PoS versions of take into account network connections or memory size.

4   Results

4.1   Rewards

In Table 2 the simulation parameters and their actual values are shown.

Table 2. Experimental setup.

Parameter	Value	Parameter	Value
Number of nodes N_0	16384	Delegate selection prob. δ_i	Eq. (13)
Node failure probability p_0	0.05	Rounds coefficient γ_0	16
Network density ρ_0	0.6	Percentage of parallelism ϵ_0	0.85
Number of links I_0	Eq. (2)	Model fit method	ML
Initial reward distribution	Fixed	Verification time T_b	Eq. (12)
Initial balance W_0	1000	Witness reward fraction τ_0	0.005
Reward limits w_l/w_h	0.05/0.1	Link capacity distribution	Lognormal
Simulation rounds R_0	Eq. (1)	Request packet length L_r	2048
Node selection distribution	Uniform	Verification packet length L_v	512
Number of delegates η_0	51	Distribution of processors p_i	Uniform
Number of runs R_1	10000	Distribution of cores s_i	Uniform

An important description of a blockchain is its reward distribution. If it is balanced enough, it may appeal to potential stakeholders seeking security. If not, it may attract high risk takers. Thus, each distribution is compatible with different behavioral stakeholder profiles, which is a key design factor.

For each node the rewards over each run and round are averaged, eliminating thus the effect of topology and keeping that of consensus protocol. To construct the empirical rewards distribution B_0 bins as in Eq. (14) will be used. This allows a large amount of bins each with a statistically safe numbers of samples.

$$B_0 \triangleq 0.25 \left\lceil \sqrt{N_0} \right\rceil \tag{14}$$

The resulting empirical mean reward distribution in logarithmic scale is shown in Fig. 1, which suggests a power law and that PoS seems to distribute network rewards more evenly than PoW.

A second way to decide whether a particular blockchain is worth joining is the probability of deviating from the expected reward. If the latter is high, then the payoff for the initial cost may be significant. The Chebyshev inequality of (15) provides upper bounds for this probability in the scale of standard deviations:

$$\text{prob}\left\{ |\mathcal{R} - \text{E}\left[\mathcal{R}\right]| \geq \xi_0 \sqrt{\text{Var}\left[\mathcal{R}\right]} \right\} \leq \frac{1}{\xi_0^2} \tag{15}$$

Table 3. Chebyshev upper bounds.

$\xi_0\sqrt{\mathrm{Var}\,[\mathcal{R}]}$	$0.2\,\mathrm{E}\,[\mathcal{R}]$	$0.3\,\mathrm{E}\,[\mathcal{R}]$	$0.5\,\mathrm{E}\,[\mathcal{R}]$	$0.75\,\mathrm{E}\,[\mathcal{R}]$	$\mathrm{E}\,[\mathcal{R}]$
PoW	$2.83\cdot 10^{-1}$	$1.45\cdot 10^{-1}$	$7.09\cdot 10^{-2}$	$1.08\cdot 10^{-2}$	$9.81\cdot 10^{-3}$
PoS I (original)	$1.83\cdot 10^{-1}$	$1.17\cdot 10^{-1}$	$4.18\cdot 10^{-2}$	$8.14\cdot 10^{-3}$	$7.79\cdot 10^{-3}$
PoS II (delegate)	$1.22\cdot 10^{-1}$	$9.62\cdot 10^{-2}$	$3.26\cdot 10^{-2}$	$7.66\cdot 10^{-3}$	$6.33\cdot 10^{-3}$

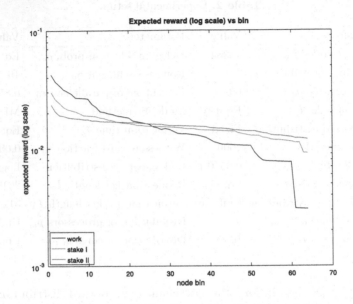

Fig. 1. Mean reward distribution for the three scenario.

From Table 3 it can be seen that PoW attains higher upper bounds, which is consistent with the less balanced reward distribution compared to the PoS variants. Therefore, a potential stakeholder may be motivated by the prospect of gaining additional rewards compared to the expected ones.

A third way to gain insight into the way the consensus protocols work is to fit a distribution to the expected network rewards. In this case more protocol properties can be derived, assuming the chosen distribution has a considerable degree of accuracy. Since from Fig. 1 the empirical distribution of the average reward appears to be a power law, three such models will be fit. Additionally, the models were selected based on the number and type of scenaria they explain.

The log-normal distribution of (16) models long scale mobile signal scatter, digital post length, and quantities made from the product of independent factors.

$$f_l\left(x;\sigma_l,\mu_l\right) \triangleq \frac{1}{x\,\sigma_l\sqrt{2\pi}}\exp\left(-\frac{(\ln x - \mu_l)^2}{2\sigma_l^2}\right) \tag{16}$$

The maximum likelihood (ML) estimators for μ_l and σ_l^2 are given in (17):

$$\hat{\mu}_l = \frac{1}{B_0} \sum_{k=1}^{B_0} \ln x_k \quad \text{and} \quad \hat{\sigma}_l^2 = \frac{1}{B_0} \sum_{k=1}^{B_0} (\ln x_k - \hat{\mu}_l)^2 \tag{17}$$

The Weibull distribution of (18) describes the time spent reading an Internet post, measuring therefore indirectly reader engagement as well.

$$f_w (x; k_0, \lambda_0) \triangleq \frac{k_0}{\lambda_0} \left(\frac{x}{\lambda_0}\right)^{k_0} \exp\left(-\frac{x}{\lambda_0}\right)^{k_0} \tag{18}$$

The ML estimators for $\hat{\lambda}_0$ and $\hat{k}_0$ are given in Eq. (19):

$$\hat{\lambda}_0 = \left(\frac{1}{B_0} \sum_{k=1}^{B_0} x_k^{\hat{k}_0}\right)^{\hat{k}_0^{-1}} \quad \text{and} \quad \frac{\sum_{k=1}^{B_0} x_k^{\hat{k}_0} \ln x_k}{\sum_{k=1}^{B_0} x_k^{\hat{k}_0}} - \frac{1}{\hat{k}_0} = \frac{1}{B_0} \sum_{k=1}^{B_0} \ln x_k \tag{19}$$

The Pareto type I distribution is frequently used to model physical and social phenomena including income distributions. It is defined for $x \geq x_0$ as in (20):

$$f_p (x; \beta_0, x_0) \triangleq \frac{\beta_0 x_0^{\beta_0}}{x^{1+\beta_0}} = \frac{\beta_0}{x_0} \left(\frac{x}{x_0}\right)^{-(1+\beta_0)} \tag{20}$$

The maximum likelihood (ML) estimators $\hat{x}_0$ and $\hat{\beta}_0$ are shown in (21):

$$\hat{x}_0 = \min\{x_k\} \quad \text{and} \quad \hat{\beta}_0 = \frac{B_0}{\sum_{k=1}^{B_0} \ln\left(\frac{x_k}{\hat{x}_0}\right)} \tag{21}$$

The Kullback-Leibler divergence $\langle f \parallel g \rangle$ between two continuous distributions $f(x)$ and $g(x)$ is shown in (22) defined over the union Ω of the their domains.

$$\langle f \parallel g \rangle \triangleq \int_\Omega f(x) \log_b \left(\frac{f(x)}{g(x)}\right) dx \tag{22}$$

In Table 4 the normalized Kullback-Leibler divergence between the empirical and the fitted models is shown. Rows were normalized to their respective minima.

Table 4. Divergence for reward models (Normalized).

Model/Protocol	Log-normal	Weibull	Pareto
PoW	1.6426	1.4318	1
PoS I (original)	1.8665	1.6612	1
PoS II (delegate)	2.0114	1.7344	1

The results of Table 4 can be interpreted based on the dependencies under-lying the node interaction, which works differently across protocols. Under PoW the verification packets of nodes closer to the initiator are more likely to reach it first. In the PoS I case only current node rewards count, while PoS II adds computing power as a factor and hence as an extra dependency layer. Therefore, given that these simulation parameters remain constant, there is dependency in the form of memory. This is better modeled by power law distributions, while memoryless interactions by exponential ones. The log-normal distribution is the closest to an exponential distribution, the Weibull distribution balances between these two cases, and the Pareto distribution is a power law. This explains the relative scores achieved by each of these three models.

4.2   Distance from the Initiator

From Fig. 2 it can be seen that under PoW nodes closer to the initiator have considerably more chances of receiving a reward. This can be attributed to the fact that packet propagation is one of the main latency factors. In sharp con-trast, the verifier selection mechanism in PoS I is topology-independent. Hence the respective curves are much different despite the round trip time being com-puted by the same branch of (12). The PoW II relies on an additional selection process for the witnesses which introduces additional skew compared to PoS I but remains also topology-independent. The distance from a network focal point is exploited in other applications such as high frequency trading (HFT).

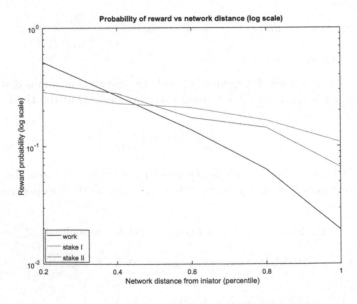

Fig. 2. Reward probability (log scale) vs network distance.

4.3   Analysis

The need for a comprehensive blockchain simulation tool is clear since to the best of the knowledge of the authors current tools focus on specific aspects. The open source SimBlock takes into consideration network parameters such as bandwidth and latency but not node reward. The very recent modular BlockSim also does not support PoS. Shadow-Bitcoin as its name suggests was created for Bitcoin simulation. Vibes as of 2017 supported only PoW. Solidity is intended only for the creation of smart contracts over the Ethereum virtual machine (EVM).

The proposed simulation has a number of limitations. A more detailed model can take into account aspects like dedicated application specific integrated circuits (ASIC) chips intended for mining rewards. Additionally, more distributions for initiator selection, rewards, and capacities can be implemented and tested.

Behavior motivation of the stakeholders and how they influence blockchain operations is vital to understanding blockchain stability. In particular, PoS can be seen as an inducement price which should be weighted against an estimate of the resources required. The reward fairness achieved by PoS may motivate stakeholders with a strong tendency for loss aversion, whereas PoW may appeal to stakeholders with powerful equipment. Furthermore, the connection of the Pareto family of distributions to the least effort principle may hint at the prospect of quick rewards as an incentive to join a blockchain.

One final note is that like any simulation the one proposed here is as accurate as the assumptions and the models allow. As real data are collected from deployed systems, their validity can be re-evaluated.

5   Conclusions and Future Work

This conference paper focuses on the probabilistic simulation of proof of work and proof of stake in blockchains. Probabilistic analysis indicates the latter achieves a more balanced reward distribution. Moreover, the probability of reward depends heavily on the distance from the initiator under the proof of work protocol.

Future research directions include more runs with a larger number of nodes and with more sophisticated consensus protocols. Moreover, failures can be extended to involve a random number of rounds, possibly relying on resiliency results from the field of temporal graphs, or neighborhoods of random radii.

Acknowledgment. This conference paper is part of Project 451, a long term research iniative whose primary objective is the development of novel, scalable, numerically stable, and interpretable tensor analytics.

References

1. Cao, B., Wang, X., Zhang, W., Song, H., Lv, Z.: A many-objective optimization model of industrial Internet of Things based on private blockchain. IEEE Netw. **34**(5), 78–83 (2020)

2. De Filippi, P., Mannan, M., Reijers, W.: Blockchain as a confidence machine: the problem of trust & challenges of governance. Technol. Soc. **62**, 101284 (2020)
3. DellaVigna, S.: Structural behavioral economics. In: Handbook of Behavioral Economics: Applications and Foundations, vol. 1, pp. 613–723. Elsevier (2018)
4. Dey, S.: Securing majority-attack in blockchain using machine learning and algorithmic game theory: a proof of work. In: CEEC, pp. 7–10. IEEE (2018)
5. Drakopoulos, G., Giannoukou, I., Mylonas, P., Sioutas, S.: The converging triangle of cultural content, cognitive science, and behavioral economics. In: Maglogiannis, I., Iliadis, L., Pimenidis, E. (eds.) AIAI 2020. IAICT, vol. 585, pp. 200–212. Springer, Cham (2020). https://doi.org/10.1007/978-3-030-49190-1_18
6. Drakopoulos, G., Kafeza, E., Al Katheeri, H.: Proof systems in blockchains: a survey. In: SEEDA-CECNSM. IEEE (2019)
7. Drakopoulos, G., Kafeza, E., Mylonas, P., Al Katheeri, H.: Building trusted startup teams from LinkedIn attributes: a higher order probabilistic analysis. In: ICTAI, pp. 867–874. IEEE (2020)
8. Drakopoulos, G., Voutos, Y., Mylonas, P., Sioutas, S.: Motivating item annotations in cultural portals with UI/UX based on behavioral economics. In: IISA. IEEE (2021). https://doi.org/10.1109/IISA52424.2021.9555569
9. Hasselgren, A., Kralevska, K., Gligoroski, D., Pedersen, S.A., Faxvaag, A.: Blockchain in healthcare and health sciences - a scoping review. Int. J. Med. Informatics **134**, 104040 (2020)
10. Khan, B.Z.: Inventing Ideas: Patents, Prizes, and the Knoweldge Economy. Oxford University Press, New York (2020)
11. Lai, K., Oliveira, H.C., Hou, M., Yanushkevich, S.N., Shmerko, V.: Assessing risks of biases in cognitive decision support systems. In: EUSIPCO, pp. 840–844. IEEE (2021)
12. Li, K., Liang, H., Kou, G., Dong, Y.: Opinion dynamics model based on the cognitive dissonance: an agent-based simulation. Inf. Fusion **56**, 1–14 (2020)
13. Liu, Y., Ai, Z., Sun, S., Zhang, S., Liu, Z., Yu, H.: FedCoin: a peer-to-peer payment system for federated learning. In: Yang, Q., Fan, L., Yu, H. (eds.) Federated Learning. LNCS (LNAI), vol. 12500, pp. 125–138. Springer, Cham (2020). https://doi.org/10.1007/978-3-030-63076-8_9
14. Marountas, M., Drakopoulos, G., Mylonas, P., Sioutas, S.: Recommending database architectures for social queries: a twitter case study. In: Maglogiannis, I., Macintyre, J., Iliadis, L. (eds.) AIAI 2021. IAICT, vol. 627, pp. 715–728. Springer, Cham (2021). https://doi.org/10.1007/978-3-030-79150-6_56
15. Ren, W., Hu, J., Zhu, T., Ren, Y., Choo, K.K.R.: A flexible method to defend against computationally resourceful miners in blockchain proof of work. Inf. Sci. **507**, 161–171 (2020)
16. Saghiri, A.M., HamlAbadi, K.G., Vahdati, M.: The Internet of Things, artificial intelligence, and blockchain: implementation perspectives. In: Kim, S., Deka, G.C. (eds.) Advanced Applications of Blockchain Technology. SBD, vol. 60, pp. 15–54. Springer, Singapore (2020). https://doi.org/10.1007/978-981-13-8775-3_2
17. She, W., Liu, Q., Tian, Z., Chen, J.S., Wang, B., Liu, W.: Blockchain trust model for malicious node detection in wireless sensor networks. IEEE Access **7**, 38947–38956 (2019)
18. Voutos, Y., Drakopoulos, G., Mylonas, P.: Smart agriculture: an open field for smart contracts. In: SEEDA-CECNSM. IEEE (2019)
19. Wan, S., Li, M., Liu, G., Wang, C.: Recent advances in consensus protocols for blockchain: a survey. Wireless Netw. **26**(8), 5579–5593 (2020)

20. Werbach, K.: The Blockchain and the New Architecture of Trust. MIT Press, Cambridge (2018)
21. Xiao, Y., Zhang, N., Lou, W., Hou, Y.T.: A survey of distributed consensus protocols for blockchain networks. IEEE Commun. Surv. Tutor. **22**(2), 1432–1465 (2020)

State-of-the-Art in Community Detection in Temporal Networks

Kostas Christopoulos$^{(\boxtimes)}$ and Kostas Tsichlas

Computer Engineering and Informatics Department, University of Patras,
Patras, Greece
{kchristopou,ktsichlas}@ceid.upatras.gr

Abstract. Community detection is a prominent process on networks
and has been extensively studied on static networks the last 25 years.
This problem concerns the structural partitioning of networks into classes
of nodes that are more densely connected when compared to the rest
of the network. However, a plethora of real-world networks are highly
dynamic, in the sense that entities (nodes) as well as relations between
them (edges) constantly change. As a result, many solutions have also
been applied in dynamic/temporal networks under various assumptions
concerning the modeling of time as well as the emerging communities.
The problem becomes quite harder when the notion of time is introduced,
since various unseen problems in the static case arise, like the identity
problem. In the last few years, a few surveys have been conducted regarding community detection in time-evolving networks. In this survey, our
objective is to give a rather condensed but up-to-date overview, when
compared to previous surveys, of the current state-of-the-art regarding
community detection in temporal networks. We also extend the previous
classification of the algorithmic approaches for the problem by discern-
ing between global and local dynamic community detection. The former
aims at identifying the evolution of all communities and the latter aims
at identifying the evolution of a partition around a set of seed nodes.

Keywords: Temporal graphs/Networks · Community detection

1 Introduction

Networks are widely used as a method for analyzing data in many scientific
fields, such as social sciences, transportation and biology. The prrocess of community detection (henceforward also referred as CD), that has its origins in graph
partitioning, is concerned with node intra-connectivity and its goal is to identify highly linked groups (communities) of nodes. For example, finding clusters
of users in social networks and functional protein complexes in bioinformatics
networks are two widely used applications of this problem.

© IFIP International Federation for Information Processing 2022
Published by Springer Nature Switzerland AG 2022
I. Maglogiannis et al. (Eds.): AIAI 2022 Workshops, IFIP AICT 652, pp. 370–381, 2022.
https://doi.org/10.1007/978-3-031-08341-9_30

In general, a static network is represented as $G = (V, E)$, where V is the set of vertices (entities) and E is the set of edges (interactions/relations between entities). An edge can be directed, such as the connection between two people where one sends an email to another or undirected, such as the connection between two collaborating peers. Lastly, edges among nodes can be associated with weights (e.g., frequency of interactions) or nodes can be associated to weights (e.g., specific properties of nodes). In many cases, real-world networks are dynamic, in the sense that new edges or nodes appear and existing edges or nodes disappear. As a result, the communities themselves change because of the evolution of the network. The appearance of a new community, the disappearance of an existing and the split of an existing into two or more, are examples of changes in the community structure.

For the purpose of representing a temporal network, it can be assumed as a sequence of static graphs (snapshots) or as a network with time annotations on its nodes/edges that represent its time evolution. The former approach requires to specify the size of our time window that defines the time instances of snapshot construction. The later, is related to events, like edge/node insertion or deletion or its existence interval. The notion of a time annotation may have different aspects/interpretations depending on the application. The following three aspects have been used in the literature [27]:

1. *Point Networks:* every link among two vertices x and y, which has been created at certain time t, can be represented as a triplet $e = (x, y, t)$.
2. *Time Interval Networks:* the time-interval connection of two nodes is represented as a quadruplet $e = (x, y, t, \Delta t)$. Δt is the duration of the link between the vertices x and y.
3. *Incremental Networks:* edges/nodes can only be added and deletions are forbidden.

In the last few years, many surveys in the field of CD in temporal networks have been published. These are discussed briefly in Sect. 2. The main contribution of this paper is in Sect. 3, which can be summarized as follows: 1) we provide an updated overview of the current state-of-the-art methods for CD in temporal networks since the last years there are quite a few new related results, and 2) we further classify the approaches in global CD and local CD in temporal networks. The latter contribution concerns the discussion on new methods related as to how a community around a given set of nodes evolves in time. This approach is appropriate in cases where one is not interested at discovering all communities, leading to large efficiency and effectiveness gains. Finally, we conclude in Sect. 4.

2   Related Work

In this section are discussed existing surveys on CD in temporal networks. In [4] a general classification of methods is proposed into two classes: 1) *Online* (real time, incremental detection) and 2) *Offline* (prior knowledge of network changes). Similarly, in [20], authors identify the same two classes but they focus on online approaches dividing them into two sub-classes: 1) *Temporal Smoothness*, where at each snapshot a static CD algorithm is run from scratch and 2) *Dynamic Update*, where the communities are updated based on the differences of two consecutive snapshots.

A very good survey is [32], where the dynamic CD algorithms have been classified based on the strategy they use for detecting meaning-full evolving communities. They propose three classes of approaches: 1) *Instant - optimal*, where the algorithms detect communities from scratch at each snapshot and then match them between consecutive snapshots, 2) *Temporal Trade - off*, where the algorithms detect communities comparing the topology of two consecutive snapshots and 3) *Cross - Time*, where the algorithms discover communities using the information of all snapshots. Similarly in [2], the authors identify three similar categories as well: 1) *Two - Stage methods* that detect the communities from scratch at each snapshot and then match them across different snapshots, 2) *Evolutionary Clustering*, that detect communities based on the changes in the topology between two consecutive snapshots and 3) *Coupling Graph* that creates an aggregate network containing all snapshots and then uses a static CD algorithm.

In [12] the authors classified the dynamic CD algorithms into four classes: 1) *Independent Detection*, here the communities are detected from scratch at each snapshot and then they are matched among consecutive snapshots, 2) *Dependent Detection*, where communities are identified based on the changes of the topology between two consecutive snapshots, 3) *Simultaneous Detection*, where communities are detected by using the information from all snapshots and 4) *Dynamic Detection*, where the communities are updated based on the network updates. Additionally, in [17] four classes of evolving clustering methods are provided that are similar to the preceding classification: 1) *Sequential mapping-driven*, 2) *Temporal smoothing-driven*, 3) *Milestone detection-driven* and 4) *Incremental adaptation-driven*.

In [7], a survey is conducted exclusively for incremental (online) CD methods in temporal networks. The proposed classification contains two subcategories of incremental methods: 1) *Community Detection in Fully Temporal Networks*, where insertions and deletions of nodes and edges are permitted and 2) *Community Detection in Growing Temporal Networks*, where only insertions of nodes and edges are permitted.

Finally, it is worth mentioning that multilayer networks can be used for dynamic community detection [23]. In particular, a multilayer network is a network made of multiple networks, called layers, where each layer has the same number of nodes, but different edge connections. The multilayer network model is commonly employed in the study of temporal networks, in which each snapshot is represented as a layer and all layers are interconnected based on their time relationship.

3 Detecting Communities in Temporal Networks: Classification

In this section, is provided a classification of dynamic CD methods. At first, the different versions of the dynamic CD problem are discerned into two: *Global* and *Local*. The former concerns the identification of all communities and their evolution in the temporal network, while the latter concerns the identification of a community around a given set of seed nodes and its evolution in the temporal network. This corresponds to the division between global and local CD in static graphs. The main body of the literature concerns the global version of the problem, however there is recently an admittedly small number of publications on the local version. Although the local version uses techniques especially from the global online dynamic CD category we believe that it constitutes a class by itself since there are many differences in terms of efficiency as well as effectiveness of the methods. Thus we identify the following 5 classes of methods:

1. Global:
   (a) Community Detection from scratch and match
   (b) Dependent or Temporal Trade - off Community Detection
   (c) Simultaneous or Offline Community Detection
   (d) Online Community Detection in fully Temporal Networks and in growing Temporal Networks
2. Local: Community Detection in Temporal Networks using Seed Nodes (Table 1)

Table 1. Overview of the proposed temporal community detection classification.

Global temporal community detection		
Class	Description	References
From scratch and match	Static algorithm at each snapshot and matching	[10, 24, 30, 31, 40]
Dependent or temporal trade-off	Based on the topology of two adjacent snapshots	[13, 18, 26, 34–36, 43]
Simultaneous or offline	Creation of single graph - run static algorithm on it	[15, 16, 22, 28, 29, 39]
Online community detection	Update in proportion to network modifications	[1, 6, 9, 11, 19, 33, 38, 41, 42, 46–48]
Local temporal community detection		
Class	Description	References
Using seed nodes	Update only the area around the seed node	[3, 14, 21, 44, 45]

In the following, we present in detail these five classes by discussing recent representative methods.

3.1 Community Detection from Scratch and Match

In this class, a static CD algorithm is applied on each snapshot from scratch and then the communities that have been found at snapshot $t + 1$ are matched (by using a similarity metric like Jaccard similarity) with the communities found at snapshot t. The advantage is that communities can be detected in parallel and existing methods for static CD can be used. On the other hand, instability (the communities may have a lot of changes between consecutive snapshots) and inefficiency (in each snapshot a static community detection algorithm is invoked) are its main two drawbacks. In the following, we discuss some representative methods of this category (more such methods can be found in [24,31,40]).

In [10], given as input a sequence of snapshots of a network, they initially find the network representatives based on the common nodes between two consecutive snapshots and list the communities. Then, the community representatives are identified and consequently, the relation of communities between different snapshots (G_t, G_{t+1}, G_{t+2}) is established by finding the predecessor(s) and successor(s) for each community. Finally, the dynamic CD is performed by looking at six different events that may happen to a community (Grown, Merged, Split, Shrunken, Born and Vanished). For all the events they track forward the network sequence of snapshots with the exception of the shrunken and split communities where a backtracking process is applied.

In [30] the authors use sliding windows to track the dynamics by computing partitions for each time slice and by modifying the community description at time t using the structures found at times $t - 1$ and $t + 1$. More specifically, the data set is divided into time windows and for each one a static CD algorithm is used. Then, the similarity scores between communities at times $t - 2, t - 1, t, t + 1, t+2$ are computed. This information allows to easily distinguish noise from real evolution. Consequently, this information is used to smooth out the communities evolution. Then, communities which have been generated by unduly splits are merged, while communities that have been generated by artificial merges are separated. At the end of the procedure, a description of the network evolution is obtained.

3.2 Dependent or Temporal Trade-off Community Detection

Methods in this class process repeatedly network changes. Initially, by using a static CD algorithm they find partitions for the initial state (first snapshot) of the network, and then they find communities at snapshot t by using information from both the current snapshot (t) and previous snapshots $(< t)$. Methods in this subcategory don't suffer from the instability problem and are faster than those from the previous category. On the other hand, the avalanche effect[1] and the fact that this method is not parallelizable are its two main drawbacks. Global and multiobjective optimization methods are the most common subcategories

---

[1] The avalanche effect describes the phenomenon when communities can experience substantial drifts compared to what a static algorithm would find on the static network at a particular time instance.

in this class. In the following, we discuss some representative methods of this category (more such methods can be found in [13,34,35]).

In [18] they detect evolutionary community structure in a weighted dynamic network. For each snapshot the follow process is iteratively applied: i) Firstly, the initial partition is detected (using the input matrix that describes the previous) and then ii) the community is expanded based on the assumption that the nodes are attached to the cluster that provides the highest modularity gain. Finally, in the last phase, the merging process starts if and only if the modularity of the merged community is higher than each partition separately. Another recent dynamic community detection algorithm is proposed in [36]. This method utilizes all the past information from the network and by using the algorithm C-Blondel, which is a modification of the Louvain algorithm, manages to compress the Network. Thus, the compressed network consists of all the historical snapshots and the changes which have been occurred on the network.

In [26], a multi-objective optimization approach has been adopted. Initially, the probability fusion method is adopted and two different approaches (neighbor diversity and neighbor crowd) are used. In this way, suitable communities are created in a fast and accurate way. Moreover, by utilizing a progression metric, the authors can detect the similarities of formed communities between two successive snapshots. The same approach has also been used by [43]. Their method, called DYN-MODPSO, is suitable for large-scale dynamic CD. Like the previous method, they use two different approaches optimizing NMI (Normalized Mutual Information) and CS (Community Score) metrics.

3.3 Simultaneous or Offline Community Detection

Methods in this class discover partitions by considering all states of the temporal network at the same time. A single multilayer network is created from all snapshots using edges based on the relationship between nodes at the same snapshot and at adjacent (preceding and succeeding) snapshots. Then, the communities are detected by using an appropriately modified static algorithm on the multilayer network. Methods in this category don't suffer from instability and the avalanche effect. On the other hand, they have certain limitations like a requirement for a fixed number of communities, or lacking a mechanism to determine operations between temporally successive partitions (like merge), etc. In the following, we discuss some representative methods of this category (more such methods can be found in [15,28,29,39]).

A significant study of the fundamental limits of discovering community structure in dynamic networks is done in [16]. The authors analyze the boundaries of detectability for a Dynamic Stochastic Block Model (DSBM) that nodes affiliations can change over time (from one community to other), and edges are created separately at each time step. The method exploits the powerful tools of probabilistic generative models and Bayesian inference, and by utilizing the cavity method, they obtain a clearly defined detectability threshold as a function of the rate of change and the communities strength. Below this threshold, they claim that no efficient algorithm can identify the communities better than chance. Then, they give two algorithms that are optimal in the sense that they succeed in detecting the correct communities up to this up to this threshold. The first algorithm utilizes belief propagation, which provides an asymptotically optimal accuracy, while the second is an efficient spectral algorithm, founded on linearizing the belief propagation equations.

Another algorithm based on clique enumeration is proposed in [22]. They use an adaptation for temporal networks of a well-known recursive static back-tracking algorithm, Bron-Kerbosch [8]. The parameter "Δ-slice degeneracy" is introduced, which is a modification of the degeneracy parameter that is often used in static graphs, and it is an easy way to measure the sparsity of the network.

3.4 Online Community Detection

In these methods, the temporal network is not considered as a sequence of snapshots, but as a succession of network transformations instead. The methods are initialized by discovering partitions at time 0 and then the community structure is updated in each update of nodes/edges. This class of methods is further divided into two main subcategories of incremental methods: 1) *Community Detection in Fully Temporal Networks*, where insertions and deletions of nodes and edges are allowed and 2) *Community Detection in Growing Temporal Networks*, where only insertions of nodes and edges are allowed. In addition, the methods of this class can either handle network updates in batches of arbitrary size (one extreme is to consider batches of size 1, that is after each update the community structure is updated). One advantage of this method is that algorithms for static CD can be used with easy modifications. Moreover, this method does not suffer from instability, and it is quite efficient since updates for the community structure are usually applied locally. In the following, we discuss some representative methods of this category (more such methods can be found in [1,9,47,48]).

In [46], a filtering technique is introduced, which is called "Δ-Screening". The technique of Δ-Screening captures in each time step, new inserted/deleted nodes (V_t) that impact the structure of the network. Initially, a static algorithm discovers the communities at time $t = 0$. Then, for each time step, all the added nodes are assigned a new community label. Then Δ-Screening captures a subset R_t ($R_t \subseteq V_t$) of these nodes. Consequently, the static algorithm (mentioned above) is invoked in order to detect the evolution of the communities, visiting only the subset of nodes R_t, of the most significant changes.

An incremental, modified Louvain algorithm [5] is proposed in [11]. Nodes and edges are inserted in or deleted from the network as time evolves, and Louvain is implemented only for those communities that are affected. The local modularity metric is applied only in a part of the network, where the changes are taking place. As a result, stability and efficiency are the two main advantages of the method. A dynamic CD algorithm, which is a modified version of the static algorithm in [37], based on distance dynamics is proposed in [19]. By utilizing the local interaction model, based on the Jaccard distance, the method in [19] overcomes the well-known disadvantages of modularity-based algorithms by detecting small communities or outliers. This is achieved regardless of the processing order of the increment set and the algorithm can achieve the same community partition results in near-linear time.

One recent, efficient and parameter-free incremental method, based on the Matthew effect, is proposed in [42]. Unlike other incremental approaches, changes are processed in batches. Between two consecutive snapshots, deletion and insertion of nodes and edges are performed. The degree of nodes as well as node and group attractiveness for the purpose of the changed sub-graph to be extracted are used. Then, the affected and non-affected communities are calculated iteratively between each pair of consecutive snapshots. The same dynamic CD framework, based on information dynamics, is used in [41].

An online version of the Clique Percolation Method (CPM), combined with the Label Propagation Algorithm (LPA) is presented in [6]. The proposed algorithm OLCPM (Online Label Propagation Clique Percolation Method) is a two step framework which firstly uses the Dynamic CPM to update the communities locally by utilizing a stream model, in order to improve the efficiency. Then, by using LPA it solves the problem of nodes affiliation while a node can be allocated to one or more communities. Finally, in [33], the algorithms named Tiles is presented. Tiles is a streaming algorithm, treating each topological perturbation as a domino tile fall: whenever a new interaction emerges in the network, Tiles first updates the communities locally, then propagates the changes to the surrounding nodes modifying the neighbors' partition memberships.

3.5   Local Community Detection in Temporal Networks

Given a set of seed nodes Z, our goal is to detect the community which includes Z. The main assumption in this case is that Z is of high importance (e.g., high degree centrality) and act as the community reference point. This problem differs from general temporal CD approaches since our objective is to discover the community defined around the set of seed nodes. Notice that the online methods described in Sect. 3.4 are global in the sense that they maintain a partition of the network in communities. The algorithms in this class are very efficient since it is required from them to maintain a single community.

In [21] a hierarchical algorithm is presented. This method discovers communities in temporal networks based on hubs (nodes of high degree centrality) by grouping nodes in their vicinity. Each node carries hub information (e.g., distance between nodes, hub and parent nodes, threshold level, etc.) and the idea is based on propagating this information through the network. Then, the intra-node hubs transfer the information (message) to the outer nodes and in this way, all non-hub nodes are assigned to the closest hub and the fuzzy membership of each node is calculated. This method can be readily adopted for the case of a set of seeds propagating the information only in their vicinity. An advantage of this method is that only a small number of processing steps (adding or removing edges) have to be performed too update the partitions while at the same time is parameter-free.

A dynamic algorithm for local community detection using a set of seeds is proposed in [44]. Initially, a greedy static algorithm is used in order to discover the local community. During this process, the community initially contains only the seed node and in each iteration one neighbor node is added maximizing a chosen fitness score. At the end of this step there is a collection of sequences (vertex, interior/border edge sum and fitness score), in increasing order of fitness score. Then, the next phase start and in each network change, the algorithm modify the collection of sequences. If after the modification the fitness score of a position is higher than the fitness score of the next position, then the node is removed and interior/border edges are modified as well. When this step is finished, the collection of modified sequences is scanned and if in one position the increasing order of the fitness score is violated then the set from this position until its end is removed. Finally, the static algorithm is used one more time in order to add new nodes to the local community. A full streaming version of the seed set expansion method is described in [45].

Another approach is Evoleaders [14] that employs leader nodes with followers, in order to identify the evolution of the communities. The "Top leaders" algorithm [25] initialize D leader nodes, one for each community, and associate the nodes of the network to an appropriate leader. In this way, the communities are constructed and, by utilizing the highest centrality node, a new leader is picked and the old one is replaced. Then, in each time step, for the initialization of the leader nodes, their common neighbors from the previous and the current time step is taken into consideration and the Top leaders algorithm is used iteratively. Consequently, the process of community splitting starts and then all small communities can be merged, in an appropriate manner, so that the quality (in terms of modularity) of the communities is improved. Finally, very recently, [3] described a framework that strengthens the vicinity of the seed set (called anchors) exploiting the fact that the seed set is of central importance for the evolving community.

4   Conclusion

Our aim in this survey is to reexamine all the recent surveys in the field of CD in temporal networks and to propose a new category of methods based on local community detection. Thus, we propose five classes of algorithms and discuss some representative methods. The advantages and drawbacks of each class are also discussed. In future work, it will be beneficial to delve into, in more detail, the local community detection class and to enrich the current survey with more literature.

Acknowledgment. This research was supported by the Hellenic Foundation for Research and Innovation (H.F.R.I.) under the "2nd Call for H.F.R.I. Research Projects to support Faculty Members & Researchers" (Project Number: 3480).

References

1. Akachar, E., Ouhbi, B., Frikh, B.: ACSIMCD: a 2-phase framework for detecting meaningful communities in dynamic social networks. Futur. Gener. Comput. Syst. **125**, 399–420 (2021)
2. Aynaud, T., Fleury, E., Guillaume, J.-L., Wang, Q.: Communities in evolving networks: definitions, detection, and analysis techniques. In: Mukherjee, A., Choudhury, M., Peruani, F., Ganguly, N., Mitra, B. (eds.) Dynamics on and of Complex Networks, vol. 2, pp. 159–200. Springer, New York (2013). https://doi.org/10.1007/978-1-4614-6729-8_9
3. Baltsou, G., Tsichlas, K.: Dynamic community detection with anchors (2022)
4. Bansal, S., Bhowmick, S., Paymal, P.: Fast community detection for dynamic complex networks. In: da F. Costa, L., Evsukoff, A., Mangioni, G., Menezes, R. (eds.) CompleNet 2010. CCIS, vol. 116, pp. 196–207. Springer, Heidelberg (2011). https://doi.org/10.1007/978-3-642-25501-4_20
5. Blondel, V.D., Guillaume, J.-L., Lambiotte, R., Lefebvre, E.: Fast unfolding of communities in large networks. J. Stat. Mech: Theory Exp. **2008**(10), P10008 (2008)
6. Boudebza, S., Cazabet, R., Azouaou, F., Nouali, O.: OLCPM: an online framework for detecting overlapping communities in dynamic social networks. Comput. Commun. **123**, 36–51 (2018)
7. Bouhatem, F., Hadj, A.A.E., Souam, F., Dafeur, A.: Incremental methods for community detection in both fully and growing dynamic networks. Acta Universitatis Sapientiae Informatica **13**(2), 220–250 (2021)
8. Bron, C., Kerbosch, J.: Algorithm 457: finding all cliques of an undirected graph. Commun. ACM **16**(9), 575–577 (1973)
9. Chen, Z., Sun, A., Xiao, X.: Incremental community detection on large complex attributed network. ACM Trans. Knowl. Discov. Data (TKDD) **15**(6), 1–20 (2021)
10. Chen, Z., Wilson, K.A., Jin, Y., Hendrix, W., Samatova, N.F.: Detecting and tracking community dynamics in evolutionary networks. In: 2010 IEEE International Conference on Data Mining Workshops, pp. 318–327 (2010)
11. Cordeiro, M., Sarmento, R.P., Gama, J.: Dynamic community detection in evolving networks using locality modularity optimization. Soc. Netw. Anal. Min. **6**(1), 1–20 (2016). https://doi.org/10.1007/s13278-016-0325-1
12. Dakiche, N., Tayeb, F.B.-S., Slimani, Y., Benatchba, K.: Tracking community evolution in social networks: a survey. Inf. Process. Manage. **56**(3), 1084–1102 (2019)
13. Folino, F., Pizzuti, C.: An evolutionary multiobjective approach for community discovery in dynamic networks. IEEE Trans. Knowl. Data Eng. **26**(8), 1838–1852 (2013)
14. Gao, W., Luo, W., Bu, C.: Evolutionary community discovery in dynamic networks based on leader nodes. In: 2016 International Conference on Big Data and Smart Computing (BigComp), pp. 53–60 (2016)
15. Gauvin, L., Panisson, A., Cattuto, C.: Detecting the community structure and activity patterns of temporal networks: a non-negative tensor factorization approach. PLoS ONE **9**(1), e86028 (2014)
16. Ghasemian, A., Zhang, P., Clauset, A., Moore, C., Peel, L.: Detectability thresholds and optimal algorithms for community structure in dynamic networks. Phys. Rev. X **6**(3), 031005 (2016)
17. Giatsoglou, M., Vakali, A.: Capturing social data evolution using graph clustering. IEEE Internet Comput. **17**(1), 74–79 (2013)

18. Guo, C., Wang, J., Zhang, Z.: Evolutionary community structure discovery in dynamic weighted networks. Phys. A **413**, 565–576 (2014)
19. Guo, Q., Zhang, L., Wu, B., Zeng, X.: Dynamic community detection based on distance dynamics. In: 2016 IEEE/ACM International Conference on Advances in Social Networks Analysis and Mining (ASONAM), pp. 329–336 (2016)
20. Hartmann, T., Kappes, A., Wagner, D.: Clustering evolving networks. In: Kliemann, L., Sanders, P. (eds.) Algorithm Engineering. LNCS, vol. 9220, pp. 280–329. Springer, Cham (2016). https://doi.org/10.1007/978-3-319-49487-6_9
21. Held, P., Kruse, R.: Detecting overlapping community hierarchies in dynamic graphs. In: 2016 IEEE/ACM International Conference on Advances in Social Networks Analysis and Mining (ASONAM), pp. 1063–1070. IEEE (2016)
22. Himmel, A.-S., Molter, H., Niedermeier, R., Sorge, M.: Enumerating maximal cliques in temporal graphs. In: 2016 IEEE/ACM International Conference on Advances in Social Networks Analysis and Mining (ASONAM), pp. 337–344. IEEE (2016)
23. Huang, X., Chen, D., Ren, T., Wang, D.: A survey of community detection methods in multilayer networks. Data Min. Knowl. Disc. **35**(1), 1–45 (2020). https://doi.org/10.1007/s10618-020-00716-6
24. Mohammadmosaferi, K.K., Naderi, H.: Evolution of communities in dynamic social networks: an efficient map-based approach. Expert Syst. Appl. **147**, 113221 (2020)
25. Khorasgani, R.R., Chen, J., Zaiane, O.R.: Top leaders community detection approach in information networks. In: 4th SNA-KDD Workshop on Social Network Mining and Analysis. Citeseer (2010)
26. Li, W., Zhou, X., Yang, C., Fan, Y., Wang, Z., Liu, Y.: Multi-objective optimization algorithm based on characteristics fusion of dynamic social networks for community discovery. Inf. Fusion **79**, 110–123 (2022)
27. Liakos, P., Papakonstantinopoulou, K., Stefou, T., Delis, A.: On compressing temporal graphs (2022)
28. Matias, C., Miele,V.: Statistical clustering of temporal networks through a dynamic stochastic block model series B statistical methodology (2017)
29. Matias, C., Rebafka, T., Villers, F.: A semiparametric extension of the stochastic block model for longitudinal networks. Biometrika **105**(3), 665–680 (2018)
30. Morini, M., Flandrin, P., Fleury, E., Venturini, T., Jensen, P.: Revealing evolutions in dynamical networks. arXiv preprint arXiv:1707.02114 (2017)
31. Palla, G., Barabási, A.-L., Vicsek, T.: Quantifying social group evolution. Nature **446**(7136), 664–667 (2007)
32. Rossetti, G., Cazabet, R.: Community discovery in dynamic networks: a survey. ACM Comput. Surv. **51**(2), 1–37 (2018)
33. Rossetti, G., Pappalardo, L., Pedreschi, D., Giannotti, F.: Tiles: an online algorithm for community discovery in dynamic social networks. Mach. Learn. **106**(8), 1213–1241 (2016). https://doi.org/10.1007/s10994-016-5582-8
34. Rozenshtein, P., Tatti, N., Gionis, A.: Discovering dynamic communities in interaction networks. In: Calders, T., Esposito, F., Hüllermeier, E., Meo, R. (eds.) ECML PKDD 2014. LNCS (LNAI), vol. 8725, pp. 678–693. Springer, Heidelberg (2014). https://doi.org/10.1007/978-3-662-44851-9_43
35. Safdari, H., Contisciani, M., De Bacco, C.: Reciprocity, community detection, and link prediction in dynamic networks. J. Phys. Complex. **3**(1), 015010 (2022)
36. Seifikar, M., Farzi, S., Barati, M.: C-Blondel: an efficient Louvain-based dynamic community detection algorithm. IEEE Trans. Comput. Soc. Syst. **7**(2), 308–318 (2020)

37. Shao, J., Han, Z., Yang, Q., Zhou, T.: Community detection based on distance dynamics. In: Proceedings of the 21th ACM SIGKDD International Conference on Knowledge Discovery and Data Mining, pp. 1075–1084 (2015)
38. Xing, S., Cheng, J., Yang, H., Leng, M., Zhang, W., Chen, X.: IncNSA: detecting communities incrementally from time-evolving networks based on node similarity. Int. J. Mod. Phys. C $31(07)$, 2050094 (2020)
39. Sun, J., Faloutsos, C., Papadimitriou, S., Yu, P.S.: GraphScope: parameter-free mining of large time-evolving graphs. In: KDD 2007, pp. 687–696. Association for Computing Machinery, New York (2007)
40. Sun, Y., Tang, J., Pan, L., Li, J.: Matrix based community evolution events detection in online social networks. In: 2015 IEEE International Conference on Smart City/SocialCom/SustainCom (SmartCity), pp. 465–470. IEEE (2015)
41. Sun, Z., Sheng, J., Wang, B., Ullah, A., Khawaja, F.R.: Identifying communities in dynamic networks using information dynamics. Entropy $22(4)$, 425 (2020)
42. Sun, Z., et al.: Dynamic community detection based on the Matthew effect. Physica A Stat. Mech. Appl. 597, 127315 (2022)
43. Yin, Y., Zhao, Y., Li, H., Dong, X.: Multi-objective evolutionary clustering for large-scale dynamic community detection. Inf. Sci. 549, 269–287 (2021)
44. Zakrzewska, A., Bader, D.A.: A dynamic algorithm for local community detection in graphs. In: ASONAM 2015, pp. 559–564 (2015)
45. Zakrzewska, A., Bader, D.A.: Tracking local communities in streaming graphs with a dynamic algorithm. Soc. Netw. Anal. Min. $6(1)$, 1–16 (2016). https://doi.org/10.1007/s13278-016-0374-5
46. Zarayeneh, N., Kalyanaraman, A.: A fast and efficient incremental approach toward dynamic community detection. In: Proceedings of the 2019 IEEE/ACM International Conference on Advances in Social Networks Analysis and Mining, ASONAM 2019, pp. 9–16. Association for Computing Machinery, New York (2019)
47. Zardi, H., Alharbi, B., Karamti, W., Karamti, H., Alabdulkreem, E.: Detection of community structures in dynamic social networks based on message distribution and structural/attribute similarities. IEEE Access 9, 67028–67041 (2021)
48. Zhuang, D., Chang, J.M., Li, M.: Dynamo: dynamic community detection by incrementally maximizing modularity. IEEE Trans. Knowl. Data Eng. $33(5)$, 1934–1945 (2019)

Machine Learning and Big Data in Health Care (ML@HC) Special Session

Machine Learning and Big Data in Health Care (ML@HC)

In the present era, Machine Learning (ML) has been extensively used for many applications to real world problems. ML techniques are very suitable for Big Data Mining, to extract new knowledge and build predictive models that given a new input can provide in the output a reliable estimate. On the other hand, healthcare is one of the fastest growing data segments of the digital world, with healthcare data increasing at a rate of about 50 % per year. There are three primary sources of big data in healthcare: providers and payers (including EMR, imaging, insurance claims and pharmacy data), -omic data (including genomic, epigenomic, proteomic, and metabolomic data), and patients and non-providers (including data from smart phone and Internet activities sensors and monitoring tools).

The growth of big data in oncology, as well as other severe diseases (such as Alzheimer's Disease, etc.) can provide unprecedented opportunities to explore the biopsychosocial characteristics of these diseases and for descriptive observation, hypothesis generation, and prediction for clinical, research and business issues. The results of big data analysis can be incorporated into standards and guidelines and will directly impact clinical decision making. Oncologists and professionals from related medical fields can increasingly evaluate the results from research studies and commercial analytical products that are based on big data, using ML techniques. Furthermore, all these applications can be Web-based, so are very useful for the post treatment of the patients.

The aim of this special session was to serve as an interdisciplinary forum for bringing together specialists from the scientific areas of Computer & Web Engineering, Data Science, Semantic Computing, Bioinformatics-Personalized Medicine, clinicians and caregivers. The focus of this special session is on current technological advances and challenges about the development of big data-driven algorithms, methods and tools; furthermore, to investigate how ML-aware applications can contribute towards Big Data analysis on post treatment follow up.

The stimulus to this scientific forum was the presentation of the ONCORELIEF project (H2020-GA No. 875392): *A Smart Digital Guardian Angel Enhancing Cancer Patient Wellbeing and Health Status Improvement Following Treatment.* ONCOR-ELIEF aims to deliver a framework that consists of three main sub-systems: 1) a *back-end data platform* where data are securely collected from heterogeneous sources, anonymized, annotated and stored, etc., 2) an Artificial Intelligence (*AI) engine* built on top of the back-end platform, which consumes and analyses data, extracts important features, produces meaningful AI models and updates them accordingly, produces correlations, etc.) a *downloadable application (ONCORELIEF Guardian Angel)* available for portable devices, which will be connected with the ONCORELIEF platform and with patients' sensing devices. It runs locally and uses models produced by the AI engine to extract insights on the patient life and condition and make suggestions. The GA may optionally send data back both for research-related reasons (another source of big data) and for computation offloading reasons (AI engine not powerful enough on the mobile phone). These models are then downloaded to personal, portable devices in order to locally analyze individual data and to generate *QoL (Quality of Life) indices*, recommendations and warnings for the patients using the application. The application has been implemented and a pilot phase is running. The first results, with real data obtained from cancer patients, were reported and they are very promising.

Furthermore, a variety of Machine Learning methods have been presented insight the special session, such as explainable interactive image classification and deep learning techniques in order to train predictive models, using big data. Finally, these methods have been used for medical image classification, big -omics data analysis, supportive recommendations to cancer patients, neurological disorder patients and dementia risk prediction.

We are grateful to the various authors that trusted their work with this special issue. Many thanks are also due to Prof. L. Iliadis and Dr A. Papaleonidas, program co-chair and organizing – publication & publicity co-chair respectively at AIAI 2022, who have greatly helped us to organize this special session. They could not have done a better job at administering all publishing details and letting us focus on the academic part. We are also obliged to the people that have served as members of the editorial review board (in alphabetical order): Prof. E. Georgopoulos, Dr I. Kalamaras, Dr S. Koussouris, Dr D. Koutsomitropoulos, Dr A. Scherrer, Prof. S. Sioutas, Prof. K. Tsichlas and T. Zimmerman. Their eager participation in the review process, the sharing of their time and the contribution of their expertise have been of outmost importance for realizing this Special Session.

Funding: This special session received partial funding by the ONCORELIEF project - CERTH/ITI.

Organization

Program chairs

Spiros Likothanassis   University of Patras, Greece
K. Votis   Researcher B', CERTH/ITI, Greece

Program Committee

S. Sioutas   University of Patras, Greece
K. Tsichlas   University of Patras, Greece
E. Georgopoulos   University of Peloponnese, Greece
D. Koutsomitropoulos   University of Patras, Greece
I. Kalamaras   CERTH/ITI, Greece
A. Scherrer   Fraunhofer Institute for Industrial Mathematics,
                                        Germany
S. Koussouris   Suite5, Cyprus
T. Zimmerman   Fraunhofer Institute for Industrial Mathematics,
                                        Germany

Machine Learning and Big Data in Health Care (ML@HC) (Invited SPEECH)

Smart Digital Guardian Angel Enhancing Cancer Patient Wellbeing and Health Status Improvement Following Treatment

S. Athanassopoulos, Gabrielle Oestreicher and S. Likothanassis

Abstract. ONCORELIEF aims to deliver a framework that consists of three main sub-systems: 1) a **back-end data platform** where data are securely collected from heterogeneous sources, anonymised, annotated and stored, etc., 2) an **AI engine** built on top of the back-end platform, which consumes and analyses data, extracts important features, produces meaningful AI models and updates them accordingly, produces correlations, etc., 3) a **downloadable application (ONCORELIEF Guardian Angel)** available for portable devices, which will be connected with the ONCORELIEF platform and with patients' sensing devices. It runs locally and uses models produced by the AI engine to extract insights on the patient life and condition and make suggestions. The GA may optionally send data back both for research-related reasons (another source of big data) and for computation offloading reasons (AI engine not powerful enough on the mobile phone). These models are then downloaded to personal, portable devices in order to locally analyze individual data and to generate **QoL (Quality of Life) indices**, recommendations and warnings for the patients using the application. The application has been implemented and a pilot phase is running. The first results, with real data obtained from cancer patients, were reported and they are very promising.

CAIPI in Practice: Towards Explainable Interactive Medical Image Classification

Emanuel Slany[1]([✉]), Yannik Ott[1], Stephan Scheele[1], Jan Paulus[2], and Ute Schmid[1]

[1] Fraunhofer IIS, Fraunhofer Institute for Integrated Circuits IIS, Project Group Comprehensible Artificial Intelligence, Bamberg, Germany
{emanuel.slany,yannik.ott,stephan.scheele,ute.schmid}@iis.fraunhofer.de
[2] Faculty of Electrical Engineering, Precision Engineering, Information Technology, Nuremberg Institute of Technology Georg Simon Ohm, Nuremberg, Germany
jan.paulus@th-nuernberg.de

Abstract. Would you trust physicians if they cannot explain their decisions to you? Medical diagnostics using machine learning gained enormously in importance within the last decade. However, without further enhancements many state-of-the-art machine learning methods are not suitable for medical application. The most important reasons are insufficient data set quality and the black-box behavior of machine learning algorithms such as Deep Learning models. Consequently, end-users cannot correct the model's decisions and the corresponding explanations. The latter is crucial for the trustworthiness of machine learning in the medical domain. The research field explainable interactive machine learning searches for methods that address both shortcomings. This paper extends the explainable and interactive CAIPI algorithm and provides an interface to simplify human-in-the-loop approaches for image classification. The interface enables the end-user (1) to investigate and (2) to correct the model's prediction and explanation, and (3) to influence the data set quality. After CAIPI optimization with only a single counterexample per iteration, the model achieves an accuracy of 97.48% on the Medical MNIST and 95.02% on the Fashion MNIST. This accuracy is approximately equal to state-of-the-art Deep Learning optimization procedures. Besides, CAIPI reduces the labeling effort by approximately 80%.

Keywords: XAI · Interactive learning · CAIPI · Image classification

1 Introduction

Medical diagnostics based on machine learning (ML), such as Deep Learning (DL) for visual cancer detection, have become increasingly important in the last decade [7]. However, on the one hand, clinicians are rarely experts in implementing ML models, on the other hand, even if the data sets are of high quality, they

© IFIP International Federation for Information Processing 2022
Published by Springer Nature Switzerland AG 2022
I. Maglogiannis et al. (Eds.): AIAI 2022 Workshops, IFIP AICT 652, pp. 389–400, 2022.
https://doi.org/10.1007/978-3-031-08341-9_31

are rarely intuitive for ML engineers. Additionally, many state-of-the-art DL algorithms are black-boxes to end-users. For ML in critical application domains like medical diagnostics, it is crucial to close the gap between clinical domain expertise and engineering-heavy ML methods.

This paper aims to enable domain experts such as clinicians to train and apply trustworthy ML models. Based on the ML pipeline, starting from data preparation to the decision-making process, we formulate three core requirements for the domain of medical diagnostics: 1) First, it is important to keep the quality of the data under control. 2) Secondly, it is necessary that the decisions of the ML model are disclosed in a transparent way - known as explainable machine learning (XAI) - where it is crucial in critical applications that models make the right decisions for the right reasons. 3) Finally, the clinical expert should be able to be involved in the optimization process [3] to allow *interactive* correction of both, explanations and decisions. Such interactive ML methods are closely related to active learning [15], in which instance and label selection occur in the interaction between algorithm and agent. By meeting these requirements, the user gains end-to-end control over the entire ML process, involving the clinical expert *interactively* in the ML process (human-in-the-loop).

We aim to combine both, explainable and interactive machine learning, denoted by *eXplainable Interactive Machine Learning* (XIML) [16]. Our domain of interest is the classification of medical images from diagnostics in everyday clinical practices, such as classifying computer tomography scans into their corresponding categories like e.g. abdomen, chest, brain, etc. For our use case, we are interested in providing a visual explanation for such a categorical classification and furthermore allow the user to correct both, the classification and the explanation.

Our core contribution focuses on four research questions about improving the applicability and efficiency of the CAIPI [16] algorithm, exemplary applied to the domain of medical diagnostics. CAIPI enables model optimization to be performed while interactively including user feedback using generated counterexamples for predictions and explanations:

(R1) Do explanation corrections enhance the model's performance [16]?
(R2) Do explanation corrections improve the explanation quality?
(R3) Does CAIPI benefit from explanation corrections for wrong predictions?
(R4) Is CAIPI beneficial compared to default DL optimization techniques?

We will outline the benefits of XIML for the medical domain in Sect. 2, recap the most important of CAIPI's core concepts and our extensions in Sect. 3, and describe our experimental setting in Sect. 4. We will answer the research questions in Sect. 5. Section 6 will discuss the results. Finally, Sect. 7 will conclude our work and summarize future research questions.

2   Related Work

Human-in-the-loop approaches provide benefits for the application of ML in the medical domain. Even if ML systems for medical diagnostics account for expert knowledge, they can still suffer from a lack of trust, since knowledge bases can be manipulated [5]. The authors [5] propose an architecture that allows an authorized user to enrich the knowledge base while protecting the system from manipulation. Although we do not provide an explicit architecture, our scope is closely related, as we aim to enable experts to control the data quality, and to monitor and correct the behavior of the ML system. Apart from trustworthiness, another major benefit of interactive ML algorithms lies in their efficiency. For instance, extracting patient groups is more efficient when using sub-clustering with human expert knowledge compared to traditional clustering [4].

A central explanatory method, which CAIPI is based on, is called *Local Interactive Model-agnostic Explanation* (LIME) [10], which samples local interpretable features to fit a simplified and explainable surrogate model where the surrogate model's parameters become human interpretable. Although LIME is one of the most famous local explanation methods, there are alternatives such as the *Model Agnostic suPervised Local Explanations* (MAPLE) method [9] that relies on linear approximation of Random Forest models for explanations.

It is worth noting that local explanation procedures are limited to explain single prediction instances only. Also, they require additional explanatory models, which also introduce uncertainty [11]. The models do not explain the black-boxes per se, since they are ML models with different optimization objective for themselves. In contrast to local explanations, global explanations aim to explain the prediction model in general. This can be achieved by approximating the complex black-box model by a simpler interpretable model. An algorithm to approximate complex models with decision trees is proposed by [1]. The major benefit of global explanations is that the interpretable model mimics the explicit complex model. However, even if the resulting models are simpler, their interpretation still requires basic ML knowledge, which apart from the computational complexity is the major drawback for global explanations.

The authors of [14] also extend the CAIPI algorithm specifically for DL use cases. They introduce a loss function with additional regularization term. Large gradients in regions with irrelevant features are penalized. Explanations for DL models for medical image classification can also be generated with inductive logic programming [13]. The connection of this paper with both of the previous papers appears to be interesting for future research.

3 Practical, Explainable, and Interactive Image Classification with CAIPI

In this section, we first recapitulate the mathematical foundations of LIME and the operation of the CAIPI algorithm. Secondly, we will discuss our extension of the CAIPI algorithm for application to complex and large image data.

The extensions will be derived by solving two problems that frequently occur with CAIPI in practice: First, default CAIPI only receives explanation corrections, if the prediction is correct but the explanation is wrong [16]. This seems to be inefficient, as wrong predictions are also made during the optimization.

Therefore, we extend CAIPI such that users can also correct explanations if the prediction is wrong. Secondly, a major contribution of our work lies in the simplification of the human-algorithm-interaction. In practice, optimization procedures are too complex for domain experts such as physicians when they depend on human interaction. To overcome this issue, we provide an universally applicable user interface.

LIME [10] exploits an interpretable surrogate model to construct explanations for predictions of a complex model. The representation of an instance is defined by $x \in \mathbb{R}^d$. The features of an instance are transformed into an interpretable representation $x' \in \{0,1\}^d$, where 0 indicates the absence and 1 the presence of a super-pixel. Super-pixels are contiguous patches of similar pixels in an image. Correspondingly, z is a sample generated around the original representation and z' a sample around the interpretable representation. The term $\pi_x(z)$ is a proximity measure between x and z. The complex model is denoted by $f(x)$ and the local explanatory model by $g \in G$, respectively, where G represents the aggregation of local explanatory models for $f(x)$. The term $\Omega(g)$ penalizes increasing complexity of the explanatory model. The objective function of LIME in (1) aims to minimize the sum of the loss function and the penalty.

$$\xi(x) = \operatorname*{argmin}_{g \in G} L(f, g, \pi_x) + \Omega(g) \tag{1}$$

The locality-aware loss is defined in (2). Locality-awareness means to account for the sampling region around the representation. This is ensured by $\pi_x(z)$, which is calculated by an exponential normalized distance function.

$$L(f, g, \pi_x) = \sum_{z, z' \in Z} \pi_x(z)(f(z) - g(z'))^2 \tag{2}$$

We make use of the Quick Shift algorithm [17] to partition an input image into super-pixels and the Sparse-Linear Approximation algorithm [10] together with the loss function (2) to generate explanations.

CAIPI [16] distinguishes between a labeled data set L and an unlabeled data set U. It uses four components: 1) The *Fit* component trains a model with L. 2) *SelectQuery* selects a single instance from U. Typically, the label belonging to this instance maximizes the loss reduction for the next optimization step. For that, we predict the instances of U and choose the instance with the lowest prediction score. 3) *Explain* applies the LIME algorithm and shows the prediction with its corresponding explanation. 4) Depending on the user input, the *ToCounterExamples* component generates counterexamples. The selected instance is removed from U and added to L together with the generated counterexamples.

We propose an image-specific data augmentation procedure. Figure 1 shows decisive features of a computer tomography scan of the chest. We scale, rotate, and translate the decisive features. The order of the augmentation is fixed. Their parameters are random with the constraint that the resulting image must fit

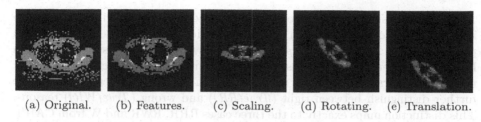

(a) Original.   (b) Features.   (c) Scaling.   (d) Rotating.   (e) Translation.

Fig. 1. Data augmentation for counterexamples. Relevant features (b) are extracted from the original image (a). The features are scaled (c), rotated (d) and translated (e).

Algorithm 1. CAIPI algorithm [16]

Require: labeled examples L, unlabeled examples U, iteration budget T
 1: $f \leftarrow Fit(L)$
 2: **repeat**
 3:     $x \leftarrow SelectQuery(f, U)$
 4:     $\hat{y} \leftarrow f(x)$
 5:     $\hat{z} \leftarrow Explain(f, x, \hat{y})$
 6:     Present $x, \hat{y}$ and $\hat{z}$ to the user
 7:     Obtain y and explanation correction C
 8:     $\{(\overline{x}_i, \overline{y}_i)\}_{i=1}^{c} \leftarrow ToCounterExamples(C)$
 9:     $L \leftarrow L \cup \{(x, y)\} \cup \{(\overline{x}_i, \overline{y}_i)\}_{i=1}^{c}$
10:     $U \leftarrow U \backslash (\{x\} \cup \{\overline{x}_i\}_{i=1}^{c})$
11:     $f \leftarrow Fit(L)$
12: **until** max. number of iterations T or min. quality of f is reached
13: **return** f

---

completely into the original frame. The augmentation is performed with Albumentations [2]. Within CAIPI, this procedure is applied to the decisive features once when the image from U is appended to L.

In the CAIPI optimization process in Algorithm 1, the user provides feedback to the most informative instance in each iteration. The model is then retrained with the additional information. The procedure terminates when reaching a certain prediction quality of f or the maximum number of iterations.

CAIPI distinguishes between three prediction outcome states: right for the right reasons (RRR), right for the wrong reasons (RWR), and wrong (W) [16]. Whereas RRR does not require additional user input, CAIPI asks the user to correct the label for W, and to correct the explanation for RWR. RWR results in augmented counterexamples, which only contain the decisive features.

At this point, we propose the following adjustment: We require the user to provide the correct label as well as the correct explanation for case W. Theoretically, this adjustment makes the optimization process more efficient, as counterexamples are generated in each iteration if either the label or the explanation or both are wrong.

Figure 2 illustrates our proposed user interface. The depicted example image is a computer tomography scan of the chest and is displayed together with its prediction (Fig. 2a). Button *Explanation* displays the LIME result as shown in Fig. 2b. The user can then choose whether the image was predicted correctly or not (buttons *True* or *False(W)*, respectively). In case of a correct prediction, we further distinguish between right (*True(RR)*) and wrong (*True(WR)*) reasons. This distinction maps exactly to the three cases RRR, RWR and W from CAIPI.

Figure 2a shows that the image was predicted correctly. However, as Fig. 2b indicates, the explanation is at least partly wrong, i.e., the instance can be considered as RWR. The corresponding button *True(WR)* opens the annotation mode (Fig. 2c), where the user can correct the explanation. Afterwards, a newly generated explanation can be evaluated as depicted in Fig. 2d. Confirming a correction starts CAIPI's *ToCounterExamples* method, which is in our case the proposed data augmentation procedure (Fig. 1). Note, that the same interaction applies to the W case, where the interface additionally asks for the correct label. For RRR, contrary, the correction mode (Fig. 2d and 2d) is concealed from the user. The remaining procedure is constant with the slight modification that no counterexamples are generated.

The extension we propose offers great benefits for CAIPI. First of all, CAIPI can be operated by end-users. Secondly, it fulfills all essential requirements defined in the Introduction, Sect. 1. CAIPI shows its prediction and explanation to the end-user in each optimization iteration, and if necessary the end-user can correct both. Furthermore, the end-user (which typically is a domain expert) is directly responsible for the data set quality, as CAIPI asks to add instances to the training data set iteratively and the end-user can ensure correct labels and emphasize correct explanations.

4   Experiments

For our experiments, we use two classes of the Medical MNIST data set [8, 18] (chest and abdomen computer tomography scans) and two classes of the Fashion MNIST data set [19] (pullover and T-shirt/top). By this selection, we want to emphasize a challenging binary classification task. The extension to categorical data is left as future work due to simplicity during the evaluation process.

We use a fairly simple convolutional neural network (CNN) as DL model in all experiments. It has a single convolutional layer with only 2 filters, a 9x9 kernel size, and stride parameter 1. It is followed by a pooling layer with kernel-size 8x8 and stride parameter 8. It follows a single linear layer with 98 neurons, a dropout layer with 0.5 dropout-rate, and two fully-connected layers with 16 and 2 neurons. All training procedures use batch size 64 and 5 epochs. We use a binary cross entropy loss function, the Adam optimization algorithm [6], and a learning rate of 0.001. The CNN corresponds to the function f in CAIPI.

Each CAIPI optimization starts with 100 preliminary labeled instances L_0. The maximum number of iterations is set to 100. We do not specify any other stop criterion. R1 until R3 are evaluated with an alternating number of counterexamples c. The number of counterexamples per iteration is $c = \{0, 1, 3, 5\}$.

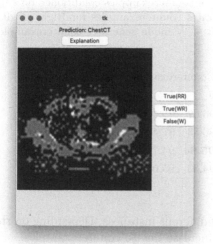

(a) Prediction of the classifier.

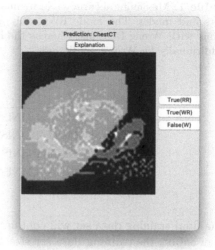

(b) LIME explanation.

(c) Correction.

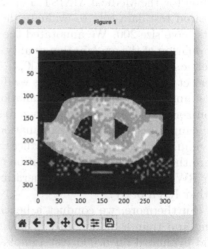

(d) Corrected instance.

Fig. 2. User interface. The prediction (a) and the explanation (b) is presented to the user. The user can correct the model's prediction and explanation in the annotation mode (c). The corrected instance can be displayed (d).

We show results on a domain-related data set, the Medical MNIST, and on the Fashion MNIST, a well-known benchmark data set. We ensure balanced classes in both data sets. Since CAIPI has 100 iterations, and L_0 has 100 instances,

Table 1. Maximum accuracy (%) by number of counterexamples conditioned on data sets and modes. The mode RWR only generates counterexamples for Right predictions with Wrong Reasons, whereas the RWR + W mode generates counterexamples additionally for Wrong predictions.

Mode	Data	Counterexamples c			
		0	1	3	5
RWR	Medical MNIST	96.02	95.42	94.51	96.75
RWR + W	Medical MNIST	96.83	97.48	96.92	**97.52**
RWR	Fashion MNIST	**95.64**	94.79	95.40	94.95
RWR + W	Fashion MNIST	94.33	95.02	94.24	94.10

the final training data set will contain 200 different instances. Depending on the user input, the training data set size will increase due to counterexamples.

We evaluate the prediction quality of our model in each optimization iteration with CAIPI with the accuracy metric on dedicated test data sets with size 6,000 for the Medical MNIST and size 4,200 for the Fashion MNIST. We also created test data sets to evaluate the explanation quality. Here, both test data sets have size 200. We annotated the true explanation for all instances. For the evaluation of the explanation quality, we use the *Intersection over Unions* (IoU) metric. IoU lies in the interval $[0, 1]$, where 0 is a completely incorrect and 1 a perfect explanation. This means we divide the intersection of the LIME explanation and the ground truth explanation by their union. We consider the average non-zero explanation score. Non-zero stands for excluding false predictions, since we cannot assume correct explanations for false predictions, and average means dividing by the number of instances with non-zero explanation score. We compare the prediction and explanation ability for generating counterexamples only for RWR predictions versus generating counterexamples for predictions that are either RWR or W.

Furthermore, we conduct a benchmark test by using the identical DL setting and train a model with 14,000 training instances for the Medical MNIST and evaluated on 6,000 test samples. Correspondingly, we trained with 9,800 instances from the Fashion MNIST and tested with 4,200 instances.

5 Results

Table 1 clearly shows that the prediction quality of our model does not benefit from an increasing number of counterexamples, as the maximum accuracy is approximately stable over the runs. Also, Table 2 shows no clear trend towards an increasing explanation quality for greater numbers of counterexamples. Thus, R1 and R2 can be negated based on the experimental setting in Sect. 4. Similarly, for R3, the adjustment of providing explanation corrections also for wrong predictions does not have positive impact on either the explanation nor the prediction quality.

Table 2. Maximum average non-zero explanation score (%) by number of counterexamples conditioned on data sets and modes. The mode RWR only generates counterexamples for Right predictions with Wrong Reasons, whereas the RWR + W mode generates counterexamples additionally for Wrong predictions.

Mode	Data	Counterexamples c			
		0	1	3	5
RWR	Medical MNIST	41.59	**44.74**	40.36	42.87
RWR + W	Medical MNIST	39.64	42.37	41.12	40.47
RWR	Fashion MNIST	65.24	64.41	64.40	65.48
RWR + W	Fashion MNIST	64.43	65.76	63.10	**66.38**

For state-of-the-art DL optimization, we achieve an accuracy of 94.67% for the Medical MNIST and 95.26% for the Fashion MNIST. This accuracy is approximately equal to the CAIPI results in Table 1. Besides, CAIPI requires significantly less training data (200, plus counterexamples) than traditional optimization ($14,000$, respectively $9,800$). With respect to R4, this is clear evidence that CAIPI influences the optimization process positively.

6   Discussion

R1 and R2 show no clear trend in favor of an increasing number of counterexamples, despite [16] states otherwise. Teso and Kersting [16] induce decoy pixels with colors corresponding to the different classes into their training data set and they randomize the pixel colors in the test set. Whenever they create counterexamples, they also randomize the decoy pixel color. We investigate R1 and R2 without prior data set modification. Table 1 shows that default active learning ($c = 0$) positively influences the learning behavior to such an extent that there is hardly space for improvement by extending it to XIML. This means that for future evaluations the use cases must be sufficiently complex so that default active learning does not provide satisfactory results.

We evaluate R2 by a dedicated test set containing annotated true explanations. We use IoU to estimate the quality of the explanation in percent by dividing the area of intersection by the area of union. The idea is, if predicted and annotated explanations are congruent to each other, the explanation is perfect. We frequently observe perfectly negative explanations, meaning that the predicted explanation highlights all image parts apart from the annotated explanation. From a human perspective, this explanation is perfect, for IoU it is a completely wrong explanation. Determining the quality of explanations is a prominent research field and future work should evaluate additional metrics.

For R3, Table 1 and 2 show that explanation corrections for RWR and W do not differ significantly compared to explanation corrections for only RWR. We argue that including more counterexamples (RWR + W) can be a chance to build more robust data set. The robustness from a statistical perspective was not addressed in this paper. It must be included in future evaluations besides accounting for the priory mentioned discussion points. Similar to earlier discussion points, R4 can be re-evaluated in more complex use cases.

The data augmentation procedure plays also a major role. The procedure defined in Fig. 1 will create training data, which are fundamentally different to the test data, since both data sets, Medical MNIST and Fashion MNIST, contain relatively centralized images. The idea behind the proposed procedure is to force the model to account for the decisive features without considering the feature position. This can be enhanced by random transformations in every epoch compared to a single transformation when the counterexamples are generated. We also expect improvement by including further constraints to make the resulting counterexamples more realistically.

Finally, our main contribution is the simplification of the human-algorithm-interaction with the introduced interface. We support this on theoretical basis, as the application of CAIPI with our interface fulfills requirements, which we defined in the Introduction, Sect. 1. Furthermore, we give practical evidence via demonstration in Sect. 3. From a psychological point of view, this is insufficient. Therefore, our interface should be subject of psychological studies in future.

7   Conclusion and Future Work

We extended the CAIPI algorithm by accounting additionally for explanation corrections if the predictions are wrong. Moreover, we introduced an user interface for a human-in-the-loop approach for image classification tasks. The interface enables the end-user (1) to investigate and (2) to correct the model's prediction and explanation, and (3) to influence the data set quality.

The experiments show that the predictive performance of state-of-the-art DL methods is met, even though the required training data set size decreases. According to our findings, the correlation between an increasing amount of counterexamples and higher predictive and explanatory quality does not hold. The introduced extension that creates counterexamples also for wrong predictions can help to build more robust data sets but does not increase the predictive nor the explanatory quality. The proposed interface is a promising extension for medical image classification tasks using CAIPI. The interface appears to be transferable to every XIML approach exploiting local explanations. Evidently, CAIPI as well as the proposed interface is transferable to any other image classification task.

The most obvious improvement is the generalization to categorical image data. This appears to be a minor adjustment. It was neglected in this paper for the sake of simplicity during evaluation of the experiments. Future research should also address wrong explanations. This can be accomplished by connecting this paper with [14]. Another prominent research subject is the CAIPI algorithm for itself. As the CAIPI algorithm can be considered as feedback-reliable data augmentation procedure, it could be continuously adjusted and modified. Here, research subjects can be instance selection, local explanation, or data augmentation methods. More sophisticated methods than simple IoU are necessary to estimate the visual explanation quality more accurately.

Further adjustments can be separated into three groups. First, the interface can be evaluated in psychological studies. Second, the computational efficiency of XIML methods can be increased by connecting them with online learning algorithms such as [12]. And third, the connection of inductive logic programming like in [13] with human-in-the-loop ML procedures is a promising research area.

References

1. Bastani, O., Kim, C., Bastani, H.: Interpreting blackbox models via model extraction (2017). http://arxiv.org/abs/1705.08504
2. Buslaev, A., Iglovikov, V.I., Khvedchenya, E., Parinov, A., Druzhinin, M., Kalinin, A.A.: Albumentations: fast and flexible image augmentations. Information **11**(2), 125 (2020). https://doi.org/10.3390/info11020125
3. Holzinger, A.: Interactive machine learning for health informatics: when do we need the human-in-the-loop? Brain Inform. **3**(2), 119–131 (2016). https://doi.org/10.1007/s40708-016-0042-6
4. Hund, M., et al.: Analysis of patient groups and immunization results based on subspace clustering. In: Guo, Y., Friston, K., Aldo, F., Hill, S., Peng, H. (eds.) BIH 2015. LNCS (LNAI), vol. 9250, pp. 358–368. Springer, Cham (2015). https://doi.org/10.1007/978-3-319-23344-4_35
5. Kieseberg, P., Schantl, J., Frühwirt, P., Weippl, E., Holzinger, A.: Witnesses for the doctor in the loop. In: Guo, Y., Friston, K., Aldo, F., Hill, S., Peng, H. (eds.) BIH 2015. LNCS (LNAI), vol. 9250, pp. 369–378. Springer, Cham (2015). https://doi.org/10.1007/978-3-319-23344-4_36
6. Kingma, D.P., Ba, J.: Adam: a method for stochastic optimization. In: Bengio, Y., LeCun, Y. (eds.) 3rd International Conference on Learning Representations, ICLR 2015, San Diego, CA, USA, 7–9 May 2015, Conference Track Proceedings (2015). http://arxiv.org/abs/1412.6980
7. Kourou, K., Exarchos, T., Exarchos, K., Karamouzis, M., Fotiadis, D.: Machine learning applications in cancer prognosis and prediction. Comput. Struct. Biotechnol. J. **13** (2014). https://doi.org/10.1016/j.csbj.2014.11.005
8. Lozano, A.P.: Medical MNIST Classification (2017). https://github.com/apolanco3225/Medical-MNIST-Classification
9. Plumb, G., Molitor, D., Talwalkar, A.S.: Model agnostic supervised local explanations. In: Bengio, S., Wallach, H.M., Larochelle, H., Grauman, K., Cesa-Bianchi, N., Garnett, R. (eds.) Advances in Neural Information Processing Systems 31: Annual Conference on Neural Information Processing Systems 2018, NeurIPS 2018, Montréal, Canada, 3–8 December 2018, pp. 2520–2529 (2018). https://proceedings.neurips.cc/paper/2018/hash/b495ce63ede0f4efc9eec62cb947c162-Abstract.html
10. Ribeiro, M.T., Singh, S., Guestrin, C.: "Why should I trust you?": explaining the predictions of any classifier. In: Krishnapuram, B., Shah, M., Smola, A.J., Aggarwal, C.C., Shen, D., Rastogi, R. (eds.) Proceedings of the 22nd ACM SIGKDD International Conference on Knowledge Discovery and Data Mining, San Francisco, CA, USA, 13–17 August 2016, pp. 1135–1144. ACM (2016). https://doi.org/10.1145/2939672.2939778
11. Rudin, C.: Stop explaining black box machine learning models for high stakes decisions and use interpretable models instead. Nat. Mach. Intell. **1**(5), 206–215 (2019). https://doi.org/10.1038/s42256-019-0048-x

12. Sahoo, D., Pham, Q., Lu, J., Hoi, S.C.H.: Online deep learning: learning deep neural networks on the fly. In: Lang, J. (ed.) Proceedings of the Twenty-Seventh International Joint Conference on Artificial Intelligence, IJCAI 2018, Stockholm, Sweden, 13–19 July 2018, pp. 2660–2666. ijcai.org (2018). https://doi.org/10.24963/ijcai.2018/369

13. Schmid, U., Finzel, B.: Mutual explanations for cooperative decision making in medicine. Künstliche Intelligenz **34**(2), 227–233 (2020). https://doi.org/10.1007/s13218-020-00633-2

14. Schramowski, P., et al.: Making deep neural networks right for the right scientific reasons by interacting with their explanations. Nat. Mach. Intell. **2**(8), 476–486 (2020). https://doi.org/10.1038/s42256-020-0212-3

15. Settles, B.: Active Learning. Synthesis Lectures on Artificial Intelligence and Machine Learning. Morgan & Claypool Publishers (2012). https://doi.org/10.2200/S00429ED1V01Y201207AIM018

16. Teso, S., Kersting, K.: Explanatory interactive machine learning. In: Conitzer, V., Hadfield, G.K., Vallor, S. (eds.) Proceedings of the 2019 AAAI/ACM Conference on AI, Ethics, and Society, AIES 2019, Honolulu, HI, USA, 27–28 January 2019, pp. 239–245. ACM (2019). https://doi.org/10.1145/3306618.3314293

17. Vedaldi, A., Soatto, S.: Quick shift and kernel methods for mode seeking. In: Forsyth, D., Torr, P., Zisserman, A. (eds.) ECCV 2008, Part IV. LNCS, vol. 5305, pp. 705–718. Springer, Heidelberg (2008). https://doi.org/10.1007/978-3-540-88693-8_52

18. Yang, J., Shi, R., Ni, B.: MedMNIST classification decathlon: a lightweight AutoML benchmark for medical image analysis. In: IEEE 18th International Symposium on Biomedical Imaging (ISBI), pp. 191–195 (2021)

19. Zalando SE: Fashion MNIST (2017). https://www.kaggle.com/zalando-research/fashionmnist

Digitally Assisted Planning and Monitoring of Supportive Recommendations in Cancer Patients

Alexander Scherrer[1(✉)], Tobias Zimmermann[1], Sinan Riedel[1], Fihmi Mousa[2], Isa Wasswa-Musisi[2], Robert Zifrid[2], Hartmut Tillil[2], Philip Ulrich[2], Thanos Kosmidis[3], Joaquim Reis[4], Gabrielle Oestreicher[5], Markus Möhler[5], Ilias Kalamaras[6], Konstantinos Votis[6], Stefanos Venios[7], Maria Plakia[8], and Sotiris Diamantopoulos[8]

[1] Fraunhofer Institute for Industrial Mathematics (ITWM), Fraunhofer-Platz 1, 67663 Kaiserslautern, Germany
{alexander.scherrer,tobias.zimmermann,sinan.riedel}@itwm.fraunhofer.de
[2] MCS Data Labs GmbH, Bismarck-Straße 10-12, 10625 Berlin, Germany
{fihmi.mousa,isa.wasswa-musisi,robert.zifrid,hartmut.tillil,
philip.ulrich}@mcs-datalabs.com
[3] Care Across Ltd, 1 Kings Avenue, N21 3NA London, UK
thanos.kosmidis@careacross.com
[4] FCiências.ID - Associação para a Investigação e Desenvolvimento de Ciências, Campo Grande, edifício C1, piso 3, 1749-016 Lisboa, Portugal
jdcreis@fc.ul.pt
[5] University Medical Center of the Johannes Gutenberg-University Mainz, Langenbeckstraße 1, 55131 Mainz, Germany
{gabrielle.oestreicher,markus.moehler}@unimedizin-mainz.de
[6] Centre for Research and Technology Hellas, Charilaou Thermi Road 6km, 57001 Thermi Thessaloniki, Greece
{kalamar,kvotis}@iti.gr
[7] Suite5 Data Intelligence Solutions Ltd, 1 Archiepiskopou Makariou III Mitsi Bu, 1065 Nicosia, Cyprus
stefanos@suite5.eu
[8] EXUS Software Ltd, Old Broad Street 25 Tower 42, EC2N 1PB London, UK
{m.plakia,s.diamantopoulos}@exus.co.uk

Abstract. This publication presents a solution approach for digitally assisted planning and monitoring of supportive recommendations in cancer patients. This solution approach shall support patients in overcoming the after-effects of therapy effectively without extensive involvement of health professionals. Health professionals and patients are provided with a web application and a mobile application respectively, which use methods from mathematical decision support and artificial intelligence. This technological basis facilitates a closed-loop workflow for the cooperation of health professional and patient in oncological aftercare. The solution approach is illustrated for an exemplary case scenario of colorectal cancer.

© IFIP International Federation for Information Processing 2022
Published by Springer Nature Switzerland AG 2022
I. Maglogiannis et al. (Eds.): AIAI 2022 Workshops, IFIP AICT 652, pp. 401–411, 2022.
https://doi.org/10.1007/978-3-031-08341-9_32

Keywords: Oncological aftercare · Supportive recommendation planning · Patient monitoring · Decision support · Artificial intelligence

1   Introduction

1.1   Oncological Follow-Up Care

With about 492000 newly diagnosed cases and about 230000 deaths per year, cancer is one of the most common diseases and the second most common cause of death in Germany [12]. Clinical cancer treatment is widely based on surgery, system therapy, radiotherapy and their combinations [11]. Cancer therapy in addition to the immediate effects may also entail significant aftereffects for patients. They often suffer from a reduced well-being and quality of life for a long time after leaving the clinic [9]. However, patients can receive only limited medical support outside of the highly specialized clinical environment. To a major extent, they are left to their own devices to overcome the aftereffects of treatment. Even regular consultation hours allow only limited exchange of information between health professional and patient at certain intervals. The individualized planning of tailored recommendations based on little information is in turn a major challenge for health professionals. And the correct independent implementation of recommendations is also a challenging and possibly error-prone task for patients.

1.2   Planning and Monitoring of Supportive Recommendations

The main health goal of the EU project *ONCORELIEF* is to support cancer patients in aftercare in regaining their well-being and quality of life [5]. This goal is achieved by establishing a closed-loop workflow that connects health professionals and patients by means of assisting digital solutions. This workflow allows intensive cooperation beyond consultation hours and software-supported individualized planning and close monitoring of supportive recommendations. The health professional uses a web application for the planning of recommendations and the patient uses a mobile application for their documentation and monitoring. The collected information goes through a data analysis, the results of which provide the basis for recommendation planning. *ONCORELIEF* follows a division-of-labor approach to recommendation planning and monitoring. The potentially time-consuming and error-prone process steps of analyzing health data and searching for suitable recommendations are performed using artificial intelligence (AI) methods. In contrast, the result-critical step of recommendation planning is performed by the health professional with the help of mathematical decision support methods. With this solution approach, *ONCORELIEF* follows the recommendations for an ethically correct use of AI on health topics [6].

1.3   Contents

This paper presents in Sect. 2 the methods used for recommendation planning and monitoring. Section 3 describes the practical application for an illustrative

case scenario of colorectal cancer. Section 4 assesses the achieved research and
development results.

2   Material and Methods

Figure 1 schematically depicts the digitally assisted closed-loop workflow of post-
treatment supportive patient care. The results obtained with AI-based data analysis of the considered patient case form the starting point. With this information,
the health professional performs recommendation planning in the web application. The planned recommendations with all their contents are transferred to
the patient's mobile application. There, the patient obtains information about
the supportive recommendations and documents them during implementation.
Based on the documented information, the mobile application does the monitoring, provides feedback to the patient and transfers the collected information to
the data analysis. From a planning perspective, this closed-loop workflow follows
the principles of sequential decision making [10].

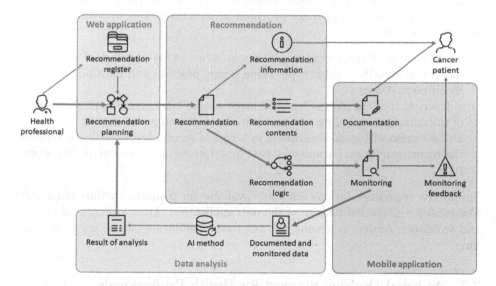

Fig. 1. Solution approach with the core components and main information flows: Recommendation planning with the web application (green) by the health professional,
supportive recommendations with their contents (red), documentation and monitoring
with the mobile application (blue) used by the patient and AI-based data analysis of
the progress achieved with the recommendation (grey). The thick arrows indicate the
main process steps of the approach. (Icons: Line Icons (iconsmind.com), Windows 8
Icons (icons8.com)). (Color figure online)

2.1 Digitally Supported Workflow

Results of AI-based Data Analysis. The planning of individually suitable supportive recommendations for a patient case is based on analysis results generated with AI methods on the case data. The choice of the appropriate method in each case depends on the nature of the considered case data and the reference data available for method training. However, the solution approach followed here is in principle independent of the choice of method and uses only the obtained results. This flexibility is achieved by using a data interface based on a generic information format. The imported data contains a listing of the performance indicators used by the AI method and a listing of the supportive recommendations with their scores in these performance indicators. This concept also follows the general objective of Explainable Artificial Intelligence (XAI) methods of providing more insight into the origin and quality of results of analysis [7].

Register of Supportive Recommendations. The imported results of analysis are matched with the contents of a recommendation register based on the recommendation names. This register contains templates for the recommendations available for planning, which are provided as structured files with the following information contents:

- a description of the recommendation in terms of its parameters with their individual identifier, value type, value range, position and multiplicity in the recommendation;
- a description of the parameter visualization with label, surrounding text, type of initialization including optional initial values and access rights;
- a description of logical conditions in terms of second-level predicate logic on the recommendation parameters, text descriptions and optional quality scores [1].

Supportive recommendations are made available for planning by importing such files with a registration feature of the web application. After a successful import and validation against a schema file, the recommendation can be used for planning.

2.2 AI-based Decision Support for Health Professionals

Selection of Recommendations. The search for suitable recommendations and their selection is treated as a multi-criteria decision problem in the web application [4]. Here, the supportive recommendation name and the performance indicators from the AI method form the planning criteria and the AI results provide the evaluations in the criterion space. The health professional in charge can use search, sort and filter functionality on these criteria to determine the suitable recommendations. The web application as a whole thus implements a division-of-labor approach. The potentially time-consuming and error-prone search for relevant recommendations is handled by AI methods. But the outcome-critical decision about which recommendations to implement is up to the health professional. With this approach, recommendation planning follows the preferable approach for the ethically correct use of AI by keeping the human in the loop [6].

Adaptation of Recommendations. The health professional can then adapt the selected recommendations to the patient's individual needs by means of the parameters that are released for this purpose. These parameters shall inform the patient how to implement the recommendations, but they are also used in the logical conditions for monitoring. Modification of these parameters thus allows for an easy individualization of recommendations, which again follows the preferable approach for the use of AI methods [6]. An explicit editing of conditions would have required an advanced understanding of certain concepts from formal mathematics and computer science. Once these adaptations are complete, the recommendations are exported back into proprietary file structures and transferred to the patient's mobile application.

2.3   Knowledge-based Decision Support for Patients

Configuration of the Mobile Application. The mobile application has methods for the retrieval and interpretation of these files and the processing of their contents. This processing includes the visualization of recommendations, the provision of features for their documentation and methods for the evaluation of the entered information in monitoring. The mobile application is thus generic over the application-specific content. This separation allows for a configuration of the mobile application also with newly registered recommendations without any software update.

Documentation of Recommendations. The display and processing of supportive recommendations in the mobile application for the patient takes place analogously to the web application. The patient documents the implementation of the recommendation via the parameters released for this purpose. Most of these parameters have predefined value ranges and only a few support entries of free text. This allows for a easy usability based on value selection, guarantees a high quality of the crucial data and their comparability in data analysis. The information entered is stored in the mobile application and transferred to the data analysis upon the patient's request. This ensures the patient's sovereignty over his or her own data.

Monitoring of Recommendations. Monitoring features a rule-based system based on an application of the logical conditions contained in the supportive recommendations to the information entered by the patient [13]. This ensures a clearly predictable behavior of the mobile application according to the instructions of the health professional and enables patient care without permanent involvement of the health professional. After each editing in a recommendation, the corresponding logical conditions are evaluated on the entered information, which again corresponds to the principle of sequential decision making. A fulfilled condition triggers a text message to the patient, following the XAI objective to communicate results in a transparent way [7]. This information is optionally combined with ratings on multiple quality scales for multi-criteria decision making by the patient during implementation of the recommendations [4]. Negative evaluations for an ongoing recommendation or also completion of a recommendation are at the patient's behest followed by a transfer of information to the health professional. This would then trigger an adaptation of the ongoing supportive recommendations by the health professional and thereby close the loop shown in Fig. 1.

3   Results and Discussion

3.1   Planning of Supportive Recommendations

Exemplary Patient Case and Results of Analysis. The methods described above are illustrated for an artificial case scenario in which a patient treated for colorectal cancer suffers from the aftereffects of anxiety, depression and fatigue. This information enters a data analysis, which here uses Random Forest classification [3]. This method uses singular decision trees for the classification of data samples, in this context the applicability of a recommendation for a case scenario. They then aggregate the classification results obtained from a forest of decision trees to a majority vote with some percentage indicating its validity. The obtained results are transferred to the web application and displayed there as can be seen in Fig. 2. A combination with another AI method would give this table another view with different column labels for the performance indicators specific to the method.

Registered Supportive Recommendations. A review of medical guidelines for the considered disease patterns of colorectal cancer and acute myeloid leukemia has so far led to the specification of altogether 24 supportive recommendations [9]:

- *Acupuncture*
- *Anti-depressant therapy*
- *Group therapy*
- *Healthy nutrition*
- *Intervention for sleep disturbances*
- *Medical treatment*
- *Mindfulness-based stress reduction*
- *Nutrition consultation*
- *Physical activity*
- *Positive social relationships*

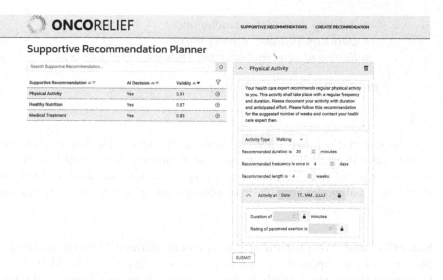

Fig. 2. Recommendation planning with the web application: survey of the available recommendations, corresponding results of data analysis and planning features (left) and display of the selected recommendation with adaptation features (right).

- *Psychiatric consultation*
- *Psycho-educational therapy*
- *Psychological consultation*
- *Recommendations against appetite loss*
- *Recommendations against hair loss*
- *Recommendations against the hand foot syndrome*
- *Recommendations against lack of sexual interest*
- *Recommendations against sleep problems*
- *Recommendations against sore mouth*
- *Recommendations against weight changes*
- *Recommendations against weight loss*
- *Scrambler therapy*
- *Supportive care*
- *Treatment of medical causes*

These recommendations have parameter structures like the following one of the exemplary supportive recommendation *Physical Activity*:

- *Physical Activity (node)*
  {
  - *Activity type (ordinal, exactly once)*
  - *Duration recommendation (integer, exactly once)*
  - *Frequency recommendation (integer, exactly once)*
  - *Length (integer, exactly once)*
  - *Activity entry (node, arbitrary)*
    {

o *Activity date (date, exactly once)*
o *Duration (integer, exactly once)*
o *Rating of perceived exertion (integer, exactly once)*
}
o *Recommendation result (ordinal, exactly once)*
o ...
}

The indentation and brackets represent the hierarchical tree structure with nodes and leafs. The items represent the parameters with their identifier, value type and multiplicity. Supported value types are *text, nominal, ordinal, integer, float, date* and *node*. Feasible multiplicities are *at most once, exactly once, at least once* and *arbitrary*.

Selection and Adaptation of Recommendations. The web application first displays all the supportive recommendations analyzed by the AI method with their respective ratings. With the help of the available search, sort and filter functionality, the health professional can narrow down the recommendation options to the relevant ones. In the considered case scenario, these are the recommendations that were identified by the AI presumably suitable. These recommendations therefore carry a *Yes* in the criterion *AI Decision* and a high value close to one in the *Validity* criterion. In Fig. 2, the health professional has therefore performed filtering operations on these two criteria and sorted the remaining recommendations by *Validity*. The health professional then selects one or more desired recommendations, in this case the previously mentioned recommendation *Physical Activity*. Selected recommendations are displayed in the web application according to their specifications from the recommendation register. In these views, the health professional can adapt recommendations to the individual needs of the patient via the parameters released for editing. For the displayed *Physical Activity*, these are most prominently the *Activity type, Recommended duration, Recommended frequency* and *Recommended length*. At the end of planning, the adapted recommendations are transferred to the patient's mobile application. This happens by means of regular requests for new information from the mobile application to the web server.

3.2 Processing of Supportive Recommendations

Documentation of Recommendations. The mobile application shows the patient an overview of the progress of previous and current supportive recommendations as shown in Fig. 3 (left). After selecting a recommendation, it switches to a full-screen view for this recommendation, see Fig. 3 (right). In this full-screen view, the patient receives the general information entered by the health professional about the recommendation provided with input options for its documentation. The patient documents the considered recommendation *Physical Activity* by adding instances of the node parameter *Activity Entry*, which in turn contain the parameters *Activity date, Duration* and *Rating of Perceived exertion*

(RPE) [2]. These parameters have predefined value ranges, making the information entered clearly interpretable and comparable among multiple instances of themselves. The same applies to the parameter *Recommendation result*, which is filled in after completion of a recommendation to document the perceived success.

Fig. 3. Processing of recommendations with the mobile application: survey of supportive recommendations (left), monitoring feedback on a single recommendation (middle) and full-screen view of a recommendation for information and documentation (right).

Recommendation Monitoring. Every edit of a recommendation automatically triggers an evaluation of the associated logical conditions. For the considered recommendation *Physical Activity* there are 15 such conditions, which have the following exemplary form

(NOT (EXISTS (Activity entry) FULFILLS ((Activity entry).(Activity date) GREATEROREQUAL ((CURRENT DATE) MINUS (Frequency recommendation)))))

This condition checks whether there is no node entry *Activity entry*, whose date *Activity date* lies within the period determined by *Frequency recommendation* and the *CURRENT DATE*. *CURRENT DATE* and the other key words written in capital letters represent operators in the used logic language. The point between *Activity entry* and *Activity date* is another operator for switching from a node to one of its children. Many logic languages like the Arden syntax encode conditions in a procedural format, which is difficult to comprehend for users without knowledge in formal mathematics and computer science [8]. The logic language used in this context encodes conditions in a readable format, which can be easily understood and validated by health professionals.

In the considered case scenario, this condition is met and yields the quality score

(Evaluation ASSIGN Bad)

The supportive recommendations specified for the considered disease patterns use the two quality scales *Evaluation* and *Urgency* with optional value assignments depending on the specific condition. Quality scores are displayed in the recommendation overview with colored symbols, see Fig. 3 (left). The colors feature a traffic-light scheme and are computed from the relative position of a quality score on the value range of the quality scale. They allow the patient to quickly identify the most important or urgent information and react on it. The fulfilled condition also triggers a text message to the patient, which is displayed on top of the recommendation view after clicking the colored symbol as shown in Fig. 3 (middle).

4   Conclusions

This work presents a solution approach for providing a digitally assisted aftercare service to cancer patients. The approach is developed for the exemplary disease patterns of colorectal cancer and acute myeloid leukemia. The obtained results shall enter a comprehensive medical evaluation for these fields of application in the near future. The generic concept of the approach, however, allows for a transfer into other medical and non-medical fields of application. This concept features digital assistance for the involved stakeholders with separate technological components, which nevertheless combine to an integrated closed-loop workflow. A web application featuring AI-based data analysis and multi-criteria decision making allows for an efficient planning of individualized supportive recommendations by health professionals. A mobile application featuring a rule-based system and sequential decision making assists cancer patients in the documentation and monitoring of ongoing supportive recommendations. The regular information transfer between these two components supports patients in effective aftercare guided by health professionals without their permanent involvement and beyond regular attendance of medical consultation hours.

Acknowledgments. The research work presented herein is part of the EU Horizon 2020 project *ONCORELIEF* (Grant Agreement ID 875392) [5].

References

1. Boolos, G.S., Burgess, J.P., Jeffrey, R.C.: Computability and Logic 4 (edn.) Cambridge University Press (2002)
2. Gunnar, V.A.: Borg: psychophysical bases of perceived exertion. Med. Sci. Sports Exerc. **14**(5), 377–381 (1982)
3. Breiman, L., Friedman, J., Stone, C.J., Olshen, R.A.: Classification and Regression Trees. Chapman and Hall/CRC Press (1984)
4. Ehrgott, M.: Multicriteria Optimization. Springer-Verlag, Berlin Heidelberg (2005)
5. EU Horizon 2020 Project ONCORELIEF: ONCORELIEF website. www. oncorelief.eu (2020)
6. European Parliament: EU Guidelines on ethics in artificial intelligence: Context and implementation. www.europarl.europa.eu/thinktank/en/document/EPRS$_$ $BRI(2019)640163 (2019)
7. Gunning, D., Stefik, M., Choi, J., Miller, T., Stumpf, S., Yang, G.Z.: XAI - Explainable artificial intelligence. Sci. Robot. **4**(37), eaay7120 (2019)
8. Hripcsak, G.: Writing Arden syntax medical logic modules. Comput. Biol. Med. **24**(5), 331–363 (1994)
9. Jordan, K., Feyer, P., Höller, U., Link, H., Wörmann, B., Jahn, F.: Supportive treatments for patients with cancer - clinical practise guideline. Deutsches Ärzteblatt Int. **114**, 481–487 (2017)
10. LaValle, S.M.: Planning Algorithms. Cambridge University Press (2006)
11. National Cancer Institute: Types of cancer treatment. www.cancer.gov/about-cancer/treatment/types (2020)
12. Robert-Koch-Institut: Cancer in Germany 2015/16. 12 edn. www.edoc.rki.de/handle/176904/8320 (2020)
13. Spreckelsen, C., Spitzer, K.: Wissensbasen und Expertensysteme in der Medizin (Knowledge-bases and Expert Systems in Medicine). Verlag Vieweg + Teubner (2008)

Monitoring Neurological Disorder Patients via Deep Learning Based Facial Expressions Analysis

Muhammad Munsif[1,3], Mohib Ullah[2], Bilal Ahmad[2], Muhammad Sajjad[2(✉)], and Faouzi Alaya Cheikh[2]

[1] Islamia College University Peshawar, 25000 Peshawar, Pakistan
[2] Norwegian University of Science and Technology, 2815 Gjøvik, Norway
muhammad.sajjad@ntnu.no
[3] Sejong University, Seoul 143–747, South Korea

Abstract. Facial expression (FE) is the most natural and convincing source to communicate human emotions, providing valuable insides to the observer while assessing the emotional incongruities. In health care, the FE of the patient (specifically of neurological disorders (NDs) such as Parkinson's, Stroke, and Alzheimer's) can assist the medical doctor in evaluating the physical condition of a patient, such as fatigue, pain, and sadness. ND patients are usually going through proper observation and clinical tests, which are invasive, expensive and time-consuming. In this paper, an automatic lightweight deep learning (DL) based FEs recognition framework is developed that can classify the facial expression of ND patients with 93% accuracy. Initially, raw images of FEs are acquired from publicly available datasets according to the patient's most common expressions, such as normal, happy, sad, and anger. The framework cropped images through a face detector, extract high-level facial features through the convolutional layers and fed them to the dense layers for classification. The trained model is exported to an android based environment over a smart device and evaluated for real-time performance. The qualitative and quantitative results are evaluated on a standard dataset named Karolinska directed emotional faces (KDEF). Promising results are obtained of various NDs patients with Parkinson, Stroke, and Alzheimer that show the effectiveness of the proposed model.

Keywords: Neurological disorder · Convolution neural network · Parkinson · Alzheimer · Emotion recognition

1 Introduction

Human facial expressions (FEs) play a significant role in human-to-human interactions and human behaviour analysis. According to Mehrabian et al. [1], for effective oral communication, body language, including FEs, contributes up to

I. Maglogiannis et al. (Eds.): AIAI 2022 Workshops, IFIP AICT 652, pp. 412–423, 2022.
https://doi.org/10.1007/978-3-031-08341-9_33

55% of total importance, while voice tons and words contribute 38% and 7% respectively. Apart from this, FEs reflects common symptoms of various medical conditions like NDs including Parkinson's [2], Stroke [3], Alzheimer, and Bell Palsy [4] diseases. Most of the time, medical experts diagnose patients with ND problems through strict overtime monitoring and various invasive and expensive medical tests, which can be challenging and painful [5]. Thus, developing an alternative, cost-effective and endurable system is essential. An automatic FEs recognition system can assist a doctor in evaluating the ND patients' overall behaviour. Such a system can efficiently differentiate and identify various FEs to identify patients' conditions (e.g., feeling well, bad, normal) associated with clinical-related FEs features. These FEs linked with clinical features can be combined with the diagnostic process as biomarkers to evaluate the performance of therapeutic response toward an ND patient.

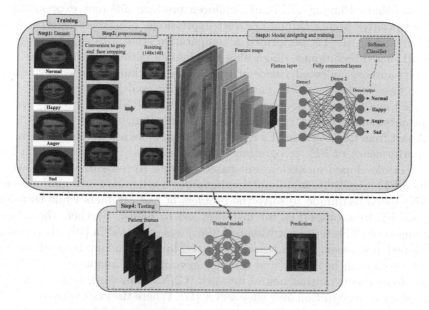

Fig. 1. Proposed framework, Broadly divided into two steps which include training and testing. Further, the training step consists of, dataset, pre-processing, and model designing, while the testing step contains real-time testing on real data of ND patients.

Various studies have been conducted to study the relationship between FEs and different NDs. Kohler et al. [6] conducted a study on Alzheimer patients' behaviour, and they found a deficit of FEs in Alzheimer patients. Similarly, Authors in [7] analyzed the behaviour of neurodegenerative disorder patients. They identified deficiency in most patients toward positive FEs such as happiness due to high subjectiveness to negative emotions such as anger and sadness. Ferndez et al. [8] observed impairment in the abilities of positive FEs recognition in frontotemporal dementia and Alzheimer patients. To identify neurologically disordered by utilizing FEs, Authors in [9] developed a method to detect NDs using FEs. In their study, a photo/video containing different expressions is shown to the patients with NDs, and the patients are advised to mimic the expressions. The tool used in this study further decodes the expression of the patients by calculating the intensity of the imitated expression. Based on the calculated intensity, the system proposed in [9] predicts the state of the disease. In addition, Dantcheva et al. [10] proposed a computer vision-based framework to monitor severely demented people and their FEs during musical therapy, classifying activities and expressions during talking, singing, happy, and normal conditions. Similarly, authors in [11] proposed a machine learning (ML)based 3D mobile game application called JEMlmE to improve the expression skills of children with autism spectrum diseases. In this study, an ML model is trained over children's expressions (sadness, happiness, anger, and natural, etc.) and is integrated with JEMlmE. Playing JEMLmE, children produce different expressions and certain positive points through correct expressions, otherwise negative points. Further, Jin et al. [12] performed a comparative study of deep learning (DL) and ML-based techniques, diagnosing Parkinson's patients through FEs analysis. The authors collected videos of healthy and Parkinson patients containing smiley faces in this study. In Face++ API, traditional ML (such as SVM, DT, LR, RF) and DL based sequence learning (such as RNN and LSTM) are used for preprocessing, feature extraction and classification.

Apart from this, various FEs recognition techniques are developed to improve the performance of FEs recognition methods such as [13]. Among them Liang et al. [14] developed an action unit-based network to recognize 33 various fine-grained FEs. Similarly, in [15] authors proposed a generative adversarial network (GAN) based technique to solve the problem of bad artefacts while transforming one FE to another FE, for instance, sad to happy. Further, the adaptive learning-based FEs representation technique was proposed in [16] where authors developed a knowledgeable teacher and self-taught student network to learn facial emotions in both easy and complex environments adaptively. In addition, a cloud-based convolution neural network (CNN) framework was developed to recognize FEs recognition over edge server [17], Where the system captures a face image using a smartphone, transmitting it to the server for preprocessing and classification. State of the arts (SOTA) discussed high computational resources for training, testing, and deployment. The FEs in SOTA are not explicitly associated with the facial emotions of NDs patients for diagnostic purposes, only focusing on security and data quality applications. To cope with the critical challenges of computation, accuracy, and association of FEs with NDs patients for diagnostic purposes, we proposed a lightweight FEs recognition framework to assist the medical experts in early diagnosing of NDs patients. In a nutshell, the contributions of the proposed framework are three folds:

1. Developed a DL-based FEs analysis framework that can monitor early-stage NDs patients, including Parkinson's, Alzheimer's, and stroke patients.

2. The model of only 9 MB is achieved which is deployable in resource-constrained devices such as smartphones and tablets for the practical use of medical practitioners.
3. Achieved the highest accuracy of the model on NDs patients data collected from YouTube containing faces carrying numerous expressions belonging to different gender and age.

The rest of the paper is organized in the following order. Section 2 presents the data preparation step, including the details of the dataset, data pre-processing and augmentation. The model architecture and the training strategy is elaborated in Sect. 3. The experimental setup and the implementation details are given in Sect. 4. The quantitative results and ablation study is also presented in Sect. 4. Section 5 concludes the paper and gives potentials future research directions.

2   Data Preparation

Dataset collection, annotation, and arranging, especially in the case of FEs of ND patients, is a very challenging task. It requires a large number of patients suffering from ND or special skilled professional actors that can make a genuine expression like the ND patients. Both cases require substantial financial resources and substantial human efforts from the researcher, doctors, and patients. So instead of making a dataset from scratch, we have explored various publicly available datasets like the Japanese female facial expressions database JAFF [18], and KEDF [19]. Further details of dataset and its preparation for the DL model are listed below.

2.1   Dataset

KEDF is a publicly available dataset developed by the psychological section of the department of clinical neuroscience, Karolinska Institute, Sweden. It contains universal human facial expressions (Normal, happy, sad, surprised, afraid, angry, and disgusted) images having the size of 562×762 of 70 participants (35 males and 35 females) obtained from five different angles with various cameras. We selected the KEDF dataset for the training of the proposed model because it contains clear, varied, and high-resolution images. Further, in Neurological disorders, patients mainly express four expressions: normal, happy, anger, and sad. So, we chose only these classes of data from the KDEF and arranged them in four classes as shown in step 1 of Fig. 1 accordingly. The arranged data consists of 900 RGB images in each of the four classes split between the training and validation set. Due to this split, 80% of the data is used for training and 20% for evaluation. Further, for real-time testing on real patients' we collected a full-length video from the YouTube platform for each mentioned NDs patient by searching in different well-known channels like Michigan Medicine, 60 min Australia BAYSTATEHEATH. After collection, we extract frames from each video and select frames or parts of the video to pass from the trained model for real-time evaluation based on the expression and age of the patients.

Table 1. Hyper-parameters of the proposed model

Layer	Kernel size	No of kernels/Neurons	Activation	Dropout rate(%)
Conv2d_1	3 × 3	32	Relu	–
B-norm1	–	–	–	–
Conv2d_2	3 × 3	32	Relu	–
B-norm2	–	–	–	–
Max-pool1	2 × 2	–	–	–
Conv2d_3	3 × 3	64	Relu	–
B-norm3	–	–	–	–
Max-pool2	2 × 2	–	–	–
Conv2d_4	3 × 3	64	Relu	–
B-norm4	–	–	–	–
Max-pool3	2 × 2	–	–	–
Conv2d_5	5 × 5	128	Relu	–
B-norm5	–	–	–	–
Max-pool4	2 × 2	–	–	–
Conv2d_6	5 × 5	128	Relu	–
B-norm6	–	–	–	–
Dropout1	–	–	–	–
Max-pool5	2 × 2	–	–	–
Flatten	-	–	–	–
Dropout2	–	–	–	30
Dense1	–	64	Relu	–
B-norm7	–	–	–	–
Dense2	–	64	Relu	–
Dropout3	–	–	–	30
Output Dense	–	4	Softmax	–

2.2   Pre-processing

Preprocessing is one of the critical steps to improve the learning capabilities of the model during training. Preprocessing aims to remove unessential pixels from the raw images and keep only region of interest (ROI) for processing. The first step is to detect the face and then crop it, as shown in Fig. 2. Face detection is a challenging task due to angles and illumination variations. To avoid such variations, a popular algorithm in terms of accuracy for face detection called viola jones [20] is used. RGB images are converted to grey before feeding them to the viola jones algorithm. Further, to reduce the computational cost, the cropped images are downsampled to 148 × 148 before feeding them into the proposed training model.

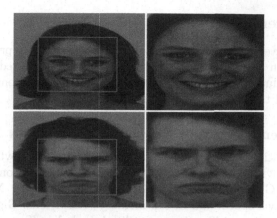

Fig. 2. Face detection and cropping

3   Model Architecture

In order to design an efficient DL model that is easily deployable on resource-constrained devices such as smartphones, it is essential to have a minimal number of trainable and non-trainable parameters. These parameters are directly related to the different components of the model and its hyper-parameters. The broad graphical depiction of our proposed model is given in Fig. 1. It consists of various components, including convolution, pooling, batch normalization, dropout, and dense layers. The model accepts a grayscale image of 148×148 as input and provides predicted probabilities as output for four facial expressions categories. The architecture contains six convolutions layers (CLs) with various numbers of 3×3 and 5×5 filters in the first four and last two layers, respectively. Relu activation function is used in each CL, which helps the model avoid high vanishing gradient problems and learn complex nonlinear functions while training. Five max-pooling layers (MPL) are utilized with the kernel size of 2×2 after each CL except the first one to reduce the dimensions of resulting features maps from CLs and leave only high weighted features as output. Further, seven batch normalization layers (BNLs) are kept after each layer for standardization of the input batches for CLs and to smooth convergence during the model's training. In last, two hidden layers have 64 neurons with the relu activation function in each, and one dense output layer contains four neurons and a SoftMax activation function used to acquire probability for four classes as an output of the model. Besides this, the dropout @ of 30% regularization technique is utilized before each of the last three dense layers to avoid overfitting and achieve high accuracy on validation samples. Further, the final model contains a total of 1.3 million parameters. A visual view of our proposed model is shown in Fig 1 and hyper-parameters parameters of various layers are tabulated in Table 1.

4   Experiment

In this section, we present the evaluation performance of the proposed method. First, we explain the experimental setting, then datasets used in the model's training and evaluation, followed by evaluation metrics, ablation study, and real-time testing. All these steps are discussed below in detail.

4.1   Experimental Setup and Implementation Details

The implementation and experiments were carried out in python version 3.7 based virtual environment that is installed on a personal computer with the specification of GTX GeForce 1070 GPU, intel(R) Xeon(R) X5560 processor with 2.80 GH clock speed, and Install memory (RAM) 8.00 Giga bite. Further, different frameworks and libraries are utilized, including TensorFlow-GPU version 2.0.0 with the frontend of Keras-GPU for designing, training, and evaluating the DL model. Categorical cross-entropy loss function and Adam optimizer with an initial learning rate of 10^{-4} are used to calculate the loss of the model and update its weights while training, respectively. In addition, we trained the proposed model on 32 minibatch sizes for 150 epochs which took almost one and half hours. Apart from this, NumPy is used for various mathematical operations like reshaping and concatenation, and Matplotlib is utilized to visualise different evaluation graphs.

Fig. 3. Real-time testing, the first row is of the Parkinson, second is Alzheimer and the last one shows the result of our framework on stroke patients

4.2   Evaluation Metrics

A total of six matrices are used to evaluate the performance of models. The confusion matrix is shown in Table 3. Time inference is used to check the model's speed and evaluate the model's weight after training. Model loss is used to show the model performance verification during training. In addition, for a better and more accurate comparison, all these metrics are calculated using the Keres functions.

4.3   Confusion Matrix

For better evaluation and observing the class-wise performance of the proposed, we draw the confusion matrix of the model, which is depicted as a Fig. 4. It can be observed that the performance of the model is 96% for each happy and neutral. However, performance for the Angry and sad class is low, which is 88% and 89% respectively.

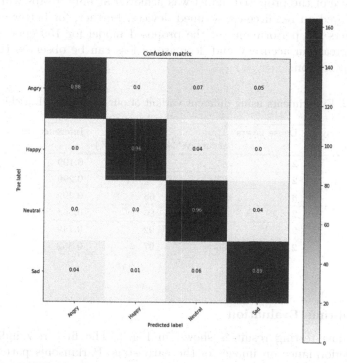

Fig. 4. Confusion matrix of proposed FER model

4.4   Ablation Study

We have done experiments on two different datasets. First, the model is trained and evaluated on KEDF data. Secondly, the real-time evolution of the trained model on ND patients' data was collected from the YouTube platform. The results of these experiments are tabulated in Table 2. From experiments, we found that when the number of convolution layers increases, dense layers are kept constant (two), training and validation accuracies are improved gradually due to the learning capability of high-level and accurate face features extraction. However, the model's size increased due to the number of trainable parameters in convolution layers. Further, when we added more dense layers, the model becomes overfit because of the high complexity in the last layers. An example of this case is experiment 3 in Table 2, where the addition of another dense layer found the model highly overfit. Despite this, from top to bottom in Table 2, we can observe an increase in inference time. This is due to increases in features extraction layers where each CNN layer takes a specific amount of time. As a result of these extensive experiments, we achieved a high performer model having only six convolutions and two dense layers with 96.0% training and 97.0 % validation accuracies, and 0.25 training and 0.18 validation losses. In the end, the total size of the proposed model was achieved at only 9 Mbs which can be easily deployed on resource-constrained devices. Further, for better evaluation, Fig. 5 depicts the performance of the proposed model for 150 epochs where a gradual increase in accuracy and decrease in loss can be observed throughout the training session.

Table 2. Experiments using different variant of our proposed DL architectures

Conv layers	Dense layers	Train accuracy(%)	Validation accuracy(%)	Inference time (sec)
1	2	85	77	0.199
2	2	87	82	0.299
3	3	90	68	0.392
4	2	92	86	0.554
5	2	94	92	0.749
6	2	96	97	0.852

4.5   Real-time Evaluation

The real-time testing result is shown in Fig. 3. The first row indicates our model's performance on images of the early-stage Parkinson's patient getting treatment from the doctors. The rest of the two are early-stage Alzheimer's and Stroke patients, respectively. Further, all patient's expressions are recognized correctly. However, certain difficult situations are wrongly classified. For example, Alzheimer's patient is normal in actuality but classified as angry due to a very drastic change in angle and appearance of the patient face.

Table 3. Comparison with state-of-the-art methods

Model name	Testing accuracy (%)	Recall(%)	Precision(%)	F1 Score(%)
NASNet mobile	74	74	74	72
ResNet50	80	80	80	80
Mobile NetV2	73	73	73	72
Proposed	93	93	93	93

4.6   Performance Comparison with State-of the Art Models

For performance comparison with the existing state of the art model, we used a pre-trained model, including NasNet mobile, Mobile Net V2, and ResNet50. The performance of each model is tabulated as Table 3. The ResNet achieved 80% testing accuracy, recall, precision and F1 score. On the other hand, the proposed model achieved the highest 93% accuracy for each mentioned metric.

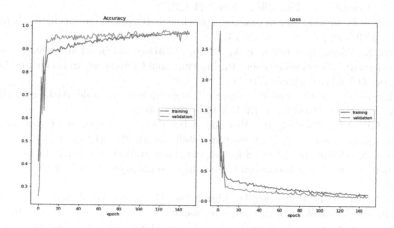

Fig. 5. Accuracies and losses of the proposed model

5   Conclusion

We presented a DL based system for automatic FEs analysis of NDs such as Parkinson's, Alzheimer's, and stroke patients. After various experiments, we achieved a lightweight and accurate model having accuracy up to 96.0% of training and 97.0% of validation. Further, tested our model in real-time using the real data of NDs patients. Besides this, the system is able successfully deploy on resource-constrained devices due its lightweight. In the future, we plan to collect more challenging datasets of the patients and improve the system through attention mechanisms and incorporating temporal information with spatial information of specific FEs.

Acknowledgement. The European Union funded this research through the Horizon 2020 Research and Innovation Programme, in the context of the ALAMEDA (Bridging the Early Diagnosis and Treatment Gap of Brain Diseases via Smart, Connected, Proactive and Evidence-based Technological Interventions) project under grant agreement No GA 101017558.

References

1. Mehrabian, A.: Some referents and measures of nonverbal behavior. Behav. Res. Meth. Instrum. 1(6), 203–207 (1968)
2. Ricciardi, L., et al.: Facial emotion recognition and expression in Parkinson's disease: an emotional mirror mechanism? PloS one 12(1), e0169110 (2017)
3. Lin, J., Chen, Y., Wen, H., Yang, Z., Zeng, J.: Weakness of eye closure with central facial paralysis after unilateral hemispheric stroke predicts a worse outcome. J. Stroke Cerebrovasc. Dis. 26(4), 834–841 (2017)
4. Baugh, R.F., et al.: Clinical practice guideline: bell's palsy. Otolaryngol.-Head Neck Surg. 149(3_suppl), S1–S27 (2013)
5. Chen, X., Wang, Z., Cheikh, F.A., Ullah, M.: 3D-resnet fused attention for autism spectrum disorder classification. In: International Conference on Image and Graphics, pp. 607–617. Springer (2021)
6. Kohler, C.G., et al.: Emotion-discrimination deficits in mild Alzheimer disease. Am. J. Geriatr. Psychiatry 13(11), 926–933 (2005)
7. Mandal, M.K., Pandey, R., Prasad, A.B.: Facial expressions of emotions and schizophrenia: a review. Schizophrenia Bull. 24(3), 399–412 (1998)
8. Fernandez-Duque, D., Black, S.E.: Impaired recognition of negative facial emotions in patients with frontotemporal dementia. Neuropsychologia 43(11), 1673–1687 (2005)
9. Bevilacqua, V., D'Ambruoso, D., Mandolino, G., Suma, M.: A new tool to support diagnosis of neurological disorders by means of facial expressions. In: 2011 IEEE International Symposium on Medical Measurements and Applications, pp. 544–549. IEEE (2011)
10. Dantcheva, A., Bilinski, P., Nguyen, H.T., Broutart, J.C., Bremond, F.: Expression recognition for severely demented patients in music reminiscence-therapy. In: 2017 25th European Signal Processing Conference (EUSIPCO), pp. 783–787. IEEE (2017)
11. Dapogny, A., et al.: Jemime: a serious game to teach children with ASD how to adequately produce facial expressions. In: 2018 13th IEEE International Conference on Automatic Face & Gesture Recognition (FG 2018), pp. 723–730. IEEE (2018)
12. Jin, B., Yue, Q., Zhang, L., Gao, Z.: Diagnosing Parkinson disease through facial expression recognition: video analysis. J. Med. Internet Res. 22(7), e18697 (2020)
13. Alreshidi, A., Ullah, M.: Facial emotion recognition using hybrid features. In: Informatics, vol. 7, p. 6. Multidisciplinary Digital Publishing Institute (2020)
14. Liang, L., Lang, C., Li, Y., Feng, S., Zhao, J.: Fine-grained facial expression recognition in the wild. IEEE Trans. Inform. Forens. Secur.16, 482–494 (2020)
15. Wu, R., Zhang, G., Lu, S., Chen, T.: Cascade ef-gan: Progressive facial expression editing with local focuses. In: Proceedings of the IEEE/CVF Conference on Computer Vision and Pattern Recognition, pp. 5021–5030 (2020)
16. Li, H., Wang, N., Ding, X., Yang, X., Gao, X.: Adaptively learning facial expression representation via CF labels and distillation. IEEE Trans. Image Process. 30, 2016–2028 (2021)
17. Shirian, A., Tripathi, S., Guha, T.: Dynamic emotion modeling with learnable graphs and graph inception network. IEEE Trans. Multimedia (2021)
18. Lyons, M., Akamatsu, S., Kamachi, M., Gyoba, J.: Coding facial expressions with gabor wavelets. In: Proceedings Third IEEE International Conference on Automatic Face and Gesture Recognition, pp. 200–205. IEEE (1998)

19. Lundqvist, D., Flykt, A., Öhman, A.: The karolinska directed emotional faces (kdef). CD ROM Depart. Clin. Neurosci. Psychol. Sect. Karolinska Institutet 91(630), 2–2 (1998)
20. Viola, P., Jones, M.: Rapid object detection using a boosted cascade of simple features. In: Proceedings of the Computer Society Conference on Computer Vision and Pattern Recognition, vol. 1, p. 1. IEEE (2001)

ParSMURF-NG: A Machine Learning High Performance Computing System for the Analysis of Imbalanced Big Omics Data

Alessandro Petrini[1,3]([✉]) [iD], Marco Notaro[1,3] [iD], Jessica Gliozzo[1,3] [iD], Tiziana Castrignanò[5] [iD], Peter N. Robinson[6] [iD], Elena Casiraghi[1,2,3] [iD], and Giorgio Valentini[1,2,3,4] [iD]

[1] AnacletoLab - Dip. Informatica, Università degli Studi di Milano, Milan, Italy
`alessandro.petrini@unimi.it`
[2] Data Science Research Center, Università degli Studi di Milano, Milan, Italy
[3] CINI - Laboratorio Nazionale Infolife, Roma, Italy
[4] CINI - Laboratorio Nazionale Big Data, Roma, Italy
[5] Department of Ecological and Biological Sciences, Universitá della Tuscia, Viterbo, Italy
[6] The Jackson Laboratory for Genomic Medicine, Farmington, CT, USA

Abstract. In the context of Genomic and Precision Medicine, prediction problems are often characterized by a high imbalance between classes and Big Data. This requires specialized tools, as traditional Machine Learning approaches may struggle with big datasets and often fail to predict the minority class with unbalanced classification problems.

In this work we present ParSMURF-NG, a High Performance Computing-oriented Machine Learning approach designed to scale well on big omics data. We measured its performance capabilities on three current-generation HPC systems and we showed its usefulness in the context of Genomic Medicine, providing a powerful model for the detection of pathogenic single nucleotide variants in the non-coding regions of the human genome.

Keywords: Parallel machine learning tool for big data · Machine learning for genomic medicine · Prediction of deleterious variants · Machine learning tool for imbalanced data

1 Introduction

The latest developments in high-throughput technologies and Artificial Intelligence have provided unprecedented tools for the development of Precision and Personalized Medicine. In particular, in recent years whole genome sequencing (WGS) has become cheap, accessible and reliable, hence making large population genome sequencing projects feasible [1,19]. Moreover, a pivotal role in the

© IFIP International Federation for Information Processing 2022
Published by Springer Nature Switzerland AG 2022
I. Maglogiannis et al. (Eds.): AIAI 2022 Workshops, IFIP AICT 652, pp. 424–435, 2022.
https://doi.org/10.1007/978-3-031-08341-9_34

analysis of the massive amount of data generated by Next Generation Sequencing (NGS) techniques [10] is played by Machine Learning (ML), as automatic learning algorithms are capable of detecting underlying patterns in data which traditional statistical methods may overlook. Advances in WGS and ML have made variant identification through the analysis of NGS data central in Genomic Medicine; however, most previous studies focus on the investigation of disease-associated protein-coding variants [2,9], and our understanding of the impact of variants located in the non-coding regions of the genome is mostly incomplete. However, several studies reported that most of the potential pathogenic variants are not in the coding areas of the genome [5].

In particular, a pivotal problem in this research field is the identification of the causal variants for the ~8000 known genetic Mendelian diseases, as one of the major problems in Genomic Medicine is the lack of a molecular diagnosis for about 50% of them, and in particular the interpretation of non-coding variants that affect coding genes [3].

Several computational approaches for the interpretation of non-coding variants have been proposed [14,15]. In particular, HyperSMURF [16] a hyper-ensemble method that constitutes the machine learning core of Genomiser (a state of the art tool for the diagnosis of Mendelian diseases [18]), achieved competitive results in the detection of pathogenic single nucleotide variants (SNV) in the non-coding portions of the human genome.

Following HyperSMURF, ParSMURF [11], introduced several improvements to the original approach: it addressed most of its computational inefficiencies, while simultaneously providing a more reliable learning model thanks to its hyper-parameter auto-tuning capabilities.

In this paper we present the following novel contributions to the above-mentioned research line:

- The release of an improved version of ParSMURF, that is the highly scalable ParSMURF-NG application[1], able to fully exploit the computational features of current supercomputers for solving relevant prediction problems in the context of Big Data and Genomic Medicine.
- The application of ParSMURF-NG to big omics data, with the aim of predicting pathogenic variants by employing an impressive number of features. We envision to achieve a significant advance in the prediction of Mendelian pathogenic variants by proposing novel breakthrough models.

2   Related Work

As briefly stated in the introduction, variant identification through the analysis of NGS data plays a pivotal role in genomic and precision medicine. Also, only in recent years the research community shifted its attention towards the understanding of the impact of variants occurring in the non-coding regions of

---

[1] https://github.com/AnacletoLAB/parSMURF-NG.

the genome, as several studies showed that most of the potential pathogenic and deleterious variants may lie there [5].

In recent years, researchers proposed several tools for the identification and prioritization of relevant non-coding variants. CADD [8] was one of the first methods that relied on machine learning strategies - logistic regression in the latest version, but originally an ensemble of Support Vector Machines (SVM) - for the prediction of pathogenic and deleterious variants in the non-coding region of the genome [14]. Part of its success was due to the precise construction of the dataset used for training the classifier, as each variant is characterized by merging in a single measure a combination of different annotations. Thanks to its dataset and the employed learning strategy, CADD is one of the most commonly used tools in this research field.

Subsequently, several other tools were developed, each one employing different learning methods, from multiple kernel learning [17] to deep neural networks [13]. Moreover, some tools based on gkm-SVM [6] or deep learning [20] trained their classifier with the actual genomic sequence. All these methods, however, are challenged by the scarcity and sparsity of known pathogenic variants, being overwhelmed in number by neutral ones. From a machine learning standpoint, the classification problem emerging from this task is very challenging: imbalance-unaware algorithms correctly classify samples belonging to the majority class only - in this case, neutral variants - due to the unbalance between classes of examples to be learned.

Recently, it has been shown that methods designed to explicitly consider the imbalance between classes provide more reliable predictions. Among these methods, GWAVA [15] exploits a modified random forest classifier, and NCBoost [4] uses gradient tree boosting with a partial rebalancing strategy.

HyperSMURF [16] addresses the imbalancing problem through the cooperation of several techniques, such as:

- improving data coverage through partitioning of the training set;
- over/under-sampling of the minority/majority classes for training set rebalancing;
- improvement of the accuracy of the learners by employing an ensemble of ensemble of random forests.

As shown in [16], HyperSMURF showed excellent performance on extremely imbalanced datasets, such those used in this field of genomic research: as a matter of fact, HyperSMURF was trained on the Genomiser dataset [18], composed of 406 manually curated pathogenic Mendelian SNVs and more than 14 million neutral SNVs, all located in non-coding regions of the human genome. Each SNV is annotated with 26 heterogeneous genomic features, including DNAse hypersensitivity, conservation scores, regulation annotations and more. In the Genomiser framework, HyperSMURF trained with this dataset is called Regulatory Mendelian Mutation (ReMM): HyperSMURF assigns a score to each SNV (ReMM score), predicting the pathogenicity of each variant. Genomiser and the ReMM scores have been widely used by the genomic diagnostics community thus motivating novel research to provide more accurate and sensitive models and software implementations able to deal with the complexity of the underlying prediction problem. Currently, however, advancements in this field of research are only feasible with the use of supercomputing systems, as computational requirements are often very high. Originally, ReMM scores were evaluated with HyperSMURF in its first software implementation, a straightforward sequential version of the algorithm. Nevertheless, next studies showed that HyperSMURF performance strongly depends on the careful tuning of its learning hyper-parameters [12], thus requiring a more efficient and parallel implementation of the original algorithm to address the computational complexity of the hyper-parameter tuning procedure.

ParSMURF [11] was developed with the goal of overcoming the limitations of HyperSMURF: its efficient parallel implementation reduces the execution times noticeably, and its hyper-parameters auto-tuning features are able to improve the quality of the learner, hence improving the predictions. Indeed, [11] shows that ParSMURF improves HyperSMURF performance when tested over the Mendelian SNV dataset by using the Cineca Marconi SKL supercomputer. Note that, by using such HPC system, ParSMURF solved in less than two weeks an hyper-parameter optimization task that, using a single core machine, would have taken 18 years to complete.

3   Methods

In this section we present ParSMURF-NG (ParSMURF - New Generation), an improved version of ParSMURF, even more suitable for tackling Big Data problems in Genomic Medicine. For this purpose, we also present its application in a project in the context of precision medicine.

3.1   ParSMURF-NG

ParSMURF-NG is a complete re-development of ParSMURF and, at the best of our knowledge, is the only High Performance Computing-oriented ML software able to process extremely imbalanced genomic dataset. The effectiveness of the learning strategy at the core of all the implementations has been shown in [16]: here the authors report that HyperSMURF learning approach outperformed all the considered alternative tools when applied to problems in the context of genomic and personalized medicine. Also, in ParSMURF-NG the underlying algorithm and approach are the same of ParSMURF and HyperSMURF; hence, for the sake of brevity, we will focus on the novelties introduced in ParSMURF-NG, reminding the reader that a complete algorithm dissertation and analysis is available on [11] and [16].

ParSMURF-NG is written in C++ for performance and optimal memory usage reasons. By using C++, we managed to finely tune the implementation depending on the target hardware: the code is optimized for standard x86-64 processors, but it also exploits the additional features of Intel XeonPhi CPUs, if available. Moreover, fine tuning of the intercommunication and synchronization between processes was possible by directly managing each MPI operation.

The master-slave programming paradigm of ParSMURF represents the major reason that limited the scalability of the approach to only a few dozens of computing nodes: under this model, pool of worker processes is orchestrated by a single master. As a consequence, the workload on the master process increases with the number of workers, thus limiting the scalability of the algorithm as, no matter how many workers are available, it is limited by the processing power of the single master.

In contrast, ParSMURF-NG new design circumvents this limitation: in its master-less parallel programming model a set of processes independently work on different subsets of the dataset. Thanks to that, synchronization happens only when the final results need to be collected, so efficiency and scalability are maximized. In this approach no orchestration by a master is required: scalability is not affected (if not marginally), and hundreds of processes - even distributed over hundreds of computing nodes - can work for quickly solving a single massive task.

In ParSMURF-NG we used nested levels of parallelization to reach a high degree of efficiency: computation is distributed across nodes of an HPC facility and the MPI library leverages process intercommunication. Inside each node, parallelization is distributed by means of threading (low-level C++ 11/14 STL threads library). Lowest level of parallelization occurs at instruction level, exploiting x86-64 vector instructions - up to AVX-512 instruction set.

Access to storage and networking happens only at the beginning and the end of each run, when each process reads the data from the shared file system, and when results need to be gathered and saved to disk, respectively. Data import can substantially stress the I/O infrastructure, as it occurs concurrently to the entire the pool of MPI processes. For this reason, I/O operations (disk read and write, network access) have been updated to rely on the MPI library, forcing the usage of underlying hardware infrastructure. Tests executed on Marconi KNL with non-MPI disk operation functions (standard C++ STL), turned into a 75× increase of import time (128 MPI processes import a dataset of 12 GB in 20 s using the MPI optimized version, and 25 min using C++ STL functions).

3.2   Improving the Detection of Pathogenic SNV with ParSMURF-NG

As a follow-up of the studies presented in [16] and [11], we leveraged ParSMURF-NG to create a learning model for the prediction of pathogenic Mendelian variants able to outperform the current state of the art. The starting point of this investigation is the very same dataset used in those works, that is a dataset of more than 14 million SNVs, out of which only 406 are pathogenic (deleterious), with each SNV annotated using 26 genomic attributes.

We attempted to boost the generalization capabilities of the previously proposed models by leveraging the more efficient architecture of ParSMURF-NG and by increasing the informativeness of the dataset. To this end, newly discovered pathogenic variants, with strong evidence from literature, were added and each SNV was better characterized gathering new features. For the former, we added 80 new pathogenic SNVs, which had the side effect of slightly decrease the imbalance between classes; the latter is done by extracting new epigenomic features from public available repositories, and adding this newly generated annotation to the 26 features of the original dataset [18]. Since ParSMURF-NG had been designed to cope with Big Data problems, we were able to extract and evaluate more than 600 new features.

Feature Extraction and Generation. Features were extracted from the International Human Epigenomic Consortium (IHEC) data portal. From there we collected up to 6 histone modification assays (H3K27ac, H3K27me3, H3K36me3, H3K4me1, H3K4me3, H3K9me3) for each of the 111 cell line considered (Assembly: hg19, Build: 2020-10). We collected assays from the following consortia: Encode, DEEP, AMED-CREST and Blueprint.

Specifically, a new annotation for each SNV is generated from each combination of these epigenomic assays and cell lines considered for this study - represented by a single cell in the IHEC data grid. If more than one experiment was present for each combination, data was aggregated considering the maximum value for each SNV. This produced more than 600 new annotations, each one representing a specific epigenomic feature for a distinct tissue/cell line.

Feature Importance and Model Selection. We applied different feature selection techniques to assess the informativeness of each newly generated feature. In particular, we used:

- the feature importance score returned by the random forests of ParSMURF-NG, based on the impurity index;
- Maximum Relevance Minimum Redundancy (MRMR), a multivariate method based on mutual information that returns the minimum set of features that, considered together, provides the highest informativeness;
- Spearman and Pearson correlation indexes, measured as correlation of a single feature with the label vector;
- Kruskal-Wallis rank sum and Mann-Whitney U tests between the two classes.

Spearman, Pearson, Kruskal-Wallis and Mann-Whitney were also evaluated by rebalancing the classes, i.e. by dividing the majority classes in subsets whose size was equal to the number of samples of the minority classes, evaluating each index for each subset and averaging the results. Those techniques were also used for evaluating the informativeness of the original 26 features for comparison and reference.

Model Selection and Generation. ParSMURF-NG was trained with the set of the most informative features selected by the above techniques. However, for

ParSMURF-NG one of the most critical task in model selection is the tuning of its hyper-parameters, as it noticeably affects the prediction capability of its trained model. Incidentally, it is also the most computing demanding task, thus specifically requiring Tier-0 HPC systems to be completed in a feasible amount of time. We chose to perform a grid search to exhaustively explore a finite space of hyper-parameters and ensure the best learning model given the selected dataset.

Finally, we train the final model using the best hyper-parameter returned by the grid selection procedure, and compared the predicting performance of the model with the one trained with the original dataset.

4   Experiments and Results

Before applying ParSMURF-NG to the prediction of pathogenic Mendelian SNVs, we performed a comprehensive evaluation of its scaling properties, by evaluating the speed-up and efficiency of the proposed parallel hyper-ensemble model on three HPC cluster systems using synthetic data.

Table 1. Summary of the specifications of the three HPC systems used for testing the scalability of ParSMURF-NG.

	Cineca Marconi A2 KNL partition	HLRS Apollo HAWK partition	LRZ SuperMUC-NG
CPU Family	Intel Xeon-Phi Knights Landing	AMD Rome	Intel Skylake Xeon Platinum 8174
CPU Specs	68 cores 4x hyper-threading 1.4 GHz	64 cores 2x hyper-threading 2.24 GHz	24 cores 2x hyper-threading 2.66 GHz
CPUs per node	1	2	2
Memory per node	96 GBytes	256 GBytes	96 GBytes
Number of nodes	3600	5632	6336
Interconnection	Intel Omnipath 2:1 Fat-tree 100GBit/s	Intel InfiniBand HDR200 Enhanced 9D-Hypercube 200 GBit/s	Intel Omnipath 2:1 Fat-tree 100GBit/s

4.1   Scalability of parSMURF-NG

The learning performance of the proposed approach has already been assessed in [16] and [11], hence to test the correctness of the new implementation, we simply replicated the tests outlined in those works, comparing the results. Additionally, we tested the improved scalability of ParSMURF-NG across three Tier-0 High Performance Computing systems: Cineca Marconi A2 Knight Landing, HLRS Apollo HAWK and Leibniz Supercomputing Centre SuperMUC-NG. A summary of the most relevant features of each system is available in Table 1

Assessment of ParSMURF-NG computing performance was accomplished by measuring the speed-up and efficiency in a strong scalability test setup, following the gold standard rules for the evaluation of parallel performance, as in [7]. To

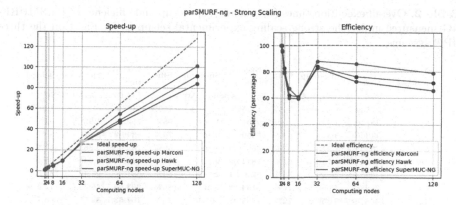

Fig. 1. Speed-up (left), efficiency (right) of ParSMURF-NG using a fixed size problem (strong scaling) on Cineca Marconi KNL partition (blue), Hawk system (green) and Leibnitz SuperMUC-NG (purple). In both graphs, x-axis shows the number of computing nodes. Efficiency is shown in percentage. ParSMURF-NG hyper-parameters used on this test: $nParts = 256$, $fp = 1$, $ratio = 1$, $k = 5$, $nTrees = 50$, $mtry = default$. ParSMURF-NG was configured to execute a 10-fold cross-validation on the dataset. (Color figure online)

insure comparability of the results, we executed the tests using the very same set-up - in terms of dataset, task specification and launch parameters - on the three systems. The only major difference between runs was in the thread count per node, as it was adjusted on each system so to match the number of actual physical cores on each node. Lastly, the software was compiled with Intel ICC on Marconi KNL and SuperMUC-NG, while on HLRS Hawk it was compiled with AMD AOCC, using the same set of optimizations (whenever possible).

Scalability tests were executed by launching the same prediction task several times, each time increasing the number of computing nodes from 1 to 128, following the power-of-2 law. For each run, we collected the overall execution time, including data loading. We used a synthetic dataset composed by a matrix of 100 columns and $30M$ rows. Out of the $30M$ samples, 2000 were marked as belonging to the minority class (1), and the rest as negatives (0), to mimic imbalance ratios of actual genomic datasets. Out of the 100 features, only 20 were informative of each sample class, and the rest were randomly generated.

Figure 1 shows a summary of the results, including speed-up and efficiency curves (See also Table 2). Test results show a remarkable speed-up on every system - up to 91× on Marconi KNL, 100× on HAWK and 84× on SuperMUC-NG - at a very high efficiency (always ≥60%). However, although the speed-up between the system being comparable, execution times on HAWK is far higher than the Intel -based system. This may be due to several factors, including the lack of 512 bit-wide vector instructions on the AMD, to different optimizations performed by the compilers. This required further investigations, but tests were performed in the context of "PRACE Preparatory Access" scalability assessment projects,

Table 2. Overall execution times (in seconds), speed-up and efficiency of ParSMURF-NG measured under the strong scaling experimental set-up as for Fig. 1 on the three HPC systems.

N of MPI processes	Execut. time	Speed-up	Effic.	Execut. time	Speed-up	Effic.	Execut. time	Speed-up	Effic.
	Marconi KNL			Apollo HAWK			LRZ SuperMUC-NG		
1	37439.7	–	100%	175526	–	100%	14080.7	–	100%
2	18726.2	1.99	100%	92015	1.90	95%	7322.7	1.92	96%
4	11300	3.31	83%	55509.9	3.16	79%	4390.92	3.21	80%
8	7525.62	4.97	62%	36569.9	4.80	60%	2625.88	5.36	67%
16	3843.57	9.74	61%	18440.9	9.51	59%	1460.85	9.64	60%
32	1395.35	26.83	84%	6246.51	28.10	88%	531.60	26.49	83%
64	769.27	48.66	76%	3194.83	54.94	86%	303.93	46.33	72%
128	408.99	91.54	72%	1735.98	101.11	79%	167.53	84.05	66%

where limited time, core/h and resources were given. Further optimization will be done as follow-up of this work.

This experiment show that the new parallel model introduced in ParSMURF-NG provides a major improvement in efficiency and scalability. Results are also impressive, considering they are obtained by simply recompiling the code.

4.2 ParSMURF-NG prediction of pathogenic SNVs in Mendelian diseases

We applied all the feature selection methods listed in the Methods section to each feature extracted from the IHEC data portal - and also on the original 26. This produced 10 different feature rankings; however, for the subsequent experiments, we only considered the rankings provided by following feature selection methods:

- ParSMURF-NG random forest impurity index
- rebalanced Spearman correlation index
- rebalanced Kruskall-Wallis rank sum test

as we assessed that all the other rankings were very similar to one of these three (data not shown). The assessment had been done by clustering the distributions of the relative differences and statistically evaluating their correlation.

For each one of these rankings, we assembled five datasets containing respectively the best 5, 10, 25, 50 and 100 features selected by each method, hence generating a total of 15 datasets.

Then we performed model selection and generation: hyper-parameter optimization was done by exploring via grid selection a space of 1440 different configurations in the context of an internal 10-fold cross validation; the best combination was used for training the final model and test it on an separate test set to evaluate its generalization performance. This procedure was performed for each one of the 15 datasets, plus for the original 26 features dataset for comparison purpose. We remark that model selection by hyper-parameter tuning was the most computing intensive task and the only that was performed on the

SuperMUC-NG HPC system. Each tuning procedure was launched over 2560 computing nodes of the infrastructure and the overall execution time of each test was, on average, 14 h. Without the aid of a system like the one we were awarded to use, each model selection test would have taken approximately 5 years, if executed on a single workstation.

Table 3. Summary of the results of the 15 selected model compared to the original dataset reference model having 26 features. The result of the best model is highlighted in bold.

Number of features	ParSMURF-NG Random Forest		Spearman rebalanced		Kruskal-Wallis rebalanced	
	AUROC	AUPRC	AUROC	AUPRC	AUROC	AUPRC
5	0.99609	0.13247	0.98103	0.24700	0.98103	0.24700
10	0.99384	0.03945	0.99501	0.24150	**0.99393**	**0.42410**
25	0.99249	0.03862	0.99135	0.14963	0.99087	0.19334
50	0.99118	0.04169	0.99369	0.16398	0.99273	0.23373
100	0.99103	0.03921	0.99345	0.14590	0.99468	0.16286

	AUROC	**AUPRC**
Old Dataset reference	0.99363	0.35041

We achieved significantly better results with respect to the models trained with the original reference data set that includes 26 features (Table 3). In particular the best results are obtained with 10 omics features selected through the rebalanced Kruskal-Wallis method. Note that in this highly imbalanced setting the AUPRC is far more informative than the AUROC. Overall, the results show that the combination of massive omics data, feature selection and fine tuning of the ParSMURF-NG hyper-parameters lead to significantly better results. Moreover the results show that feature selection plays a key role to improve the overall results and most of the considered epigenetic features are not significant in improving the prediction performance of the system.

5   Conclusions

In this work we presented ParSMURF-NG a Machine Learning approach derived from HyperSMURF, able to efficiently deal with highly imbalanced datasets of big dimension. Along with its excellent scalability performance, we showed its application in the context of Personalized and Genomic Medicine aimed to provide a more powerful model for predicting the pathogenicity or deleteriousness of non-coding SNVs.

We provide a model which improves the current state of the art in terms of generalization, and our experiments showed that the best results were obtained by using just an handful of new features, out of the ≥ 600 considered. For this reason, as a follow-up, we plan to investigate the use of a more heterogeneous set of features, adding not only histone modifications but also a wider range of genomic and epigenomic assays.

Acknowledgements. This study has been developed and performed in the context of the project "ParBigMen: ParSMURF application to Big genomic and epigenomic data for the detection of pathogenic variants in Mendelian diseases". This project had been awarded by the Partnership for Advanced Computing in Europe in its 21st Call for Proposal. We acknowledge PRACE for awarding us access to SuperMUC-NG at LRZ, Germany.

Code and Data Availability
ParSMURF-NG is distributed as source code, and it is available at https://github.com/AnacletoLAB/parSMURF-NG

References

1. Abecasis, G.R., et al.: An integrated map of genetic variation from 1,092 human genomes. Nature **491**(7422), 56–65 (2012)
2. Adzhubei, I., Jordan, D.M., Sunyaev, S.R.: Predicting functional effect of human missense mutations using polyphen-2. Curr. Protoc. Hum. Genet. **76**(1), 7–20 (2013)
3. Amberger, J.S., Bocchini, C.A., Scott, A.F., Hamosh, A.: Omim.org: leveraging knowledge across phenotype-gene relationships. Nucleic Acids Res. **47**(D1), D1038–D1043 (2019)
4. Caron, B., Luo, Y., Rausell, A.: NCBoost classifies pathogenic non-coding variants in mendelian diseases through supervised learning on purifying selection signals in humans. Genome Biol. **20**(1), 32 (2019)
5. Edwards, S.L., Beesley, J., French, J.D., Dunning, A.M.: Beyond GWASs: illuminating the dark road from association to function. Am. J. Hum. Genet. **93**(5), 779–97 (2013)
6. Ghandi, M., Lee, D., Mohammad-Noori, M., Beer, M.A.: Enhanced regulatory sequence prediction using gapped k-mer features. PLoS Comput. Biol. **10**(7), e1003711 (2014)
7. Grama, A., Karypis, G., Kumar, V., Gupta, A.: Introduction to Parallel Computing, 2nd edn. Addison Wesley, Boston (2003)
8. Kircher, M., Witten, D.M., Jain, P., O'Roak, B.J., Cooper, G.M., Shendure, J.: A general framework for estimating the relative pathogenicity of human genetic variants. Nat. Genet. **46**(3), 310–315 (2014)
9. Kumar, P., Henikoff, S., Ng, P.: Predicting the effects of coding non-synonymous variants on protein function using the sift algorithm. Nat. Protoc. **4**(7), 1073–1081 (2009)
10. Leung, M.K.K., Delong, A., Alipanahi, B., Frey, B.J.: Machine learning in genomic medicine: a review of computational problems and data sets. Proc. IEEE **104**, 176–197 (2016)
11. Petrini, A., et al.: parSMURF, a high-performance computing tool for the genome-wide detection of pathogenic variants. GigaScience **9**(5), giaa052 (2020)

12. Petrini, A., et al.: Parameters tuning boosts hyperSMURF predictions of rare deleterious non-coding genetic variants. In: NETTAB 2017, Methods, Tools and Platforms for Personalized Medicine in the Big Data Era, Palermo, Italy, October 2017
13. Quang, D., Xie, X., Chen, Y.: DANN: a deep learning approach for annotating the pathogenicity of genetic variants. Bioinformatics **31**(5), 761–763 (2014)
14. Rentzsch, P., Witten, D., Cooper, G., Shendure, J., Kircher, M.: CADD: predicting the deleteriousness of variants throughout the human genome. Nucleic Acids Res. **47**(D1), D886–D894 (2019)
15. Ritchie, G.R.S., Dunham, I., Zeggini, E., Flicek, P.: Functional annotation of noncoding sequence variants. Nat. Methods **11**(3), 294–296 (2014)
16. Schubach, M., Re, M., Robinson, P.N., Valentini, G.: Imbalance-aware machine learning for predicting rare and common disease-associated non-coding variants. Sci. Rep. **7**(1), 2959 (2017)
17. Shihab, H.A., et al.: An integrative approach to predicting the functional effects of non-coding and coding sequence variation. Bioinformatics **31**(10), 1536–1543 (2015)
18. Smedley, D., et al.: A whole-genome analysis framework for effective identification of pathogenic regulatory variants in mendelian disease. Am. J. Hum. Genet. **99**(3), 595–606 (2016)
19. Turnbull, C., et al.: The 100 000 genomes project: bringing whole genome sequencing to the NHS. BMJ **361** (2018)
20. Zhou, J., Troyanskaya, O.G.: Predicting effects of noncoding variants with deep learning-based sequence model. Nat. Methods **12**(10), 931 934 (2015)

Predicting Risk of Dementia with Survival Machine Learning and Statistical Methods: Results on the English Longitudinal Study of Ageing Cohort

Daniel Stamate[1,2(✉)], Henry Musto[1], Olesya Ajnakina[3,4], and Daniel Stahl[3]

[1] Data Science and Soft Computing Lab, Computing Department, Goldsmiths College, University of London, London, UK
[2] Division of Population Health, Health Services Research and Primary Care, School of Health Sciences, University of Manchester, Manchester, UK
daniel.stamate@manchester.ac.uk
[3] Institute of Psychiatry Psychology and Neuroscience, Biostatistics and Health Informatics Department, King's College London, London, UK
[4] Department of Behavioural Science and Health, Institute of Epidemiology and Health Care, University College London, London, UK

Abstract. Machine learning models that aim to predict dementia onset usually follow the classification methodology ignoring the time until an event happens. This study presents an alternative, using survival analysis within the context of machine learning techniques. Two survival method extensions based on machine learning algorithms of Random Forest and Elastic Net are applied to train, optimise, and validate predictive models based on the English Longitudinal Study of Ageing – ELSA cohort. The two survival machine learning models are compared with the conventional statistical Cox proportional hazard model, proving their superior predictive capability and stability on the ELSA data, as demonstrated by computationally intensive procedures such as nested cross-validation and Monte Carlo validation. This study is the first to apply survival machine learning to the ELSA data, and demonstrates in this case the superiority of AI based predictive modelling approaches over the widely employed Cox statistical approach in survival analysis. Implications, methodological considerations, and future research directions are discussed.

Keywords: Predicting risk of dementia · Survival machine learning · Survival random forests · Survival elastic net · Cox proportional hazard · Nested cross-validation · Monte Carlo validation

1 Introduction

Dementia, of which approximately two-thirds constitute Alzheimer's Disease (AD) cases [1], is associated with a progressive decline of brain functioning, leading to a significant

---

H. Musto—Joint first-author.

© IFIP International Federation for Information Processing 2022
Published by Springer Nature Switzerland AG 2022
I. Maglogiannis et al. (Eds.): AIAI 2022 Workshops, IFIP AICT 652, pp. 436–447, 2022.
https://doi.org/10.1007/978-3-031-08341-9_35

loss of autonomy, reduced quality of life and a shortened life expectancy [2]. Accumulated evidence indicates that individuals who have dementia have an excess mortality [3] and a shorter life expectancy [4] than individuals without this disease [5]. In England, dementia is now reported as being the leading cause of death for women, having overtaken cancer and cardiovascular disease [6].

The development of prognostic prediction models, built on combined effects of thoroughly validated predictors, using Machine Learning tools, can be used to forecast the probability of dementia developing within an individual. It is hoped that the availability of such prediction models will facilitate more rapid identification of individuals who are at a higher risk of dementia before the full illness onset [10]. This, in turn, would reduce time to treatment initiation, subsequently minimising the social and functional disability and thereby improving the quality of life for many people affected by these disorders. Identifying individuals at risk of developing dementia would allow the recruiting of patients at high risk for future clinical trials, thereby catalysing the assessment of new treatment or prevention programmes. Furthermore, identifying modifiable risk factors would allow the development of new prevention programmes. For example, there are already some indications that being physically active, staying mentally and socially active, and controlling high blood pressure can potentially deter onset of dementia in the general population [7].

2   Literature Review

To date, several papers have been published which seek to predict, in a binomial or multinomial classification setting, the probability that any one individual may develop dementia, using neuropsychological test scores, cerebrospinal fluid biomarkers, genetic information, neuroimaging, and demographics data within a fixed period of time. For a recent review, see [8]. These include several studies using the longitudinal Alzheimer's Disease Neuroimaging Initiative (ADNI) study. For example [9] compared several Machine Learning techniques to explore variables found in the ADNI dataset and their suitability as indicator of dementia onset. Although a good performance was demonstrated across all examined algorithms, the best model was Gradient Boosting Machine, with an internally validated area under the curve (AUC) of 0.87. On the other hand, [11] achieved a discriminative accuracy of 0.91 when using ADNI data and support vector machines (SVM) to predict dementia onset. [10] proposed an efficient prediction modelling approach to the risk of dementia based mainly on the Gradient Boosting Machines method, using a large dataset from CPRD (Clinical Practice Research Datalink) repository with data from primary care practices across UK [27], and achieving an AUC performance of 0.83.

Although the ADNI and similar longitudinal studies have as their strength a rich and varied data, the overreliance of the predictive community on these data sources has led to disappointing results when attempting to validate these models on external datasets. The problem is further compounded by the handling of the temporal aspect of the longitudinal studies. Studies that have stuck to the classification-based methodology have dealt with the temporal aspect by including time (defined as discrete time intervals since the start of the study) as a predictor in the model, rather than the outcome of interest [9]. However, by not attempting to predict these temporal aspects, we lose the opportunity to gain clinically relevant information on the expected time to a dementia diagnosis. A common problem of longitudinal studies is drop-out over time where only partial information on a person's survival time is available (Censoring). Furthermore, the standard classification approach is susceptible to instability and inaccuracy when dealing with imbalanced data. Because most subjects do not go on to develop the disease (in this case, dementia), imbalance in the classification outcome must be addressed, usually with under-sampling, over-sampling, or bootstrapping. Such approaches add further complications to a model and the interpretability of its predictions.

A possible solution is one that has in general been less explored so far within the realm of machine learning. This solution is the use of survival methodology as a tool for accounting for and predicting the temporal dynamics of receiving a diagnosis of dementia. In other words, one would seek to utilise the well-established survival techniques found in Cox Proportional Hazards or similar and build upon these frequentist approaches using modified Machine Learning tools [1]. Such an approach would preserve the potential information contained within a temporal outcome, and associated dichotomy of dementia versus no dementia whilst also strengthening the predictive power of the existing frequentist approach by overlaying modified machine learning techniques. Furthermore, it can provide an opportunity to introduce high dimensional data of the type likely to be found when predicting using clinical data. The standard Cox model struggles when confronted with such data, and thus it would be of significant benefit to clinical research if the two approaches could be combined. Finally, survival methods can provide a way to account for censored data whereby subjects are dropping out during the study or are surviving beyond study length. Thus, it can create models which are more robust than standard classification models.

Despite the scarcity of survival modelling papers in relation to dementia prediction, recent examples have shown promise in attempting to outperform the classic Cox proportional hazard model, using survival machine learning and survival deep learning on clinical datasets [12–14]. A pertinent study within the current field of interest is [15] whose authors sought to look at survival machine learning performance when applied to datasets designed for dementia investigation. They found that all machine learning models outperformed the standard Cox Proportional Hazard model. This study, along with those mentioned above, provides support for survival machine learning as a predictive tool for clinical temporal problems.

3   Methodology

This paper builds upon [16] which looked at the English Longitudinal Study of Aging (ELSA) and used an accelerated failure time (AFT) survival modelling approach to predicting the time to a subject's likely diagnosis with all-cause dementia. This work found strong evidence that certain features related to socioeconomic markers and genetics play a key role in predicting time to dementia diagnosis.

3.1 Problem Definition

In this work we propose an approach to predicting the time to a dementia diagnosis, based on survival machine learning techniques such as Survival Random Forests and Survival Elastic Net, and on a conventional statistical method such as Cox Proportional Hazard model. In order to obtain insight into the predictions, we created and assessed variable importance rankings derived from our best model in this study, which could ideally provide actionable advice for prevention.

3.2 Data Description

Data was drawn from the English Longitudinal Study of Ageing (ELSA) study, which is a nationally representative sample of the English population aged ≥ 50 years [17]. The ELSA study started in 2002 (wave 1), with participants recruited from an annual cross-sectional survey of households who were then followed up every two years until 2016. Comparisons of ELSA with the national census showed that the baseline sample was representative of the non-institutionalised general population aged 50 and above in the United Kingdom. Ethical approval for each of the ELSA waves (1–8) was granted by the National Research Ethics Service (London Multicenter Research Ethics Committee). All participants gave informed consent. In total, the dataset contained 7556 participants, 45% of which were male.

3.3 Ascertainment of Dementia Cases

To ascertain dementia cases, we used methods with validated utility in population-based cohorts [18–20]. Dementia diagnosis was ascertained at each wave using self-report participant's physician diagnosis of dementia or AD. For those ELSA participants who were unable to respond to the main interview themselves, the Informant Questionnaire on Cognitive Decline in the Elderly (IQCODE) was administered with a score above the threshold of 3.386 indicating the presence of dementia [21, 22]; the selected threshold demonstrated both excellent specificity (0.84) and sensitivity (0.82) for detection of all-cause (undifferentiated) dementia [23]. Overall, 83.5% of dementia cases were identified from reports of physician-diagnosed dementia or AD and 16.5% were identified based on the IQCODE score.

3.4 Predictors

$N = 197$ predictor variables related to participants' general health, comorbid health conditions, mental health, cognitive domains, life satisfaction, mobility, physical activity, social-economic status, and social relationships were considered for the model development. The gene APOEe4, a predictor with a well-established link to Alzheimer's risk, was also included as a predictor. For further details see [17].

3.5   Data Pre-processing

The process of model development, evaluation and validation was carried out according to methodological guidelines outlined by [24]; results were reported according to the Transparent Reporting of a multivariable prediction model for Individual Prognosis Or Diagnosis (TRIPOD) guidelines [25]. Boolean variables were created, indicating the location of missing data for each predictor. All synonyms for missing values were standardised, and duplicate variables were removed. Variables with missingness at 51% or greater of the total rows for that predictor were removed. The cut-off of 51% allowed to include the APOEe4 (a predictor with a well-established link to Alzheimer's risk), which had 50.8% missingness. The remaining predictors had a mean percentage missingness of 1.27%, with a range of 0–50.8%. Missing values were imputed using K-nearest neighbour with $K = 5$. The data was centered and scaled as part of this process.

We used two versions of the dataset on which we developed our models. The first data version excluded variable scfru which was based on a questionnaire regarding diet and particularly on evaluating a score based on fruit consumption, and the second version included this variable. Variable scrfu was among the variables that showed predictive capability, but also did its NA indicator which in certain cases as dementia may be related to the limited capacity of certain patients to respond to the questionnaire. For this reason, on one hand, we wanted to see the impact of including or excluding scfru in/from our predictive models, and on another hand we compared our models mainly using the performances on the dataset without scfru.

3.6   Model Development

A simple Cox Proportional Hazard Model (hereafter denoted simply by Cox) was constructed, which served as the baseline for comparison with two survival machine learning models:

1. Cox Penalised Regression using Elastic Net (hereafter denoted simply by ElasticNet) [15], which is similar to the base Cox Proportional Hazard Model but with Elastic Net regularisation, allows the model to shrink the coefficients of less important variables, and even to make them equal to 0, depending on the shrinkage strength and the proportion of the Lasso component in this model. This helps improving prediction accuracy and model interpretability. The main hyperparameters of the model that were tuned were *alpha*, which controls the proportion between the L1 (Lasso) and L2 (Ridge) regularisations, and *lambda*, which controls the strength of the shrinkage. In our tuning grid, the values for *alpha* varied between 0 (corresponding to Ridge regularisation) and 1 (corresponding to Lasso regularisation), with a step of 0.05, while the values for *lambda* varied between 0.05 and 0.3, with a step of 0.05.
2. Survival Random Forest (hereafter denoted simply by RF) [15], is based on the Random Forests algorithm which produces a model formed of an ensemble of trees, each of which learnt on a bootstrap copy of the training set and in the node of which a random sample of predictors of fixed size *mtry*, compete to be selected, with their best split point in order to maximise the survival difference between subsequent nodes [11]. RF has been chosen in this study for its flexibility to capture non-linear

patterns in data. Apart from the hyperparameter *mtry* explained above, we used also a hyperparameter called *min.node.size* implementing a pre-pruning criteria for the trees in the RF model to have a minimum number of instances in the terminal nodes. In the tuning grid, the values of *mtry* varied between 10 and the half of the number of columns in the dataset, with a step of 3, while the values for *min.node.size* in the grid were 1, 10, and 20. RF comprised 500 trees which is the default value. The number of trees promotes model convergence (large is better), and in general is not a hyperparameter to tune.

Model tuning was performed using 5-fold cross-validation on the training data set, as part of a nested cross-validation procedure explained below.

3.7 Model Optimisation and Evaluation with Nested Cross-validation and Monte Carlo Validation

A Nested Cross-Validation (NCV) procedure was implemented to tune and evaluate our models with precise estimates of the models' performance. NCV consisted of an outer 3-fold CV, and an inner 5-fold CV.

In order to reliably assess the models' stability, we conducted a Monte Carlo validation procedure (MC), consisting of 90 experiments per model. In each experiment, the dataset was randomly split in 2 thirds for the training data on which the models were tuned with a 5-fold CV, and 1 third for the testing set on which the models were evaluated.

To ensure representativeness of training and test samples in both procedures, NCV and MC, the data splitting was stratified based on the dementia cases variable.

3.8 Performance Metric

We used the concordance index, called also Harrell's C-index [26] and simply denoted *cindex* here, to assess and compare the prediction performance of the different models. C-index is a generalisation of the ROC AUC metric, and intuitively gives the probability that a predicted risk for dementia is higher for patients with a shorter time to event. More precisely:

$$Cindex = C/(C+D)$$

where C represents the number of concordant pairs of patients, and D represents the number of discordant pairs of patients [26]; *cindex* is a number between 0 and 1, where 0.5 signifies a random prediction, and 1 indicates that larger times to event concord perfectly with smaller predicted risks.

3.9 Software and Hardware

The data analysis was conducted using the R language. The stratified data splitting, the KNN imputation and data normalisation via centring and scaling were performed using the Caret R package. The Cox, ElasticNet, and RF survival models were all trained and tuned and evaluated under the umbrella of the MLR3 R package. The hardware consisted of 3 servers running Linux, with Intel 10 cores, AMD Ryzen 16 cores and AMD Ryzen 12 cores, and with 128 GB, 128 GB and 64 GB of RAM, respectively, which were used in our analyses including the computationally intensive tasks for tuning the models, and NCV and MC validation procedures for assessing the models' performances and their stability.

4 Results

4.1 Internal Validation Using Nested Cross-validation

The nested cross-validation cindex performance for train, inner cross-validation, and test or outer cross-validation, for each type of model are detailed below.

Table 1. Nested cross-validation results, based on the data without and with scfru variable

Survival model	Outer-CV (test) cindex	Train cindex	Inner-CV cindex
Cox	**0.776**	0.814	NA (not tuned)
+scfru	**0.791**	0.828	
ElasticNet	**0.843**	0.855	0.840
+scfru	**0.861**	0.873	0.861
RF	**0.851**	0.972	0.848
+scfru	**0.867**	0.955	0.864

The best performing model in terms of the nested cross-validation was Survival Random Forest, followed by Survival Elastic Net, followed by Cox PH model. Hence both machine learning models, RF and ElasticNet, outperformed the conventional statistical model Cox on the test set.

4.2 Monte Carlo Validation

The results for the Monte Carlo validation are outlined in Table 2 and Fig. 1 below.

Table 2. Monte Carlo validation results (90 experiments) for Cox, Survival Elastic Net and Survival Random Forest based on the data without and with scfru variable.

Survival model	Test cindex mean (SD)	Train cindex mean (SD)	CV cindex mean (SD)
Cox	**0.761** (0.03)	0.793 (0.032)	NA (not tuned)
+scfru	**0.778** (0.034)	0.807 (0.036)	
ElasticNet	**0.842** (0.011)	0.856 (0.004)	0.841 (0.005)
+scfru	**0.862** (0.01)	0.873 (0.004)	0.861 (0.005)
RF	**0.849** (0.009)	0.966 (0.01)	0.850 (0.005)
+scfru	**0.866** (0.009)	0.962 (0.009)	0.866 (0.005)

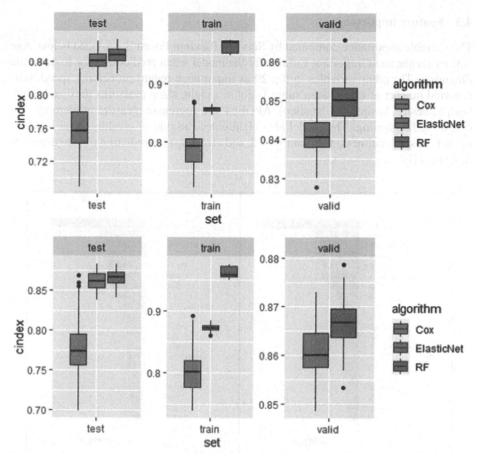

Fig. 1. Boxplots for the Monte Carlo derived cindex performances for Cox, Survival Elastic Net and Survival Random Forest. On top: results on dataset without scfru variable, and on bottom: results with scfru variable.

The results in the Monte Carlo validation reveal the following aspects: (a) the machine learning survival models based on Random Forests and Elastic Net demonstrate clearly better mean cindex on the test sets than the conventional statistical model Cox; (b) the results are close to and confirm the estimated performances obtained in the nested cross-validation in Table 1; (c) the standard deviations (provided in brackets in Table 2) for cindex performances on the test sets for Survival Random Forest and Survival Elastic Net are small, and about 3 times smaller than the standard deviations for Cox, which means that the machine learning models are very stable, and by far more stable than the conventional statistical model. This interpretation is confirmed also visually by the boxplots in Fig. 1.

4.3 Feature Importance

The variable importance computed by Survival Random Forest is provided below. Age was by far the most important variable for the model when predicting time to dementia diagnosis. The other variables in top 20 as importance regard processing speed, self-reported number of hours sleep subjects got in a night, sleep measures (heslpa, heslpd, heslpb, heslpe, heslpf, and headlco), APOEe4, the aggregate measure of memory, and executive functioning. The model also highlighted the role of wealth, social isolation (dhnch, scscc, loneliness_w2, ffamily_w2, and r1retemp) in predicting time to dementia diagnosis (Fig. 2).

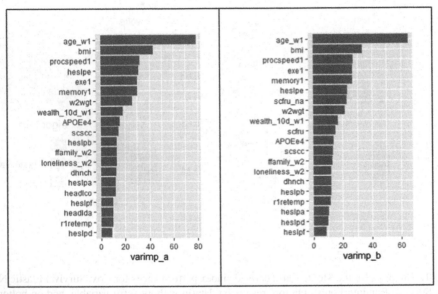

Fig. 2. Variable importance for Survival Random Forest (RF) model: on left for dataset without scfru, and on right for data with the scfru variable.

5 Discussion

To our knowledge, this paper is the first attempt to develop, evaluate and validate a prediction model for estimating an individual risk of dementia onset in the ELSA dataset using survival machine learning. Our results showed that the machine learning models herein were able to outperform the classic Cox model, with the best performing machine learning technique being the Survival Random Forest followed closely by Survival Elastic Net, as per test results in the nested cross-validation included in Table 1, and test results in the Monte Carlo validation included in Table 2, and Fig. 1. Monte Carlo clearly demonstrates the high stability of the survival machine learning models as illustrated by the same Table 2 and Fig. 1. The Survival Random Forest model achieved a mean cindex for the test dataset of 0.849 and a standard deviation of 0.009 in 90 Monte

Carlo iterations. Survival Elastic Net achieved a mean cindex for the test dataset of 0.842 and a standard deviation of 0.011. Both machine learning models outperformed and were more stable than the Cox model which achieved a mean cindex of 0.761 and a standard deviation of 0.03 (about 3 times larger than the machine learning models) in the Monte Carlo validation. This study indicates strong evidence of machine learning's utility in the field of survival prediction. As mentioned previously, the addition of machine learning paradigms to the classic frequentist survival approaches allows for more variables to be explored than would be possible in a standard Cox proportional hazard model. Moreover, as this study demonstrates, the best survival model based on Random Forests not only improved the predictive accuracy and stability but also provided a useful mechanism to infer the variables' importance, which concords with clinical interpretations of the role of the variables in dementia onset.

In this study, we used two versions of the dataset on which we developed our models. The first data version excluded variable scfru which was based on a questionnaire regarding diet and particularly on evaluating a score based on fruit consumption, and the second version included this variable. The comparisons between the models on the results without or with the scfru variable, lead to the same conclusions in terms of the ranking we established for these methods. Moreover, there is a slight performance increase for all the models on the dataset with the scfru variable, which is the reason why we included these results here. This variable made it in top 20 most important variables, but also did its NA indicator, which in certain cases as dementia, may be related to the limited capacity of certain patients to respond to the questionnaire. For this reason, we compared the three models we developed mainly using the performances on the dataset without scfru.

Although this paper presents examples of good predictive survival machine learning modelling, there are some limitations to this work. Firstly, the data contained predictors with a high percentage of missing values. Although every effort was taken to account for missingness and preserve the pattern of missingness before imputation was performed, a complete dataset may provide results that differ from this work especially if missingness is related to the outcome (not missing at random). Even though dementia and AD were ascertained using a combined algorithm based on a physician made diagnosis and a higher score on the informant reports (IQCODE), it is still reliant on a self-reported diagnosis reported by either the participants themselves or their carers and render more severe cases. Thus, we cannot exclude a possibility that some participants within the "dementia-free" group may have been the preclinical stages of dementia and who, if followed for long enough, might eventually develop dementia. Further, the ELSA dataset is a centre-based data collection study and, although extensive and varied data collection was carried out to try and account for confounding variables, it is possible that other predictors, unmeasured by the data collection procedure, could have an impact on model performance. It is therefore imperative that future work validate these models on different datasets such that the results can be well substantiated. Finally, the ELSA data uses English subjects, who were chosen because they were deemed representative of the United Kingdom at large. Therefore, these results cannot be generalised to populations in other countries. Once again, work must be done to ensure that these results are substantiated by data from subjects in differing datasets.

6 Conclusion

This paper represents a first attempt at applying survival machine learning techniques to the ELSA dataset. The intention of this work was to build and validate models which demonstrated good predictive ability on this dataset, specifically in relation to the time to dementia onset. Future work should seek to validate the findings here on other datasets that share similar predictors and outcomes. If the results are substantiated, this could prove to be a new and fruitful approach to clinical prediction modelling of dementia. Another future work will investigate the applicability of an adapted version of the survival machine learning approach we developed here, to the prediction of dementia risk using routine primary care records such as CPRD [27], by extending the machine learning based framework we introduced in [10].

Acknowledgments. Daniel Stamate is part-funded by Alzheimer's Research UK (ARUK-PRRF2017-012), the University of Manchester, and Goldsmiths College, University of London. Daniel Stahl is part-funded by the National Institute for Health Research (NIHR) Maudsley Biomedical Research Centre at South London and Maudsley NHS Foundation Trust and King's College London. The views expressed are those of the author(s) and not necessarily those of the NHS, the NIHR or the Department of Health and Social Care. Olesya Ajnakina is further funded by an NIHR Post-Doctoral Fellowship (PDF-2018-11-ST2-020).

References

1. Hendrie, H.C.: Epidemiology of dementia and Alzheimer's disease. Am. J. Geriatr. Psychiatry **6**(2), S3–S18 (1998)
2. Ljubenkov, P.A., Geschwind, M.D.: Dementia. Semin. Neurol. **36**, 4 (2016)
3. Dewey, M., Saz, P.: Dementia, cognitive impairment and mortality in persons aged 65 and over living in the community: a systematic review of the literature. Geriatr Psychiatry **16**, 751–61 (2001)
4. Hill, G.B., Forbes, W.F., Lindsay, J.: Life expectancy and dementia in Canada: the Canadian study of health and aging. Chronic Dis. Can. **18**, 166–167 (1997)
5. Brayne, G., Gao, L., Dewey, M., Matthews, F.E., Medical Research Council Cognitive Function and Ageing Study Investigators: Dementia before death in ageing societies— the promise of prevention and the reality. PLoS Med. **3**(10), e397 (2006)
6. Deaths Registered in England and Wales (Series DR), 2013. Office for National Statistics (2014). http://www.ons.gov.uk/ons/dcp171778_381807.pdf
7. Kuehn, B.M.: Nearly half of dementia cases could be prevented or delayed. JAMA **324**(11), 1025 (2020)
8. Goerdten, J., Cukic, I., Danso, S.O., et al.: Statistical methods for dementia risk prediction and recommendations for future work: a systematic review. Alzheimer's Dementia Transl. Res. Clin. Interv. **5**(1), 563–569 (2019)
9. Musto, H., Stamate, D., Pu, I., Stahl, D.: A machine learning approach for predicting deterioration in Alzheimer's disease. In: 20th IEEE International Conference on Machine Learning and Applications (ICMLA), Pasadena (2021)
10. Lanham, J., et al.: Predicting risk of dementia with machine learning and survival models using routine primary care records. In: 2021 IEEE International Conference on Bioinformatics and Biomedicine (BIBM) (2021)

11. Mathotaarachchi, S., et al.: Identifying incipient dementia individuals using machine learning and amyloid imaging. Neurobiol. Aging **59**, 80–90 (2017)
12. Moncada-Torres, A., van Maaren, M.C., Hendriks, M.P., Siesling, S., Geleijnse, G.: Explainable machine learning can outperform Cox regression predictions and provide insights in breast cancer survival. Sci. Rep. **11**(1), 6968 (2021)
13. Omurlu, I.K., Ture, M., Tokatli, F.: The comparisons of random survival forests and Cox regression analysis with simulation and an application related to breast cancer. Expert Syst. Appl. **36**(4), 8582–8588 (2009)
14. Kim, D.W., Lee, S., Nam, W., Kim, H.J.: Deep learning-based survival prediction of oral cancer patients. Sci. Rep. **9**(1), 6994 (2019)
15. Spooner, A., et al.: A comparison of machine learning methods for survival analysis of high-dimensional clinical data for dementia prediction. Sci. Rep. **10**(1) (2020)
16. Ajnakina, O., Cadar, D., Steptoe, A.: Interplay between socioeconomic markers and polygenic predisposition on timing of dementia diagnosis. J. Am. Geriatrics Soc. **16406** (2020)
17. Steptoe, A., Breeze, E., Banks, J., Nazroo, J.: Cohort profile: the English longitudinal study of ageing. Int. J. Epidemiol. **42**, 6 (2013)
18. Deckers, K., et al.: Modifiable risk factors explain socioeconomic inequalities in dementia risk: evidence from a population-based prospective cohort study. J. Alzheimer's Dis. **71**(2), 549–557 (2019)
19. Hackett, R.A., Steptoe, A., Cadar, D., Fancourt, D.: Social engagement before and after dementia diagnosis in the English Longitudinal Study of Ageing. PLoS ONE **14**, 8 (2019)
20. Rafnsson, S.B., Orrell, M., d'Orsi, E., Hogervorst, E., Steptoe, A.: Loneliness, social integration, and incident dementia over 6 years: prospective findings from the English longitudinal study of ageing. J. Gerontol. **75**(1), 114–124 (2020)
21. Cadar, D., Lassale, C., Davis, H., Llewellyn, D.J., Batty, G.D., Steptoe, A.: Individual and area-based socioeconomic factors associated with dementia incidence in England: evidence from a 12-year follow-up in the English longitudinal study of ageing. JAMA Psychiat. **75**(7), 723–732 (2018)
22. Jorm, A.F.: A short form of the Informant Questionnaire on Cognitive Decline in the Elderly (IQCODE): development and cross-validation. Psychol. Med. **24**(1), 145–153 (1994)
23. Quinn, T.J., Fearon, P., et al.: Informant Questionnaire on Cognitive Decline in the Elderly (IQCODE) for the diagnosis of dementia within community dwelling populations. Cochrane Database Syst. Rev. (4), CD010079 (2014)
24. Steyerberg, E.W.: Clinical Prediction Models. A Practical Approach to Development, Validation, and Updating. SBH, Springer, Cham (2019)
25. Collins, G.S., Reitsma, J.B., Altman, D.G., Moons, K.G.: Transparent reporting of a multivariable prediction model for individual prognosis or diagnosis (TRIPOD): the TRIPOD statement. BMC Med. **122**(2015), 434–443 (2015)
26. Harrell, F., Califf, R., Pryor, D., Lee, K., Rosati, R.: Evaluating the yield of medical tests. J. Am. Med. Assoc. **247**, 2543–2546 (1982)
27. Clinical Practice Research Datalink | CPRD. https://cprd.com

Author Index